European Banking in the 1990s

Second Edition

EDITED BY

JEAN DERMINE

© Blackwell Publishers 1990, 1993

First published 1990

Reprinted 1991 (twice)
Second edition 1993

Blackwell Publishers
108 Cowley Road, Oxford, OX4 1JF, UK

238 Main Street, Suite 501
Cambridge, Massachusetts 02142, USA

British Library Cataloguing in Publication Data

A CIP catalogue record for this book is available from
the British Library.

Library of Congress Cataloging-in-Publication Data

European banking in the 1990s/edited by Jean Dermine;
  [contributors, Jean Dermine . . . et al.]. − 2nd ed.
      p.   cm.
  Includes bibliographical references and index.
  ISBN 0-631-18843-6 (pbk.)
  1. Banks and banking−European Economic Community countries.
  2. Banking law−European Economic Community countries.
  3. Europe 1992.   I. Dermine, Jean.
  HG2980.5.A6E87   1993
  332.1′094′09049−dc20   92-26973   CIP

Typeset in 10 on 12 pt CG Times
by Advance Typesetting Ltd, Long Hanborough, Oxford
Printed in Great Britain by T. J. Press Ltd, Padstow, Cornwall

This book is printed on acid-free paper

Contents

List of Contributors

PATRICK ARTUS, *Caisse des Dépôts et Consignations*

ERNST BALTENSPERGER, *University of Bern*

CHRISTIAN DE BOISSIEU, *University of Paris I (Panthéon-Sorbonne)*

ANTONIO M. BORGES, *Central Bank of Portugal*

JORGE BRAGA DE MACEDO, *Ministry of Finance, Portugal*

FRANCO BRUNI, *Università di Brescia, Centre for Monetary and Financial Economics and Scuola di Direzione Aziendale, Università Bocconi*

RAMON CAMINAL, *Instituto d'Analisi Economica (CSIC)*

NIGEL CARTER, *Bank of England*

JEAN-PIERRE DANTHINE, *Université de Lausanne*

JEAN DERMINE, *INSEAD*

GEOFFREY FITCHEW, *European Commission*

PAUL A. GEROSKI, *Centre for Business Strategy, London Business School*

DANIEL GROS, *Centre for European Policy Studies*

JORDI GUAL, *IESE*

GABRIEL HAWAWINI, *INSEAD*

RICHARD HERRING, *The Wharton School, University of Pennsylvania*

PIERRE HILLION, *INSEAD*

BERTRAND JACQUILLAT, *University of Paris I (Dauphine)*

RICHARD M. LEVICH, *New York University and National Bureau of Economic Research*

ERNST-MORITZ LIPP, *Dresdner Bank*

COLIN MAYER, *University of Warwick*

DAMIEN J. NEVEN, *University of Liège*

RAFAEL REPULLO, *Bank of Spain*

WOLFGANG RIEKE, *Deutsche Bundesbank*

BERND RUDOLPH, *Goethe-Universität*

ANTHONY M. SANTOMERO, *The Wharton School, University of Pennsylvania*

ROY C. SMITH, *New York University*

ALFRED STEINHERR, *European Investment Bank*

ALEXANDER K. SWOBODA, *Graduate Institute of International Studies and International Center for Monetary and Banking Studies*

STEFAN A. SZYMAŃSKI, *Centre for Business Strategy, London Business School*

GREG UDELL, *New York University*

THÉO VERMAELEN, *INSEAD*

XAVIER VIVES, *Fundación de Estudios de Económia Aplicada and Universidad Autónoma de Barcelona*

INGO WALTER, *INSEAD and New York University*

CHARLES WYPLOSZ, *INSEAD and Centre for Economic Policy Research*

Introduction

Jean Dermine

Will the integration of capital markets in Europe succeed? What problems are likely to arise? What adjustments are expected in specific countries or industries? How should these developments affect the strategies of financial institutions? These are some of the key issues faced by European bankers. In February 1989, a conference 'European Banking After 1992' was held at the European Institute of Business Administration, INSEAD, Fontainebleau. Under the auspices of the International Financial Services Research Programme, 60 senior bankers, regulators and professors were invited to discuss 14 papers commissioned from specialists. Drawn from various fields of research − banking, business policy, economics, finance and industrial organization − the contributors analyse the structural effects of financial integration on specific markets or countries. More precisely, their extensive analyses concern regulation, equity markets and investment banking, banking markets in six countries, the Euromarkets, monetary policy, and, finally, the lessons that can be drawn from the current integration of interstate banking in the United States. The Fontainebleau conference was opened with a lecture by Mr Fitchew, Director General for Financial Institutions and Company Law at the European Commission. In his address, Mr Fitchew presents the objectives of the Commission, i.e. the creation of a liberalized and Community-wide competitive market in financial services.

The book is a revised and updated edition of the Fontainebleau papers. It is organized in five parts, each one addressing a specific set of issues. As the financial services industry is the most heavily regulated sector, the first part of the book concerns the pattern of regulation likely to emerge in Europe. Baltensperger and Dermine and also Mayer analyse the regulations for banks and securities firms. The starting point of their analysis is the existence of market failures in the functioning of private markets which calls for public intervention. Baltensperger and Dermine argue that the main reason for regulation in banking should not be the protection of depositors but rather the stability of banking markets. The financing of illiquid assets with deposits withdrawable at par on demand creates a potential risk of bank runs. Such destabilizing situations could happen in a deregulated Europe. Indeed, a cross-country analysis of margins and costs reveals that structural adjustments will be necessary in previously regulated countries and that, with increasing competition, more bank failures will occur − a situation unknown so far in Europe. To ensure the stability of banking markets, Baltensperger and Dermine suggest two alternatives: discretionary interventions by the lender of last resort or the adoption of new rules for liquid deposits. The incentives to withdraw funds would be offset in the new deposit contract because investors would be liable for bank losses, even if they have run. There would be no place to hide. Moreover, these authors argue that, as long as national monetary authorities and deposit insurance systems are responsible for domestic markets, there is a strong case for joint supervision by the home and host country authorities. Mayer draws the lessons to be learnt from the British regulatory system for the securities industry, the most advanced one in Europe. He calls for more flexibility and a clear distinction between systemic risk and investor protection. Capital controls should be imposed on those firms, such as brokers and dealers, which are both vulnerable to systemic risk and necessary for a smooth functioning of the economy. As far as investor protection is concerned, Mayer calls for differentiation between small investors and large investors and for a diversified range of protection ranging from disclosure of information to insurance.

The second part of the book concerns the developments in European equity markets and in investment banking. Hawawini and Jacquillat provide a complete analysis of the market structure and organization of stock markets in Europe. An empirical analysis of the gains to be expected from portfolio diversification across European stocks shows the benefits of integrated capital markets and the need to improve the international clearing and settlement systems. A key issue concerns the emergence of leading financial centres in Europe. Hawawini and Jacquillat predict a major role for London as the leading equity centre for international companies, but they argue that national stock markets will expand to service domestic companies. Walter and Smith assess the future of the investment banking industry in Europe. Backed by a wealth of original data, they predict a major growth in four activities: underwriting, corporate financial advisory services (including mergers and acquisition, break up and leveraged buyouts), secondary market trading and brokerage, and portfolio management. The acceleration of corporate restructuring will put substantial demand on European capital markets and competition in investment banking will be fierce. On the regulatory side, they call for a major international effort, possibly at the Bank for International Settlements, to harmonize regulations such as those on anti-trust, take-overs or market making.

The third part of the book concerns the structural adjustments in the banking markets of six countries. In a global assessment of the single European market, Neven applies various tools and models of imperfect competition to the European retail banking industry. In his view, the economic gains will arise not so much from integration but from competitive deregulation. From a detailed analysis of cost structure and productivity, he shows that operating expenses are substantially higher in several countries, such as Belgium, France, Italy and Spain. This is due, in part, to the ability of bank employees to obtain relatively higher salaries. Neven finds useful insights in location theory to evaluate the impact of price deregulation on branching. He shows that the strategic location of branches will be affected by price competition.

The first four countries under investigation, France, Italy, Spain and Portugal, share a common feature in that they have been regulated for many years. De Boissieu analyses France, a country that has experienced a very quick phase of innovation and deregulation in the last few years. He argues that the French securities industry is relatively well positioned in continental Europe because of progress in deregulation, technology (such as the settlement system) and the creation of a very active market in derivative products, the Marché à Terme International de France (MATIF). As far as banking is concerned, he noticed that branch competition has produced a costly intermediation structure, and that freedom of capital flows will force France to reduce taxes on capital income. This will represent a substantial financial burden for the state. Bruni explains that Italy has had one of the most 'repressed' financial systems with capital controls, a high reserve require-ment, and controls on investment to finance the budget deficit. To prepare Italy for the 'European decade', deregulation of capital and credit flows has already been accompanied by major innovations in public debt financing. The question raised in Italy concerns the likeliness or not of a 'discipline effect' of liberalization on the reduction of the budget deficit. Without it, the temptation to go back to regulation would be strong. Bruni argues that the overprotected Italian banking system is still very inefficient and, as a report of the European Community (EC) shows, it is the country where consumers may expect the most from deregulation. It is also the country where the adjustments will be the more important. The Spanish banking system described by Caminal, Gual and Vives shares similar characteristics: a high reserve requirement and portfolio constraint, protection from external competition and lack of innovations. Caminal, Gual and Vives develop a detailed analysis of the forces of competition in Spanish banking. They observe an increase in competition after the very large banking crisis of 1978–83, and potential competition coming from savings banks and new public-debt-related products. Finally, they question the wisdom for big mergers when economies of scale in retail banking are far from evident. In his analysis of Portugal, Borges insists on the tax imposed on the banking system to finance a large and persistent public deficit. He calls for privatization to reduce the financial burden and to prepare the industry for 1993.

The last two countries analysed are Switzerland and Germany. These two countries share some common features, like universal banking, low inflation, low cost structure and deregulation. Moreover, Switzerland is an interesting case as it is not a member of the EC. Swoboda analyses the sources of comparative advantage of international financial centres. Economic and political stability, a supply of universal banking services, banking secrecy and the 'self-inflicted disadvantages' of other countries help Switzerland very much. However, he warns about potential problems such as a lack of innovations due to conservatism, the decreasing importance of bank secrecy with institutional savings and the penalizing tax structure, with a 35 per cent withholding tax (not, however, on fiduciary deposits) and a stamp duty on financial transactions. Swoboda argues that the single market of the EC is unlikely to create problems for the Swiss banking system, globalization and competition issues aside. On regulatory grounds, the Swiss banks are already tightly regulated, and the only worry could be reciprocity, because of fiscal distortion and tax evasion. In this area the Swiss will be helped by current disagreement within the Community which prevents a common system of tax reporting. If common withholding taxes are imposed, the only concern will be for fiduciary deposits. Overall, Swoboda is more concerned with competition issues and the need to increase sophistication in the Swiss banking system.

Rudolph discusses a specific issue of great concern to the German banking community, the capital ratios proposed by the Bank for International Settlements and the Commission. He argues that the extremely conservative approach taken by the regulatory authorities in Germany will penalize the banks, and that the German Banking Act Principle I should be revised to include new capital categories.

The fourth part of the book concerns the Euromarkets and macro-economic policies. Levich attempts to evaluate the impact of European integration on the Euromarkets. Historically, the growth of the Euromarkets is explained by the regulatory burden imposed on domestic institutions in terms of reserve requirement, taxation and disclosure of information and secrecy. Levich argues that the freedom of capital flows will force a competitive deregulation and very probably an overall decrease of the regulatory burden in each country. Nevertheless, Levich believes that prudential regulations for domestic residents and national currencies are likely to remain heavier than for foreign currencies, and that there will still be room for a Euromarket. An important part of the analysis by Wyplosz concerns the functioning of the European Monetary System (EMS). Wyplosz challenges the conventional wisdom according to which the EMS has been an excellent tool to bring down inflation. He observes profound asymmetries in the system, and that the disinflation costs, in terms of reduction in the growth of gross national product (GNP), have been large. Wyplosz argues that the functioning of the

EMS has required capital controls in several countries, such as Italy and France. He suggests more frequent adjustments of parities, if destabilizing capital flows are to be avoided in periods of foreign exchange crisis. Finally, Wyplosz turns to the regional adjustments required by the single market and to the urgent need for efficient regional policies in the EC.

As Europe works on integrating its capital markets, the United States is experiencing interstate banking. Santomero, in the last part of the book, illustrates the lessons that can be relevant in Europe, although, as he cautions, there are substantial differences between the two banking systems. An important result of his analysis is to show that some states, like Delaware or South Dakota, have succeeded in attracting banking business through lower wages, rental costs or taxation. Citibank, the pre-eminent retail banker in the United States, does not use its headquarters location in New York for its US$18 million credit card operation. This suggests that the political process in terms of competitive deregulation, arbitrage or reregulation will play a key role in shaping the future of the European banking industry. A related political issue concerns the acceptance by smaller member countries of the acquisition of their lead banks by outside banking firms. Finally, Santomero questions the likelihood of observing a truly pan-European bank when local recognition is an issue, to say nothing of the language problems.

As the book goes to press, it is a pleasure to acknowledge the support and help from colleagues at INSEAD, namely Professors Walter, Remmers and Wyplosz. The Editor is especially grateful to Charmian Hewett for brilliant assistance in organizing the conference, and to Sally Kenyon for preparing the manuscript.

The Fontainebleau conference was repeated in New York in April 1989, at the invitation of the Salomon Brothers Center at New York University. Thanks are due to the authors for updating their chapters. We hope that readers will share our curiosity in these exciting developments.

Overview:
European Financial Markets—
the Commission's Proposals

Geoffrey Fitchew

The date 1992 has now become a familiar catch-phrase and there is no shortage of articles and conferences on the completion of the European market. I shall first define what 1992 was not. It was not the date when all planned changes in the European market would suddenly come into effect; many of the new measures were in force before 1992. Nor was it simply a date to be aimed at with no real significance; it was backed up by the legal force of the Treaty of Rome itself. It was not a panacea, a cure for all ills, nor was it an attempt to bring about complete harmonization. Equally, it was not a holiday for business; the benefits which will result are essentially for consumers. The White Paper did not in itself tell business managers what they should do; the strategy and tactics were for them to decide.

31 December 1992 was quite simply the date by which the member states of the European Community (EC) were to have removed all remaining barriers to trade within the EC, establishing a single unified market in Europe. The concept itself is not new; it goes right back to the origins of the EEC in the 1950s. The Treaty of Rome clearly envisaged from the outset the creation of a single integrated market free of restrictions on the movement of goods, services, people and capital.

Early progress in the 1960s on removing quotas and tariff barriers in the traded goods sector was good, but by the beginning of the 1980s it was clear that a new impetus was needed for a process which was running out of steam. The European economy was stagnating and there was talk of Euro-sclerosis. Hence the Commission's 1985 White Paper on Completing the Internal Market set out a detailed programme and timetable for the final completion of the framework of the single European market by 31 December 1992. The White Paper programme was approved by the EC heads of state or government the same year, and is given legislative backing by the 1986 Single European Act now incorporated into the Treaty, which defines the internal market as follows:

The views expressed in this chapter are those of the author, not necessarily those of the Commission.

An area without internal frontiers in which the free movement of goods, services, persons and capital is ensured in accordance with the provisions of the Treaty.

The aim therefore was to provide a framework for the widest possible opportunities for increased competition.

In December 1988 the Commission published its Progress Report on completing the internal market. 31 December 1988 marked the half-way point of the programme and, of the 277 proposals, over 90 per cent had been tabled. By that date too, the shape of Europe as it was to be after 31 December 1992 was apparent in its main contours. Over 45 per cent of the proposals had been adopted by the Council of Ministers at that stage.

The Progress Report noted all this as cause for satisfaction and encouragement, but it also showed that many different problems involving controversial areas remained to be solved before achieving free movement of goods, services, labour and capital within the EC. It goes on to reaffirm a commitment to build on the Declarations of both the Hanover Summit of June 1988 and the Rhodes Summit of December 1988 which stated that the major objective of completing the internal market had reached the point where it was irreversible.

The White Paper argued that, to a large extent, a common market already existed for goods and that it was important to foresee a similar development in services, and particularly financial services which play a very important role in the European economy. The financial services sector is of growing importance to the economy of the EC. In terms of output it accounts for about 7 per cent of gross domestic product (GDP) for the EC as a whole. In terms of employment the financial services sector represents about 3 million jobs or about 3.5 per cent of total employment in the EC. At present that market is still fragmented and there are very wide price differences between the cost of financial services throughout the EC.

The Commission proposals to create a single market in financial services had two main components. First, the *sine qua non* of a free market in financial services was the complete liberalization of capital movements. The final stage was adopted in June 1988 when finance ministers agreed to remove all remaining controls on movements of capital, including those of a short-term monetary nature not linked to commercial transactions. The United Kingdom, Germany and the Netherlands had already completely freed capital and five other countries did so by mid-1990. France and Italy, which had already liberalized long-term portfolio investment, acted ahead of time in liberalizing short-term transactions by commercial and industrial firms. Spain, Greece, Portugal and Ireland were allowed more time, but had to come into line by 1992. Indeed, the Irish government decided to remove all restrictions on portfolio investment over one year, as from 1 January 1989. In parallel with this the Commission published proposals on the taxation of savings in order to reduce the risks of large-scale fiscal fraud, once liberalization of capital movements had taken place. This involved the introduction of a basic withholding tax at a proposed rate of 15 per cent.

Second, the Commission aimed to open up the market for financial services by removing barriers to the cross-border marketing of financial services and the free circulation of financial products. The objective was market integration to bring down the costs of insurance, mortgage credit, consumer credit and brokerage services, which in many member states remained high because of lack of national and international competition.

Building on the basic principles of the Treaty and legislation already adopted by the EC, the general method of achieving these objectives which the White Paper adopts was as follows.

1 *The harmonization of essential or key standards* for prudential supervision of financial institutions and for the protection of investors, depositors and consumers;
2 *Mutual recognition* by the supervisory authorities of financial institutions in each member state of the way in which they apply those standards;
3 Based on the first two elements, *home country control and supervision* (i.e. control and supervision by the member state in which the financial institution is based) of financial institutions which wish to operate in other member states either by establishment or by offering their services directly across frontiers.

The White Paper talks of minimum standards, but it has been made clear that key standards are what is meant. The harmonized standards cover the following:

- solvency;
- fitness and properness;
- disclosure of information to clients;
- 'consumer protection' through guarantee funds.

We now look at the three main areas of banking, insurance and securities.

With respect to banking, the Commission put forward a proposal for a directive to allow banks to exercise across frontiers the full range of banking activities that they were allowed to exercise at home. A single licence lay at the heart of this approach. Bank operations throughout the EC would be licensed, regulated and supervised for the most part by the home country. On the basis of that single licence, they would be able to set up any number of branches in other member states without having to obtain agreement from the host country supervisors. Equally, they would be able to market and advertise their services — in principle offering the full range of financial techniques — across frontiers without having a physical presence. It was also proposed that this single banking licence should be valid for all forms of securities business. Given the diversity of national regulatory standards, however, the Commission also proposed harmonizing accounting standards and essential prudential regulation, such as minimum capital and limits on shareholdings in non-financial companies. The proposal on capital standards parallels the recommendation agreed by the Group of Ten Central Bank Governors in Basle in 1988. What was involved was a package of four measures laying down a minimum level of capital (own funds), a harmonized solvency ratio and rules for large risks undertaken by credit institutions as well as deposit guarantee schemes.

Some comments about insurance are included despite the fact that it is not dealt with in this book. This is done for two reasons.

1 It is the sector where we still have the most work ahead of us, the sector where progress has been most slow, almost a sector apart.
2 It is increasingly in competition with other types of financial institutions. In life insurance in particular the products on offer are increasingly difficult to differentiate from other savings or investment trusts offered by banks, portfolio managers and so on. One example is group pensions.

The way forward in the insurance sector was opened up in June 1988 with the adoption of a directive to open up to cross-frontier competition the market in property and damage insurance for so-called 'large risks' — i.e. for the larger commercial and industrial buyers of non-life insurance. From 1992 any large industrial firm would be able to insure directly *all* its buildings, plant and equipment throughout the Community, and indeed worldwide, with the insurer which offers it the most competitive terms. Later on the same will be done for mass risks. In December 1988 the Commission proposed to liberalize the markets in compulsory motor and life insurance. However, it was emphasized that life insurance is a complicated area, and progress was to be made in stages.

The main objectives in the securities sector were as follows:

- to make it easier for companies to treat the EC as a single market for the issue of shares and bonds for obtaining stock exchange listing; and
- to ensure by full and proper disclosure of information that all investors are provided with the information that they need to make the proper assessment of risks associated with an investment.

In the securities sector, an important agreement came into effect in October 1989. This was a directive which liberalized the activities of undertakings for collective investment in transferable securities (UCITS), better known in the United Kingdom as unit trusts or mutual funds and in France as SICAV. A UCITS authorized by its own member state can market its units to investors in any other member state.

A second major proposal covered investment services offered by non-bank investment businesses, such as brokers, dealers and portfolio managers and advisers. As in the banking sector, the aim was to create a single licence which allowed any securities firm to open branches and market a wide range of services in other member states. Home country supervisors would be responsible for the issue of licences, essential regulations (such as capital adequacy) and the acceptability of major shareholders, while host country rules would apply to the remainder. A major feature of this proposal was that it would open up stock exchange membership in all member states. It would not be possible for any stock exchange to impose a numerical ceiling on applicants from other member states.

In the field of disclosure, legislation was introduced to deal with the following:

- harmonizing the conditions for the admission of securities to official stock exchange listing (directive adopted in 1979);
- harmonizing listing particulars for issues on exchanges (directives adopted in 1980 and 1987);
- information to be published on a regular basis by companies whose shares have been admitted to official stock exchange listing (directive adopted in 1982);
- harmonization of the contents of the public offer prospectus;
- the prohibition of insider trading; and
- information to be published when major shareholdings in a company are acquired or disposed of.

By the end of 1988 the Commission had put forward all 25 of the proposals for the financial services sector foreseen in the 1985 White Paper programme but, despite rapid progress since then, it is clear that there are problems still to be tackled.

1 In the insurance field the Commission put forward proposals on group pension schemes and on mass risk insurance in both the life and non-life fields. Progress on these was delayed by problems caused by the European Court Judgement of 1986 which ruled that in future insurance legislation, there was a need for a more detailed harmonization than had been envisaged to give the mass risk − the man in the street − more security through harmonization of technical reserves and harmonization of general and special policy conditions.

2 A second major area that had to be dealt with was capital adequacy rules for secrities traders. This was linked to the proposed Investment Services Directive and had to cover systematic risk. It had to apply equally to banks and non-banks in order to level the ground between them. This was not an easy task given the two different traditions which existed in

the EC: the universal bank tradition with its requirement for 'consolidated' rules, and the Anglo-American tradition which relies on fire-breaks and separate capital adequacy and where the emphasis is on marked to market and liquidity. The dialogue between these two different traditions has begun and is taking place not only in Brussels but also in Basle. Specific problems being tackled are associated with foreign exchange, interest rate risk and position risk.

3   A third area of difficulty was the harmonization of contract law. The Commission has often been asked: 'How can you have a single market with twelve different systems of contract law?' It is clear though that full harmonization of the law of contract is not possible in the foreseeable future. To do so would be a Sisyphean task. However, a choice of contract law does exist under the Rome Convention which was signed in 1981 but has not yet been ratified. This embodies the principle of freedom of choice of contract law, but with a bias in favour of consumer unless own initiative. However, it does not cover insurance or negotiated instruments and in the case of insurance, we may have to fill the gap.

4   A dilemma also exists over the question of public law versus public interest. Exclusion clauses exist in the second banking directive and the investment services directive, but there is no definition of what constitutes public interest. As a result there is a risk of restrictions being introduced in the guise of public interest leading to interference with the free circulation of various financial products. The conundrums which have to be solved here include the restrictions which exist in France on current accounts paying interest, the laws against usury which exist in some member states and laws which exist against indexed loans or variable-rate loans. On the whole the motto we have adopted in this area is *solvitur ambulando*; in other words, to wait until the problems are thrown up and hopefully solved by the market itself. It is clear though that some forays into the field of consumer protection may be necessary.

In summary, what the Commission is trying to do is to create the framework for a liberalized and competitive EC-wide market in financial services. Therefore, the aims being followed are very much in line with the examples of deregulated financial markets elsewhere in the world. The Commission wants the single European market to be a liberalized market in three respects.

1   The barriers to cross-frontier trade in financial services between member states should be brought down.

2   The specialization rules and compartmentalization of European financial markets should largely, though not completely, disappear. Many of the restrictions on who could do what and on what kinds of financial

investment could be bought and sold will be removed. (The long list of activities for which the single banking licence would be valid is proof of this.)

3 Finally, the market should be liberalized in the sense that it will be open to the rest of the world.

On this final point, concerns are being expressed as to whether the playing field is going to be level for third-country companies wishing to compete in the European market. Unfortunately a lot of nonsense is talked about this subject. Talk of 'Fortress Europe' helps nobody and, to say the least, some of the reactions have been immoderate and unjustified by anything the Commission has said or written. This needs to be overcome by careful management of the relationship. The Commission made its position on the situation very clear on 19 October 1988 when it stated that the 'internal market should not close in on itself'. That statement was firmly endorsed by the European Council meeting in Rhodes. As global financial markets move rapidly to 24-hour trading, it is vital that the European market remains open if we are to retain a growing share of the market in services. A single market – a European financial market – open to the world will act as a stimulus for continued worldwide liberalization of banking and financial markets. At the same time, however, we quite reasonably want to make sure that European banks and other financial institutions have satisfactory access to third-country markets. That is why 'reciprocity' clauses are included in banking and other directives. We need to be well armed for the General Agreement on Tariffs and Trade (GATT) and other negotiations. However, the intention is that it would only be used as a last resort.

This brings me to the conclusion of my comments. I hope that I have shown that we have a coherent and achievable approach to the creation of a single market in financial services, that we have already made great strides towards it, but that we still have much left to do.

The Regulation of Financial Markets in Europe

European Banking: Prudential and Regulatory Issues

Ernst Baltensperger and Jean Dermine

Europeans like to refer to the European Community (EC) as the 'Common Market', but 35 years after the 1957 Treaty of Rome, the Common Market remains in many respects an aspiration yet to be realized. This is particularly true in the banking and financial services industry where differences in regulations, prior authorization to do business and restrictions on capital flow in some countries have prevented the creation of a fully integrated European banking market. It was this recognition that led to the publication in 1983 of a White Policy Paper calling for more integrated financial markets. At the Council of Ministers held in Milan in 1985, the European Commission proposed a detailed timetable for the completion of the internal market by 1993. In December 1991, the Maastricht agreement on a draft Treaty on Economic Union marked an important step in the process of European monetary and financial integration. The regulatory impulse by the European authorities has been matched on the field by a large number of domestic and cross-border mergers and acquisitions. In the Netherlands for instance, two mergers have created the ABN-AMRO bank and the financial services group ING, which combines banking and insurance activities.

To succeed in the achievement of a fully integrated banking market, the European Commission has acted along three main axes: promotion of free entry and non-discriminatory supply of financial services for EC banks, the development of fair competition and the design of an appropriate legal framework to protect consumers. The prudential issues raised by European integration are reviewed in this chapter in the light of recent developments in the banking literature. Two major questions are addressed. The first concerns the existence of failures in the functioning of private markets which call for public intervention. The second concerns specific problems raised by the integration of previously segmented banking markets.[1]

In international banking, as long as national monetary and supervisory authorities do not delegate their responsibilities to a supranational authority,

The authors are grateful to Damien Neven for helpful discussion.

the integration of banking markets raises two specific issues. The first concerns supervision and regulation. Does domestic regulation apply to other banks operating in the country ('national treatment principle') or does it apply to the foreign component of domestic banks ('home country principle')?

The second issue concerns the extent of responsibility of the domestic lender of last resort and of the domestic deposit insurance system. Do they cover branches or subsidiaries of domestic banks operating abroad? Do they cover branches and subsidiaries of foreign banks operating domestically?

The European Commission has adopted the principle of home country control for banking supervision (supervision by the parent bank's regulator on a consolidated basis), but many countries have adopted the 'national treatment principle' for deposit insurance (deposits of domestic and foreign banks are insured on a national basis). We shall argue that this approach is sound as far as the protection of consumers is concerned. However, in our view, it could create potential problems if the main concern is the stability of the financial systems and the prevention of systemic crisis leading to default of solvent banks. We argue that the protection of consumers of financial services is, in many respects, similar to the control of the safety of industrial goods. This explains the parallelism adopted by the Commission between industry and financial intermediaries and the choice for home country control. However, we argue that the production of financial services may create externalities which are borne by the host country, so that the host country authorities should keep supervisory control responsibilities. To pursue the comparison with industrial goods, we argue that the externalities in bank production are similar to pollution in industrial plants located abroad, i.e. pollution that host countries should control. Therefore as long as monetary and supervisory authorities do not delegate their powers to a supranational authority, we recommend that they keep full responsibility for domestic operations. A second conclusion concerns the need to increase private incentives for monitoring risk. We suggest dismantling the deposit insurance systems currently in place and relying exclusively on interventions by the lender of last resort to maintain the stability of banking markets. The case for stability is particularly relevant in a period of deregulation and integration of banking markets which, as our empirical evidence shows, do differ significantly.

The chapter is organized as follows. A short description of the European banking industry is given in section 1.1. The proposals by the European Commission are reviewed in section 1.2. In section 1.3 we discuss the sources of potential market failure calling for public intervention. Finally, in section 1.4 we argue that the major reason for banking regulation should be the stability of banking markets and that, as long as national monetary authorities do not delegate their power to a supranational authority, they should keep full responsibility for their domestic markets.

1.1 European Banking: Some Data

Aggregate data on the banking systems in the 12 EC member countries, the United States, Japan and Switzerland are given in table 1.1. Savings and mutual banks have been included as these institutions compete directly with commercial banks. The assets of these 'secondary' banks represent 50 per cent of the assets of the commercial banking system in the EC.

Our count of financial institutions in the EC adds up to a total of 4,661 banks, compared with about 16,000 in the United States and 1,225 in Japan. The size of banking systems relative to GDP is 170 per cent in the EC, 84 per cent in the United States and 280 per cent in Japan. 'Banked' countries in Europe include Belgium, Luxembourg, Switzerland and the United Kingdom. Data on the market share of the five largest institutions are also reported. If there is evidence of concentration at the national level, this is not the case at the EC level where the market share of the largest five institutions is 14 per cent. The process of European globalization is in its initial phase, especially in the retail market. It is being encouraged by the proposals of the European Commission.

1.2 European Banking from 1957 to 1992

To understand fully the prudential issues at stake and the process of European banking integration, it is useful to review the major actions undertaken by the Brussels Commission and the Council of Ministers. Three time periods can be distinguished: deregulation of entry to domestic markets from 1957 to 1973, various attempts towards harmonization of banking regulations from 1973 to 1983, and the recent proposal of freedom of cross-border services, single banking licence, home country control and mutual recognition. The contents of directives, recommendations and proposals by the Commission are briefly summarized below. A complete list is reproduced in the appendix.

1.2.1 Deregulating Entry, 1957–1973

The objective of the 1957 Treaty of Rome was the transformation of highly segmented national markets into a common single market. This objective was to be achieved by two types of measures: the recognition of the right of establishment and the coordination of legislation whenever necessary.[2] Proposals for directives are drafted by the Commission and must be approved by the Council of Ministers.[3]

Table 1.1   Summary statistics on selected banking systems, end 1989

	Belgium	Denmark	France	Germany	Greece	Ireland	Italy
No. of commercial banks	85	76	404	299	34	33	267
No. of savings and mutual banks	29	165	421	594[b]	–	2	813
Assets of commercial banks (billion ECU)	238.7	93.20	771	518	39	20	588
Assets of other depository institutions (billion ECU)	40.60	–	411.50	1,085	19	13.7	246
GDP (billion ECU)	141.10	92.40	868.80	1,072	48.70	26.90	783
Total assets/GDP	1.98	1	1.89	2.4	1.20	1.25	1.07
Population (millions)	9.90	5.13	56.20	62	10	3.50	57.50
Market share of five largest institutions (%)	58	77	43	26	63	45	53
ECU rate (domestic currency per ECU)	43.40	8.05	7.02	2.07	179	0.77	1,510

Sources: OECD and national sources.
[a] Includes city and regional banks.
[b] Does not include 3,225 cooperative credit institutions.

In July 1965, the Commission proposed a Directive on the Abolition of Restrictions on Freedom of Establishment and Freedom to Provide Services in Respect of Self-employed Activities of Banks and other Financial Institutions. This directive, which was adopted by the Council in June 1973, ensures the equal treatment of national and other firms of member states with regard to entry into domestic markets and the conditions under which banks can operate. It is explicitly recognized that subsidiaries of banks whose parent companies are established in non-member countries are to be regarded as EC undertakings in every way. As Clarotti (1984) noted, very little discrimination remained as to entry in member states. However, the objectives of the initial Treaty were still far from being met. Although the original Treaty and the 1973 directive called for it, international competition through the supply of cross-border services was severely limited by restrictions on capital flow. Explicitly mentioned in Article 67 of the Rome Treaty and fully incorporated in the 1960 and 1962 directives, the liberalization of capital flow should have been enforced, but several countries (France, Italy, Denmark and Ireland) have availed themselves of the right conferred in the Treaty of Rome to guard against disequilibrium in the

Table 1.1 *Continued*

Luxembourg	Netherlands	Portugal	Spain	UK	EC	USA	Japan	Switzerland
166	89	29	145	556	2,183	12,689	145[a]	236
49	53	1	188	163	2,478	3,323	1,080	214
239	345	45	400	1,745	5,002.90	2,754	4,183	399
–	222.70	–	175.30	283.40	2,497	1,033	3,100	382
5.43	203	39.40	343	764	4,387	5,720	2,623	170
44	2.80	1.14	1.70	2.65	1.70	0.84	2.80	4.60
0.37	14.80	10.50	38.90	57.20	326	247	123.50	6.50
26	84	56	39	29	14	14	25	60
43.40	2.33	173	130	0.67	–	1.10	152	1.80

balance of payment to defer this freedom. Moreover, the accession treaties for the new member states (Spain, Portugal and Greece) provide for time lags in the implementation of this directive. Only five countries out of 12 have so far fully liberalized their capital flow (Belgium, Germany, Luxembourg, the Netherlands and the United Kingdom). Furthermore, there was no coordination of banking supervision, so that banks operating in different countries could be subject to different rules. For example, capital earmarked for branches would be required in many countries. This led to the second phase of attempts to harmonize regulations.

1.2.2 Harmonization of Banking Regulations, 1973–1983

Progress in harmonization came in 1977 with the adoption of the First Directive on the Coordination of Laws, Regulation and Administrative Provisions Relating to the Taking up and Pursuit of Credit Institutions. This directive established a definition of credit institutions (Article 1): 'Undertaking whose business is to receive deposits and other repayable funds from the public and to grant credit for its own account'. The principle of home country control was established. The supervision of credit institutions operating in several member countries is gradually being shifted from the host country to the home country of the parent bank. The 1977 Directive was a first step towards the harmonization of regulation. It was a general programme which, without providing any specific regulation, called for further directives. A first result of the 1977 Directive was the creation of a Banking Advisory Committee, whose first task was to work on liquidity and solvency ratios for a trial period. Second, a directive on the Supervision of Credit Institutions on a Consolidated Basis, which was proposed in 1981, was adopted in 1983. Two other directives on a Uniform Format for Bank Account and on Consumer Protection were adopted in 1986. The 1977 Directive also initiated work on winding up and liquidation, and on the mortgage market.

After the First Banking Directive in 1977 and the directives mentioned above, the European banking markets were still far from full integration for four major reasons.

1   A bank wishing to operate in another country still had to be authorized by the supervisors of the other country.
2   The bank remained subject to supervision by the host country and its range of activities could be constrained by host country laws.
3   In most countries, branches had to be provided with earmarked endowment capital as if they were new banks.
4   Finally, the supply of cross-border services was severely impaired by the restrictions on capital flows.

The full harmonization of national regulations seemed to be a complicated task which prompted a new approach towards European integration.

1.2.3   The Completion of the Internal Market by 1992, 1983–1992

In April 1983, a White Policy Paper on financial integration called for further work to achieve a better allocation of savings and investment in the EC. Following various European Councils, at the Milan meeting in 1985 the Commission proposed its White Paper on the completion of the internal market by 1992. In short, the Paper called for the removal of the physical, technical and fiscal barriers in all industries by 1 January 1993. The content of the White Paper was incorporated into the 1986 Single European Act which, in addition to calling for the effective integration of markets, increased the consultancy role of the European Parliament and allowed qualified majority (instead of unanimity) for a large number of decisions (although not on fiscal matters).[4] The 1991 Maastricht agreement on economic and monetary union details the statute for a European system of central banks.

In the context of banking, the White Paper called for a single banking licence, home country control and mutual recognition. These principles are incorporated in the 1988 proposal for a Second Banking Directive. All credit institutions authorized in one European country were to be able to establish or supply financial services without further authorization. They were to be able to undertake all the activities listed in the annex of the Second Directive, provided that these activities are not forbidden by the home country supervisor.

The list included most activities of universal banks, except for the delivery of insurance services:

1 Deposit-taking and other forms of borrowing
2 Lending
3 Financial leasing
4 Money transmission services
5 Issuing and administering means of payments (credit cards, travellers' cheques and bankers' drafts)
6 Guarantees and commitments
7 Trading for own account or for account of the customers in
   (a) Money market instruments (cheques, bills, credit deposits, etc.)
   (b) Foreign exchange
   (c) Financial futures and options
   (d) Exchange and interest rate instruments
   (e) Securities
8 Participation in share issues and the provision of services related to such issues
9 Money broking
10 Portfolio management and advice
11 Safekeeping of securities
12 Credit reference services
13 Safe custody services.

The Directive called for home country control on solvency and large exposure but recognized explicitly that host country regulation would apply for monetary policy reasons and for market position risk. Recognizing that full competition requires a fair level playing field and harmonization of regulation, the Second Banking Directive called for minimal equity (5 million European Currency Units (ECU)), supervisory control of major shareholders and the permanent participation of banks in the non-financial sector (less than 15 per cent of equity for a single holding and less than 60 per cent in total, unless funded exclusively with equity).

The Second Directive was accompanied by two recommendations on large risk exposure and on deposit insurance and by proposals for directives on reorganization and winding up, own funds, solvency ratios and accounting for foreign branches.

Winding up and liquidation: mutual recognition by host authorities of actions taken by the home country; liquidation decided by the home country although actions could be taken by host country according to its own legislation.

Large risk exposure: credit institutions may not incur an exposure to a client or to a group of connected clients in excess of 40 per cent of own funds. In aggregate, large exposures may not exceed 800 per cent of own funds. A draft directive proposes to limit large exposure to 25 per cent of own funds.

Deposit insurance: call for deposit insurance in all countries with the requirement that branches of institutions having their head office outside national territory must join the deposit guarantee scheme of the host country.[5] As is discussed below, a draft directive on deposit insurance is under discussion.

Own funds and capital ratios: basically in agreement with the Bank for International Settlements' proposals but enforceable on all European banks.[6]

Accounting for foreign branches: branches whose parent banks are established in another member state will not need to publish separate accounts.

Accompanying this process was the proposal for full liberalization of capital flows. A directive adopted in 1986 liberalized a slightly expanded list of flows mentioned in the 1960 and 1962 directives, but in June 1988 in Luxembourg, the Council of Finance Ministers adopted a directive on the complete liberalization of capital movements by June 1990. Exceptions included Ireland, Spain and Portugal (1992) and possibly Greece (1995). By June 1989, the Commission had to come up with a proposal to harmonize fiscal laws and a reinforcement of the European Monetary System. It should be noted that this directive contains a safeguard clause authorizing member states to take the necessary measures in the event of balance-of-payments problems.

Finally, at the December 1991 Maastrict meeting, the heads of states or governments reached an agreement on economic and monetary union. A European system of central banks will be created in 1999 (possibly earlier), embracing the national central banks and headed by a new monetary institution, the European Central Bank (ECB). Although the primary objective of the European System of Central Banks is to maintain price stability, there are explicit references to regulation and supervision. 'The ECB may offer advice to and be consulted by the Council, the Commission and the competent authorities of the member states in the scope and implementation of Community legislation relating to prudential supervision of credit institutions and to the stability of the financial system. The ECB may fulfil a specific task concerning policies relating to the prudential supervision of credit institutions and other financial institutions with the exception of insurance undertakings' (Draft Treaty on Economic Union, Article 105, section 6). On a proposal by the Commission and unanimity of the Council, supervisory tasks could be given to the European Central Bank.

Although the topic is discussed elsewhere in this book, let us just mention that as far as the securities industry is concerned – an industry in which banks have been very active recently – various directives aimed at increasing information to investors have been issued. In the business of undertakings in transferable securities (the so-called UCITS, unit trust or SICAV), a 1985 directive ensured that a single licence and freedom of cross-border services with compliance with local marketing regulations came into existence by October 1989. Quite controversial and still under discussion with various national authorities is a draft directive on 'Investment Services in the Securities Field'. Like the Second Banking Directive, it calls for home country control.

From this review of the directives, recommendations and proposals for directives, it appears that the objective pursued by the European Commission is threefold: free entry and provisions of financial services throughout the EC, the establishment of a fair level playing field with a single banking licence, home country control, mutual recognition and minimal harmonization on equity, accounting, ownership and participation in the non-financial sector, and finally consumer protection. In this respect, reference (e.g. 1985 White Paper; Clarotti, 1987) is often made to the European Court of Justice case 'Cassis de Dijon' according to which control of the quality of a product is warranted but can be met fully by the home country supervisor. However, reference is also made to the 1986 non-life insurance Court case according to which control by host authorities can be accepted as long as it is justified on the grounds of 'public interest'. A second major illustration of the perceived need for consumer protection is the Directive and Recommendation on Deposit Insurance:

Member states shall ensure that the deposit-guarantee schemes that exist in their territory cover the deposits of branches of institutions having their head office in another member state. As a transitional measure, pending entry into force of a deposit-guarantee scheme in all member states, the latter shall ensure that the deposit-guarantee scheme, in which the institutions that have their head office in their territory take part, extend cover to deposits received by branches set up in host countries within the Community which have no deposit-guarantee scheme, under the same conditions as those laid down to guarantee deposits received in the home country (Article 16).

Examination of the proposals for directives suggests that one of the major reasons for public intervention in banking is the premise that consumers of financial services need to be protected. In order to assess the European framework, it is useful to review the banking literature and analyse the sources of potential market failure and the economic need for banking supervision. This is the object of section 1.3.

1.3   The Economics of Banking Regulation

Following the approach proposed by Baltensperger and Dermine (1987a), extended further by Eisenbeis (1987), we review the major services provided by banks and analyse the potential sources of market failure. Although the services provided by banks are interrelated, it is convenient to distinguish four categories: portfolio management, payment (transmission) mechanism, risk sharing and monitoring or information-related services.

Portfolio management: at low cost, investors can acquire a diversified portfolio of liabilities issued by deficit spending units. The pure case is the SICAV, mutual fund or unit trust which allows the holder of a share to have access to a diversified portfolio of liabilities.

Payment mechanism: a second role for banks in the economy is the management of the payment system, that is to facilitate and keep track of transfer of wealth among individuals. This is the book-keeping activity of banks realized by debiting and crediting accounts.

If an institution were to offer only these two services, its shares would be valued at current market price every day and shareholders would earn the market rate of return, adjusted for risk, less a fee retained by the intermediary for managing the investment pool and the payment mechanism.

Risk-sharing services: an essential function of banks is to transform the risks faced by the parties, i.e. to supply risk-sharing contracts. First, banks not only provide a diversified asset, they also organize efficiently the distribution of the risky income earned on the asset pool. The deposit holders (the depositors) receive a fixed payment while the shareholders receive the residual income. Other insurance services would include liquidity insurance (option for the deposit holder to withdraw quickly at face value), interest rate insurance (floating-rate lending with various ceilings on interest rate) and in principle any type of risk such as income variability (mortgage contract with insurance provision related to unemployment).

Monitoring or information-related services: banks perform a useful function in reducing the cost of screening and monitoring borrowers. As Diamond (1984) has shown, private information held by borrowers results in contracting problems, and the delegation of screening and monitoring to banks is an efficient allocation mechanism. In addition to the classical lending function of banks, most of the 'investment banking' activities such as underwriting and distribution of securities, trust or fiduciary services, merger and acquisition, and risk/treasury management can be included in information-related services.

As has been argued in the literature (Fama, 1980), if banks were to provide only the first two services − portfolio and transmission − there would be no special need for banking regulation. However, recent literature on insurance and monitoring services shows that the contract that emerges – *illiquid assets financed by short-term deposits* – creates a potential market failure and a need for public intervention. Three independent explanations can be advanced: the public good character of information gathering and monitoring, the macro-economic externality resulting from a bank default and the potential for bank runs and systemic crisis.

1.3.1 Information and Consumer Protection

The first argument is that the evaluation of bank risks is a costly activity which has the nature of a public good. Once it is produced, it is available to consumers at very low transfer cost. As such the monitoring and evaluation of banks should not be undertaken by each depositor but could be delegated to a public agency or a private rating firm. Furthermore, since holders of small accounts may find the cost of interpreting the rating high and/or since they care only about risk-free deposits, two alternatives could be developed. The first is to have deposit insurance. The second is to create risk-free banks, i.e. intermediaries investing all deposits in risk-free securities. Depositors would have the choice between banks offering a higher but risky return and those providing quasi-risk-free deposits.

Our view on public information is that in this respect the banking industry does not differ much from any other industry. The major difference is that a large set of depositors may prefer a risk-free deposit. As such, this does not require public intervention in addition to what is required for the securities industry in terms of disclosure of information.

1.3.2 Macro-domino Externality

The second possible source of market failure is that the insolvency of one bank or group of banks (domino effect) is costly because information on borrowers is being lost. Borrowers would need to turn to other banks at more expensive credit terms. The externality does not arise from the loss of information *per se* – this is a private cost and borrowers should deal with safe banks – but comes rather from a macro-economic effect which is not internalized by the borrower. More expensive credit terms imply lower investment and unemployment. Although it is likely that large failures in the banking industry would produce this effect (Bernanke, 1983), we find two reasons for disregarding this argument. The first is that a large failure is an extraordinary event which does not warrant permanent intervention, particularly in view of the regulatory costs involved. Second, in most cases insolvent banks are taken over by other banks, precisely to avoid the costs due to losses of information. Therefore, we have to rely on other sources of market failure to justify permanent banking regulation.

1.3.3 Bank Runs

An argument formalized by Diamond and Dybvig (1983), and further expanded by Postlewaite and Vives (1987), Jacklin and Bhattacharya (1988) and Freeman (1988), is that an important activity of banks is to finance illiquid assets with short-term deposits. This creates the potential risk that savers run to withdraw their funds. A run can be triggered by bad news about the value of bank assets or by any unexplained fear. In both cases there is a cost, since illiquid assets may have to be sold at a loss. Moreover, a bank failure could eventually trigger a signal on the solvency of other banks, leading to a systemic crisis. A market failure occurs because a cooperative solution among depositors cannot be enforced. Collectively, there is no incentive to run but individually there is the incentive to be the first in the line to collect the deposit at full face value. In our view, it is the financing of illiquid assets with short-term deposits and the potential for bank runs which explains the need for public intervention and the establishment of a safety net to guarantee the stability of the financial system.

Three features of European insurance systems make them unique. The first is that, contrary to the Federal Deposit Insurance Corporation in America, the public is totally ignorant of their existence. Publicity is even forbidden in Germany. The argument seems to be that the announcement of their creation could destabilize the confidence in the banking system. Since deposit insurance systems are unknown and the coverage is small (incomplete in the United Kingdom), they are unlikely to contribute much to stability and one would have to rely on lender of last resort interventions by central banks to ensure stability. Secondly, as shown in table 1.2, the coverage is different across countries. This could be destabilizing if depositors start to chase the best coverage. A third feature of European deposit insurance mechanisms is that they cover the deposits of domestic and foreign banks operating locally. This could create potential difficulties. Indeed, any insurance activity requires the monitoring of the risks taken by the insuree, but the principle of home supervision would not allow the control of foreign entities by the domestic deposit insurance agency.

Since European deposit insurance systems are not widely known to the public, it seems certain that they do not meet the objective of preventing runs on banks. One is left wondering about the motivation for their recent creation. European deposit insurance systems can be interpreted as a tool for creating small risk-free deposits, while putting part of the cost of bailing out on the insurance fund funded by the banking industry. As it is responsible in the end, the banking industry would act as a 'banking club' which would regulate its members (Goodhart, 1985). This motivation is understandable, but it would seem that alternative institutional mechanisms can meet the same objectives: the creation of risk-free banks would provide risk-free deposits to those who wish to hold them, and the financing of the cost of bailing out an institution by the banking sector can be enforced without recourse to a deposit insurance system.

Three different issues have to be distinguished: the supply of risk-free deposits, the responsibility of the banking industry and the promotion of financial stability.

Table 1.2 Deposit insurance systems

Country	Coverage (domestic currency)	Coverage (ECU)
Belgium	BFr 500,000	11,520
Denmark	DKr 250,000	31,056
France	FFr 400,000	56,980
Germany	30% of equity per deposit	
Ireland	£IRL 10,000	12,987
Italy	L 1 billion (100% for first 200 mil. and 75% for next 800)	662,000
Luxembourg	FLux 500,000	11,520
Netherlands	DFl 40,000	17,167
Spain	Pta 1,500,000	11,536
United Kingdom	75% of deposits up to £20,000	22,388
Greece	No system	
Portugal	No system	
Japan	Yen 10,000,000	65,789
United States	$100,000	90,909

It is our view that current European proposals do not fully address the third issue, financial stability. In this respect, three sets of questions have to be addressed. Is there any evidence of liquidity transformation and is the risk of a bank run relevant? Second, what are the various mechanisms to foster stability? Third, since bank riskiness has to be controlled, what are the best policies in this respect?

Empirical evidence on liquidity transformation is clear. In the United Kingdom, France and Belgium, only 70 per cent of deposits with less than three months to maturity are matched by liquid assets with equivalent maturity. It is symptomatic that supervisors treat retail liquid deposits as core stable funds. They will be the first to run in case of difficulties. How serious is this risk? No firm answer can be given, but it can be noted that periods of deregulation and increasing competition are likely to see the disappearance of infra-marginal firms which could potentially destabilize the banking market. We present in table 1.3 data showing differences in the structure of European banking markets for further information.

Table 1.3 Interest margins and operating expenses

	Belgium	Denmark	France	Germany	Greece	Ireland	Italy
Average margin on demand deposits[a]							
(1980−5) (%)	11.20	16.20	11.70	6.50			4.30
(1987−91) (%)	8.70	9.00	9.70	7.20			
Average margin on savings deposits[a]							
(1980−5) (%)	5.60	8.90	4.30	2.80			3.40
(1987−91) (%)	3.90	7.00	5.20	2.20			
Population per branch	1,816	1,677	2,189	1,564			3,800
Operating expenses per asset in banks[c] (%)	2.60	2.80	3.20	2.50			3.00
Operating expenses as percentage of gross margin	0.66	0.65	0.65	0.65	0.76		0.63

[a] Current short-term rate minus interest rate paid on deposits.
[b] Does not include 22,000 branches of postal savings banks.
[c] Excludes interbank assets; expenses on non-interbank is calculated as follows: total expenses minus (interbank assets × 1/8%).

The first part of the table shows evidence of substantial differences in interest margins in the retail market. High margins are observed in Belgium, Denmark, France, Spain and the United Kingdom. The joint effect of inflation, higher interest rate and deposit rate regulation is quite evident in the period 1980−5. Countries with lower margins include Germany, Italy, the Netherlands and Switzerland. However, the period of 1987−91 is indicative of a convergence process in interest rate margins. Margins are decreasing in the first group of countries, while they are going up in the Netherlands and Germany. This is due to a general movement of deregulation and a convergence of interest rate levels in the European Monetary System. As has been emphasized in the literature, if non-price competition occurs, it is likely to lead to free services, overbranching and higher operating expenses. Data on average operating expenses per asset (interbank assets excluded) and as a percentage of gross margin, and population per branch are reported in the second part of table 1.3. Although it is necessary to be cautious with aggregate data since the structure of bank assets and the size of branches could vary across countries, it would appear that operating expenses are rather high in Belgium, France, Spain and the United Kingdom, and lower in Italy, Germany, the Netherlands and Switzerland. This corresponds to the high−low margins breakdown. Entry to markets with high margins could undermine the stability of domestic institutions locked up with

Table 1.3 *continued*

Luxembourg	Netherlands	Portugal	Spain	UK	USA	Japan	Switzerland
	5.60		14.50	10.80	9.00	5.60	4.80
	6.80		6.00	7.00	7.50	5.40	6.80
	2.80		10.70	2.50	1.00	3.80	1.30
	4.70		9.00	2.00	1.00	2.00	2.60
	2,000	6,031	1,127			8,700[b]	1,622
1.00	2.50	2.50	3.50	4.20	3.50	1.00	1.95
0.41	0.65	0.47	0.60	0.65	0.61	0.61	0.55

high fixed costs. As it is well known that incentives to risk taking are the highest when a bank is close to insolvency, it would imply that supervisors need to increase their monitoring efforts in this period of deregulation. Fortunately, the recent requirement on equity standards could facilitate the restructuring of the banking industry. Indeed, infra-marginal firms will be unable to raise fresh equity to meet the new standards and will be forced to merge with sounder institutions.

A major result of the banking literature is that the need for public intervention comes from the potential instability in banking markets. The question about the best ways to achieve stability remains. Three ways can be distinguished. The first is to adapt the current framework with its deposit insurance and lender of last resort facilities. A second approach suggests relying exclusively on discretionary lender of last resort interventions, while the third suggests abandoning the safety net completely while adapting the contractual terms of the liquid deposits.

The current approach could be improved if the various deposit insurance systems offered the same coverage and if domestic supervision applied to all institutions, domestic or foreign, covered by the insurance or the lender of last resort safety nets. Also, these insurance systems should be advertised. The major weakness with this system is that it reduces private incentives to monitor risks.[7] A recent draft proposal of the Commission proposes to organize deposit insurance on a consolidated basis, along the lines of the 'home country' principle. All the deposits of a consolidated bank would be insured by the deposit insurance of the parent bank. A new issue would be raised in this case. Since deposits of foreign banks located in one country would be insured by different insurance mechanisms, there would be a need to harmonize the coverage to ensure fair competition.

The second approach would be to abandon deposit insurance and to rely exclusively on the lender of last resort. As has been argued by Tobin (1987) and Goodfriend and King (1987), this is a function of the central bank that should be used extremely rarely. Indeed, there are strong presumptions that, if problems arise, deposits tend to flow to well-managed banks so that there is no need to fear massive runs. The major advantage of a discretionary safety net as opposed to a more systematic insurance is that it increases private incentives for monitoring and evaluating bank riskiness. As in the first proposal, the safety net is still in place and would be made available only to institutions financing illiquid assets with short-term deposits (Corrigan, 1986). The cost of bailing out would be borne by the banking industry which would find it necessary to monitor its members. As central banks would be primarily concerned with the stability of their domestic market, it would seem necessary that they keep some supervisory powers on all institutions operating domestically. An alternative would be to have the ECB in charge of international banks with significant risks located abroad. This mechanism is in principle allowed by the Maastricht Treaty but requires the unanimity of member states.

The third approach, already discussed by Baltensperger and Dermine (1987a), is to attack the problem of bank runs at its root. Since it is the absence of cooperation among depositors and the hope of being the first to withdraw that causes the run, why not impose the cost of bankruptcy *ex post* on all current and former depositors. The incentives to run would be reduced since there would be no place to hide to avoid the losses. The two difficulties with this proposal are the definition of the time of failure and the enforcement of the *ex post* penalty. The time of failure needs to be defined so that the penalty falls only on those who have withdrawn their funds after the failure. Enforcement of the penalty would require the means to identify depositors and the ability to tax them. A major difference between the *ex post* penalty and a public safety net is that in the first case losses are borne by depositors while in the second case they are shifted to the public agency. The complete privatization of costs is a clear advantage.

Recognizing that under current legal systems the enforcement of the *ex post* penalty would be difficult, we favour the second proposal − a discretionary intervention system with a lender of last resort. The objective of financial stability is being met with this proposal, while the private incentives for monitoring risk still remain since public intervention is uncertain. As there would be some cases of bailing out, the public authorities would naturally want to limit their exposure. This is traditionally achieved through equity and liquidity ratios and bank inspection of credit exposure and market position risk. A useful framework in this respect is the probability of ruin theory discussed by Boyd and Graham (1988) and Saunders (1987). The probability of insolvency is lower, the larger the equity to asset ratio, the larger the profit and the smaller the variance of return.[8] This framework emphasizes two aspects. The first is that control of risk (variance) may be counterproductive if it reduces profitability. Second, only total risk matters, and therefore, as stressed by Schaefer (1987), more attention should be paid to diversification and not just to individual risks as is done by current equity standards. A special issue in this respect is the risk arising from the relationship between industry and commerce. Bankers have argued that they should be allowed to enter into new activities, such as insurance brokerage and under-writing, real estate development, management consulting and information processing, to improve their profitability. Their argument is that banks would benefit from economies of scope and reduced costs. This may come from shared inputs in production (such as financial information), reduced marketing costs or benefits from financial diversification. Quite naturally, regulators have constrained the activities of banks to reduce the size of their safety nets.

Although the extent of economies of scope has yet to be demonstrated, it has also to be shown that a relationship between banking and commerce would indeed increase risks. The proposal for a Second Banking Directive is not very explicit on this subject and leaves it to national supervisors to regulate the ownership of banks and the participations of credit institutions in non-financial firms. Holding company structures owning banks and non-banks (the case in France and Belgium) would coexist with banks having an interest in non-financial firms (Germany) or more severely restricted banks. It appears that harmonization should be enforced in this respect and that banking entities who benefit *de facto* from a safety net should be separated from other non-bank affiliates. One way is to follow the Federal Reserve regulation which prohibits various financial transactions (such as loan or sale of asset) between affiliates (Black et al., 1978; Litan, 1987). Deregulation and financial integration are pushing non-banks into banking activities and banks into non-banking; it would seem appropriate to define and limit the extent of the public safety net.

1.4 Conclusions

We argue that the main reason for public intervention in banking is the stability of financial markets. This does not imply the systematic protection of depositors. As long as national authorities do not delegate their powers to a supranational authority, we recommend that they keep full responsibility for domestic markets. This is justified because a bank failure will affect the local economy, the deposit insurance system or the lender of last resort. Supervision should not be entirely delegated to the supervisor of the parent bank. An alternative consistent with the Maastricht Treaty is to delegate the supervision of international banks with significant risk located abroad to the ECB. To increase private incentives for monitoring risk, we suggest dismantling the deposit insurance systems currently in place and relying exclusively (but in extreme cases only) on lender of last resort interventions. As some depositors will prefer risk-free deposits, it would be efficient to create risk-free banks, i.e. banks investing mostly in safe assets. Portfolio allocation by investors will show the extent of this need. Finally, it would seem that the case for the stability of banking markets is particularly relevant today with the deregulation and integration of previously segmented markets.

Appendix Directives, Proposals for Directives and Recommendations Related to the Integration of European Banking Markets

1 Directive on the abolition of restrictions on freedom of establishment and freedom to provide services in respect of self-employed activities of banks and other financial institutions, 28 June 1973, Directive 73/183, O.J.L. 194/1 of 16 July 1973.
2 First directive on the coordination of laws, regulations and administrative provisions relating to the taking up and pursuit of the business of credit institutions, 12 December 1977, Directive 77/780, O.J.L. 32/30 of 17 December 1977.
3 Financial Integration, Communication from the Commission to the Council, 1983.
4 Directive on the supervision of credit institutions on a consolidated basis, 13 June 1983, Directive 83/350, O.J.L. L193/18 of 8 July 1983.
5 White Paper on the completion of the internal market, 14 June 1985, COM (85) 310 final.
6 Directive on the annual accounts and consolidated accounts of banks and other financial institutions, 8 December 1986, Directive 86/635, O.J.L. L372/1.
7 Directive on the coordination of laws, regulations and administrative provisions relating to consumer credit, 22 December 1986, 87/102, O.J.L. 42/48, 12 February 1987.
8 Proposal for a directive on the obligations of branches established in a member state by credit institutions having their head offices outside the member state regarding the publication of annual accounting documents (amended proposal), 7 March 1988, COM (88) 118 final.

9 Proposal for a directive concerning the reorganization and the winding up of credit institutions and deposit guarantee schemes (amended proposal), 11 January 1988, COM (88) 4 final.

10 Proposal for a directive on the own funds of credit institutions, 15 January 1988, COM (88) 15 final.

11 Recommendation concerning the introduction of deposit guarantee schemes in the community, 87/63, O.J.L. 33/16 of 4 February 1987.

12 Recommendation on monitoring and controlling large exposures of credit institutions, 22 December 1986, 87/62. O.J.L. L33, 10 of 4 February 1987.

13 Proposal for a directive on solvency ratios for credit institutions, 20 April 1988, COM (88) 194.

14 Proposal for a second directive on the coordination of laws, regulations and administrative provisions relating to the taking up and pursuit of the business of credit institutions and amending Directive 77/780/EEC, 16 February 1988, COM (87) 715.

15 Proposal for a directive on the freedom of establishment and the free supply of services in the field of mortgage credit, 22 May 1987, COM (87) 255.

16 Directive revising the first directive of 11 May 1960, 86/566, 17 November 1986, O.J.L. 332/22 of 26 November 1986.

17 Directive on the implementation of Article 67 of the EEC Treaty, June 1988.

18 Treaty on Economic Union, 1992, Europe document No. 1759/60.

Notes

1 We shall not address macro-monetary issues such as the control of money supply. For a discussion, see Baltensperger and Dermine (1987a,b).

2 Articles 52−66 deal with the Right of Establishment and Article 57 relates to the Coordination of Legislation.

3 Directives are binding on member states as to the result to be achieved but leave the choice of form and method to national authorities. A timetable for implementation is included in a directive. Breaches can be pursued by injured individuals or institutions, by authorities of other member states or by the Commission before national courts or the European Court of Justice. Recommendations have no legal force but member states can choose to implement them by national legislation.

4 A qualified majority requires 54 votes out of 76 and the distribution is as follows: Germany, ten; Belgium, five; Denmark, three; Spain, eight; France, ten; Greece, five; Ireland, three; Italy, ten; Luxembourg, two; Netherlands, five; Portugal, five; United Kingdom, ten.

5 Belgium, Germany, Spain, France, the Netherlands, Italy and the United Kingdom have a deposit insurance system. Denmark, Ireland and Portugal have plans to introduce such a system. Greece and Luxembourg have not yet prepared any plans.

6 A study by the Economist Advisory Group (1986) showed that harmonization of capital ratios was a major concern for many European banks.

7   It has frequently been suggested that we should rely on flexible insurance premiums to price risk (Baltensperger and Dermine, 1987b). So far, no one has succeeded in putting this proposal into practical use and we do not intend to discuss it further in this chapter.

8   If we denote by r the return on asset (net income/asset), normally distributed with mean m and standard deviation s, and by E/A the equity-to-asset ratio, the probability of default $P(r < -E/A)$ is given by $N(E/As + m/s)$ where N is the cumulative normal distribution.

References

Baltensperger, E. and Dermine, J. (1987a) Banking deregulation in Europe. *Economic Policy*, 4, 63–109.

Baltensperger, E. and Dermine, J. (1987b) The role of public policy in insuring financial stability: a cross-country comparison perspective. In R. Portes and A. Swoboda (eds), *Threats to International Financial Stability*. Cambridge: Cambridge University Press.

Bernanke, B. (1983) Non-monetary effects of the financial crisis in the propagation of the Great Depression. *American Economic Review*, 73, 257–76.

Black, F., Miller, M. and Posner, R. (1978) An approach to the regulation of bank holding companies. *Journal of Business*, 51, 374–411.

Boyd, J. and Graham, S. (1988) The profitability and risk effects of allowing bank holding companies to merge with other financial firms. *Federal Reserve Bank of Minneapolis, Quarterly Review*, Spring, 3–20.

Clarotti, P. (1987) Comment batir l'Europe des Banques. *Revue Banque*, 475, 758–70.

Clarotti, P. (1984) Progress and future developments of establishment and services in the EC in relation to banking. *Journal of Common Market Studies*, 22, 199–226.

Corrigan, E.G. (1986) Financial market structure, a longer view. Annual Report, Federal Reserve Bank of New York.

Diamond, D. (1984) Financial intermediation and delegated monitoring. *Review of Economic Studies*, 51, 393–414.

Diamond, D. and Dybvig, P. (1983) Bank runs, deposit insurance and liquidity. *Journal of Political Economy*, 91, 401–19.

Economist Advisory Group (1986) An evaluation of the consequences of the existence of different prudential ratios for competition between credit institutions in the European Community. Report, European Economic Community.

Eisenbeis, R.A. (1987) Eroding market imperfections, implications for financial intermediaries, the payment system and regulatory reform. *Symposium on Restructuring the Financial System*. Kansas City, MO: Federal Reserve Bank.

Fama, E. (1980) Banking in the theory of finance. *Journal of Monetary Economics*, 6, 39–57.

Freeman, S. (1988) Banking as the provision of liquidity. *Journal of Business*, 61, 45–64.

Goodfriend, M. and King, R. (1987) Financial deregulation, monetary policy and central banking, Research Paper, Rochester.

Goodhart, C.A. (1985) *The Evolution of Central Banks*. London: London School of Economics and Political Science.

Jacklin, C.J. and Bhattacharya, S. (1988) Distinguishing panic and information-based bank runs: welfare and policy implications. *Journal of Political Economy*, 96, 568–97.

Litan, R. (1987) *What Should Banks Do?* Washington, DC: Brookings Institution.

Pecchioli, R. (1987) *Prudential Supervision in Banking*. Paris: OECD.

Postlewaite, A. and Vives, X. (1987) Bank runs as an equilibrium phenomenon. *Journal of Political Economy*, 95, 485–91.

Saunders, A. (1987) Bank holding companies, structure, performance and reform, Mimeo.

Schaefer, S. (1987) The design of bank regulation and supervision, some lessons from the theory of finance. In R. Portes and A. Swoboda (eds), *Threats to International Financial Stability*. Cambridge: Cambridge University Press.

Tobin, J. (1987) The case for preserving regulatory distinctions. *Symposium on Restructuring the Financial System*. Kansas City, MO: Federal Reserve Bank.

Comment

Richard Herring

Baltensperger and Dermine present a lucid survey of the path towards integration of the European banking market. Their strategy of contrasting actual (and proposed) European regulation with the theory of prudential regulation is illuminating and provocative. They argue that the most persuasive rationale for regulation stems from the structural vulnerability of banks to a contagious collapse of confidence. This structural vulnerability arises because banks finance illiquid assets with liabilities which they promise to redeem at par on short notice.

As theorists, Baltensperger and Dermine prefer a fundamental remedy which would correct the problem of instability at its source. They propose a modification of the deposit contract to include a sort of 'clawback clause' which would allocate losses proportionately across all depositors when a bank becomes insolvent. However, they regretfully conclude that it would be unworkable because of difficulties in establishing the time of failure and enforcing the *ex post* penalty on depositors who flee after the failure occurs. I would not dispute this conclusion. Indeed, I would register an additional concern. Although the clawback proposal is designed to eliminate the motive for a run by dispensing with the first-come, first-served method of paying out bank assets, the solution would only push the problem back one stage. It is true that depositors would no longer have an incentive to run *after* a bank is insolvent, but they would have an even greater incentive to run *before* a bank becomes insolvent in order to avoid being a depositor of record when failure occurs and losses are allocated.

Because Baltensperger and Dermine believe that their clawback proposal is unworkable, they consider other ways of protecting the stability of the banking system. One traditional mechanism is the chartering function. Many countries — including some of the countries now committed to achieving an integrated European market — rely heavily on high entry barriers to ensure that only institutions which are very well capitalized and prudently managed control banks. Perhaps equally important, high barriers generate monopoly profits, the capitalized value of which may exercise a restraining influence on risk-taking. However, continued reliance on high entry barriers conflicts fundamentally with the main thrust of integration.

The aim of the principle of mutual recognition and the adoption of a single banking licence is to increase competition by reducing barriers to entry. This is likely to succeed and greater competition will undoubtedly reduce the cost of financial services and increase the pace of financial innovation; however, it will also inflict losses on inefficient or incompetently managed banks. This creative destruction is a crucial part of the integration process and, as Baltensperger and Dermine note, it is likely to increase the risk of financial instability. Banks which find their going-concern value eroded by intensified competition will have less to lose and may be tempted to take greater risks to maintain profitability. This puts greater pressure on the supervisory process.

Prudential supervision endeavours to restrain risk-taking by constraining a bank's choice of assets and limiting leverage through capital adequacy requirements. Higher capital requirements reduce a bank's incentives to take risks. More capital also increases protection for depositors and the public in the event that losses occur. Baltensperger and Dermine seem optimistic that the 1988 Basle initiative to establish a common set of capital adequacy guidelines for banks in all major countries will strengthen prudential supervision. I am less sanguine.

The Basle initiative is an impressive feat of diplomacy, but it is not a very effective mechanism for controlling risk. The risk classification scheme is really a standardized accounting format rather than a plausible technique for evaluating a bank's risk of failure. For example, the risk weight applied to claims on banks in the OECD area is a fifth of that applied to claims on all other private sector borrowers. This is a much more optimistic view of the relative creditworthiness of many banks than the market seems to hold. Moreover, it seems to give official sanction to the notion that banks should be exempt from the usual standards of credit analysis because they have access to the safety net.

The authorities have recognized that the proposed guidelines are not designed to deal with liquidity, interest rate and exchange risk; however, the guidelines suffer from an even more fundamental limitation. The emphasis on the book value of capital and the measurement of risk on an instrument-by-instrument basis generates the wrong information to guide prudential supervision. What ultimately matters for the safety and soundness of a bank is not the characteristics of particular asset or off-balance-sheet commitment, but rather the *market* value of the portfolio of all the bank's activities. Unfortunately, the guidelines given by the Bank for International Settlements (BIS) do not enhance the ability of the authorities to monitor the market value of bank capital even though structural changes which are eroding the capital of some institutions render the task more urgent.

The termination function could reduce the risk of a contagious collapse by assuring creditors that a bank would be recapitalized, merged or put into receivership before it could cause loss to creditors. But, since the BIS guidelines do not improve the quality of information available to the authorities, there is little hope that the termination function can be performed more efficiently.

Deposit insurance is sometimes viewed as a useful additional safeguard. Deposit insurance in the United States was originally designed to protect small savers, but it has become an important means of protecting the system against a contagious loss of confidence. Unfortunately, it is a very costly means, as evidenced by the current dilemma of how to fund losses at one of the insuring agencies which may reach $100 billion – roughly $400 for every man, woman and child in the United States. Baltensperger and Dermine reject the Second Banking Directive's call for the adoption of deposit insurance in all European countries. Indeed, they advocate the dismantling of the systems currently in place on grounds that they undermine market discipline. I found this rather surprising since I was thoroughly persuaded by their earlier analysis that existing deposit insurance in Europe is so limited in coverage that it offers negligible comfort to the large creditors who are best situated to exert market discipline.

Baltensperger and Dermine are undoubtedly correct, however, to insist that safe deposits could be provided at lower potential cost to the public but, rather than dispense with deposit insurance, I would prefer to institute reforms which would render deposit insurance wholly superfluous. In addition to the risk-free bank which Baltensperger and Dermine advocate, the same goal could be accomplished by establishing a depository institution that holds only marketable assets which are marked to market daily or by requiring that insured deposits be collateralized by marketable assets.

Baltensperger and Dermine conclude that the best hope for safeguarding the banking system is to place sole reliance on a discretionary lender of last resort (LLR). This is a very beguiling solution. In principle, uncertainty over whether the LLR will act will intensify market discipline, while the LLR stands by to protect stability if market discipline should run amok. Improved market discipline, however, depends crucially on uncertainty about LLR intervention. We could imagine a mechanism to implement this – for example, the LLR could determine whether it would intervene in any given situation by spinning a roulette wheel. But, just as Einstein believed that God would not play dice with the universe, market participants are unlikely to believe that central bankers would play roulette with the banking system. Genuinely uncertain LLR assistance is as unworkable as the clawback proposal.

Since the LLR cannot make a credible commitment to behave randomly, market participants will do what they have always done and proceed on the basis of expectations about which institutions are most likely to receive LLR assistance. (Indeed, several private rating firms provide assessments of the likelihood that a bank will receive official assistance along with an evaluation of its creditworthiness.)

It is very easy to identify the banks most likely to receive assistance. The *ad hoc* cost—benefit analysis which central banks customarily undertake includes many factors — the condition of the bank, why the bank is in trouble, its prospects for recovery, and the state of the economy — but the overriding consideration is the potential spill-over cost if support is not forthcoming. This leads to the conclusion that creditors are most likely to be protected at a large bank because failure of a large bank is likely to cause a greater drop in aggregate demand, interrupt more credit relationships and pose greater threats to the payments system than the failure of a small bank. Even more important, the failure of a large bank is more likely to undermine confidence in the banking system generally and to lead to runs on other banks.

It can be argued that no bank will be so large relative to the European market that this will be a serious problem. (Baltensperger and Dermine indicate that the five largest European institutions will account for only 14 per cent of the market.) However, LLR assistance will continue to be the province of *national* central banks, and so until restructuring is accomplished the relevant notion of size will continue to be the size of a domestic institution relative to the domestic market. In this regard, the concentration ratios of Baltensperger and Dermine are more worrisome. In all European countries the share of the five largest banks is well above that in Japan and the United States. The number of banks regarded as too large to fail — or, more precisely, too large to be permitted to cause loss to creditors — is very great.

Reliance on discretionary LLR assistance gives these banks a wholly unwarranted competitive advantage. Moreover, it weakens market discipline on precisely those institutions which, by virtue of their size, pose the greatest potential threat to the stability of the banking system. Thus, although I have learnt much from analysis of the problem by Baltensperger and Dermine, I am uncomfortable with their solution.

2

The Regulation of Financial Services: Lessons from the United Kingdom

Colin Mayer

The 1986 Financial Services Act (FSA) introduced a comprehensive system of regulating financial services in the United Kingdom that had not previously existed. With it came a plethora of rules relating to the activities of investment businesses that distinguishes financial services from most other sectors of the British economy.

One justification that may be sought for the regulation of this but not other sectors of the economy is that investors are at greater risk than consumers of other products. In fact, according to Franks and Mayer (1989), the losses that clients of investment management firms have suffered on account of financial failure appear to be small, probably well below those in other industries, such as the building industry where entry and exit of firms is commonplace. Why then has an extensive system of regulation been imposed on investment managers but not on builders?

An obvious answer comes from comparing investment managers with banks, not builders. Banks are vulnerable to risks of runs and the concern exists that runs could spread through a banking system in a contagious manner. The regulation of banks is therefore justified by the systemic risks to which the banking system is liable. It might then be thought that the rationale for the FSA came from similar considerations. In fact, there are good reasons for believing that this was not the case. As described in section 2.1, the FSA emerged as a response to the Gower Report (1984) which in turn was prompted by the financial failure of a number of investment businesses. The concern of the Gower Report was investor protection not systemic risks, and the objective of the FSA was to correct deficiencies in existing legislation relating to investor protection.

While the justification for regulation of non-banks was different from that of banks, the form that it has taken is quite similar. The regulation of financial

This chapter draws on research performed with Professor Julian Franks on the regulation of investment managers. I am very grateful to him for detailed comments on this paper. I am also grateful for comments from participants at the INSEAD conference on European Banking after 1992. The chapter was written while the author was Houblon–Norman Fellow at the Bank of England. The views expressed in this chapter are those of the author, not those of the Bank or any other institution with which the author is associated. Any errors are the sole responsibility of the author.

services in the United Kingdom is described in section 2.2. This raises two questions. Firstly, is the regulation of non-banks justified at all and, secondly, has the right system of regulation been enacted?

The principles of regulating financial institutions are set out in section 2.3. It distinguishes between market failures created by problems of asymmetric information and systemic risks. It suggests that the appropriate responses to these two types of risk are very different. Furthermore, since asymmetries in information afflict some investors and firms more than others, the level of protection offered against asymmetric information should be allowed to vary across institutions. This heterogeneity stands in marked contrast with the uniformity that is required of regulation for systemic risks. The principles described in section 2.3 are used to evaluate the regulation of financial services in the United Kingdom in section 2.4.

While these are important considerations for the UK authorities, the issues raised are of much wider interest. The principle of 'home country authorization' which lay at the heart of EC proposals to complete the internal market by 1992 attributed the primary task of supervising financial institutions to the relevant authority of the member state of origin. However, both levels and forms of regulation differ considerably across countries and in financial services, more than in banking, conflicts have emerged between the objectives of different regulators. Such is the degree of disagreement that as yet, as section 2.5 describes, there remain many unresolved issues. Section 2.6 concludes the chapter.

2.1   The History of Regulation of Financial Institutions in the United Kingdom

There have been significant developments in bank regulation in the United Kingdom over the past decade. Following the secondary banking crisis of 1973 and the EEC Banking Directive of 1977, the Banking Act was passed in 1979. Before the Act, any partnership, company or individual could take money on deposit. No licence was needed and no undertaking had to be given about the assets of the business or the way in which the business was conducted. Whether a particular deposit-taking business was a bank depended on the privileges granted to it by the Bank of England and its reputation among the established members of the banking community.

Following the Act, deposit-takers had to be classified as either 'recognized banks' or 'licensed institutions'. The minimum conditions that a bank had to fulfil were that[1], (a) it enjoyed a 'high reputation and standing in the financial community', (b) it provided 'either a wide range of banking services or a highly specialized banking service', (c) the business was performed 'with integrity and prudence', (d) it was under the direction of at least two individuals and (e) it met minimum net asset requirements that were stipulated in the Act but also had to be considered appropriate by the Bank of England. Licensed deposit-takers had to satisfy the equivalent of (c) to (e), but instead of (a) merely had to demonstrate that all directors, controllers and managers were 'fit and proper' to carry out the business. Following the collapse of Johnson Matthey Bankers, an institution of supposedly high status, new legislation was introduced in 1987 that created a single category of authorization and required all institutions to be able to satisfy 'fit and proper' tests.[2]

The Act also introduced a Deposit Protection Fund under which 75 per cent of sterling deposits were protected up to a maximum deposit, excluding interest, of £10,000, which was raised to £20,000 by the 1987 Act.[3]

While the Act has clearly altered the process by which UK banks are regulated, legislation was designed to interfere as little as possible with the informal supervisory procedures that had previously existed. The broad criteria listed above leave the Bank of England with a wide measure of discretion in interpreting the law. While its authority derives from statute, the running of the system still depends to a large degree on moral suasion.[4]

In many ways the more significant regulatory changes that have occurred over the past decade have affected non-banks rather than banks. In part this reflects the composition of structural developments that have taken place in the City of London. While commercial banking has altered, it is the non-deposit-taking financial services that have experienced fundamental changes. The ending of several restrictive practices amongst financial institutions in 1986 and the introduction of new financial instruments during the 1970s and 1980s have combined to transform the way in which the financial service sector is structured and operated. In particular, the entry of a large number of new, frequently foreign, institutions convinced the authorities that the regulation of financial services had to be tightened.

Following the collapse of several institutions at the end of the 1970s and in the early 1980s,[5] the UK government commissioned a broad review of the regulatory structure (Gower Report, 1984). This led to the publication of a White Paper in 1985 that proposed a new framework for investor protection which formed the basis of the 1986 FSA. Prior to the Act, the principle statute governing securities investment was the Prevention of Fraud (Investments) Act of 1958. This required dealers in securities (with some exceptions) to be licensed and to be subject to conduct of business rules. The scope of the Fraud Act was limited and, in particular, did not relate to a serious concern that existed at the time about the sale of life insurance policies. Furthermore, the Fraud Act was felt to emphasize honesty of investment business to the exclusion of broader questions of competence.

Perhaps as a consequence, it failed to prevent the collapse of several small investment management firms.

The response was the enactment of a comprehensive system of regulating financial services. Save with a few exceptions, any person performing investment business comes under the terms of the FSA. The Act provides for rules regarding the 'conduct of business', 'fit and proper' tests, capital requirements, cold-calling, clients' monies and disclosure of information. There is an elaborate system of authorization of firms, a compensation scheme and a complaints and arbitration procedure. There are several regulating organizations that monitor the activities of firms and separate bodies that prosecute fraud. In all, according to one estimate (Lomax, 1987), the direct costs of the regulatory bodies are around £20 million per annum and the costs to financial institutions of complying with the Act are over £100 million. In contrast, Franks and Mayer (1989) report that over the whole of the period 1979—87 investors lost approximately £15 million as a result of financial failure in the investment management business.[6] The UK regulatory system has been described as ill considered (Veljanovski, 1988), unduly costly (Lomax, 1987) and stifling for competition and innovation (Goodhart, 1988). Are the costs justified? Is regulation (beyond prevention of fraud and theft) warranted at all? Has the United Kingdom enacted an appropriate form of regulation?

2.2   Regulation of Financial Services in the United Kingdom

The first thing that strikes the reader of the FSA (apart from its complexity and length) is the broad terms in which much of it is couched. For example, if one looks up capital requirements under the Act all that one finds is the following:

The Secretary of State may make rules requiring persons authorised to carry on investment business by virtue of sections 25 or 31 above to have and maintain in respect of that business such financial resources as are required by the rules

and may

make provision as to assets, liabilities and other matters to be taken into account in determining a person's financial resources for the purposes of the rules and the extent to which and the manner in which they are to be taken into account for that purpose.[7]

This level of generality reflects the distinctive blend of statutory and self-regulation that characterizes the UK system. The regulatory powers conferred by the Act are transferred to a designated agency called the Securities and Investments Board (SIB). The agency was required by the

Act to stipulate a set of rules and regulations regarding the conduct and operation of investment businesses. However, unlike most regulators, it is not the primary function of this agency to regulate businesses directly (save in a few exceptional cases). Instead, the primary function of the agency is to certify a number of clubs (called Self-Regulating Organizations (SROs)) whose membership derives from different parts of the investment business. Certification requires acceptance by the agency of the rules of the clubs and the way in which the rules operate. The primary relevance of the agencies' rules is therefore to act as a benchmark or more accurately a minimum to which the rules of the clubs have to conform. The clubs do not have any direct powers under the Act except to sanction members who do not comply with their rules and ultimately to expel them. The importance of this stems from the fact that any business that is designated as an investment business under the terms of the FSA has to be a member of a club (or, in the exceptional circumstances mentioned above, directly authorized by the agency).[8] Therefore the operation of an investment business is inconsistent with rejection or expulsion from a club.

This blend of statutory and self-regulation is by no means exceptional in the United Kingdom. Unqualified solicitors, patent agents, midwives, dentists, pharmacists and veterinary surgeons are prohibited by statute from practising. Unqualified doctors are not debarred but must not parade as medical practitioners and are not allowed to practise within the National Health Service. The blend of statutory and self-regulation is thought to be more flexible than a statutory system and more effective than self-regulation (which is, for example, used to regulate take-overs in the United Kingdom). It can respond to the needs of investors and firms without requiring the ratification of Parliament but at the same time provides regulatory authorities with powers to force compliance and prosecute for fraud.

It is not clear how such a system balances risks of regulatory 'capture' by members of the club against the provision of excessive investor protection. The latter is likely to be a feature of systems where politicians and government officials, who are sensitive to the political consequences of fraud and financial failure, administer the regulatory process. This is an important issue, and it raises questions about the organization of regulatory bodies, hierarchical relations between governments and regulated industries, and the role of clubs. We shall have little further to say on this, save to cite examples of where over-regulation may have resulted from statutory requirements.

Investment businesses are defined as those businesses involved in the dealing, managing or advising on investments. There are five SROs and the broad allocation of businesses between SROs is shown in table 2.1. A firm that performs more than one activity is frequently a member of more than one SRO. In that case it is assigned a lead regulator, who is usually responsible for the largest part of the firm's business.

Table 2.1 The structure and membership of the self-regulating organizations

Securities and Investments Board (SIB)			
Financial Intermediaries, Managers and Brokers Regulatory Association (FIMBRA)	Investment Management Regulatory Organization (IMRO)	Life Assurance and Unit Trust Regulatory Organization (LAUTRO)	The Securities and Futures Authority (SFA)
Independent investment managers and advisers	Investment managers that are part of larger companies	Companies selling life assurance and unit trust investments	Brokers and dealers

In applying to an SRO for membership, a firm has to demonstrate the following.

1   It is *fit and proper* to carry on investment business. In its assessment, an SRO will take account of an applicant's proposed line of business, financial position, expertise and past record.
2   It has *adequate capital* to run the business. Capital requirements are related to annual expenditures by firms, their volume of business,[9] and the position in investments that they take on their own account.
3   It complies with certain rules regarding the *conduct of its business*. These relate to advertising, unsolicited approaches to individuals (cold-calling), published recommendations, written agreements with customers, investment advice offered, churning of clients' accounts, independence and the disclosure of material interests. Firms are expected to 'know their customers' in the sense that they should have reasonable grounds for believing that recommendations made are suited to the circumstances of particular clients.
4   It holds *clients' money* in separate bank accounts from those of the firm.

In addition to being screened when first applying for membership, firms are monitored regularly and on an *ad hoc* unannounced basis. The frequency of monitoring depends on the nature of the business: more complex and risky businesses are subject to more frequent monitoring. For example, while firms that are acting on a purely advisory basis are generally only audited annually, those that are involved in dealing and clearing transactions may be subject to monthly monitoring.

In the event of a default, investors are eligible for compensation in respect of the defaulting firm's liabilities up to a maximum amount of £48,000 subject to the limitation that compensation payments in total should not exceed £100 million in any one year.[10]

2.3 The Principles of Regulating Financial Institutions

The case for regulating banks rests on two propositions.[11] The first is that banks are central to the smooth functioning of an economy; widespread failures amongst banks could seriously disrupt other sectors of an economy. The second is that banks are vulnerable to runs. The shortfall of the net realizable value of bank assets (loans) below that of liabilities (deposits) creates a risk of default in the event of depositors choosing to withdraw their funds. If the risk of depositors withdrawing their funds from one bank is increased by the failure of another bank, then the banking system may be threatened by individual failures. An externality is therefore created by a combination of interrelationships between banks' solvency levels and the role of banks in an economy.

In the case of non-banks, it was noted above that one of the requirements of the FSA is that clients' money be held in separate bank accounts. Clients' funds are therefore threatened by failure of deposit-taking banks but not by those of investment businesses. The market failures that justify bank regulation do not in general apply to investment businesses. However, there are two that appear relevant to investment firms: systemic risks and imperfect (or strictly asymmetric) information.

2.3.1 Systemic Risks

By analogy with banks, a *prima facie* case for regulation exists where the functioning of one part of the financial system is essential to the rest of the system or the economy as a whole *and* where interlinkages exist between the performance of different financial institutions. Whether a particular class of financial institution and activity is central to economic activity is a subject on which opinions differ. However, few would deny that widespread failures amongst brokers and dealers could seriously jeopardize the operation of a securities market. The liquidity of a market relies on efficient procedures for dealing in securities and settling and clearing transactions. Furthermore, significant interlinkages exist between brokers, dealers and other financial institutions. The failure of one firm can have serious consequences for others. Respondents to a survey of 32 UK investment managers in 1988, reported by Franks and Mayer (1989), stated that the average loss that their firm would have suffered if one of their counter-parties (brokers or dealers) had defaulted on 31 March 1988 was £3.9 million. If all their counter-parties had defaulted they would on average have lost £35 million.

In view of their central role in a security market and the interlinkages that exist between firms, there is a *prima facie* case for the regulation of brokers and dealers. The position of investment managers (mutual funds, pension funds, life assurance firms, private client firms) within an economic system is less certain. While they permit investors to diversify portfolios at low cost and possibly benefit from the expertise of others, investment managers can be bypassed by direct investment. Many security markets operate with rudimentary forms of investment management. Furthermore, interlinkages between investment managers and other firms are less pronounced than those between brokers and dealers. Provided that investment managers do not hold client funds, then, in the absence of fraud, costs to investors of financial failure are limited to interruption of business. These are probably small since the assets of failed firms that have not been subject to fraud are usually transferred at low cost to other firms. Other creditors may be affected but, provided that investment managers do not borrow to take investment positions on their own account, the value of an investment manager's debts should be restricted to those that are required to run the business. As a consequence, extensive protection of investment managers against systemic risks is probably not justified. As the limitations on compensation schemes described above suggest, systemic considerations were not at the forefront in the design of the FSA in the United Kingdom.

2.3.2   Asymmetric Information

The second class of market failure results from asymmetric information. There are three types of risk to which the uninformed investor is exposed: uncompensated wealth transfers (in particular fraud and theft), incompetence and negligence. Attempts to compensate for these risks by raising prices for finance and services provided create adverse selection and moral hazard problems. The fraudulent, incompetent and negligent drive out the honest and the competent (adverse selection) and encourage dishonesty and negligence (moral hazard).

Financial markets are likely to be particularly prone to information problems for two reasons. Firstly, unlike the sale and purchase of goods, financial services involve ongoing relations between client and firm. Investment managers, for example, provide advisory and portfolio services over an extended period of time. Secondly, the quality of services supplied is frequently difficult to evaluate. It is widely thought that much fraud and misappropriation remain undetected. In the absence of sensitive benchmarks against which to evaluate performance, detailed monitoring will be required to detect losses.

Market failure due to asymmetries in information is usually discussed in relation to bank lending (e.g. Jaffee and Russell, 1976; Stiglitz and Weiss, 1981). In fact, granted that the function of a bank is to screen and monitor borrowers, it is far from evident that this is the most relevant or pervasive example in financial markets. The area in which asymmetries in information are likely to be more pronounced is at the interface between private investors and institutions. The incentives on and abilities of institutions to evaluate quality of borrowers is likely to exceed those of individuals. Free-riding on information collection will be more prevalent amongst a large group of private investors than a small number of large institutions. Market failures due to asymmetric information are therefore more serious in institutions serving private clients, deposit-taking banks and investment managers with a private clientele (retail markets), than in those primarily transacting with other institutions and companies − broker−dealers and investment managers with an institutional clientele.

Drawing together the two classes of market failure, table 2.2 summarizes the failures that are associated with banks, brokers, dealers and investment managers with private and institutional clients. Systemic risks are a real concern in banks, brokers and dealers. They are less serious in the investment management business.[12] Asymmetric information creates market failures in banks and investment managers that service private clients, but not in brokers, dealers and investment managers that primarily transact with institutions.

Table 2.2 Market failures in financial services

Asymmetric information	Systemic risks	
	Yes	No
Yes	Banks	Private client investment management
No	Brokers, dealers	Institutional client investment management

2.3.3 Responses to Market Failures

What is the appropriate response to these market failures? In looking to regulation to correct them economics warns us that regulators will be prone to capture (Stigler, 1971) and self-regulatory professions will raise members' income by imposing barriers to entry (Shaked and Sutton, 1981). The setting of minimum standards may worsen the welfare of those who wish to consume cheap low quality service, and result in overinvestment in training and the provision of high quality services (Shapiro, 1986). The scope of regulation should therefore be limited to areas where there is a clear case of market failure. Elsewhere, the proper functioning of markets should be encouraged.

In determining the scope and form of regulation, the first point to note is that the two classes of market failure described above are very different. Systemic risks are essentially financial in nature. Bank runs result from shortfalls of realizable asset values below those of liquid deposits; brokers and dealers face risks of insolvency from losses on own positions. A central component of the regulation of banks, brokers and dealers is therefore the requirement that these institutions hold sufficient capital to reduce risks of financial failure to acceptably low levels.

In contrast, the risks arising from asymmetric information do not primarily relate to financial performance. Instead they reflect the nature and activities of a business and the type of individuals that it employs. Therefore, in correcting for failures arising from asymmetric information, financial requirements are unlikely to play a major role except in so far as they are indirectly related to the nature and activities of firms and the individuals within those firms. Instead, the correction of asymmetric information will primarily rely on the screening and monitoring of firms and individuals.[13] Adverse selection is diminished by imposing 'fit and proper' tests, and moral hazard is diminished by monitoring the 'conduct of business'.

Table 2.3 relates regulation to the three classes of institutions described in table 2.2. Capital requirements should be required of banks, brokers and dealers but not of investment managers. 'Fit and proper' tests and 'conduct-of-business' rules should be required of banks and investment managers that service private clients but not of brokers, dealers and investment managers that primarily transact with institutions. The imposition of uniform regulation for different classes of financial institution is therefore inappropriate.[14]

Table 2.3 Investor protection in financial services

Fit and proper, conduct-of-business tests	Capital requirement	
	Yes	No
Yes	Banks	Private client investment management
No	Brokers, dealers	Institutional client investment management

Tables 2.2 and 2.3 and the above discussion deliberately exaggerate the distinction between different classes of firms. Some institutions will not be able to evaluate the quality of firms with which they transact any better than individuals. Some individuals may feel competent to screen and monitor firms themselves. Some forms of systemic risk are more serious than others. The consequences of a collapse of a banking system cannot be equated to

those of a broker—dealer system in a bank-based financial system in which security markets are small and insignificant. There is therefore in practice a continuum of failures from financial collapse to minor disruption and from serious information deficiencies to minor asymmetries. This heterogeneity argues further against uniformity of regulation.

There are two forms that investor protection may take. It may be limited to information disclosure or may provide explicit guarantees against financial failure in the form of insurance. The credit rating of corporate bonds and commercial paper is an example of pure information disclosure. Credit-rating agencies provide no guarantees against the financial failure of firms that they have rated highly. Similarly, financial institutions could be rated in terms of the quality of their organizational arrangements and the quality of personnel employed. These ratings could be provided by private sector agencies. Rules regarding the criteria by which institutions are rated could be made explicit so that the performance of the monitoring agency could be evaluated. This form of protection may be quite adequate for institutions that are primarily transacting with professionals.

Other investors may prefer the higher degree of protection afforded by insurance. In the case of firm-specific risks, private sector insurance may be available. In the case of systemic risks, losses are by definition correlated across firms and insurance will only be available to the extent that risks can be internationally diversified.[15] Systemic risks that cannot be diversified will require underwriting by the government as the lender of last resort.

To summarize, regulation should range from requirements on information disclosure to insurance. Where market failures reflect risks that are correlated across firms, then governments may have to intervene. But where market failures result from risks that are essentially firm specific (fraud, negligence and incompetence), then private provision of monitoring and insurance will frequently be adequate. The criteria by which private agencies monitor the performance of firms is a proper concern of public agencies, just as the government lays down disclosure rules for the auditing of company accounts. Beyond that the role of government is limited.

There is an important exception to this. Where wealth transfers, in particular fraud, occur, then enforcement frequently requires the imposition of criminal penalties. These are appropriately prosecuted by a public agency, such as the police, and not a private institution. The *ex post* imposition of criminal penalties should, however, be distinguished from *ex ante* monitoring of the quality of firms and institutions which can frequently be delegated to the private sector. The more severe are *ex post* penalties and the greater the incidence of detection, the lower are the *ex ante* requirements. The United States, for example, emphasizes *ex post* detection and deterrence more than the United Kingdom, and as a consequence requires less *ex ante* screening and monitoring of certain classes of financial institutions.

One form of *ex post* penalty is the erosion of a firm's or individual's reputation. Established firms have more to lose from a revelation of malpractice than a new entrant, and *prima facie* there is a case for more extensive *ex ante* screening ('fit and proper' tests) of new firms than of established ones. However, as the Johnson Matthey case and the amendments to the 1979 Banking Act illustrate, reputation is not always a reliable defence against wealth transfers. In particular, where client balances are held, not only are systemic risks increased but also fraud is easier to perpetrate.

If malpractice is not easily identified by (at least certain classes of) investors then *ex post* monitoring ('conduct-of-business' rules) will still be required, even of the most reputable firms, to ensure that investors are duly compensated for losses sustained. Where the quality of services is readily established but the quality of individuals or firms is not, then 'fit and proper' but not 'conduct-of-business' tests are warranted. The stringent testing of prospective new entrants to most non-financial professions (for example, medicine, the law and accountancy) but the lax evaluation of established practitioners suggests that this is frequently encountered outside financial services.[16] It may also apply to investment businesses that do not handle client assets and merely perform advisory services.

This suggests a third set of considerations − the nature of firms − to be included with the type of investor and the scale of systemic risks in designing a regulatory framework. Table 2.4 illustrates. Banks that hold client balances and less well-established investment businesses (except those that merely provide advice) require 'fit and proper' and 'conduct-of-business' tests. Established private client investment businesses need only comply with 'conduct-of-business' rules, and established investment businesses that only transact with professional investors may escape regulation altogether. Since asymmetries of information create a barrier to entry, some of the costs of conducting 'fit and proper' tests should be borne by established firms.

Table 2.4 Screening and monitoring of investment businesses

Fit and proper tests	Conduct-of-business rules	
	Yes	No
Yes	Banks, less well-established investment businesses	Less well-established investment advisers
No	Established private client investment businesses	Established institutional client investment businesses

Enhanced competition diminishes the costs of regulating excess profits of established firms.

These principles will be applied in the next section to an evaluation of the regulation of financial services in the United Kingdom.

2.4 An Evaluation of the Regulation of Investment Managers in the United Kingdom

The first point to note about regulation in the United Kingdom, as described in section 2.2, is that it satisfies many of the principles set out in section 2.3. Firstly, there is variety in the regulation of financial institutions as reflected in differences in the rules of the SROs. Secondly, self-regulation distances the execution of regulation from the government. There are, however, several respects in which it diverges. This will be illustrated in relation to the regulation of one class of financial institutions − investment managers.

As shown in table 2.1 there are two SROs that regulate the investment management business: Financial Intermediaries, Managers and Brokers Regulatory Association (FIMBRA) and Investment Management Regulatory Organization (IMRO). The distinction between the two is that the former draws its membership from independent investment advisers and the latter from firms that are usually part of larger corporate entities. FIMBRA is primarily concerned with institutions that deal with private clients; IMRO's members often have institutional investors. However, the distinction between the two is not precise. Several members of IMRO have private clients. As a consequence, while there are significant differences in the way in which the two bodies operate, 'fit and proper' tests and 'conduct-of-business' rules are required of both memberships. Even institutions that just transact with other professionals are subject to an onerous system of regulation. Investors are therefore not offered the alternative of transacting at lower cost on mutually acceptable terms with unregulated firms.

Investment managers are required to satisfy the four sets of rules described in section 2.2. These include a requirement that investment managers separate client balances from their own. Some investment managers are parts of licensed deposit-takers in which case, quite appropriately, they are subject to the Banking Acts, including quite onerous capital requirements. More surprisingly, investment managers that do not hold client balances are also required to hold capital.

Capital requirements are set in relation to the value of expenditures of investment managers over a particular period of time.[17] In the cases of large firms with high expenditures these requirements can be substantial. At one stage, there was also a proposal that requirements be related to the volume of business of firms, in which case even small firms that actively managed portfolios on behalf of clients would have been required to hold substantial amounts of capital.[18] In the event, volume of business has not been used as a criterion for determining capital requirements.

The objective of the capital requirements was to diminish the risks incurred by investors. Negligence or incompetence could cause an investment manager to execute transactions on behalf of clients incorrectly, in which case firms would require resources to compensate investors. In addition, perhaps through no fault of their own, investment managers might encounter delays in the settlement of transactions, or still worse a failure of a counter-party to settle at all, in which case the investment manager may be liable for losses sustained by investors.

These risks are very real. The survey of UK investment managers mentioned in section 2.1 revealed that five firms reported errors amounting to 30 per cent of the value of transactions over the six months October 1987 to March 1988.[19] One firm reported a loss of over £0.5 million. It was recorded in section 2.1 that counter-party default could be even more serious.

Although investors are clearly at risk from execution errors, settlement delays and counter-party default, the appropriate response is not to require firms to hold capital. Large execution errors are very infrequent. Only nine of the 32 respondents reported significant execution errors. Very few firms have ever encountered counter-party default. The risks are small probabilities of large losses. As a consequence, large amounts of capital would be required to provide complete protection against these risks at substantial costs to firms. For example, the capital requirement on the 32 respondents to the survey would have had to have been on average five times higher than existing requirements to meet the losses sustained by one counter-party default and 28 times higher to protect against a simultaneous collapse of all counter-parties.

More effective protection can be provided at lower cost by pooling risks and insuring firms against the idiosyncratic losses of execution errors, settlement delays and counter-party default.[20] Professional indemnity insurance is widely used as a method of providing protection against execution errors. Firms arrange lines of credit with banks to secure short-term finance of settlement delays. Until recently, investment managers looked to the Stock Exchange Compensation Fund as a form of protection against counter-party default.[21] In the presence of uncorrelated risks, the total amount of capital that has to be held by insurers who pool risks is substantially below that which would be required of investment managers.

The other risk to which the investor is exposed is purely financial. An investment manager may become insolvent merely because it is unable to pay its fixed overheads or because it has sustained losses on investments made on its own account. Capital would appear to be more relevant to these. But again capital is only appropriate if serious losses can be sustained and these are correlated across the industry as a whole.

As mentioned in section 2.3.1, the costs of investment managers becoming insolvent are probably small. Most investment managers (that have not been fraudulent) which encounter financial distress are readily taken over by other firms. This is not an infrequent occurrence, and for the most part it does not impose costs on investors beyond the disruption and inconvenience of interruption of business. These on their own certainly do not justify onerous regulatory requirements.

Risks of financial collapse could be correlated across firms if they held significant own positions. That would give investment managers some of the features of brokers and dealers. However, in section 2.3.1 it was suggested that the consequences of systemic problems in investment management may be less severe than those in broking and dealing. Less onerous capital requirements should therefore be required of investment managers than of brokers and dealers, and those requirements should only be related to the own positions of investment managers. Alternatively, the imposition of capital requirements on investment managers could be avoided altogether by requiring separation of own positions.[22]

The distinction between broker–dealers and investment managers appears to be recognized in the United States. Brokers and dealers are subject to stringent capital requirements. Investment companies that issue securities to the public (e.g. mutual funds) are required to hold a fixed amount of capital ($100,000).[23] Investment advisers that do not issue securities and just invest in other firms' quoted and unquoted securities are not required to hold capital under the Investment Advisers Act 1940.[24]

Investment managers should not be required to hold capital. Some types of investment manager should probably not be subject to onerous 'fit and proper' or 'conduct-of-business' tests. Some businesses should therefore be largely unregulated and others only regulated in limited ways. This stands in marked contrast with the onerous requirements that have been imposed on all investment managers in the United Kingdom.

Where has the United Kingdom gone wrong? The main deficiencies of UK regulation come from trying to impose too great a degree of uniformity across the financial system as a whole. The distinction between systemic risks and investor protection and the association of different classes of risk with different forms of protection has not been made sufficiently precise. It was noted in section 2.1 that there is a presumption in the FSA that investment businesses should hold capital. This is appropriate for some but not all. There is the requirement that individuals be 'fit and proper' and businesses conducted appropriately. Some investors will welcome these requirements; others will not, at least once they become aware of the costs that they are being indirectly forced to bear.

Elimination of capital requirements will not reduce the level of investor protection. Insurance can provide more protection than capital at lower cost. Furthermore, current investor compensation schemes are, as described above, very limited. Savings from reduced capital requirements could, at least in part, be used to augment existing levels of compensation.

2.5   An Evaluation of the Harmonization of Regulation in the EC

Harmonizing regulation in the EC is still evolving. A directive on investment services was published in December 1988. This proposed that principles of home country authorization that have been applied to banks in the Second Banking Coordination Directive should extend to investment businesses. Under this principle a firm that is authorized in one member state should be able to establish branches or provide services elsewhere in the EC without requiring further authorization. Furthermore, access to host security markets and membership of stock exchanges should be available to overseas firms where appropriate.[25]

The Directive proposed that rules relating to prudential supervision ('fit and proper' tests), 'conduct of business' and financial soundness be within the exclusive jurisdiction of home member states and that a compensation fund be administered by home countries. However, at present it is felt that harmonization of rules relating to 'conduct of business' and compensation schemes is not feasible. For the moment, it is suggested that 'conduct-of-business' rules continue to be enforced by the host country and the *host* compensation schemes apply to branches of investment businesses. In the longer term it is envisaged that a uniform system of rules will apply to 'fit and proper' tests, 'conduct-of-business' tests, and capital requirements and compensation schemes.

This uniformity across nations is as misconceived as uniformity across institutions in the United Kingdom. Like the UK authorities, the Commission is failing to distinguish adequately between the avoidance of systemic risks and investor protection. Where only investor protection is at issue, a diverse range of levels of protection can and should coexist. It is quite appropriate that some investors should be able to purchase investment management services with low levels of protection at relatively low cost from any country inside (or indeed outside) the EC. Other investors will seek higher levels of protection from firms, irrespective of their country of origin. Conversely, investment management firms should be able to supply services offering particular levels of protection anywhere within the EC. What is required is a system by which investors know the level of protection that they are being offered. To meet this end, there could be various categories of authorization corresponding to recognized levels of protection. This could be implemented through an extension of the club principle described above to an international setting: the authorization of investment management firms by different (self-)regulatory authorities. Alternatively, private agencies could be used to evaluate the degree of protection offered to investors.

Where there are systemic risks, the coexistence of several degrees of protection is not feasible. The public-good element of the financial system means that different levels of risk cannot in general be tolerated. In contrast with regulation of investment management, competition between national authorities threatens *under-regulation* of banks, brokers and dealers. The response in banking has been international harmonization of regulatory rules, in particular those pertaining to capital adequacy. Likewise, if the principle of home country authorization is to apply, a uniform system of regulating brokers and dealers throughout the EC will be required.

However, it is questionable whether the principles set out in the Second Banking Directive should be extended to investment businesses. The payments system is central to the operation of all countries' economies. In contrast, there is appreciable variation in the relevance of security markets to different members of the EC. Security markets (bond or equity) play a less central role in bank-based systems, such as in Germany, than in market-based systems, such as in the United Kingdom. There is therefore little justification for applying the same level of protection to security markets in all countries in Europe.

Even if home country principles of authorization are accepted, diversity in the regulation of investment managers should be tolerated. Furthermore, while capital should appropriately be required of brokers and dealers to protect against systemic risks, it should not be required of investment managers. As described in the previous section, the risks involved in investment management are primarily non-financial in nature and where there are financial risks the costs associated with them are comparatively small.

2.6 Conclusions

In this chapter we have described regulation of investment businesses in the United Kingdom and considered current proposals to harmonize regulation of investment services in Europe.

We noted that there are several appealing features of the current regulatory system in the United Kingdom. The mixture of self-regulation and statutory regulation offers considerable scope for effective and flexible regulation. The multiplicity of regulatory organizations is appropriate in view of the different risks involved in the provision of financial services. Unfortunately, the heterogeneous nature of investment businesses has not been fully recognized. The notions of 'fitness and properness' and the requirement that businesses satisfy rules of conduct have been too readily accepted as requirements of all firms. Most seriously of all, capital requirements have been expected of firms where financial risks are small or absent.

Principles have been set out by which investor protection should be designed. The first consideration was whether investment businesses were prone to systemic risks in the sense that, firstly, there were significant interactions between the financial performances of firms and, secondly, their continued operation was essential to the functioning of an economy. On this basis, a distinction was drawn between banks, brokers and dealers on the one hand and investment managers on the other. The systemic risks present in the former group justified the imposition of capital requirements. In contrast, the risks in investment management relate primarily to fraud and the conduct of business for which screening and monitoring are required.

The second consideration that was discussed above was the nature of the investor. Asymmetries of information give rise to market failures that undermine the operation of certain industries. Asymmetries are likely to be prevalent in the investment business because of the continuing nature of the relation between client and firm and the difficulties involved in evaluating the performance of firms. Within the investment business, asymmetries in information will be pronounced where there are large numbers of small uninformed investors. Market failures will therefore be particularly serious in retail businesses. Professional investors may feel more competent to evaluate performance. Different regulatory rules, ranging from information disclosure to insurance, will be appropriate depending on the nature of the investor. In the absence of systemic risks, there will be considerable opportunities for delegating regulation to private sector auditors and insurers.

The European Commission is proposing extending the principles of home country authorization from banking to financial services. It is questionable whether this is appropriate. Unlike the payments system, the relevance of investment business to the functioning of economies differs appreciably between member states. Thus the costs of systemic collapse and the appropriate level of protection also differ.

Leaving this point of principle aside, the European Commission is following the UK authorities in trying to impose too great a degree of uniformity across financial institutions and investors. Capital requirements should not be required of all financial institutions. The same levels of protection should not necessarily be provided to all classes of investors.

As the internationalization of security markets progresses, the system-wide role of particular national markets will diminish. This is already in evidence in Europe with Eurobond markets operating alongside domestic markets and offering investors and firms choices between relatively regulated domestic and unregulated international markets. Likewise, international listing of shares has diminished the reliance of companies on domestic equity markets. Once internationalization is taken to the point at which companies can be quoted in several different markets, competition between markets in terms of the protection that they offer and the prices that they charge will be possible. There will then be more scope for a return to the decentralization of regulation to individual markets which currently prevails without the associated barriers to international trade.

Notes

1 Schedule 2 of the Banking Act 1979 amended in the Banking Act 1987.
2 Rules were also changed regarding ownership of institutions, permissible exposures, the function of auditors and the power of the Bank of England to obtain information.
3 The maximum amount payable to any one depositor is therefore £15,000.
4 Peter Cooke, the Head of Banking Supervision at the Bank of England, discusses recent developments in bank supervision at greater length in Gardener (1986). The failure of Johnson Matthey Bankers in 1983 resulted in a tightening of the 1979 Act in 1987.
5 The most significant was the investment management firm Norton Warburg in 1981.
6 However, Franks and Mayer (1989) are careful to emphasize that since malpractice tends only to be revealed when financial failure occurs, actual losses may be substantially in excess of reported losses.
7 Section 49 of the FSA.
8 Alternatively a firm may be a member of a recognized professional body (such as one of the accountancy associates) or authorized under the Insurance Companies or Friendly Societies Acts.
9 Proposals to introduce volume-of-business requirements have in some cases been shelved.
10 Claims not exceeding £30,000 are paid in full; thereafter 90 per cent of claims are paid up to £50,000.
11 For a more extensive discussion of these issues see Diamond and Dybvig (1986), Bernanke and Gertler (1987), Bhattacharya and Gale (1987), and Jacklin and Bhattacharya (1988).
12 Note that in distinguishing between investment managers and other types of financial institutions, only pure investment managers that neither hold client balances nor take own positions are being assumed. Firms that hold client balances have some of the features of banks, and firms that take own positions may create similar systemic risks to brokers and dealers. This is discussed further below.

13 See Leland (1979) for the case for setting minimum standards.

14 It might be thought that the default of a fraudulent or incompetent institution could have wider implications by threatening the solvency of others. However, this is no different from the normal risks of investment. The appropriate response is to require institutions to hold sufficient capital to be able to weather isolated defaults and to relate capital requirements to the riskiness of counter-parties.

15 However, there may be other reasons for the failure of insurance markets to develop (see for example Rothschild and Stiglitz, 1976).

16 A less favourable interpretation would echo the warnings of the economic literature that self-regulating professions erect barriers to entry to preserve monopoly rents.

17 Firms are subject to the maximum of an absolute minimum capital requirement of £5,000 and an expenditure-based requirement which is either six weeks' or three months' worth of expenditure depending on whether they act as principals in transactions or take counter-party risk.

18 The proposal was that capital requirements be the maximum of the absolute minimum requirement and the expenditure requirement that were described in note 17 and either 0.1 per cent or 0.3 per cent of the previous quarter's value of purchases and sales depending on whether firms were acting as principals or taking counter-party risk.

19 While this includes the stock market crash, execution errors are not restricted to such exceptional periods.

20 Of course, counter-party default may be part of a systemic collapse. However, there is a serious danger of double counting if protection against systemic risk is provided at the level of brokers and dealers as well as investment managers.

21 Compensation is now only available to private investors.

22 Separation of own positions is in the spirit of structural regulation that is advocated by Kay and Vickers (1988), but for a critique of this see Mayer (1988).

23 Subject to certain stipulated minima, these are computed in relation to either a firm's aggregate indebtedness or its customer receivables after applying a 'haircut' (of 15−30 per cent) to the market value of its equity positions.

24 California imposes a minimum capital requirement of $25,000.

25 This does not apply to credit institutions in countries that do not accept credit institutions as members of their stock exchanges.

References

Bernanke, B. and Gertler, M. (1987) Banking and macroeconomic equilibrum. In W.A. Barnett and K.J. Singleton (eds), *New Approaches to Monetary Economics*. Cambridge: Cambridge University Press.

Bhattacharya, S. and Gale, D. (1987) Preference shocks, liquidity and central bank policy. In W.A. Barnett and K.J. Singleton (eds), *New Approaches to Monetary Economics*. Cambridge: Cambridge University Press.

Diamond, D. and Dybvig, P. (1986) Bank runs, deposit insurance and liquidity. *Journal of Political Economy*, 91, 401−19.

Franks, J.R. and Mayer, C.P. (1989) *Risk Regulation and Investor Protection: The Case of Investment Management*. Oxford: Oxford University Press.

Gardener, E.P.M. (1986) *UK Banking Supervision*. London: Allen and Unwin.

Goodhart, C. (1988) The costs of regulation. In A. Sheldon (ed.), *Financial Regulation — or Over-Regulation*. London: Institute of Economic Affairs.

Gower Report (1984) *Review of Investor Protection*, Cmnd 9125. London: Her Majesty's Stationery Office.

Jacklin, C.J. and Bhattacharya, S. (1988) Distinguishing panic and information-based bank runs: welfare and policy implications. *Journal of Political Economy*, 96, 568–97.

Jaffee, D.M. and Russell, T. (1976) Imperfect information, uncertainty and credit rationing. *Quarterly Journal of Economics*, 90, 651–66.

Kay, J.A. and Vickers, J. (1988) Regulatory reform in Britain. *Economic Policy*, 7, 285–343.

Leland, H.E. (1979) Quacks, lemons and licensing: a theory of minimum quality standard. *Journal of Political Economy*, 87, 1328–46.

Lomax, D. (1987) *London Markets after the Financial Services Act*. London: Butterworths.

Mayer, C.P. (1988) Discussion of Kay and Vickers: Regulatory reform in Britain. *Economic Policy*, 7, 344–6.

Rothschild, M. and Stiglitz, J.E. (1976) Equilibrium in competitive insurance markets: an essay on the economics of imperfect information. *Quarterly Journal of Economics*, 90, 629–50.

Shaked, A. and Sutton, J. (1981) The self-regulating profession. *Review of Economic Studies*, 48, 217–34.

Shapiro, C. (1986) Investment, moral hazard and occupational licensing. *Review of Economic Studies*, 53, 843–62.

Stigler, G.J. (1971) The theory of economic regulation. *Bell Journal of Economic and Management Science*, 2, 3–21.

Stiglitz, J.E. and Weiss, A. (1981) Credit rationing in markets with imperfect information. *American Economic Review*, 71, 393–410.

Veljanovski, C. (1988) Introduction. In A. Sheldon (ed.), *Financial Regulation — or Over-Regulation*. London: Institute of Economic Affairs.

Comment

Pierre Hillion

In an interesting paper, Colin Mayer investigates the various sources of risk that financial services in the United Kingdom are exposed to, evaluates the adequacy of regulation in the United Kingdom and makes some proposals about the regulation of financial services in Europe.

One of his conclusions is that 'the main deficiencies of UK regulation come from trying to impose too great a degree of uniformity across the financial system as a whole'. The European Commission should therefore avoid making the same mistake. He argues forcefully that regulation should be flexible across countries, across financial services and across investors to minimize the high costs of regulation. I certainly do not disagree with his conclusions. An interesting issue which should be addressed in the last section of the paper pertains to the impact of European integration on the different sources of risk to which financial services are exposed.

The two sources of risk identified by Mayer are systemic risk and specific risk arising from asymmetries in information. Systemic risk is essentially financial in nature, and originates from the interrelationship between bank solvency levels and the role of banks in the economy. Specific risks, arising from asymmetries in information, do not relate to financial performance. Rather, they reflect the nature and activities of a business and the type of individuals that it employs. Mayer suggests that banks, dealers and brokers are more likely to be exposed to systemic risk, whereas asymmetries in information are more likely to affect banks and investment managers that service private clients. Since financial services are exposed to different sources of risk, regulation should be flexible.

An interesting issue is therefore the impact of European integration on these two sources of risk. It is not clear to me how European integration could affect the specific risks arising from asymmetries in information. Could enhanced competition increase this source of risk? I do not know. The impact of European integration on systemic risk is more interesting. The issue is important since, as suggested by Mayer, the higher (the lower) is the systemic risk, the higher (the lower) are the capital requirements and therefore the higher (the lower) are the costs to the banking system and thus investors.

European integration might possibly affect the systemic risk in two different ways which could be referred to as the diversification effect and the competition effect. Unfortunately, these two effects seem to work in opposite directions.

The diversification effect: financial theory suggests that, provided that risks are not perfectly correlated across banks, brokers and dealers of different European countries, the amount of systemic risk in any given country before 1992 should decrease now 1992 has passed. I am not saying that systemic risk should disappear, but simply decrease. This should imply a decrease in the required reserves and hence imply lower costs to the financial community.

The competition effect: this works in the opposite direction. Mayer warns us in section 2.4 that 'competition between national authorities threatens under-regulation of banks, brokers and dealers'. Under-regulation increases the probability of default and therefore should increase systemic risk. This should imply an increase in the required reserves and hence higher costs to the financial community.

Which of these two effects, the diversification effect or the competition effect, will dominate? I do not have an answer to that question. It would have been interesting to see these problems addressed in the last section of the chapter, i.e. the impact of European integration on the different sources of risks to which financial services are exposed.

Part II

European Equity Markets and
Investment Banking

3

European Equity Markets in the 1990s

Gabriel Hawawini and Bertrand Jacquillat

Up to the mid-1980s, two discernible factors of change affected national European equity markets: the worldwide advances in technology and telecommunication applications in most aspects of the securities industry, and competition among key European financial centres in vying for a role as the European 'link' in the increasingly global issuance and trading of securities. Over the past seven years, an additional, and indeed equally significant, change factor emerged in the form of vigorous legislative efforts on the part of the European Commission to create an integrated European financial sector to serve as the basic thread for weaving together the 12 nations into a single European economy after 1992.

Among the various opinions, recommendations and directives issued by the Commission concerning all subsectors of the financial services industry, the 1988 directive (an extension of a 1986 Commission directive) concerning the liberalization of capital movements is noteworthy here in so far as it has served as a necessary backdrop for legislative reforms that are more specific to the securities subsector. The fundamental aim of this 'core' directive was to remove exchange controls and allow the free movement of capital throughout the European Community (EC) without any discrimination between residents and non-residents.[1]

In most respects the specific directives relevant to the securities industry were designed around the same basic principles that affect the banking and insurance subsectors: minimum harmonization of essential standards, mutual recognition in the application of these standards, and home country control and supervision. These principles were filtered by the Commission into a small number of key directives (see the appendix), the essence of which is examined briefly in the next section.

We acknowledge the research assistance of Christian Agossa, Eric Rajendra, Michael Schill and Robert Whitelaw. We have benefited from the comments made by Jean Dermine and Théo Vermaelen. We thank Marie-Laure Guérin and Marieke Hilarion for typing several versions of this manuscript.

This chapter has three sections, and begins with an examination of the current (albeit rapidly evolving) structure and operations of European equity markets, assesses their informational efficiency, and summarizes the European Commission's key reforms specific to the securities industry. In section 3.2 we examine various issues in pan-European portfolio diversification and provide empirical evidence to support the argument that large risk-reduction benefits accrue to investors as they diversify their portfolios across European equities. We further argue that any decline in risk-reduction opportunities due to European economic integration should be more than offset by gains from increased informational–operational efficiency and enhanced market liquidity. Several hypotheses as to the possible structure and dynamics of European equity markets beyond 1992 are presented in section 3.3. A number of obstacles on the road to the integration of European equity markets are also identified.

3.1   European Equity Markets: Current Structure, Operations and Reforms

Despite significant historic inter-European economic linkages, the single most striking feature of Europe's stock markets, taken as a whole, is their diversity in size, structure, regulation, taxation, trading practices and operational efficiency. While the EC's legislative efforts attempted to remove some of these differences through harmonization of various standards, certain market peculiarities remain.

However, this diversity can be characterized as both a strength and a weakness. The strength resides in the opportunity for European markets to specialize in the delivery of particular products and services. The weakness lies both in the possible inability of European markets to play a unified and significant role in the global equity market and in the obstacles that this diversity could impose on the integration process fostered by the EC.

In this section we examine the range of structures, activities and organizations represented by the individual equity markets, compare their operational efficiencies and end with an assessment of their informational efficiencies within the perspective of the efficient market hypothesis.

3.1.1   Size and International Activity

The significant differences in market size and activity among individual European equity markets are summarized in table 3.1. The International

Table 3.1 European equity markets: size and activity

	Market capitalization[a] 31 Dec 1990	Market capitalization[b] 31 Dec 1990 (ECU million)	Market capitalization/ GDP[c] 1990 (%)	Listed stocks[d] Dec 1990	Foreign stocks[e] Dec 1990	Volume of transactions[f] 1990 (ECU million)	Turnover ratio[g] Dec 1990	No. of sections[h]
Belgium	2,027,809	48,071	31.5	341	159	7,567	0.16	OM, SM, OTC
Denmark	225,600	28,620	27.8	282	9	8,944	0.31	OM, SM, TM, OTC
France	1,561,217	224,632	24.1	669	226	93,737	0.42	OM, SM, OTC
Germany	530,834	259,971	22.1	647	234	405,498	1.56	OM, SM, TM, OTC
Italy	168,134,800	109,160	12.9	220	0	32,917	0.30	OM, SM, TM, OTC
Luxembourg	323,944	7,679	111.1	732	182	169	0.02	OM, OTC
Netherlands	251,054	108,974	49.4	498	238	32,285	0.30	OM, SM, TM
UK	445,045	628,772	81.0	2,559	613	430,683	0.68	OM, SM, OTC
Portugal	1,183,000	–	–	143	0	–	n.a.	OM, OTC
Spain	10,796,152	82,663	21.6	429	2	28,381	0.34	OM, SM, OTC

[a] In millions of local currency; values are for domestic capitalization only.
[b] Translations in ECU are based on year-end 1990 exchange rates given by the Fédération Internationale des Bourses de Valeurs (FIBV).
[c] OECD National accounts – main aggregates.
[d] Total number of listed stocks (domestic and foreign), excluding investment funds.
[e] Number of foreign listed stocks.
[f] Translations in ECU based on year-end 1990 exchange rates given by the FIBV.
[g] Annual volume of transactions (f) divided by total market capitalization (b).
[h] Markets are official market (OM), second market (SM), third market (TM) and over-the-counter market (OTC).

Note: Data for Portugal as at 31 December 1987

Sources: Fédération Internationale des Bourses de Valeurs (1990); OECD

Stock Exchange of London (ISE), formerly the London Stock Exchange, is clearly the leading market in terms of both market capitalization and the number of domestic and foreign stocks listed. ISE's domestic market capitalization of approximately ECU 0.6 trillion at year-end 1990, places it third internationally after Tokyo (ECU 2.1 trillion) and New York (ECU 2.0 trillion).[2]

In so far as the number of foreign stocks listed is a fair indicator of the level of 'internationalization' of Europe's equity markets, ISE again holds the leading position with 613 foreign stocks listed. Amsterdam follows, trading a relatively large number of foreign equities since 1980 through the Amsterdam Securities Accounting System (ASAS), and now lists 238 foreign issues. However, in terms of market capitalization, the second ranking market in Europe is Frankfurt (ECU 260 billion). Frankfurt is also the first in terms of sheer annual transaction volumes owing to its high turnover ratio compared with London (1.56 compared with 0.68).

Numerous factors converge in enabling London to have reached, and to continue to maintain and enhance, its premier position among European equity markets including a historical head start in terms of capital accumulation and trading of shares stemming from early industrialization, a long-standing technology interchange with New York and Tokyo in the fields of telecommunications, settlement systems and product innovation, positive linkages with other areas of capital markets in which London maintains a key role − especially debt and foreign exchanges − and progressive self-initiated reforms (as evidenced by Big Bang in 1986).

3.1.2 Market Structure and Organization

All European equity markets, with the exception of the ISE, maintain official floor trading and hours (see table 3.2). Strictly speaking, London no longer has an organized equity market because independent market-making activities by intermediaries, coupled with the rise in the use of electronic quotation systems, have rendered London's trading floor obsolete. Today, the ISE is essentially an over-the-counter market similar to New York's National Association of Securities Dealers and its automated quotation system (NASDAQ). Off-floor trading for large blocks of shares tended to drive increasingly large amounts of trade out of Continental stock exchanges towards broker−dealer offices or towards the ISE where the liquidity of large blocks of foreign shares is often higher than on the local market of origin.[3] In hopes of restrengthening their position, some of the Continental exchanges have begun screen-trading systems. Opened in 1991, Germany's Integrietes Börsenhandels und Informationssystem (IBIS) plans to expand from its current trading of Frankfurt's 30 leading stocks and bonds. Copenhagen,

Table 3.2 European equity markets: structure and organization, December 1991

	Official trading hours[a]	Floor trading[b]	Off-floor trading[c]	OTC market[d]	Continuous market[e]	Screen trading[f]	Physical delivery[g]	Central settlement and clearing[h]	Margin trading[i]	Daily limit on price[j]
Belgium	12h50–14h30	Yes	Yes	Yes	Yes	Yes	Yes/no	No	No	Yes
Denmark	09h00–15h30	No	Yes	Yes*	Yes	Yes	No	Yes	No	No
France	10h00–17h00	Yes	Yes	Yes*	Yes	Yes	No	Yes	Yes	Yes
Germany	11h30–13h30	Yes	Yes	Yes	Yes	Yes	Yes/no	Yes	No	No
Italy	10h00–13h45	Yes	Yes	Yes	Yes	Yes	Yes/no	Yes	Yes	No
Luxembourg	11h15–13h15	Yes	Yes	Yes	No	Yes	Yes/no	Yes	No	Yes
Netherlands	09h30–16h30	Yes	Yes	No	No	Yes	No	Yes	No	No
UK	08h30–16h30	No	Yes	Yes*	Yes	Yes	Yes/no	Yes	Yes	No
Portugal	10h00–13h00	Yes	Yes	No	No	No	Yes/no	Yes	No	Yes
Spain	09h30–17h00	Yes	Yes	No	Yes	No	Yes/no	Yes/no	No	Yes

[a] Netherlands, there is a 16h30–22h30 session for the most active domestic securities to coincide with New York Stock Exchange; Spain, there is also a later session to coincide with the New York Stock Exchange; London allows trading outside of hours.
[b] Introduction of continuous markets usually makes the floor less active; floor trading continues to exist for small trades in Denmark and France.
[c] Off-floor trading hours for selective markets: France, 10h00–17h00; Germany, 08h00–17h00.
[d] Unofficial and non-regulated OTC markets unless indicated by an asterisk; asterisk indicates a regulated OTC market.
[e] Off-floor computerized centralized market.
[f] Off-floor decentralized electronic market, e.g. London's Stock Exchange Automated Quotation market and Germany's IBIS.
[g] Securities are hand delivered to settle the deal (as opposed to 'dematerialized' book-entry transfer systems that are generally operated by a central clearing authority; see (h)). 'Yes/no' indicates a central depository system with physical delivery possible if desired by the investor.
[h] The book-entry system is operated by a central authority in France, Luxembourg, the Netherlands and Spain. However, settlement and delivery delays vary between countries and depend on whether the transaction occurs in the cash or the forward delivery market. The TAURUS electronic book system will eliminate physical delivery in the UK after 1993–4.
[i] Margin trading is the process of buying securities with money borrowed from brokers. This is forbidden in most countries or regulated as in Denmark. Where margin trading is allowed, foreigners can also deal on margin.
[j] Limits for selected countries are as follows: France, ranges from ±5% for less liquid securities to +21.20% to −18.75% for more liquid, and currently includes only the stock market; Germany, no limits in principle but a change of ±5% from the last fixed price should be reported to the Managing Committee of the Stock Exchange before trading resumes; Portugal, ±15% in consecutive sessions; Belgium ±10% in 'Corbeille' cash market, ±5% in 'Parquet' and second market and no limit in the forward market; Luxembourg, ±10% for equities.

Note: Data for Portugal as at 31 December 1987

Source: Data from Amsterdam, Brussels, Copenhagen, Frankfurt, Luxembourg, Milan, Paris Stock Exchanges; Audihispana, Madrid; Touche Ross, London; Spicer & Oppenheim (1988)

Paris and Milan also maintain continuous screen-based markets. Though the current list of securities is limited, most of the Official List was expected to be included by the end of 1992. Regulations that prevent the intermediaries from trading on their own account and engaging in market-making activities have reduced the relative liquidity of Continental exchanges. This prohibition has traditionally been justified on the grounds that it protects investors (since intermediaries act as agent—broker as opposed to principal—dealer) and limits the risks borne by intermediaries. Recent reforms in Italy have replaced individual brokers with security investment firms (SIMs). The SIMs, many part-owned by banks, are now also allowed to trade on their own account, as well as for third parties. While it can be argued that increased competition may eventually force all Continental exchanges to allow intermediaries to perform market-making activities if they wish to augment the liquidity and flexibility of their markets, the present state of undercapitalization of most Continental intermediaries (with the exception of banks) would indeed lead to precarious financial situations in the event of sharp declines in stock market prices.

3.1.3 Price-setting Mechanisms

There are various price-setting mechanisms in the European equity markets, with the periodic call system (or batch system) in a dominant position. Under this system, orders coming in over an interval of time are not transacted immediately, but are stored and transacted together in a multilateral transaction. Batch systems can function in verbal, written or auction forms.[4]

The batch system approach followed by most exchanges is expected increasingly to be replaced by a continuous market system, similar to that which prevails in London, with computer-assisted trading and quotations. In a continuous market system, a transaction occurs whenever two traders' orders cross. Continuous market systems are now also available in Brussels (CATS), Copenhagen, Frankfurt (IBIS), Lisbon (TRADIS), Madrid (CATS), Milan (BORSAMAT) and Paris (see table 3.2).

Currently, more than one price-setting mechanism may operate in the same market. For instance, in Paris an auction form of the batch system is used to determine the price of some of the stocks that trade in the cash market, whereas a continuous system is employed for all other stocks.

3.1.4 Price-stabilization Techniques

Closely related to price-setting mechanisms is the issue of price-stabilization techniques, with the most frequently employed being the imposition of a maximum daily limit on price changes (see table 3.2). For instance, in the Paris market opening prices of liquid shares are not allowed to change by more than 10 per cent from the previous day's closing price. Moreover, the price after an exchange trading break may not change by more than 5 per cent. The total price change for the day's closing price cannot increase by more than 21.20 per cent or decrease by more than 18.75 per cent.

Other price-stabilization techniques include trading halts with indicative prices, the refusal to accept destabilizing orders (both employed in Brussels), stabilizing speculation by market makers (employed in Amsterdam and Brussels), and the affirmative obligation stabilization method as employed in the United States and not currently used by any European stock exchange.[5] Furthermore, it is important to note that the majority of European exchanges do not employ any administrative stabilization techniques such as 'circuit breaking'.[6]

Trading halts with indicative prices are less drastic than maximum price limits since in the former case stabilizing orders can enable trading to resume after a short break. Unfortunately, few exchanges use this technique. Stabilizing speculation by market makers is encouraged in some markets by offering participants a trading advantage through lower trading costs and/or preferred access to some market information. The range of stabilization techniques employed indicates the need for harmonization of standards in this area to enable individual European markets to respond to sharp stock price movements in a coordinated fashion as economic integration proceeds.

3.1.5 Clearing and Settlement Systems

There are as many settlement systems as there are countries within the EC (see table 3.2), and this fact perhaps presents one of the prime obstacles to an integrated equity market in Europe. Most countries have a centralized system of clearing and settlement such as France's Société Interprofessionnelle de Compensation des Valeurs Mobilières (SICOVAM), whereas Italy maintains a network of multiple settlement and clearing systems.

The situation in the United Kingdom is of particular interest because it illustrates an important aspect of a clearing and settlement system: how to be operational at both the international and national levels. Currently, there are two systems in different stages of operation in the United Kingdom; if coordinated, they could give rise to the first instant settlement system for international equities in the world. London's Transfer and Automated Registration of Uncertificated Stock (TAURUS) system, which is to be introduced by 1993 or 1994, is designed to eliminate the share certificates that change hands after each stock market deal in international equity, and also to serve as an automated trade confirmation system. The Institutional Net Settlement (INS) system enables a single payment after the exchange has netted out all the business with member firms. Up to now, these two systems have not been combined.

On the international level, the ISE has initiated a centralized clearing system for world stock exchanges called GLOBALCLEAR. This has not been a success because, among other reasons, neither New York nor Tokyo consented to surrender business to London. A similar prior attempt at becoming the international equity settlement centre for Europe and Scandinavia had also met with the same lack of enthusiasm from participating national stock exchanges which had their own aspirations in attracting foreign business. It is evident that all European exchanges realize that the exchange with the widest and most efficient international settlement and clearing system will hold the competitive advantage.

The integration process may in part assist in the establishment of bridges between major Continental stock exchanges and the ISE. For instance, links now exist between France's SICOVAM and Germany's AUSLAND-KASSENVEREIN. In a larger context, the on-going Interbourse Data Information System (IDIS) project, which attempts to link together Europe's major stock exchanges, ought to be mentioned as it is highly favoured by the European Commission itself. The principal point here is that without a reliable pan-European settlement and clearing system, it is hard to imagine a truly integrated European equity market.

3.1.6   Exchange Membership and the Protection of Intermediaries and Investors

Unlike the United States and Japan, stock exchange membership in Europe does not require the purchase of a 'seat'. Membership is usually granted by the public or private authority of the ruling stock exchange. Usually, membership comes with a stockbroking monopoly, except in the United Kingdom where entry in the market is free, even for foreign firms (see table 3.3). Most markets (Belgium, Luxembourg and Spain being the exceptions) have now been opened to foreign firms.[7]

All countries have established minimum capital requirement for firms and a few countries have done so for individuals. (Only London's ISE has established detailed capital requirements according to the nature and scale of business.) Similarly, all countries require an annual financial report for listed companies, but most also require a more frequent, semi-annual (Italy), quarterly (Belgium, Denmark, Netherlands and United Kingdom) or monthly (United Kingdom) report. In terms of investor protection, half

Table 3.3 European equity markets: membership and regulation, December 1991

	No. of brokers	Broker's monopoly[a]	Seat holding[b]	Minimum commission[c]	No. of exchanges[d]
Belgium	335	Yes	No	Fixed	3 (Brussels)
Denmark	29	Yes	No	Negotiable	1 (Copenhagen)
France	57	Yes	No	Negotiable	1 (Paris)
Germany	1,303	Yes	No	Fixed	8 (Frankfurt)
Italy	255	Yes	No	Negotiable	10 (Milan)
Luxembourg	84	Yes	No	Negotiable	1 (Luxembourg)
Netherlands	150	Yes	No	Negotiable	1 (Amsterdam)
UK	403	No	No	Negotiable	1 (London)
Portugal	12	Yes	No	Fixed and negotiable	2 (Lisbon)
Spain	87	Yes	Yes	Fixed	4 (Madrid)

[a] Only authorized brokers can engage in the brokerage activity in these countries.

[b] Brokers can be required to hold a seat on the trading floor to perform their activities. In Spain the seat is granted.

[c] For more information, see table 3.5.

[d] Number of stock exchanges in a given country with the location of the principal exchange given in parentheses.

Note: Data for Portugal as at 31 December 1987

Source: Amsterdam, Brussels, Copenhagen, Frankfurt, Luxembourg, Milan, Paris Stock Exchanges; Audihispana, Madrid; Touche Ross, London; Spicer & Oppenheim (1988)

the EC countries have investor insurance while the other half do not (see table 3.4).

The legislation efforts and reforms of the European Commission that concern the European equity markets directly are threefold in nature (see appendix) and should have a benign effect in terms of establishing uniform standards and greater harmonization of the current diverse set of regulations.

Offering securities products and/or services

Firms authorized in their home country will be permitted under the Investment Services Directive (under final consideration) to offer a specified list of investment services throughout the EC. Supplementing this major directive is the Directive on Capital Adequacy which harmonizes the capital requirements for investment firms. Unit trusts or mutual funds authorized in one member state and meeting basic standards set by the UCITS Directive ('Collective investment in transferable securities') can sell their units throughout the EC without further approval.

Table 3.4 European equity markets: membership and regulation, December 1991

	Access to foreign firms	Additional require-ments for foreigners	Annual financial state-ments	Other financial state-ments	Investor insurance or guarantee	Regulatory body[a]
Belgium	No	–	Yes	Quarterly	Yes	CBF
Denmark	Yes	No	Yes	Quarterly	No	DSAFA
France	Yes	Yes	Yes	Yes	Yes	COB/CBV
Germany	Yes	No	Yes	No	No	
Italy	Yes	No	Yes	Semi-annual	No	CONSOB
Luxembourg	No	No	Yes	Yes	Stockbrokers	LMI
Netherlands	Yes	No	Yes	Quarterly	Yes	SBN
UK	Yes	No	Yes	Monthly/Quarterly	Yes	SFA
Portugal	No	–	Yes	No	No	Bank of Portugal
Spain	No	–	Yes	Yes	No	CNMV

[a] CB, Commission Bancaire et Financiare; DSAFA, Danish Supervisory Authority of Financial Affairs; COB, Commission des Operations de Bourse; CBV, Conseil de Bourses de Valeurs; CONSOB, Commissione Nazionale per la Societa e la Borsa; LMI, Luxembourg Monetary Institution; SFA, Securities and Futures Authority; CNMV, Sociedad Rectora Bolsa y Comision Nacional Mercado de Valores.

Note: Data for Portugal as at 31 December 1987

Source: Amsterdam, Brussels, Copenhagen, Frankfurt, Luxembourg, Milan, Paris Stock Exchanges; Audihispana, Madrid; Touche Ross, London; Spicer & Oppenheim (1988)

Company listings on various exchanges
The Admissions Directive coordinates minimum standards for company listings on stock exchanges (individual countries can make their own more stringent conditions to 'protect the public'). The Listings Directive specifies which authorities are competent to check and approve listing particulars for multi-country admission.

Reporting and disclosure requirements
The Interim Reports Directive sets minimum standards for interim reports of listed companies, and the two prospectus directives extend the scope and arrangements for mutual recognition of public offer prospectuses and their distribution. The Large Shareholdings Directive

ensures that investors and regulators are informed about major share stakes changes, and the Insider Trading Directive harmonizes existing rules on this subject.

3.1.7 Commissions and Taxation

Until the recent wave of deregulation that affected European financial markets beginning with London's Big Bang in October 1986, fixed commissions were the common practice in European equity markets. Since then, commissions have become negotiable in most European exchanges even though a dual system still persists in some markets with the existence of a ceiling on fixed commissions. Although Belgium, Germany and Portugal continue to maintain a fixed-type commission structure, each allows some degree of flexibility (see table 3.5).

Table 3.5 European equity markets: commission structures, December 1991

	Commission type	
	Negotiable[a]	Fixed[b]
Belgium	No	Yes
Denmark	Yes	
France	Yes	
Germany	No	Yes[c]
Italy	Yes[d]	
Luxembourg	Yes	
Netherlands	Yes	
UK	0.0%–0.2%	
Portugal	No	0.1%–0.6%
Spain	Yes	0.8 pts per share price 1.5 pts under 500 pts
		0.25% for share prices above 500 pts

[a] Commissions may be fully negotiable or negotiable within specified ranges. The data in this column indicate the usual range of observed commission rates.
[b] Commissions can be fixed or fixed within a specified range or fixed up to a certain amount above which they become negotiable.
[c] German specialists require 0.06% of net value for shares, banks charge 1.0% for shares.
[d] Italy, maximum limit of 0.7% but most banks asking only 0.1%.

Note: Data for Portugal as at 31 December 1987

Source: Amsterdam, Brussels, Copenhagen, Frankfurt, Luxembourg, Milan, Paris Stock Exchanges; Audihispana, Madrid; Touche Ross, London; Spicer & Oppenheim (1988)

Commissions are only one part of the cost of trading, and taxation of capital gains, dividends and transactions should also be taken into account. Capital gains are normally taxed where the investor resides, regardless of the national origin of the investment (this ensures that domestic and international investments are taxed similarly). Dividend payments are sometimes the subject of a withholding tax, although in recent years many countries have removed it in order to attract foreign investments. Transactions tax is usually proportional to the amount transacted or to the commission charged by brokers (as is the case for the value-added tax on commissions charged which is prevalent in most EC countries).[8] Currently, these taxation practices vary across European countries and lead to distortions in the flow and allocation of capital. The harmonization of these taxes can be expected to remain a thorny issue well beyond January 1993, especially in so far as tax issues among member states are still decided by the unanimity rule rather than the qualified majority rule.

3.1.8   Derivative Markets

In 1992 seven markets traded equity-related derivative securities: the London International Financial Futures Exchange (LIFFE), the European Options Exchange (EOE) of Amsterdam, the Financial Futures Amsterdam (FTA), the Marché des Options Negociables de Paris (MONEP), the Marché à Terme International de France (MATIF) and the Mercado de Futuros Financieros (MEFF) in Madrid and Barcelona. Equity-related derivative securities can be option and futures contracts on stock market indices. Option contracts are traded on the EOE and the MONEP, while futures contracts are traded on the MATIF and FTA (see table 3.6). With the merger of the LIFFE and the previous London Traded Option Market (LTOM) in March 1992, the new LIFFE provides trading for both option and futures contracts. Despite some efforts to introduce a screen-based trading system for derivative instruments, such as on the Deutsche Termin Börse (DTB), the traditional outcry system continues to be the dominant method for the most actively traded contracts. The German market was slow to develop due to the prohibition by gambling laws of derivative markets until 1988. The recent creation of the Belgian Futures and Option Exchange (BELFOX) provided Belgium's entrée into derivative instrument trading. The exchange began trading a future on a national government bond but began option trading during 1992. Spain has also recently begun derivative trading and Milan began futures trading in 1992.

3.1.9   Informational Efficiency

A review of the evidence on the informational efficiency of European equity markets (Hawawini, 1984) concluded that they could be considered informationally efficient on the three forms of the efficient market hypothesis (EMH): weak form, semi-strong form, and strong form. The key findings are as follows.

1   European equity markets are weak-form efficient regardless of their size
    even when price changes are measured over daily time intervals. A

Table 3.6 Derivative securities markets in Europe, December 1991

	Stock option	Number listed	Stock index option	Stock index future	Option on stock index future	Trading market
Belgium[a]	No	0	No	No	No	BELFOX
Denmark	Yes	6	No	KFX	KFX	Copenhagen Stock Exchange
France	Yes	23	CAC 40/ MONEP	CAC 40/ MATIF	CAC 40/ MATIF	MATIF (futures); MONEP (options)
Germany	Yes	67	DAX	DAX	No	Deutsche Termin Börse
Italy	Yes	–	–	–	–	MIFF
Luxembourg	No	–	No	No	–	–
Netherlands	Yes	23	XMI	FTAA	XMI	EOE
UK[b]	Yes	75	FTSE 100	Yes	Yes	LIFFE
Portugal	No	0	No	No	–	–
Spain	Yes	0	Ibex 35	No	–	–

[a] BELFOX opened trading of mainly government bond futures December 1991; began option trading in 1992.
[b] LIFFE (London International Financial Futures and Options Exchange) houses merged LTOM and LIFFE since March 1992.
Note: Data for Portugal as at 31 December 1987
Source: Amsterdam, Brussels, Copenhagen, Frankfurt, Luxembourg, Milan, Paris Stock Exchanges; Audihispana, Madrid; Touche Ross, London; Spicer & Oppenheim (1988)

weak-form efficient market is a market in which current prices fully and instantaneously reflect all the information implied by the historical sequence of prices. Past prices cannot be employed to earn abnormal profits and the best forecast of tomorrow's price is today's price.

2   Most European equity markets are also efficient in the semi-strong form, implying that prices adjust rapidly and fully to publicly available information, limiting the use of such information to consistently earn above-normal profits.

3   Various research efforts revealing the inability of European institutional portfolios to outperform the market also indicate that many European equity markets may be strong-form efficient. The assumption here is that the inability of these institutional investors to earn abnormal returns, even with possible access to relevant information before it is widely disseminated, is consistent with the strong form of market efficiency.

The above findings should not be interpreted to mean that stock price manipulation and insider trading do not take place in the various European equity markets. In fact, the widely held view is that some individuals and institutions do manage to earn abnormal profits by trading on privileged information, especially in the smaller European equity markets (Hawawini, 1984, p. 148). Therefore the issue is not whether the problem of asymmetric information exists but how European regulators could make their individual markets more efficient and encourage insiders to reveal their superior knowledge.

In a study of Belgian legislative efforts aimed at improving Belgium's capital markets by encouraging information disclosure, Vermaelen (1986, p. 436) argues that effective responses to this problem could be classified in two categories: the regulatory approach, which through regulations forces firms to disclose information, and the free-market approach, which attempts to create market-induced disclosure incentives and information-signalling systems which lead to voluntary disclosure by insiders. The former is the approach pursued in the United States, while the latter is embodied in the UK model of self-regulation and supervision.

Vermaelen points out that, despite its good intentions, the goal of the regulatory approach, in increasing market efficiency by reducing insider trading, is unlikely to be met (as confirmed by the Belgian experience) and indeed may reduce market efficiency by slowing down the speed with which information will be reflected in security prices. Nevertheless, on a Europe-wide basis, the effective integration of the individual equity markets may necessitate the adoption of a minimum set of laws and regulations covering insider trading and stock price manipulation, coupled with a strong law enforcement agency in each country. This should build consistency across markets and foster a level playing ground for investors, intermediaries and exchanges alike.

3.2   Potential Benefits of Portfolio Diversification across European Equity Markets

International portfolio investment has a much longer tradition in Europe than in other major financial centres such as the United States or Japan. Although the benefits of international portfolio investment have been obvious for quite some time (Levy and Sarnat, 1970; Jacquillat and Solnik, 1978) little work has been done on the extent of these benefits within a particular subset of the world's stock markets, e.g. European equity markets.

In this section we examine empirically the major gains which can be achieved from the diversification of European equity markets.[9] We first describe the data and the methodology we employ and then present and discuss our findings.

3.2.1 Data and Methodology

Monthly stock index returns, market capitalization data and exchange rate data (with the exception of data on the ECU) were obtained from the *Morgan Stanley Capital International Perspective*, a monthly publication. The data begin in January 1980 and end in July 1988. All stock returns include gross dividends and each stock index contains the following number of stocks: Belgium, 22; Denmark, 27; France, 83; Federal Republic of Germany, 58; Italy, 68; the Netherlands, 24; Norway, 18; Spain, 31; Sweden, 38; the United Kingdom, 136. The data on the ECU were obtained from *International Financial Statistics*, a monthly publication of the International Monetary Fund.

All calculations were performed using arithmetic monthly returns, and annualized returns are simply 12 times the relevant monthly figures. Annualized risk measures (standard deviation) are monthly figures multiplied by the square root of 12. Total returns for each month are computed from equity returns and exchange return using the formula:

$$R(\text{total}) = \{1 + R(\text{equity}) \}\{1 + R(\text{exchange rate}) \} - 1$$

Total risks (standard deviations) are then computed from these time series of total returns. All frontier graphs in the risk − standard deviation space display annualized figures, and no short-sales constraints are imposed.

3.2.2 Risk Diversification and Market Correlation

The well-known argument about risk diversification is that it lowers risk without necessarily sacrificing return. For this to happen, it is a prerequisite that the various capital markets behave independently of one another.

The degree of independence of a stock market is directly linked to the independence of a country's economy and government policies and regulations. To some extent, common world and European factors affect the expected cash flows of all European firms and therefore their stock prices. However, purely national as well as firm-specific factors do play an important role in asset returns, leading to sizeable differences between markets. Table 3.7 presents the correlation matrix for a selected group of countries from 1980 to 1988, with returns denominated in the local currencies. For example, this table shows that the correlation coefficient between the French and the German markets is 0.517. The square of this correlation coefficient, usually called R^2, indicates the percentage of common variance between the two markets. Here, close to 27 per cent of stock price movements are common to the French and the German markets.

Table 3.7 Correlation matrix of equity returns for a selected group of countries (local currency), 1980–1988

	Belgium	Denmark	France	Germany	Italy	Japan	Netherlands	Norway	Spain	Sweden	UK	USA
Belgium	1.000	0.233	0.562	0.500	0.278	0.399	0.486	0.498	0.230	0.281	0.468	0.407
Denmark	0.233	1.000	0.226	0.238	0.291	0.204	0.352	0.301	0.206	0.212	0.234	0.363
France	0.562	0.226	1.000	0.517	0.373	0.311	0.453	0.433	0.271	0.237	0.428	0.481
Germany	0.500	0.238	0.517	1.000	0.259	0.268	0.574	0.417	0.289	0.283	0.405	0.430
Italy	0.278	0.291	0.373	0.259	1.000	0.276	0.384	0.139	0.344	0.270	0.298	0.233
Japan	0.399	0.204	0.311	0.268	0.276	1.000	0.359	0.261	0.315	0.177	0.415	0.317
Netherlands	0.486	0.352	0.453	0.574	0.384	0.359	1.000	0.589	0.316	0.400	0.660	0.630
Norway	0.498	0.301	0.433	0.417	0.139	0.261	0.589	1.000	0.215	0.387	0.487	0.536
Spain	0.230	0.206	0.271	0.289	0.344	0.315	0.316	0.215	1.000	0.271	0.347	0.333
Sweden	0.281	0.212	0.237	0.283	0.270	0.177	0.400	0.387	0.271	1.000	0.397	0.410
UK	0.468	0.234	0.428	0.405	0.298	0.415	0.660	0.487	0.347	0.397	1.000	0.637
USA	0.407	0.363	0.481	0.430	0.233	0.317	0.630	0.536	0.333	0.410	0.637	1.000

Table 3.8 Correlation matrix of equity returns for a selected group of countries (common currency for pairs), 1980–1988

	Belgium	Denmark	France	Germany	Italy	Japan	Netherlands	Norway	Spain	Sweden	UK	USA
Belgium	1.000	0.371	0.610	0.584	0.318	0.317	0.569	0.575	0.330	0.338	0.497	0.455
Denmark	0.371	1.000	0.324	0.366	0.239	0.160	0.453	0.398	0.270	0.270	0.383	0.490
France	0.610	0.324	1.000	0.587	0.388	0.245	0.519	0.527	0.353	0.287	0.461	0.445
Germany	0.584	0.366	0.587	1.000	0.276	0.190	0.647	0.481	0.346	0.352	0.440	0.465
Italy	0.318	0.239	0.388	0.276	1.000	0.265	0.351	0.201	0.334	0.304	0.360	0.280
Japan	0.317	0.160	0.245	0.190	0.265	1.000	0.282	0.207	0.273	0.155	0.272	0.221
Netherlands	0.569	0.453	0.519	0.647	0.351	0.282	1.000	0.648	0.372	0.450	0.690	0.696
Norway	0.575	0.398	0.527	0.481	0.201	0.207	0.648	1.000	0.314	0.477	0.562	0.541
Spain	0.330	0.270	0.353	0.346	0.334	0.273	0.372	0.314	1.000	0.315	0.424	0.365
Sweden	0.338	0.270	0.287	0.352	0.304	0.155	0.450	0.477	0.315	1.000	0.489	0.496
UK	0.497	0.383	0.461	0.440	0.360	0.272	0.690	0.562	0.424	0.489	1.000	0.618
USA	0.455	0.490	0.445	0.465	0.280	0.221	0.696	0.541	0.365	0.496	0.618	1.000

Few markets exhibit correlation coefficients with other markets that are higher than 0.500. The following pairs can be seen in table 3.7: France–Belgium, 0.562; Germany–Belgium, 0.500; France–Germany, 0.517; Germany–the Netherlands, 0.574; the Netherlands–Norway, 0.589; the United Kingdom–the Netherlands, 0.660.

The same conclusion holds when returns are measured in a common currency. Table 3.8 presents the correlation matrix for the same group of countries from 1980 to 1988. Using the Belgium–Germany example, this table should be read as follows: the correlation coefficient of Belgian equity returns with German equity returns measured in Belgian francs is 0.584. It is obviously the same as the correlation coefficient of Belgian equity returns with German equity returns measured in Deutschemarks (DM). Although correlation coefficients appear a little higher in table 3.8 than in table 3.7, large risk-reduction benefits still seem to exist when investors diversify their portfolios within European equity markets.

3.2.3   Portfolio Volatility

Foreign equity markets are often perceived as more volatile than the home market, especially if currency risk is taken into consideration. Supporting evidence of this volatility is found in tables 3.9–3.11 for French, German and UK investors respectively.[10] The average annual domestic return for each equity market is given in column 1. Column 2 is the exchange gain component of the return for the German investor (table 3.10) investing outside Germany. Column 3 is the total DM-denominated return. The total risk, measured by the standard deviation of DM rates, is presented in column 6. Total risk has two components, the domestic equity risk and the exchange risk, which are given in columns 4 and 5 respectively.

The objective of a risk-diversification policy is to reduce the volatility of a portfolio. The total risk of all stock markets (with the exception of Denmark) is larger than that of the German market when the DM is used as the base currency, even though the domestic risk of some markets might be lower than the risk of the German market. Because of the exchange rate component, the same conclusion holds true from the French or the UK investors' perspective (tables 3.9 and 3.11 respectively). Nevertheless, the addition of more risky foreign countries to a purely domestic portfolio still reduces its total risk if the correlation coefficient of the foreign equity market with the domestic market is not too large.

Table 3.9 Risk and return from the perspective of France, 1980 – 1988 (per cent)

Country	1 Domestic return	2 Exchange gain	3 Total return	4 Domestic risk	5 Exchange risk	6 Total risk
Belgium	27.34	1.89	29.27	21.49	6.56	22.60
Denmark	20.08	2.03	22.21	19.04	3.34	19.78
France	21.54	0.00	21.54	23.01	0.00	23.01
Germany	15.16	4.43	19.67	20.30	4.01	20.95
Italy	30.51	−0.93	29.58	28.90	3.68	29.22
Japan	22.37	12.73	35.49	17.51	10.91	21.75
Netherlands	21.38	4.19	25.67	19.89	3.83	20.55
Norway	15.47	1.81	17.30	27.92	6.61	28.67
Spain	31.03	−1.80	29.18	22.63	6.33	23.56
Sweden	33.15	0.59	33.78	23.71	8.01	25.18
UK	23.14	2.73	25.82	19.89	10.52	22.12
USA	16.34	6.05	22.44	16.88	12.32	20.67
World[a]	18.32	6.15	24.61	14.33	8.85	16.83
Europe[a]	20.88	2.70	23.58	15.38	4.92	16.09
World[b]	18.43	6.70	25.28	14.18	9.12	16.86
Europe[b]	21.40	2.73	24.12	15.42	5.34	16.34
World[c]	20.08	7.98	28.27	13.57	8.24	16.10
Europe[c]	22.06	2.63	24.41	15.32	5.18	16.21

[a] Index calculated using capitalization weights as of 30 June 1980.
[b] Index calculated using capitalization weights as of 29 June 1984.
[c] Index calculated using capitalization weights as of 30 June 1988.

Table 3.10 Risk and return from the perspective of Germany, 1980 – 1988 (per cent)

Country	1 Domestic return	2 Exchange gain	3 Total return	4 Domestic risk	5 Exchange risk	6 Total risk
Belgium	27.24	−2.49	24.74	21.49	5.89	22.04
Denmark	20.08	−2.34	17.76	19.04	2.42	19.46
France	21.54	−4.27	17.21	23.01	3.84	23.29
Germany	15.16	0.00	15.16	20.30	0.00	20.30
Italy	30.51	−5.27	25.25	28.90	3.66	29.52
Japan	22.37	8.38	31.08	17.51	11.25	21.96
Netherlands	21.38	−0.22	21.16	19.89	1.79	19.97
Norway	15.47	−2.54	13.03	27.92	6.53	29.03
Spain	31.03	−6.12	24.83	22.63	6.48	23.86
Sweden	33.15	−3.75	29.37	23.71	8.02	25.24
UK	23.14	−1.58	21.52	19.89	10.87	22.57
USA	16.34	1.73	18.10	16.88	12.64	20.93
World[a]	18.32	1.83	20.27	14.33	9.25	17.22
Europe[a]	20.88	−1.65	19.20	15.38	4.88	16.26
World[b]	18.43	2.37	20.93	14.18	9.51	17.24
Europe[b]	21.40	−1.62	19.74	15.42	5.30	16.53
World[c]	20.08	3.65	23.91	13.57	8.66	16.48
Europe[c]	22.06	−1.98	20.04	15.32	5.26	16.46

[a] Index calculated using capitalization weights as of 30 June 1980.
[b] Index calculated using capitalization weights as of 29 June 1984.
[c] Index calculated using capitalization weights as of 30 June 1988.

Table 3.11 Risk and return from the perspective of the United Kingdom, 1980 – 1988 (per cent)

Country	1 Domestic return	2 Exchange gain	3 Total return	4 Domestic risk	5 Exchange risk	6 Total risk
Belgium	27.34	0.05	27.45	21.49	10.56	24.31
Denmark	20.08	0.34	20.10	19.04	10.44	20.35
France	21.54	−1.64	19.97	23.01	10.45	25.55
Germany	15.16	2.75	18.01	20.30	10.87	23.48
Italy	30.51	−2.59	27.31	28.90	10.85	28.98
Japan	22.37	10.60	33.50	17.51	11.72	22.95
Netherlands	21.38	2.43	23.62	19.89	10.08	21.33
Norway	15.47	−0.23	15.27	27.92	8.46	29.10
Spain	31.03	−3.69	27.29	22.63	9.88	25.00
Sweden	33.15	−1.48	31.63	23.71	9.42	25.67
UK	23.14	0.00	23.14	19.89	0.00	19.89
USA	16.34	3.85	20.32	16.88	12.17	21.11
World[a]	18.32	3.98	22.48	14.33	9.03	17.35
Europe[a]	20.88	0.59	21.45	15.38	6.15	16.61
World[b]	18.43	4.52	23.15	14.18	9.21	17.41
Europe[b]	21.40	0.56	21.93	15.42	5.70	16.47
World[c]	20.08	5.82	26.18	13.57	8.65	16.91
Europe[c]	22.06	0.21	22.23	15.32	5.79	16.39

[a] Index calculated using capitalization weights as of 30 June 1980.
[b] Index calculated using capitalization weights as of 29 June 1984.
[c] Index calculated using capitalization weights as of 30 June 1988.

3.2.4 Currency Risk

Although the European Monetary System (EMS) protects any European investor against wide currency fluctuations, currency risk is often put forward as an argument against European equity diversification. Indeed, currency risk might affect the reduction in security risk achieved by European equity diversification. Currency fluctuations affect both the total return and the volatility of any foreign currency denominated investment. In fact, and particularly over short periods of time, the impact of currency fluctuations on investment returns may exceed that of capital gains or dividend income. Over a long period of time, however, currency fluctuations have never been the major component of total return on a diversified portfolio.

Since exchange rates are difficult to forecast, we shall focus on the contribution of exchange rate uncertainty to the total risk of a portfolio rather than its contribution to expected returns. Empirical studies have shown that currency risk, as measured by the standard deviation of exchange rate movement, is smaller than the risk of the corresponding market. This can be shown by comparing columns 4 (domestic risk) and 5 (exchange risk) of tables 3.9, 3.10 and 3.11. The exchange risk component of total risk is far smaller than the domestic risk component for every country. Furthermore, comparison of the last three columns shows that market and currency risks are not additive. This would only happen if both were perfectly correlated.

In fact, as shown in table 3.12, there is very weak, sometimes negative, correlation between the two. Table 3.12 gives the correlation coefficients between stock returns and returns on foreign exchange from the perspective of each investor's nationality. For example, row 1 indicates the correlation coefficients of the Belgian stock market with each foreign exchange rate displayed on that row. Thus 0.12 is the correlation between the Belgian equity market and the Italian lira−Belgian franc rate. It implies that the Belgian equity market tends to go up when the Italian lira appreciates (the Belgian franc depreciates). Various economic theories have been proposed to explain the influence of real exchange movements on domestic economies. They lead to opposite conclusions (Dornbusch, 1980; Lucas, 1982) and the empirical evidence is somewhat puzzling. Exchange rate fluctuations seem to have only a small systematic influence on stock prices.[11]

However, the contribution of currency risk should be measured for a portfolio that is diversified across both markets and currencies, since part of the risk is diversified away by the cocktail of currencies represented in the portfolio. This can be seen by looking at the world and European data in tables 3.9−3.11. European portfolios exhibit a total risk which is almost the same as the domestic risk, whether the perspective is for UK, French or German investors.

3.2.5 Risk-adjusted Returns

The risk reduction benefit is the most frequently used argument in favour of international investment and European diversification. It is not, however, the sole motive for European diversification. If it were, it could easily be achieved by investing part of the assets in Treasury bills. However, while the inclusion of Treasury bills lowers portfolio risk, it also lowers its expected return. In the framework of the capital asset pricing model,[12] the expected return on a security is equal to the risk-free rate plus a risk premium. In an efficient market, reducing the risk level of a portfolio by adding less risky investments implies reducing the expected return.

It seems that diversification across European equity markets lowers risk without sacrificing return, as shown in tables 3.9−3.11. Whereas the risk of a European portfolio (16.34 per cent annualized standard deviation from the French investor's perspective with the index calculated using the capitalization weights as of end June 1984) is significantly lower than the

Table 3.12 Correlations between stock returns and returns of foreign exchange

Stock Market	Belgium	Denmark	France	Germany	Italy	Japan	Netherlands	Norway	Spain	Sweden	UK	USA
Belgium	–	0.02	0.00	0.04	0.12	0.00	0.00	0.10	0.01	0.14	-0.03	0.06
Denmark	0.14	–	-0.11	-0.12	-0.16	0.14	-0.01	0.21	-0.11	0.13	0.16	0.21
France	0.04	-0.01	–	-0.02	0.08	0.00	0.00	0.16	-0.01	0.04	-0.04	-0.05
Germany	0.05	0.07	-0.02	–	0.13	0.02	-0.06	0.10	-0.12	0.11	-0.03	0.07
Italy	0.07	-0.08	-0.03	-0.13	–	0.27	-0.11	0.23	0.00	0.24	0.19	0.18
Japan	-0.09	-0.07	-0.08	-0.09	-0.05	–	-0.10	-0.10	-0.03	-0.02	-0.16	-0.04
Netherlands	0.12	0.12	-0.03	-0.01	0.03	0.11	–	0.19	-0.04	0.19	0.12	0.25
Norway	0.06	-0.05	0.00	-0.08	-0.02	-0.06	-0.04	–	-0.04	0.04	-0.02	-0.01
Spain	0.06	0.02	0.00	-0.05	0.00	0.09	-0.04	0.10	–	0.05	-0.01	0.05
Sweden	-0.03	-0.02	0.00	-0.02	0.01	0.11	-0.03	0.13	-0.01	–	0.02	0.19
UK	0.04	0.05	0.05	0.00	0.06	-0.07	0.01	0.15	0.07	0.17	–	0.07
USA	0.07	0.02	0.01	-0.01	-0.02	-0.03	0.00	0.03	-0.10	-0.04	-0.04	–

risk of any specific market (Denmark has the lowest standard deviation with 19.78 per cent and Italy the highest with 29.22 per cent), the return of a European portfolio, which is a weighted average of the return for individual countries, is comparable with the equity return of the various countries that make up our sample.

It should be stressed that there is no guarantee that the past will repeat itself. Indeed, over any given period, one national equity market is bound to outperform the others — as a specific stock or a specific industry sector is bound to do within any particular national equity market — and with perfect hindsight, the best strategy would be to invest solely in the top performing market. However, as the markets are fundamentally efficient and since it is a formidable task to forecast them, it is better to spread risk over several European equity markets. The results from tables 3.9−3.11 show that such a strategy ensures a higher expected return.

Of course, the same argument applies to world equity diversification. It should be noted, however, that during the period 1980−8 world diversification did not bring a significantly higher risk−return trade-off than a purely European diversification. For the German investor, world diversification brought a small advantage (20.93 per cent compared with 19.74 per cent, using end 1984 capitalization weights) with a somewhat higher risk (17.24 per cent versus 16.53 per cent).

3.2.6 Optimal International Asset Allocation

In this section we examine the *ex post* efficient frontier (with no short-selling constraints on any investments) using a mean-variance Markowitz optimization framework (Markowitz, 1959).

The risk and return curves for *ex post* investment strategies are given in figures 3.1, 3.2 and 3.3 for France, Germany and the United Kingdom respectively. Computations are performed using each of the three local currencies for each of those countries. The set of optimal strategies represents the portfolio of market indexes that could have maximized returns for different levels of risk (standard deviation). The world indexes using three sets of market capitalization weights, end June 1980, end June 1984 and end June 1988 (note that only the first weighting scheme could have been implemented in practice), are also included in the figures.

According to modern financial theory, the market portfolio should be efficient in a risk−return sense, i.e. the market portfolio should be on the efficient frontier. Internationally, according to figures 3.1−3.3, market portfolios seem far from efficient, at least judging from historical data. This implies that there is plenty of room for an asset allocation strategy different from market capitalization weights.

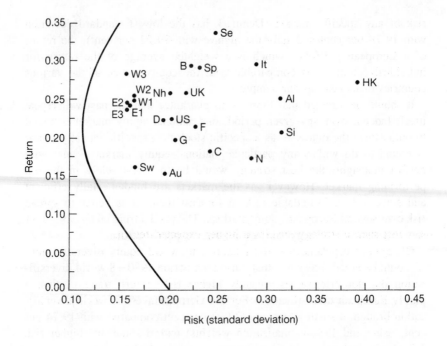

Al	Australia
Au	Austria
B	Belgium
C	Canada
D	Denmark
E1	Index of European countries using capitalization weights as of 30 June 1980
E2	Index of European countries using capitalization weights as of 29 June 1984
E3	Index of European countries using capitalization weights as of 30 June 1988
F	France
G	Germany
HK	Hong Kong
It	Italy
Jp	Japan
N	Norway
Nh	The Netherlands
Se	Sweden
Si	Singapore
Sp	Spain
Sw	Switzerland
UK	United Kingdom
US	United States
W1	World index using capitalization weights as of 30 June 1980
W2	World index using capitalization weights as of 29 June 1984
W3	World index using capitalization weights as of 30 June 1988

Figure 3.1 Efficient frontier for France.

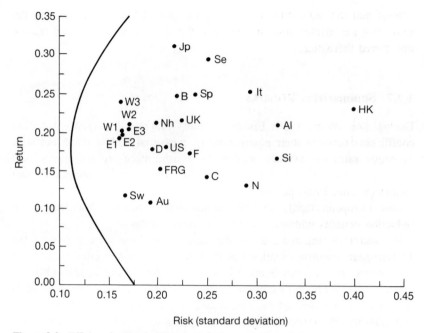

Figure 3.2 Efficient frontier for Germany: for key, see figure 3.1.

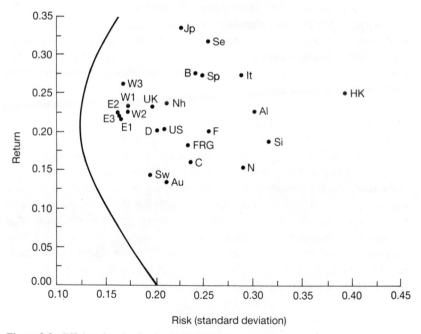

Figure 3.3 Efficient frontier for the United Kingdom: for key, see figure 3.1.

Note that the asset allocation strategies applied here are passive in the sense that the market weights are set at the start of the period and remain unchanged thereafter.

3.2.7 Summarizing Remarks

During most of the 1980s European equity markets. displayed correlation coefficients between their equity returns, measured both without and with exchange rates, of average magnitude. Furthermore, equity returns and exchange rates exhibited almost no correlation, as found in other empirical studies (Solnik, 1988, pp. 47–8). Hence a dynamic asset allocation strategy across European equity markets would have brought about high risk reduction benefits without a sacrifice in total returns.

We can raise the issue as to the validity of these conclusions as the 12 European countries continue their efforts at economic integration. Will this process place equity returns in these countries more in line with one another? Will increased exchange rate stability among European currencies be a further outcome of ongoing monetary integration? In other words, assuming that the response to these two questions is in the affirmative, will the correlation coefficients discussed above increase by any significant measure, and consequently reduce portfolio diversification opportunities?

It is quite possible that European integration may result in statistically significant increases in correlation coefficients between major European equity market returns over the next five to ten years. Despite this possibility, it could be argued that any decline in diversification opportunities from a risk reduction standpoint will be more than offset by certain key factors such as increased operational and informational efficiency as well as more opportunities for 'focused diversification'. Increased operational efficiency should lead to greater liquidity ('depth') in each major market as well as greater fluidity ('scope') across markets. In other words, as markets integrate, many of the current operational obstacles, such as clearing and settlement, should greatly diminish, encouraging more foreign listings and expanding the choice for investors. In addition, focused diversificaton opportunities should arise as markets integrate. By this we mean that increased opportunities for 'industry sector', 'company size' or 'economic/ geographic pockets' diversification approaches on a Europe-wide basis should present themselves, similar to those available in a fully integrated market such as the United States.

3.3 Future of European Equity Markets

A forecast of the future is always a difficult and precarious exercise. In this concluding section we discuss a number of key issues which should affect the evolution of European stock exchanges.

3.3.1 Various Economic, Deregulation, Integration and Competitive Factors Prevalent in the late 1980s should Foster Equity Funding as an Efficient Financing Alternative

On the whole in the lead up to 1992 the major industrial economic blocks, including Europe, experienced economic growth and stability. The practical benefits of this in the European context have been lower inflation rates, a narrowing of interest rate differentials, more stable exchange rates within the EMS and a steady increase in economic productivity, which in turn have favourably affected the overall performances of the various European equity markets.

In addition, Europe saw an acceleration of the integration process in the late 1980s, especially in the financial sector, in preparation for the unified economic market of 1993. A direct effect of these efforts has often been attributed to the rise in domestic and cross-border mergers and acquisitions, partly reflecting a consolidation process (see chapter 4). While it can be argued that this reduces the number of listed companies on the various exchanges, it should be noted that an ancillary effect of the trend in mergers and acquisitions may be a gradual increase in average equity prices because most firms are acquired at a premium from their market value.

In the securities industry, more specifically, the positive benefits clearly lie in the ongoing harmonization of the vast panoply of regulations, practices and attitudes in each of the national markets which in turn should allow firms to access multiple currency equity funding, with less administrative and operational obstacles, assisted by pan-European securities houses in the distribution and trading of their securities (see section 3.1).

In addition to the positive fall-out of the integration process, continuing national equity market reforms have further assisted in stimulating the modernization of often archaic Continental trading arrangements (see section 3.1). The national reforms, especially in major Continental markets (Germany, France and the Netherlands) could in many ways be termed a competitive reaction to the rapid liberalization and modernization efforts of London, New York and Tokyo and a realization that once an 'intangible' market consolidates itself in one location, the competitive lead time of that location will be hard to recapture in a market characterized by rapid technological evolution.

A related factor driving the positive growth predictions for European equity markets is the continued trend of privatization of hitherto government-owned corporations. This has a threefold effect on European equity markets: it creates new supplies of stock, it raises awareness of equity markets among local investors and it forces governments into assuming a more constructive view of their national equity markets.

3.3.2 'Piggy-backed' to the Development of Equity Financing, Equity-linked Derivative Products should also Demonstrate Strong Evolution

The market for equity-linked options and futures contracts in Europe should develop more rapidly over the next decade stimulated by the need of institutional fund managers (see below) and European multinational corporate finance managers and treasurers for more sophisticated risk – return management tools. In the past, the derivatives market was hindered by various factors such as the lack of investor sophistication and poor liquidity in the underlying equity markets, as well as outright mistrust on the part of certain public and regulatory authorities (we saw in section 3.1 that Germany banned public trading in futures and options until 1989 under the argument that they violated gambling laws).

The key European financial centres will continue the current competition for leadership in developing and maintaining an edge in the European derivatives market. Until 1992 France and the United Kingdom were the only two EC countries with futures and option contracts on their respective stock market indices, but the others have competitively followed suit.

3.3.3 The Importance of Institutional Investors in European Equity Markets should Develop, Necessitating New Skills and Capabilities on the Part of Intermediaries

Institutional investors have begun to play a key role in most of the major European equity markets. The main impetus for this trend is derived from the continued growth of mutual and pension funds. Pension funds are increasingly shifting towards a capitalization system and away from a redistribution system. In the former, funds collected from individuals are invested for future distribution according to certain investment criteria whereas, in the latter, contributions made by individuals currently working are immediately redistributed to current pensioners. These government reforms are partly based on the fact that rapidly ageing populations are increasingly exerting pressures on limited public retirement funds coupled with the fact that government liberalization in many European countries now permits an increased percentage of equity holdings in those funds.

Moreover, equity mutual funds are ideal vehicles for individual investors seeking to capture the potential gains from diversification which we discussed in section 3.2. Furthermore, there has also been a growing interest from individuals in investing part of their savings in the stock market through mutual funds to supplement their compulsory pension plans. Recent government liberalization efforts in this area have even enabled individual investors to deduct from their taxable income a set level of the funds invested (as in the UK Personal Equity Plans, the French Plan d'Epargne Retraite and the Belgian Pension Savings Plan).

The above institutionalization trend in European equity markets has gone hand in hand with the increasing need for equity market intermediaries (brokers−dealers) to have an 'own-book' positioning and market-making capability. The importance of building this capability across European markets cannot be stressed sufficiently. Unlike individual investors, institutional investors buy, hold and trade in enormous blocks and utilize extremely sophisticated portfolio management techniques. Successful intermediaries will be called upon, not only for their execution capability, but also for their 'information' capability, i.e. their knowledge of who the buyers and sellers are.

3.3.4 A Continuation of Current European Equity Market Dynamics should Result in a Two-tiered Market Structure

As reviewed in earlier sections, numerous factors indicate that the continuation of current developments in European equity markets should lead to the formation of a two-tiered market, with London as the key European 'hub' centre and the various Continental exchanges as satellite centres of differing importance.

Of the prime factors that will enable London to be the European link in the global equity market, four clearly need to be cited: (a) the sheer size and level of concentration of activity (number of listings, amounts of new issuance/distribution/trading and the number of major well-capitalized intermediaries); (b) existence and importance of cross-linkages to other major capital markets (bonds, bank debt syndication and foreign exchange) in which London has maintained a lead position; (c) heavy investment made over the past decade in data processing and telecommunications equipment that enables rapid execution and effective settlement of equity trades (London has been the traditional absorbing centre for most of the technological innovations that have emanated from New York and Tokyo);

(d) the very fact that points (a), (b) and (c) exist leads to London's competitive advantage in developing an equity-linked derivatives market and being capable of supporting block trading and other market-making activities which in the post-1992 period will be vital competitive factors (see the earlier discussion of the institutionalization trend and the trans-European equity issuance practices of major European corporations).

If major corporations in the next decade, having 'outgrown' their home markets, tend to issue (and subsequently trade) their equities in London, what role can be foreseen for Continental exchanges and intermediaries that up to the present have been hampered by a lack of each of the above four factors? The answer probably lies in the path followed by certain smaller US exchanges and regional intermediaries that have tended to focus on 'middle-market' companies and flotations of regional start-ups, and serve as satellite exchanges for smaller trades and occasional 'packaged trades' (similar to the role Frankfurt plays *vis-à-vis* other local German exchanges).

As mentioned above, there will be significant differences in importance even among these Continental 'satellite' exchanges, with Paris and Frankfurt holding the competitive edge (despite the strong efforts of Amsterdam), partly because of the scale and scope of their operations. Paris appears to have a slight advantage over Frankfurt as a result of its rapid modernization and its attempts at developing equity-linked derivative markets. Frankfurt is hindered by archaic regulations, a traditional official distaste for most forms of derivative products and a stifling dominance of the universal banks that have little incentive to change the current relatively protected situation. If they do plan any changes, it is more likely that German universal banks, supported by their vast capitalization, will transfer their equity trading skills and undertake equity market activities in London.

3.3.5   Several Impeding Factors may Limit the Favourable Outlook for the Development of European Equity Markets

The above favourable outlook for the continued growth and development of European equity markets presupposes limited obstacles in its path, be they market initiated or operational — structural. Two key potential obstacles need to be highlighted and serve to temper our positive views: the strong 'crowding-out' effect that may arise from the traditionally vibrant debt markets, and the high possibility that, despite the integration process, an interconnected clearing and settlement system on a pan-European basis may be an extremely long-term prospect.

Debt markets (broadly defined to include private and government bonds, syndicated loans, note issuance facilities etc.) in European countries, as elsewhere, are generally larger and more developed than equity markets and are growing at faster rates (OECD, 1992).

Over the past two decades, global equity financing has steadily declined as a percentage of all financing forms. Key reasons for this relative decline are the faster growth rate of debt financing, the steadily increasing levels of government debt financing, the increasingly shorter-term perspectives of institutional and individual investors, and the rapid level of technological innovations associated with the bond market. The last reason has enabled enormous advances in 'financing flexibility' for corporate issuers and 'investment portfolio flexibility' for investors. A continuation of this trend may result in a 'crowding-out' of financing in the equity form, with relative market pricing of the two forms adjusting to reflect the changes in supply and demand conditions.

In addition to the competition from debt markets, the future of integrated European equity markets depends strongly on effective interconnected clearing and settlement systems (this is not the case with unsecuritized debt, where the 'suppliers' of funds are financial intermediaries). While legislative efforts to obtain 'harmonization' and 'mutual recognition' in the EC will enable investors to capture diversification opportunities and intermediaries to expand their area of operations, a pan-European interlinked clearing and settlement system will require both private market efforts (of the various exchanges working jointly) as well as supranational support from EC and non-EC European states. It is most likely that the final functioning (the efforts have already begun, as seen in section 2.5) of these telecommunications and operations interlinkages will be forthcoming only when the various national equity markets feel that a status quo in market structure and 'roles' for exchanges have been established (see section 3.3.4). Until that point, the changing dynamics and the aspirations, however far-fetched, of certain national exchanges may preclude such mutual efforts.

Appendix   Key Directives Concerning the European Securities Industry

Name/subject	Aim	Status/comments
Directive on Investment Services	Similar to the Second Banking Directive, it allows firms to carry out specified investment services (investment advice, broking, dealing or portfolio management) throughout the EC if they have authorization in their home country; home member state must ensure that the investment firm follows conduct of business rules. Introduces procedure for reciprocity with third countries; Commission may initiate negotiations to secure comparable competitive opportunities for Community investment firms in third country	Amended Proposal stage; passed Council agreement
Directive on Capital Adequacy	Supplements the Directive on Investment Services by harmonizing the capital requirements for investment firms; subjects bank and non-bank investment firms to equivalent legislation requirements so as to ensure fair competition	Amended Proposal stage; awaiting decisions by BIS Basle and IOSCO in order to keep legislation compatible with international standards
Directive on UCITS (1985, amended 1988)	Coordinates laws and rules for collective investment undertakings (UCITS); principle is that a unit trust approved in one state and meeting basic standards set by the directive can sell its units anywhere in the EC without further approval	Deadline: 1/10/89, except for Greece and Portugal which had until 1/4/92; in force in all but Italy
Directive on Special Measures for Certain Investments by UCITS (1985, amended 1988)	Enables UCITS to treat certain bonds neither issued nor guaranteed by the state as offering similar security to state-guaranteed bonds; extends the limiting amount UCITS may invest in one specific class of security	Same as Directive on UCITS

Appendix *continued.*

Name/subject	Aim	Status/comments
Directive on Admissions to EC Stock Exchanges (1979, amended 1982)	Coordinates minimum standards for companies on stock exchanges with the goal of making it easier for companies to raise capital on a pan-European basis	In force in all markets; countries cannot refuse a listing on the grounds that the company has not been listed on another exchange first but they can turn it down for investor 'protection' reasons
Directive on Listing Particulars for Securities Issuance on Official Exchange (1980, amended 1987, 1990)	Specifies which authorities are competent to check and approve listing particulars in cases where an application for admission to official listing is made in more than one member state; establishes the principle of reciprocal agreements with non-EC countries	Deadline: 17/4/91; 1980, Directive in force in all countries except for France and Italy; 1987, accepted by all but Greece; 1990, accepted by all but Belgium and France
Directive on Interim Reports (1982)	Sets minimum standards for interim reports of listed companies; established that interim reports must be published within four months of end of each six-month period	In force in all member states
Directive on Scrutiny and Distribution of Prospectuses (1989)	Aims to harmonize rules for publishing and distribution of prospectuses	Deadline: 17/4/91; in force in all but France, Greece, Ireland, and Italy
Directive on Mutual Recognition of Public Offer Prospectuses (1990)	Extends the scope and arrangements for mutual recognition by recognizing public offer prospectuses as listing particulars	Deadline: 17/4/91; implemented in all but Belgium, France, Ireland, Portugal, and Spain
Directive on Large Shareholdings Disclosure (1988)	Ensures that investors/regulators are aware of major changes in ownership; shareholder must inform company and/or regulator within seven days when holding goes above or below 10%, 20%, 33.3%, 50%, 66.6%	Deadline: 1/1/91; main problem should prove to be enforcement – for example, the UK has a system where shares are registered by a company, while France and Germany have bearer securities cleared electronically through SICOVAM and Deutsche Kassenverein (DKV)

Appendix   *continued.*

Name/subject	Aim	Status/comments
Directive on Insider Trading (1989)	Prohibits insider dealing, whereby investors who are in possession of inside information take advantage of that information at the expense of others who are not, and thus ensures that all investors are placed on an equal footing; includes cooperation among national authorities	Deadline: 1/6/92; accepted by France, Ireland, and Luxembourg
Directive on Securities Transaction Tax (1976)	Aims to abolish indirect taxes (stamp duties) on securities transactions; does not apply to VAT on commissions	Proposal stage; this directive is part of the overall tax programme of the EC

Source: Compiled from various sources, including *The Banker*; the European Commission Directorate General XV, *Completing the Internal Market: A Common Market for Services*; and *EC Financial Newsletter*, Clifford Chance.

Notes

1   A safeguard clause allows exchange controls to be imposed where 'exceptional' short-term capital movements would seriously disrupt monetary and exchange rate policies.

2   See *F.I.B.V. Statistics 1990*, Fédération Internationale des Bourses de Valeurs, Paris, p. 15.

3   These and other factors have permitted London to consolidate further its key position among European equity markets. For instance, approximately 25 per cent of the capitalization of the most active French shares are traded in London rather than Paris. This also appears to hold true in the case of large block trading of other Continental shares. See Hawawini (1984, p. 155).

4   The auction form of batch system is utilized to establish the opening price in some continuous markets such as Amsterdam and Frankfurt (see Cohen et al., 1986, p. 17).

5   The affirmative obligation stabilization gives the US specialist the responsibility of stabilizing prices if transaction-to-transaction price changes or price changes over each thousand shares traded exceed certain limits set up for each stock according to its size. The size is measured by the stock's price and transaction volume.

6   'Circuit breaking' refers to the halting of transactions if the stock market index rises over a specified limit during the trading session. It is an example of an administrative stabilization technique.

7   Reforms in France enable foreigners to hold a majority interest in local brokerage houses; similar reforms are also under way in Belgium and Spain. These trends are significant in that the emergence of broker–dealer houses with a majority interest in several European domestic firms, providing an effective linkage among European markets, should hasten the movement towards integration.

8   The securities transaction tax is part of the overall tax reform programme and aims to abolish indirect taxes on securities transactions.

9   In so doing, we perform an analysis using a format which is similar to the one utilized by Solnik (1988) and Jacquillat and Solnik (1989).

10 Owing to space shortage, we have presented results on portfolio volatility for these three countries only. However, they represent 66 per cent of total European equity capitalization. Similar tables for the other European countries are available from the authors on request.

11 The low correlation between stock returns and exchange rate movements has been documented in various studies. See, for example, Adler and Simon (1986) and Solnik (1988).

12 This model was developed by Sharpe (1964); see also Alexander and Francis (1986).

References

Adler, M. and Simon, D. (1986) Exchange rate surprises in international portfolios. *Journal of Portfolio Management*, 12(2), 44–53.

Alexander, G. and Francis, J.C. (1986) *Portfolio Analysis*. London: Prentice Hall.

Cohen, K., Maier, S., Schartz, R. and Whitcomb, D. (1986) *The Microstructure of Securities Markets*. Englewood Cliffs, NJ: Prentice Hall.

Commission of the European Communities (1990) *Completing the Internal Market: A Common Market for Services*. Brussels: December 1990.

Dornbusch, R. (1980) *Open Economy Macroeconomics*. New York: Harper and Row.

Fédération Internationale des Bourses de Valeurs (1990) *F.I.B.V. Statistics 1990*. Paris: FIBV.

Hawawini, G. (1984) European equity markets: price behavior and efficiency. Monograph Series in Finance and Economics, Salomon Brothers Center for the Study of Financial Institutions, New York University.

Jacquillat, B. and Solnik, B. (1978) Multinationals are poor tools for international diversification, *Journal of Portfolio Management*, 4, 8–12.

Jacquillat, B. and Solnik, B. (1989) *Marches Financiers: Gestion de Portefeuille et des Risques*. Paris: Dunod.

Levy, H. and Sarnat, M. (1970) International diversification of investment porfolios. *American Economic Review*, 60(4), 668–75.

Lucas, R. (1982) Interest rates and currency prices in two-country world. *Journal of Monetary Economics*, 10(3), 335–60.

Markowitz, H. (1959) *Portfolio Selection: Efficient Diversification of Investments*. New York: Wiley.

OECD (1992) *National Accounts Main Aggregates*, Volume 1. Paris: OECD.

Sharpe, W. (1964) Capital asset prices: a theory of market equilibrium under conditions of risk. *Journal of Finance*, 19(3), 425–42.

Solnik, B. (1988) *International Investments*. Reading, MA: Addison Wesley.

Spicer and Oppenheim (1988) *Guide to Securities Markets Around the World*. New York: Wiley.

Vermaelen, T. (1986) Encouraging information disclosure. *Tijdschrift voor Economie en Management*, 31(4), 435–50.

Comment

Théo Vermaelen

This chapter starts with a discussion of the factors which made 1992 possible in equity markets. The authors emphasize the role of the EC bureaucracy. I personally would have put more emphasis on the leading role of the UK in liberalizing Continental stock exchanges. As the authors point out, the UK equity market had most of the features of the 'idealized' market before 1992: negotiated commissions, free entry into the market-making business, a sophisticated trading system, etc. I believe that the enthusiasm of the Continent for stock market reform has been largely fuelled by the competitive pressure from the UK. As the authors point out, it is today cheaper to buy large blocks of French stocks in London than in France. Hence the deregulation of financial markets is an example of deregulation through competition. The problem with the 1992 initiative has been that, while promoting competition between firms, it was at the same time trying to eliminate competition between regulators by imposing uniform regulatory standards. As usual, this was done under the questionable assumption that regulators rather than market forces should determine what investors need.

Take, for example, the authors' proposal to impose uniform price-stabilization techniques across Europe. There is no evidence to support any beneficial effects from trading suspensions or price limits. For example, an extensive study by Professor Richard Roll from the University of California at Los Angeles found that the existence of price-stabilization techniques made no difference to the long-term price response of security markets during the October 1987 crash. Price limits only create short-term inefficiencies.

Another popular example of misguided government regulation was the outcry for restrictions on insider trading. The argument was that insider trading makes the market inefficient and makes investors reluctant to trade. The argument confused insider trading with inside information. Markets *are* inefficient and investors may be unwilling to trade because they believe that prices do not reflect all available information. Even in a world without insider *trading*, inside *information* will still exist. If, for example, M. Mitterrand and his friends decide to take over Triangle at a tender price five times the market price, the market is inefficient between the moment of the decision and the time of the announcement of the public bid. We could argue that, by encouraging insider trading, the market would become more efficient. If, for example, all friends of M. Mitterrand were free to benefit from insider trading, prices of Triangle shares would increase much faster because each insider has an incentive to reveal his information as soon as he or she takes a position. Competition between insiders will reduce insider trading profits and in the process eliminate insider information. The only argument against insider trading is that people with a competitive advantage (in information acquisition) can make a lot of money. However, that is true for others with a competitive advantage such as tennis players, rock stars and perhaps some university professors.

The second part of the chapter is devoted to a rather unqualified recommendation to diversify internationally. The theoretical arguments for international diversification (or for any diversification for that matter) are based on two assumptions: (a) asset returns are not perfectly correlated (which is, of course, true), and (b) markets are fully integrated so that only world market (non-diversifiable) risk is compensated by higher expected returns.

If markets are not fully integrated it may be that international diversification will not only reduce risk, but also expected return. For example, if Japanese investors are reluctant to invest abroad, they will ask for compensation for domestic risk and not just for world market risk. This means that a European investor should not fully diversify, but tilt his portfolio towards Japanese companies. Only if markets become more integrated could an argument be made for international diversification. This leads to the 'Catch 22 of international diversification': it only pays to diversify if 'everyone else' is already diversified.

Hence, whether international diversification pays is an empirical issue: do we sacrifice expected return when we reduce variance? The authors claim to test this by comparing the historical rate of return and variance on a set of domestic markets with the corresponding values of a diversified European portfolio. It is stated that 'whereas the risk of a European portfolio (16.34 per cent) . . . is significantly lower than the risk of any specific market (between 19.78 and 29.22 per cent) . . . the return on a European portfolio . . . is comparable with the equity return of the various countries'. Are (in table 3.9) the 35 per cent Japanese return and the 33.78 per cent Swedish return 'comparable' with the 23.58 per cent return of the European index? The only way to test the international capital asset pricing model is (a) to compute stock market price sensitivities (βs) of particular stocks to economic shocks relative to the world market portfolio and (b) to test whether average domestic returns are a positive function of their world market β. Without performing such a test, casual empiricism allows us to reject the hypothesis: the market with the lowest world market β (Japan) has also the largest historical rate of return. Moreover, during recent years, various 'anomalies', such as the fact that small firms beat large firms on a risk-adjusted basis, have shown up in empirical studies. Hence, rather than diversifying inter-nationally, investors should concentrate on these anomalies (e.g. buying small firms in countries where the small firm effect is most pronounced).

In summary, while this chapter is interesting and informative, I would have preferred to see a more critical assessment of (a) the benefits of international diversification and (b) the ambiguous role of the European Commission which, behind the banner of free enterprise, attempts to eliminate competition between regulatory bodies.

4

European Investment Banking: Structure, Transactions Flow and Regulation

Ingo Walter and Roy C. Smith

The 1992 initiatives in Europe portend significant risks and opportunities for the investment banking industry, rivalling and perhaps surpassing the US deregulation of the 1970s, the UK Big Bang of 1986, Japan's liberalization of the later 1980s, and even the possible repeal of the Glass–Steagall provisions of the Banking Act of 1933 in the United States and its counterpart in Japan, Article 65 of the Securities and Exchange Act of 1947.

The 1992 initiatives do not constitute a discrete 'event' so much as a series of deregulations that accompany and validate fundamental economic policy changes that have occurred in Europe since about 1980. These changes include a retreat from popular socialism and state interference in industry aimed at achieving full employment, and movement toward free-market policies that attempt to remove the stifling inefficiencies that accompany public-sector management of industry in the absence of effective competition.

Our task requires that we speculate about the future. We are aware of how difficult this is while in the middle of many changes and developments that will have a profound effect on outcomes during the 1990s. We have tried therefore to look at the larger forces driving the marketplace for financial services, and have attempted to analyse the extent to which these forces will continue to shape events in the future.

The most powerful of these forces, as judged by experiences with financial deregulation in other countries, has been that of free competition among established investment banking players seeking to protect their entrenched market positions and a plethora of newcomers from both domestic and foreign quarters seeking to develop new opportunities for themselves. New and old competitors alike are striving to improve the investment banking services they offer and to demonstrate superior performance capabilities. This tends to upgrade the quality and lower the prices of the services offered. Pressures develop on profitability, and a survival-of-the-fittest mentality ensues. The fittest do survive, but as a stronger more competitive species.

This is part of a larger study by the authors entitled *Investment Banking in Europe: Restructuring for the 1990s* (Oxford: Basil Blackwell, 1989).

This somewhat Darwinian view applies both to investment bankers and their principal clients in the 1992 European environment. The power of competition to effect changes to a post-deregulation setting has been underestimated in the past. We give it full rein. We believe that forces already unleashed by the 1992 initiatives will ultimately be formidable and, indeed, irreversible.

On the whole our view is that the 1992 initiatives, as imperfect and delayed as they may ultimately prove to be, will nevertheless eventually lead to a substantial reordering of the investment banking business in Europe. This will take place in an environment in which demand for all investment banking services will be increased by invigorated industrial activity, although stiff competition will ensure that the benefits of enhanced performance and lower costs will mainly flow to the users of the services. Such an environment will test the abilities of many banks to operate profitably on a larger, but unprotected, European regional basis. Shifts in strategies will be required, and the timeliness and effectiveness with which they are implemented will affect the reordering of the investment banking industry that we expect to take place in Europe and, indeed, worldwide. The 1990s will be interesting times for investment bankers.

In this chapter we consider the specific implications of the 1992 initiatives for the three principal areas of investment banking activity − capital raising, corporate financial advisory services (including mergers, acquisitions, breakups and leveraged transactions), and secondary-market and brokerage trading. We devote considerable attention to the evolving rules of the game in securities market regulation. This is an area in which much is yet to be done, and our observations are accompanied by some specific policy suggestions.

4.1   Investment Banking Services

4.1.1   Underwriting New Issues of Securities

Most visible among all European investment banking services is the management of underwriting syndicates for new issues of securities. 'League tables' showing each underwriter's performance as a lead manager of issues appear frequently in various financial publications. These depict a broad array of different types of securities and markets in which they are sold. The best-known and largest single market in Europe is the Eurobond (and Euro-equity) market, used extensively by governments and corporations worldwide. Most securities sold by European corporations, however, are *domestic* issues in their own national markets with banking and financial companies comprising about 62 per cent of all such issues. Nevertheless, the data suggest that European non-financial corporations, historically infrequent issuers of securities, are increasing their usage of capital markets (as opposed to bank borrowing) as the markets have become more active and accommodating and as companies have become more experienced in using them.

As of the end of 1987, the total volume of all intra-European capital market new issues by European corporations had reached levels equal to approximately 76 per cent of comparable corporate financing activity in the United States, and 81 per cent of the level of activity in Japan – see table 4.1. This volume of financing indicates that the European markets had achieved a comparatively mature state of development in relation to the world's two other principal capital markets. The amounts shown under 'Europe' represent the consolidated volume of financing by European corporations in the Eurobond markets plus the volume of domestic capital market issues and those in other European national markets.

Domestic capital markets have been especially important for new issues of debt securities in Germany, France and Italy, and for equity securities in France and the United Kingdom – where large privatization programmes occurred in 1986 and 1987. Altogether, European domestic new issues totalled $240 billion in 1987. To this amount, European corporations (including public-sector incorporated entities) added a further $50 billion of new issue financing from transactions in the Eurobond and equity markets and issues floated in the domestic markets of other European countries (i.e. European 'foreign' issues). The 1987 total of all European capital market issues, including privatization issues, was $291 billion – $201 billion in debt and $90 billion in equity (table 4.2). European non-financial corporations accounted for 38.28 per cent of all European issues in 1987, although they accounted for 46 per cent of all Euromarket and foreign-market issues (table 4.3).

By comparison, corporate new issues of securities in the United States in 1987 totalled $381 billion, of which 53 per cent represented issues by non-financial corporations. In Japan, corporate new issues totalled $359 billion, of which about 35 per cent was accounted for by non-financial corporations. The total amount of capital market new issue activity in the three regions, on a per dollar of gross national product (GNP) basis, shows a reasonable degree of similarity. There is a substantial difference between them, however, with regard to non-financial corporate use of capital markets for new issues in relation to GNP. European non-financial corporations appear to be lagging behind their counterparts in the United States and Japan in this respect by a ratio of 1 to 1.7, as shown in table 4.1.

We know, of course, that the United States experienced an extremely active period of mergers and acquisitions and financial restructuring which precipitated substantial amounts of debt and equity financing by corporations

Table 4.1 Volume of capital market financing by regional corporations in their respective regional markets 1987 (US$ million of proceeds at average exchange rates)

	USA			Europe			Japan[a]		
	Financial	Non-financial	Total	Financial	Non-financial	Total	Financial	Non-financial	Total
Equities	34,500	33,900	68,400	163,593	73,986	237,579	4,400	23,600	28,000
Bonds	145,600	167,100	312,700	239,019	37,470	276,489	227,900	103,100	331,000
Total	180,100	201,000	381,100	402,612	111,456	514,068	232,300	126,700	359,000
GNP (US$ billion)		4,700			5,300			2,400	
Financing per $ GNP	0.038	0.043	0.081	0.042	0.026	0.068	0.097	0.053	0.150

[a] Includes short-term discount debentures sold by banks.
Sources: OECD; EC; Securities Data Corporation.

Table 4.2 Capital market financing by all European companies, 1985–1988 (US$ million of proceeds at current exchange rates)

	Total debt issues				Total equity issues				Total issues			
	Euro-bonds	Foreign bonds	Domestic bonds	Total bonds	Euro-equities	Foreign equities	Domestic equities	Total equities	Euro-issues	Foreign issues	Domestic issues	Total issues
1985												
No. of issues	340	93			45	6			385	99		
Volume	33,588	3,478	110,432	147,498	3,253	156	29,233	32,642	36,841	3,634	139,665	180,140
Average issue size	99	37			72	26			96	37		
1986												
No. of issues	449	95			107	17			556	112		
Volume	49,465	4,582	142,509	196,556	13,943	2,297	57,570	73,810	63,408	6,879	200,079	270,366
Average issue size	110	48			130	135			114	61		
1987												
No. of issues	337	165			109	26			446	191		
Volume	29,239	6,465	165,845	201,549	11,924	3,377	74,306	89,607	41,163	9,842	240,151	291,156
Average issue size	87	39			109	130			92	52		
1988												
No. of issues	511	208			43	11			554	219		
Volume	53,931	9,401	n.a.		5,921	740	n.a.		59,852	10,141	n.a.	
Average issue size	106	45			138	67			108	46		

n.a., not available.

Sources: European and foreign data, Securities Data Corporation; domestic data, OECD.

Table 4.3 Capital market financing by European non-financial corporations (US$ million of proceeds at average exchange rates)

	Non-financial debt			Non-financial equities			Total non-financial issues			Non-financial as a percentage of total issues
	Eurobonds and foreign bonds	Domestic bonds	Total bonds	Euro-equities and foreign equities	Domestic equities	Total Equities	Euro-issues and foreign issues	Domestic issues	Total issues	
1985	11,779	12,249	24,028	2,660	23,610	26,270	14,440	35,859	50,299	27.92
1986	25,314	19,122	44,436	13,112	45,886	58,998	38,426	65,008	103,434	38.26
1987	13,576	23,894	37,470	9,873	64,113	73,986	23,449	88,007	111,456	38.28
1988	31,996	n.a.		6,351	n.a.		38,347	n.a.		n.a.

n.a., not available.

Sources: European foreign data, Securities Data Corporation; domestic data, OECD.

that had a long experience in using capital markets. Japanese capital market activity is dominated by banks, which issue substantial quantities of interest-bearing and short-term discount debentures. Japanese non-financial corporations show the least use of their own capital markets as a percentage of total financing in the three regions. Japanese non-financial corporations, on the other hand, were the largest issuers of equity securities in the three regions relative to total issues. This no doubt reflects the high stock prices prevailing in Japan at the time. Japanese corporations have also been the most frequent issuers in the Euromarkets, where they have been able to finance freely and opportunistically, without regard to Japanese domestic regulatory and procedural constraints.

In Europe, the long tradition of reliance on the part of non-financial corporations on banks, and the relatively poorly developed state of capital markets in several countries, prevented companies from gaining experience with securities transactions. This condition changed significantly as a result of the rapid development of the Euromarkets and of the market in Switzerland, and the effects of privatization sales of equities by several European governments. Indeed, European non-financial corporations increased their participation in the capital markets considerably after 1985. During the period 1985−7 intra-European debt and equity issues by European non-financial corporations exceeding $265 billion were sold. The volume data are given in table 4.3.

The market for European corporate debt and equity issues undertaken in Europe thus developed substantially. It achieved a level of activity sufficient to supply competitively the capital requirements of European firms. Industry, in turn, began to decrease its reliance on the banking system and overseas markets for its funding requirements. Only comparatively small amounts of financing were done by European companies during the 1985−8 period in the United States or Japan. Nor was it any longer necessary for European corporations to rely on financings denominated in non-European currencies when financing outside their own markets. In 1988, 74 per cent of all European corporate Euromarket and foreign financing was denominated in European currencies or European Currency Units (ECUs), compared with only 39 per cent in 1985 (table 4.4).

Table 4.4 Volume of non-domestic European capital market issues of all European corporations, by currency of issue (US$ million of proceeds at current exchange rates)

	European currencies	ECUs	Other currencies	European currencies and ECUs as a percentage of total
1985	12,707	3,004	24,764	38.82
1986	33,982	2,531	33,773	51.95
1987	36,984	2,681	11,339	77.77
1988	46,567	5,489	17,937	74.37
Total	130,240	13,705	87,813	62.11

Source: Securities Data Corporation.

Equity new issues and secondary sales of privatization issues showed the most rapid growth during the period, from a combined volume of US$32.6 billion in 1985 to US$89.6 billion in 1987. The equity markets were disrupted by the worldwide stock market crash of October 1987, and did not fully recover in 1988.

Privatization programmes raised approximately $40 billion for European governments between 1985 and 1987 from the sale of shares in public-sector corporations. This extraordinary achievement demonstrated a latent investment capacity of European Community (EC) capital markets that had not been called upon before. Although structured as domestic market issues, many of the large privatizations involved substantial distributions of shares in other parts of Europe, in the United States and in Japan. These issues helped to stimulate demand for cross-border investment within Europe, and indeed led to the emergence of a new invigorated European marketplace for equities.

Except for US and Japanese tranches of privatization issues, almost all were offered to a mixed intra-European ('Euro-equity') market that had developed as a much larger and more efficient vehicle than any of the individual domestic equity markets within the EC. For almost all issues – except perhaps initial public offerings or issues of unusually small size – the larger intra-European market offered the most economic alternative to issuers in terms of issue size, cost of issuance and net realized cost of funds. In many respects, the internal European market for equity capital raising envisioned by the 1992 initiative had already begun to show impressive signs of life by the end of 1986.

4.1.2 The Influence of Competition on European Financial Markets

Banks and other financial institutions in Europe have for many years been shrewd and aggressive seekers of low cost funds. They were quick to learn of the newer financing techniques that began to flood the market in the early 1980s. Often they would underwrite their own issues, or arrange syndicates for such issues from among other institutions with whom they enjoyed profitable reciprocal business arrangements. They also subscribed to the principle that any bank or investment bank bringing an attractive new idea to the market would be rewarded with the lead managership for the issue. Thus, competition based on performance and innovation developed. With it developed the skills of the institutions' lending and client relationship officers who carried many of the new financial technologies to their customers for whose businesses they were increasingly having to compete.

As noted earlier, European non-financial corporations had not traditionally been substantial users of the capital markets, preferring to rely upon banks for loans when they needed them. By the mid-1980s, however, these corporations had developed extensive requirements for funds for new investments, financial restructuring, acquisitions and other needs associated with industries undergoing structural change. They had also become more aware of the markets around them and had been called on by aggressive investment bankers offering new financing ideas. They learnt about Eurobonds, Euronote programmes in the form of note issuance facilities (NIFs), revolving underwriting facilities (RUFs) and multi-options facilities (MOFFs), Eurocommercial paper, swaps and synthetic securities, and a variety of hedging techniques. They also learnt about Euro-equity markets and observed an increasing number of international investors showing interest in, and acquiring, their outstanding equity securities in the secondary market.

In addition to equities and equity-linked debt, companies were also offered a variety of alternative ways to raise low-cost working capital through the issuance of commercial paper in dollars or other currencies that could be swapped into whatever currency they needed at a significant interest rate saving. Working capital, medium-term debt, longer-term debt and equity finance were suddenly available to European companies on attractive terms from the 'market'.

Attracted by these offerings, many European corporations broke away from their traditional exclusive 'Hausbank' relationships of long standing in order to open themselves up to new ideas, proposals and solicitations from other financial institutions. For example, Caesare Romiti, President of Fiat, has pointed out that 'finance is a prime strategic resource of industry' and that industrialists had to look for the 'best brains' to work with them in 'active, innovative and flexible partnership arrangements with their banks' (Romiti, 1988).

4.1.3 The Intra-European Market for New Issues after 1992

A loosely integrated three-market structure of (a) Eurosecurities, (b) foreign bonds and equities and (c) domestic issues is still in place in Europe. As a consequence of the changes and the competitive energies associated with the EC 1992 initiatives, these markets can be expected to converge into a single European capital market comprising institutional investors such as pension funds, insurance companies, investment companies, the portfolio managers of continental European banks which manage private funds, and retail investors acting independently. After 1992 there is less reason for this three-market construction to continue − subject to how the regulatory issues regarding prospectus disclosure, withholding taxes and other matters are resolved.

From the perspective of both their institutional and their retail aspects, we believe that the new issue markets in the period after 1992 will become deeper and more varied. A broader spectrum of investors can be expected to develop, which will in time lead to a filling in of the gaps in the Euromarkets and most European domestic markets that have existed for some time. This includes lack of interest and activity in European markets for maturities over ten years, securities backed by mortgages or real estate assets (some of which have been issued in the Euromarkets and in the UK domestic market but without high levels of acceptance) or non-investment grade ('junk') securities.

Furthermore, as the gaps are closed, additional market support services will be created. These comprise bond rating services (some Eurobond issues are already rated by Moodys and Standard & Poor (S & P)), improved custody and clearing procedures and improved methods for financing securities inventories such as through repurchase agreements. These services will materially assist the market liquidity and growth of new issue volumes.

As deregulation has occurred in financial markets throughout Europe and as further changes following the EC 1992 initiatives appear to be inevitable, some observers have come to believe that national capital market activity will displace the Euromarkets which, in effect, will no longer be needed − the financing business that was generated in the Euromarkets in the past because of exchange controls and other regulations will no longer have to be done outside the home market.

We do not agree. After 25 years of activity the Euromarket has become the single most important market for corporate issues in Europe. Development of the Euromarket has been a special situation, driven by regulatory considerations. In the process, however, it has become the most technically developed market in Europe. The free flow of capital envisioned by the 1992 initiatives should lead towards a single integrated European capital market rather than back to the fragmented collection of separate markets that existed before. Institutional investors will operate within Europe as a whole, seeking the most viable and interesting opportunities. Borrowers and bankers alike will tap into the common pool of funds, as they always have, to build a market in various real and 'synthetic' securities that suit their needs.

Access to this important market after 1992 will, we assume, continue to be free and unregulated in the EC 1992 context. Although the markets themselves will perhaps be more highly integrated, regulatory drag in the national markets may well continue to be greater than in the Euromarket, especially if initiatives for EC withholding taxes on national market issues of securities are carried through. Given a choice, most participants will prefer an unregulated market to a regulated market, particularly if both can be accessed simultaneously. In any case retail investors, still representing the major part of the Euromarket, will prefer to remain beyond the view of tax collectors or other authorities that they have always sought to avoid.

Much more likely than decline and collapse of the Euromarket as a consequence of the 1992 initiatives is therefore the emergence of a new intra-European integrated financial marketplace that is built upon and encompasses both the various EC domestic markets and the London-based Euromarket. In such an integrated financial market, issues aimed at national investors can also be sold to Euro-investors at the same time, as indeed has been the case in the past. Larger regional issues normally targeted at the Euromarket should come to be marketable to individuals in national markets as well, once common prospectus requirements, issuing procedures and withholding tax matters have been harmonized. The distinctions between national markets and the Euromarkets will fade, and non-national investment banks will compete − on a performance basis and on an understanding of how European investors behave − for the business of national companies and periodically win new issues assignments.

It is also likely, we believe, that a substantial increase in the overall level of Euro-capital market activity will occur as a result of the wave of corporate restructuring, discussed in the next section. Active capital markets are necessary to effect such corporate restructurings. Funds have to be raised by buyers of corporations and reinvested by sellers. New types of financings will have to be developed to suit transactions being put together in Europe, and new types of securities − including perhaps Euro-junk-bonds − may emerge. A centralized capital market that draws from all parts of Europe, from the national markets as well as from the Euromarkets, will be the most efficient way to marshal capital resources. It seems logical to expect the markets to evolve in this way in an essentially deregulated environment. Of course, the extent to which the concurrent development of regulatory and tax questions may affect these expectations remains open to question.

4.1.4 Corporate Financial Advisory Services

A major component of investment banking activities consists of fee-based advisory services associated with corporate finance transactions. These include fees derived from mergers and acquisition (M&A) transactions which involve acquisition of control of companies or minority stakeholdings in them, take-over defence, leveraged buyouts (LBOs) by management and outsiders, dispositions of unwanted units, and other financial restructurings.

The market for M&A services within Europe differs considerably between the United Kingdom, where M&A activity has been active along US lines for many years, and continental Europe, where until recently it has not been. Corporations in the United Kingdom have been able to benefit from a well-developed market for corporate control since the 1950s. A comparatively large number of publicly owned corporations exist in the United Kingdom and these have been, and continue to be, mainly owned by financial institutions. Share markets in the United Kingdom (compared with the rest of Europe) are active, and prices of shares are held to be fair representations of the value of corporations. Take-over transactions are governed by the Take-over Panel, a self-regulatory organization which is authorized to determine the rules of fair play. Next to the US market, the UK market is the largest in the world for M&A transactions.

On the Continent, different conditions exist. There are far fewer publicly owned companies in each of the continental countries than in the United Kingdom. Instead, there are relatively more privately owned enterprises, partnerships and closely held companies. Despite the fact that there are many large world-class continental European corporations, most companies are considerably smaller in size than those traded in the London market. Fleuriet's study (1989) showed that in France, for example, about 900 companies were listed on the Bourse, comprising a market capitalization equal to about 29 per cent of French GNP, a percentage that was about the same in Germany, Italy and Spain: in the United Kingdom at the same time the market capitalization of listed companies was approximately 88 per cent of GNP; in the United States, which has a very large number of small listed companies, the percentage was about 50 per cent.

Accordingly, the environment on the Continent for M&A transactions is quite different from that of the United Kingdom. Information is not as readily available, transactions tend to be negotiated face to face by controlling parties, stakeholdings and corporate alliances are common, hostile activity is scorned and sophisticated tactical and financial manoeuvres are regarded with suspicion. Notwithstanding these traditions and attitudes, however, conditions are changing in the M&A business on the Continent, and larger numbers of transactions have been completed in recent years.

One reason for the increase in Continental M&A activity since about 1983 has been the growing recognition of the need for industrial restructuring in Europe. This powerful economic drive has superseded traditional concerns in a number of countries and, of course, the aforementioned increasing liquidity of European capital markets has made non-traditional alternatives possible. No longer must an entrepreneur look for a friendly bank or competitor to buy all or part of his holdings upon his retirement. He can now sell shares at a decent price in the open market, or hire an investment banker to find a wealthy stranger to buy the company. No longer must a company suffering structural difficulties be forced to hold on to businesses that no longer fit. It can now dispose of them in the market. And, of course, no longer must a healthy firm seeking to expand across European borders build up new businesses in other countries step by step. It can now purchase a complete going-concern business from someone else at a market price.

Consequently, it is likely that the market for corporate control and related M&A services will continue to grow rapidly throughout Europe − in the

EC countries and the non-EC European countries as well. Several factors shape this outlook.

First, the emerging internal market will require larger more competitive enterprises able to reap significant economies of scale and economies of scope, particularly in such sectors as transportation, information technology, telecommunications, financial services, food products, consumer electronics and pharmaceuticals. Like the wave of mergers and acquisitions that has from time to time rolled over the United States − driven by underlying industry economics, global competitive shifts and the perceived need to diversify − European M&A activity is following along similar lines.

The greater are managements' convictions about the specific competitive impact of the 1992 initiatives, the more aggressive will be their drive to develop a market presence throughout the EC, a presence that is competitively viable on a global basis. For many, the conviction that their objectives can only be achieved in the short run through acquisition activity will be powerful. Consequently, as has been the case in the United States and the United Kingdom, a determination to pursue acquisitions despite objections of the target company will introduce, to a much greater extent than previously, predatory actions on the part of acquirers. Unless opposed by public policy − which, although much more relaxed on the matter of hostile offers than in the past, is still a very complex area and differs widely from country to country − the hostile take-over attempt can be expected to become much more prevalent in the Europe of the 1990s.

Second, acquisitions of brand names and manufacturing facilities in an internal market for highly competitive products may be a cheaper alternative than *de novo* investments in Europe, as they have been in the United States.

Third, the growing concentration of shareholdings in institutional portfolios subject to a progressively higher performance orientation serves to increase the emphasis on realizing underlying equity values. More competition among investment managers, more liquidity and greater room to manoeuvre will require all financial managers to become more performance oriented than they have been in the past. Thus, investment managers should be more inclined than in the past to favour take-overs and short-term returns in preference to maintaining long-term holdings out of either loyalty or inertia. This change has already occurred to a significant degree in the United Kingdom. Such shifts in continental European investor behaviour are likely to develop − though perhaps not as much, for example, as in the United States, where performance orientation appears to be at a maximum.

Fourth, ample financing continues to be available from banks anxious to earn large fees and spreads on M&A transactions. Under the new Bank for International Settlements (BIS) risk-based capital adequacy standards that lump all corporate lending into one category, M&A loans are advantageous for most banks, which can earn significantly increased spreads in take-over financings without any increased charge against capital than for a straight loan to an AAA-rated corporation such as Unilever. In addition to the banks, liquidity for M&A financings is available from investment funds that purchase high-yield bonds and 'mezzanine' debt issues (i.e. quasi-equity) of acquiring corporations. Such funds have been widely sold to private, institutional and corporate investors in the United States and in Europe.

Finally, sufficient M&A 'technology' is in place, both home grown in Europe and developed in the United States and adapted to European conditions, to facilitate such transactions. The nature of this technology is discussed below.

Among the constraints holding back M&A activity in the EC are limited and often fragmented public shareholdings and heavy concentrations of voting stock in the hands of management or parties friendly to management, such as banks or investment companies. Because of national differences among the EC countries concerning the ways in which the market for corporate control is regulated, and the unpredictability of national or EC anti-trust intervention, risk arbitrage markets in Europe have not fully developed. Until new and transparent EC-wide regulations covering anti-trust considerations and take-over behaviour on the part of principals − and those connected with them − are promulgated, the various markets will remain fragmented and comparatively inefficient. In contrast, once the new regulations are agreed, as is anticipated, the markets should become integrated and comparatively efficient. This will enable risk arbitrage activities to flourish and, in general, ease the process of M&A completion considerably.

Between 1985 and 1991 the pattern of worldwide M&A activity − broadly defined to include mergers, acquisitions, tender offers, purchases of stakes, divestitures and LBOs − has changed considerably. Transactions in the United States appear to have peaked, while both US cross-border transactions and transactions entirely outside the United States have grown much faster.

Table 4.5 shows combined M&A activities on a worldwide basis for the period 1985−91. During this period, approximately 17,200 transactions involving mergers, tender offers, purchases of stakes, divestitures and LBOs with a market value of $2.4 trillion were completed. Of these transactions, approximately half were transactions between US companies. Nearly $760 billion, or 30 per cent, were transactions entirely outside the United States − i.e. in which only non-US companies (or non-US subsidiaries of American companies) were involved − and $327 billion, or 14 per cent, were cross-border transactions in which US parent companies acted as buyers and sellers with non-US counterparts.

Table 4.5 Volume of completed international merger and corporate transactions in the United States, 1985–1991 (US$ million)

Year	Domestic US (no.)	Domestic US ($m)	Cross-border Buyer from USA (no.)	Cross-border Buyer from USA ($m)	Cross-border Seller from USA (no.)	Cross-border Seller from USA ($m)	Cross-border Total (no.)	Cross-border Total ($m)	Cross-border Outside US (no.)	Cross-border Outside US ($m)	Global total (no.)	Global total ($m)
1985	804 (868)	192,863.2	25 (57)	3,854.9	76 (109)	9,999.1	101 (163)	13,854.0	143 (106)	20,721.3	1,048 (1,137)	227,438.5
1986	1,178 (1,288)	203,985.7	39 (50)	2,918.4	164 (144)	31,126.8	203 (194)	34,045.2	296 (203)	38,728.9	1,677 (1,685)	276,759.8
1987	1,311 (1,311)	205,814.3	52 (89)	8,492.5	187 (135)	36,940.3	239 (224)	45,432.8	586 (366)	86,602.5	2,136 (1,901)	337,849.6
1988	1,580 (1,249)	294,429.7	81 (127)	6,687.6	247 (175)	61,450.9	328 (302)	68,138.5	1,452 (858)	124,230.1	3,360 (2,409)	486,798.3
1989	1,872 (1,705)	244,793.3	149 (213)	25,336.3	405 (236)	52,393.2	554 (449)	77,729.5	1,832 (1,575)	203,032.9	4,258 (3,729)	525,555.7
1990	1,564 (2,332)	106,802.1	143 (237)	20,896.8	398 (325)	50,458.2	541 (562)	71,355.0	1,986 (1,565)	204,448.1	4,091 (4,549)	382,605.2
1991	1,139 (1,666)	48,032.8	133 (228)	8,268.5	212 (187)	8,152.8	345 (415)	16,421.0	1,354 (1,299)	83,237.8	2,838 (1,752)	147,691.9
Total	9,448 (10,419)	1,296,721.1	622 (1,001)	76,455.0	1,689 (1,311)	250,521.3	2,311 (2,309)	326,976.3	7,649 (5,972)	761,001.6	19,408 (17,162)	2,384,699.0

Sources: Large, Smith & Walter; Securities Data Corporation.

The overwhelming predominance of US–US transactions obscures important changes that have been occurring outside the United States. As table 4.6 shows non-US volume has overtaken US volume by a significant margin. Deals completed outside the United States grew by a factor of ten between 1985 and 1991 – or a factor of 14 if the much higher 1990 volume is considered.

During this period, cross-border transactions accounted for 20 per cent of all M&A transactions involving US corporations, and 77 per cent of these deals were inward investments, most of which involved European buyers. Clearly, European corporations were not interested only in the EC internal market. For many years they had recognized the importance of deploying more of their business activities in the United States, where the domestic economy had been expanding rapidly, the dollar had declined sharply after 1985, and fears of possible protectionism interrupting market access through imports were rising.

Of the transactions entirely outside the United States between 1985 and 1991, approximately 28 per cent have been intra-European deals, of which transactions in the United Kingdom accounted for the substantial majority. Table 4.7 presents European M&A activity for the 1985–91 period. As recently as 1985, 87 per cent of all European M&A transactions consisted of mergers, tender offers, tender–mergers and purchases of stakes in companies.

Table 4.6 Merger activity declines and moves to Europe

	1991	1990	1989	1988
US domestic transactions	48.0	106.8	244.8	294.5
US cross-border transactions	16.4	71.4	77.7	68.1
Intra-European transactions	47.9	110.0	121.8	79.0
Other transactions outside US	35.3	94.4	81.2	45.2
Global total	147.7	382.6	525.6	486.8
US as % of global	32.5	27.9	46.6	60.5

Sources: Large, Smith & Walter; Securities Data Corporation.

Table 4.7 Volume of completed international merger and corporate transactions in Europe, 1985–1991 (US$ million)

			Cross-border					
Year	Intra-Europe (no.)	($m)	European buyer (no.)	($m)	European seller (no.)	($m)	Total (no.)	($m)
1985	72 (43)	10,613.7	45 (46)	6,267.4	29 (44)	2,342.3	74 (90)	8,609.7
1986	195 (101)	18,985.2	106 (66)	18,631.7	44 (36)	6,082.5	150 (102)	24,714.2
1987	416 (220)	48,965.3	132 (75)	28,161.4	63 (82)	12,314.6	195 (157)	40,476.0
1988	1,091 (613)	78,996.0	209 (139)	38,389.0	133 (138)	13,566.8	342 (277)	51,995.8
1989	1,359 (1,037)	121,830.3	306 (167)	40,129.7	212 (284)	25,091.8	518 (451)	65,221.5
1990	1,296 (896)	109,994.7	261 (180)	47,672.6	297 (333)	50,129.7	558.0 (513)	97,802.3
1991	788 (828)	47,903.6	142 (130)	6,324.0	211 (253)	13,935.3	353.0 (383)	20,259.3
Totals	5,217 (3,738)	437,288.8	1,201 (803)	185,575.8	989 (1,170)	123,463.0	2,190 (1,973)	309,078.8

Table 4.8 presents a more detailed summary analysis of data for both European domestic and cross-border transactions exceeding $50 million in value involving mergers, acquisitions, stakes and divestitures where the seller firm is located in one of the 12 EC countries. The data cover the years from 1985, when the 1992 initiative was announced, through 1991. Note the large share of intra-European and intra-UK transactions during this period.

Based on type of transaction, about 25 per cent by value of the deals during 1985–91 involved stakes, compared to 13 per cent in the United States, which confirms the idea that European firms have given significantly more precedence to the acquisition of stakes in Europe than American firms have done (see table 4.9). By contrast, leveraged buyouts played a much smaller role in Europe, as table 4.10 shows.

Nevertheless, the high proportion of stake acquisitions in Europe, certainly compared with the United States experience, indicates a uniquely European *modus operandi*. European companies appear to favour stakes for several reasons, including the concept of forging an alliance for a common purpose – offensive or defensive – without giving up their own independence, the idea that a gradual commitment to a final arrangement is wiser, cheaper and reversible, and because in many situations a substantial minority

Table 4.8   Volume of completed intra-European M&A transactions by country, 1985–1991 (US$ million)

Country of buyer	Year	Country of seller company					Totals Buyer
		UK	France	Italy	Germany	Other European	Totals Buyer
UK	1985	8,363.9	0.0	0.0	0.0	12.2	8,376.1
	1986	12,401.1	23.8	0.0	1.0	70.0	12,495.9
	1987	29,859.4	124.5	125.9	216.5	520.5	30,846.8
	1988	39,537.9	1,172.8	480.8	201.6	1,012.3	42,405.4
	1989	54,204.9	1,261.3	290.2	361.9	3,125.3	59,243.6
	1990	26,905.8	2,561.0	115.1	1,109.4	4,049.3	34,740.6
	1991	13,202.4	385.5	3.9	233.2	540.7	14,365.7
	Total	184,475.4	5,528.9	1,015.9	2,123.6	9,330.3	202,474.1
France	1985	0.0	10.7	0.0	0.0	0.0	10.7
	1986	5.9	222.0	520.9	0.0	32.1	780.9
	1987	316.6	1,674.4	207.3	0.0	0.0	2,198.3
	1988	3,137.0	7,355.1	35.7	310.2	1,056.2	11,894.2
	1989	5,211.9	15,145.6	602.4	1,989.7	3,331.9	26,281.5
	1990	3,149.0	9,498.8	3,380.9	502.9	4,421.7	20,953.3
	1991	509.8	3,736.0	285.0	756.0	2,193.7	7,480.5
	Total	12,330.2	37,642.6	5,032.2	3,558.8	11,055.6	69,599.4
Italy	1985	16.8	0.0	165.0	0.0	0.0	181.8
	1986	0.0	0.0	1,199.4	129.0	0.0	1,328.4
	1987	0.0	20.4	7,876.3	0.0	1,050.8	8,947.5
	1988	0.0	325.0	1,314.2	429.3	887.7	2,956.2
	1989	7.9	294.4	7,007.8	63.1	0.0	7,373.2
	1990	55.4	602.8	11,801.2	500.6	482.1	13,442.1
	1991	59.1	320.1	2,344.2	356.1	76.2	3,155.7
	Total	139.2	1,562.7	31,708.1	1,478.1	2,496.8	37,384.9
Germany	1985	0.0	0.0	0.0	898.5	445.0	1,343.5
	1986	425.0	0.3	887.4	980.0	0.0	2,292.7
	1987	159.6	330.6	0.0	425.6	0.0	915.8
	1988	59.2	154.0	866.1	2,227.3	39.6	3,346.2
	1989	817.8	1,341.3	37.5	2,221.3	1,475.3	5,893.2
	1990	1,269.7	2.2	53.2	2,124.5	1,304.7	4,754.3
	1991	626.1	8.7	0.0	4,411.9	1,884.9	6,931.6
	Total	3,357.4	1,837.1	1,884.2	13,289.1	5,149.5	25,477.3
Other European	1985	209.2	0.0	0.0	0.0	492.4	701.6
	1986	828.6	0.0	0.0	0.0	1,258.7	2,087.3
	1987	558.5	169.1	0.0	239.0	5,090.3	6,056.9
	1988	7,469.1	1,026.6	2,491.7	0.0	7,384.6	18,394.0
	1989	1,759.6	3,975.1	305.9	826.6	15,371.6	22,238.8
	1990	6,673.7	1,434.5	392.8	2,762.4	24,841.0	36,104.4
	1991	1,534.1	496.5	259.7	233.3	13,446.5	15,970.1
	Total	19,052.8	7,103.8	3,450.1	4,061.3	71,885.1	101,553.1
Totals Seller	1985	8,589.9	10.7	165.0	898.5	949.6	10,613.7
	1986	13,660.6	246.1	2,607.7	1,110.0	1,360.8	18,985.2
	1987	30,894.1	2,319.0	8,209.5	881.1	6,661.6	48,965.3
	1988	50,223.2	10,035.5	5,188.5	3,168.4	10,380.4	78,996.0
	1989	62,002.1	22,017.7	8,243.8	5,462.6	23,304.1	121,030.3
	1990	38,053.6	14,099.3	15,743.2	6,999.8	35,098.8	109,994.7
	1991	15,931.5	4,946.8	2,892.8	5,990.5	18,142.0	47,903.6
	Total	219,355.0	53,675.1	43,050.5	24,510.9	95,897.3	436,488.8

Sources: Large, Smith & Walter; Securities Data Corporation.

Table 4.9 Partial ownership positions as a percentage of all completed US and European M&A transactions[a,b] 1985–1991 (in percentage terms)[c]

Year	US[d] seller	European seller[e]		Intra-European deals[f]	
		UK	Rest of Europe	UK	Rest of Europe
1985	5.820	15.494	22.410	5.598	23.024
1986	14.591	9.770	43.234	6.266	36.827
1987	12.651	40.712	4.888	31.807	3.357
1988	9.582	27.279	35.701	13.590	28.549
1989	20.909	26.866	33.124	30.019	28.081
1990	10.007	25.588	4.221	4.913	9.695
1991	15.471	49.450	5.216	5.622	11.917
Average 1985–91	12.719	27.880	21.256	13.974	20.207

[a] Partial ownership positions involve open or privately negotiated stake purchases of stock or assets.
[b] Data include only completed transactions. Data are classified according to the announcement date of a transaction, not taking into consideration when a transaction is completed.
[c] Percentage values denote the fraction of total transaction volume which involves partial stakes.
[d] Completed partial stakes as a percentage of total dollar volume of completed M&A transactions in which the seller is a US company.
[e] Completed partial stakes as a percentage of total dollar volume of completed M&A transactions in which the seller is a European company.
[f] Completed partial stakes as a percentage of total dollar volume of completed M&A transactions in which the buyer and the seller are European companies.
Sources: Large, Smith & Walter; Securities Data Corporation.

stake-holding can aassure *de facto* control of a company. In the United States, by comparison, acquirers are motivated by tax, accounting and legal reasons to prefer 100 per cent ownership, although American companies often recognize that when in Rome, Brussels, Lyon or Dusseldorf, they may find it preferable to abide by local customs, at least for a while.

Besides source and type of transaction, the data have also been broken down by Standard Industrial Classification (SIC) codes identifying the primary business of firms on both sides of each transaction. Tables 4.11 and 4.12 indicate the flow of European M&A deals valued at $50 million or more by major industry category (a) of the firm undertaking the transaction and (b) of the target. Investment and holding companies (including industrial conglomerates such as Hanson Trust and BTR of the United Kingdom) accounted for a large but declining share of the value of M&A transactions during the 1985–91 period. Industries most heavily involved as principals included food products, oil and gas, chemicals, banks and electronics and electrical equipment, while those most heavily involved as targets comprised oil and gas, food products, chemicals, banks and transportation equipment.

Table 4.10 Leveraged buyouts as a percentage of all completed US and European M&A transactions[a,b] 1985–1991 (in percentage terms)[c]

Year	US[d] seller	European seller[e]		Intra-European deals[f]	
		UK	Rest of Europe	UK	Rest of Europe
1985	13.520	5.613	0.000	0.966	0.000
1986	16.436	2.373	1.038	3.691	0.000
1987	17.326	5.360	0.618	6.924	0.646
1988	25.817	6.769	3.622	9.668	3.214
1989	11.104	9.764	2.473	13.965	2.374
1990	6.634	1.321	0.153	2.663	1.674
1991	4.496	4.999	0.049	4.227	6.492
Average 1985–91	13.619	5.171	1.136	6.015	2.057

[a] Leveraged buyout (LBO) is defined as a transaction in which an investor group, investor, or investment/LBO firm acquires a company, taking on an extraordinary amount of debt, with plans to repay the debt with funds generated from the company or with revenue earned by selling off the newly acquired company's assets. An acquisition is considered an LBO if the investor group includes management or if newspaper articles or press releases describe the transaction as a buyout.
[b] Data include only completed transactions. Data are classified according to the announcement date of a transaction, not taking into consideration when a transaction is completed.
[c] Percentage values denote the fraction of total transaction volume which involves LBOs.
[d] Completed LBOs as a percentage of total dollar volume of completed M&A transactions in which the seller is a US company.
[e] Completed LBOs as a percentage of total dollar volume of completed M&A transactions in which the seller is a European company.
[f] Completed LBOs as a percentage of total dollar volume of completed M&A transactions in which the buyer and the seller are European companies.
Sources: Large, Smith & Walter; Securities Data Corporation.

At the SIC two-digit level of aggregation, about 40 per cent of the number and 34 per cent of the value of transactions during the 1985–91 period were intra-industry, with food products, oil and gas, chemicals and banks most heavily involved. Of intra-European transactions, almost 50 per cent were intra-industry the rest being inter-industry. Note the similarity of the transaction-flow structure with that of the United States – it is evident in the capitalization-weighted Spearman rank correlation figures shown in table 4.13. The data show that an active and rapidly growing EC market for corporate control has developed since 1983, a market that promises to have a significant catalytic impact on the further economic restructuring of Europe, especially when (or as) remaining institutional and regulatory obstacles are eased. The industry segments so far subject to restructuring through M&A transactions in the EC are similar to those subject to M&A

activity in the United States. This is not surprising, as the underlying economic forces affecting these industries are similar on both sides of the Atlantic.

4.1.5 The Emergence of Hostile Transactions in Europe

With only a few exceptions, hostile deals in Europe have been few and far between outside the United Kingdom. Indeed sentiments on the Continent against such transactions appear to be strong. In February 1989, the French President Mitterrand decried the 'roving bands of predatory capital' that threatened ownership of French companies, noting that he could be counted on to prevent such abuses in France. Alfred Herrhausen, Chairman of the Deutsche Bank, has also commented that hostile deals are 'missteps of American capitalism' and to be avoided in Europe. Even so, rumblings deep within the earth can be heard.

There are many misconceptions about hostile bids, and these have taken years to work their way through the American economy. Before 1974 hostile bids in the United States were limited to mainly non-establishment entrepreneurs and conglomerateurs, most of whom were regarded by institutional shareholders as 'raiders' and 'asset strippers', whose behaviour was destructive to the economy and the financial system. In 1974, however, a blue-chip company, International Nickel, made an unwanted tender offer for an old Philadelphia company, Electric Storage Battery (ESB). The distinguished firm of investment bankers, Morgan Stanley & Co., represented International Nickel. Arguments were raised about ESB management's poor performance and their efforts to entrench themselves. In the end, International Nickel won, and before long other blue-chip companies were attempting to make opposed acquisitions. These are quite common in the United States today. There is still a lively debate as to whether unfriendly acquisitions are profitable investments for the acquiring companies, and anxieties still exist among the general public about hostile take-overs, but serious arguments are rarely heard any longer among financial and corporate executives concerning whether unsolicited offers are inappropriate or out of line.

In the end, this argument in the United States today is left to be resolved by the shareholders, who ultimately decide whether existing management can be relied upon to improve the value of the company to a level equal to or higher than an offer made by someone else. Efforts by acquirers to 'steal' the company, or by management to entrench themselves through actions clearly not in their interests, can be rejected or opposed by shareholders – who sometimes need the law courts to adjudicate matters. In freely competitive markets, management groups that are not competitive will be replaced, either by the company's own board of directors or by the management of another company.

Table 4.11 Rankings of industry groups of US and European M&A buyer companies by SIC code[a,b] 1985–1991 (US$ million)[c]

Buyer Description SIC		US transactions			European transactions		
		Ranking[d]	Number	Value[c]	Ranking	Number	Value
67	Holding & other inv't. offices	1	2,660	357,438.0	1	792	74,311.3
28	Chemicals & allied products	2	378	95,991.0	2	303	51,030.4
13	Oil & gas extraction	3	432	80,269.3	6	145	28,695.8
48	Communications	4	408	66,571.5	23	64	7,057.0
60	Depository institutions	5	689	65,857.5	4	172	40,869.3
27	Printing & publishing	6	220	44,868.8	8	229	20,074.0
20	Food & kindred products	7	230	44,111.5	3	290	47,048.5
35	Industrial machinery & equip.	8	391	43,413.5	16	293	10,502.8
36	Electronic & other elect. equip.	9	317	39,619.2	7	279	27,300.2
21	Tobacco products	10	15	38,185.7	56	5	487.3
37	Transportation equipment	11	140	37,923.6	9	134	16,835.1
38	Instruments & related prods.	12	256	31,142.3	35	79	3,531.7
63	Insurance carriers	13	273	30,072.9	5	169	32,262.1
62	Security & commodity brokers	14	315	25,682.4	10	242	15,659.7
53	General merchandise stores	15	58	22,440.1	28	30	5,011.3
49	Electric, gas & sanitary servs.	16	210	21,233.6	20	64	9,384.6
61	Non-depository institutions	17	141	20,415.2	36	43	3,457.8
78	Motion pictures	18	107	20,162.8	33	30	4,145.4
73	Business services	19	321	19,336.6	18	230	9,887.2
40	Rail transportation	20	37	18,414.0	66	1	78.4
45	Air transportation	21	76	17,291.6	41	22	2,722.4
26	Paper & allied products	22	87	15,858.5	14	84	11,090.1
33	Primary metal industries	23	110	14,395.9	19	172	9,654.2
32	Stone, clay & glass products	24	92	12,934.2	13	160	12,958.8
54	Food stores	25	48	11,896.4	31	29	4,851.3
34	Fabricated metal products	26	111	11,061.4	32	122	4,613.4
10	Metals mining	27	72	10,948.0	24	33	6,722.0
65	Real estate	28	123	10,359.9	25	138	5,485.1
70	Hotels & other lodging places	29	61	10,035.1	17	97	10,260.4
30	Rubber & misc. plastic prods.	30	84	9,582.3	21	100	7,292.5
80	Health services	31	171	7,740.4	50	23	971.6
24	Lumber & wood products	32	36	7,271.7	38	35	3,272.9
58	Eating & drinking places	33	73	6,670.4	15	70	10,659.6
23	Apparel & other textile prods.	34	45	6,026.1	34	60	3,893.7
64	Insurance agents, brokers & servs.	35	22	5,920.8	29	46	5,001.0
50	Wholesale trade, durable goods	36	111	5,356.4	26	210	5,414.8
51	Wholesale trade, non-durables	37	82	5,226.0	12	164	13,406.3
59	Miscellaneous retail	38	69	5,091.7	39	45	2,797.7
0	Unknown	39	56	4,184.7	47	38	1,047.2
87	Engineering & mgmt. services	40	116	3,809.2	22	226	7,062.1
15	General building contractors	41	35	3,714.7	30	94	4,869.3
12	Coal mining	42	35	3,373.5	46	15	1,108.3
39	Misc. manufacturing industry	43	52	3,272.7	59	34	333.3

Table 4.11 *continued.*

Buyer Description SIC		US transactions			European transactions		
		Ranking[d]	Number	Value[c]	Ranking	Number	Value
29	Petroleum & coal products	44	25	2,209.1	37	29	3,450.9
46	Pipelines, excl. natural gas	45	20	2,198.6	0	0	0.0
22	Textile mill products	46	41	2,066.2	42	89	2,333.1
52	Building & garden materials	47	11	2,059.8	55	8	752.4
42	Trucking & warehousing	48	27	1,976.1	57	18	383.6
44	Water transportation	49	30	1,865.7	27	62	5,360.7
75	Auto repair, serv. & parking	50	12	1,809.6	58	18	358.3
25	Furniture & fixtures	51	26	1,449.4	52	32	873.0
56	Apparel & accessory stores	52	25	1,384.9	44	20	1,513.9
47	Transportation services	53	14	1,277.3	53	24	813.9
79	Amusement & recreation services	54	26	1,218.0	49	24	1,028.1
14	Non-metallic minerals, excl. fuels	55	11	1,132.5	63	11	158.1
41	Local & passenger transit	56	6	934.5	68	1	12.1
55	Auto dealers & serv. stations	57	9	774.8	61	32	264.5
72	Personal services	58	18	773.2	51	62	909.7
8	Forestry	59	5	731.1	40	21	2,730.4
16	Heavy construction, excl. building	60	24	729.1	43	45	1,623.2
82	Educational services	61	14	617.4	60	8	288.2
1	Agricultural production, crops	62	13	440.3	54	9	806.8
31	Leather & leather products	63	9	356.3	11	33	13,673.6
83	Social services	64	9	353.4	71	1	1.3
57	Furniture & home furnish. stores	65	20	290.9	48	24	1,038.2
9	Fishing, hunting & trapping	66	3	272.1	67	2	58.4
17	Special trade contractors	67	13	99.7	45	37	1,119.2
2	Agricultural production, livestock	68	2	90.5	70	1	4.1
96	Admin. of econ. programmes	69	2	70.0	0	0	0.0
86	Membership organizations	70	3	49.9	0	0	0.0
76	Misc. repair services	71	5	26.9	64	9	110.3
89	Services, nec	72	3	16.8	69	2	8.1
81	Legal services	73	1	1.0	0	0	0.0
95	Environmental housing/quality	74	1	1.0	0	0	0.0
94	Admin. of human resources	0	0	0.0	62	1	234.2
7	Agricultural services	0	0	0.0	65	1	90.0

[a] Completed transactions include: mergers, tender-mergers, tender offers, purchases of stakes, divestitures, recapitalizations, exchange offers and LBOs.
[b] The volume data are classified according to the announcement date of a transaction, not taking into consideration when a transaction is completed.
[c] Million dollars of purchase price − excluding fees and expenses − at current exchange rates.
[d]Ranking is based on total dollar value of acquiring industry.

Sources: Large, Smith & Walter; Securities Data Corporation.

Table 4.12 Rankings of industry groups of US and European M&A seller companies by SIC code[a,b] 1985–1991 (US$ million)[c]

Seller SIC	Description	US transactions			European transactions		
		Ranking[d]	Number	Value[c]	Ranking	Number	Value
28	Chemicals & allied products	1	519	143,943.1	5	236	25,361.0
13	Oil & gas extraction	2	546	90,013.1	3	128	33,385.4
20	Food & kindred products	3	297	84,640.1	1	301	54,034.0
48	Communications	4	526	84,244.3	28	78	4,317.6
36	Electronic & other elect. equip.	5	572	78,849.8	7	257	22,172.3
60	Depository institutions	6	808	70,830.9	2	135	36,299.6
35	Industrial machinery & equip.	7	634	63,400.8	14	284	13,570.3
27	Printing & publishing	8	310	46,886.5	11	217	16,929.3
53	General merchandise stores	9	102	45,280.4	19	36	9,321.3
37	Transportation equipment	10	214	40,448.2	6	176	23,978.2
78	Motion pictures	11	150	39,907.3	43	48	2,320.9
73	Business services	12	553	38,186.4	13	372	14,466.9
38	Instruments & related prods.	13	443	36,108.1	36	112	3,485.7
21	Tobacco products	14	15	35,860.4	57	4	560.7
61	Non-depository institutions	15	175	33,446.1	21	64	7,447.4
54	Food stores	16	115	31,646.3	15	46	10,497.9
49	Electric, gas & sanitary servs.	17	237	31,258.5	12	75	16,497.4
70	Hotels & other lodging places	18	160	29,435.2	16	109	9,673.1
63	Insurance carriers	19	306	29,341.9	4	97	32,300.5
32	Stone, clay & glass products	20	138	27,057.2	22	123	6,315.7
30	Rubber & misc. plastic prods.	21	157	24,904.3	37	120	3,334.9
33	Primary metal industries	22	191	24,895.2	24	142	5,993.8
26	Paper & allied products	23	100	24,695.0	9	126	18,207.5
58	Eating & drinking places	24	155	23,537.8	23	91	6,216.6
40	Rail transportation	25	58	23,304.3	69	1	24.1
45	Air transportation	26	133	23,034.5	34	34	3,549.7
80	Health services	27	259	21,679.5	53	36	1,225.8
65	Real estate	28	185	19,342.7	8	212	18,237.8
34	Fabricated metal products	29	232	18,888.4	18	178	9,400.0
62	Security & commodity brokers	30	164	16,764.2	17	133	9,480.0
23	Apparel & other textile prods.	31	91	16,002.4	41	69	2,664.0
10	Metals mining	32	81	14,662.0	26	15	4,861.2
59	Miscellaneous retail	33	147	13,454.7	39	73	3,145.1
87	Engineering & mgmt. services	34	251	12,959.0	32	213	3,856.1
22	Textile mill products	35	97	11,231.0	30	108	4,038.9
51	Wholesale trade, non-durables	36	143	11,031.5	25	153	5,795.0
50	Wholesale trade, durable goods	37	233	9,275.7	20	305	8,226.9
75	Auto repair, serv. & parking	38	34	8,860.2	49	26	1,753.9
64	Insurance agents, brokers & servs.	39	30	7,597.7	40	46	2,734.5
67	Holding & other inv't. offices	40	178	7,590.9	10	128	17,169.5
42	Trucking & warehousing	41	58	6,727.8	44	37	2,231.4
46	Pipelines, excl. natural gas	42	25	6,616.9	71	3	22.6

Table 4.12 *continued.*

Seller SIC	Description	US transactions			European transactions		
		Ranking[d]	Number	Value[c]	Ranking	Number	Value
29	Petroleum & coal products	43	50	5,801.1	35	22	3,510.9
79	Amusement & recreation servs.	44	75	5,363.7	31	47	3,857.2
39	Misc. manufacturing indust.	45	103	5,115.8	52	67	1,255.4
24	Lumber & wood products	46	60	5,113.8	45	40	2,099.0
56	Apparel & accessory stores	47	64	5,018.7	54	29	1,000.8
25	Furniture & fixtures	48	66	4,964.2	55	51	693.5
12	Coal mining	49	48	4,269.5	61	14	389.1
57	Furniture & home furnish. stores	50	57	4,005.9	33	35	3,801.4
44	Water transportation	51	48	3,798.7	29	57	4,182.8
52	Building & garden materials	52	32	3,541.3	56	15	677.2
14	Non-metallic minerals, excl. fuels	53	27	3,518.5	60	19	401.5
8	Forestry	54	22	2,412.2	62	4	229.3
1	Agricultural production, crops	55	25	2,238.9	46	16	1,989.6
15	General building contractors	56	54	1,997.3	42	93	2,573.5
2	Agricultural production, livestock	57	8	1,942.5	74	2	4.2
55	Auto dealers & serv. stations	58	24	1,797.4	47	56	1,788.8
16	Heavy construction, excl. building	59	38	1.782.9	48	31	1,785.4
47	Transportation services	60	28	1,735.7	50	39	1,689.0
31	Leather & leather products	61	30	1,663.4	51	32	1,351.9
0	Unknown	62	45	1,523.3	38	65	3,329.9
72	Personal services	63	28	1,241.3	58	39	530.3
41	Local & passenger transit	64	4	514.3	68	8	49.6
89	Services, nec	65	8	445.8	65	3	117.0
17	Special trade contractors	66	19	445.1	27	51	4,347.9
7	Agricultural services	67	3	417.1	70	3	22.7
82	Educational services	68	12	397.6	63	13	171.1
83	Social services	69	9	360.1	67	3	67.1
76	Misc. repair services	70	7	171.3	59	6	530.1
9	Fishing, hunting & trapping	71	1	27.0	66	4	108.8
81	Legal services	72	1	5.0	73	1	4.9
91	Exec., legislative & general	0	0	0.0	72	1	10.2
88	Private households	0	0	0.0	64	1	152.9

[a] Completed transactions include: mergers, tender-mergers, tender offers, purchases of stakes, divestitures, recapitalizations, exchange offers and LBOs.

[b] The volume data are classified according to the announcement date of a transaction, not taking into consideration when a transaction is completed.

[c] Million dollars of purchase price − excluding fees and expenses − at current exchange rates.

[d] Ranking is based on total dollar value of target industry.

Sources: Large, Smith & Walter; Securities Data Corporation.

Table 4.13 Spearman rank correlation of US and European industries participating in M&A transactions[a] 1985–1991

		SIC of buyer	SIC of seller
Number of deals	r	0.8043	0.8463
	N	(69)	(72)
	p	0.0000	0.0000
$ volume	r	0.7416	0.7532
	N	(69)	(72)
	p	0.0000	0.0000

[a] Correlations are based on the number of transactions and the dollar volume of US and European industries (two-digit SIC codes).

Data from tables 4.11 and 4.12.

Much the same situation exists in the United Kingdom, where unsolicited take-overs have played a prominent role in the London market since Reynolds Metals, advised by S.G. Warburg, bid for British Aluminum in 1957. Since then the UK M&A market has grown and become frantic with activity, much of it hostile. Many of the transactions have been valued at more than $1 billion. The UK practice is to resolve merger disputes not through litigation but instead through rulings of the Take-over Panel, which perhaps accounts for the fact that hostile bidders win less often in the United Kingdom than they do in the United States. Nevertheless, hostile bidders win often enough that managers that are perceived to be underperforming can expect to attract unwanted attention.

There is evidence to suggest that the practice of unsolicited M&A transactions is rapidly making its way into continental Europe. After at least two decades of observing such transactions in the United Kingdom and the United States, and in many cases profiting handsomely from them, European institutional investors are becoming conditioned to act in their own best interests when presented with a specific situation. This does not necessarily apply to tied-in relations with, for example, a large and friendly minority investor. But in most arm's length situations it does. With such large shareholders willing to look at take-over offers objectively, the onus falls on management to demonstrate how it will outperform the offer, a task which goes beyond the capabilities of many managements.

Large European companies seeking to get on with their own restructuring activities have watched the attitudes of investors change, and have acted accordingly. Seven UK companies, for example, have been targets of large

Swiss and German concerns. In 1980 Allianz bid for Eagle Star Insurance, driving it into the arms of BAT Industries. In 1987, Nestlé acquired Rowntree Mackintosh in an unwanted bid, and in 1988 Siemens together with GEC bid for Plessey, a UK electronics firm. And there have been many others. In 1991 and 1992 such hostile transactions as Perrier-Nestlé and Continental-Pirelli made headlines.

However, the bidders have not been restricted to large well-established European companies, nor to UK targets. A new class of aggressive financial entrepreneurs has emerged in recent years. These individuals have demonstrated their willingness to launch controversial unfriendly take-over bids for seemingly protected Continental European businesses. They have not always succeeded in the bids that they have launched, but they have almost always made money and generated more than a token amount of support from institutional investors and from bankers willing to finance their bids.

Table 4.14 provides data for transactions opposed by targets for the period 1985–91. As indicated, hostile transactions in the United Kingdom are common, and it is clear that their volume has been rising along with the volume of M&A transactions in general. Non-UK Europeans appear to be more willing to initiate such efforts because they have found ways to achieve limited success, e.g. by provoking a higher bid, even if the tender offer is ultimately withdrawn.

The early stages in the growth of hostile bidding activity in Europe were reflected in such transactions as Carlo de Benedetti's efforts to acquire (together with other European partners) Société Générale de Belgique (Belgium) in 1987, Georges Pebereau's efforts with respect to Société Générale (France) in 1988 and Elders IXL's bid for Scottish and Newcastle Breweries (UK) in 1988. Despite de Benedetti's failure to take over Société Générale de Belgique, its share price rose sufficiently for the position of its market capitalization to increase from 143 to 47 in Europe for 1988, and this led to a fundamental financial restructuring of the company, issuance of major new share capital and a total change of management.

The underlying forces anticipated by the EC 1992 initiatives are now unleashed and are working in the market. It is apparent that a boom period of further economic restructuring in Europe will provide a major source of fee income for investment banks, as well as many highly profitable related opportunities in special financings.

This activity has just begun and will no doubt continue for some years. It will create a very attractive area of potential business for the investment bankers that are capable of competing effectively in this arena. Table 4.15 gives an impression of its value by depicting European M&A advisory assignments and comparing them with the United States.

Table 4.14 Unsolicited or hostile offers as a percentage of all completed US and European M&A transactions[a,b] 1985–1991 (in percentage terms)[c]

| | United States | | | Intra-European transactions | | | |
| | | | | United Kingdom | | | |
Year	Domestic[d]	US Cross-border[e] US buyer	US seller	Domestic[f]	UK/rest of Europe[g] UK buyer	UK seller	Rest of[h] Europe
1985	9.983	0.000	16.168	71.800	0.000	0.000	4.889
1986	5.823	0.000	15.781	7.615	0.000	20.786	0.000
1987	3.513	2.120	9.859	22.274	0.000	0.000	0.000
1988	21.617	2.025	29.914	17.227	7.658	60.663	4.310
1989	3.797	0.000	2.888	13.754	0.000	0.000	11.140
1990	0.000	0.000	0.000	14.721	0.000	0.000	0.266
1991	0.000	0.000	0.000	2.671	0.000	0.000	0.000
Average 1985–91	5.633	0.592	10.659	21.437	1.094	11.636	2.943

[a] Hostile offers are defined as those transactions in which the acquiring company proceeds with its offer against the wishes of the target company's management.

[b] Data include only completed transactions. Data are classified according to the announcement date of a transaction, not taking into consideration when a transaction is completed.

[c] Percentage values denote the fraction of total transaction volume which involves hostile offers.

[d] Completed hostile deals as a percentage of total dollar volume of completed M&A transactions in which both buyer and seller are US companies.

[e] Completed hostile deals as a percentage of total dollar volume of completed M&A transactions in which either the buyer or the seller is a US company and the counterpart is a non-US company.

[f] Completed hostile deals as a percentage of total dollar volume of completed M&A transactions in which both buyer and seller are UK companies.

[g] Completed hostile deals as a percentage of total dollar volume of completed M&A transactions in which either the buyer or the seller is a UK company and the counterpart is a Continental European company.

[h] Completed hostile deals as a percentage of total dollar volume of completed M&A transactions in which both buyer and seller are Continental European companies.

Sources: Mergers and Corporate Transactions database; Securities Data Corporation.

4.1.6 Secondary Market Brokerage and Trading

There are various forms of secondary market transactions in European securities that will be affected by the evolution of an integrated intra-European financial market in the 1992 context. These include secondary transactions in Eurobonds, government securities of the various EC countries, stocks and bonds listed on national exchanges and non-European securities, as well as financial instruments other than stocks and bonds, such as futures and options contracts. In some European countries these transactions are conducted by banks as a part of their securities investment business on behalf of clients. In others, they are conducted by market wholesalers and by brokers acting as agents for their clients. At present, there is a broad array of different types of banks, brokers and securities dealers serving the European domestic and international securities markets.

Table 4.15 US and European corporate use of financial advisers as a percentage of all completed merger and acquisition transactions[a] 1985–1991 (in percentage terms)[b]

| | Adviser to buyer frequency[c] | | | | | Adviser to seller frequency[d] | | | | |
| | European seller | | | Intra-European deals | | European seller | | | Intra-European deals | |
Year	US seller	United Kingdom	Rest of Europe	United Kingdom	Rest of Europe	US seller	United Kingdom	Rest of Europe	United Kingdom	Rest of Europe
1985	17.270	36.583	100.000	33.391	89.412	18.561	12.871	0.000	3.843	0.000
1986	15.734	54.895	97.380	39.801	78.550	31.198	10.468	2.620	10.669	0.881
1987	12.361	50.282	56.128	41.846	42.351	33.708	16.959	5.490	17.956	3.551
1988	18.116	40.093	65.827	33.988	44.714	23.006	9.077	19.200	10.469	8.409
1989	19.017	39.988	67.923	40.074	57.901	27.270	15.895	24.080	15.875	17.153
1990	5.889	46.849	7.502	26.688	10.584	32.886	4.412	2.302	6.204	1.323
1991	4.026	46.302	6.840	19.431	12.376	36.267	2.894	1.300	4.641	1.361
Average 1985–91	13.202	44.999	57.371	33.603	47.984	28.985	10.368	7.856	9.951	4.668

a Data include only completed transactions. Data are classified according to the announcement date of a transaction, not taking into consideration when a transaction is completed.
b Percentage values denote the fraction of the total number of transactions that involves the presence of financial advisers.
c Presence of financial advisers to the buying company as a percentage of the total number of attempted M&A transactions.
d Presence of financial advisers to the selling company as a percentage of the total number of attempted M&A transactions.

Source: Large, Smith & Walter; Securities Data Corporation.

Parts of the overall European market, such as the United Kingdom, have already undergone substantial restructuring. Other national markets are in various stages of reform. Commission structures, dealing rules, settlement procedures and other market practices vary widely throughout Europe. As markets converge in a post-1992 environment, many changes will have to take place – at the stock exchange level and at national and EC-wide regulatory levels.

In the preceding sections of this chapter, we point to probable expansion and further development of intra-European markets for capital raising as a direct consequence of the 1992 initiatives, and a wave of M&A and corporate restructuring activity. These developments will create a requirement for a comparable expansion and rationalization of secondary markets for intra-European securities transactions.

Intra-European trading in securities has increased considerably since 1985 and the beginning of the world stock market boom. Market values of extant securities have increased considerably, even after taking the effect of the 1987 crash into account. Privatization has added billions of dollars of value to the stock of publicly held securities in Europe. Such holdings require access to liquidity, which has been provided with varying degrees of efficiency by banks and brokers in various countries. Where indigenous securities markets are inefficient, or impaired by regulation, foreign markets will spring up in the 1990s, as they have in London.

As deregulation and competitive forces push their way through Europe – which the 1992 reforms and an increasingly performance-oriented marketplace will undoubtedly assure – movement towards linking national markets into a common intra-European securities market can be expected, and indeed should be expected.

London has already begun to function as an intra-European trading centre. In French stocks, for example, London secondary market trading in 1988 accounted for the equivalent of about 20 per cent of the daily volume on the Paris Bourse (*The Economist*, 1988b). In this respect, London has several advantages. It is the home not only of the Euromarket and many large globalized institutional investors, but also of the Stock Exchange Automated Quotation (SEAQ) system and a related (but different) system, International SEAQ, for the trading of shares attractive to international investors.

Efforts by French and Dutch securities firms to become part of the SEAQ system met strong resistance from London. There is every reason to believe, however, that the system will ultimately be expanded further to include the principal stocks from all the major European financial centres. Many of these stocks are already traded on International SEAQ. Incorporating broker–dealers from other countries into the system would not be difficult technically. For many European stocks (and virtually all international bonds) the market linkages are already in place. The technology and the know-how for a major market expansion exists, has been debugged and is relatively easy to install.

If markets are to be made abroad in the internationally popular stocks of a country, it seems reasonable for that country to take steps to recapture a substantial proportion of that business. Expanding an existing intra-European SEAQ system to include national market makers, not only in the stocks that the foreigners want to buy, but also in the foreign stocks that national investors wish to purchase, would seem a practical way to begin the process of forming an active pan-European secondary market in equities.

Whether or not an organized single intra-European secondary market in securities evolves, we can certainly expect greater linkages between the securities markets of the EC countries in the future. This being the case, it becomes essential that common regulatory principles be agreed and adhered to so as to prevent Gresham's law from applying to European securities markets. Poorly regulated markets should not be allowed to drive out those that are well regulated.

4.2 Securities Industry Regulation in the European Economic Community

We have implied in earlier sections of this chapter that the investment banking industry in Europe will be shaped to a significant degree by the evolving rules of the game, the design of which is to a large extent the responsibility of the Commission's Directorate General 15 (DG XV).

Some areas of EC public policy will affect the industry *indirectly*, notably general tax and anti-trust policies as well as rules governing take-overs and related transactions in the 12 EC member states. Public policies *directly* affecting the investment banking industry concern (a) the conditions under which securities firms may do business throughout the EC, (b) capital adequacy for investment banking firms, (c) securities taxation and (d) conduct-of-business standards governing various financial transactions in EC markets.

The criteria against which each of these will be measured centre on efficiency, transparency and stability. Efficiency refers to the all-in cost of investment banking services, as well as the quality and embedded technology of the products they provide – heavily influenced by the EC-wide competitive structure of the industry. Transparency refers to disclosure of securities, market and firm information that is sufficiently accurate and complete for investors to make informed decisions, wherein an appropriate distinction is made between professional or institutional investors, and individual or retail investors. Stability means that securities market activities of firms do not of themselves generate 'excessive' volatility on their own, and that problems of individual firms are adequately contained before they can damage the overall financial system.

As in the case of banking, design of regulatory systems is difficult, at best. In part, this is because the benefits, costs and risks associated with regulatory alternatives are inordinately difficult to assess – not least because regulatory deficiencies usually become apparent after it is too late. In part too, the EC regulatory structure must be imposed on national regulatory structures that have evolved in very different ways and have large vested interests linked to them. Not least important, EC regulation must be seen in the context of an increasingly global capital market in which there are many alternatives for both issuers and investors and in which non-EC firms and institutions play a determining role.

The general outline of the Commission's thinking with respect to firms involved in the investment business became evident in 1988, with publication of a draft directive covering the securities business scheduled to go into effect in January 1993 (Commission of the European Communities, 1988a). It is essentially modelled on the United Kingdom's 1986 Financial Services Act, and can be divided into six major aspects.

First, EC 'home' and 'host' countries and forms of commercial presence by investment firms are carefully defined. The securities business itself is specified to encompass commission brokerage; securities dealing as principal; market making; portfolio management; broker–dealer activities in transferable securities, money market instruments, financial futures, options, foreign exchange transactions and interest rate instruments such as interest rate swaps, caps and floors; securities underwriting; safekeeping of securities; and activities related to the above, presumably including financial advisory and take-over related business.

Second, investment firms are defined as those registered and functionally home based in one of the EC member states, and actively engaged in one or more of the above activities. Home country agencies (public authorities or professional associations appointed by public authorities) hold licensing and regulatory power regarding appropriate capitalization, ownership and management certification. Regulation of securities activities of credit institutions are covered under the EC Banking Directive and home country bank regulators (Commission of the European Communities, 1988a). Thus far, the EC approach to regulation of the securities industry, despite common licensing, has been separate from banking regulation, even with regard to matters of capital adequacy. Securities business and banking are *not* integrated for regulatory purposes, although in many commercial and managerial aspects they are highly integrated indeed.

Third, investment firms duly registered and supervised by EC home countries may establish a commercial presence (subject to prior notification of home and host country authorities) and are free to supply securities services in any EC member country without separate authorization.

Fourth, investment firms that hold membership in stock exchanges in their home countries will be free to apply for full trading privileges on all EC stock, options and futures exchanges either via a branch or subsidiary or by acquiring an existing member firm. An exemption is provided in the case of host countries that do not permit credit institutions to hold memberships in stock exchanges or other organized securities markets, the latter pending further harmonization.

Fifth, authorities in all EC countries and the Commission itself must be kept informed of new authorizations of firms as well as acquisitions of and participations in existing firms. Home country authorities are exclusively responsible for monitoring changes in investment firm ownership and participations, capital adequacy and risk management, compliance with prudential rules, managerial integrity and conflicts of interest, accounting procedures, and adequacy of investor protection (based on home country standards), and are responsible for injunctions, sanctions and suspensions in the event of regulatory irregularities. Exemption from some of these rules is possible in cases where they are inappropriate or where professional investors are involved. Non-compliance with securities regulations in host countries based on local investigations must be reported to home country authorities for corrective measures, which in turn are notified to all EC authorities and the Commission. In the case of a securities firm's non-compliance with a host country's directive to cease illegal activities and if, despite attempted home country corrective measures, the violation continues, the host country can take action on its own – including shutting down the offending firm's activities in its market. In addition, securities firms must comply with compensation funds and other investor protection measures in host countries. Firms and individuals retain the right to prompt notification and recourse to the courts in the event of dispute. All pre-existing activities can continue, provided that they meet the standards contained in the directive.

Sixth, securities firms home based outside the EC must be authorized to do business in one of the member states through subsidiaries – by EC home country authorities as well as by the Commission – whereupon they effectively become indigenous investment firms subject to equal (but not more favourable) treatment with firms home based in any of the EC countries. Authorization of foreign-based firms presupposes that all investment firms based in any EC country receive full reciprocal treatment in the firm's home country. In the case of failure to meet the reciprocity test during the Commission's three-month evaluation period, authorization can be refused; Commission proposals to the EC Council of Ministers on achieving reciprocity with the country in question can then follow.

Finally, there is close collaboration between the EC Commission, authorities responsible for securities markets and institutions, and banking and insurance authorities, and all regulators are held to high standards of professional confidentiality in carrying out their work. The Commission's DG XV is assisted by a committee of member state representatives. In effect, DG XV has the right to countermand host country restrictions on firms from other member countries, and can make certain future changes in the directive of its own accord, thereby achieving significant discretionary power.

4.2.1 The Reciprocity Issue and the Common Passport

Controversial aspects of the draft directive included the reciprocity provisions, which were viewed especially by the United Kingdom and Luxembourg as essentially protectionist in character and potentially damaging to their respective roles as open and fully competitive financial centres – with some even arguing that more liberal establishment rules should apply to London and Luxembourg than to the rest of the EC. France, however, took a hard line on the reciprocity issue, possibly in the hope that this could improve the competitive position of Paris against London. In some ways the issue reflected weak liberal home country establishment regulation versus tough host country rules governing the creation of a viable commercial presence.

Under full implementation of reciprocity, firms from a given country are excluded from the entire EC if the home country of the applicant is found to discriminate in any respect against firms from *any* EC member country. The home country so concerned can retaliate and exclude from its markets firms from *all* EC members. The dangers of reciprocity are readily apparent, although they are somewhat ameliorated by the provisions for any firm established in the EC by the end of 1992. Nevertheless, reciprocity remains an important feature of the single passport and is likely to be raised when new authorizations are requested, and perhaps with requests from established non-EC firms to conduct new kinds of investment banking activities.

Universal banking practices in the EC versus the separation of commercial banking from investment banking in the United States and Japan gives rise to a potentially major reciprocity issue. If reciprocity is waived by the EC, it could result in exceptional pressure on the US Congress to repeal Glass–Steagall, or become a matter of serious dispute between the EC and its US and Japanese trading partners. According to one observer, reciprocity is '. . . a missile aimed at Tokyo which will land in New York and explode on Capitol Hill' (Plender, 1988).

Realistically, US financial institutions, some of which have been established in Europe longer than many European institutions, probably have little to fear from the reciprocity issue. Informed Europeans recognize the contributions these American firms have made to the evolution of the financial system, the importance of the United States to their own financial institutions, and the potential costs of de-linking Europe's financial system from markets that have become truly global in nature. Japanese firms may have more cause for concern, given the perceived lack of reciprocity shown to European institutions in their attempts to establish a viable presence in Japanese financial markets. Consequently, Japanese firms have rapidly increased their presence in the EC, broadening their networks especially in the United Kingdom and Germany. In late 1988 18 leading international bankers, mainly American and Japanese, issued an appeal for open access to European financial markets in the 1992 context (Wagstyl, 1988).

With respect to reciprocity, the securities draft directive is consistent with the EC Second Banking Directive, wherein the Commission specifies conditions under which foreign banks are permitted to operate on a level playing field with their EC competitors under a single banking licence. Under the banking reciprocity provisions, non-EC institutions' home countries are likewise required to offer EC institutions reciprocal or 'non-discriminatory' access to their own market. By attaching reciprocity conditions, the EC Commission thus fell short of *de jure* 'national treatment' (whereby foreign and domestic firms are treated identically, and therefore there is the general equivalent of liberal trade in regulated industries) in both the banking and securities industries as the operating standard for financial services under the 1992 initiative (Walter, 1988).

As in the case of the EC banking directive, governments were urged by the Commission to apply reciprocity tests immediately, both to facilitate later implementation of reciprocity at the EC level and to preclude an end-run around reciprocity, a suggestion evidently aimed at Japan. Despite the tough language, reciprocity is likely to be implemented with considerable discretion on the part of the Commission. Rather than insisting on full reciprocity, the Commission is likely to pressure third countries for treatment of EC players on a par with indigenous firms, and therefore effectively apply a national treatment standard to a significant extent.

In part, the final story on reciprocity will depend on the outcome of the ongoing Uruguay Round of trade negotiations under the auspices of the General Agreement on Tariffs and Trade (GATT). For the first time, multilateral trade negotiations include financial services, with national treatment representing the financial services industry's equivalent of the GATT most-favoured-nation principle. This standard implies equality of opportunity in market access, including the right to establish a viable commercial presence no less favourable than that accorded to local firms − as opposed to treatment no less favourable than foreign firms receive in the applicant's home country (*The Economist*, 1988a). If national treatment is accepted in any future GATT agreement, the reciprocity issue for EC investment banking should effectively disappear for all countries that become signatories.

4.2.2 'Regulatory Arbitrage'

The EC securities draft directive implied that, whereas the EC single passport would be under the control of home country authorities, conduct-of-business rules would be the exclusive responsibility of host country authorities. British regulators in particular feared that complete reliance on home country regulation of securities firms could place London at a serious competitive disadvantage in the light of the relatively stringent Financial Services Act. At worst, home country regulation could lead to 'regulatory arbitrage' among firms seeking the most permissive home country environment as well as competitive laxity in supervision and control of securities firms on the part of countries seeking to attract such firms.

For example, the International Stock Exchange (ISE) in London argued that exclusive reliance on home country control represented a major competitive threat to London, and that split authority between home and host countries could lead to investor and issuer confusion, regulatory loopholes and erosion of investor protection, and market inefficiency. It argued instead for principal reliance on host country control, except for capital requirements and authorization of firms to do business (*The Economist*, 1988a). ISE is a product of combining the London Stock Exchange and the International Securities Dealers Association into an integrated self-regulatory organization. It has not replaced the London Stock Exchange, but is considered a part of it for regulatory purposes.

Still, it seems likely that a gradual convergence in EC regulation of securities firms will emerge, with players based in the more heavily regulated countries successfully lobbying for liberalization and the emergence among regulators and the EC authorities of a consensus on minimum acceptable standards that will eventually be accepted by home countries with substandard regulatory regimes. The objective is to optimize the balance between market efficiency and regulatory soundness, so that market forces are the sole determinants of what investment banking activities are carried out, where and by whom in the integrated EC financial market.

Equally controversial was the omission of investment advice and secondary market making from the draft directive, as were the complaints procedures specified in the directive in the event of infractions of host country rules. For some, inclusion of non-governmental self-regulatory organizations as competent authorities was also objectionable. The draft directive likewise omitted any reference to capital adequacy harmonization for investment firms, taxation of investments and investment-related transactions, and conduct-of-business principles.

4.2.3 Capital Adequacy

In order to create a level playing field in financial services, the EC will eventually have to come to grips with the capital adequacy issue. For banks, this has largely been accomplished through the BIS risk-based capital standards and EC banking harmonization. No comparable standards exist for securities firms, yet required capitalization will clearly affect the competitive positioning of players home based in different EC member countries.

The alternatives range from matching capital against position (market) risks, to minimum levels of firm capital covering all eventualities and EC-wide enforcement of maximum exposure limits. Whatever emerges will also have to be aligned with capitalization requirements of banks in order to achieve regulatory parity, in part because the banking and securities business is fully integrated in most EC countries and is likely to become increasingly so. The argument is that implementation of the investment services directive in the absence of a capital directive could lead to significant competitive dislocations among securities firms and between securities firms and banks.

4.2.4 Investment Taxation

Likewise to be settled is the matter of securities taxation in the face of continuing differences in national tax systems with respect to assets, interest and dividend income, capital gains and losses, and securities transfers (stamp) taxes. This is potentially significant with the development of EC-wide marketing of investment funds under the common passport, with Luxembourg the logical tax base for such activity. Such tax rates have differed widely among EC member countries. For example, France has imposed up to 45 per cent tax on interest income and a 25 per cent tax on dividend income, while Luxembourg imposes a 15 per cent tax on stock dividends and no taxes at all on bond and bank deposit interest payments. Withholding taxes in interest income of each EC member country are given in table 4.16.

A dramatic example of the sensitivity of the tax issue in 1988 was an estimated $10.7 billion flow of German investment funds into the Luxembourg bond market following the announced imposition of a German 10 per cent withholding tax as from January 1989. Investor reactions to the German tax bid up the price of Euro-DM issues to the point where in early 1989 it was cheaper for PepsiCo to borrow than the German government to do so. The German authorities were subsequently induced to allow 'coupon washing' − permitting investors to sell bonds immediately prior to the interest payment date and buy them back immediately afterwards to escape the tax (*The Banker*, 1988a; de Jonquières, 1989).

Table 4.16 Base withholding tax rates, 1988, for most non-resident individual bank-account holders

	Dividends %	Bond Income %	Savings Interest %
Luxembourg	0[a]	0	0
Netherlands	25	0	0
Portugal	12	12	15
Belgium	25[b]	25[b]	25[b]
Denmark	30	0	0
France	25	0	0
Ireland	0	0[c]	0
Spain	20	0	20
UK	0	25	0
Greece	42–53	0	0
Germany	25	10/0[d]	10/0[d]
Italy	32.4	12.5	30

[a] Except on dividends of Luxembourg corporations, usually 5%.
[b] Exempt under certain circumstances.
[c] Government intends to introduce 10% withholding tax.
[d] As of 1 January 1989. Repealed 1 July 1989.

Source: European tax authorities, as reported in *European Wall Street Journal*, 15 February 1989.

A decision on narrowing or eliminating intra-EC differentials in taxation of capital earnings has been of great interest to such high tax countries as Denmark and France, which vigorously advocated full harmonization of national taxes on interest, including imposition of a common withholding tax. The United Kingdom just as vigorously resisted direct tax harmonization on the grounds that it would represent a step in the direction of monetary unification and fiscal integration and, in addition, was probably unnecessary anyway to avoid serious tax evasion (*The Banker*, 1988a).

The withholding tax issue was also related to the sensitive question of financial confidentiality, where both Luxembourg and Switzerland have high stakes, although serious controversy surrounding common policies on financial insight and regulation in the OECD suggested limited progress in this area as well (Walter, 1989). Finally, there is the harmonization of corporate profits taxes, with little apparent pressure to move ahead rapidly despite the fact that cross-border M&A transactions are exposed to significant tax complexity within Europe.

In February 1989 the European Commission proposed a minimum 15 per cent withholding tax (administered at source) on interest income of investments (bonds and bank deposits) by Community residents in other EC countries. Eurosecurities and non-EC residents were exempted from the withholding tax proposal. Also exempted were savings accounts of young people and small savers that are already exempt from national tax systems, although countries would be free to impose withholding taxes above the 15 per cent floor. Governments could exempt interest income subject to tax withholding at source from declaration for tax purposes. Also exempted were countries that already apply equal or higher withholding taxes on interest income. Additional aspects of the proposal concerned cooperation in enforcement and exchange of information among EC fiscal authorities. Dividends were omitted because they are generally less heavily taxed by EC member countries and because national tax systems were thought to capture this type of income relatively effectively (Buchan, 1989; Buchan and Dixon, 1989; *The Economist*, 1989; Greenhouse, 1989).

Supporters of abolishing tax havens within the EC argued that tax harmonization was essential if a common capital market were not to lead to widespread tax evasion after the final removal of intra-EC capital restrictions on 1 July 1990. The effort was led by France, together with Belgium, Italy and Spain. All four countries argued that absence of tax harmonization would weaken their currencies in relation to those of other EC members. All four have tax collection systems that are relatively weak in other respects.

Opponents, mainly the United Kingdom and Luxembourg as well as the Netherlands, argued that tax harmonization was both unnecessary and harmful to the functioning of efficient capital markets, and that substantial investments would subsequently flow outside the EC, especially to Switzerland and Caribbean tax havens. Indeed, they argued that the proposal failed to recognize that Europe is part of a global capital market and that EC interest rates would have to be raised in order to prevent capital outflows from becoming a serious problem. The United Kingdom was also concerned about the special role of the Isle of Man and the Channel Islands (which are 'semi-detached' from the EC) and their treatment in the withholding tax initiative.

Any single EC country had the power to veto the EC withholding tax initiative. In this case, attention focused on the United Kingdom and Luxembourg. According to Jacques Delors, President of the EC Commission, 'If Luxembourg does not agree, it will have to choose between that and its European calling. Everyone has to make sacrifices and concessions for each other' (*New York Times*, 1989). Nevertheless, in a subsequent meeting of EC finance ministers every country other than France raised specific objections to the plan – ranging from UK and Luxembourg objections in principle, to German objections to the proposed 15 per cent rate, which was felt to be excessive, as well as the erosion of banking confidentiality.

The withholding tax proposal was finally defeated in June 1989. However, it appeared likely that the EC would eventually come up with some sort of watered-down withholding tax arrangement as well as possibly disclosure requirements for tax purposes.

4.2.5 Conduct-of-Business Rules

Much more difficult than design of a common passport for the securities business in the context of the 1992 initiatives has been progress towards a uniform set of rules governing the conduct of business. This includes share registration and new issues procedures and securities prospectuses, investment management and mutual funds, investor protection rules, transparency, insider trading and related market practices.

Whereas intra-EC differences in conduct-of-business regulations in banking are limited and converging due to international initiatives such as the Cooke Committee of the BIS, no similar conditions exist in investment banking. The implication is that these are to be left largely to the host countries where the activities actually occur – with the unwelcome results that securities firms would have to deal with 13 different sets of rules (including the Eurobond market) and the possibility of rule-based protectionism against foreign firms would be left open.

Insider trading rules

A dramatic example highlighting conduct-of-business issues was the Pechiney–Triangle insider trading scandal early in 1989, reaching into high levels of the French government, following a request for information from the US Securities and Exchange Commission (SEC). The insider transactions in Triangle shares were evidently carried out through institutions in Switzerland, Luxembourg and Anguilla in the Caribbean. The French regulatory body, and Commission des Operations de Bourse (COB), did not have the independence or enforcement powers of the SEC, and could only turn the matter over to the judiciary along with the available evidence. Ordinarily, that might have been the end of the affair, had it not been for a steady flow of information from the SEC and French investigative journalism that kept the COB activity alive despite strong political pressures to suppress it (Neher, 1989).

The power and investigative enthusiasm of the COB to pursue insider trading cases, which have evidently been endemic to the French equities market, were greatly strengthened as a result of the nature and magnitude of the Triangle scandal. It was necessary to make French trading more equitable and transparent if the Bourse was to hold its own in the future EC capital market (Revsin, 1989; *The Economist*, 1989). Under a new law, the COB can bring charges and assess penalities, as well as refer its findings to the courts and initiate prosecutions. Lack of political independence, however, continues to hamper its effectiveness and confidence in its objectivity.

In the United Kingdom, the Securities Investments Board (SIB) did not seek responsibility to investigate insider trading under the Financial Services Act, and this issue continues to be the responsibility of the Department of Trade and Industry and the insider dealing unit of the London Stock Exchange. Prosecutions have come under criminal law since 1980, but it has been difficult for the London Stock Exchange and Department of Trade and Industry to put together airtight cases. Moreover, the penalties involved have been extremely light (Wolman, 1989). However, in 1988 the Serious Fraud Unit, established with strong investigative powers under the 1987 Criminal Justice Act and reporting directly to the Attorney General, obtained the human and financial resources to bolster the UK effort in this regard significantly (Murphy, 1988; Walter, 1989).

Insider trading rules continue to be widely divergent across the EC, even with significant tightening in France and the United Kingdom. Comparable tightening in such non-EC countries as the United States, Switzerland and Japan will eventually force alignment across the EC capital markets for competitive reasons.

Share registration

As early as 1982 the EC Commission floated a proposal on content and distribution of prospectuses covering issues of equities and bonds, including Eurobonds, to be sold to individual and institutional investors in the member countries. All new stock and bond issues were to be covered by prospectuses meeting the EC disclosure standards, which would have required translation into nine languages and distribution in advance to the relevant authorities in the 12 countries and to the EC Commission for pre-approval. No distinction was made between the needs of institutional and individual investors.

The proposals were strongly supported by Belgium, Spain, Italy and the Netherlands on the grounds of investor protection but, apart from harmonizing bond and stock issuing procedures for domestic and foreign issues in the various national markets, the inclusion of Eurobonds in the proposals had the potential of substantially reducing speed and flexibility, increasing costs, and forcing unwanted disclosure on issuers in a professional market that had been lightly regulated from its beginnings in the 1960s and therefore had become highly efficient – with competitive forces in effect self-regulating the market to prevent questionable securities practices and preclude shoddy firms.

The proposals triggered strong opposition from the securities industry, and from the United Kingdom and Luxembourg responding to the possible flight of new issue business to other financial centres outside the EC. The proposals were stonewalled from the beginning by both countries, subsequently joined by Ireland to form a blocking minority. In 1988 the United Kingdom formally asked the Commission to exclude Eurobonds from the directive, against the threat of indefinite stonewalling. Various spokesmen advocated the adoption of the existing Euromarket offering circular as a simple and effective solution, although the question remained whether it should be published before or after the offering (Hennessy, 1988).

The EC disclosure directive was finally put forward in late 1988. All Eurosecurities will be exempt from the disclosure rules if they are 'not the object of a generalized advertising or canvassing campaign'. The prospectus directive came into force in 1992.

Curiously, the EC debate on information disclosure points in a direction quite different from that taken in the United States, where greater differentiation between institutional and individual investors is made. After long experience of requiring full disclosure of all public offerings of securities, as required by the Securities Act of 1933, progress has been substantial in reducing the difficulty and complexity of issuing securities in the US market for larger more frequent issuers. In 1985, Rule 415 was adopted by the SEC which permitted issuers to 'include by reference' a majority of the information required to be disclosed in a new issue. Subsequently, greater scope was afforded to the 'private placement' exemption from registration to the extent that under proposed Rule 144A (circulated late in 1988) virtually any security offered to institutional investors who control assets of more than $100 million could be regarded as exempt from registration, subject to certain conditions. Such practices, which recognize that sophisticated financial investors have access to information filed by corporations annually with the SEC, will allow some of the ease-of-marketing attributes characteristic of the Eurobond market to be put into practice in the United States, especially for non-US issuers. This direction is one which the EC Commission would be wise to consider adopting in Europe.

The argument is that institutional investors (specifically, those having in excess of $100 million of assets) can fend for themselves in decisions on securities purchases and have no need for the disclosure required under the 1933 Securities and Exchange Act. Resale of unregistered securities to the general public in the United States would continue to be restricted, anti-fraud and civil liability provisions of securities laws would continue to hold, and bearer securities resold in the United States would incur tax sanctions (Federal Register, 1988).

New issues practices

Other than the proposals for an EC common prospectus, no conduct-of-business rules had made their appearance at the EC level by the end of 1988. Foreign securities issues in national capital markets in the EC continue to face widely differing rules, while Eurobond practitioners have expressed concern that any EC initiatives should be fully consistent with self-regulation in that market. This is based largely on precedent rather than formal rules. The relatively loose guidelines published by the Association of International

Bond Dealers (AIBD) have focused more on transactions reporting than market practices such as post-offering price manipulation (stabilization). Again, Eurobond practitioners argued that more rigorous attempts to prevent such practices are inappropriate for a market composed entirely of some 800 professional participants (Lascelles, 1988). Nevertheless, as of 3 April 1989 all AIBD members based in the United Kingdom must report all transactions in international securities to the AIBD, as the designated exchange for Eurosecurities. This requires the approximately 200 members to subscribe to TRAX, the AIBD's proposed computerized trade matching and risk management system.

Mutual funds and investment management

The EC directive governing the operation and sale of mutual funds – Undertakings for the Collective Investment of Transferable Securities (UCITS) – was the first set of conduct-of-business rules on investments to go into effect in the EC. UCITS specifies general rules for the kinds of investments that are appropriate for mutual funds and how they should be sold. The regulatory requirements for fund management and certification are again left to the home country, while specific rules for adequacy of disclosure and selling practices are left to the host country.

Consequently, funds duly established and monitored in any EC member country such as Luxembourg, and that are in compliance with UCITS, could be marketed to investors EC-wide as of October 1989, as long as local selling requirements were met. This includes high performance 'synthetic' funds, based on futures and options, not permitted in some financial centres such as London. Under UCITS, 90 per cent of assets must be invested in publicly traded companies, no more than 5 per cent of the outstanding stock of any company may be owned, and there are limits on investment funds' borrowing rights.

Beyond UCITS, no action has been taken with respect to investment management, and the presumption is that any regulation in this regard will be left to the host country in the near term. In the future, however, national conduct-of-business rules in this area may be subject to harmonization as well.

4.2.6 Trading Conduct

Being left to host countries, trading conduct has not so far been addressed at the EC level and continues to evolve in the member countries. The 93 principles embodied in the proposed conduct-of-business rules of the UK Securities Investments Board (SIB), announced in late 1988, represent a good example of an integrated approach to this issue that may eventually influence the EC rules on investor transactions (Cohen, 1988).

The SIB principles include independence of the investment adviser and adequacy of client information (including risk preference) suitable to a fiduciary relationship, warnings against tied sales and exploitation of conflicts of interest, self-dealing, the presence of material interest in customer transactions, front-running, overcharging, churning of portfolios and insider trading, as well as effective dissemination of research, prompt and timely execution and execution at best price. Regarding information disclosure they include an emphasis on transparency with respect to clients and regulators, including periodic statements and clarity of agreements (complementing a 'standard customer agreement'), deceptive advertising, as well as disclosure of material interest of the firm in client transactions. Also included are rules governing management of discretionary accounts, pressure tactics, staff supervision, compliance and complaints procedures, inclusion in client accounts of securities subject to stabilization, buy-back obligations, custody procedures and segregation of client securities.

The stated objective of the SIB rules is that they should be 'user friendly' and keep *de jure* regulation as limited as possible, consistent with the principle of self-regulation and investor protection but sufficiently broad and flexible to capture violations in spirit. They make no distinction between professionals and ordinary investors in terms of rights, except for omission of professionals and securities market practitioners from the right to sue. A further objective was to make the rules adaptable to each of the self-regulatory organizations that are responsible for different segments of the non-bank financial services industry.

Parts of the SIB proposals, such as the segregation of client accounts, are already captured in the EC draft directive on the common passport. Others are required of all markets that pretend to be equitable to participants. Despite the likelihood of disagreements as the EC conduct-of-business rules emerge, therefore, there would already appear to be broad areas of agreement.

Among non-EC countries, Switzerland and Japan are probably the most affected by the emerging EC securities regulation. Swiss firms will receive the same treatment as US or Japanese firms, although there is greater pressure to bring Swiss regulations into alignment in areas such as admission to stock exchanges, taxation of stock transactions and take-over rules. In the case of Japan, the emergence of a single market for investment banking in Europe provides a much stronger lever to pry open the Japanese capital market, especially given the importance of Europe for Japanese financial firms.

4.3   Conclusions and Policy Implications

On the basis of the foregoing discussion, we can draw a number of conclusions about the probable impact of the 1992 initiatives on the investment banking business in Europe.

(1) We anticipate that a wave of corporate restructuring will occur in Europe similar to the wave that has enveloped the United States. Many basic industries in Europe are badly in need of restructuring and revitalization which, government assistance or ownership having failed to make them competitively viable on a global basis, will be possible only through the intervention of private-sector entrepreneurs. Increasing competitive pressures − together with increasingly available financial resources and know-how − can be expected to result in the further acceleration of activity in domestic and cross-border mergers and acquisitions, divestitures and even LBOs in Europe. As this process has just begun, it can be expected to last for many years, as has been the experience in the United States.

(2) The acceleration of corporate restructuring activity will create attractive sources of business to investment banks during the post-1992 era in Europe. Competition among investment banks for this business will be intense, with many long-standing relationships being supplanted by new competitors. US firms, fresh with highly sophisticated skills in the take-over and restructuring fields, have already been aggressive in the United Kingdom in attempting to penetrate that market. Together, US and UK firms will do the same for the rest of Europe, alongside Continental and Japanese players. European transactions will be done according to an evolving European style, not as copies of US transactions, and hence investment banking firms will have to adapt their own practices to the European environment.

(3) The unfolding merger and corporate restructuring boom will place substantial demands on European capital markets, creating a need for greater financial capacity. This capacity already exists within an intra-European capital market comprising domestic, European foreign-based and Eurobond markets, and is already comparable with markets in the United States and Japan with respect to its ability to finance the governmental as well as the banking and finance sectors. The corporate sector in Europe has been substantially less active in capital markets than in the United States or Japan. However, with the financial needs accompanying the coming wave of restructuring, the market for corporate transactions should expand to meet the increasing need for finance. Clearly such a prospect is welcome to investment banks operating in Europe, although much reshuffling of clients can be expected as relationship banking begins to be eroded by the desire to have access to the latest types of corporate finance transactions. Over time, investment bankers capable of offering integrated financial services of various types and with substantial trading capabilities, as in the United States, will emerge among the market leaders. Hausbank relationships will be more difficult to maintain.

(4) Increasing corporate activity in capital markets should lead to deeper more efficient operations of secondary markets as well and, with their improved performance, a greater willingness on the part of European financial institutions to trade their portfolio holdings.

(5)   More active and efficient markets will lead to competition among institutional portfolio managers based to a much greater extent on their investment performances. Brokers will make sophisticated research and trading products available to investment managers, and competition for the business of serving the portfolio managers will become intense.

(6)   Those seeking to offer investment banking services within the EC will consist of major European banks and financial services companies of all types from the United States and Japan. In terms of not limiting qualified competitors from participating, Europe will be the most competitive financial market in the world. This in itself may result in greatly improved market efficiencies and financial innovation, relative to markets in the United States and Japan, and therefore has the potential for attracting business from the other markets to Europe. Such a prospect may accelerate the pace of US and Japanese reforms of laws and regulations preventing banks from competing for investment banking services.

(7)   The European regulatory environment for securities will have to be addressed as a priority matter, specifically with respect to three main areas: (a) the establishment of EC-wide anti-trust regulations and rules governing the conduct of take-over activity; (b) the rules governing the behaviour of market participants, including insider trading, market making and other activities in the secondary market; (c) the rules governing new issue disclosures and procedures. Early initiatives in all three areas have already been implemented. Beyond this, however, arrangements need to be provided for enforcing the new regulations and for resolving disputes and conflicting claims arising from them. The EC itself may be too cumbersome and inexperienced a body to bring forward workable recommendations in these extremely difficult areas within the next few years.

Accordingly, it may make the most sense to ask the BIS to undertake another important mission, a mission similar to its successful Basel Committee work on bank capital adequacy. Such a committee, consisting of the most experienced securities regulators in Europe under the chairmanship of a knowledgeable and distinguished public servant, could come forward with specific recommendations aimed at establishing minimal standardized regulations for home country supervisors. The pressures on the financial markets will soon become very great, as various parties affected by the 1992 movements begin to position themselves for the future. It is essential that adequate uniform regulations, which do not exist today even in preliminary form, be in place soon. Without them, either the markets will fail to develop adequately in Europe or, perhaps more likely, the possibilities of acute misbehaviour will become too great for anyone's comfort.

Markets have a way of developing quickly, on their own. They do not wait until regulators are ready for them, as UK regulators learned in conjunction with Big Bang. The effects of the 1992 initiatives on securities markets and investment banking activities will have as profound an impact on the financial environment in Europe as Big Bang had on the markets in the United Kingdom. Even now, the markets remain uncertain as to what sort of regulatory structure will exist when the 1992 reforms fully take hold. It is hardly too soon to move ahead on the regulatory issues.

References

The Banker (1988a) Papering over the Euro-cracks, November.

The Banker (1988b) Future perfect?, November.

Buchan, D. (1989) Plans for EC minimum savings tax get rough ministerial ride. *Financial Times*, 14 February.

Buchan, D. and Dickson, T. (1989) Commission tax proposal meets hostile reception. *Financial Times*, 2 February.

Cohen, N. (1988) SIB relents on Eurobond pricing. *Financial Times*, 5 December.

Commission of the European Communities (1988a) *Proposal for a Council Directive on Investment Services in the Securities Field*, COM (88) 788-S4N 176. Brussels: Commission of the European Communities.

Commission of the European Communities (1988b) *Proposal for a Second Council Directive on the Laws, Regulations and Administrative Provisions Relating to the Taking-up and Pursuit of the Business of Credit Institutions*. Brussels: Commission of the European Communities.

The Economist (1988a) Euro-gloom, 10 September.

The Economist (1988b) Boursemanship, 8 October.

The Economist (1989) A pungent French tale of stocks and shares, 4 February.

Federal Register (1988) *Securities and Exchange Commission, Securities Act of 1933, Rule 144A and Amendments to Rule 144 and 145*, November.

Fleuriet, M. (1989) Mergers and acquisition: the French experience, Chase Manhattan SA, mimeo.

Greenhouse, S. (1989) Withholding tax plan on investments likely in Europe. *New York Times*, 11 February.

Hennessy, J.M. (1988) The American View of 1992. *International Economy*, July – August.

de Jonquières, G. (1989) A new landscape takes shape. *Financial Times*, 11 January.

Lascelles, D. (1988) The new SIB rule book. *Financial Times*, 17 November.

Murphy, P. (1988) The same old ball game. *The Banker*, December.

Neher, J. (1989) Why Paris insider flap cheers outsiders. *International Herald Tribune*, 27 January.

New York Times (1989) Plan to end Europe havens, 6 January.

Plender, J. (1988) Towards a bigger bang. *Financial Times*, 28 October.

Revsin, P. (1989) U.S. SEC turns small-stakes scandal into a major political affair in France. *Wall Street Journal*, 4 February.

Romiti, C. (1988) Remarks at a conference of the Ticino Bankers Association, Lugano, Switzerland, 19 October.

Wagstyl, S. (1988) Japanese decide to hedge bets. *Financial Times*, 19 December.

Walter, I. (1988) *Global Competition in Financial Services*. Cambridge, MA: Ballinger and Harper & Row.
Walter, I. (1989) *Secret Money*, 2nd edn. London: Unwin-Hyman.
Wolman, C. (1989) UK treads carefully over insider dealing. *Financial Times*, 7 February.

Comment

Nigel Carter

The chapter by Ingo Walter and Roy Smith on European investment banking is a wide-ranging and thorough analysis of the subject; it is clearly presented and contains many useful statistics and other data (some not previously published). The broad picture and the general thrust of the conclusions are convincing. However, a number of qualifications should perhaps be made and some points might usefully have been amplified. They are indicated in these notes which do not attempt a comprehensive critique of a generally impressive paper.

The paper's basic message is that the outlook for investment banking in Europe is very bullish. This is based on the view that a prolonged wave of corporate restructuring in Europe is virtually an inevitable result of existing economic fundamentals, that the wave has indeed begun and that it will produce a boom in merger, acquisition and related activities which will create substantial opportunities for investment bankers – probably through the 1990s.

The argument that there will be a prolonged M&A boom based on a surge in corporate restructuring merits examination. In support of the authors' argument there is a lot of anecdotal evidence from activity in the late 1980s and many European industrial and commercial firms have indicated that they are contemplating restructuring involving mergers or acquisitions in the future. In the paper itself, table 4.8 'Volume of completed intra-European M&A transactions by country' shows an increase in such transactions from roughly $10.6 billion in 1985 to $47.9 billion in 1991. However, two questions arise: How prolonged will this phenomenon be? May the peak even have been passed? To deal with these questions, table 4.8 itself shows that the 1991 and 1990 figures are below the peak of 1989. One is at least compelled to ask whether the boom is faltering or to seek some explanation for this dramatic downturn in activity as a possible guide to future developments.

Even if one accepts that the data run in table 4.8 may be too short to show a significant trend, one has to ask whether the M&A boom is likely to continue far into the 1990s as Walter and Smith expect. It would be normal to see a flurry of restructuring activity in anticipation of such a major change as the creation of the single European market, much of the activity perhaps prompted by 'fear of missing the boat'. But it is arguable that the restructuring fever could subside substantially as the initial panic passes and as a few well-publicized mistakes perhaps begin to emerge.

There are other reasons too for suggesting that M&A activity could slow down significantly. In particular there are numerous entrenched barriers to take-overs in many European countries (the United Kingdom being the major exception). Barriers include complex cross-shareholdings, restrictive voting arrangements, lack of transparency of shareholdings, and, in some countries, a culture which is deeply hostile to anything of the nature of a contested take-over. While there is some pressure (not least from the United Kingdom) for a remedy for this situation, it is questionable how successful such efforts to open up the European take-over market will be. In the meantime, we are probably seeing many (may have already seen most) of the easier friendly M&A opportunities. We may be entering the area of contested take-overs which is likely to put a severe brake on the process. For all the reasons indicated above the restructuring boom, while likely to continue for some years, may not be as active or prolonged as is suggested in the chapter.

The other theme on which these notes focus is the outlook for competition for investment banking business in Europe. It would have been illuminating, given the knowledge and experience of the authors, if they had analysed in more depth the prospects for competition in Europe between EC and non-EC (particularly US and Japanese) investment banking organizations.

The paper rightly stresses the strengths of the non-EC institutions such as highly developed traditional securities markets skills, innovative capacity, aggressive marketing and substantial capital bases. They are, and will continue to be, formidable competitors.

It would have been interesting, however, if the paper had compared them with local European organizations and had analysed in depth the features of the European market which could inhibit entry from outside − in particular, the strength of traditional bank−corporate relationships, securities placing power and the role of the European universal banks.

It is argued strongly in the chapter that traditional bank relationships are being eroded and that this will give investment banks the opportunity to break in. It is true that the increasing sophistication of many corporate treasurers means that they are looking more critically at financing options. But the analysis needs to be refined. For example, a distinction should probably be drawn between banks' large and small corporate clients. The former are less likely to be firmly embedded in existing banking relationships, not only because of the sophistication of their management, but also because of their relative bargaining power and the strength of competition for their custom. Smaller firms, in contrast, are generally more likely to feel committed to a particular bank. They may well judge that what they might at times lose in terms of cost or flexibility of financing is more than compensated over the longer term by the benefits of an established banking relationship.

A key success factor in the issue and underwriting of securities is, of course, placing power. In general the US and Japanese investment banks and securities houses have a clear competitive edge in placing securities, including those issued by European corporations, in their home markets. However, European investment bankers compete much more strongly in terms of placing power in Europe and often retain a significant advantage (even if this is now under attack). If the predicted M&A boom leads to a large growth in securities issues by smaller less well-known corporations, the placing power of European investment bankers should come even more into its own, since investors outside Europe will be less willing to buy such paper and a large proportion of the securities will have to be placed in Europe.

Finally, the role of the universal bank, which may be seen as the basic model in European banking, is relevant to the question of banking relationships and to placing power. The range of in-house products and services which can be offered by the large European universal banks gives them certain strengths which non-EC investment banks do not have. The major European banks can now offer a wide variety of investment services to their corporate customers and help them to access both national and international capital markets, while at the same time offering more traditional banking facilities. Thus under one roof they can offer not only the services which form the core of most established banking relationships, but also the capacity for innovative financial techniques. They are therefore generally well placed to handle any corporate restructuring that their clients may require. Given this kind of competition, it may not be so easy for a narrowly focused investment bank (whether from inside or outside Europe) to extract, say, even a large German corporation from its established relationship with a major local universal bank.

Part III

Banking in Six European Countries

5

Structural Adjustment in European Retail Banking: Some Views from Industrial Organization

Damien J. Neven

The objective of the European Commission's White Paper was to dismantle barriers to intra-European flows of goods, services and factors of production. In this context, the European Commission put forward a number of directives which were specific to the banking industry. The objective of this chapter is to assess the impact of the proposed changes in regulation, in the light of the pre-1992 structure and organization of the European banking industry. Attention will also be focused on retail banking.

The completion of the 'internal market' in the banking sector has been the subject of a number of studies. Most important was a study of the European financial sector undertaken by Price Waterhouse on behalf of the European Commission. This study was part of the so-called Cecchini report which tried to estimate the benefits which should accrue from a more integrated Europe. Price Waterhouse's objectives were (a) to assess the importance of the financial sector, (b) to identify the barriers to trade in financial services and (c) to estimate the consequences (the benefits?) of integration. With respect to this last objective, the study proceeded as follows. A number of financial services was selected and the prices of those services were compared across the various member countries. It was then assumed that integration would increase trade, allow more arbitrage and foster competition, so that prices of financial services in Europe would reach a common level, close to the lowest existing levels. The benefits from integration could then be quantified as the increase in consumer surplus resulting from the fall in prices expected to occur in countries where prices were currently high.[1] This exercise certainly provided an interesting and simple benchmark. Yet the assumption that prices would converge to some 'low' level (however defined) seems questionable.

I wish to thank the participants of the Conference 'European Banking After 1992', European Institute of Business Administration, INSEAD, Fontainebleau, for helpful discussions and M. Burda, J. Dermine and C. Wyplosz for insightful comments.

Presumably, it was thought that a 'perfect' market for a homogeneous commodity with a large number of small profit seeking banks might achieve such convergence. Casual observation does not suggest that the banking industry fitted the picture particularly well, however, at least in its form then; banking products were differentiated in the sense that consumers would not switch from one bank to another in response to small price differences; players were and still are sometimes few; regulation will stay for prudential (and other) reasons; banks in some countries have historically also been notorious for their collusive behaviour. That is, the structure of the banking market looked likely to be imperfectly competitive. In this chapter, I attempt to apply to the European banking industry various concepts and models of imperfect competition, borrowed from industrial organization. These tools are used to get some insight into the structure of the European banking industry that will emerge after 1992. Particular attention will be given to the structural conditions of the industry in terms of cost and demand. The type and degree of competition between banks will be emphasized.

I shall proceed as follows. In the first section, the Commission's directives on the banking sector are reviewed, in the light of the objectives of the White Paper. A distinction is drawn between 'classical' trade involving flows of services across borders and the movement of factors of production. It is found that, for the banking industry, the liberalization of factor movement is of particular importance. Next, it is argued that the current directives amount to the inception of a process of competitive deregulation, which is more important than harmonization *per se*. Hence, in section 5.2, I try to identify the areas in which deregulation will be significant; it seems that the banking industry is characterized by a lack of price competition, either because regulation in this area has been captured or because of some collusive behaviour. One can thus expect deregulation to induce more price competition and the deregulation of interest rates is identified as particularly important. Therefore I try to analyse (making references to the industrial organization literature) how the intensification of price competition will modify banks' strategies and market structure. The banking industry is assessed in terms of the incentive of individual banks to achieve productive and allocative efficiency. It is argued that the incentive for productive efficiency should be improved in terms of a more effective market for corporate control. It might be difficult for this to come about, however, because even under the most liberal directive proposed by the Commission mergers and acquisitions in banking would still be monitored (at least potentially) by national authorities. In addition, even if banking was not given a special status with respect to mergers and acquisitions, significant problems could still arise in this area. Indeed, there is a wide variety of legislation, regulatory bodies and corporate law which rule on take-over bids and procedures. This situation would make some European banks particularly vulnerable, while others are protected, and there is not, for the time being, any plan to harmonize these rules. In terms of allocative efficiency, a distinction is drawn between the type of competition between banks and the intensity of competition. With respect to the type of competition, it is argued that where interest rates were regulated, banks had an incentive to compete through quality. As a result, banks have 'overinvested' in quality, especially in terms of branch density and automatic teller machines. The impact of interest rate deregulation, which amounts to adding an additional competitive (price) variable, is then assessed with particular reference to the number of branches and their location. Some indirect evidence is also gathered with respect to the intensity of competition. Finally, section 5.3 presents some conclusions.

5.1 European Integration and Deregulation in the Banking Sector

As indicated above, the objective of the White Paper on the completion of the internal market was to remove the barriers to intra-EC trade in goods and services and allow for the free movement of factors of production. At the outset, it is important to notice that 'trade' can arise in several ways; first, trade can arise, in the classical sense, through the cross-border movement of a good or service. In the banking sector, this would occur if a resident of one country obtains (and pays for) services[2] performed by a bank established in a foreign country. Alternatively, rather than supplying its customer from abroad, the bank could choose to open a subsidiary or a branch in the customer's country. This alternative arrangement would require the bank to make an investment abroad, i.e. to move capital, and presumably to move some labour (at least initially) to staff the subsidiary. All this means that there is an alternative to the movement of goods and services – the movement of factors of production (capital and labour). As indicated below, this alternative seems to be particularly relevant in the banking sector. One reason might be that trust, confidence and reputation which are important in banking will be easier to establish when there is geographical proximity of the supplier and the receiver of the service (Sampson and Snape, 1985).

The directives on banking and capital flows put forward by the European Commission bear on both alternatives of trade. In what follows, I shall (a) discuss the effect of integration on 'classical' trade and (b) turn to 'trade' involving factor movements.

5.1.1 Integration and the Flows of Banking Services

The main constraint on the flow of banking services in the old environment stemmed from the restrictions on capital movements. Indeed, a resident of one country who wanted to contract a loan or make a deposit abroad needed to make a capital movement between his home base and the foreign country. The Commission's action on the liberalization of capital flows is in two steps. The first wave of liberalization (which came into force on 1 March 1987) dealt primarily with capital movements related to the flows of goods and non-financial services. In June 1988 the Council adopted the second wave of liberalization, which will be implemented by the mid-1990s. Targets of the directives include short-term capital movements linked to the acquisition and trading of monetary instruments, short-term financial credit, the opening and use of bank deposits and the placing of part of mutual funds (October 1989). The directive on the placing of mutual funds is particularly important for the flow of banking services across countries, which should be greatly facilitated.

Integration should thus affect trade flows between countries and it is useful to think of the current integration in terms of the theory of customs unions. A customs union is said to be formed when a group of member countries reduce (or remove) the barriers to trade between members and adopt a common trade policy with the rest of the world. More generally, the formation of a customs union amounts to the creation of more liberal or easier trading conditions between members than between a member and the rest of the world. Hence, given that the (common) external trade policy of the EC is not due to change (at least formally and officially), the completion of the internal market, which amounts to the reduction of non-tariff barriers to intra-EC trade, is equivalent to the completion of a customs union. In principle, two effects arise when a customs union is formed. On the one hand, trade can be diverted. This will happen when a member country, which has previously imported some commodity from the rest of the world, because of the lower protection starts to import from another member country instead. This is presumably not desirable, given that in this case the rest of the world is the efficient source of supply.[3] On the other hand, trade can be created. This happens when a country has previously produced some commodity while being protected by some trade barriers. When barriers are removed, the country prefers to stop domestic production and to import from a member country. This is presumably desirable given that the production is shifted from the inefficient domestic industry to a more efficient locus.

What about banking services? To what extent is trade in banking services important? Should we expect more trade diversion or more trade creation? Table 5.1 presents the export earnings from banking services as a percentage of the total banking output and the import of banking services as a percentage

Table 5.1 Trade in banking services, 1984

Country	Export/output	Import/apparent consumption
Belgium and Luxembourg	6.80	4.50
Germany[a]	1.90	1.90
Spain	0.54	0.31
France	2.04	2.26
Italy	5.55	7.23
Netherlands	3.41	2.40
UK[b]	9.70	7.50

[a] Data refer to financial services (banking and insurances).
[b] Output refers to London clearing banks only.
Sources: Statistical Office of the EEC (SOEEC); OECD, 1987; own calculations

of apparent consumption for the then eight EEC countries.[4] It is clear from this table that trade in banking services is limited, at least relative to other industries (the average import share in gross domestic product (GDP) for these countries ranges from 22.2 per cent in Spain to 76.1 per cent in Belgium). It is only in the United Kingdom that trade in banking services accounts for a significant share of output. In addition, trade in banking services for any particular country tends to go both ways (import and export). Hence trade is of an intra-industry type. Table 5.2 provides data on the trade balance and intra-EEC exports and imports at the same time (as a percentage of total exports and imports respectively). It appears that, with the exception of France and Italy, the countries of the EEC then had a trade surplus in banking services. In addition, it seems that the bulk of trade took place with the rest of the world, rather than between EEC countries. This last observation suggests that trade diversion could very well occur as a consequence of integration; as indicated above this effect is not desirable from the point of view of an efficient allocation of world resources. Trade

Table 5.2 Trade balance and direction of trade, 1984

Country	Inter-EEC exports / total exports	Intra-EEC imports / total imports	Trade balance (million ECUs)
Belgium and Luxembourg	35	45	132
Germany	n.a.	n.a.	n.a.
Spain[a]	36	36	30
France	14	30	−56
Italy	25	23	−293
Netherlands	36	50	58
UK	n.a.	n.a.	n.a.

n.a., not available.
[a] Data refer to 1985.
Sources: SOEEC, as quoted by Price Waterhouse, 1988; own calculations

diversion could also positively harm Europe's trading partners. Given the relatively low importance of the banking trade, however, diversion is not likely to be a major issue for these partners. Still, diversion could be avoided by applying to extra-EC trading partners the conditions that will apply to intra-EC trade.

5.1.2   Integration, the Movement of Factors and the Right of Establishment

As indicated above, the alternative to the export of services for a bank is the establishment of branches or subsidiaries in foreign countries. The impediments to 'trade' in this case stem from (a) restrictions to foreign direct investments, (b) restrictions to the movement of labour and (c) the rules governing market access. General restrictions to intra-EC labour movement have, by and large, now been lifted as have most restrictions to the movement of capital. In addition, it does not seem that 'there is any specific restriction on the employment of foreign EC national or special discriminatory rules in terms of professional qualifications or degree of competence and management experience' (Price Waterhouse, 1988). The rules governing market access are particularly relevant in the banking industry, however, given that market access is regulated for prudential reasons. Access to foreign markets can take place through either the *de novo* establishment of a subsidiary or the acquisition of a foreign bank. With respect to the establishment of banking subsidiaries, it does not seem that the conditions of market access discriminate against foreign banks. According to the survey of national regulations undertaken by Price Waterhouse, 'with the temporary exception of Spain, the entry and establishment rules for foreign banks are essentially the same as for domestic institutions'. One could presumably argue that the extent of actual discrimination against foreign banks is underestimated by this study, which focuses on the legal framework. The significance of some of these regulations depends on the margin of discretion with which they are applied. Still, the *prima facie* case points to the absence of overt discrimination. More restrictions do apply with respect to the acquisition of domestic banks by foreign institutions, however; formal restrictions apply in France, Italy, and Spain. In all countries, an authorization is required from the competent supervisory institution. In addition Portugal, which is not covered by the Price Waterhouse study, seems to have significant restrictions to foreign penetration and acquisitions.

In practice, the degree of penetration by foreign banks varies substantially across Europe. As table 5.3 indicates, the market share absorbed by foreign institutions ranges from 1 per cent in Denmark to 91 per cent in Luxembourg. Comparing countries of similar size, large differences appear between say Belgium (46 per cent) and the Netherlands (10 per cent), or the United

Table 5.3 Market share absorbed by foreign institutions (end of 1987, percentage of total assets)

Country	Market share
Belgium	46
Denmark	1
France	16
Germany	4
Ireland[a]	11
Italy	3
Luxembourg	91
Netherlands	10
Portugal	3
Spain	11
UK	60

[a] End of 1986.
Sources: Steinherr and Gilibert, 1988

Kingdom (60 per cent) and Germany[5] (4 per cent). This is somewhat puzzling given that, in principle, there is no overt discrimination against foreign establishments anywhere. The differences could be explained in several ways; first, it might be that foreign penetration is high in the markets which are attractive in terms of profits. Looking at the correlation between the market share of foreign firms and the rate of return on assets (see table 5.10 later) provides little support to this hypothesis[6] (corr = −0.36). Alternatively, one could presume that, in countries where market concentration is high, foreign penetration would be low. This would occur because foreign firms would prefer to penetrate rather unconcentrated markets, given that the potential retaliation from a very concentrated industry would be more severe (see Schmalensee, 1978). Indeed, some support can be found for this hypothesis, with a correlation between foreign penetration and market concentration (measured by the C5 concentration ratio − see table 5.9 later) equal to −0.58. On the whole, given the discrepancies in foreign penetration indicated above, one might still be tempted to conclude that 'hidden' restrictions exist or that existing rules are used with much discretion, particularly in Germany, Denmark, Italy and Portugal.

The European Commission has taken very concrete steps with respect to the issue of market access; the so-called Second Banking Directive, which was presented to the Council in February 1988, introduces a list of bank activities for which the principle of mutual recognition applies. This principle simply states that, if a banking service can be legally performed under some conditions in one country, it cannot be forbidden under the same conditions in another country. The list of services covered includes underwriting and trading, for customers or for own account, of practically any type of security, the participation in share issues, money brokering, leasing and issuing of credit cards. More importantly, this directive also establishes a *single banking licence*, valid across the EC. It is enshrined in the principle that, once a bank is authorized to undertake activities in its home country (according to the rules prevailing there), it may conduct the same activities in any member countries irrespective of whether or not these activities are allowed in the host country and without the need to obtain local authorization. It fact, the implementation of this principle amounts to the mutual recognition of regulatory bodies for the list of activities covered by the directive. The implications of this new principle are wide ranging: foreign banks might be able to gain some competitive advantages by supplying domestic customers with products that domestic banks cannot offer (and vice versa). The story does not end there, however. Clearly, the regulatory body of the domestic market will have an incentive to change its own regulations in order to put local banks on the same level as foreign banks. As a result, some harmonization of the regulations across countries can be expected as the various national regulatory bodies attempt to 'level the playing field'.

Moreover, one could very well imagine that the national regulatory agencies could use their power to provide their domestic banks with a competitive advantage abroad. Indeed, it would suffice for these agencies to allow a banking product which is forbidden in other countries (or allow an existing product under weaker conditions). Since one can expect all regulatory agencies to respond by relaxing their own regulation, a process of competitive deregulation will ensue, i.e. a process in which regulatory agencies compete through their rulings (which *de facto* have EC standing) to provide their domestic banks with some competitive advantage.

The outcome of such a process will surely be a harmonized regulation. Yet it might be a minimum of regulation and, indeed, might be a lack of regulation. In order to avoid such an outcome, the Commission has recognized that some basic rules should be harmonized. These basic rules include the process of prudential supervision (size and composition of funds, solvency and liquidity coefficients, concentration of credit risks) and the definition of common standards of investor protection.

One can wonder whether the Second Banking Directive and especially the mutual recognition of regulatory bodies were at all necessary, at least in principle, to obtain some benefits from integration. Indeed, just imagine a world in which the various national markets would be efficient, made of a large number of cost-efficient small firms. Assume in addition that regulation differs across countries but does not discriminate against foreign operators. Regulation differs across countries simply because of a diversity of national (or regulator's) preferences. In such a world, the Second Banking Directive and the mutual recognition of regulatory bodies would be positively harmful! Indeed, the process of competitive deregulation would lead to the establishment of a common regulation, which for all (except possibly one) members would differ from their original, most preferred, model. In other words, the new outcome would be Pareto dominated by the original outcome. That is, if there is a diversity of preferences, a variety of regulations which accommodate those preferences is desirable. Of course, variety might also entail production (in terms of duplication and unexhausted scale economies) and transaction costs. These have to be weighed against the benefits from diversity.

Still, it is unrealistic to consider the European banking market as 'efficient'. To the extent that regulation has been captured to some degree and to the extent that firms' behaviour is somewhat collusive, a competitive deregulation should a priori lead to more competition and more efficient banks (as discussed in section 5.2). Some benefits should thus accrue from this process, but the benefits will stem from deregulation and not harmonization *per se*.[7] In order to assess these gains, one should thus (a) identify the areas in which either regulation has been captured or where banks have a tendency to collude and (b) analyse how deregulation will modify banks' strategies and market structure. This is the objective of section 5.2.

5.2 Price Competition in the Banking Industry

As indicated above, in order to assess the impact of deregulation, it is useful to identify the areas in which either regulation has been captured or collusion among banks is apparent. The study by Price Waterhouse referred to above is particularly informative in this respect. Indeed, the study provides evidence on the level of prices for a number of standard banking products across the EC. These products include commercial loans, consumer credit, credit cards, mortgages, commercial draft, traveller's cheques, current accounts and letters of credit. For every single product, large differences are observed in prices across countries, as indicated in table 5.4. The question then arises of whether such price differences indicate varying degrees of price competition. One should be careful in interpreting the data since several

Table 5.4 Prices of standard banking products, 1987 (ratio of highest to lowest observed price)

Mortgage[a]	2.76
Consumer credit	3.29
Credit card	5.00
Commercial draft	5.46
Traveller's cheque	1.44
Letter of credit	1.71
Commercial loan	1.57

[a] 1986

Source: Price Waterhouse, 1988

factors can possibly explain such price differences. First, it might be very likely that, even though we observe price differences for every single product, the cost of the bundle of products is still approximately the same in every country. Price differences would then reflect different types of discrimination across products. Still, even if this were the case, the possibility of discriminating in price is itself a strong sign of a lack of price competition. Second, it might be that differences in prices reflect differences in costs. In turn, differences in costs might reflect differences in factor prices, differences in scale or sheer inefficiency (assuming that all banks have access to the same technology). Sheer inefficiency would not be inconsistent with the hypothesis of a lack of price competition (which would allow banks to be inefficient). With respect to scale economies, there is a large body of empirical literature which tries to estimate the degree of scale economies in banking. It seems that by and large there is now a consensus that scale economies are unimportant and exhausted at a low level of activity (for example, see Benston et al., 1982). Finally, with respect to factor prices and especially the price of labour, one would only expect systematic differences between Spain on the one hand and the rest of the Community on the other hand (Portugal is not included in the study). Yet the highest prices are often observed in Spain. Hence, one is led to conclude that possible cost differences are not likely to invalidate our presumption that price differences reflect different degrees of price competition.

Some more direct evidence can also be obtained in a survey by the Organization for Economic Cooperation and Development (OECD, 1987). This study shows that in several European countries interest rates were still regulated or subject to cartel-like agreements (table 5.5). Interestingly, regulation in Belgium has even been strengthened since this study was completed (see Baltensperger and Dermine, 1987). Finally, the persistent size of average margins on demand and savings deposits presented in table 5.6 is a strong indication of a lack of price competition. All in all, it

Table 5.5   Deposit rate regulation

Country	Market rate paid on demand deposits	Market rate paid on savings deposits
Belgium	No	No
France	No	No
Germany	No	Yes
Greece	No	No
Ireland	No	No
Italy	Yes	Yes
Netherlands	No	Yes[a]
Spain	No	No
UK	Yes	Yes

[a] Concerted pricing.

Sources: Bingham, 1985; Baltensperger and Dermine, 1987

Table 5.6 Margins on deposits (per cent, average 1980–1985)

Country	Margins on demand deposits	Margins on savings deposits
Belgium	11.2	5.6
Denmark	16.2	8.9
France	11.7	4.3
Germany	6.5	2.8
Italy	4.3	3.4
Netherlands	5.6	2.8
Spain	14.5	10.7
UK	10.8	2.5

Source: Chapter 1

seems that a lack of price competition is an important characteristic of the banking market in Europe. At the same time, the process of competitive deregulation outlined above should make price competition more intense. In what follows, we shall concentrate on the effect of price competition on bank strategies and market structure. This does not mean that other dimensions of deregulation will be unimportant. At the same time, new far-reaching developments are taking place independently of deregulation (the emergence of mutual funds as substitutes for traditional savings, or the securitization of debts). Still, the introduction of price competition should be, in my opinion, particularly significant.

A priori, intuition suggests that, if price competition increases, prices should fall and banks should become more efficient. Indeed, prices should fall as banks start to undercut each other. As discussed below, it is not so clear that efficiency will necessarily be improved, however. In addition, the existence of price competition might also reduce profitability and should have an impact on other bank strategies, so that the market structure will be deeply affected. We shall take both issues in turn.

5.2.1 Deregulation and Incentives for Efficiency

At the outset, one should distinguish between productive and allocative efficiency. Productive efficiency requires that whatever is done should be achieved at minimum cost; allocative efficiency implies that what is done meets consumer needs at prices which reflect the cost of provision. The incentives to be efficient will come from both the capital and the product market. A firm in competitive product markets has in general incentives to allocative efficiency since otherwise consumers will shift to other firms. However, the main incentive to productive efficiency will be the threat of bankruptcy or the threat of a hostile take-over. The possibility of going bankrupt and/or an efficient market for corporate control are thus necessary conditions for productive efficiency. Yet, in the banking market, none of these conditions is fully satisfied. Indeed (as documented by Baltensberger and Dermine, 1987), European countries have deposit insurance schemes which are designed precisely to reduce the risk of bank failures. While aiming at protecting depositors, these schemes also in fact protect the banks.[8] The treatment of take-overs is not fully effective either, since foreign participations in banks are still subject to approval by the appropriate regulatory body (even if the Second Banking Directive is fully implemented). In addition, even if the system of approval applicable to banks is lifted, questions can be raised in general about the efficiency of the market for corporate control in Europe (Yarrow, 1986). The survey by Armstrong et al. (1988) also points to important differences between European countries in the nature and strength of the rules governing take-overs. As a result, banks in some countries (like the Netherlands) would be completely protected while banks in other countries (like the United Kingdom) would be much more vulnerable.

On the whole, deregulation by introducing competition in the product markets should improve allocative efficiency. However, much less can be expected in terms of incentives for productive efficiency.

5.2.2   Deregulation, Bank Strategies and Market Structure

It is useful, at the outset, to characterize competition between banks in the pre-1992 situation. Two separate issues can be distinguished. First, if banks are not competing in price, in what areas are they competing? In other words, what is the *prevailing type of competition*? Second, are banks, while colluding on price, vigorously competing in these other areas? That is, what is currently the *competitive pressure*? The issues will be taken in turn.

Prevailing type of competition

In what follows, we review some characteristics of current competition and try to assess how it will be affected by the introduction of price competition.

Network and quality competition

Clearly, when banks do not compete in price for customer deposits they have an incentive to overinvest in equipment designed to collect these deposits; in general banks will invest in equipment (branches) to collect deposits to such a point that the marginal cost of deposits, equal to the interest on deposits plus the marginal cost of equipment, is equivalent to the interbank rate (which is an alternative source of funds). Hence, when interest rate spreads are high, the interbank rate is much above the deposit rates and banks have a stronger incentive to expand their facility. This is illustrated in table 5.7, which presents a weighted average[9] of the margins on demand and savings deposits along with the number of inhabitants per branch and the density of

Table 5.7 Branch networks and interest spreads

Country	Number of inhabitants per branch	Interest spread (weighted average)	Population density
Belgium	1,807	7.000	323
Denmark	1,497	10.725	119
France	2,176	6.150	101
Germany	1,530	3.720	245
Italy	4,192	3.620	190
Netherlands	1,978	3.500	427
Spain	1,191	11.650	76
UK	1,896	4.570	231

Sources: OECD, 1987; chapter 1; UK, Steinherr and Gilibert, 1988.

population. The latter variable is included because, other things being equal, one would expect countries with low densities to show a higher number of inhabitants per branch. The reason is that the marginal benefit from opening a branch is lower when density is low. In addition, the marginal cost of branches is presumably invariant to density. As a result, the optimal number of branches (i.e. the number for which marginal cost is equal to marginal benefit) will be lower when density is low and hence the number of inhabitants per branch will be higher. By and large, our presumption seems confirmed that countries with low price competition also have very dense branch networks.

Next, the decision to open branches should not be seen as a bank's decision which is independent of its competitors' decisions. For any customer, the distance from his residence (or workplace) to the nearest branch is an important aspect of banking service. The density of the network can thus be seen as an aspect of the quality of the banking service provided to the customers. This is also an area of the service which is not heavily regulated and over which there is no apparent collusion. It is thus reasonable to consider that banks actually compete in this area. In short, not only do banks have an individual incentive to 'overinvest' in branches, but competition will also lead them to extend their network. Yet, branch density is only one aspect of the service quality. Some other aspects, like the quality of the premises or the quality of the staff, are difficult to quantify but casual observation suggests that banks compete in these areas. The density of automated teller machines (ATMs) is also presumably valued by the consumers and is therefore likely to be used as a competitive strategy. Table 5.8 presents the number of ATMs per million inhabitants. We observe again that countries like Germany and Italy, where average margins are low, have a low density of ATMs. By contrast, Belgium and Spain, with high margins, have high densities of ATMs. France and the United Kingdom, which have

Table 5.8   Density of automated teller machines

Country	No. of ATMs per million inhabitants
France	130
UK	120
Spain	70
Germany	35
Italy	30
Ireland	50
Belgium	70

Source: Batelle as quoted by *The Economist*, 1988

very high densities of ATMs with average margins, are also interesting, given that these two countries have experienced a strong competition between networks.

The evidence reviewed so far suggests that banks do compete in quality areas. How will quality competition be affected by the introduction of price? To answer this question, reference to the analysis of Dixit (1979) is useful. Dixit builds a model in which firms sell differentiated products and have two strategic variables, namely price and quality. He allows firms either to compete or to collude over either or both variables and compares the outcomes of these various competitive scenarios. For our purpose, the relevant comparison is between the outcome of price collusion and quality competition and the outcome of competition on both quality and price. This comparison yields unambiguous conclusions: if an industry competes on quality alone, the resulting quality level will exceed that when price is competitive as well. Interestingly, it will also exceed the level achieved when there is collusion in both areas. In a way, quality is used to overcompensate for the absence of price competition. Hence, one can expect that (a) banks will have to adjust downwards the level of quality they offer, particularly in terms of branch networks, and that (b) the adjustment will be less important in those countries where banks collude on both price and quality. It is also useful to think of the results in terms of individual banks; presumably banks have competed in quality with a varying degree of success. As a result, banks have achieved different levels of quality, e.g. in terms of the density of their network. This accords with intuition and casual observation. As price competition increases, those banks that were successful in terms of quality will also be in the worst position to compete in the new environment. Indeed, the adjustment which will be required, e.g. in scaling down the branch network, will be particularly important for those banks. The winners of the quality game might thus be (at least initially) the losers of the price and quality game.

Some more insights into the economics of branches can be gained from location theory. To keep the illustration simple, assume that banks are competing in some geographical space, represented by a segment of unit length. Consumers are evenly spread along this segment and will decide which bank to visit on the basis of geographical proximity and price. Assume that initially banks only compete through the location of their branches. From the analysis of Eaton and Lipsey (1975) we can conclude that competing banks will then have an incentive to locate their branches back to back, or at least very close to one another. For example, if two banks each have to locate one branch, they will both find it optimal to go to the centre. The reason is simply that banks will split equally the interval between them, whereas they will obtain the entire custom from their 'long' market. Banks thus have an incentive to reduce the interval between them and, as a result, will pair at the centre (any pairing outside the centre would be unstable, since branches would have an incentive to leapfrog). This type of analysis can be generalized to more complex situations, with more banks and with several branches per bank; when there is no price competition, there is a tendency towards spatial agglomeration. This result also accords with the casual observation that banks often gather in particular neighbourhoods.

As price competition arises, location incentives will be modified in the following way; if banks stay in the same neighbourhood, consumers who decide on the basis of price and proximity will easily be attracted by some price reductions, since banks are basically undifferentiated in terms of geographical proximity. Price will be the main variable according to which consumers choose. As a result, price competition between geographically concentrated branches is likely to be very intense. In order to relax this competition, banks will then have an incentive to move away from one another (d'Aspremont et al., 1979). By so doing, banks will be able to charge higher prices, since customers around their locations will trade off high price against the inconvenience of going to a bank much further away. Isolated branches could thus obtain some local monopoly power. All this means that the optimal locations of branches are deeply affected by the existence of price competition. The strategy of branch concentration which has often been implemented will no longer be appropriate in the new competitive environment. Banks might have to consider relocating their branches. Some further insight can be obtained by looking at the optimal number of branches in this simple paradigm. In the absence of price competition, banks will determine the optimal number of branches by trading off the fixed cost of an additional branch against the additional market share that can be obtained. When there is price competition, the matter is not as clear. Indeed, as a bank opens new outlets, on average branches will also be closer to the competitors' branches and accordingly price competition will be more intense. The incentive to expand the network is therefore reduced (Martinez-Girault and

Neven, 1988). In a way, this result is also a particular application to a spatial context of the result by Dixit (1979) (see above), that non-price competition leads to excessive quality (branches).

Finally, the argument is sometimes put forward that entry barriers in the banking industry are high because a new entrant has to set up a branch network. In principle, the mere size of the investment required to set up the network should not constitute a barrier to entry; what matters is whether the operation of the new firm, after entry at whatever appropriate scale, is profitable. Efficient capital markets should provide the necessary funding for entry at whatever size if indeed operations can be anticipated to be profitable. It is only to the extent that capital markets are not efficient in allocating funds that there might be a barrier to entry. One could also be concerned, however, about the behaviour of incumbent firms. What matters is whether incumbent firms can credibly threaten the entrant to react aggressively in the event of entry to such an extent that entry will turn out to be unprofitable. If such a credible threat can be implemented, the entrant will prefer to stay out, so that entry will be effectively deterred. There is also an entry-deterring strategy which is particularly relevant to the banking industry: by extending their network further than they would otherwise, incumbent banks could effectively 'crowd in' the market, to such an extent that entry with an additional network (or even branch) would become unprofitable (Schmalensee, 1978). Unfortunately, no evidence could be gathered to assess whether such entry-deterring strategies are used in the banking industry. It is still interesting to notice that, in general, it will take fewer branches to deter entry effectively when there is price competition than when there is no price competition (Corstjens et al., 1988). This suggests that entry deterrence through the extension of branch networks might become more of a concern.

Price discrimination

It is commonly observed that banks offer some services free, such as the maintenance of a current account, as in Belgium and the Netherlands (as reported by the Price Waterhouse study). Transactions on current accounts are also often carried out without charge, as in Belgium, the Netherlands, France or Spain. This suggests that in order to maintain an overall level of profitability banks charge prices in excess of costs for other services. In other words, banks discriminate in price across products and, to the extent that different types of consumers buy different products, banks also discriminate across consumers. In the United States, where the same practices are observed, it is estimated that elderly and affluent consumers subsidize the transaction accounts of low income customers by as much as $4 billion (in 1981) (Bryan and Allen, 1988). The extent of cross-subsidization of services is difficult to estimate, however, and, according to Steinherr and Gilibert (1988), most banks have not been able to set up a reliable analytical cost accounting system to estimate product-specific costs. The reason is that many banking services are jointly produced. For example, there is no obvious way to allocate the fixed costs of branches across loans, deposits and other services. The problem is particularly acute because the share of total cost which has to be allocated across products is very high. According to a study by McKinsey of the American banking industry, up to 80 per cent of total costs have to be 'shared' by a range of products. In general, less than 30 per cent of total costs are unique to specific products (Bryan and Allen, 1988).

As price competition increases, one would expect the extent of price discrimination to be reduced, so that prices will reflect cost more closely. Still the question arises of how this will happen. What is the mechanism that will ensure that prices reveal cost, given that in the current situation a large proportion of costs have to be 'shared' by a range of services? The answer depends to a large extent on whether there are economies of scope in banking services, i.e. whether the unit cost of a service can be reduced if another service is provided at the same time. If not, then there is no compelling reason to produce services jointly; to illustrate, consider two services which are currently jointly produced by a bank. If there are no economies of scope, the possibility of competing in price should provide new banking institutions with the opportunity of supplying each service separately without incurring any cost disadvantage. These institutions should thus reveal the cost of the individual services. If, by contrast, there are important economies of scope, these new specialized institutions cannot be expected to emerge and there is no obvious mechanism to reveal the cost of individual services. Hence, the question of whether 'universal' or 'specialized' banks will emerge depends to an important extent on the existence of economies of scope. The econometric evidence on this is somewhat limited. Gilligan et al. (1984) report that there are some economies of scope between personal deposits and loans, and between consumer deposits and other revenues like service charges or fee income (see also Gilligan and Smirlock, 1984 and Switzer et al., 1988). Still, the methods used to estimate cost complementarities in these studies are not entirely satisfactory. Some indirect evidence can be obtained by observing the successful operation of some new specialized institutions, particularly in the United States; e.g. it seems that non-mortgage credit can be dissociated from other branch activities and shifted to point-of-purchase locations without any significant cost disadvantage. In 1975, 44 per cent of non-mortgage debt was branch based in the United States, but this figure declined to 32 per cent by 1985 (Bryan and Allen, 1988). This tendency towards the dissociation of services can be expected to be particularly relevant for consumer durable loans (especially for cars).

On the whole, it seems that more price competition should lead to the dissociation of the services for which there are no significant economies of scope with other branch-based activities. When there are significant diseconomies of scale as well, joint production of services in branches might thus be an inefficient mode of production which will not be sustainable as price competition reveals the true costs.

Bank loyalty, product differentiation and price competition

In general, within the two broad classes of absorption of savings on the one hand and release of savings on the other hand, banking products seem to be highly substitutable. The conditions for loans and deposits (leaving the price aside) tend to be fairly standard, at least for the majority of consumers. The scope for differentiation also seems limited, given that banking products are rather simple items which can be defined by a few characteristics. There is one form of product differentiation which seems to be important, however; given that depositing money with a bank will always involve a risk, consumers who are risk averse will attach a particular attention to the reputation of the bank they deal with. In addition, given that money matters are still seen as private affairs, a relationship of trust and confidence with bankers will also be highly valued. Since it takes time to build both reputation and trust, private customers will have a tendency to be loyal to their bank and cannot be expected to switch bank immediately in response to a perceived price difference. It is also noteworthy that the cost of changing banks is typically a fixed cost. According to a study by the American Banking Institute, it takes an interest differential of $1-3$ per cent for private customers to switch bank. von Weizsacker (1984) has investigated the characteristics of competition when there are once and for all costs of switching from a product to its substitute. He assumes that there is no price competition. Quite surprisingly, he finds that the existence of switching costs tends to increase the degree of substitutability between products. The reason is as follows: when prices are fixed and future preferences for banks are uncertain (a good bank today might be a bad bank tomorrow), little weight will be given to current preferences in choosing a bank, and this is precisely when switching costs are high. Hence, the higher the switching cost, the less weight is given to current preferences, which is another way of stating that products are perceived as more substitutable. Interestingly, this result also suggests that individual banks should have an incentive to reduce switching costs!

When firms compete in price, another effect comes into play; banks will have an incentive to attract new customers (often young ones) by reducing price. They will do so, knowing that higher prices can be charged in the future when the customer price elasticity will be low, owing to switching costs. Klemperer (1987) analyses such a situation. He finds that, when customers have chosen a bank, the competition between banks is reduced by the existence of the switching costs. Each bank has some market power over its stock of loyal customers. This accords with intuition. In the initial period when banks try to attract new customers, one could expect competition to be more intense, however, with banks competing for high market shares (i.e. for a large stock of future loyal customers). However, this is not necessarily the case; if the customers are forward looking, they will realize that banks are trying to lure them. As a result, they will not respond to the attractive initial offers of the banks, which in turn will have less incentive to compete vigorously. In general, it is unclear whether competition will be initially more or less intense than without switching costs.

On the whole, there is thus an interaction between price competition and bank strategies with respect to customer loyalty. When there is no price competition, banks cannot gain much from customer loyalty. When competition in price is allowed, banks will have an incentive to use price in order to attract customers. This will be beneficial later, when customers are indeed captured, but it might be very costly in the initial period. Casual observation suggests that banks already try to attract young customers by offering them gifts and special facilities. As price competition increases, we would expect to see gifts for youngsters but also better interest rate conditions.

The competitive pressure

So far, we have reviewed a number of bank strategies which are likely to be affected by deregulation. We have seen that banks have engaged in various forms of non-price competition and the question remains whether competition along those dimensions was intense. In principle, non-price competition could eliminate excess profits in the same way as price competition. At the same time, one could presume (see below) that banks which were subject to intense competition would be better positioned to cope with the new environment. Hence, it is useful to assess the intensity of competition in the pre-1992 environment.

Various indicators of competition can be used. First of all, we look at the degree of concentration. In general, one would expect collusion to be easier between a small number of large players than in a more atomistic industry. Table 5.9 presents two concentration measures, namely the market share

Table 5.9 Concentration

Country	Market share absorbed by five largest firms (%)	Herfindahl index (1983)
Belgium	70	0.119
Denmark	78	n.a.
France	50	0.086
Germany	44	0.046
Greece	83	n.a.
Italy	55	0.050
Luxembourg	30	0.086
Netherlands	84	0.177
Portugal	78	n.a.
Spain	46	0.086
UK	36	0.036

n.a., not available.
Sources: chapter 1; Price Waterhouse, 1988

absorbed by the five largest firms and the Herfindahl index (as projected by Price Waterhouse — this second measure seems rather unreliable). It appears that the market is very concentrated in Belgium, the Netherlands, Greece and Portugal and relatively unconcentrated in the United Kingdom and Luxembourg, with the other countries falling in between.

One would expect that a low competitive pressure would translate into high profits. Table 5.10 presents the rate of return on assets (before tax) for most European countries. It is immediately apparent that profits are particularly high in Denmark, Germany, Spain, Italy and the United Kingdom, and particularly low in Belgium, France and Portugal. The rate of return on deposits, excluding the interbank deposits, is also presented in table 5.10. This second measure of profitability might be more directly related to the activity of collecting funds since the interbank rate is competitively priced and hence interbank deposits generate little profit. According to this second measure, the relative profit performance of Belgium and Luxembourg is markedly improved.

Table 5.10   Profitability, 1984

Country	Rate of return on assets	Rate of return on deposits (excluding interbank)	Inflation rate
Belgium	0.34	1.29	6.30
Germany	0.76	1.34	2.40
Denmark	1.00[a]	n.a.	6.30
Spain	0.80	1.03	11.30
France	0.30	0.85	7.40
Greece	0.43	0.45	18.50
Italy	0.77	1.33	10.60
Luxembourg	0.30	1.29	6.30
Netherlands	0.51	1.02	3.30
Portugal	0.34	0.40	29.30
UK	0.85	0.87	5.00

n.a., not available.
[a] Adjusted.
Sources: OECD, 1987; own calculations

These profit figures can be related to the concentration data presented above. It turns out that high concentration does not lead to higher profits, as one could expect (the correlation between profits and the five firms' concentration ratio is equal to −0.12). One explanation behind this might be that the profit figures are a poor representation of the economic rent accruing to banks. The rent can be dissipated in several ways and, in general, can be shared between capital and labour. Rent sharing with labour could result in excess staff and/or higher wages. In order to examine this, table 5.11 presents the level of asset (excluding the interbank assets) per employee and the ratio of the remuneration per employee in banking to the national average. The results are striking; in all countries, remuneration in banking is higher than the national average. This could be explained by higher human capital in banking, or rent sharing. Assuming that the adjustment for human capital would be approximately the same across countries, a large difference appears between Germany and the rest of Europe, with a very low level of remuneration in Germany, together with a high level of assets per employee. Hence, it seems that relative to other countries there is no rent sharing (neither through staff nor wages) in German banking. The situation in the Netherlands is similar, but not as striking as the German one. By contrast, remunerations in Spain and Italy are particularly high, with low to average assets per employee. The United Kingdom seems to have very high remunerations, which are to be contrasted with a high level of assets per employee, however. France and Denmark have moderately high wages but a very low level of assets per employee (see also table 5.12).

Table 5.11 Wages and productivity, 1984

Country	Remuneration per employee national average	Assets employee (thousand ECUs)
Belgium	1.856	916.54
Germany	1.099	1,022.16
France	1.559	787.85
Italy	2.134	939.63
Netherlands	1.193	1,034.90
Luxembourg	1.904	3,701.10
Spain	1.699	821.73
Greece	1,827	874.12
Denmark	1.259	749.56
UK	1.994	1,387.30

Sources: OECD, 1987; SOEEC; own calculations

Table 5.12 Remuneration per employee in banking, relative to the national average

Country	1980	1981	1982	1983	1984
Belgium	1.81	1.86	1.91	1.85	1.86
Germany	1.08	1.08	1.09	1.10	1.10
France	n.a.	n.a	1.55	1.57	1.56
Italy	2.00	2.09	2.00	2.18	2.13
Netherlands	1.04	1.06	1.16	1.18	1.19
Luxembourg	1.70	1.77	1.84	1.94	1.90
Spain	1.56	1.56	1.63	1.69	1.69
Greece	1.80	1.77	1.79	1.83	1.83
Denmark	1.17	1.19	1.23	1.25	1.26
UK	1.72	1.81	1.93	1.92	1.99

Sources: OECD, 1987; SOEEC; own calculations

On the whole, the following picture emerges: Germany seems a profitable banking market, with relatively average concentration and no rent sharing. It is apparently the country which is best positioned to compete in the new environment. The absence of rent sharing might be particularly important to the extent that adjustments in wages and/or the labour force tend to be difficult. At the other extreme, Spain and Italy are highly profitable but have extensive rent sharing. The competitive pressure should be lowest in those countries. Figures for the United Kingdom should be interpreted cautiously, but on the whole it combines a high return with high productivity and high wages, so that the extent of rent sharing is difficult to estimate. Belgium, France and the Netherlands have a low profitability with evidence of some rent sharing, especially for Belgium and France.

Overall, competition seems to be most intense in Germany, the Netherlands and, possibly, the United Kingdom. A factor which might have contributed to fostering competition in these countries is the absence of capital control; indeed, these countries have not had capital controls for some time, and so banks have had access to the international capital market to obtain funds at competitive prices. Large corporate clients presumably have had the same opportunity. As a result, there was a ceiling on the interest rate that could be charged to these clients. At the same time, there was a limit on the amount that banks could spend in order to gather domestic funds, so that marginal inefficient banks could not survive. On both accounts, access to capital markets thus presumably has the effect of increasing competition. Interestingly, Germany and the Netherlands have also experienced low levels of inflation since the early 1980s. This might also be significant because bank profitability increases with inflation (mostly because of interest rate ceilings on deposits). Hence, most European countries have experienced a period in the early 1980s of high inflation and high profits, with the exception of Germany and the Netherlands. Some rent has thus accrued to banks in these other countries, rent which has been shared with labour. This has not happened in Germany and the Netherlands, which had much less rent to share.

5.3 Conclusion

In this chapter, it has been argued that little benefit can be expected to accrue from European integration of the banking market. What matters is that the European integration will give rise to a process of competitive deregulation. This should affect the banking industry in a significant way. As price competition starts to emerge, bank strategies in terms of branches, networks, quality, price discrimination and product range should be modified. To the extent that some national markets have enjoyed a high degree of protection and that the resulting rents have been shared with labour, the adjustment might require difficult job reductions and salary cuts. This should be of particular concern in Spain and Italy.

In preparation for European integration and deregulation, much attention was given to bank mergers, acquisitions and cross-participations. This is indicated, for example, by the acquisition of the Italian subsidiary of Bank of America by Deutsche Bank, the agreement between Midland and the Hong-Kong and Shanghai Corporation or the participation of Commerzbank in Banco Hispano Americano of Spain. At the same time, a wave of mergers and acquisitions was observed in the United States, following deregulation. In this respect, the American experience should be particularly instructive for Europe, because deregulation in the United States concerned similar areas to Europe, namely interest rates and geographical coverage. In this sense, the United States could be a laboratory experiment for European deregulation. One can thus wonder about the motives behind those mergers and acquisitions. Of course, one motive might simply be to gain market power but this should be discarded from a public policy perspective. Apart from market power, the *prima facie* case should also be against mergers and acquisitions given that, as indicated above, there are apparently no significant economies of scale in banking. Notice, however, that there are important network externalities in credit card and payment systems, such that consumers will prefer to hold a credit or charge card which is widely acceptable. This might be a motive for increasing size. However, in the European context, credit card and payment systems are (by and large) either carried out by independent non-bank institutions or have been subject to cooperative agreements. To the extent that small banks can join an existing network at non-discriminatory terms, network externalities should thus not be a rationale for size. A closer look at the American experience suggests (a) that mergers and acquisitions occurred between small to medium-size banks and (b) that the main benefit from those operations stemmed from cost reductions in cheque clearing and processing and from the economies of throughput with respect to marketing and software development (see *The Economist*, 1988). Interestingly, most banks kept a decentralized organization. With respect to the European context, it is interesting to note that the potential for cost savings in cheque processing is likely to be more limited than in the United States, given that most European countries have an efficient centralized clearing system. Second, even if cost can be reduced, the majority of the savings will occur within rather than across countries, for the simple reason that a majority of transactions take place within rather than across countries. As a result, mergers between banks of the same country seem to make more sense than mergers across countries. If one looks at the second motive for mergers and acquisitions revealed by the American experience, one reaches the same conclusion; indeed marketing tends to be specific to countries and software is specific to languages, so that avoiding duplication of marketing and software expenditures is more realistic within rather than across countries.

Another motive for mergers and acquisitions could be to achieve a better diversification of risk, given that business cycles are not fully synchronized. The relevance of this motive should decline, however, as Europe becomes more integrated.

On the whole, given that mergers and acquisitions are often difficult to realize because of managerial, cultural and organizational problems, one is left rather agnostic about the benefits of cross-border mergers in banking, apart from market power. Hence, from a public policy perspective, it does not seem that such mergers should be encouraged. In more general terms, one can wonder whether the process of deregulation will lead to the entry and exit of a lot of firms. As mentioned above, exit in the sense of bankruptcy has less significance in banking than in other industries, while exit through mergers should occur mainly for small to medium-size institutions. Entry of new firms is conceivable but it might not even be necessary; to the extent that some banking services can be dissociated from a branch network (as discussed above), the barriers to entry and exit in the supply of those services seem rather small. As a result, the market for those services is to some extent contestable, so that the mere threat of competition should discipline the existing firms. Competition in the supply of those services could thus increase without substantial entry. Finally, the entry of new banks with a branch network is conceivable, but it will depend on the perceived barriers to entry and exit. As mentioned above, the barriers to entry should not be formidable if new banks can join the existing payment and credit card networks at favourable conditions. To the extent that capital in banking is not too specific to the industry, barriers to exit, or at least the costs of scaling down, should not be over-riding . Still, the analysis presented above suggests that there is in many countries an excessive number of branches. Hence, a reallocation of the existing capacity between different players is more likely than a net increase in the total number of branches.

Notes

1   One should ideally also have taken into account the change in producer surplus. This was difficult to assess, however, given the variety of outcomes which might stem from an increase in competition (in terms of market shares, firm sizes, etc.).

2 This would include bank deposits that we regard as banking products (and not as inputs).
3 Trade diversion is certainly harmful, even to the members, when production is competitive and trade is of the inter-industry type. With imperfect competition and/or inter-industry trade, one can build scenarios where trade diversion has ambiguous effects in terms of welfare.
4 'Output' is measured as gross income (including interest earnings). Apparent consumption is equal to domestic output − exports + imports.
5 It is commonly argued that the high reserve requirement in Germany makes this market unattractive to foreign banks. This is not entirely convincing, however, given that one cost component (reserve) does not unambiguously determine profitability.
6 Ideally, one should correlate foreign penetration with some past (and not current) profitability. Differences in profitability across countries are rather stable over time, however.
7 Notice that this is not necessarily the case for all industrial sectors. When economies of scale and/or the existence of a large strategic home base are important, some benefits can flow from integration *per se*.
8 A system of 'lender of last resort', as an alternative to deposit insurance, would have the same effect.
9 Where the weights represent the typical proportions of demand and savings deposits in the money supply.

References

Armstrong, T., Haspeslagh, P. and Neven, D. (1988) Note on the harmonisation of European takeover and merger regulation, INSEAD, mimeo.
d'Aspremont, C., Gabsezwicz, J. and Thisse, J.-F. (1979) On Hotelling stability in competition. *Econometrica*, 47, 1145−50.
Baltensperger, E. and Dermine, J. (1987) Banking deregulation. *Economic Policy*, 4, 63−109.
Benston, G., Hanweck, G. and Humphrey, D. (1982) Scale economies in banking: a restructuring and reassessment. *Journal of Money, Credit and Banking*, 14, 435−56.
Bingham, T. (1985) *Banking and Monetary Policy*. Paris: OECD.
Bryan, L. and Allen, P. (1988) The changing world of banking: geographic strategies for the 1990s. *McKinsey Quarterly*, 52−71.
Corstjens, M., Matutes, C. and Neven, D. (1988) Brand proliferation and entry deterrence, INSEAD, mimeo.
Dixit, A. (1979) Quality and quantity competition. *Review of Economic Studies*, 46, 587−99.
Eaton, B. and Lipsey, R. (1975) The principle of minimum differentiation reconsidered: some new developments in the theory of spatial markets. *Review of Economic Studies*, 42, 27−50.
The Economist (1988) Banking survey, March 22.

Gilligan, T. and Smirlock, M. (1984) An empirical study of joint production and scale economies in commercial banking. *Journal of Banking and Finance*, 8, 67–77.

Gilligan, T., Smirlock, M. and Marshall, W. (1984) Scale and scope economies in the multi-product banking firm. *Journal of Monetary Economics*, 13, 319–405.

Klemperer, P. (1987) Markets with consumer switching costs. *Quarterly Journal of Economics*, 102, 375–94.

Martinez-Girault, X. and Neven, D. (1988) Can price competition dominate market segmentation. *Journal of Industrial Economics*, 36, 431–42.

OECD (1987) *Rentabilité des Banques*. Paris: OECD.

Price Waterhouse (1988) The cost of non-Europe in financial services. In *Research of the Cost of Non-Europe*, vol. 9. Brussels: Commission of the European Communities.

Sampson, G. and Snape, R. (1985) Identifying the issues in trade in services. *World Economy*, 8, 171–81.

Schmalensee, R. (1978) Entry deterrence in the ready to eat breakfast cereals industry. *Bell Journal of Economics*, 89, 1228–38.

Steinherr, A. and Gilibert, P. (1988) The impact of freeing trade in financial services and capital movements on the European banking industry, European Investment Bank, mimeo.

Switzer, L., Doukas, J. and Lauzon, M. (1988) Economies of scale in branch banking: evidence from Canada, paper presented at the European Economic Association Meetings in Bologna, Italy, mimeo.

von Weizsacker, C. (1984) The costs of substitution. *Econometrica*, 52, 1085–116.

Yarrow, G. (1986) Privatization in theory and practice. *Economic Policy*, 2, 324–71.

Comment

Paul A. Geroski and Stefan A. Szymański

One of the most interesting dilemmas associated with 1992 is that of separating the wheat from the chaff. 1992 has been a major exercise in European public policy which has also turned into a major exercise in pure public relations hype, and it is not at all evident where myth takes over from reality. There is a real need for substantive sober analyses of the likely effects of 1992, and Damien Neven's analysis of European retail banking is a most welcome example of the kind of work that is needed.

We feel it is worth drawing two lessons from Neven's paper – one relating to the issue of productive efficiency (ensuring that what is done is done at least cost) and the other to the issue of allocative efficiency (ensuring that the price to consumers reflects no more than the costs of the producer). Productive efficiency, Neven argues, can best be ensured by the existence of an effective market for corporate control. That is, inefficient managers should be faced with the threat of take-over whether they are inefficient merely from indolence or because they are operating below the minimum efficiency scale. Allocative efficiency, in contrast, can be secured through price competition. Price competition between retail banks will ensure that economic profits are driven to zero, whilst at the same time there will be no opportunities for cross-subsidization of banking services in a market where each 'product' can be individually priced. The deregulation of 1992 will in principle ensure both productive and allocative efficiency in the manner described above. Neven goes on, however, to hedge these arguments with some warnings about the possible pitfalls, and it is these we would like to emphasize.

First, as far as the market for corporate control is concerned, it is difficult to be sanguine about the prospect of increased concentration or cooperation between operators in European industry, either in retail banking or elsewhere. Increasing concentration may allow the opportunity to exploit economies of scale; however, it also increases market power and may well add to X-inefficiency rather than decreasing it. We know of very little evidence, either in the United Kingdom or elsewhere, that shows that increasing scale generates organizational or managerial efficiencies, and there is a good deal of anecdotal evidence to suggest that it achieves the reverse. Certainly, there is little evidence to be found in the Cecchini report to suggest that there are significant economies of scale in banking.[1] In addition, both Neven and de Boissieu (chapter 6) find little evidence for the existence of economies of scale in European and French banking. However, people tend to believe what they want to believe and the existence of fairly clear evidence on scale economies does not mean that we shall not see banks at least attempting to increase concentrations through take-overs and market sharing agreements, thus increasing market power. This is a development which we strongly believe will be to the detriment of the European consumer, and we look to the regulatory authorities – either nationally or in Brussels – to prevent it.

Turning to allocative efficiency, we again find ourselves in broad agreement with Neven's views. Price competition is the most likely mechanism by which allocative efficiency will be achieved. However, it is still possible to ask whether price competition will really be enhanced by the changes in 1992. Consider first the demand side. When are prices a decisive element in the choices of consumers? One might think of three possible circumstances.

1   When goods are homogeneous price is the only way in which products are differentiated – and one expects that consumers will generally choose the lowest-priced good. Now this may be a fair characterization of certain basic retail services – cheque accounts or savings deposits – but in general we feel that customers value the long-term aspects of their relationship with a bank (Neven's evidence in switching cost) suggesting that homogeneity may be limited.
2   When goods are search goods their characteristics are unknown prior to purchase (in contrast with experience goods whose quality can only be ascertained after purchase). Again, long-term banking relationships tend to be of the experience kind, suggesting that the relevance of price competition is limited.
3   When consumers are well informed they are able to compare effectively the prices of services offered. Here the evidence goes both ways. On the one hand, consumers are becoming increasingly sophisticated in their approach to financial matters; on the other hand the range and complexity of financial instruments is growing all the time. On the whole, it might be argued that price competition will not become really intense until the product range stabilizes (if it ever does).

Therefore we find reasons to be sceptical about the relevance of price competition on the demand side.

However, price competition might still be generated from the supply side. Here we find Neven's arguments intriguing, particularly his suggestive application of location theory to retail banking. His arguments are based on

Hotelling's (1929) story of competition between two firms for the custom of consumers spaced evenly along a line of unit length each with unit demand for the product. If firms do not compete on price then they will compete on location, with the result that each firm will locate at the centre. Hotelling uses the story of two ice-cream sellers on a beach as his metaphor, but casual observation of the location of retail banks on High Streets suggests that this metaphor is perfectly apt in the banking market. Drawing on the work of d'Aspremont et al. (1970), Neven points out that the introduction of price competition within this model will give the two firms incentives to move apart so as to weaken the effects of price competition, and, in the same way, the liberalization of constraints in 1992 may indeed be expected to increase price competition and hence cause some separation in the location of services, not necessarily in terms of physical distance but in terms of quality of service. Of course this is only a metaphor and not meant for literal interpretation. In addition, models of spatial competition (for an excellent survey see Tirole, 1988) can be quite sensitive to changes in specification. Nonetheless, the general conclusion to which Neven points seems to us likely to be quite robust.

We would like to extend this metaphor to competition between retail banking services in member countries in general. Prior to 1992 one may think of retail banks as positioned at either end of the line. For whatever reasons, retail banks in the United Kingdom do not compete directly with French banks and so on. Now introduce price competition and ask what is likely to happen. Banks generate monopoly rents prior to the introduction to competition because they are separated, and they have local market power. Any movement towards the centres will diminish this market power and, for reasonable specifications, this cost to the firm will dominate any gains that might accrue from moving towards the centre. The consequence is that nothing changes and deregulation is ineffective. But there is one element missing in this story, and that is the threat of entry. Outsiders to the market do have incentives to enter and acquire a share of the monopoly rents, in the process driving prices down towards competitive levels. The threat of entry, in our view, is vital to stimulating competition. But will this be forthcoming in the years after 1992? This remains an open question: talk of reciprocity (see elsewhere in this volume) may seriously inhibit entry from outside the EC (it seems fanciful to suppose that there would be new entrants from within). We see this as a very serious threat to the potential gains in consumer surplus which may arise from the deregulation of 1992.

One final point needs to be made on spatial competition. In these models there is also a general result that completely free entry generates excessive competition, a tendency to concentrate at the centre. It is interesting to speculate that this may leave the regulatory authorities with an important role in controlling the flow of entry. It is possible to imagine a situation where the conditions for entry from inside the EC are sufficiently stringent to deter excessive entry, but also weak enough to ensure that the threat stimulates the optimal level of competition.

Notes

1   More generally, we believe the Cecchini report to be excessively bullish on the prospects for economies of scale in European business. For a general discussion see Geroski (1989) and for the relevance to retail banking see Davis and Smales (1989).

References

d'Aspremont, C., Gabsezwicz, J. and Thisse, J.-F. (1979) On Hotelling stability in competition. *Econometrica*, 47, 1145–50.

Commission of the European Communities (1988) The economics of 1992. *European Economy*, 35, 91–2.

Geroski, P. (1989) The choice between diversity and scale. In P. Geroski (ed.), *1992: Myths and Realities*. London: Centre for Business Strategy, London Business School.

Davis, E. and Smales, C. (1989) The integration of European financial services. In P. Geroski (ed.), *1992: Myths and Realities*. London: Centre for Business Strategy, London Business School.

Hotelling, H. (1929) Stability in competition. *Economic Journal*, 39, 41–57.

Tirole, J. (1988) *The Theory of Industrial Organization*. Cambridge, MA: MIT Press.

6

The French Banking Sector in the Light of European Financial Integration

Christian de Boissieu

The purpose of this chapter is to provide an overview of the situation of the French banking sector on the eve of the implementation of the ambitious financial liberalization decided by member countries of the European Community (EC). In the financial sphere, 1992 began in 1989 with the application of important directives concerning the marketing of unit trusts and mutual funds and the insurance business. The complete removal of capital controls was effected by July 1990 (for the most advanced member countries). Some of the comparative advantages and handicaps of the French banking sector facing new competitive conditions are emphasized in this chapter. Three points are discussed: recent developments in the French financial system; the growth of bank profitability in France; and the consequences of financial liberalization for the regulatory and fiscal framework and for the strategy of French banks.

6.1 Recent Developments in the French Financial System: An Overview

6.1.1 Characteristics of the French Financial System in the 1960s and 1970s

Until the end of the 1970s, the French financial system could be (and has been) analysed by reference to the model of the 'overdraft economy'. Many studies (especially at the Bank of France) have elaborated on a distinction drawn by Hicks (1974) between the 'overdraft economy' and the 'auto-economy' (or, more appropriately, between the overdraft sector and the auto-sector). In an overdraft economy, deficit units do not borrow from the capital markets (which are non-existent or only residual) but rely on bank credit. 'Indirect finance' (i.e. financial intermediation) predominates and 'direct finance' plays a marginal role. In Hicks' words: 'In a pure overdraft economy, where firms kept no liquid reserves, they would be wholly dependent, for their liquidity, on the banks' (Hicks, 1974, p. 54).

Indirect finance procedures were dominant in France until the end of the 1970s. Capital markets were underdeveloped compared with the United States, the United Kingdom, Canada etc. The money market was the opposite of an 'open market', and the role of the Paris stock exchange was marginal in the savings–investment adjustment process. In 1981, financial inter-mediation still represented, on a flow-of-funds basis, close to 80 per cent of total financing in the French economy. Other features, some substantially and others more superficially associated with the overdraft economy model, have been stressed in France: the certainty of commercial banks concerning their refinancing by the Bank of France, the consequent low level of banks' excess reserves, the high rigidity in nominal interest rates etc.

In the 1960s and 1970s diversification in the menu of financial instruments was limited compared with the United States or the United Kingdom. Among the few financial innovations during this period, we must refer to the development of open-ended unit trusts (*sociétés d'investissements à capital variable* (SICAV)), beginning in 1963, and to a successful diversification of savings instruments with financial intermediaries (particularly contractual savings for housing financing, under the names of *plans d'épargne-logement* and *comptes d'épargne-logement*, which have been and still are very attractive to French households).

During the 1960s and 1970s the credit market in France was structurally 'overdetermined': the monetary authorities were controlling both the quantities of credit available, through credit ceilings (first applied dis-continuously in 1958–9, 1963–5 and 1968–70, and then permanently during the period 1973–84), and the interest rates. The first shock of deregulation came in 1966–7 with the reform implemented by M. Debré, then Minister of Finance, and consisted of several important steps.

1   The complete liberalization of bank lending rates, the only remaining constraint being the legal definition of a ceiling for these rates (the ceiling is the usury rate), while deposit rates were kept under tight control by monetary authorities.
2   The liberalization of branch banking, which created intense competition for market shares. Many large banks opened new branches – the so-called *course aux guichets* – and this phenomenon, which reached a peak in the early 1970s had, and still has today, negative effects on bank productivity and the cost of intermediation. Since 1986, some French commercial banks have been closing branches in 'over-branched' areas in an attempt to reduce the cost of intermediation and to restore labour productivity.
3   The distinction between commercial and investment banking, traditional in France since the Banking Act of 1941 and the post-war legislation, was kept in force but somewhat relaxed.

6.1.2 **Financial Innovation**

Preliminary remarks

In most recent publications financial innovations (especially product innovations) are considered as instruments used by private agents to circumvent discretionary measures taken by the monetary authorities. Financial innovation is then regarded as a challenge to monetary policy. This view, which is well summarized by the 'regulatory dialectic' between regulation and innovation (Kane, 1981) is useful when describing the experience of all Organization for Economic Cooperation and Development (OECD) countries, particularly the Anglo-Saxon countries. In France we saw some examples of financial innovation introduced to circumvent regulations. For instance, in September 1981 M. Delors, the Minister of Finance, tightened the regulation on deposit rates in such a way that many savers who, until this reform, were in a position to have rates indexed to money market rates could no longer do so. These savers were encouraged to invest in new financial instruments offered by all financial intermediaries, namely short-term open-ended unit trusts and mutual funds (unit trusts and mutual funds are the two forms of what are called 'undertakings for collective investment in transferable securities' (UCITS)).

Even if the 'regulatory dialectic' is also valid in the French case, it appears that in France, as in Italy, *public* financial innovation predominates. Rather than a challenge, financial innovation is considered as a tool for economic policy.

The distinction between private and public financial innovation

Private financial innovation comes from non-governmental sectors (banks, firms, households etc.) and arises in a decentralized way. *Ex ante* control over these new financial instruments by the monetary authorities is absent or extremely limited. The authorities only intervene *ex post*, possibly to monitor the phenomenon, to adapt the definitions of monetary aggregates and reserve requirements etc.

On the contrary, public financial innovation results from the initiative of the public decision-makers who either introduce the new financial instruments themselves or place restrictions on other parties.

In France, most of the new financial instruments have been created in the form and at the time chosen by the monetary authorities (i.e. the Bank of France and the Treasury Department). Even if the new instruments were associated with demand, either explicit or latent, by private operators, they resulted from a centralized process. This has been very clear since the starting point: in 1978, the Monory Act (named after the Minister of Finance) promoted, through tax deductions, the development of the stock market, and this confirms that, in France as in many other countries, financial innovation has sometimes been a tax innovation. A rather paradoxical outcome of the public innovation process is the creation, by the public decision-makers, of the commercial paper market in December 1985. Generally speaking, a commercial paper market gives private agents (lenders and borrowers) some autonomy *vis-à-vis* the banking system and the central bank, and it may reduce the efficacy of monetary policy by inducing large swings in the velocity of money. Thus it could be seen as a paradox that monetary authorities took the initiative in this case.

The French experience also confirms that the distinction between private and public financial innovation is only applicable up to a certain limit. Over a certain threshold of development, a new financial instrument introduced by the monetary authorities is totally subject to market forces (in France, the market for certificates of deposit provides an interesting example of this contention).

The reasons for the acceleration in the pace of financial innovation

The acceleration of the financial innovation process in France after 1978 can be explained not only by factors common to all OECD countries but also by more specific factors.

In the first set, in addition to general technical progress, we find the arguments developed in the model proposed by Silber (1975, 1983): innovation is a way of loosening constraints whose adhesion price becomes high (the increase in the adhesion price must be related, in particular, to the inflation rate etc.). Traditional constraints − regulations, competition among financial institutions, increasing risks (exchange risk, interest rate risk etc.) − have been active in generating a demand for and a supply of new financial instruments and markets.

In countries like France, where public financial innovation dominates, other constraints must also be taken into account.

1 The external constraint on the French banking and financial system: at the end of the 1970s France had to catch up with the leading countries in the field of financial innovation (the United States, the United Kingdom, Canada etc.) in order to maintain the competitiveness of the French banking system and the role of Paris as a financial centre.
2 The government budgetary constraint: an important aspect concerns coordination between monetary policy and fiscal policy. The constraint associated with monetary targeting by the central bank has led the French Treasury Department to issue new instruments (*obligations renouvelables du Trésor* (ORT), *obligations assimilables du Trésor* (OAT) etc.) in order to finance public sector deficits through non-monetary means.

3   Constraints of financing bearing on certain categories of firms: nationalized firms, and small and medium enterprises (SMEs). The Delors Act of January 1983 created several financial instruments (*titres participatifs, certificats d'investissement* etc.) tailored to nationalized enterprises and SMEs since they serve to increase the capital of the firm without changing the structure of property rights (these instruments completely separate pecuniary from voting rights).

The use of new payment technologies in the French banking sector

The French banking sector has recently gone through a rapid computerization process. While it represents 4 per cent of the GNP, it accounts for 20 per cent of total computer expenses. The use of electronic money increased very rapidly in France in the late 1980s, as can be seen in table 6.1.

Table 6.1 Automatic cash dispensers and automatic teller machines (end of year)

	1978	1983	1987	1988 forecast
France				
No. of machines	1,000	5,100	10,000	12,000
Population per machine	54,800	10,940	5,470	4,600
USA				
No. of machines	9.750	48,118	76,231	n.a.
Population per machine	22,513	4,896	3,222	
Germany				
No. of machines	n.a.	1,600	7,500	n.a.
Population per machine		38,500	8,147	
UK				
No. of machines	2,189	5,653	11,500	n.a.
Population per machine	24,852	9,659	4,930	

n.a., not available.
Source: Bank for International Settlements (BIS)

In international comparisons, France is close to the United Kingdom and far ahead of Germany. The diagnosis is confirmed by looking at the density of the point-of-sale systems. In France, the number of these systems increased to 70,000 at the end of 1987 (which corresponds to 780 people per terminal) from 10,000 at the end of 1983 (5,470 people per terminal). This technological dimension has to be kept in mind when looking at the open competition associated with the implementation of the Single European Act.

6.1.3   Recent Evolution in the Regulatory Framework

Main characteristics of the new Banking Act (1984)

From the end of the Second World War until the early 1980s banking activity in France was governed by a set of regulations adopted in 1941 and largely confirmed in 1945. These regulations, in contrast with the German 'universal banking' system, favoured a high degree of specialization and compartmentalization in the French financial system. They established a rather clearcut classification of credit institutions and bank activities according to several criteria; the main distinction between commercial and investment banking was supplemented by taking into account the average maturity of the credits, the field of intervention (agriculture, export financing etc.), the degree of control exercised by the monetary authorities etc. In view of the increased opening up of the French economy, the development of 'direct finance' and a progressive tendency towards universal banking, it was clear in the early 1980s that the 1941−5 legislation had to be updated.

The 1984 Banking Act introduced more uniformity in the French banking sector, by referring to the notion of 'credit institution' (*établissement de crédit*) already introduced in the European Directive adopted in December 1977. Under French law, a credit institution is defined as an institution that engages in at least one of the following three banking operations: (a) collecting deposits from the public; (b) granting credit; (c) issuing the system means of payment (e.g. credit cards, traveller's cheques, bankers drafts).

Without exception, all credit institutions are subject to the same rules (e.g. the same liquidity ratio, solvency ratio etc.). The broad definition of credit institutions implies that there is no incentive for the development of 'non-bank' banks in France. A firm which only grants credit *or* only collects deposits is subject to the same regulations as a full-service banking firm.

There are several categories within the class of credit institutions, the main distinction being between financial institutions which can collect demand and short-term deposits (ordinary banks, which belong to the French Bankers Association (Association Française des Banques (AFB)), mutual and cooperative banks, savings banks etc.) and others. However, some important agents are excluded from the coverage of the Banking Act: The Treasury, the Bank of France, the Caisse des Dépôts et Consignations (which centralizes the deposits with the *caisses d'épargne* and invests them in the financing of social housing, municipalities etc.) and the postal financial services. As in Germany, Italy and some other countries, French postal financial services are a part of the postal administration. They are allowed to offer a wide variety of financial instruments to collect resources, but are not permitted to grant credits.

While preserving the distinction between financial institutions and non-financial organizations, the new Banking Act authorizes credit institutions to find a better equilibrium between the opposing forces of specialization and diversification. Credit institutions are allowed to engage in activities collateral to their main functions, but various ceilings are imposed to limit the extent of diversification. For example, under a rule adopted by the Committee for Banking Regulation in November 1986, the net income derived from accessory activities (insurance business etc.) may not be greater than 10 per cent of the global net product of a credit institution.

The deregulation – reregulation dialectic

The deregulation of interest rates, commissions and fees

As stated earlier, lending rates were deregulated in 1967. As far as deposit rates are concerned, the deregulation process has been more gradual and controversial. Since May 1986, interest rates on time deposits with a maturity over three months have been freely determined, and they follow money market rates closely.

Interest payments on demand deposits have been prohibited since 1967. In the present discussion between the banks and their customers, the zero interest rate on demand deposits is seen as the counterpart of free access to many bank services (cheque books, no penalty for small denomination cheques etc.). In France, as elsewhere, this regulation has been circumvented by financial innovation. The UCITS, the Marché à Terme International de France (MATIF) and all kinds of cash-management techniques generate market interest rates on financial instruments that are a close substitute for demand deposits.

The regulatory framework is one aspect to be complemented by the study of concrete procedures of financing. Traditionally, the financing of the French economy has been carried out, to a large extent, through subsidized interest rates. The proportion of subsidized credits – which involve agriculture, housing, exports and some investment expenditures – in the total amount of credits was 42 per cent in 1975 and 44.6 per cent in 1984. The stock-flow dimension means that there is great inertia, despite the implementation of financial deregulation and liberalization. Although the rate of growth of subsidized credits has been negative since 1986 (see table 6.2), the proportion was still about 42 per cent at the end of 1987.

Table 6.2 Medium- and long-term credits to firms and households with concessionary interest rates

	Rate of growth (%)					
	1982	1983	1984	1985	1986	1987
Subsidized credits	+19.8	+15.6	+ 8.2	+ 0.4	−13.2	− 3.9
Total credit to firms and households	+15.0	+12.7	+10.8	+10.3	+ 7.5	+ 9.0

Source: Conseil National du Crédit

The aggregate data conceal a significant change in the structure of subsidized credits. Not only has the subsidy of the privilege (i.e. the gap between market interest rates and interest rates on housing credits, export credits etc.) been reduced during recent years, but also the proportion of credits with subsidized interest rates *de facto* (i.e. through a procedure of revision) or *de jure* indexed on market interest rates has risen dramatically. No doubt, behind the apparent stability in the proportion of subsidized credits, the share of the French financial system indexed on market rates has increased significantly.

Bank commissions and fees have been completely deregulated since 1986, and are now subject to full competitive pressures.

The deregulation of volumes

As already indicated, the removal of credit ceilings at the end of 1984 (but actually at the end of 1986) is a major component of the deregulation process.

Branch banking in France

Branch banking in France is a good illustration of a cycle of deregulation–reregulation. Between 1945 and 1967 any new branch had to be authorized by an individual decision of the National Council of Credit (Conseil National du Crédit). The full liberalization of branch banking in 1967 was effective until 1982, and the period 1982–6 was characterized by reregulation of branch banking and some rationing of the demand presented by financial intermediaries. Since 1986, French credit institutions have not needed an authorization from the public decision-makers to open new branches. Only a few financial intermediaries, keeping some form of privilege (e.g. the savings bank A passbook deposit or the mutual credit 'blue book', both exempted from taxes, and the privilege of Crédit Agricole in the allocation of credits with subsidized interest rates) need this authorization. To be sure, the residual regulation of branch banking is less of a constraint for the banks under present circumstances, since French credit institutions are closing some branches rather than opening new ones in order to reduce their overheads.

The rapid growth in the number of branches during the 1970s is illustrated in table 6.3. This table also documents the more recent slow-down, and even decline (in 1986), in the branch banking process.

Table 6.3 could be usefully complemented by the OECD data concerning the average number of branches per institution, which gives joint information about branching and banking concentration. The figure for France − close to 60 branches per institution in 1986 − is much higher than the comparable figure for Germany (nine) or Switzerland (nine), but much lower than for

Table 6.3 Number of permanent branches (end of year)

	1966[a]	1970	1975	1980	1985	1986	1987
Ordinary banks (belonging to AFB)	4,483	6,426	9,508	9,664	9,908	9,917	9,939
Mutual and cooperative banks		6,361	8,580	10,365	11,095	11,125	11,175
Savings banks (*caisses d'épargne*)		2,250	2,989	3,630	4,626	4,374	4,378
Other		n.a.	n.a.	n.a.	47	47	58
Total		15,937	21,077	23,659	25,674	25,463	25,550

n.a., not available.
[a] Before 1967, there is no official record concerning the number of branches of Crédit Agricole and *caisses d'épargne*.
Source: Banking Commission

Table 6.4 Number of inhabitants per branch (permanent or occasional), 1983

Belgium	968	Germany	1,541
Switzerland	1,300	Canada	1,934
France	1,524	UK	2,283
		USA	2,310
		Japan	2,780

Source: BIS

Japan or the United Kingdom. By international standards, taking into account not only permanent but 'occasional' branches (i.e. branches that are open only during certain seasons or on certain days), France is second to none in the group of the seven most industrialized countries. The ratio given in table 6.4 is quite stable in France. At the end of 1987, it was equal to 1,535 inhabitants per branch.

In the light of the European financial integration process, extended branch banking could be both an asset and a handicap. On the asset side, it may create barriers to entry opposed to domestic and foreign competitors which would have to be circumvented through acquisitions, take-over bids, etc. A large branch network also gives a comparative advantage in the field of 'proximity services', which will remain active despite the new payment technologies and the use of the principle of 'free supply of cross-border financial services' by many foreign institutions. However, an extensive network implies large overheads, and this may jeopardize the search for productivity and efficiency.

The Big Bang in Paris

The deregulation of commissions and fees has been, in Paris as in London, an important aspect of the Big Bang. In addition, a major change results from the adoption of the Act of January 1988 which adapts the status and functions of stockbrokers to the new environment. Before the reform, there were rigid 'Chinese walls' between banks and stockbrokers, and the latter had a monopoly of negotiation and intervention on the stock market. As the January 1988 Act was gradually implemented, the stockbrokers became specialized brokerage firms (*sociétés de bourse*) and they were induced to increase their capital in order to cope with the challenges of 1992. In most cases the recapitalization of the *sociétés de bourse* implies close cooperation between banks and stockbrokers and the participation of the former in the capital of the latter. By July 1988, 31 out of 61 *sociétés de bourse* had opened their capital mainly to credit institutions but also to other organizations (e.g. the holding Compagnie du Midi, which controls insurance companies and also some non-financial firms, holds shares of Meeschaert–Rousselle). The proportion is much higher if we consider only Paris stockbrokers: 29 agreements out of 45 *sociétés de bourse*. These agreements were made with domestic financial institutions (e.g. Crédit National invested in Dupont-Denant), and with foreign institutions (e.g. Warburg controls Bacot-Allain, James Capel controls Dufour–Koller–Lacarrière). 'Chinese walls' have been displaced rather than completely removed. For example, the *sociétés de bourse* (brokerage firms), which, under the January 1988 Act, are now open both to other financial intermediaries and to non-financial agents, retain their monopoly on the trading of securities.

Adjustment in the tools of prudential control

In France, as in other countries, financial innovation and financial fragility (associated with the crisis of international debt, but also with the large indebtedness of French firms during the 1970s) have led to new definitions for the different categories of prudential ratios (liquidity ratio, solvency ratio etc.). The reregulation involves extending the area of prudential control (a logical consequence of the new concept of banking embodied in the Banking Act of 1984) and adapting the concrete definition of the ratios (taking into account off-balance-sheet operations and other items). Greater consideration has been given to deposit insurance, even though the issue is less topical in France than in Anglo-Saxon countries because of the low rate of banking mortality in France and the direct guarantee given by the state to deposits collected by the *caisses d'épargne*, the Caisse des Dépôts et

Consignations or the nationalized banks. The Banking Act gave an official extension to the agreement initiated by the French Bankers Association, which involves reciprocal support between bankers in the case of a major difficulty (up to FFr 400,000 per account). Article 52 of the 1984 Banking Act has given a legal recognition to interbank solidarity. It states: 'Where such action appears justified by a credit institution's situation, the Governor of the Banque de France shall call upon the shareholders or members of the institution to provide the latter with the support it needs. The Governor of the Banque de France may also arrange for the assistance of the credit institutions as a group with a view to taking the measures needed to protect the interests of depositors and third parties, ensure the smooth functioning of the banking system and safeguard the reputation of the financial centre.'

The procedure of Article 52 was applied to the case of Al Saudi Bank in the autumn of 1988. In October 1988, the Bank of France organized a complex bail-out plan to save this bank from bankruptcy. The solution which was implemented raised some controversy, since it discriminated between domestic and foreign depositors, the latter having been reimbursed in full. A different message was sent to the market in March 1989, with the decision to close down the Banque de Participations et de Placements (BPP), which was smaller than the Al Saudi Bank but faced comparable difficulties. In France, as elsewhere, the line between bankruptcy and bail-out is rather pragmatic.

6.1.4 The Financing Structure of the French Economy

Financial innovation and deregulation were the main forces behind the dramatic change in the financing structure. The rapid development of 'direct finance', disintermediation and securitization has to be assessed in a macro-economic framework.

The macro-economic framework

From a national accounting viewpoint, the change between 1983 and 1986 is characterized by a progressive reduction in the financing deficit of non-financial firms and a relative stability (in nominal values) of household surplus (table 6.5). The progressive improvement in the firms' net position

Table 6.5 Deficits (−) and surpluses (+) (billion French francs)

	1983	1984	1985	1986
Households	+157	+154	+152	+169
Non-financial firms	−108	− 98	− 84	− 76

Source: national accounts

resulted from several factors, the most important of which was the policy of wage disindexation that was initially implemented in 1982. The figures for 1987 show a slight deterioration in the net position of the firms and a reduction in household surplus. When the nominal values are converted into ratios, they exhibit two significant changes: (a) a marked decrease in the household savings rate; (b) a continuous improvement in the self-financing ratio of firms since 1982.

The drop in the household savings rate (table 6.6, second column) took place despite the dramatic increase in real interest rates, which after having frequently been negative in the 1970s became strongly positive in the 1980s. Most econometric publications explain the decline in the household savings rate by the wages disindexation policy and its impact on the time profile of real incomes.

Table 6.6 Household, financial and non-financial savings rates (per cent)

	Household savings rate	Non-financial savings rate	Financial savings rate
1980	17.6	12.5	5.1
1981	18.0	11.3	6.7
1982	17.3	11.0	6.3
1983	15.9	10.4	5.5
1984	14.5	9.6	4.9
1985	13.8	9.3	4.5
1986	13.3	9.2	4.1
1987	12.0	9.2	2.8

Two important factors must be kept in mind in interpreting the aggregate data. First, the drop in financial savings has been more pronounced than the decrease in non-financial savings (housing etc.), especially since 1985. This phenomenon means that, in France, the financial savings of households have borne most of the burden of the adjustment not only of disindexation but also of financial instability. Growing uncertainty before and after the crash of October 1987 explains the dramatic drop in the financial savings rate in 1987. Second, the drop in the household savings ratio has occurred concomitantly with the institutionalization of savings through the development of SICAVs and other types of mutual funds. The success of institutional savings is confirmed by the data: the funds invested in UCITS managed by French financial institutions are up to 50 per cent of total UCITS in EC member countries.

As for corporate savings, the rapid rise in the self-financing ratio since 1982 (see table 6.7) has been the consequence of disindexation (and the related increase in firms' margins) and, in the early 1980s, of the low rate of investment. Since 1985, it has coincided with a significant increase in the investment rate (defined as the ratio of investment to added value).

Table 6.7 Self-financing and investment ratio (excluding large nationalized corporations) (per cent)

	Self-financing ratio	Investment rate
1979	83.2	14.8
1980	66.3	15.8
1981	60.3	15.4
1982	64.2	15.3
1983	71.2	14.5
1984	76.0	14.2
1985	76.5	14.7
1986	93.4	15.1
1987	91.0	15.9

With increased liquidity, French firms first reduced their net debt to the banking sector. Thereafter they have invested in physical equipment and some of them, as elsewhere, were attracted to financial assets because of high real interest rates and expectations of a further drop in nominal rates.

An assessment of disintermediation in France

There are several competing measures for the intermediation ratio. Here I refer to the series of the National Council of Credit (Conseil National du Crédit) which takes the viewpoint of borrowers (how deficit units satisfy their needs) and considers the UCITS as pure channels of disintermediation (clearly, this is a controversial issue since most UCITS, directly or indirectly, are managed by credit institutions).

Figure 6.1 presents the rate of intermediation in terms of flows. The flows are very sensitive to short-run movements (e.g. the drop in intermediation during 1987 before and after the financial crash). The stock approach raises many difficult issues, however, including complex problems of valuation.

Turning to the structure of corporate financing, we see a parallel development of 'direct finance'. It appears, from a flow-of-funds perspective, that 'direct financing' (i.e. financing through domestic or international capital markets) jumped to 80 per cent in 1986 from 36 per cent in 1981. For 1987,

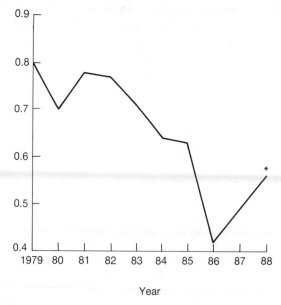

Figure 6.1   The intermediation ratio. The asterisk represents the value in the first semester. *Source:* Bank of France.

we see the same slow-down — 'direct financing' is close to 64 per cent — which began well ahead of the October crash.

The securitization process in France

A global securitization ratio, which considers from a flow approach the proportion of securities in total financing, has been calculated by Montfront (1988). The ratio, which was stable at around 15 per cent during the period 1970–9, jumped to 60 per cent in 1986 and then dropped significantly in 1987 to only 42 per cent.

Securitization began later in France than in the United States or the United Kingdom, but it has developed very rapidly under the influence of a 'catch-up' effect. This phenomenon is illustrated by the percentage of commissions and fees in aggregate bank net income (table 6.8). Between 1984 and 1988, the share of commissions increased markedly. For large commercial banks, it was close to 25 per cent in 1987, and some were close to figures seen in the Anglo-Saxon countries (for instance, Crédit Commercial de France had a ratio of 37 per cent in 1987).

Another proxy variable for disintermediation and securitization is given by the growth of off-balance-sheet operations (back-up lines, standby commitments and letters of credit, swaps etc.). Off-balance-sheet operations

Table 6.8 Ratio of commissions in bank net income, 1980−1984 (per cent)

Japan	15.1
France	15.4
USA	24.4
Germany	27.4

correspond to 26.2 per cent of the total of balance-sheet operations as of December 1987, compared with 22.8 per cent at the end of 1980 (for banks reporting to the French Bankers Association).

Securitization will accelerate with the gradual implementation of the December 1988 Law creating specialized *fonds communs de créances*. Through such institutional changes, French monetary authorities want to extend competitive pressures in the banking sector and to induce downward adjustments in the intermediation cost. Nevertheless, because of macro-economic constraints, the authorities have decided to exclude short-term consumer credits from the securitization process, which will primarily concern medium- and long-term housing credits.

6.1.5 Elements of Continuity and Change in the French Banking Sector

Market structures

The observer is struck by the low variability in the number of banks belonging to the French Bankers Association (since 1950, the number has fluctuated around 400). Another permanent feature is that the French banking sector remains highly concentrated: in December 1987, the three large depository institutions nationalized in 1945 (Crédit Lyonnais, Société Générale and the Banque Nationale de Paris) accounted for 49 per cent of total bank credit and 55 per cent of demand and time deposits (including certificates of deposit) with commercial banks. If we add to these figures Crédit Agricole (the largest French depository institution by the size of the balance sheet), Crédit Industriel et Commercial, Banque Indosuez, Banque Paribas and Banques Populaires, we arrive at close to 90 per cent of the banking activity in France. The concentration ratio did not change significantly during the period 1960−87. The high concentration ratio in the banking sector is not an idiosyncrasy of the French system. Even higher ratios are observed in the Netherlands and Denmark, let alone countries like Portugal, Greece and Ireland (Steinherr and Gilibert, 1989).

The high degree of concentration means that, until the opening of the French banking sector to external competition, it was necessary to resort to oligopoly theory in order to model the functioning of this sector. Oligopolistic competition and also collusion are the basic ingredients when we analyse the market for financial services and the determination of bank base lending rate (*taux de base bancaire*) in France until the early 1980s. Two consequences must be emphasized.

1 The high concentration explains, at least partially, the low rate of banking mortality in France. Some mortality exists, but it involves only small local and regional banks. Owing to the constraints of the 'systemic risk', the Bank of France could not allow a nationwide bank to fail.
2 The risk of diseconomies of scale is well understood by large depository institutions, which have been closing some branches and reducing the number of employees since the mid-1980s.

The stability in the concentration ratio coincided with a significant change in market shares. The banks that are members of the French Bankers Association lost ground in the mobilization of liquid savings (their market share fell to 35 per cent in 1987 from 43 per cent in 1950) to the benefit of mutual and cooperative banks (particularly Crédit Agricole) and, to a lesser extent, savings banks (*caisses d'épargne*). From the viewpoint of credit allocation, the shrinkage in the market share of the AFB banks is similar (from 35 per cent in 1978 to 30 per cent in 1987), but it has mainly benefited specialized financial institutions (Crédit National and Crédit d'Equipement des Petites et Moyennes Entreprises (Credit for the Equipment of Small and Medium Enterprises)).

The permanence of sizeable interbank operations

For all credit institutions, interbank operations represent a high proportion of the total balance sheet: 32 per cent in December 1987 (the figure is quite stable over time). The share of interbank operations is much higher for cash management banks (*banques de trésorerie*) and for discount houses; it is much lower for local and regional banks. Even when large depository institutions such as Crédit Lyonnais or Banque Nationale de Paris (BNP) are considered, sizeable interbank operations appear not only on the asset side but also on the liability side of the balance sheet. For example, in December 1987, resources from other financial intermediaries amounted to 27 per cent of total liabilities of BNP.

The extent of maturity transformation

In the 1960s French policy-makers encouraged maturity transformation by banks in order to facilitate the financing of rapid real growth. The French monetary authorities changed their mind in the 1970s, perhaps because of the extension of interest rate risk (mainly due to the international environment, as the credit ceilings were maintained), but also because some economists were arguing that maturity transformation could speed up inflation. On this controversial issue, no rigorous proof has ever been given. Nevertheless, monetary policy resorted, and is still resorting, to incentives that encourage credit institutions to extend their equity and quasi-equity base (*titres participatifs, certificats d'investissement,* etc.) and therefore the average maturity of the liability side of their balance sheet. The coefficient of term transformation, computed by calculating the average maturity of the asset side and of the liability side (a ratio above unity means the existence of maturity lengthening through transformation) fell to 1.6 at the end of 1987 from 2.2 in December 1980. This figure covers only bank operations in French francs, but a parallel change is observed for operations denominated in foreign currencies.

Foreign banks in France and French banks abroad

The market share of foreign banks in the French market has been fairly stable over the last 10 years, with a moderate and gradual increase to 17.1 per cent at the end of 1987 from 14.7 per cent in 1976. By European standards, the market share absorbed by foreign institutions is high in France: the corresponding figures were (in 1987) 4 per cent for Germany, 10 per cent for the Netherlands and 3 per cent for Italy, but 60 per cent for the United Kingdom, 91 per cent in Luxembourg (Steinherr and Gilibert, 1989). Because of the importance of interbank operations in the activities of foreign banks, their market share is lower in terms of credit (10.7 per cent in 1987) and deposits (9.2 per cent in 1987).

As regards the position of French banks abroad, the data collected by the Banking Commission indicate a more rapid growth in their investment abroad than in their domestic activities (the total assets of French banks in foreign countries increased from FFr 6.8 billion in 1978 to FFr 48 billion at the end of 1987). A significant switch from the US and Asian markets to the EC market and Switzerland has taken place since 1984.

The heterogeneity of the French banking sector

The concept of heterogeneity has been widely used since the 1960s to characterize some features of the French banking sector. It has various meanings. At first, it was (and still is in certain circumstances) referred to when pointing out the coexistence of permanent lenders (i.e. banks with large branch networks) and structural borrowers (i.e. credit institutions without a branch network) on the money market. For a long time, this coexistence was put forward as an argument to justify credit ceilings and to show the difficulties of the transition to flexible interest rates, which would create large and perhaps unsustainable transfers between lenders and borrowers.

Nowadays the analysis of heterogeneity has several dimensions. An interesting study by the Banking Commission (1988) selects 100 criteria to approach the notion of heterogeneity (among these criteria, we find many ratios concerning the structure of the balance sheet, the conditions of production, profitability etc.) and develops a typology with fairly homogeneous subcategories.

1   The three largest depository institutions (other than Crédit Agricole): BNP, Crédit Lyonnais and Société Générale.
2   Other large and diversified banks with branch networks.
3   Small and medium-size diversified banks.
4   Small local and regional banks.
5   Cash-management banks (*banques de trésorerie*).
6   Banks dealing mainly with non-residents and in foreign currencies.

It is very difficult to present international comparisons on banking heterogeneity. Perhaps, because of the conjunction of several factors – historical legacy, government intervention, the traditional specialization of some bank networks (e.g. Crédit Agricole, Banques Populaires, etc.) – the banking sector is more heterogeneous in France than in many other OECD countries. However, with extended competition, the picture is changing rapidly.

6.1.6   The Issue of Ownership in the French Banking Sector

The two waves of the nationalization process, the first in 1945 and the second in 1982–3, were followed by the privatization programme initially implemented at the end of 1986 by the Prime Minister Jacques Chirac and the Minister of Finance Edouard Balladur. Privatization of banks stopped at the end of 1987, after the October financial crash and the change in political majority in June 1988.

In 1982 the socialist government justified the nationalization of banks by its desire to influence the objective function of the banking firm in a direction more favourable to the financing of small and medium enterprises and by the need to articulate industrial and monetary policy more clearly. The results have been rather disappointing. In 1986 the conservative government justified privatization by the pressures of competition and the need for French credit institutions to raise their capital. It is too early to assess the fulfilment of these goals. The question of ownership is relevant when analysing the distribution of resources and profit among activities and agents. It does not always give accurate information about the distribution of power. This is one lesson to be drawn from the French experience. Before the implementation of the 1982 nationalization programme, the actual control of the banking sector by the monetary authorities was already stringent through the 'moral suasion' exercised by the Bank of France, the Ministry of Finance (particularly the Direction du Trésor) and other public bodies. The change in ownership resulting from privatization does not necessarily mean less influence for the monetary authorities. Everything depends on the practical use of 'moral suasion'. As stated earlier, for a long time the French financial system has been exposed to 'overdetermination', since policy-makers were, at the same time, influencing the determination of interest rates and, through credit ceilings, both the volume of credit and its intersectoral allocation. Perhaps overdetermination has been reinforced by nationalization, but institutional features give only one side of the picture. They need to be complemented by a functional perspective.

6.2   Bank Profitability in France

Despite the recent disintermediation process, commercial banks have remained the centrepiece of the French financial system and, notwithstanding macro-economic and structural developments, they have managed to improve their profitability dramatically since 1985. However, since the timing of this improvement coincides roughly with major structural and macro-economic developments, considerable uncertainties persist as to the nature and durability of the recent strengthening in banking profitability. Furthermore, the recent structural changes have raised questions about the viability and profitability of certain types of traditional banking activities. Yet, whether they are private or state owned, commercial banks must remain profitable in order to perform smoothly their essential role in the payment and financing systems.

In this section (which draws heavily on Szymczak, 1990), we assess the recent trends in the costs, margins and profits of commercial banks, propose an international comparative analysis of bank performances and examine the various causative factors of these developments. For this purpose, we use consolidated figures on the operations and profitability of French commercial banks over the last two decades. However, owing to database limitation, we shall restrict ourselves to the traditional commercial banks, the so-called 'Banques AFB' (i.e. the banks which are members of the Association Française des Banques, or the former 'Registered Banks') and exclude mutualist and cooperative banks.

6.2.1   Traditional Features of Bank Profitability in France

Bank profitability is assessed at various levels of analysis. Bank income and profit formation are broken down in consecutive stages in order to evaluate bank costs and margins on the basis of the balance sheets and profit and loss accounts. Relevant aggregates are systematically calculated and divided by business volume indicators to allow historical and international comparisons.

In order to provide a broad picture of the traditional features of costs and margins in French banking, two complementary sources of data are used. The data collected and compiled by the French Banking Commission are used to assess the major developments over the period 1972−84, whereas the international comparisons of costs and margins rely mainly on bank accounting series compiled and harmonized by the OECD (1985, 1987).

Since most of the analysis is undertaken in terms of ratios, and since bank costs and margins can be constructed as interest rates, the choice of the business volume indicator is crucial. For this purpose, the balance-sheet total is no doubt the standard indicator, and will therefore be used extensively in this study. However, the balance-sheet total includes all interbank transactions. Therefore it introduces a systematic bias, especially in the international comparisons. Indeed, French commercial banks have experienced a relatively atypical balance-sheet structure. During the early 1980s, more than 45 per cent of their assets consisted of interbank loans, compared with 25 per cent for the London clearing banks, 23 per cent for all German universal banks, and 11 per cent for all US banks (for more details on international comparative analysis of bank costs and margins, see Revell, 1980; Szymczak, 1987a).

In order to correct this bias, a second business volume indicator, the funds committed to non-financial entities, is used to supplement the balance-sheet total. This aggregate is obtained by deducting from the balance-sheet total all self-contained interbank transactions unrelated to a net funding requirement or capacity generated by transactions with non-financial entities. As such, the new aggregate constitutes a more accurate indicator of the volume of final intermediation carried out by banks, which is of primary importance from an analytical standpoint. International comparisons of costs and margins are made systematically for all banks as well as for the largest banks alone at two separate levels of aggregation in each country. Finally, since international comparisons aim at highlighting major structural features of bank profitability in France compared with other major industrial countries, only the average ratios calculated for the years 1980−4 are listed below.

Wide, distorted and vulnerable gross margins

Traditionally, gross margins in France had three major characteristics: a high level of interest spread, an unusual net banking income structure, reflecting an over-reliance on the interest margin, and finally a vulnerability of the interest margin to disinflation and to changes in the level and structure of interest rates.

Wide interest margins

One of the most usual indicators of intermediation cost is the interest margin, i.e. the difference between interests received and interests paid out by the banks.

If the balance-sheet total is chosen as an indicator of the volume activity of the banks, the traditional interest margin of all French banks appears much wider than that of Swiss, Japanese and German banks, but compares favourably with that of the US, Italian and Spanish banks (Table 6.9). With the same indicator, the largest French banks had an interest margin comparable with that of major Italian, US and German banks, but significantly lower than those of the UK clearing banks and the largest Spanish banks. However, this ranking is distorted by the atypical proportion of interbank transactions in the balance sheets of French banks. This can be corrected by assuming that the volume of bank activity is best reflected by the restricted aggregate 'funds committed to non-financial entities'. Use of this new indicator suggests a substantially different picture. It now appears that the interest margin of French banks outranked that of all the other major banking systems. The same apparently applied for the margin of the largest banks; the London clearing banks and the largest Spanish banks were the only ones to outperform their French competitors during the early 1980s.

Table 6.9 Interest margin: average ratios 1980–1984

All commercial banks				Top commercial banks			
Interest margin/ FCNFE		Interest margin/ balance-sheet total		Interest margin/ FCNFE		Interest margin/ balance-sheet total	
Switzerland	1.6	Switzerland	1.3	Japan	1.5	Japan	1.2
Japan	1.8	Japan	1.5	Switzerland	1.8	Switzerland	1.3
Belgium	3.1	Belgium	1.8	Italy	2.8	Italy	2.6
Germany	3.3	Germany	2.3	USA	3.2	USA	2.7
USA	3.7	France	2.7	Germany	3.8	Germany	2.7
Italy	3.8	USA	3.2	France	4.7	France	2.7
Spain	4.8	Italy	3.2	UK	4.7	UK	3.4
France	4.9	Spain	4.1	Spain	5.7	Spain	4.9

FCNFE, funds committed to non-financial entities.
Source: OECD, 1987

If the interest margin is undeniably an important indicator, its significance should not be overstated in comparative international analysis since the structure of gross margins varied significantly from country to country.

The unusual structure of gross margins

In France, as well as in many other industrial countries, commercial banks were the subject of extensive regulations and price controls that gradually shifted the locus of competition in the banking industry. Because they forced banks to suspend explicit pricing of payments and ancillary services in an attempt to retain their deposit base, price controls and interest rate regulation (especially the prohibition of interest payments on demand deposits imposed since 1967) thrust competition into various forms of implicit interest payments. Thriving non-price competition took the form of free financial services, such as free checking, underpriced capital market transactions on behalf of customers and, particularly in the late 1960s and 1970s, additional branches to provide customers with free convenience services. Furthermore, banks themselves generally had a poor knowledge of the sectoral net income generated by their various types of operations, since analytical accounting systems were long neglected.

In order to compensate for the underpricing of numerous ancillary and payments services, and to achieve an overall operating equilibrium, French banks systematically overcharged intermediation operations. This led to extensive cross-subsidization between various types of operations and between different types of customer (Faulhaber, 1975; Conseil National du Crédit, 1987).

Partial information is available because the Banking Commission published useful data based on a very broad categorization of bank activities. According to these analytical accounting data, payment services and various ancillary financial services generated 48.8 per cent of overheads and depreciation, but directly generated only 8.5 per cent of net banking income. Consequently, these activities generated a net operating deficit estimated at FFr 17.9 billion in 1983, which had to be supported by the interest margin (Szymczak, 1986). Consequently, traditional pricing policy carried out by French banks imposed an overpricing of intermediation services estimated at more than 30 per cent of what would have been charged if each type of operation had been priced proportionally to its costs of production.

In order to take into account distortions induced by extensive cross-subsidization, the overall margin, defined as the ratio of net banking income to an indicator of volume of bank activity, must be considered. Again, if the balance-sheet total is used as volume indicator, the overall margin of French banks occupies a median rank (table 6.10). However, if funds committed to non-financial entities alone are used as an indicator for bank activity, the overall margin was higher for all French banks than for banking systems in most other major OECD countries except Spain.

Endowment effect and vulnerability of interest margin

Because changes in market interest rates used to induce changing spreads between assets and liabilities, the general level and structure of interest rates had an important impact on bank profitability. During the late 1970s and early 1980s, as the market rates shot up, so did spreads. Consequently, the profitability of traditional intermediation activities was boosted. Since 1982, however, rapid disinflation and the associated gradual decline in interest rates

Table 6.10 Overall gross margin: average ratios, 1980−1984

All commercial banks				Top commercial banks			
Net banking income/ FCNFE		Net banking income/ balance-sheet total		Net banking income/ FCNFE		Net banking income/ balance-sheet total	
Japan	2.1	Japan	1.8	Japan	1.9	Japan	1.5
Switzerland	3.1	Belgium	2.2	Switzerland	3.6	Switzerland	2.5
Belgium	3.9	Switzerland	2.5	Italy	4.3	France	3.2
Germany	4.5	Germany	3.2	USA	4.6	Germany	3.8
USA	4.9	France	3.2	Germany	5.4	USA	3.8
Italy	5.2	USA	4.2	France	5.5	Italy	3.9
France	5.8	Italy	4.5	UK	6.9	UK	5.0
Spain	5.9	Spain	5.1	Spain	6.9	Spain	5.9

FCNFE, funds committed to non-financial entities.
Source: OECD, 1987

have imposed a squeeze on bank interest margins, further damaging bank profitability. This rate sensitivity resulted from the existence of an indexation differential between bank assets and liabilities. Indeed, when the money market rate moved by one percentage point, the average yield on loans moved in the same direction by 0.57 percentage points, but the average cost of deposits moved, also in the same direction, by only 0.4 percentage points. Consequently, during the period 1972−84, when the money market rate changed by 1 percentage point, the spread moved in the same direction by 0.17 percentage points on average.

Since this indexation differential was the major feature of the rate-sensitivity profile of the French banking system, the underlying balance-sheet characteristics that accounted for such a repricing gap must be identified. In this regard, it is possible to construct a somewhat crude but useful indicator of the degree of mismatch on bank balance sheets. The difference between assets and liabilities scheduled to be repriced or to mature within a year, which is commonly referred to as the one-year pricing gap, is the usual proxy for both the direction and order of magnitude of the near-term interest rate sensitivity of the banks. Such an indicator, based on the transactions with non-financial entities and denominated in French francs, shows that in 1984 the balance sheets of the commercial banks were characterized by a significant repricing gap which resulted from a structural disequilibrium between short-term assets (in terms of repricing or maturities) and short-term liabilities (Szymczak, 1987b). Within a year, a change in money market rates could alter the yield of 57 per cent of bank assets, but modify the cost of only 42 per cent of their liabilities. In a period of accelerating inflation and rising interest rates such a balance-sheet structure generated significant 'endowment profits' which were partly regulatory induced. Since 1982, disinflation has engendered a gradual decline in interest rates which squeezed these endowment profits and has exerted a downward pressure on the profitability of intermediation operations.

High operating costs

From an accounting standpoint, international differences in the level of gross margins reflect the respective levels of operating costs and of gross profits, the relative importance of which differs significantly from one country to the other. As regards the comparative level of operating costs, French banks were once again in a median position, and the largest banks rank very favourably when the balance sheet is chosen as the volume indicator (table 6.11).

Table 6.11   Operating costs: average ratios, 1980–1984

All commercial banks				Top commercial banks			
Operating costs/ FCNFE		Operating costs/ balance-sheet total		Operating costs/ FCNFE		Operating costs/ balance-sheet total	
Japan	1.5	Japan	1.3	Japan	1.3	Japan	1.0
Switzerland	1.7	Switzerland	1.4	Switzerland	2.1	Switzerland	1.5
Germany	3.0	Belgium	1.9	USA	3.2	France	2.2
Belgium	3.2	Germany	2.1	Italy	3.3	Germany	2.6
Italy	3.4	France	2.2	Germany	3.7	USA	2.6
USA	3.4	USA	2.9	France	3.8	Italy	3.0
France	3.9	Italy	2.9	Spain	4.4	UK	3.5
Spain	3.9	Spain	3.4	UK	4.8	Spain	3.8

FCNFE, funds committed to non-financial entities.
Source: OECD, 1987

In contrast, in terms of funds committed to non-financial entities, French banks traditionally appear as burdened with higher operating costs than their foreign counterparts, except for Spanish banks. The largest French banks had operating costs comparable with those of the largest German banks and lower than those of their UK and Spanish counterparts. However, these costs were still higher than those of Japanese and US banks.

Since banking is traditionally a labour-intensive industry, the ranking by operating costs reflects to a large extent the ranking by staff costs. The staff costs of French banks used to represent two-thirds of total operating costs and, in terms of funds committed to non-financial entities, they have been far higher than those in the other industrial countries, again with the exception of Spain. For the largest banks, these costs were comparable with those of

German and Italian banks, but still far higher than for Japanese and US banks.

More generally, the degree and nature of competition prevailing in French banking shaped costs and margins. As a consequence of extensive regulation, significant public ownership and a traditional oligopolistic structure, which allowed the occurrence of collusive behaviour on some occasions, French banking markets were imperfectly contestable. To a certain extent, the method of monetary management (the so-called *encadrement du crédit*) and other regulations discriminated against new entrants. Furthermore, the very structure of the industry, dominated by an oligopoly of four major banking groups which could benefit from significant economies of scale in their retail banking operations, also protected these banks from entry. Indeed, a new entrant would have required an important quasi-irreversible outlay of capital, i.e. significant sunk costs, in order to create from scratch a branch system sufficiently widespread to imply effective competition in retail banking. Hence, in this concentrated industry, threat of entry was not a strong constraint on pricing. Banks could charge monopoly prices and gross margins were probably higher than would have been sustainable in a perfectly contestable industry. In this context, because the market power of the firms relieved them from some pressures to minimize costs, certain patterns of expense preference behaviour and of X-inefficiency were likely to emerge and to become pervasive. In this regard, in addition to possible risk avoidance, imperfect competition allowed overstaffing, excessive extension of branch networks, slack in organizational structures and, as a consequence, inefficient resource use in significant portions of the French banking industry. All this contributed to maintaining intermediation costs at a high level in France.

A dramatic increase in provisions for risks

During the period 1972−84, actual and anticipated loan losses contributed to put downward pressure on bank profitability and to raise base lending rates. In France, non-performing assets rose throughout the period from 1.4 per cent of total loans to non-financial entities in 1972 to 2.6 per cent in 1980 and 4.1 per cent in 1984. Consequently, banks strove to build up loan loss reserves, especially on sovereign debts. Annual appropriations to provisioning accounts increased from 0.2 per cent of total credits in 1972 to 1 per cent in 1980 (after 0.5 per cent in 1979) and to 1.4 per cent in 1984.

A low and stagnating profitability

Traditionally, French banks were considered to be far less profitable than their foreign competitors. Analysis of the data compiled by the OECD tends to corroborate this general opinion broadly, but not fully. Indeed, it appears that the return on assets i.e. after-tax profits as a ratio of the balance-sheet total for French banks was fairly meagre in the early 1980s, outranking only those of the Belgian and Japanese banks (table 6.12). However, when the return on assets is calculated as the ratio of after-tax profits to funds committed to non-financial entities, French banks rank somewhat higher.

Table 6.12   Return on assets: average ratios, 1980–1984

All commercial banks				Top commercial banks			
Post-tax profits/ FCNFE		Post-tax profits/ balance-sheet total		Post-tax profits/ FCNFE		Post-tax profits/ balance-sheet total	
Japan	0.26	Belgium	0.19	Italy	0.17	France	0.13
Belgium	0.34	Japan	0.22	France	0.23	Italy	0.15
Germany	0.34	France	0.23	Japan	0.24	Japan	0.20
Italy	0.37	Germany	0.24	Germany	0.36	Germany	0.25
France	0.41	Italy	0.32	Switzerland	0.62	Switzerland	0.43
Spain	0.58	Switzerland	0.48	USA	0.70	USA	0.57
Switzerland	0.60	Spain	0.50	UK	0.90	UK	0.65
USA	0.84	USA	0.71	Spain	0.94	Spain	0.80

FCNFE, funds committed to non-financial entities.
Source: OECD, 1987

Various factors account for the traditionally low profitability and the deterioration experienced over the period 1981–4. On the one hand, macro-economic developments were particularly adverse. Domestic dis-inflation imposed a squeeze on interest margins and impaired the ability of borrowers to service their debts. On the other hand, worldwide disinflation and recession contributed to the advent of the debt crisis in the less developed countries which, alongside a structural intensification of competition in international markets, contributed to an unprecedented slump in the profitability of international operations. The pre-tax profits of overseas branches shrank by about 47 per cent over the period 1982–4.

Clearly, such macro-economic developments do not completely account for the traditionally low level of bank profitability. In this respect, two major structural and interconnected factors contributed to what was an integral feature of French banking. Oligopolistic and imperfectly contestable market structures, on the one hand, and widespread public ownership and control of banks, on the other, contributed to the low level of bank profitability, despite the high level of interest margins imposed on customers.

6.2.2 Bank Profitability in a Changing Environment

In order to highlight the major recent developments in bank profitability, the various significant stages in bank profit formation are discussed. Developments in gross margin, operating costs, loan loss provisions and profitability over the period 1985−7 are reviewed in turn.

Improvement and restructuring of bank gross margins

Since 1984, gross margins have improved and have experienced a dramatic change in their internal structure. Net banking income increased by 8.6 per cent in 1985 and by 11 per cent in 1986. In real terms, net banking income increased by 2.6 per cent in 1985 and by 8.3 per cent in 1986, against only 1 per cent in 1984. This development is explained by a significant improvement in gross margins on domestic operations, since net banking income stemming from overseas branches further declined by 7.8 per cent in 1985 and by 6.8 per cent in 1986.

In 1987, however, the positive trend in gross margins was interrupted. Net banking income declined by 2.3 per cent in nominal terms, and by 5.4 per cent in real terms. This development is entirely accounted for by deterioration in gross margins on domestic operations, with domestic net banking income deteriorating by 2.7 per cent in 1987 while overseas branches net banking income increased by 1.8 per cent. This setback was unprecedented as it was the first decline in nominal net banking income since the beginning of the 1970s. The decline in net banking income in 1987 was due to the continuation of the adverse trend in net interest margin, which declined by 4.6 per cent, and also a quasi-stagnation in net non-interest income, which increased by only 0.9 per cent.

Because of the increased contestability of the various banking markets, traditional intermediary activities stagnated in terms of volume and declined in terms of profitability. Consequently, traditional cross-subsidies proved unsustainable. Indeed, it became increasingly difficult to finance production of underpriced and therefore unprofitable services by overcharging inter-mediation activities and levying high interest margins.

Reduction in the growth of operating costs

Since 1984 the growth in operating costs has been significantly reduced. In nominal terms, the growth rate in operating costs decreased from 11.2 per cent in 1984 to 7.1 per cent in 1985, 5.2 per cent in 1986 and 3.9 per cent in 1987. In real terms, growth declined from 3.2 per cent in 1984 to 2.6 per cent in 1987 (i.e. a decrease of 0.6 per cent in real terms). Here as well, domestic operations largely account for such positive developments. In order to achieve effective cost containment, banks attempted to limit the rate of growth of staff costs by restricting hiring, except for their then fast-growing and highly profitable investment banking departments. As a consequence, in 1987 the total number of employees declined by 1.1 per cent to 226,700, compared with declines of 0.7 per cent in 1986 and 0.1 per cent in 1985.

A further strengthening of loan loss reserves

During the period 1985−7, French banks continued to build up weighty loan loss reserves against foreign debt. Net provisions peaked in 1986 when French banks increased loan loss reserves by FFr 30.9 billion compared with FFr 25.2 billion in 1985. In 1987, this effort was slightly reduced, with provisions amounting to about FFr 28 billion essentially for sovereign risks. In view of this continuous and important provisioning effort, French banks managed to improve dramatically the provisioning level of their domestic and international risks. As a result, by the end of 1986, risky loans, estimated at FFr 306 billion for the 44 major banks, were globally provisioned to the extent of 40 per cent. Private risks were provisioned to the extent of 57 per cent by the end of 1986. The provisioning ratio for sovereign risks reached 31 per cent by the end of 1986, against 23 per cent by the end of 1985, while domestic risks were considered heavily provisioned. According to preliminary estimates, the provisioning ratio for sovereign risks reached 40 per cent by the end of 1987.

Improved profitability

French banks have made dramatic strides with regard to declared profits. They managed to post hefty gains in 1985 and 1986, with net profits increasing by 66.2 per cent in 1985 to FFr 8.4 billion (against FFr 4.9 billion in 1984), and by 36.5 per cent in 1986 to FFr 11.4 billion. Despite adverse developments in operating income and because of lighter loan loss provisions and exceptional earnings, banks managed to post further gains in 1987, with net profits estimated at about FFr 13.5 billion, i.e. an increase of 18 per cent compared with 1986. As a consequence, profitability increased significantly for commercial banks. In 1986, return on equity reached 10.9 per cent, against 10.3 per cent in 1985 and 7.4 per cent in 1984 for the so-called 'Banques AFB'. In 1987, return on equity was estimated to have reached about 10 per cent.

Despite such positive developments the usual bank profitability indicators and capital-to-assets ratios, with the possible exception of those for 1987, are still low by international standards. In a comparison of the five largest banks in the major industrial countries in 1986, French banks still performed rather poorly in terms of pre-tax profits per employee, capital-to-assets ratio and return on assets, ranking just ahead of Belgian and Japanese banks.

In 1987, the picture appeared quite different. The relative profitability of the largest French banks improved significantly. They ranked at a median level in terms of pre-tax profits per employee and pre-tax profit on assets and were very well positioned in terms of pre-tax return on equity, just behind the largest Spanish and Japanese banks.

6.3 The Consequences of Financial Liberalization for the Regulatory and Fiscal Framework and the Strategy of Banks

6.3.1 Preliminary Remarks on the Programme of Financial Liberalization

European financial liberalization is taking place gradually. The significant moves occurred well before the end of 1992, with the full liberalization of UCITS by October 1989 and the removal of capital controls by July 1990. Several questions are relevant when looking at the dynamics of European financial systems.

1 Is the programme credible? A long discussion is required to answer this crucial question. No doubt the gap between the rapid financial integration and the rather slow monetary solidarity among EC partners could not be maintained in the long run. Elsewhere (de Boissieu, 1988) we have differentiated three possible scenarios for the development of the European Monetary System (EMS) (particularly its exchange rate mechanism) depending on the way that this gap is reduced (through monetary cooperation or financial reregulation or any combination of cooperation and conflict). Europe is still exposed to a sequence of deregulation and reregulation waves, and it is likely that some countries with weak currencies will reactivate exchange controls if faced with external or domestic shocks.

2 Which concept of financial liberalization will prevail? There is still a debate concerning the relationships between the European internal market and the rest of the world. Compared with the period 1985−6, recent developments indicate that the European Commission, under pressure from several EC member states and as a result of the attitude of the US administration, is willing to make use of the reciprocity clause. In this game of strategy between Europe, Japan and the United States, the outcome is still uncertain. Nevertheless, it is clear that the debate *erga omnes vs reciprocity* conditions the market area and the form and intensity of competition, and consequently the optimal micro-economic strategy, since the main challenge to French financial institutions may come from Japanese and US competitors rather than from other Europeans.

3   Will financial liberalization constitute a shock for the French economy? Let us take the case of capital controls. The wholesale market has been completely deregulated. As far as exchange restrictions are concerned, it remains to deregulate the retail market by phasing out the last restrictive measures: the banning of residents from opening accounts abroad and accounts in France denominated in foreign currencies (except in ECU). For some experts, the French financial system has already been liberalized, since people can buy foreign securities abroad without any restriction. We depart from this view, since we believe that the complete removal of capital controls will create new space for international portfolio diversification and capital movements. The complete deregulation of the retail market may induce a 'qualitative jump'.

6.3.2   Adjustments in the Regulatory Framework and the Tax System

The level of adjustment and the risk of competitive deregulation

Deregulation is endogenous. As Kane (1987, pp. 111–12) wrote: 'Deregulation is not something like an ideological infection that develops inexplicably among swing voters. It is spread by programmed responses to changes in the political and economic landscapes that regulators (including politicians) face.' The same author attributes regulatory relaxations to increasing competition in what he refers to as the 'market for financial services regulations'.

Competition between regulators can take place at the domestic and the international level. Competitive deregulation in the EC, resulting from the desire of national authorities to attract funds and activities (offensive strategy) or to avoid an adverse shift in the location of savings (defensive strategy), means in many cases an adjustment on the 'short side' of the market for regulation (the minimum level for taxation, the maximum for deposit interest rates etc.) and the application of the clause of the 'least-regulated country'. This could be welfare improving, but in some circumstances may also be detrimental to stability. A satisfactory trade-off between efficiency and stability implies that in some cases (e.g. prudential control), the adjustment should not be on the 'short side'.

The deregulation of deposit rates and the new structure of bank revenues

In order to avoid the flight of sight and time deposits, France will have to phase out all regulation concerning deposit rates. Clearly, in this matter the 'short side' of the market for regulation is going to be reached. As far as demand deposits are concerned, table 6.13 suggests that three groups of countries coexist. First, we have a few countries with no explicit interest

Table 6.13 Interest payments on demand deposits, December 1988 (per cent)

France	0
Germany	0−2 (dominant values, 0.25 and 0.5)
Netherlands	0.55 (average value)
Belgium	0.50 (average value)
Spain	7.00 (average value)

payments on demand deposits (France, United States). Second some countries have had deregulated interest rates for a long time, but the bank cartel and also 'moral suasion' by the central bank explain the low level of deposit rates (Germany). Lastly, in some southern countries (e.g. Spain, Italy) real interest rates on demand deposits are positive, but this is combined with high interest rates on bank reserves with the central bank. Given the degree of bank concentration and the 'moral suasion' exercised by French monetary authorities and despite recent aggressive moves by some British banks, we expect France to join the second group, namely to show modest interest payments on demand deposits ('modest' means deposit rates which are significantly negative in real terms).

1 Complete deregulation of deposit rates will be one aspect of a package consisting of a radical change in bank revenues. French banks cannot continue to underprice numerous ancillary and payment services and to overcharge intermediation operations, since payment services will be difficult to attract from abroad (inertia effects may be powerful in this case), whilst it is quite certain that overpricing of intermediation operations in a world of perfect capital mobility exposes France to the risk of a flight of financial activities abroad.

2 The lessons to be drawn from the period 1987−8 and the unsuccessful tentative efforts by the French Bankers Association to fix market prices for payment services are interesting. To be socially and politically acceptable, the change must be profit-neutral for the main categories of agents. Globally speaking, the level of net banking income will not be changed *ceteris paribus*. Only the structure of net banking income will be modified, with a higher proportion coming from commissions and fees. Likewise, consumers' organizations will accept the move only if it is globally welfare-neutral.

3 Behind global neutrality, significant distribution effects will appear. The losers of the present combination of underpriced payment services and overpriced intermediation operations (e.g. the small and medium enterprises which have only indirect access to disintermediated financing) are going to be the winners of the structural change. A welfare perspective

would have to refer to compensation criteria and also study the macro-economic feedback consequences of these distribution effects.

4   The deregulation of deposit rates will be a catalyst for the development of a market for deposits and for the extension of liability management by banks. Despite the removal of credit ceilings and most foreign exchange restrictions, the French system of financial markets remains 'incomplete'. With a real market for deposits, other elements which have traditionally been neglected (deposit insurance, etc.) would have to be taken into account.

The outlook for 'two-speed' finance in France

Is the present place of tax-exempt passbook accounts (such as the A passbook accounts with the savings banks) and of subsidized credits consistent with the Single European Act and the internal market? From a legal viewpoint, the question seems controversial: European regulations are consistent with privileged financial procedures provided that this financing is earmarked for specific collective projects. In France, the financing of municipalities and cheap housing (*logement social*) has been based on the recycling of A passbook accounts. Could the system survive without a dramatic change?

The French Bankers Association recently asked for a generalization of A passbook accounts (namely to enable banks to collect tax-exempt deposits). The extension of 'two-speed' finance (the conjunction of two sectors, one exposed to and the other sheltered from market forces) would be a somewhat paradoxical consequence of the search for fair competition. Instead of a generalization of tax (and other) privileges, we expect a progressive shrinkage and the adjustment of the French system to less segmented financial structures. 'Two-speed' finance will not disappear, since it exists in some form or another in most EC countries. However, it will decrease to well under the present threshold. Accordingly the financing structure of the savings banks and of the Caisse des Dépôts et Consignations will have to be adjusted.

Adjustments in financial taxation

Delocalization of savings and financial activities will depend on comparisons of financial packages rather than on piecemeal comparisons. Individual investors, institutional investors, banks and insurance companies are going to compare the quality of financial services and the level of return for different financial centres. As usual, taxation is a crucial variable for the determination of comparative advantages. Official reports by the Boiteux Committee (Boiteux, 1988) and the Lebegue Committee (Lebegue, 1988) have shown that, in order to curb the risk of delocalization, financial taxation has to be adjusted downwards. The adjustment applies to taxes on both financial instruments and financial institutions.

Taxation of financial institutions

The French banking sector was and still is largely subject to specific taxes: on wages, on the outstanding amount of credit etc. This idiosyncratic situation is due to the fact that the extension of value-added tax (VAT) in 1968 did not apply to the banking sector. Up to now, as far as bank net income is concerned, only commissions and fees are subject to VAT. The removal of the remaining tax idiosyncrasies requires a general application of VAT to banks (or the implementation of a specific tax on French banks which would integrate the piecemeal measures prevailing at present).

Taxes on financial instruments

In France, there is a wide range of tax rates on income derived from financial instruments: zero on tax-exempt passbook accounts such as *livrets A* with the *caisses d'épargne* and *livrets bleu* with *crédit mutuel*; 26−7 per cent on bonds; 33 per cent on negotiable claims; 47 or 52 per cent on non-negotiable savings certificates issued by banks, the Treasury etc., depending on whether or not anonymity is preserved. Moreover, given the corporate income tax rate on distributed profits (42 per cent) and a 50 per cent face value for the tax credit, the actual tax credit on dividends (*avoir fiscal*) is equal to 69 per cent, compared with 100 per cent in Germany. Most of the distortions had to be corrected by July 1990. In addition to the complete removal of the special tax on stock market transactions (*impôt de bourse*), which is necessary to equalize Paris conditions with external (especially London) conditions, the French system has to adjust in three further directions.

1 Average and marginal tax rates have to be reduced. This applies to interest rates, dividends, capital gains etc. The Lebegue Committee has presented very precise recommendations for the taxation of UCITS, the gradual abolition of discrimination between income and capital gains, and the generalization of withholding taxes at rates chosen after coordination between the member states. Withholding taxes reduce, or even delete, the tax gap between residents and non-residents, provided that they are not supplemented by other income taxes. As far as the tax credit on dividends is concerned, we must expect a gradual drop in the corporate income tax to 33 per cent (rather than an increase in the face value of the tax credit) and the abolition of the discrimination recently introduced between the tax rates on distributed profits (42 per cent) and retained profits (39 per cent).
2 Control procedures have to be harmonized. This is crucial because it clearly affects delocalization of savings and because there are persistent gaps within the EC. For instance, the rather inquisitorial system in place

in France is far removed from the German procedure. The very concept of the great internal market implies adjustment to liberal solutions, but not always on the 'short side'. Withholding taxes will constitute the optimal cooperative solution in many cases, since they provide a satisfactory balance between control and liberalism.
3 Tax-exempt passbook accounts have to be gradually phased out (see above).

Constraints in adjusting financial taxation

The bulk of the adjustment took place in 1990, and was integrated in the 1990 budget. The special tax on bank credit was removed in January 1989, and other measures were implemented in 1989 (e.g. a more favourable tax rule regarding coupons on UCITS and the removal of the 5.15 per cent tax on life insurance contracts). The downward adjustment had to cope with two major constraints.

1 Government budgetary constraint: the calculations made by the Boiteux Committee and the Lebegue Committee indicated a loss of income for the budget of close to FFr 30 billion. When added to the drop in taxes due to a significant downward move of VAT, it represented an impressive figure (between FFr 110 billion and FFr 150 billion). Clearly, given the time schedule of deregulation, adjustment in financial taxation had to be given first priority. However, the budgetary constraint on the French government has been tight and became tighter still with the slow-down in real growth. Accordingly, the authorities will have to compensate for the reduction of financial taxation (through an extended income tax base? through other means?).
2 General political constraint: it would be difficult for any French government, but particularly for a socialist government, to alleviate the taxation of capital incomes while implementing rather stringent controls regarding the taxation of labour incomes and the growth of real wages.

Adjustment in quasi-taxes

Any banking regulation can formally be interpreted as a tax on the banking sector without prejudging who will be the final taxpayer (the banks? the depositors, because of lower deposit interest rates? the borrowers, because of higher lending rates?). The set of quasi-taxes is rather heterogeneous, since it includes reserve requirements, deposit insurance premiums, liquidity ratios, the tax regime for bank provisioning etc. However, all these elements of the regulatory framework may induce or speed up some delocalization of financial activities.

Reserve requirements

Table 6.14 suggests that France is in an intermediate situation as far as reserve requirements are concerned. Clearly, some elements of table 6.14 must be related to the interest payments on demand deposits (see table 6.13);

Table 6.14 Reserve requirements, December 1988 (per cent)

		Ratio		Interest payments
		Residents	Non-residents	
France	Demand deposits	5	0	No
	Time deposits, savings accounts and related financial instruments	2.5	0	No
Germany	Demand deposits	6.6−12.1 (according to the size of the deposit)	12.1	No
	Time deposits	4.95	4.95	No
	Savings accounts	4.15	4.15	No
USA	Demand deposits and other checkable deposits	3−12 (according to size)	0 (in principle)	No
	Time deposits	0−3 (according to maturity)	0 (in principle)	No
Spain		16.5	0	An interest rate (7.5%) is paid on a fraction of reserves (11.5% out of the global ratio of 16.5%)
Italy	25% of the variation in the outstanding amount of demand deposits, time deposits and related financial instruments			5.5%
Japan	Time deposits and CDs	0.125−1.75 (according to size)		No
	Other deposits	0.25−2.5 (according to size)		No
UK	No reserve requirements			
	'A cash ratio deposits scheme', the ratio is equal to 0.45% of eligible liabilities (0.25% in some particular cases)			No

for instance, the high deposit rates on demand deposits are, for the banks, partially offset by the high interest rate on compulsory reserves. In most EC countries, as in the USA and Japan, reserve requirements are no longer an active tool of monetary policy. They are low and are seldom changed.

In a world of rapid financial innovation and tough competition between direct financing (disintermediation) and banking financing, monetary authorities could not resort to significant manipulations of the reserve requirement ratio. In this matter, France could remain in an intermediate position provided that it follows possible adjustments in the main EC countries.

Liquidity ratio

In many EC countries there is nothing equivalent to the liquidity ratio implemented in France and altered in February 1988. The purpose of the 1988 reform was to extend the application of the liquidity ratio to all credit institutions (including the *maisons de titres* defined by Article 99 of the 1984 Banking Act), to branches settled abroad and to all currencies (monitoring is no longer limited to operations in francs, but also concerns operations in foreign currencies). Through the moral suasion of the Bank for International Settlements (BIS) and the intervention of the European Commission, it is likely that many European countries (including Germany) will have to implement a liquidity ratio close to that prevailing in France.

Deposit insurance

With enlarged competition and the gradual development of a market for demand and time deposits, the present deposit insurance scheme will have to be changed from an unfunded and purely contractual regime to something similar to the funded regimes in place in most Anglo-Saxon countries.

Provisioning

The regulations concerning provisions on sovereign debt and the associated ta deductions are relatively liberal in France compared with other OECD countries. The attitude of the authorities has favoured the high provisioning ratio of French banks. In this field, there is no adjustment to implement in the light of new competitive pressures.

The deregulation of UCITS

Despite the 50 per cent market share of French UCITS in total European UCITS, monetary authorities will have to alleviate present rules concerning open-ended unit trusts and mutual funds. For instance, constraints on portfolio management by UCITS, such as the floors and the ceilings concerning the holding of bonds (*l'obligation de l'obligation*), will have to be removed. It is likely that money market funds (i.e. funds totally invested in money market instruments) will be authorized before long.

6.3.3 The Implications of the Financial Liberalization Programme for the Strategy of French Banks

Preliminary remarks on the development of the market for financial instruments and services

The paradigm of perfectly contestable markets seems to be a relevant benchmark when looking at the dynamics of the market for financial services: the new entrants in this market have no handicap in terms of costs, and they can avoid the large overheads faced by large depository institutions; it is likely that exit out of the market has a low, even negligible, cost since a major proportion of the costs are reversible (sunk costs are low).

In a situation where the ratio of private savings is diminishing in France as in other developed countries – the drop in the savings ratio of households from 17.6 per cent in 1980 to 12 per cent in 1988 has been only partly offset by the restoration of the savings ratio of firms – new competitors will erode bank profitability. Will generalized competition mean the end of the packaging era? With more educated and informed clients, there will be some tendency towards depackaging, since the rule of comparative advantage will concern every element in the package. To apply this general observation to the French situation, some financial institutions will be able to cope with more intense competition despite their limited range of financial services because of regulatory restrictions (e.g. the Post Office financial services which are not allowed to grant credits given their administrative status) if they develop some of their comparative advantages (e.g. 'proximity services' may represent an interesting 'niche' for the financial services of the Post Office). Depackaging means the return to specialization, natural 'habitats' and 'niches'. In the new environment, packaging could survive only if financial packages are competitive in many segments of the range of financial services and not in just a few.

Effect of extended competition on size in the French banking sector

In order to study the possible impact of extended competition on banking concentration, we must try to answer at least two questions:

1   Are there potential scale economies in the French banking sector?
2   If the answer to the preceding question is positive, what is the role of the scale economies argument for banking concentration and cooperation?

Scale economies

Several sources of scale economies, which are now well known, can be identified for financial firms (e.g. Lewis and Davis, 1987, p. 201). Most of the empirical difficulties derive from the multiproduct nature of bank activities. To be sure, there is no justification for a global approach to returns to scale. A functional split between bank activities is required. For instance, we know that some activities in banks are undoubtedly subject to scale economies: direct marketing, the use of computers, direct interventions on capital markets etc. Since empirical estimates are generally presented in terms of products, we would need some rule of thumb for the correspondence between *functions* and *products*.

Until now, the functioning of the French banking sector has rarely been described using the tools of industrial economics. This may be due to several reasons, some of which clearly result from the idiosyncrasies of the French banking sector (state intervention reinforced by the implementation of the nationalization programme which was only slightly reduced by the partial privatization process in 1986−8 etc.). As far as the relationship between size and profitability is concerned, Steinherr and Gilibert (1989) have shown that it is not significant in most EC countries. The Spearman correlation index calculated for the 15 largest French banks for the year 1987 is not significantly different from zero (0.034).

Two studies present interesting and complementary conclusions for the years 1974 and 1986.

1 Levy-Garboua and Renard (1977) have carried out a cross-sectional analysis of 94 banks for 1974. Combining the production approach and the intermediation approach (to use the terminology due to Humphrey (1984) which was introduced later), they have shown the existence of increasing returns to scale as far as the production approach is concerned. From the best estimates (a log-linear operating costs function, with funds committed to non-financial entities (FCNFEs) taken as the scale variable), it appears that, for 1974, the elasticity of operating costs with respect to FCNFEs was significantly less than unity (around 0.5).

2 In a recent study, Dietsch (1988) presented a cross-sectional analysis of 243 banks for the year 1986. Emphasizing the intermediation approach more than the production approach, Dietsch takes into consideration the overall bank costs (operating costs plus financial costs). The use of the well-known translog cost function, which is well adapted to multiproduct activities and to the estimation of U-shaped average cost curves, leads to separate estimates of global (or ray) and partial economies of scale. As far as ray economies of scale are concerned, it appears that the elasticity of total bank costs with respect to total output

is close to unity (0.97). At the global level, i.e. without splitting bank activities, the 'reservoir' of scale economies seems to be rather limited. In contrast, for some bank products, there are significant potential economies of scale (the partial elasticities of costs with respect to credits and deposits are equal to 0.56 and 0.23 respectively).

The impact of potential scale economies on banking concentration

As usual, it is rather artificial to isolate size effects. As Lewis and Davis (1987, p. 199) put it: '. . . size differences between financial firms rarely (if ever) involve purely a scaling factor'.

Looking at the French experience during 1987−8, we feel that the search for scale economies was of secondary importance in the move towards larger units and financial conglomerates. In many cases, the external growth of French banking firms came from the willingness to increase diversification and to reach critical levels for market shares.

Concentration could be, in certain circumstances, an answer to extended competition. Cooperation could be another answer, and the recent agreements between insurance companies and banks (more specifically, between Union des Assurances de Paris and BNP and between Groupe des Assurances Nationales and Crédit Industriel et Commercial) indicate its success. Cooperation could be the right way to take advantage of economies of scope without being exposed to the risk of diseconomies of scale. Could it be a permanent solution to the challenge of 1992, or will it be mainly conceived as a transition leading to mergers, acquisitions and larger units? It appears clearly that cooperation could be, in many cases, the optimal steady-state adjustment to the new environment.

It is very likely that, during the first stages of the implementation of the liberalization programme, banking will undergo the same evolution as the industrial sector did in the 1960s: after a first period where actual and expected competition induces overconcentration (the 'big is beautiful' era), there is a spontaneous tendency to reduce the diseconomies of scale and to return to smaller units. The scenario of overshooting in size effects, followed by a gradual return to the optimal size, seems plausible.

The impact of financial liberalization on diversification

The perspective of the great internal market is accelerating the diversification process which has taken place during recent years. With the removal of regulations and the gradual dismantlement of privileged financing circuits, the French banking sector is much less specialized than in the 1960s, and a trend towards universal banking is prevailing here as elsewhere.

On empirical grounds, the study by Dietsch (1988) indicates the existence of economies of scope for some bank products. With four categories of operations ((a) deposits, (b) credits, (c) market operations (except operations on securities) and (d) operations on securities), it appears that, for the year 1986 and the 243 banks in the sample, there existed significant economies of scope for several pairs of products, with the exception of the pairs (a, b), (a, c) and (b, c). Therefore the marginal cost of production for some products may be reduced by the extension of some other activities.

Beyond the econometric approach, many bankers feel that there are large potential economies of scope in distribution activities: once a nationwide (or international) network has been created, enlarging the range of financial instruments and services generates only marginal costs at a low level. This aspect must be considered because competition, after having mainly concerned production (financial innovations), will also and perhaps predominantly concern the sector of distribution.

The scenario of greater diversification provokes at least two comments.

1 We expect some overshooting in the diversification process, similar to the overshooting phenomenon already mentioned for the size effect. In order to cope with the new competitive conditions, French banks are going to propose to their customers a menu of financial products and services beyond the optimal diversification level (the optimal variety of menu). In the medium and long term, a spontaneous tendency to return to habitats and niches will prevail.

2 From the viewpoint of monetary authorities, it is crucial to adapt the content and tools of monitoring and control to the new situation resulting from cross-diversification. As banks engage more and more in insurance operations, with insurance companies developing bank operations and with non-financial entities such as La Redoute, Carrefour etc. entering the market for financial services, it would be relevant to substitute a functional control (i.e. the control of *activities*) for the institutional control (i.e. the control of *institutions*). The difficulty that we find in France, as elsewhere, is due to the fact that, in order to respect the unity of the decision-making process (for instance, the unity within a bank holding company), it is necessary to maintain the institutional approach while combining it with some functional dimensions.

Capital adequacy in the perspective of 1992

By international standards, French banks are less undercapitalized than is usually expected, particularly when interbank operations are not considered (Szymczak, 1987a). However, a sufficient level of capital equity will be crucial for French banks, as for other banks, to abide by the Cooke ratio, to finance mergers and acquisitions in a context where financial institutions will try to offset the erosion of profit margins by significant increases in their market share and to resist unfriendly take-overs. In the French environment, two aspects must be emphasized: the general issues raised by the adjustment to the Cooke ratio and the corresponding EC capital ratio, and the specific problems arising from the capitalization of state-owned banks.

Adjustment to the Cooke ratio

At the global level, the French banking sector had not much to adjust in order to comply with the Cooke ratio (7.25 per cent at the end of 1990 and 8 per cent at the end of 1992). A sample of large French banks in June 1987 revealed a risk-based capital ratio (calculated using the weights of the Cooke ratio) of 7.5 per cent. However, the standard deviation around this average figure seems significant. The European Commission prepared a directive which adapted the Cooke proposal to the EC area. Some French banks found it more difficult to comply with the 4 per cent subratio (which concerns genuine equity, i.e. capital and reserves) than to respect the global 8 per cent ratio. By international standards, the rate of provisioning is high in the French banking sector, and resorting to quasi-equity such as participating debt (*titres participatifs*, etc.) has been extensive not only on the part of state-owned banks but also by private banks. As provisions and quasi-equity count for the global ratio but not for the 4 per cent subratio, many banks were more embarrassed to comply with the latter.

The frontier between core capital and quasi-equity is still controversial. *Certificats d'investissement* belong to tier I of the Cooke ratio (equity), whilst *titres participatifs* (only issued by state-owned or cooperative firms) are classified in tier II (quasi-equity) on the basis of the fact that there is a strictly positive floor to the return on the latter instruments. Accordingly, French banks will continue to issue *certificats d'investissement* within the limits introduced by regulation. A case concerning the status of the capital notes issued by Crédit Lyonnais in November 1988 is still pending. Since these notes are a type of perpetual subordinated debt, it is likely that the BIS commission will classify them in tier II. Consequently, at the end of 1988, the BNP gave up its plan to issue such financial instruments.

Not only do the Cooke ratio and its EC equivalent put a ceiling on the operations of banks in relation to their capital – they constitute the new version of credit ceilings which is adapted to financial deregulation, the implementation of indirect monetary policy (i.e. interest rate policy) and the growth of off-balance sheet operations – but the risk-based capital ratio also fixes a limit to leverage. This aspect is particularly important in France, where the leverage effect has been extensively used by banks to restore or at least maintain their profitability. With a ceiling on leverage, it becomes crucial to improve the productivity record and to boost unit profit margins by cutting some operating expenses.

Capitalization of state-owned banks

Like private banks, large state-owned depository institutions need to raise capital not only to increase their capital ratio but also to fund domestic and foreign acquisitions. For that purpose, they may resort to one of the following means (or any combination of them).

1   The sequential accumulation of profits: for the reasons already indicated which concern the dynamics of the market for financial services, there is not much leeway in this direction.

2   New money brought in by the shareholder (the state): given that the government budgetary constraint will remain tight during the next few years − in a world of perfect capital mobility, the credibility of French economic policy will be more dependent on the medium-run stance of monetary and fiscal policy − the degrees of freedom are rather limited. Since the early 1980s, the French Treasury has reduced the *dotations en capital* granted to state-owned firms (both industrial and banking firms). The financial disengagement of the state will speed up in the future, and resorting to quasi-equity (such as *titres participatifs*) cannot be seen as a lasting substitute for equity.

3   Financial assets given by the state to nationalized banks: instead of new money, the state would transfer a portion of shares in nationalized industrial firms in order to raise the capital of nationalized banks.

4   Gradual and partial privatization of state-owned banks: as the Cooke ratio is calculated on a consolidated basis, the privatization of some subsidiaries of state-owned banks could be equivalent from the financial viewpoint but politically easier to implement.

Despite the formal commitment by President Mitterrand during the 1988 presidential campaign not to shift the frontier between the state-owned sector and the private sector, the last option is the most satisfactory in the medium run. Whatever the political environment, the implementation of financial liberalization will accelerate the transition from a 'hard' to a 'soft' concept of nationalization. Banks such as the BNP or Crédit Lyonnais will acquire sufficient capital by attracting private shareholders (the state holding the majority and the control), provided that the buyers − either individual or institutional (open-ended unit trusts, mutual funds, private insurance companies etc.) − exist.

6.4   Concluding Remarks

The main ingredients for a cost−benefit analysis of the French banking sector in the single European market have been presented in this chapter.

The relative strength of French banks comes from various sources: the rapid change in the macro-economic and financial environment; a lead (compared with other EC countries) in the implementation of new financial technologies; the relatively large internationalization of French banks. However, several factors could be seen as handicaps under the new competitive conditions. Two of them must be emphasized: the persistent and not always consistent intervention of the state in the French banking sector, and a relatively high cost of intermediation. In a cost−benefit analysis, the extended branch banking in France is ambiguous. On the one hand, it could be a powerful barrier to entry and an asset for 'proximity services' and personal relationships with customers. On the other hand, it could jeopardize efficiency and productivity records in circumstances where they will be more crucial.

References

Banking Commission (Commission Bancaire) (1988) *Rapport Annuel pour 1987.*

de Boissieu, C. (1988) Financial liberalization and the evolution of the EMS. *European Economy*, 136, 53−70.

Boiteux, M. (1988) *Fiscalité et Marché Unique Européen*. Paris: Documentation Française.

Conseil National du Crédit (1987) *L'Indice des Technologies Nouvelles sur l'Activité des Intermediaires Financiers.*

Dietsch, M. (1988) Economies d'échelle, économies d'envergure et structure des coûts dans les banques de dépôts françaises, unpublished paper.

Faulhaber, G. (1975) Cross-subsidization: pricing in public enterprises. *American Economic Review*, 65, 966−77.

Hicks, J. (1974) *The Crisis in Keynesian Economics*. Oxford: Basil Blackwell.

Humphrey, D. (1984) The US payments system: costs, pricing, competition and risk. Monograph Series in Finance and Economics, Salomon Brothers Center for the Study of Financial Institutions, New York University.

Kane, E. (1981) Accelerating inflation, technological innovation, and the decreasing effectiveness of banking regulation. *Journal of Finance*, 36, 355−67.

Kane, E. (1987) Competitive financial reregulation: an international perspective. In R. Portes and A. Swoboda (eds), *Threats to International Stability*. Cambridge: Cambridge University Press.

Lebegue, D. (1988) *La Fiscalité de l'Epargne dans le Cadre du Marché Intérieur Européen*. Paris: Conseil National du Crédit.

Levy-Garboua, V. and Renard, F. (1977) Une étude statistique de la rentabilité des banques en France en 1974. *Cahiers Economiques et Monétaires*, Vol. 5. Paris: Bank of France.

Lewis, M. and Davis, K. (1987) *Domestic and International Banking*. Oxford: Philip Allan.

Montfront, R. (1988) L'évolution du système financier français à travers le TERF. Bank of France, unpublished paper.

OECD (1985) *Costs and Margins in Banking, Statistical Supplement (1978–1982)*. Paris: OECD.

OECD (1987) *Bank Profitability*. Paris: OECD.

Revell, J. (1980) *Costs and Margins in Banking: an International Survey*. Paris: OECD.

Silber, W. (1975) Towards a theory of financial innovation. In W. Silber (ed.), *Financial Innovation*. Lexington, CT: D.C. Heath.

Silber, W. (1983) The process of financial innovation. *American Economic Review*, 73, 89–95.

Steinherr, A. and Gilibert, P. (1989) The impact of freeing trade in financial services and capital movements on the European banking industry. Research Report, no. 1, January, Center for European Policy Studies Financial Markets Unit.

Szymczak, P. (1986) La réforme de la tarification bancaire. Direction de la Prévision, Ministry of Finance, Paris, December.

Szymczak, P. (1987a) Eléments de comparaison internationale des coûts et marges bancaires. *Revue d'Economie Financière*, 1, 51–74.

Szymczak, P. (1987b) Taux d'intérêt et système bancaire. *Economie et Prévision*, 77, 3–39.

Szymczak, P. (1990) Bank profitability in France. In C. de Boissieu (ed.), *Banking in France*. London: Routledge.

Comment

Patrick Artus

Christian de Boissieu has presented a complete and detailed analysis of the issues that French banks are facing, and has provided us with original and interesting data concerning profitability, financial innovation, the structure of financing and of the banking sector in France, regulatory issues etc. As he gave a very comprehensive discussion of all the important questions, this discussion is limited to seven points which seem to be of particular importance.

The complexity of the French banking sector

The complexity of the French banking sector stems first from the coexistence of nationalized and private banks (Société Générale, Crédit Commercial de France, Paribas, Suez), as well as of large public financial institutions (Caisse des Dépôts et Consignations, Crédit National, Crédit Foncier etc.), secondly from the fact that most subsidized credits and tax-exempt savings accounts can be distributed only by some intermediary, namely the Crédit Agricole, the *caisses d'épargne* and the postal financial services, and finally the huge differences in tax rates on income derived from the different financial assets (from zero to 52 per cent).

The dispersion of the ownership of the capital of private banks

The ownership of the capital of the banks that were privatized in 1986 and 1987 is not very concentrated. For instance, in the case of Paribas, Suez or Société Générale, the investors who are members of the *noyaux durs* (stable shareholders) and the employees of the banks own about 15 per cent of the capital, whereas the public holds between 40 and 70 per cent. This means that French private banks could not resist unfriendly take-overs. A quick calculation shows that, at current market values, the cost of taking a majority stake in the capital of the four privatized banks would amount to $8 billion, which is less than half the annual total of mergers and acquisitions in the banking sector in the United States. The solution to this problem may be an increased share for institutional investors in the ownership of the capital of those banks.

The degree of inertia in the behaviour of French investors

The last capital control (namely, that French residents cannot open an account abroad or lend in francs to non-residents) was removed by July 1990. What, then, will be the degree of portfolio diversification of French residents? All existing studies show a large degree of inertia in the behaviour of French investors: differences in taxation or in yields which do not compensate for differences between financial assets do not lead to large changes in portfolio composition. Non-interest-bearing demand deposits still represent a large share of money holdings; people do not easily change banks and concentrate all their assets (deposits, securities, initial funds etc.) in the same one. It is clear that at present only the customers of a given bank invest in its equity or in its initial funds. Econometric tests like those performed by Feldstein and Horioka show that the international mobility of capital is still very low in the French case. The impression would therefore be that financial integration and liberalization in Europe will not lead to large shifts in the currency composition of the financial wealth of French residents; however, behaviour can change quickly, and there is still a major uncertainty concerning this point.

The structure of bank balance sheets

As de Boissieu has stressed, a major feature of the structure of bank balance sheets is the fact that the apparent interest rate on bank assets is indexed much more on market interest rates than on the apparent interest rate on bank liabilities. This is of course due to the importance of non-interest-bearing demand deposits, or of saving accounts with regulated (non-indexed) interest rates. This means that the French banking sector benefits substantially from interest rate increases, but that its exposure to interest rate risk is very large. The second interesting point is that French banks have limited holdings of securities (Treasury Bills or bonds), which makes the implementation of open-market procedures very difficult for the monetary authorities.

The cost of harmonization and liberalization for the budget

Many observers agree that tax harmonization is a necessity. If it is assumed that the various tax rates on financial income are replaced by a uniform withholding tax at a rate of 15 per cent, and that various special taxes (on insurance contracts, bank credit etc.) are suppressed, the loss of income for the budget amounts to about FFr 25 billion. However, we must also consider the effects of the suppression of the remaining credits made at interest rates lower than market rates. In particular the financing of local administrations and of the agencies that build low-rent houses by the Caisse des Depôts et Consignations is based on very long term credit (more than 30 years) at a very low interest rate (5.8 per cent at present indexed on the rate paid on A savings accounts which is currently 4.5 per cent). If this financing had to be done under market conditions, the cost for the borrowers (who are public or quasi-public borrowers) would amount to about FFr 35 billion per year. The total loss of income for the budget would therefore be as high as FFr 60 billion per year, i.e. 1.2 per cent of GDP, which would be very difficult to bear.

Welfare and distribution effects

de Boissieu has suggested that France will have to suppress all regulations concerning deposit rates, while banks will have to price bank services at normal levels in order to stabilize their total profits. The fact that this would certainly be welfare improving for people on high incomes, who would benefit from an increased yield on their liquid assets, and would penalize people on low incomes, with few savings and who use payment services intensively, should not be ignored. The same problem will occur for the reduction in the taxation of financial income, which will lead to an average level of taxation well below that on wage income.

Uncertainty concerning the potential economies of scale

The existing econometric results (which are very scanty) show that the returns to scale are very close to unity. This implies that no large movement of concentration is to be expected in the French banking sector. However, the measure of production seems rather unsatisfactory in these studies and the actual degree of returns to scale by type of activity is quite uncertain.

7

Banking and Financial Reregulation: The Italian Case

Franco Bruni

The process of change of the Italian monetary and financial system towards 1992 and a higher degree of international integration started at the beginning of the 1980s and developed along the following four main lines: European Monetary System (EMS) discipline; liberalization of capital movements and removal of exchange controls; internal financial deregulation (and reregulation); changes in the structure and organization of the financial industry. The fourth line also included developments at the strictly micro-level of the individual firm, which can be quite independent of what is considered in the third line. It is important to recognize that, in addition to exchange rate discipline and external liberalization, internal deregulation and structural changes were also mainly caused by the international political and market pressure that came from the 1992 perspective.

If we look at the relative importance of the four lines of change, it turns out that the last one, structural changes in the financial industry, has been the least important up to now. Organizational changes were slow and are probably behind schedule. To some extent this is normal and physiological, as the first three lines of change were a prerequisite and a stimulus for the micro-transformation of the financial industry leading up to 1992. However, the latter can also be suspected of being too late and irresolute. Three reasons can be cited for this delay: the managerial and technical inefficiency of the banking sector, which has found it hard to move out of the climate of protection; the fact that several crucial pieces of reregulation were absent and the debate about them was confused and incomplete (e.g. procedures for lay-offs in banking, privatization of public banks, anti-trust legislation, acquisition of banks by non-banks, stock exchange regulations, closed-end investment funds and tax treatment of new instruments); a credibility problem as a result of which many of the steps made (along the first three lines of change) away from high inflation and from financial protection and repression were sometimes considered potentially reversible in view of the persistence and the worsening of the main disease suffered by the Italian economy, i.e. the level of debt and the public sector deficit.

The disequilibrium of Italy's public finance is so large that it can offer a unified interpretation of many of the country's economic problems and, in particular, of those that have arisen during its international integration. In the Italian case it is particularly appropriate to consider administrative controls on financial markets and operators as forms of implicit taxation. From this point of view liberalization tends to increase the deficit, and thus the latter appears as the main obstacle to the achievement of the former. It is interesting, in this respect, to contrast Italy with France where, during the 1970s, financial *dirigisme* and protectionism were even stronger but much less related to the needs of public finance, so that no serious public debt problem can be cited in discussing the rapid and strong liberalization efforts made during the 1980s.

The introductory remarks in the present section justify the plan of the rest of this chapter. The main regulatory steps towards 1992 are summarized in section 7.1 in which we concentrate on both external and internal financial liberalization. In section 7.2 we comment on some structural aspects of the Italian financial industry, and then turn to the issue of implicit taxes connected with financial controls. While the approach of the previous sections is that of a broad overview of the issues, in section 7.3 we look at a single specific type of control: compulsory reserve requirements. Its cost for the banking system and its relevance for the collection of seigniorage are illustrated and the problem posed by the forced disappearance of that source of implicit taxation as a consequence of European financial integration is discussed. Some concluding comments are presented in section 7.4.

7.1   Financial Liberalization and Reregulation

A major process of 'internal' and 'external' financial deregulation, reregulation and innovation can be considered to have started in Italy in 1983, when there was also a change in monetary policy, which became tighter with higher real interest rates and stronger exchange rate discipline.

Some important changes in financial rules had been made earlier. For example, the portfolio constraint, whereby banks were obliged to buy certain categories of bonds issued by public special credit institutions, which did not completely disappear until 1987, had already been weakened in 1979, and again in 1982. Moreover, in 1981 the so-called 'divorce' (between the central bank and the Treasury) was crucial in changing to more indirect forms of monetary control: the obligation which imposed on the central bank the role of residual purchaser of Treasury Bills was abolished. During the second half of the 1970s several moves were made towards the modernization of the money market, which was also necessary for developing an effective method of open-market operation: among other things, reserve requirements were reformed and new types of instruments were promoted as banks' certificates of deposits.

After 1983, internal reform and the abolition of financial protectionism became more serious parallel processes. The complementarity of internal and external financial liberalizations is important: to be successful, they must maintain approximately the same speed (Bruni and Monti, 1986, pp. 89–101).

On the internal front, the main step was the abolition of the ceiling on bank loans in June 1983. On the external front, the crucial measure was the phasing out of the requirement of a non-interest-bearing deposit against the holding of foreign assets; it had been as high as 50 per cent since 1973, and was decreased to 40 per cent in 1984, 25 per cent in October 1985 and 15 per cent in August 1986, and was abolished in May 1987. In 1983, the government had proposed a bill for a general reform of foreign exchange regulations based on the principle that everything is allowed which is not explicitly forbidden. The reform was approved in 1976–7 and came into force during 1988. In 1985 the First European Economic Community (EEC) Directive on Banking (issued in 1977!) was approved by parliament; as a consequence, freedom of entry into the banking industry substantially increased.

Regulatory steps on the 'internal' and 'external' fronts turned out to be parallel even when they both slowed down or reversed their direction. This happened at the beginning of 1986, when controls were temporarily reinforced: the ceiling on bank loans was re-established for the first semester and, at the same time, the compulsory foreign currency financing of exports was increased. A similar reversal of the liberalization process took place at the end of 1977.

However, the basic trends towards deregulation re-emerged with new important measures. Full convertibility of lira banknotes was restored, leads and lags in the payment of imports and exports were liberalized, the permitted holding period of foreign currency proceeds from exports was lengthened, and banks were allowed to maintain unbalanced cross-currency positions to increase the extent of their forward positions in foreign currency and to purchase foreign currency options abroad against lire. Several innovations started to produce substantial changes in the internal structure of the financial system. In 1983 the establishment of open-ended mutual investment funds had been allowed and regulated by law. These new intermediaries developed very rapidly, competing with banks in the collection of savings. The issuance of banks' certificates of deposit was liberalized (starting in 1976) and a secondary market was organized. Money market mutual funds, directly linked to bank checking accounts, were introduced in 1988. The merchant banking activities of commercial banks were officially allowed and regulated in 1977. Minimum capital requirements have been prescribed for banks, and an interbank fund for the mutual insurance of deposits was established in September 1987. Many types of new instruments have been introduced in the market for Treasury securities, a withholding tax on interest from new issues has been imposed, substantial reforms of the issuing procedures (as the marginal auction system) have been adopted, and a secondary market has been organized (since May 1988) with committed primary dealers and real-time video connections.

New changes planned for the lead up to 1992 included a reform of reserve requirements (see section 7.3), a complete reorganization of the interbank deposit market, the introduction of closed-end mutual funds, interest rate options and financial futures, and the reform of the stock exchange with the creation of a new type of intermediary to operate on it (ending the monopoly of stockbrokers).

The general reform of foreign exchange regulations, prepared during the previous five years, came into force on 1 October 1988. The general principle was thus established by which every financial operation abroad is allowed which is not explicity controlled, and controls can be introduced only temporarily to cope with balance-of-payments difficulties and to avoid exchange rate crises. However, two important exceptions to this principle remained, which had to be removed before 1992: the 'foreign exchange monopoly' which in practice permanently forced the channelling of foreign exchange operations through the banking system, and the supply of financial products and services by non-residents which required specific authorization. Among the individual items of the wide-ranging liberalization that occurred after 1 October 1988, the following can be cited: the forward exchange market can now be used independently of 'real' imports and exports to cover risks from financial operations; foreign exchange loans can be provided by banks with no constraint on their destination; investment by residents in listed and non-listed foreign securities with residual maturity longer than 180 days is completely liberalized; exports of Italian and foreign banknotes by residents is almost completely liberalized and cheques in lire on Italian banks can be drawn abroad.

It is therefore evident that on both the 'internal' and the 'external' fronts, a lot of progress towards liberalization and modernization has been made in a relatively short time. The macro-economic consequences have been relevant. The country's financial openness and the role of capital movements in external equilibrium have been increasing very fast. Figure 7.1 shows the impressive growth since 1983–4 of an index that we have called the degree of 'financial intensity' of Italy's international payments. Moreover, consider the relationship between the domestic and international levels of interest rates. Before 1983, both the nominal covered differential and the real *ex post* interest differential were largely negative, about −3.5 per cent on the

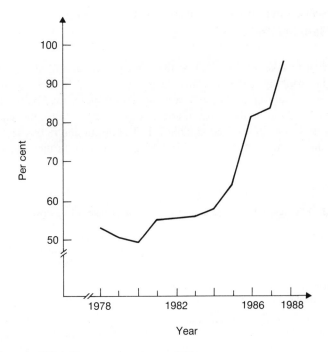

Figure 7.1 Financial intensity of Italy's international payments: the ratio of gross inflows and outflows of non-bank capital to imports and exports of goods.

average for the period 1977−82. At the beginning of 1989, the covered differential, which captures the effect of exchange controls, was not significantly different from zero, while the real differential was large and positive (more than 3 per cent with Germany) because the freedom of capital movement requires a risk premium on Italian rates. This impressive change has produced a large increase in the cost of the public debt and in the Treasury deficit, as the tax that was previously implicit in the controls has disappeared. However, while the short-term impact of liberalization worsens the conditions of public finance, it also puts a lot of pressure on adjustment of the deficit net of interest expenses, which should be considered as an endogenous variable, which also depends on the degree of monetary discipline (Bruni, 1988). The situation is now very uncertain and rather risky: there are contradictory symptoms of the working of this 'discipline effect', and it is possible that the public debt problem will halt or reverse the process of financial liberalization.

7.2   Some Structural Problems in the Italian Banking Industry

If we want to take a broad look at the comparative structural conditions of the Italian banking and financial industry in view of the unification of the European capital market in 1992, a good starting point may be the findings of the EEC Report on the 'Cost of non-Europe' (EEC, 1988); the data which refer to Italy are summarized in table 7.1. The discussion in this section will follow the framework of that table, while providing further evidence on various points of the analysis.

Table 7.1   EEC research on 'The cost of non-Europe in financial services': some findings for Italy

	Italy	European average	Italy's rank
Employment in banking and insurance, 1985 (% total employees)	2.50	3.50	8th out of 8
Rate of growth in employment in banking and insurance, 1978−85	25.50	14.70	2nd out of 8
Value added in credit and insurance (branch), 1985 (% GDP)	5.60	6.70	5th out of 8
Insurance premiums, 1984 (% GDP)	2.20	4.60[a]	8th out of 8
Bank loans outstanding, 1984 (% GDP)	96.00	130.00[a,b]	7th out of 8
Stock market capitalization, 1986 (% GDP)	75.00	103.00[a,b]	7th out of 8
Profit before tax on banks, 1982 (% GDP)	1.03	0.66[a]	2nd out of 8
(% loans outstanding)	1.80	0.69[a]	1st out of 8
Value added in banking, average 1978−84 (% loans outstanding)	6.30	3.50[a]	1st out of 8
Household consumption, 1980 (% total uses of output of the credit and insurance sector)	4.10	16.40[a,c]	6th out of 6
Claims on general government, end 1985 (% total financial assets of banking institutions)	20.80	11.70[d]	1st out of 7
Claims on the rest of the world, end 1985 (% total financial assets of banking institutions)	8.40	27.60[d]	6th out of 7
Claims of the rest of the world, end 1985 (% total liabilities of banking institutions)	13.80	28.20[d]	5th out of 7

Table 7.1 *continued*.

	Italy	European average	Italy's rank
Total imports, 1980 (% total resources of the credit and insurance sector)	6.60	2.80[c]	1st out of 6
Total exports, 1980 (% total uses of resources of the credit and insurance sector)	6.10	4.20[c]	3rd out of 6
Potential price fall of a basket of financial products resulting from the completion of the European market (%)	14.00	11.00[a]	2nd out of 8
Potential price fall of a basket of banking services resulting from the completion of the European market (%)	9.00	10.00[a]	4th out of 8
Estimated gains in consumer surplus resulting from integration of the European credit and insurance market (million ECUs)	4.00	22.00	3rd out of 8
Estimated gains in consumer surplus resulting from the integration of European banking market (million ECUs)	3.50	15.00	3rd out of 8

[a] Unweighted.
[b] Excluding Luxembourg.
[c] Excluding Belgium and Luxembourg.
[d] Excluding France.
Source: EEC, 1988

The Italian financial services industry emerges from the EEC study as one of the most exposed to the shocks and benefits of European financial integration.

Of the eight countries surveyed, Italy is the one where the financial industry appears small. This is particularly true for employment as a percentage of total employees, but the country is also in or near the last place when several 'output' measures of the industry (bank loans, insurance premiums and stock market capitalization) are related to gross domestic product (GDP). In table 7.2 we compare the number of bank branches, which also appears small in Italy as a result of several years of strict control on new openings. The same indication is given by the number of checking accounts and cheques drawn. The higher number of employees of Italian bank branches may depend on their larger average size, but the data in table 7.2 may also indicate that the technology used by the branches to supply their services has a low capital intensity and/or a low productivity.

Table 7.2 The supply of banking services: an international comparison, 1983 or 1984

	Bank branches	Bank branches (% of population)	Bank employees per bank branch	Bank checking accounts (% of population)	Average balance in checking accounts (million lire)	Bank cheques drawn per year per person
Italy	12,913	0.023	22.7	28	14.5	10
France	35,898	0.066	10.4	70	3.6	58
Germany	39,836	0.065	13.3	84	2.4	11
UK	24,574	0.044	11.9	189[a]	2.6[a]	46
Switzerland	4,986	0.043	27.3	–	–	–
USA	102,000	0.043	16.3	153	5.8	157
Japan	42,648	0.036	–	203	2.8	4

[a] Some time-deposit accounts are included.

Sources: Bank of Italy, Bank for International Settlements (BIS), EEC, OECD; for further information see Banca d'Italia, Libro bianco sul sistema dei pagamenti, *Italia*, April 1987

Italy's banking system appears much larger if it is measured using the value of bank deposits. However, this can obviously be a deceptive way of measuring the supply of banking services, and it is also an effect of the relative underdevelopment of Italy's financial structure. Moreover, a rapid process of bank disintermediation has been going on for several years in Italy, where the nominal size of the banking system is becoming closer to the average of the other major countries.

It is tempting to interpret the relatively small size of the banking and financial sector as an indicator of a lack of competitiveness resulting from past protective controls and direct and indirect barriers to entry. This would be consistent with the 'dual' finding that the Italian banking sector is very profitable: the most profitable when profits are measured in relation to loans outstanding, and second only to Spain when they are taken as a percentage of GDP. There are reasons for believing that the EEC Report, by referring to 1982 Organization for Economic Cooperation and Development (OECD) data, overestimates the relative profitability of Italian banks: Bank of Italy statistics on bank earnings have since been revised downwards, while the GDP new series is more than 15 per cent higher than the old series. However, profits have risen substantially since 1982, mainly because of lower depreciation and provisions for loan losses. Therefore the profitability of Italian banks must still rank among the highest in Europe (table 7.3). It is important to note that this is entirely due to the earnings of small and medium-sized institutions; the margins of the larger banks do not look systematically larger in Italy than elsewhere. In fact Italian data show a very strong negative

Table 7.3 Indexes of bank profitability[a]

	Rate of return on equity (before tax)	Average rate of inflation	Real rate of return on equity (before tax)
Belgium	14.25	4.87	9.38
Denmark	10.83	5.20	5.63
France	12.93	5.83	7.10
Germany	19.06	2.27	16.79
Ireland	12.84	6.27	6.57
Italy	19.27	9.53	9.74
Luxembourg	9.06	6.10	2.96
Netherlands	17.12	1.60	15.52
Portugal	5.06	21.67	−16.61
Spain	9.95	10.60	−0.65
UK	22.78	4.70	18.08

[a] In percentages. Averages for the period 1984−6. The inflation rate has been approximated with the GDP deflator at market prices.
Sources: OECD; Financial Statements of Banks; Commission of the European Communities

correlation between size and profitability (even when the latter is measured in proportion to the net worth of the banks, so that the effect of the higher average ratio of capital to assets of smaller institutions is taken into account − see table 7.7) which is difficult to regard as resulting from negative economies of scale; it must also be a consequence of the fact that smaller banks receive a greater benefit from protective regulations and enjoy a strong local market power.

Another striking feature of the Italian financial industry is the very small part of its output absorbed by households. The percentage reported in the EEC study (table 7.1, row 9) is based on 1980 input−output tables, referring to both banking and insurance, and looks extremely low: it is nearly a factor of 3 greater in Spain, a factor of 3.5 greater in France and nearly a factor of 6 greater in Germany, the United Kingdom and the Netherlands. We could object to the statistics used for the comparison. Moreover, the situation has certainly changed in recent years: the percentage of bank loans to households, for instance, is increasing. But the fact remains that the consumers' market for financial services is still underdeveloped in Italy. It is a market where domestic financial institutions can be thought to have a comparative advantage but, at least in an indirect way, the competitive pressures of the post-1992 era should contribute to its expansion.

While private consumption absorbs a small part of the output of Italy's financial industry, a distinguishing characteristic of the country's banking sector is that a large part of its activity is devoted to financing the public sector. The input–output tables cited above, which were used in the EEC Report, set the percentage of financial products consumed by the government to zero for all countries. However, in the analysis of the demand for bank assets (table 7.1, row 10) Italy is shown to have the highest percentage of bank claims on government. Table 7.4 has been prepared to investigate this further (Bruni et al., 1982) using more recent International Monetary Fund (IMF) data; in recent years, Spain seems to have taken the first position.

Table 7.4 Claims on government as a percentage of the total assets of commercial banks

	1970	1979	1984	1987	Including reserves 1987
Italy	10.3	20.3	22.3	21.6	35.4
France	5.1	2.7	5.0	4.2	5.8
Germany	7.5	12.9	14.3	13.5	16.6
UK	8.8	3.0	1.2	1.1	1.6
Belgium	20.1	14.7	16.9	19.3	19.6
Spain	18.1	10.6	18.6	24.3	37.4
USA	12.1	7.5	9.3	7.7	10.2

Calculations are based on IMF–IFS data. 'Total assets' are obtained as the sum of reserves, foreign assets and claims on the private sector, government and other financial intermediaries. The percentages refer to the claims on central government only. By including claims on local government and on other official entities a significant increase in the ratio is obtained for Germany (1987, about 18 per cent) and the USA (1987, 14.4 per cent). In the Italian case the definition of credit to the public sector can be broadened in various stages: in its broadest definition, including reserves at the central bank, public bank credit takes more than 50 per cent of the banks' balance sheet (Bruni et al., 1982, in particular table 3, p. 131).

Comparison of the composition of bank balance sheets in European countries reveals another important feature of the Italian case (table 7.1, rows 11 and 12): the country has the least open banking system apart from Spain. The percentage of assets and liabilities with respect to the rest of the world is low, and the international market share of the Italian banking system is much lower than it was at the beginning of the 1970s before the substantial strengthening of exchange controls. Regulations and financial protectionism caused a drastic reduction in the weight of foreign assets in the balance sheet of the whole private sector and have been the main obstacle to the growth of international activity by Italian banks. The latter is given in table 7.5 in proportion to the value of international trade (i.e. the degree of 'real openness' of the country), and Italy is the only country where the ratio is now

Table 7.5 Degree of openness of the banking system

| | Average of foreign assets and liabilities as percentage of: | | | | | | | |
| | Average value of imports and exports of goods and non-factor services | | | | Banks' total assets | | | |
	1970	1979	1984	1987	1970	1979	1984	1987
Italy	62	44	52	49	13	11	15	13
France	49	91	136	129[a]	16	27	41	34
Germany	26	37	37	49	6	9	9	11
UK	145	239	484	429	47	66	74	65
Belgium	49	81	148	162[b]	40	52	68	64
Spain	22	51	59	53[b]	4	8	12	8
USA	43	60	51	61	6	11	9	10

IMF–IFS data on 'Deposit Money Banks' have been used; total assets are defined as in the footnote to table 7.4. Exports and imports are IFS lines 90c and 98c.
[a] June.
[b] 1986.

lower than in 1970. Table 7.6 gives the market shares and shows that, if banking systems are defined according to the nationality of ownership of banks, Italy's share of the international bank credit market is more than twice the share obtained if bank units are classified according to the country of

Table 7.6 International market share of the banking system

| | Foreign assets[a] | | | | |
| | Country[b] | | | Nationality[c] | |
	Dec 1970	Dec 1980	Jun 1988	Jun 1985	Jun 1988
Italy	9.8	2.5	1.9	4.1	4.5
France	8.6	8.4	8.0	9.3	8.8
Germany	12.1	6.3	5.7	6.9	8.0
UK	31.4	26.2	26.1	7.8	5.8
Belgium	4.2	4.5	4.6	1.7	2.4
Luxembourg	3.1	7.7	5.4	0.4	0.5
Netherlands	4.5	4.6	3.6	2.8	2.9
Spain	0.8	1.3	0.7	1.2	0.9
Switzerland	18.8[d]	10.3	3.8	3.9	4.4
USA	10.0	15.0	15.7	26.5	15.0
Japan	5.6	4.9	19.5	24.8	37.9

[a] Foreign assets of banks in individual countries as a percentage of total international assets of banks in industrial countries.
[b] Country where banks, branches or subsidiaries are located.
[c] Nationality of ownership of banks.
[d] 1971.
Source: 1970, 1980, IMF–IFS; 1985, 1988, BIS

location. This must be partly an effect of regulations, and may mean that Italian banks are ready to profit from the liberalization in 1992; they seem capable of producing a much larger amount of international services than is at present possible and convenient for them to undertake from their home country. Only Japan shows similar characteristics; the opposite is observed for the United Kingdom, Belgium and Luxembourg. However, the network of foreign branches and subsidiaries of Italian banks is small: the average number of countries where foreign branches of each of the top seven Italian banks are located is 18 (end of 1987), while it is 22, 23, 35 and 43 respectively for the top seven Spanish, German, UK and French banks.

Although the rest of the world has a small share of Italian bank balance sheets, the EEC Report seems to show (table 7.1, line 13) that in Italy imports take a larger share of the resources in the credit and insurance sector. This could be a serious sign of weakness in domestic production, even if, surprisingly, the same statistical source (1980 input−output tables) shows that the country's share of exports on the total uses of the sector is higher than the European average.

After its overview of the regulatory barriers to trade and establishment in banking in various countries, the EEC Report ends by stating that what counts is 'not so much overt, discriminatory rules and regulations, but rather national practices that apply equally to both domestic and foreign-controlled banks' (EEC, 1988, p.76). In this general conclusion, Italy is often identified (together with Spain) as the country where protection is most evident. This occurs, for instance, when minimum capital requirements, 'comfort letters' from parent institutions and ceilings on some types of loan (individual and medium-term) are considered for branches of foreign banks, or when the public ownership of banks is considered as a potential obstacle to foreign acquisition of indigenous banks.

The effects of protective regulation and the potential impact of 1992 are quantified in the EEC Report by looking at the differences in prices of a given basket of banking, insurance and securities services. Apart from Spain, Italy was identified as the country with the greatest number of products priced above the free-trade equilibrium level and with the largest potential overall price reduction in the financial services sector in 1992. If banking services only are considered, Italy's potential price fall comes fourth, after Spain, Germany and France. The gain in consumer surplus resulting from integration of the European credit and insurance market is estimated at around 4 million European Currency Units for Italy; this is third, after the gains estimated for Germany and the United Kingdom in absolute terms, and after the gains for Spain and the United Kingdom when measured in proportion to gross national product. More than 80 per cent of these gains could result from the integration of the banking market alone.

To understand the impact of this disrupting integration process on the Italian banking industry, it is also important to consider the capital ratio and the riskiness of banks. Table 7.7 shows that the average degree of capitalization of Italian banks (which, on average, is higher for smaller banks) is not low by international standards, being higher than in France, Germany and Japan. Moreover, the fact that reserves and claims on the central government account for more than 35 per cent of their total assets (as shown in table 7.4) suggests that (at the cost of a much more rigid balance sheet) Italian banks have a low average riskiness (this is taken into account, at least in part, by the Bank for International Settlements (BIS) weighting method used to calculate the capital-to-asset ratio in the last column of table 7.7). The very small exposure to countries with high indebtedness is also a sign of the comparatively low risk of Italy's banking system: its claims on the Baker countries were less than 6 billion dollars at the end of 1987, i.e. 2 per cent of the total debt of these countries with BIS reporting banks, a little more than 4 per cent of the aggregate value of Italy's foreign assets, and about 40 per cent, 20 per cent and 15 per cent of the corresponding claims of German, French and UK banks respectively.

Table 7.7 Capital-to-asset ratio of banks

	Average of top five banks 1987	Average of all banks 1986	Average of top seven banks weighted using BIS method
Italy	4.03	5.30	11.5
France	3.10	2.71	10.8
Germany	3.10	3.69	8.0
UK	5.29	5.19	13.2
Belgium	2.04	–	–
Luxembourg	3.33	–	–
Denmark	6.25	–	–
Netherlands	3.97	–	–
Spain	6.00	7.95	13.2
Switzerland	5.53	–	–
USA	4.55	5.70	9.1
Japan	2.47	2.29	3.8

Sources: top five, *The Banker*, July 1988; all banks, OECD, *Bank Profitability*, 1988; top seven, data provided by *Credito Italiano*

However, new sources of risk for Italian banks are emerging: the expansion of their international activity, which is necessary to keep up with financial globalization; the gradual weakening of the implicit deposit insurance for bank failures, which has been provided by the government for many years; the growing possibility of mismatch between the maturity and the currency composition of assets and liabilities. Moreover, with stronger competition in the domestic bank credit market, a larger share of loans is going to smaller and riskier borrowers; in the period 1978–87 non-performing loans grew from 3 to more than 8 per cent of performing loans, and from 35 to nearly 40 per cent (with a peak of 44 per cent in 1982) of the banks' net worth. The management of credit, interest and exchange rate risks is a new challenge for Italian banks; it will require a significant increase in the capital ratio of several institutions.

A large bank size can help in facing a wider integrated risky market, even if standard economies of scale do not play an important role (Revell, 1987). This is another relevant point to consider in looking at the strengths and weaknesses of Italy's banking system in the process of financial globalization. Table 7.8 shows that the largest Italian banks and the corresponding concentration index of the system are significantly smaller in Italy than in the other major European countries. There is less difference if the average size of all banks is examined. A considerable concentration process is probably needed as well as an acceleration of the complete dynamics of the banking structure and of the replacement of old with new institutions. EC directives and recent liberalizations (see section 7.1) will favour these developments. Table 7.9 gives the number of mergers, acquisitions, entries and exits in the system; change appears to have been much faster since 1988.

However, in order to increase capitalization and concentration in Italian banking, some important rules of play need to be changed and/or clarified. Major debates are now starting on several issues such as anti-trust regulations, privatization and mergers of public banks, the possibility of industry buying banks and the rules that constrain banks in the labour market as far as dismissals and labour mobility are concerned. The results of these discussions will be crucial for the restructuring of Italian banking and its success after 1992. In addition the whole process of reregulating the non-bank financial sector and its relation with banking will be very important. The 'cost of non-Europe' has been shown to be particularly high for Italy in insurance and securities services, which are two industries with which banking will probably develop increasing synergy.

Table 7.8 Bank size

	Total assets of top five banks (% of total assets of Italy's top five)	Herfindhal concentration index (×100)	No. of banks in world top				Average world rank of top five of country : 3[a]	Estimated average size of all banks[b] (billion ECUs)
			500	100	50	25		
Italy	100	3.7	33	8	1	0	19	1.6
France	232	10.2	20	10	5	4	5	2.0
Germany	165	3.3	44	11	7	2	9	1.5
UK	155	15.0	15	5	4	2	13	1.9
Belgium	64	14.8	9	4	0	0	29	2.2
Luxembourg	16	18.2	6	0	0	0	98	1.4
Denmark	22	12.7	8	0	0	0	77	–
Netherlands	90	22.4	5	4	3	0	22	2.3
Spain	53	9.4	13	2	0	0	35	0.7
Switzerland	105	18.6	15	3	3	0	26	–
USA	150	1.9	–	11	4	1	12	–
Japan	338	1.2	–	28	21	16	1	–

Data on the top 500 banks in the world are from *The Banker*, July 1988. Data are for 1987 except for the last column, where calculations have been performed using information contained in the EEC Report (EEC, 1988) using 1986 data for Germany and the UK, 1985 for Belgium and 1984 for other countries.

[a] So that the best possible rank is $(1+2+3+4+5)/5 : 3 = 3 : 3 = 1.$

[b] Germany, 240 commercial banks; France, 435 commercial banks and credit cooperatives; Italy, 401 commercial and savings banks; UK, 660 statistical banks; Belgium, 119 banks, private savings banks and public credit institutions; Luxembourg, 111 banks; Netherlands, 86 universal banks; Spain, 363 banks.

Table 7.9 Mergers, acquisitions and changes in the number of Italian banks

	In	Out			Total change	No. of banks at end of period
	new banks	liquidations	mergers	acquisitions		
1982	+18	−2	−4	−6	+6	1,085
1983	+18		−4	−7	+7	1,092
1984	+13		−5	−4	+4	1,096
1985	+16	−1	−2	−8	+5	1,101
1986	+14	−1	−2	−10	+1	1,102
1987	+20	−1	−4	−8	+7	1,109
1988[a]	+14	−1	−8	−9	−4	1,105

Data are from the Bank of Italy and the Italian Bankers' Association and include all commercial and savings banks, and cooperative, rural and handicrafts banks. The changes mainly refer to small institutions, except in 1988 when two new banks were established as joint stock companies.

[a] January–June.

7.3   Reserve Requirements

Italian banks could be at a considerable competitive disadvantage after 1992 if the present compulsory reserve requirements are maintained. This is obvious from table 7.10 where Italy's reserve coefficient can be seen to be the highest. As regards this aspect of banking regulation, the following questions are worth discussing.

1   How large is the effective cost associated with reserve requirements?
2   Who really bears that cost: the depositors, the borrowers, or the banks themselves?
3   If the requirements and their costs stay at their present level, what will happen to Italian banks after 1992?
4   Why are reserve requirements so high in Italy, i.e. what is their economic function?
5   Given the answer to question 4, what would be the consequences of reducing the requirements in view of 1992?

Table 7.10   Coefficients of reserve requirements (percentage of deposits)

	Mid-1988	Average	
		1976−80	1987
Italy[a]	25[b]	14.8	20.6
Germany	6.6−12.1	8.2	5.8
France	2.5−5.0	1.7	2.7
UK	0.5		
Belgium	0		
Denmark	0		
Netherlands	0[c]		
Ireland	10		
Luxembourg	0		
Greece[a]	7.5		
Portugal	15.0		
Spain[a]	18.5		
USA	3[d]		

[a] Required reserves remunerated to some degree.
[b] Marginal rate on increase in deposits, while only 22.5 per cent of deposit decreases is given back to the bank.
[c] A small, variable and remunerated reserve requirement was introduced in May 1988.
[d] 12 per cent on demand deposits greater than US$40.5 million.

Sources: Morgan, *World Financial Markets*, issue 5, 1988; Banca d'Italia, 'La mobilizzazione della riserva obbligatoria: motivazioni e implicazioni', October 1988

By combining the answers to questions 3 and 5, we could also try to forecast the future development of regulation.

7.3.1 How Large is the Cost?

In Italy, as in some other countries, reserves are remunerated. This must be taken into account in answering the first question: the interest on them does not depend on market rates and is fixed at 5.5 per cent, except for reserves against certificates of deposits on which the central bank pays 8.5 per cent. Let r_R be the average remuneration of reserves. A rigorous measure of the implicit cost would require an estimate of the difference between the yield that the bank receives on its compulsory asset holdings and the yield that it would receive with no reserve requirements regulation. This can be difficult to obtain as it involves counter-factual simulations. However, approximate measures can be calculated by an appropriate choice of opportunity cost of funds, say r. If K is the average reserve coefficient on deposits, the implicit cost of reserves is then $(r-r_R)K$ per unit of deposit or $(r-r_R)K/(1-K)$ per unit of funds lent. Note that in this last definition, when the reserve coefficient is increased the unit cost of the requirements grows more than proportionally. The two definitions measure how much the deposit or lending rates would have to be decreased or increased to transfer the whole implicit cost on depositors or borrowers of the banks. Table 7.11 shows that the

Table 7.11 Implicit cost of reserve requirements

Country	Calculated using an opportunity cost of funds equal to the average interest rate on	As percentage of	1976−80	1981−84	1985	1986	1987
Germany	Government securities	Deposits	0.5	0.5	0.3	0.3	0.3
		Funds lent[a]	0.5	0.5	0.3	0.3	0.3
France	Government securities	Deposits	0.2	0.2	0.1	0.2	0.2
		Funds lent[a]	0.2	0.2	0.1	0.2	0.2
Italy	Government securities	Deposits	1.3	2.2	1.7	1.3	1.0
		Funds lent[a]	1.5	2.6	2.1	1.6	1.3
		GDP	−	1.3[b]	1.1	0.8	0.6
	Funds lent[c]	Deposits	−	2.3[b]	2.1	1.9	1.5
		GDP	−	1.4[b]	1.3	1.1	0.9

[a] Deposits minus reserves.

[b] 1983−4.

[c] Weighted average of unit interest income earned on domestic assets, net of reserves: loans, securities and interbank accounts.

Sources: Banca d'Italia, 'La mobilizzazione della riserva obbligatoria: motivazioni e implicazioni', October 1988, p. 10; calculations using data from the Bank of Italy's Annual Report

implicit cost for Italian banks was halved beetween 1985 and 1987 as a consequence of the sharp decrease in interest rates, but in 1987 it was still 1 per cent of deposits (and somewhat higher for 1988, showing an abrupt arrest of the descent), 1.3 per cent of funds lent and 0.6 per cent of GDP, if the opportunity cost is measured with the average interest rate on government securities. This is a factor of 3 −5 higher than the cost of reserve requirements for German and French banks, for which, because of the low average ratio of reserves to deposits, there was no significant difference between the measures of the cost as a percentage of deposits or of funds lent. If the average interest rate on domestic assets, net of reserves, is used as the opportunity cost, the implicit cost of the requirements was 50 per cent higher and reached almost 1 per cent of GDP. We can conclude that the cost is still very high, not far from the total pre-tax profits of the banks, and may represent a serious competitive disadvantage for the Italian banking system: with fixed remuneration of reserves, the decrease in the opportunity cost of compulsory asset holdings has been in part compensated by the substantial increase in the average ratio of reserves to deposits, which is now about 1/5, nearly 5 percentage points higher than in 1982. In January 1989 a project for reforming of reserve requirements was approved: partial short-term with-drawals of reserve funds were made possible because only the average monthly balance of compulsory deposits were to be considered. This should greatly improve the efficiency of the market for overnight funds and interbank deposits (Banca d'Italia, 1988), but will not significantly reduce the cost of the constraint.

7.3.2 Who Bears the Cost?

The answer to the second question depends on the relative power of the banks in the various markets where they operate. If there is high competition in all of them and substitutability of bank by non-bank instruments, the whole cost would be borne by the banks themselves. In the Italian case imperfections seem larger in the deposit market, where banks have a stronger power to fix the rates, and certificates of deposit and wholesale forms of collection of funds still play a limited role (Fama (1983) shows that the cost of reserves on certificates of deposit is paid by bank borrowers). We can therefore assume that the major part of the cost of reserve requirements is paid by retail depositors, even if nothing precise can be stated without a difficult econometric study of the behaviour of demand and supply functions for both deposits and loans. However, the situation is changing and the market power of depositors is increasing; banks are finding growing competition in all the markets where they operate, and their ability to transfer the cost of reserve requirements to their clients will probably decrease. These developments have been reinforced by 1992.

7.3.3 What will happen to Italian Banks in the Post-1992 Era?

This leads to the third question. If reserve requirements stay at their present level, they could be a cause of disintermediation of Italian banks in the integrated European market. The worst case would be if foreign banks were allowed to enter Italy with their home country reserve regulations. This will not happen if the Commission keeps considering reserve requirements as instruments of monetary policy (for which there are no plans of harmonization and host country regulations will apply), a view that we shall dispute in answering the fourth question. But even with host country regulations the freedom of short-term capital movements will cause disintermediation; in this respect, the 1990 liberalization, allowing residents to keep deposits with banks abroad, is even more important than 1992. Its effect will also depend on the answer to question 2: a slower and feebler disintermediation will result to the extent that banks will be able to keep transferring the implicit cost of reserve requirements in a very uneven way to their weaker clients (small depositors and borrowers), for whom access to foreign banking markets will remain more difficult and costly.

7.3.4 Why are Reserve Requirements so High in Italy?

To answer the fourth question, the various possible functions of reserve requirements need to be briefly recalled.

They were originally introduced in various countries (in 1926 in Italy) for prudential purposes to guarantee the convertibility of deposits into legal tender. Although 100 per cent reserves would still make deposits safer assets, the requirements have obviously been losing this meaning almost everywhere, particularly since the adoption of modern prudential controls, implicit and explicit (or 'discretionary' and 'contractual' (Baltensperger and Dermine, 1987)) forms of deposit insurance, capital and liquidity ratios etc. In any case, prudential reasons could not explain the difference between Italy's reserve coefficient and those of other countries. However, it has sometimes been suggested that part of the original purpose of the instrument could be recovered: the enormous pool of reserves with the Bank of Italy could be utilized as a mutual deposit insurance fund, so that the implicit cost of reserves could be considered as an insurance premium (Monti, 1979, pp. 109–11). However, the recently established interbank insurance fund has no connection with compulsory reserves (Merusi, 1986).

Reserve requirements can also be used as a mechanism for selective credit controls. This happens when specific assets other than monetary base are accepted in satisfaction of the reserve obligation, or if the level of the coefficient, or the remuneration of the reserve, for individual banks are determined in such a way as to reward those banks which give privileged treatment, in the composition of their assets, to securities regarded as worthy by the authorities. In Italy, the regulation of reserves used to have some selective purpose, but in 1975 this function was completely eliminated (Banca d'Italia, 1988, p. 6) by a reform providing that the requirements could be satisfied only with monetary base and organizing the mechanism to obtain a gradual equalization of the average reserve coefficients of all the banks.

The third possible function of compulsory reserves is embedded in the textbook model of the money multiplier: by limiting the level and variability of the ratio of deposits to monetary base, reserve requirements constrain money and credit creation and allow monetary policy to control the fluctuations in prices and other macro-economic variables. A particular application of this model is often stressed by the Bank of Italy (e.g. Banca d'Italia, 1988, pp. 5, 7), which states that a high reserve coefficient is required to check the multiplication of the excess of monetary base created to finance the Treasury's deficit. In fact, there are countries that apply a successful monetary policy with zero or very low compulsory reserves. This should suffice to prove that the multiplier model is not a good explanation of the existence of the constraint and cannot justify the very high level of Italy's coefficient, even when the special difficulties of the country's monetary control mechanism are taken into consideration. Moreover, the monetary policy function of reserve requirements has been seriously questioned in recent years in the theoretical literature. Several arguments have been offered to support the idea that monetary control can also be effective without this type of regulation. Even with no compulsory reserves, there is a positive demand for base money and, provided that the government keeps an effective monopoly in base money production, banks voluntarily hold a certain amount of reserves for precautionary reasons, so that the money multiplier is larger but determinate, finite and related to other variables, such as interest rates, in fundamentally the same way as with reserve requirements (e.g. Fama, 1983; Baltensperger and Dermine, 1987, pp. 67–9). With a larger multiplier, it may be more difficult to achieve short-run stability of the money stock, but monetary policy will generally remain effective in controlling its ultimate objectives, i.e. in stabilizing aggregate demand and the price level. The simple mechanism of the money multiplier is really only applicable when at least two conditions are met: the true operational target of the central bank is the stock of monetary base or reserves, and commercial banks are tightly constrained in their ability to respond to a cash surplus or deficiency by varying interest rates charged on loans and offered on deposits (Goodhart, 1989). However, if bank rates are deregulated and if the central bank's day-to-day target is the money market interest rate, the model of monetary control is different and is much less dependent on the level of reserve requirements. Central bank operations relate to the demand and supply of excess reserves, while required reserves are predetermined and do not influence the relevant market; the operational target is the interest rate because the demand for excess reserves is highly interest inelastic and any attempt to peg their quantity rigidly would result in extreme interest rate instability (Goodhart, 1989, p. 2). As Horrigan (1988, pp. 104–5) concludes: 'if the central bank adjusts the interest elasticity of the supply of reserves' to various real and monetary shocks 'or if it pegs the interest rate, the required reserve ratio is irrelevant for economic stabilization. Reserve requirements may have a valid role in generating revenue for the Government, but they have no necessary role in stabilizing the economy.' In the case of the Bank of Italy, for instance, the excess monetary base created by the Treasury's operations can be technically sterilized on the open market, independently of the level of reserve requirements, provided that the authority is willing to pay the market rate and give up the tax on compulsory reserves which is implicit in their lower remuneration.

We are therefore left with the fiscal function of reserve requirements, which appears to be the only important one, especially if an explanation is sought for international differences of reserve coefficients. The EC should recognize this fact, and the harmonization of reserve regulations should appear on its agenda: this type of structural constraint on banking should cease to be considered an autonomously usable instrument of short-run monetary policy. Compulsory bank reserves provide a way of artificially increasing the private sector's demand for monetary base, thus permitting the Treasury to collect a larger amount of seigniorage (Bruni et al., forthcoming). The higher reserve coefficients imposed in Italy, Spain, Portugal and Greece correspond to what has been called the 'fiscal asymmetry' of Europe (Giavazzi, 1988, p. 11, table 1) whereby southern countries have lower explicit tax revenues and more seigniorage. There may be reasons to think that this mix is in some sense 'optimal' (because the social cost of collecting explicit taxes is higher than in northern countries and the presence of a larger underground economy reduces the base for explicit taxation) and, in particular, that higher reserve requirements, by widening the inflation tax base, facilitate 'a policy shift aimed at stabilizing the price level' (Giavazzi, 1988, p. 17–18). However, the lower political cost of implicit taxes (especially when collected with low inflation by means of scarcely known direct financial controls) can push their use beyond what is socially optimal, contributing to the persistence of public deficits which are too wide and public expenditure which is too large and insufficiently productive. In any case, fiscal asymmetry is a serious obstacle to further progress in European monetary unification (to the extent that seigniorage is collected via inflation) and/or capital market integration (if constraints like reserve requirements are used that affect the relative competitiveness of national financial systems).

7.3.5 **What are the Consequences of Reducing Reserve Requirements?**

Let us therefore deal with our fifth question: if 1992 will require a sharp reduction of the reserve coefficient of Italian banks, what will the macro-economic consequences be? In other words: how important is the source of implicit taxation provided by compulsory reserves? Unfortunately, the answer cannot simply be derived from the answer to question 1. The implicit cost for the banks and their clients (which, as we noted, is itself difficult to define and measure in a rigorous way) is not necessarily identical with the implicit revenue for the Treasury (Porta, 1984). These two factors are usually calculated in very different ways: we can only mention here some of the difficulties that arise in understanding the relationship between the two concepts. First, seigniorage takes the inflation tax into account, and if inflation is non-neutral, affecting (decreasing) the real rate of interest, the opportunity cost of compulsory reserves will be different from (lower than) the tax revenue implicit in the constraint. Secondly, when the cost is transferred to bank clients, general equilibrium adjustments take place which influence in complicated ways the amount of implicit tax that reaches the public sector. Another problem is the following: must the accounts of the tax collector, i.e. the central bank, be consolidated with Treasury accounts? Suppose, for instance, that in the balance sheet of the former the counterpart of bank reserves is constituted by foreign assets; the profits of the central bank, i.e. the seigniorage that will be transferred to the Treasury, will then depend on the yield on foreign assets and on the behaviour of exchange rates, and part of the seigniorage could be collected by a foreign central bank. If the central bank is not consolidated with the Treasury, only the monetary base created to finance the latter will directly enter the calculation of seigniorage, the amount of which will change with the ratio of the Treasury monetary base to the total monetary base (Bruni et al., forthcoming, section 2, appendix). Finally, consider what happens in a period when there is a change, say an increase, in the average reserve coefficient. In a 'cash-flow definition' of seigniorage we should include the amount of monetary base that has been added to reserves, while in an 'opportunity cost definition' only the unpaid interest on that amount would have to be included (Gros, 1988). In the Italian case the two procedures give a very different result if seigniorage is calculated for the last few years, when the reserve coefficient increased rapidly, hypothesizing a gradual decrease in the coefficient towards a much lower common European level.

Despite these differences and complications, reasonable estimates of the seigniorage on compulsory reserves in Italy turn out to be of the same order of magnitude as the implicit cost of the constraint discussed in section 7.3.1 and reported in table 7.11. From 1984 to 1987 the average yearly amount of total seigniorage was approximately 2 per cent of GDP (Bruni et al., forthcoming, tables 2 and 3), of which more than 70 per cent came from compulsory reserves. The tax collected with the constraint thus reduced by a third the increase in the ratio to GDP of the public debt held outside the central bank, which had been around 4.5 percentage points per year. It is important to note that the amount of seigniorage relative to GDP had about the same average value during the high inflation period from 1976 to 1981; the increase in the reserve coefficient has compensated for the decrease in the inflation tax rate. In the period 1987−8 seigniorage was lower, with probably less than 1 per cent of GDP coming from compulsory reserves; its contribution to the slowing down of public debt is also smaller because the monetary base is now created mainly by the foreign sector.

Seigniorage on bank reserves is therefore still significant, even if it is lower than a few years ago. The steady increase in the average reserve coefficient which is built into the present regulations is nearing its end, and this will further depress seigniorage if inflation remains low. We conclude that the reduction in reserve requirements, which, from the point of view of the banking system, was essential to cope with 1990−2 (as discussed in section 7.3.2), would not mean a very strong marginal burden for the country's public finance. (Obviously, the reduction has had to be performed with the right timing and an appropriate mix of decreases in the marginal coefficient, increases in the remuneration of reserves and reimbursements of the stock of reserves sterilized, if necessary, with open-market operations.) The real issue probably lies with the current level of seigniorage. Considering the importance that it has had in the recent past, its current decrease is seriously hindering the stabilization of the debt-to-income ratio. In fact, the lower revenue from the implicit tax nearly completely balances the difficult reduction in the deficit net of interest. An optimistic scenario would emphasize the help that could come from the behaviour of interest rates. If 1990−2 brings a much stronger commitment by the authorities to keep inflation low and the exchange rate constant, and if further steps are made in the process of European monetary union, the expected depreciation, as well as the inflation and exchange rate risk premiums that are now built into Italian interest rates, could disappear. This would bring about a substantial reduction in the public sector's interest bill and a much lower deficit, which could then manage without the seigniorage revenue. In the meantime, the decrease in interest rates would reduce the implicit cost of reserves for the banking system. The problem is obviously one of credibility: will it be possible to believe a programme of rigorous monetary stability at a time when the accounts of the public sector will still be in a state of emergency?

7.4   Conclusions

As Steinherr and Gilibert (1988, p. 32) put it, 'the potential gain [from European financial integration] is largest for the most distorted economies, [but] needless to say, there is a price to be paid: adjustment will be all the more painful'.

At the beginning of this decade Italy's financial system was certainly very distorted. A serious process of change was then started: it would have been necessary, even if painful, regardless of 1992, but as it was mainly caused by the economic, political and cultural pressure of the international community, we can view this action as a preparation for the next 'European' decade.

First, monetary and exchange rate policies were adjusted. Despite the sharp decrease in inflation, and in inflation differentials relative to other industrial economies, EMS discipline caused a steady revaluation of the real exchange rate with the other currencies of the system: since 1979, the average yearly increase in its effective value has been greater than 1.5 per cent. Second, internal financial deregulation started, stimulating competition among banks, eliminating direct credit controls and portfolio constraints, and introducing important innovations in public debt instruments and management, in the organization of the money market and in the techniques used for monetary control. These first two lines of action made possible the third crucial step: a rapid liberalization of capital movement and a general reform of foreign exchange regulations. Some important controls (such as the prohibition on holding foreign bank deposits) were removed in 1990, and impressive progress was made with substantial macro-economic consequences on the rules governing exchange rate determination, on the relationship between domestic and international interest rates, on the cost of the public debt and on the Treasury's deficit. The latter development is particularly dangerous: if the 'discipline effect' of liberalization does not work sufficiently fast on influencing political decisions, it is possible that the public finance problem will cause the reintroduction of financial protectionism.

The difficult 'macro-changes' in the country's monetary and financial system that we reviewed above were a prerequisite and a stimulus for the micro-transformation of the structure and organization of the financial industry that was required to cope with 1992. Progress on this latter front, which also involves 'purely internal recasting of banks' organizational structures, both geographical and sectorial' (Steinherr and Gilibert, 1988, p. 53), has been much slower in Italy. Among the causes of this delay we can include the following: managerial inefficiency in the banking sector, which finds it hard to move out of the climate of protection; the fact that several crucial pieces of reregulation that would stimulate and help the structural changes are still not in place; a credibility problem as a result of which deregulation is sometimes considered potentially reversible.

Therefore several distortions and inefficiencies remain in the Italian financial services industry, which emerges as one of the most exposed to the shocks of adjustment and to the benefits of European financial integration. Because of a lack of competitiveness resulting from past protective controls, Italy's banking and financial sector appears relatively small and very profitable. The consumers' market for financial services is still under-developed. Much bank activity is still devoted to the financing of the public sector, while the degree of openness of the banking system is very low: the percentage of assets and liabilities relative to the rest of the world is small, the network of foreign branches and subsidiaries of Italian banks is probably inadequate, and their share of the international market is much smaller than it was at the beginning of the 1970s. EEC research on the cost of non-Europe (EEC, 1988) found that Italy is the country with the highest number of financial products priced above the free-trade equilibrium level even if, when only banking services are considered, Italy's potential price fall comes fourth after Spain, Germany and France. The average degree of capitalization of Italian banks is not low by international standards, and the structure of their balance sheets seems to indicate a low average riskiness; however, with liberalization and international integration, new sources of risk are emerging that will require a significant increase in the capital ratio of several Italian banks. Also, the size of Italian banks and the degree of concentration of the banking industry seem insufficient to face a wider risky international market. A considerable acceleration of the whole dynamics of the industry is probably needed, with more mergers, acquisitions and replacement of old with new institutions.

These 'micro-developments' will obviously require the continuation of the progress at the 'macro-institutional' level. Strong competitive pressures have to be maintained with *de*regulation, but important *re*regulations are also needed, clarifying the rules of the game in several areas, such as anti-trust, privatization and merger programmes for public banks, the possibility of enabling industry buy banks, the rules that constrain banks in the labour market as far as dismissals and labour mobility are concerned, and the whole regulatory framework for the non-bank financial sector and its relation with banking. The debates that are now developing on these issues have to be followed carefully to understand how the Italian financial industry will be able to compete in the post-1992 era.

In the last part of this chapter we looked at a specific problem that could cause a considerable competitive disadvantage for Italy in the European market: compulsory reserve requirements. The implicit cost of this constraint was halved during 1985−7 as a consequence of the sharp decrease in interest rates, but, given the substantial increase in the average ratio of reserves to deposits, the cost is still very high and is not far from the total pre-tax profits of the banks. The major part of this cost is probably paid for by retail depositors, but the banks' ability to transfer the burden to their clients is decreasing. From this point of view, 1992 could be terrible if foreign banks are allowed to enter Italy with their home country reserve regulations. However, this will not happen if the Commission continues to consider the requirements as instruments of short-term monetary control, for which there are no plans for harmonization and host country regulations will apply. We have disputed this view, arguing that the main function of compulsory reserves is neither prudential nor connected with monetary policy: it is the collection of a large implicit tax for the needs of public finance. The importance of this source of implicit taxation has been decreasing in recent years: the reduction in reserve requirements that, from the point of view of the banking system, was essential to cope with 1990−2 has not meant a very strong marginal burden for the country's public finance. The real issue is the fact that the current decrease in the seigniorage on bank reserves is seriously hindering the stabilization of the debt-to-income ratio. Some help could come from the behaviour of interest rates in 1990−2, if the inflation and exchange rate risk premiums built into Italian rates have disappeared, causing a sharp decrease in the cost of public debt. However, this will happen only if the market has been successful in supporting a programme of rigorous monetary stability and complete exchange liberalization at a time when the accounts of the public sector were in a state of disarray.

References

Baltensperger, E. and Dermine, J. (1987) Banking deregulation in Europe. *Economic Policy*, 4, 64−107.

Banca d'Italia (1988) La mobilizzazione della riserva obbligatoria: motivazioni e implicazioni.

Bruni, F. (1988) Costs and benefits of liberalization of capital flows: some theoretical and policy issues with special reference to the Italian case. In D.E. Fair and C. de Boissieu (eds), *International Monetary and Financial Integration: The European Dimension*. Dordrecht: Martinus Nijhoff.

Bruni, F. and Monti, M. (1986) Protezionismo valutario e integrazione internazionale. In T. Padoa-Schioppa (ed.), *Il Sistema dei cambi, oggi*. Bologna: Mulino.

Bruni, F., Monti, M. and Porta, A. (1982) Bank lending to the public sector: determinants, implications and outlook. In D.E. Fair and L. de Juvigny (eds.), *Bank Management in a Changing Domestic and International Environment*. The Hague: Martinus Nijhoff.

Bruni, F., Penati, A. and Porta, A. (forthcoming) Financial regulation, implicit taxes and fiscal adjustment in Italy. *Proceedings of the Conference on Fiscal Policy, Economic Adjustment and Financial Markets, Milan, 27–30 January 1988.*

EEC (1988) Research on the cost of non-Europe. *Basic Findings*, Vol. 9. Luxembourg: Price Waterhouse.

Fama, E. (1983) Financial intermediation and price level control. *Journal of Monetary Economics*, 12, 7–28.

Giavazzi, F. (1988) The exchange rate question in Europe (revised), University of Bologne, mimeo, December.

Goodhart, C. (1989) Bank reserve requirements and monetary control, presented at the Conference on La Modifica della Riserva Obbligatoria: Aspetti Teorici e Problemi Operativi, Turin, 20 January, mimeo.

Gros, D. (1988) Seigniorage in the EEC: the implications of the EMS and financial markets integration, European Economic Association, Bologna Meeting, August, mimeo.

Horrigan, R. (1988) Are reserve requirements relevant for economic stabilization? *Journal of Monetary Economics* 23, 97–105.

Merusi, F. (1986) In La tutela dei depositanti: dalla riserva obbligatoria al Fondo Interbancario di Garanzia. *Note Economiche*, 3–4, 233–8.

Monti, M. (1979) Intervento. In *La tutela del Risparmio Bancario*, pp. 99–111. Bologna: Mulino.

Porta, A. (1984) L''imposta implicita' sulla riserva obbligatoria e il suo gettito per lo Stato: alcune riflessioni sul caso italiano. *Bancaria*, 7, 652–60.

Revell, J. (1987) Mergers and the role of large banks, Research Monograph in Banking and Finance no. 2, University College of North Wales, Bangor.

Steinherr, A. and Gilibert, P.L. (1988) The impact of freeing trade in financial services and capital movements on the European banking industry, European Investment Bank, mimeo.

Comment

Alfred Steinherr

1992 has exerted a major influence on the financial industry and on research on the implications of financial integration. In this process we have all benefited greatly from understanding better the specific characteristics of the national financial markets in the EC.

This chapter by Franco Bruni is a good example: it provides wide-ranging information and an analytical view of the risks and opportunities that confronted the financial sector in Italy on the road to 1992 and beyond. Like other contributions to the subject, his chapter raises at least as many questions as it tries to answer for obvious reasons. The data at hand are fairly incomplete and mostly of limited quality, and the issues of concern are to a large extent not amenable to satisfactory modelling. Hence contributions to this area are characterized by an important dose of analogy to exploit theoretical or empirical knowledge in other areas of research, paired with judgemental elements and commonsense impressions.

The title of the chapter uses 'reregulation' instead of 'deregulation'. In my view this choice overemphasizes Europe-wide scope for harmonized regulation. It is fair to assume that only a few key areas, such as capital requirements, accounting conventions and presentations etc., will be regulated on an EC basis. The difficulties of harmonization are such that it will be attempted only for major key issues. Hence, the dominant feature of 1992 will be deregulation with some reregulation on a national basis to adjust to 1992, and some reregulation in the form of harmonization.

A major conclusion of the chapter is that Italy is one of the EC countries most exposed to the 'shocks and benefits of European financial integration'. This conclusion is suggested by the following structural features. First, Italy has a relatively underdeveloped market and hence there is untapped market potential. If the value-added of financial services is taken as a share of GDP, this claim is not supported. Since financial products are a luxury good, GNP per capita and the uneven regional income distribution may explain residual differences. The fact that financial intermediation is smaller in an economy with a large underground economy could also be relevant.

Second, the high profitability of Italian banks, which rank among the highest in Europe, is stressed. In table 7.3, Italy is ranked second after the

United Kingdom in terms of return on equity before tax. However, a more appropriate measure is provided by real rates of return, and here Italy ranks on par with Belgium, and after the United Kingdom, Germany and the Netherlands. Thus real profitability is nearer the average rather than exceptionally high. However, even this requires an explanation.

Neven (chapter 5) suggests that the compensation of employees in the Italian banking sector is exceptionally high: the average compensation in banking is three times the economy-wide average compensation. Hence Franco Bruni is still correct in assigning a major explanatory role to protection, even though the variable to be explained is not high profitability alone but high returns on capital and labour. The future implications are, of course, quite different: high profits are a buffer (but also an attraction) to foreign competition; high returns to labour are a competititve disadvantage.

This changes the evaluation of the sector's potential to some extent. Bruni suggests that regulations have protected but also restrained growth of banking and therefore that deregulation would provide great opportunities. This may neglect the high employment costs and high rigidity of employment in Italian banking as well as other weak features such as suboptimal infrastructure (transport, mail, telephone etc.), the cost of building a reputation in the international market etc.

Bruni argues that among the measures required to improve efficiency, 'a considerable concentration process is probably needed . . .'. The basis for this suggestion is the fact that the largest Italian banks are significantly smaller than those in other European countries. However, neither the evidence nor the conclusions are totally convincing. Size and efficiency or profitability are not correlated. Steinherr and Gilibert show that in Belgium, Greece, Ireland, Italy and the United Kingdom size and profitability are negatively correlated for the major banks, whereas in all other EC countries the correlation index is positive but close to zero. In Italy it is not clear what bank mergers could achieve as long as the public sector remains the main shareholder in the banks. I believe that the most fruitful approach would consist in privatizing banks and allowing unrestrained entry of foreign banks. This would ensure a profit-oriented bank management and hence greater efficiency. Whether this process will lead to more concentration is of secondary importance.

However, is it really true that Italy has an excessively low degree of concentration? As measured by the share in bank assets by the top five institutions, market concentration in Italy is higher than that in Germany. Examination of different types of banking institutions suggests that there may be a need for greater concentration among savings banks, but otherwise Italy's market structure does not seem to be fundamentally out of line with other European countries.

The question of reserve requirements is given considerable space because Italy has the highest reserve requirements in the EC. Reserves are remunerated at fixed rates which, at least in the past, have been far below market rates. Bruni argues that this puts Italy at a serious competitive disadvantage, at least as long as market rates remain well above the rates on reserves. However, as is argued later, the implicit tax is mostly borne by consumers so that banks may feel the effects only when consumers shift to other products. I would not attach too much importance to his element of competitive disadvantage because, unlike more structural features, in the single European financial market either excessive amounts of reserves or below-market rates will be corrected.

Of course, there is the problem of financing the public debt. In this respect I feel tempted to disagree to some extent with Bruni's estimation of the implicit costs of reserve requirements as close to 1 per cent of GDP. This is very large for an industry that only accounts for 4.9 per cent of GDP, including insurance. The benefit goes to Banca d'Italia which provides a very large current account overdraft to the Treasury (100,000 billion lire in 1988) at highly subsidized rates and distributes a major share of its profits to the Treasury (however, this is a relatively small amount). A question I would like to raise is whether banks receive some subsidized refinancing.

Finally, some of the opportunities and strengths of the Italian banking industry are not stressed in the chapter. Italy has the largest savings rate in the EC, and this is the basis for the high growth of banking. Italy has the largest market for government securities in Europe and therefore great potential for investment banking. The only problem is efficiency. However, efficiency can be increased when government reduces its control over banks and when foreign competition is admitted. A last weakness, the low international role of the lira, is also likely to disappear as Europe moves towards monetary union.

8

Competition in Spanish Banking

Ramon Caminal, Jordi Gual and Xavier Vives

Our purpose in this chapter is to assess the state of competition in the Spanish banking system in the run-up to the integration of the European financial market.

Banking in Spain has undergone a major liberalization process in the last fifteen years, which has recently accelerated and has developed from a situation of tight regulation and protection from competition. The outcome of this process is a changing sector in which the recent merger attempts are the most visible phenomena.

The work that is reported here is in the spirit of what could be called the industrial organization (IO) of banking. This is certainly a developing field since finance and banking theory and IO have evolved quite separately.[1] Probably the most important contribution that IO can make to banking theory is the consideration of strategic aspects previously neglected by providing a box of tools for analytical purposes.[2] In financial markets the weight of the competitive paradigm is still very large even in situations where the capacity of individual players to influence market outcomes is not negligible. It should also be pointed out that the very existence of financial intermediaries is linked to market imperfections.

When trying to study competition in Spanish banking two types of problem are encountered: firstly, the lack of a fully developed theoretical model of banking competition that takes into account the complexities of banking as a multiproduct concern in a strategic framework;[3] secondly, the lack of a body of empirical evidence on the Spanish financial sector and on banking in particular. With these limitations our objectives are rather modest: provide basic evidence, pose some fundamental issues and problems, survey and extend wherever possible the existing work, and attempt to draw a coherent picture of Spanish banking.

This paper is part of a larger project, under the direction of Xavier Vives at the Fundación de Estudios de Economía Aplicada (FEDEA), to study the banking sector in Spain. We are grateful to Xavier Freixas, Rafael Repullo and Joan E. Ricart for helpful comments, and to Josep Comajuncosa, Marisa de la Torre, Belén Mateos, Xavier Ramirez and Jesús Saurina for research assistance.

The plan of this chapter is as follows: in section 8.1 we describe the Spanish banking system and its development during the 1980s, and make some international comparisons; in section 8.2 we collect more systematic and theoretically based empirical evidence on the main issues; in section 8.3 we attempt a competitive analysis of the sector; some speculative remarks are made in section 8.4; and we conclude with a review of developments after 1989.

8.1 The Spanish Banking System in the Run-up to European Integration

Spanish banking was traditionally a closed system, heavily regulated, protected from external competition, conservative in terms of innovations and controlled by the large banks, who also own substantial portions of industry. Since the Spanish financial system and private agents were very unsophisticated, banks were able to obtain their main input (deposits) at a very low (deposit rate) cost and were required to finance public expenditure cheaply through investment requirements. In exchange large banks were allowed to coordinate their market actions in the context of complete regulation of interest rates.

The banking system was subjected to a strong shock because of the protracted industrial crisis that the country suffered after the oil price increases in the 1970s. Many banks failed and had to be rescued. The banking crisis temporarily reversed a trend towards lower concentration and slowed down the deregulation process started in the mid-1970s (since authorities were worried about the solvency of the system). After the crisis concentration decreased again until two of the largest banks decided to merge. The outcome was a banking system with concentration and profitability levels roughly similar to European standards, which did not look very efficient but was nevertheless capitalized, and a country which appeared, perhaps paradoxically, overbanked.

We shall now try to support the above claims by describing the main facts about regulation and the development of competition (with particular emphasis on the crisis and the changes in concentration), and by comparing the Spanish system with international standards. However, before doing that, we shall briefly describe the state of the financial system.

8.1.1 The Financial System

At the end of 1988 the characteristics of the Spanish financial system, compared with other EC countries, were unusual. On the one hand, the relative weight of the banking industry was very important,[4] although declining. On the other hand, there was a sophisticated organized market for public debt and money markets, in sharp contrast with an underdeveloped stock market (although currently under reform, as we shall see later).

The market for public debt has developed very rapidly in the mid to late 1980s, partly because of the needs of public debt financing and partly for monetary policy reasons. In 1984 the government decided to obtain a large part of its financial resources at market rates. Given the high and volatile inflation rates prevailing in that period the demand was oriented towards short-term Treasury notes (*Pagarés del Tesoro*) that, in addition, offered an attractive fiscal opacity.[5] Precisely because of this, these notes were not suitable for monetary control purposes, and in 1987 a new instrument appeared: Treasury bills (*Letras del Tesoro*). At the same time it was crucial to make the market deeper to allow for the volume of transactions required by the intervention of the Bank of Spain.

Thus in April 1987 the new market was organized around a centralized compensation system (Central de Anotaciones en Cuenta), run by the Bank of Spain. The Central de Anotaciones issues the Treasury bonds and makes payments by a simple accounting settlement. Also, it registers all exchanges of bonds, without the need of a public notary (the role played by the *agentes de cambio y bolsa*). Thus transaction costs were drastically reduced. In addition, the system of continuous bidding reduced the interest rate spread and increased the liquidity of these bonds.

The Spanish interbank market had its origin in 1971 after the setting of a reserves requirement two years earlier. However, in the last decade the volume of transactions in this market grew at a dramatic pace. Three main elements have contributed to this fact: (a) the development of a policy of monetary control; (b) the high interest rates in the 1980s, providing a high opportunity cost for idle resources; (c) the entry of foreign banks after 1978, with major limitations in the deposits market.

Traditionally, the Spanish stock market has been very thin, lacking in transparency and inefficient, with a highly protected system of stockbroking dominated by a small number of families. Stockbrokers ran a very lucrative business. They needed no capital backing since they were not allowed to act as market makers, but collected high proportional commissions; share transactions could only be validated by a licensed stockbroker. Insider trading was not regulated until very recently and was considered standard behaviour in the market coupled with very little information disclosure on the part of the firms. The inefficiency of this system of stockbroking was exacerbated by problems of liquidity, price manipulation and crowding out due to public debt financing.

It is very easy to illustrate the thinness of the Spanish stock market. For example, the number of quoted companies in 1986 was only 312,[6] but only about 60 stocks currently listed are considered sufficiently liquid for any major investor to contemplate buying them. In 1987 non-bank Spanish firms obtained only 9 per cent of their financial resources in the stock and securities markets (Trujillo et al., 1988, p. 125). Also, the capitalization of stock listed in the four Bolsas (Madrid, Barcelona, Bilbao and Valencia) at the end of 1986 was about 11 per cent of gross domestic product (GDP) compared with about 65 per cent in the United Kingdom, 25 per cent in Germany and 17–18 per cent in France and Italy (OECD, 1988, p. 61; capitalization for Spain in 1987 was substantially higher). The composition of traded assets is also very significant: in 1987 about 75 per cent of traded assets were those of banking firms and public utilities. With trading concentrated in a relatively small number of stocks and an even smaller number of sectors the market is inevitably volatile with plenty of room for large-scale shareholders to manipulate prices. The large accumulated public deficits in the 1980s and their financing needs also hindered the development of an efficient stock market.

Several changes were introduced in the 1980s such as credit transactions (through *Sociedades instrumentales de agentes de cambio y bolsa*), which increased the market's liquidity, and a second market for small and medium-sized businesses which has not been very successful. A drastic reform of the stock market was begun in 1988 (see the appendix).

8.1.2 Regulation

The Spanish banking system has traditionally been heavily regulated in terms of interest rates, entry, branching, and investment and reserve requirements. Furthermore, these regulations put different constraints on different institutions, such as banks and savings banks, for example. Liberalization advanced significantly in the 1970s and has accelerated recently, transforming banking into a free-market business.

From complete regulation to liberalization

In 1962 the *Ley de Ordenación Bancaria* allowed the establishment of new banks and tried to separate commercial from so-called 'industrial' banks. Nevertheless banks tended to follow the tradition of universal banks. During the 1960s deposit and loan rates were regulated and so were the investments of financial institutions through investment requirements. Spanish banks have been required to provide loans to specific priority sectors (traditionally, agriculture, housing, export-oriented activities etc.) or to hold public debt, both at below-market rates.

In 1969 the process of liberalization of the financial system started. The discount rate of the Central Bank became the reference rate to fix deposit and credit rates according to certain margins, with the exception of deposits of more than two-year maturity in industrial banks, loans of more than three-year maturity, deposits in foreign currency and interbank transactions, which are freed, and checking accounts, which have a fixed rate. Reserve requirements for the purposes of monetary control were introduced in 1970 and 1971 for banks and savings banks. In 1974 the process received a major impulse with the authorization of new banks and free branching (backed by enough capital), making the operations that industrial, commercial and savings banks were allowed to perform more homogeneous, reducing the investment coefficients and completely liberalizing interest rates for operations of more than two-year maturity. Monetary control was rationalized using reserve requirements, credits from the Central Bank to the banking system and open-market operations.

In 1977 interest rates of more than one-year maturity were freed and the process of setting all banking institutions on the same footing continued tending to equalize investment (down) and reserve coefficients across institutions and allowing savings banks increasingly to perform the same operations as others (including participation in the Central Bank money auctions). Nevertheless, until very recently savings banks were restricted to investing mostly in their own geographic region, thus cutting down the possibilities of diversification.

Savings banks traditionally suffered stricter regulations in terms of geographical limits to their operations, higher investment coefficients and distribution of profits. It is only since 1973 that they have been able to operate in the market for time deposits of more than two years; since 1975 they have been allowed to expand their number of branches but only within their own geographic region.

Foreign bank entry was regulated in 1978 with a view to restricting its participation in the retail market. Foreign banks were subjected to three restrictions. They could not obtain financing (through deposits, for example) in Spain for more than 40 per cent of the credits given to Spanish residents (the interbank market was excluded from this restriction). They could not open more than three branches, including the main office, and their portfolio of securities had to be of government issues. These restrictions remained in place till 1986.

In 1981 several interest rates were liberalized, including loan rates of all maturities and deposit rates of more than six months' maturity for more than a million pesetas. Bank dividends were also liberalized. In 1985 freedom of branching was complete except for foreign banks and for the geographical limits imposed on savings banks which have recently been removed. In 1987 all interest rates and service charges were liberalized.

The present situation and EC regulations

Entry

Spanish regulations discriminate against foreign banks. After joining the EC in 1986 Spain volunteered to suppress immediately the foreign bank requirement of holding exclusively public assets. It also established a gradual adjustment schedule for the period 1986–92 to deregulate the number of branches that an EC bank could open and the composition of its liabilities: (a) the upper bound on the ratio of domestic liabilities to loans to Spanish residents increased by 10 per cent each year, from 50 per cent in 1988 to 90 per cent in 1992; (b) foreign banks were allowed to open an extra branch in 1990 and two more in 1992.

Spanish regulations with respect to authorizing new banks are more concerned with guaranteeing the solvency of the entrant than with the degree of competition in the market. Thus, financial regulators not only require a set of objective conditions for the potential entrant (national or foreign) but also maintain a large degree of discretion. In particular, the candidate is required to argue convincingly for the necessity of the new bank in terms of showing that its activities are needed in a certain geographic area, depending on its population, economic characteristics, existence of other banks etc. This discretionary power was already forbidden by the early regulations of the EC (First Coordination Directive, December 1977), and even more clearly by the Second Coordination Directive, January 1988, which laid down the basic principle that any bank authorized by its home member state could provide a wide set of banking services in any EC country – the so-called 'single banking license' provision.[7] Therefore, after 1992, Spanish authorities had to authorize any bank, Spanish or EC, as long as the candidate satisfied the given conditions, and their discretionary power was abolished.

Reserve requirements

In 1988, Spanish private and savings banks were required to keep 18 per cent of a subset of their liabilities as deposits in the Bank of Spain. An 11.5 per cent share of these deposits received a rate of return of 7.75 per cent. The level of the coefficient as well as its return was changed quite frequently by the Bank of Spain. This requirement played an important role in financing the public deficit since a higher coefficient allowed a higher increase in the monetary base for a given rate of growth of an arbitrary monetary aggregate. Like other measures related to monetary policy, this requirement has not been affected by EC regulations. However, since the return on bank reserves is much lower than the market return and the reserve requirements of other

European countries were much lower, maintaining these percentages would jeopardize the competitive position of Spanish banks. Therefore, the government lowered the reserve coefficient to between 5 and 6 per cent by 1992, essentially suppressing the 11.5 per cent with yield.

Investment requirements

Since 1987, investment requirements have affected public debt holdings almost exclusively. In October 1988 the investment coefficient was 11 per cent (10 per cent devoted to public debt). The government in January 1989 committed itself to a gradual phasing out of the coefficients, with them disappearing completely by 1 January 1993.

Capital requirements

Since May 1985, Spain has regulated the solvency of financial intermediaries in a similar way to the Basle Agreement with respect to the recommended procedure. However, the level of the coefficient was substantially higher, 5 per cent of equity over average assets in 1987 (see Termes, 1988), and was one of the highest in the world. Also, the 1985 legislation eliminated the discrimination among different types of financial intermediaries and established a uniform solvency coefficient for all types (*coeficiente de garantia*). This coefficient required a certain level of capital depending on a risk-weighted measure of total assets; the weights included not only solvency risk but also interest rate and exchange rate risk. It distinguished six risk classes: from assets without solvency risk (which were given a weight of 0.25 per cent) to fixed tangible assets (which were given a weight of 35 per cent). Similarly to EC regulations, the solvency coefficient applied to the consolidated financial group, i.e. to the set of financial intermediaries (excluding insurance companies) that constitute a decision unit. In 1987, Spain adapted to the EC recommendations by requiring that no risk could exceed 40 per cent of capital. Loans to group firms (or board members) are penalized.

8.1.3 Crisis

From 1978 until 1983−5 the banking system experienced a severe *crisis*. Between 1978 and 1983, 51 banks (representing 46 per cent of the existing banks in 1977) involving 20 per cent of total 1983 non-equity liabilities were affected. The peak of the crisis was in 1982 (12 banks failed) and 1983 (21 banks, basically the Rumasa group which consisted of 18 banks). Five more banks were affected in 1984 and 1985.

The causes of the crisis were diverse but generally coincided with the experience of other countries.[8] First, the industrial crisis derived from the increase in the oil price in 1973 and 1979. Spain suffered the impact of the crisis more severely than other industrialized countries. The consequences for the banking system were more profound owing to the close links between banks and industrial firms. The industrial portfolio of banks was substantial and was not well diversified. Banks usually controlled several firms to which lines of credit were extended, leaving market criteria aside, because they were part of the group. The second cause was bad management and fraud. Apart from the phenomenon of risk concentration, banks in a bad situation, as is well known, have a tendency to take too much risk (attract deposits with very high rates and make very risky investments) because of either limited liability constraints or because they believe that the government will come to their rescue. This brings us to the third cause – the lack of monitoring of banks in trouble by the Central Bank. In fact, in Spain a Deposit Guarantee Fund (Fondo de Garantía de Depósitos (FGD)) was instituted only in response to the crisis, and was not consolidated until 1980. It has two main functions: (a) insurance of deposits up to 1.5 million pesetas and (b) intervention in cases of trouble. The FGD was not affected by the EC recommendation of December 1986, which encouraged those EC countries that did not have a Deposit Guarantee Fund at that time to create one according to certain criteria.

The crisis had an effect on the structure of the market, leading to a noticeable increase in concentration over the period 1980–4 and slowing down the liberalization process since the authorities were worried about the solvency and stability of the system.

8.1.4 Evolution of Competition

The evolution of competition in banking is marked by the slow loosening of the severe regulatory environment and the disintermediation process. This process has been going on for a long time, particularly since 1982 when the public sector started competing with financial institutions to finance the growing deficit through the public auction of Treasury notes (*Pagarés del Tesoro*). Large firms followed suit in issuing commercial paper. Nevertheless banks have kept control over the process by acting as underwriters for most of the issues. Savings banks have been less affected.

After the liberalization of branching in 1974 there was a large geographic expansion of banks competing through proximity to the customer and service instead of prices, which were regulated.[9] In two years the number of branches doubled from 5,600 in 1975 to 10,200 in 1977. Until 1982 they continued to increase at an annual rate of 8 per cent until the process stopped in 1985. Savings banks expanded more slowly since they were constrained by the higher investment coefficients that they had to meet. As coefficients eased they increased branching and had already caught up with the banks in

1984. In 1987 there were about 16,500 bank offices and 11,750 savings bank offices. In any case it appears that their expansion was more cost effective than those of banks.

Assets, liabilities and the disintermediation process

The development of securities markets, mainly public debt but also commercial paper, jointly with the (slower) development of the stock market and the role (minor up to now) played by new non-bank financial institutions (such as mortgage societies and Sociedades Mediadoras del Mercado del Dinero (SMMD)) has substantially increased the supply of substitute products of the traditional bank offer. In this way bank liabilities with respect to the private sector developed from being 84 per cent of total private financial assets in 1981 to 68.4 per cent in 1987 (Gutiérrez and Campoy, 1988).

Banking institutions have reacted by putting products (liabilities) in the market to match the competition of the public sector and firms, and have acted as underwriters for those securities in a substantial way. Nevertheless the increased competition shows mainly in the upper segment of customers (who have access to the new instrument) and does not have a drastic effect on margins. However, the endorsement and intermediary activity of banks gives them control of the market and has resulted in increased revenues for services and fees.

As for the development of the asset structure (see table 8.1), the percentage of financial investment in loans decreased dramatically for private banks and moderately for savings banks. The portfolio of securities decreased substantially for savings banks but only slightly for banks. Investment in the interbank market and in monetary assets increased for both. In particular, after 1984 investment in Treasury notes (*Pagarés del Tesoro*) increased substantially, even above what was compulsory owing to the lack of other investment opportunities. The disintermediation process was on its way.

Table 8.1 Asset structure for private and savings banks (per cent)

	Private banks		Savings banks	
	1982	1987	1982	1987
Bank of Spain and monetary assets	7.2	22.0	9.3	25.4
Interbank market	5.1	14.1	9.2	11.3
Loans	74.7	51.4	52.3	46.2
Securities	12.9	12.6	29.2	17.1

The numbers do not add up to 100 because of rounding.
Source: Trujillo et al., 1988, p. 301

On the liability side the most important fact was the decrease in the proportion of cheap deposits (see table 8.2). Long-term deposits were almost stable for savings banks and decreased by 20 points for banks. Initially (1980−3) they increased somewhat as customers attempted to obtain a high return. In the second period (1983−5) there was a movement towards negotiable liabilities (*pagarés bancarios*) and finally (1985−7) to endorsements of Treasury notes (*cesiones de pagarés del tesoro*). Changes were drastic for banks and moderate for savings banks. These movements could be explained in terms of tax and were also linked to the recovery in the demand for credit from 1985 onwards. Since then, institutions, rather than financing the government (purchasing Treasury notes), have been financing the private sector and transferring the notes to their clients.

Table 8.2   Liability structure for private and savings banks (per cent)

	Private banks		Savings banks	
	1982	1987	1982	1987
Checking and savings accounts	41.1	37.5	57.6	50.3
Term deposits and credit deposits	48.4	28.9	40.6	36.7
Negotiable liabilities	4.2	5.5	0.1	0.6
Asset endorsement	−	23.3	−	6.2
Other	6.4	4.8	1.5	6.2

The numbers do not add up to 100 because of rounding.
Source: Trujillo et al., 1988, p. 303

Players and lines of business

Banking institutions are of three main types: private banks, savings banks and credit cooperatives. The first have consistently lost ground in aggregate terms in favour of the second. In 1976, in percentages of total assets, the proportions were 71.6 to 25.9 per cent, while in 1987 they were 64.3 to 32.5 per cent (Trujillo et al., 1988, p. 294). Credit cooperatives account for the remainder (around 3 per cent) but we shall not deal with them any further. One of the reasons for the relative decline of banks is that they are more affected by the disintermediation process.

Banks are multiproduct businesses, but some institutions concentrate more on retail banking and others more on wholesale. Typically, savings banks concentrate on the retail business while industrial banks and foreign banks concentrate on wholesale business. Commercial banks concentrate on both. Indicators of bank specialization (Trujillo et al., 1988, pp. 296−7) show quite different behaviour of market participants. In 1987 the total assets per branch were 1,682 million pesetas for private banks, 16,644 million pesetas for foreign banks and 1,359 million pesetas for savings banks. Loans to individuals as a percentage of total assets were 4.6 per cent for banks and 15.8 per cent for savings banks. Another difference is that savings banks carry out very few operations in foreign currency. This is because they could not expand abroad before 1984. In 1987 private banks had about 14 per cent of their assets in financial instruments in foreign currency compared with 2 per cent for savings banks.

Savings banks are net lenders and banks, particularly foreign banks because of their restrictions, are net borrowers in the interbank market. Loan and discount operations, particularly with variable interest rates, are more important for banks than for savings banks, and the portfolio of securities held and mortgage credits is less important. Part of this situation was due to the increased restrictions (now abolished) in the operation of savings banks (the larger portfolio of securities, for example). Savings banks have a higher proportion of short-term deposit liabilities (checking and savings accounts), while banks have a larger proportion of temporary endorsement of assets.

The average financial cost per deposit for savings banks has been lower than that of banks since 1978, maintaining a two-point differential for a few years and reducing further in the late 1980s (see figure 8.1). This may reflect the convergence in the operations of both types of institution. For several years savings banks could not compete on price but, rather, had to attract clients by proximity to customers and offering services to a traditionally less price-conscious clientele.

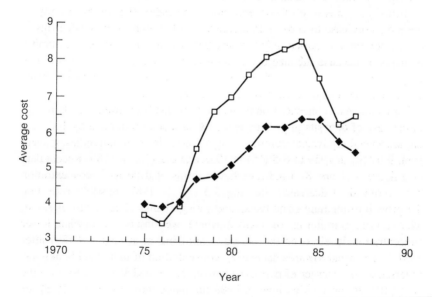

Figure 8.1 Average financial cost of deposits for banks (□) and savings banks (♦).

It is worth noting that, owing to regulations, savings banks concentrated their expansion in their regions of origin. Savings banks show consistently higher profits (both in terms of returns on assets and returns on equity) and higher net interest income, at least since 1980, and do not show the tendency of banks to decrease their operating expenses (mostly labour) as a proportion of assets (see table 8.3). In fact, the tendencies in staff costs seem to be the reason for this process.

Foreign banks are subject to severe legal restrictions on expansion in the retail market but, probably because of the strong position of national institutions in this market, they have not exhausted its limited possibilities. Foreign banks obtain financing mainly in the interbank market (60 per cent versus 16 per cent for national banks in 1987) and give credit mainly to large corporate clients; they specialize in variable-rate credits (up to 35 per cent of the market) and merchant-bank-type activities. Their share in the deposits market is small but increasing. Similarly, they increased their share in terms of assets up to 1986, to 6.85 per cent, and then declined to 6.4 per cent in 1987.[10] The reason seems to be the increased competition faced from national banks in the markets for variable-rate and syndicated loans, and because of the lower fixed rates given for other loans. The high levels of the interbank rates in 1987 also contributed to this relative decline.

Concentration

We shall use the Herfindahl index H, i.e. the sum of squares of market shares of firms, as a measure of concentration. The index H goes from unity in the monopoly case to zero in an atomistic market with many small firms.[11] Concentration in a market may increase because of a decrease in the number of firms or because the size distribution is more unequal. It helps to view the levels of H in terms of the equivalent number of symmetric firms corresponding to a particular value of H, i.e. $n = 1/H$.

For many years concentration in the industry had been going slowly down. In the case of deposits in private banks the H index (multiplied by 100) and the associated equivalent number of symmetric firms (in parentheses) went from 9.9 (10) in 1959 to 6.5 (15) in 1973 and 6.2 (16) in 1980. Recent data (see figures 8.2 and 8.3) indicate that in terms of deposits,[12] concentration has continued to decrease, reaching 5.5 (18) in 1987, possibly reflecting the growth of medium-sized banks and foreign banks. The picture is somewhat different in terms of loans[13] where we observe somewhat lower concentration levels over the period, stabilizing at around 4.9 (20) after 1981.[14] The trend towards decreasing concentration of individual banks was reversed by the merger of two large banks, Bilbao and Vizcaya, to form the new BBV. It can be seen how in 1988 the index moved to 6.45 (15.5) for deposits and 5.85 (17) for loans.

Table 8.3 Comparative analysis of commercial banks and savings banks in Spain

	1981		1983		1985		1986		1987	
	Commercial banks	Savings banks	Commercial banks	Savings banks	Commercial banks	Savings banks	Commercial banks	Savings banks	Commercial banks	Savings banks
Net interest income/assets	4.15	4.73	3.95	5.28	3.57	4.28	3.73	4.68	3.89	4.87
Operating expenses/assets	3.42	3.55	3.09	3.61	2.80	3.39	3.00	3.83	3.04	3.51
Profit before tax/assets	0.75	1.03	0.65	1.06	0.72	1.04	0.81	0.91	1.00	1.22
Staff costs/assets	2.31	2.36	2.08	2.35	1.88	2.20	2.10	2.65	2.12	–
Equity/assets[a]	6.48	6.04	5.94	5.82	5.52	5.51	5.68	5.38	–	–
Profit before tax/equity	11.54	17.10	10.94	18.19	13.04	18.92	14.36	16.89	16.69	22.27
Correction for inflation	−3.00	2.50	−1.20	6.00	4.20	10.10	5.60	8.10	11.50	17.10
Rates of inflation used	14.6		12.2		8.8		8.8		5.2	

[a] Equity equals capital plus reserves minus provisions (arithmetic average of years $n-1$ and n).

Sources: Bank Profitability, Statistical Supplement; Financial Statements of Banks 1982–6; OECD, 1988; Boletín Económico, Banco de España, March 1988

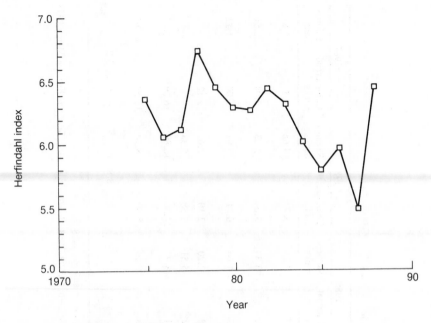

Figure 8.2 Herfindahl index for banks: deposits.

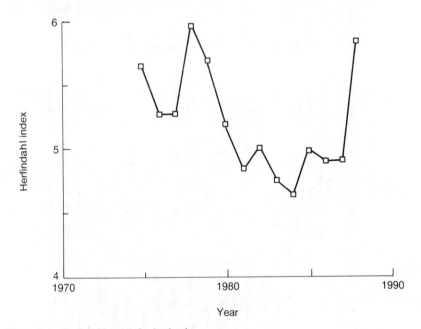

Figure 8.3 Herfindahl index for banks: loans.

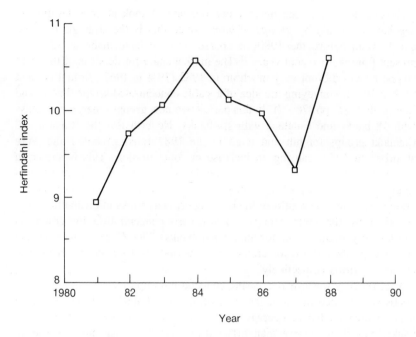

Figure 8.4 Herfindahl index for banks consolidated in groups: deposits.

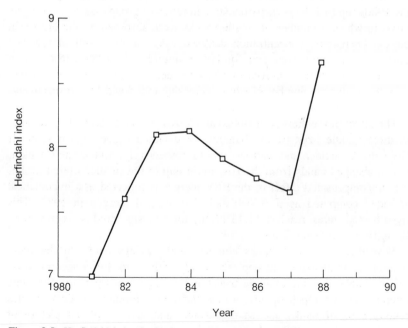

Figure 8.5 Herfindahl index for banks consolidated in groups: loans.

Nevertheless, it seems much more relevant to look at concentration in deposits (or loans) by *groups of banks* since this is the strategic decision unit.[15] Data before the 1980s is sparse, but we have made an effort to present figures for recent years.[16] The market share for deposits of the eight largest groups did not vary much up to 1982 (79.4 in 1967, 78 in 1980 and 81.2 in 1982), conveying the idea of a stable concentrated sector (Fanjul and Maravall, 1985, pp. 76–7). In this period two new groups emerged: Rumasa with 18 banks and Catalana with six banks. Nevertheless the Rumasa and Catalana groups (eighth and tenth in the 1982 ranking) failed and were absorbed in 1983, causing an increase in concentration. This is shown in figures 8.4 and 8.5, where we can see that the decline in concentration of single banks in 1981–4 is matched by an increase in concentration by groups, showing the results of the banking crisis as banks in difficulties were absorbed by the main groups. In any case concentration by groups is substantially higher than for individual banks. The *H* index was around 10 for deposits and 7.6 for credits in the period 1981–7, corresponding to 10 and 13 firms respectively.

The tendency towards decreasing concentration up to the beginning of the 1980s is explained by the higher rate of growth of small and medium-sized banks which tended to decrease the inequality in the size distribution of banks. This factor more than offset the increase in concentration due to mergers in the period. However, concentration increased at the beginning of the 1980s (up to 1984–5), particularly in terms of groups, as a result of the crisis in which a number of smaller banks were absorbed by the big seven banks. Thereafter, concentration declined again as the result of renewed growth of medium-sized and foreign institutions. In 1988 concentration increased: the *H* index moved to 10.57 for deposits and to 8.66 for loans, with the equivalent number of firms decreasing to 9.5 and 11.5 respectively. The reversal of the trend in concentration is clear.

The effect of the merger of Bilbao and Vizcaya was moderated by changes in three middle-sized banks: Bankinter and Guipuzcoano, which spun off from the Santander and Banesto groups respectively, and Urquijo-Union, which changed hands from the Hispano group to the smaller March group. The uncompensated effect of the BBV merger is reflected in a hypothetical *H* index computed as if Bilbao and Vizcaya had merged in 1987. This hypothetical index reaches 11.43 (9.36) for deposits (credits) representing 8.7 (10.7) equivalent firms.

Nevertheless, private banks compete with savings banks in the retail market for both loans and deposits. Deals with firms are concentrated on private banks, but increasingly banks and savings banks perform the same operations and compete openly. A final and more relevant index thus includes both groups of banks and savings banks and gives a global picture of development in the 1980s. It can now be seen that concentration levels are slightly higher in the loan market. Again, there is increased concentration up to 1984, with a decline thereafter for both loans and deposits (see figures 8.6 and 8.7). For deposits the index increases from 4.2 in 1981 to 4.6 in 1984, and then decreases to 4.1 in 1987. These represent the equivalent number of firms moving from 24 down to 22 and up again to 25, during that period. For loans these numbers are 23, 21 and 25. To explain the even stronger decline in concentration in recent years we would have to add to the growth of medium-sized and foreign banks, the above-average growth of savings banks, which in general are smaller than banks, that eat up market share of private banks. In 1988 concentration increased moderately with the equivalent number of firms falling to 24 in the case of deposits and to 23 in the case of loans.[17]

Concentration figures were not very high overall, not even after the 1988 merger. For example, taking as benchmarks the 1984 US Department of Justice Merger Guidelines, a market is deemed unconcentrated if H (multiplied by 100) is below 10, highly concentrated if it is above 18 and moderately concentrated for values between these extremes. Post-merger levels below 10 are not challenged, since implicit coordination among firms is assumed to be difficult and explicit collusion can be dealt with directly (through Section I of the Sherman Act). When considering competition among groups of Spanish banks H exceeds 10 only for deposits. In this case the BBV merger could have only been challenged in the deposits market (according to the Guidelines, since it increases the H index by more than one point) if the relevant market did not include savings banks.

Market shares

The changes in concentration are better understood in relation to the growth of the market shares of the different types of institutions involved: the large private banks (Bilbao, Vizcaya, Central, Banesto, Hispano, Santander and Popular, with the two first merging in 1988), the medium-sized banks (Bancotrans, Herrero, March, Pastor, Sabadell and Zaragozano, with the addition of Bankinter and Guipuzcoano in 1988), the foreign banks[18] and other banks, the two largest savings banks (La Caixa and Cajamadrid), and the remainder of the savings institutions. Figures 8.8 and 8.9 confirm the fact noted above that private banks are losing their overall market share to savings institutions both in capturing deposits and in the loan market.

Figures 8.10 and 8.11[19] show how the large banks started losing their market share after the absorption of banks during the crisis was complete (notice the large loss in the market share of 'other banks' between 1981 and 1984) and when the process of financial liberalization in Spain speeded up. They lost 6 per cent of the market in deposits and 5 per cent of the market in loans between 1984 and 1987. Most of the loss in the deposit market was due to the gain in market share by the two leading savings banks

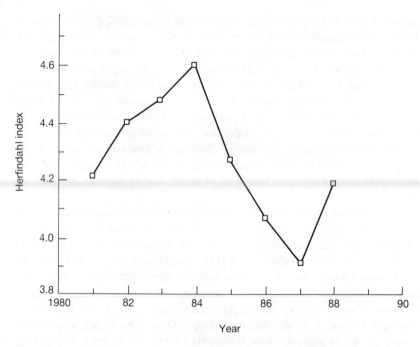

Figure 8.6 Herfindahl index for banks consolidated in groups and savings banks: deposits.

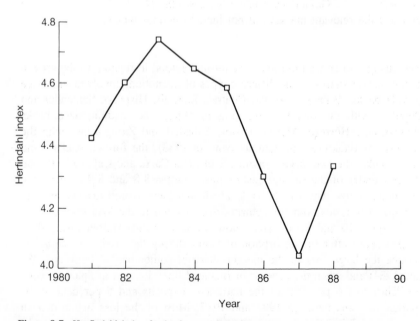

Figure 8.7 Herfindahl index for banks consolidated in groups and savings banks: loans.

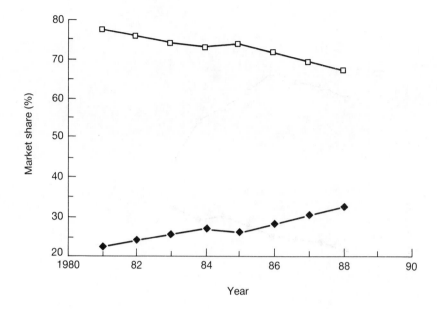

Figure 8.8 Market shares for banks (□) and savings banks (♦): deposits.

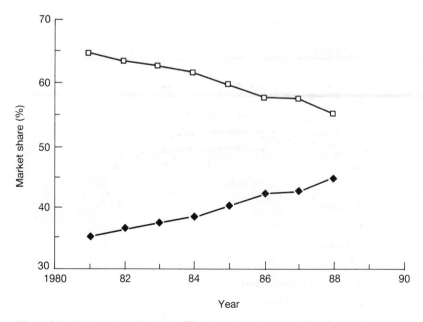

Figure 8.9 Market shares for banks (□) and savings banks (♦): loans.

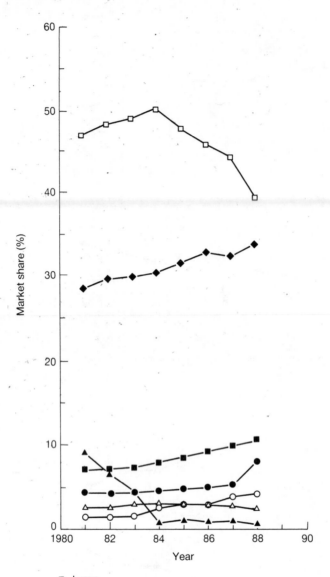

Figure 8.10 Market shares for banks and savings banks by group: deposits.

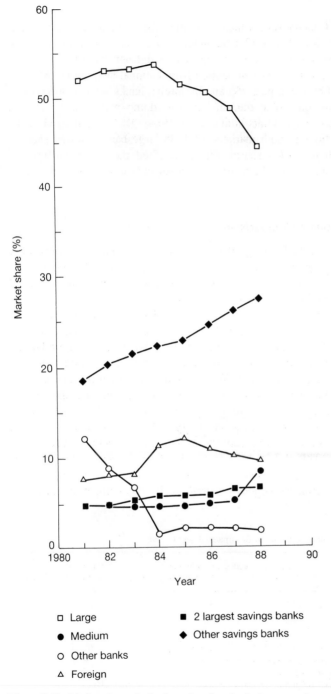

Figure 8.11 Market shares for banks and savings banks by group: loans.

(La Caixa and Cajamadrid), which accounted for more than 2 percentage points, other savings banks (2 percentage points), and the foreign banks (more than 1 percentage point). Foreign banks did not perform so well in loans, as they faced stronger competition from national institutions. Most of the business lost by the large banks and by foreign banks went, in aggregate, to savings institutions, with the smaller ones doing particularly well (an increase of 4 percentage points in the period 1984−7). Medium-sized banks held better positions in both markets. In 1988 large banks showed sharper reductions in their market shares which benefited the medium category, because of the spin-off of the three medium-sized banks mentioned above.

8.1.5   International Comparisons

In comparison with the banking systems of other industrialized countries the Spanish system appears oversized, sound, less open in terms of foreign trade, overpriced and not very efficient. Profitability and concentration levels are not very different from the international norm.

The Spanish financial system, defined as including credit and insurance institutions, appears to be of above average economic dimensions for EC standards (table 8.4), and is only surpassed by Luxembourg and the United Kingdom, which are international financial centres. This could either be due to overpricing (because of inefficiencies and/or market power) or be an indication of extensive financial services provided to domestic and foreign clients. The latter seems not to be the case. Table 8.4 provides some information on observed labour productivity. Column 1 divided by column 2 gives the ratio of labour productivity in the financial sector relative to the whole economy. This is 2.29 for Spain and 1.7 for the rest of the EC. This overperformance of Spain could arise because the human and physical capital employed in the industry is above average or by non-competitive pricing.

Table 8.4   Economic dimensions of the financial sector, 1985

	Gross value-added (% GDP)	Employment (% total employment)	Wage bill (% total for economy)
Luxembourg[a]	14.9	5.7	12.2
UK	11.8	3.7	8.5
Spain	6.4	2.8	6.7
Average of rest of EC[b]	5.1	3.0	5.0

[a] Data for Luxembourg correspond to 1982.
[b] Rest of EC includes Belgium, Germany, France, Italy and the Netherlands.
Source: Emerson et al., 1988

The ratio of column 3 to column 2 shows that the Spanish financial sector also enjoys an above average remuneration per employee relative to the rest of the economy. The ratio is close to that of a sophisticated financial sector like that of the United Kingdom which employs higher quality human capital, and indicates the possibility of non-competitive wages in the industry, possibly appropriating some of the oligopolistic rents that could explain high observed productivity (Steinherr and Gilibert, 1988).

The concentration levels of banking institutions in Spain do not seem to differ substantially from the European norm. They tend to be higher than for large countries like Italy, Germany or the United Kingdom and lower than for smaller countries like Belgium, Holland, Sweden and Switzerland. The market share of the ten largest institutions (in terms of assets in 1985) in Spain was just above the eight-country average (with data of 1984 and adding France to the countries listed above): 58.2 per cent compared with 57.5 per cent.[20]

According to 1986 data Spanish banking institutions (private banks and savings banks) compare favourably with Organization for Economic Cooperation and Development (OECD) countries in terms of return on assets. In terms of return on equity they do not fare so well.[21] This is probably because of the higher provisions of Spanish institutions as a result of the banking crisis which is manifested as a lower leverage. This is shown in table 8.5. Spain has tough equity requirements (a minimum equity-to-assets ratio of 5 per cent in 1987). Returns tended to fall during the crisis, particularly in 1982, but recovered later on. In fact real returns for banks adjusted for inflation, were negative until 1984 (see table 8.3) but were still much higher than average industrial returns, maintaining a differential of about 10 percentage points between 1981 and 1985. Only the United Kingdom showed a larger difference in favour of banks (Ballarín et al., 1988, pp. II-21, II-28).

Spanish banking institutions have very high intermediation margins, for example as measured by the ratio of net interest income to assets. They also have very high ratios for labour costs and about the highest operating expenses. This can be interpreted as evidence of inefficiencies derived from the regulated and protected environment but it may also indicate a retail-oriented banking system.

It is also worth pointing out that the interest rate spread for Spanish financial institutions is almost the highest in the EC, and is only exceeded by Denmark. In April 1988, the interest rate spread for Spain was 6.1 and the EC-12 simple average was 4.1.[22] This should be corrected by the different reserve requirements in different countries; Spain is a country with a high coefficient (18 per cent in 1988) to which the investment coefficient previously mentioned (11 per cent) would have to be added.

Table 8.5 Comparative analysis of banking systems, 1986

	1	2	3	4	5	6	7	8	9	10	11
	Pre-tax profit/ assets	Assets/ equity	Pre-tax profit/ equity	Operating expenses/ assets	Net interest income/ assets	Staff cost/ assets	Credits per branch (thousand ECUs)	Population per branch	No. of branches	Credits per worker (thousand ECUs)	Interest rate spread (1988)
Banks											
Spain	0.81	17.61	14.36	3.00	3.73	2.10	6,040	2,342	16,498	632	6.1
EC average[a]	0.65	25.02	15.36	2.23	2.56	1.44	29,776	4,988	5,396	1,348	4.1
OECD average[b]	0.68	26.63	18.03	2.22	2.40	1.28	–	–	–	–	
Savings banks											
Spain	0.91	18.59	16.89	3.83	4.68	2.65	2,782	2,960	13,062	500	
Four-country average[c]	0.83	23.78	19.97	2.62	3.42	1.65	7,097	5,362	13,769	780	
Eight-country average[d]	0.84	29.18	19.44	2.87	3.23	1.52	13,805	5,758	7,423	1,345	

In using data for comparative purposes it is worth referring to the methodological country notes published by the OECD.
Equity: capital and reserves (arithmetic average of years $n-1$ and n). In the case of Spain 'provisions' are eliminated from 'capital and reserves'.
The data for banks in columns 7–10 have been taken from the report of the Asociación Española de Banca Privada, March 1988. The data for Spain, Luxembourg, the Netherlands and the United Kingdom refer to 1987. The data for savings banks have been calculated using data from *Bank Profitability*, OECD, Paris, 1988. They refer to domestic branches, foreign branches of domestic banks (in the case of Germany and Belgium) and branches of foreign banks in domestic territory (in the case of Spain, Belgium and Italy). Italian data refer to 1985.
[a] Columns 1–6 include all EC countries except Denmark, Greece and Ireland, and columns 7–11 include all EC countries.
[b] Columns 1–6 include all OECD countries except Denmark, Greece, Ireland, Austria, Iceland, Turkey, Australia and New Zealand.
[c] Spain, Germany, Belgium and Italy.
[d] The four above plus Finland, Norway, Sweden and Switzerland.

Sources: Exchange rates at December 1986, *Boletín Económico, Banco de España*, March 1988; Asociación Española de Banca Privada, March 1988; *Bank Profitability*, OECD, Paris, 1988; population, *Labour Force Statistics 1966–1986*, OECD, Paris, 1988

Table 8.5 shows that banking institutions in Spain, particularly private banks, have, relative to other countries, a high number of branches of low 'productivity' as measured by credits per branch and population per branch (and also credits per worker). In terms of the density of automated teller machines (ATM) Spain, with 70 ATM per million population ranks above Germany and Italy, similar to Belgium and below the United Kingdom and France.[23]

According to 1986 data the large Spanish banks are substantially smaller than their European, US or Japanese counterparts. The largest Spanish bank before the merger, Central, was then 103 in world ranking in terms of assets and 47 in Europe. It was more than five times smaller than the largest bank in Europe and more than eight times smaller than the largest in the world. Relative to GDP, the large Spanish banks, before the mergers, were comparable with German or Italian banks for example. The largest bank in each of these countries represents, in terms of assets, between 11 and 15 per cent of GDP. The new Bilbao−Vizcaya ranks approximately 80 in the world and represents almost 19 per cent of the Spanish GDP.

Spain was one of the least open European countries in terms of trade in banking services, with ratios of exports over output or imports over apparent consumption of less than 0.6 per cent in 1984, compared with 2 per cent for France and Germany, and much higher percentages in Belgium, Italy and the United Kingdom. Like other EC countries, the trade in financial services concentrated mainly on non-EC partners (about two-thirds of the total trade) (Neven, 1989, tables 1 and 2). As for penetration by foreign banks, Spain did not differ from European standards, despite its protectionist and regulatory tradition. Excluding Luxembourg and the United Kingdom, the simple average market share of foreign banks in EC countries was 11.7 per cent, just above the 11 per cent of Spain.[24]

The interpretation of international comparisons must be treated with care. For example, the relative inefficiency of the Spanish system may have different interpretations. It may mean that the same levels and qualities of outputs and services are produced at a higher cost. It may also reflect the fact that Spanish banking is more retail oriented and that clients receive higher quality in terms of convenience (high number of branches), in which case the output composition is not the same and costs should be higher. Nevertheless it should also be taken into account that Spanish banks probably offer fewer financial products, particularly the more sophisticated ones, than their European counterparts. Ideally, indexes of the composition of output and quality of the different services are needed for relevant comparisons to be made.

8.2 Efficiency, Size and Market Power

In the previous section we have highlighted the fact that, at least by some criteria, the Spanish banking industry has shown higher rates of return than other Spanish industries in recent times. At the same time it has been argued that this is the case notwithstanding the evidence of high transformation costs arising from overmanning and the inefficiencies inherited from past protectionist and regulated environments. In view of the recent merger proposals two issues seem prominent: the relationships between size and efficiency, and size and profitability, and the extent of market power.

The purpose of this section is to explore more systematic evidence available on the relation between size and efficiency (economies of scale and of scope), size and profitability, and market power for the Spanish banking industry. Other issues will be dealt with in a summary manner.

8.2.1 Cost Structure

Even though there is circumstantial evidence to suggest that the Spanish banking industry, in the context of an overly regulated and comfortable business environment, has been fairly inefficient − in the sense of not striving to minimize costs and not operating on the frontier of production possibilities − we will not deal with such non-optimizing behaviour here. Neither will we characterize the inefficiency alluded to in the discussion of international comparisons. This inefficiency can be understood from two points of view: social and private. It is worth noting that what may be inefficient from the social point of view may well be efficient from a private perspective. A case in point is the extensive branch network of Spanish banks, potentially a source of social inefficiency, which may serve as a formidable barrier to entry for foreign banks. In this section we shall focus on the more manageable issue of the presence of size advantages derived from scale economies in the industry.

The results of international research in this area are not yet conclusive. Most recent studies using US data do not find economies of scale for banks beyond $100 million and they even report slight diseconomies of scope (Gilligan and Smirlock, 1984; Gilligan et al., 1984; Humphrey, 1985; Berger et al., 1987; Mester, 1987). Nevertheless it is well known that banking studies based on economies of scale suffer from a series of research design weaknesses. In some of these studies the joint production of deposits and credits by banking institutions is considered, but other lines of business (such as underwriting and foreign exchange dealing) are left out and banks with more than a billion dollars in assets are not considered. An exception is the work of Shaffer and David (1986) who estimated cost functions for the 100 largest US commercial banks. They found that the efficient bank scale ranged between $15 billion and $37 billion. This contrasts with earlier findings limited to smaller banks.

There is, however, a certain consensus that banking is not the sort of economic activity where one expects to find relevant economies of scale, particularly in the retail and small and medium-sized firms. Humphrey (1987) argues that the observed average cost variation between banks of different sizes is much smaller than the existing dispersion of average costs in banks of the same class. Consequently economies of scale cannot be very important in conferring competitive advantages.

In Spain, the most comprehensive analysis of this issue was presented by Fanjul and Maravall (1985) who estimated cost functions for the Spanish banking industry.[25] They used a simple Cobb–Douglas approach with cross-section data for a sample of 83 banks in 1979. A similar approach was used for savings institutions with a sample size of 54. The equations derived by Fanjul and Maravall use alternative measures of costs. Basically, they use operating costs (TOC), but also total costs (which include TOC plus financial costs (FC)) and that part of TOC (labour costs plus general expenses) which corresponds to TOC minus depreciation.

Output is the main explanatory variable and in the monetary version it is made up of the product of the number of branches (NB), the number of accounts per branch (AB) and the size of deposit per account (DA) as separate regressors. Additional explanatory variables include salary, measures of asset and liability structures, and dummies to capture institutional differences in the case of private banks (industrial versus commercial banking; local versus national focus). A second set of regressions are run with a physical definition of output: number of accounts N. Two new regressors are included: deposit per branch and the average value of checking accounts. This is not the case for savings banks where regressors other than output stay unchanged. Furthermore, the number of accounts per branch and the size of deposit per account are included as additional explanatory variables unrelated to output.

Estimation is undertaken using ordinary least squares and the authors reach an overall conclusion that diminishing returns are absent. Significant economies of scale are found with respect to both AB and DA, with independent increases of both variables by 10 per cent, leading to cost increases between 6 and 8 per cent. No such result is found for the number of branches but the evidence seems to indicate constant returns in this instance. The authors note that DA does not result in economies of scale when the dependent variable includes financial costs. In contrast, results do not change significantly when depreciation is deducted from the dependent variable TOC. Equations with a physical measure of output also show significant scale economies. Finally, statistical work with savings bank data confirms the results obtained for commercial banks, except for the case of a physical measure of output where constant returns to scale are found. Returns to scale are even more relevant for the case of DA. Most results reported by Fanjul and Maravall establish strong economies of scale with cost elasticities with respect to output of between 0.60 and 0.77. Only for the variable number of branches do we find values around 0.96, close to constant returns to scale.

These results show even stronger economies of scale than those obtained by similar previous studies for the United States (Gilbert, 1984). In those studies elasticities of operating cost with respect to output range from 0.803 to 1.036, depending on the output category (number of accounts) specified. The results obtained by Fanjul and Maravall using their physical measure of output are typically in that range, with values of 0.761−0.914 for private banks and 0.949−0.986 for savings institutions.

The study by Fanjul and Maravall is subject to the same criticisms as for all studies using a Cobb−Douglas approach: it cannot capture either the U-shaped average cost curves or the existence of joint costs. Their conclusion that overall the Spanish banking industry does not face diminishing returns to scale might be questioned by an approach that allows average cost curves with both downward- and upward-sloping parts (as shown by Benston et al. (1972) in the United States). Alternatively, allowing for joint production of several outputs might provide evidence in favour of size (Gilligan et al., 1984). Nonetheless this need not be the case, as shown for the United States by Berger et al. (1987). Preliminary evidence from the estimation of a multiproduct translog cost function for Spanish banks and savings banks by Delgado (1989) shows that increases in output per branch, keeping the number of branches fixed, would decrease average costs, while at the firm level there are no signs of economies of scale. In terms of economies of scope there is some evidence that they exist for certain classes of banks (foreign banks) but not in general.

8.2.2 Size and Profitability

The empirical literature on the impact of market structure on the performance of the banking industry has focused on the standard analysis of the relationship between profitability and concentration measures, generally using cross-section samples of local market areas (fundamentally for the United States) where such a statistical design is possible. The idea is that concentrated markets are more conducive to high price−cost margins and collusive behaviour. Gilbert (1984) presents a comprehensive survey of work up to the early 1980s for the banking industry, noting the measurement problems involved, and the general conclusion is that the positive relationship between profitability and concentration is weak.

As with the general empirical literature testing the IO structure − conduct − performance (SCP) paradigm, work on the banking industry has ignored the alternative efficiency hypothesis (Demsetz, 1973) for some time, and only recently has any attempt been made to test the competing collusion and efficiency theories. The efficiency hypothesis explains the potential relationship between concentration and profitability in terms of cost advantages of larger firms. Concentrated markets have large firms that are more efficient and therefore have higher profits.

One such study by Smirlock (1985) concludes that market share is a significant explanatory variable of bank profitability (which is interpreted in favour of the efficiency hypothesis), and that when this is accounted for concentration plays no role in explaining profitability differences between markets. Nevertheless the discrimination between the two hypotheses is not easy. Tests of this sort have been critically assessed by Schmalensee (1987) in a more general framework. Special care is needed to interpret the results of this type of regression in a structural fashion. For this reason, we shall next review the evidence for the Spanish banking industry only with respect to the correlation between market share and profitability.

Early empirical results for estimates of the relationship between size and profitability for the Spanish banking industry are provided by Lafuente and Salas (1983). They estimate, using a sample of 15 publicly quoted banks, a simple semilog − linear relationship between accounting profitability (returns on assets) and size as measured by the volume of sales for several cross-section samples in the 1970s. Their results do not show any correlation between profitability and size. The same exercise, but with returns on sales as the dependent variable, yields a significant negative relationship for samples corresponding to 1972 and 1976. Lafuente and Salas also report the relationship between size and profit variability as a performance measure. Randomness in profit is approximated by the estimated standard deviation of returns on assets and the idea is to test whether larger banking firms perform better in the sense that they show less erratic profitability. The results reported do not indicate any relationship between size and this additional performance measure.

More recent work (Ballarín et al., 1988) finds no statistical relationship between profitability and firm size for a sample of 135 private banks (and alternatively for 78 savings banks) in 1985. Returns on assets are regressed on market share as measured by the share of assets on total assets of the banking system. The results replicate those obtained by Schuster (1984) for several other countries and hold for both private banks (national or local) and savings banks. No relationship is found between the selected market share variable and accounting profitability.

8.2.3   **Market Power**

The data presented in section 8.1, in particular the international comparisons, are not inconsistent with a relatively high degree of market power in the Spanish banking sector. This hypothesis is reinforced by the fact that Spanish banks have been receiving much higher returns than other firms in the industrial sector. Is there any evidence that Spanish banks collude in terms of their quality offer or to keep prices above the competitive level, or that there are significant departures from competitive behaviour?

The few studies that have been made concentrate on pricing behaviour. Casual observation of the large expansion process of branches after deregulation in 1974 seems to indicate that banks in a strongly regulated price context competed along the quality dimension, providing convenience through proximity and free services to customers. An important issue in this respect is analysis of how the extension of the branch network and the location pattern compares with what would be optimal from a social point of view. Some theoretical location models suggest that, with fixed prices, competition in location tends to produce too much agglomeration. In other words, the spatial distribution of branches would not be optimal from the welfare point of view (Neven, 1989).

The first problem encountered by the analyst is the definition of 'competitive pricing' in banking. Banking is a multiproduct business in which products and services are jointly offered. We are thus in a differentiated product context in which pricing at marginal cost could entail not recovering the fixed costs of operation. A more appropriate benchmark may then be Bertrand pricing, in which prices are above marginal costs. In any case, as far as we know there is not yet a full-fledged model of banking competition which incorporates all the main relevant features of the banking business: multiproduct competition on the different products (both on the asset and on the liability side) and services, taking into account regulatory restrictions like reserve requirements and restrictions arising from the term and risk structure of assets and liabilities. With these limitations in mind let us proceed with the available evidence.

There is a temptation to read performance results in concentration indices following the IO SCP paradigm. However, it is now well known this is not without problems. Higher concentration tends to be associated with a higher probability of collusion to maintain prices above competitive levels or simply with a higher degree of market power. The Cournot model, for example, associates concentrated markets with high mark-ups over marginal costs. Nevertheless, Bertrand-type models seem to suggest that 'two is enough for competition', a point stressed in recent contestability literature. Potential competition may discipline even a monopolist if there is free and costless entry and exit from a market. One of the reasons that we have chosen the Herfindahl index H to measure concentration is because performance results can be read from this index, at least in one plausible scenario (and this is still arguable in the context of banking competition): Cournot competition. Then H is proportional, with a factor depending on the elasticity of demand to the sum of the relative mark-ups over marginal cost of the different firms weighted by market shares. A higher H then implies larger departures from marginal cost pricing.

For example, and only for illustrative purposes, according to the previous model and assuming that market elasticities are constant, the Herfindahl concentration indices presented in section 8.2 suggest that average mark-ups in 1988 industry, in both the deposit and the loan markets, could have increased by more than 13 per cent when considering competition among groups of banks or by more than 7 per cent when savings banks are included. If it were not for other deconcentration movements in 1988, the recent Bilbao–Vizcaya merger could have resulted in a noticeable increase in aggregate mark-ups. This increase, according to our 1987 hypothetical H index which simulated the BBV merger but did not incorporate later developments, would have ranged from 17 to 22 per cent depending on whether we looked at groups of banks only (22.5 per cent for deposits and 22.3 per cent for loans) or at both groups of banks and savings banks (17.65 per cent for deposits and 20.30 per cent for loans).[26]

A possible measure of market power of a firm is given by Tobin's q ratio, which is the ratio of the market value of the firm to the replacement value of its assets. This replacement value is in practice approximated by the book value of the firm (Lindenberg and Ross, 1981). A ratio of close to unity implies competitive behaviour, while larger ratios are taken to be evidence of market power since, according to the valuation of the market, the firm is expected to earn supranormal returns. The q ratio has the advantage of incorporating an adjustment for risk, but it is not free from accounting measurement problems when using approximations and relies heavily on the efficiency of the stock market as a pricing mechanism.

The ratio q for the seven big banks in Spain from 1978 to 1985 was (slightly) above unity only in 1978 and 1981, probably because of the effect of the severe banking crisis during that period. Nevertheless international comparisons of averages over the period 1974–82 show Spain, with a ratio of 1.62, above France, Germany and the United Kingdom (table 8.6). After 1985 q ratios for the big Spanish banks are well above unity. Even after the October 1987 crash they ranged from 2 to 4 (Ballarín et al., 1988). The evidence provided by the stock market prices must be treated with some caution, given that, as we have seen, the stock market was under-developed and generally controlled by the large banks. In particular the price of the stock of a bank was typically manipulated by the same institution buying or selling in the market.[27] The market value of the big Spanish banks is very high indeed. For some, it may represent between 50 and 70 per cent of the market value of much larger banks such as Citibank, Deutsche, National Westminster or Barclays (Gutiérrez and Campoy, 1988, p. 61). This can be understood as implying that profitable growth in the Spanish market, or from a Spanish base, is estimated to be very high by the market, or perhaps that the break-up value of Spanish banks is very high, or, as hinted before, that prices tend to be manipulated. A mixture of the three factors, with less weight on the second, is probably not far from the truth.

Table 8.6 *q*-ratios

Countries	Market price/book value (average 1974−82)	Market price/book value (1978)
France	0.89	0.94
Switzerland	1.65	1.61
Germany	1.34	1.43
UK	0.59	0.68
Japan	1.92	1.62
USA	0.90	0.87
Spain	1.62	1.10

Sources: Aliber, 1984; Ballarín et al., 1988

The report 'The Economics of 1992' (Emerson et al., 1988) includes some research on the prices of financial services in Europe. The percentage differences of prices of selected financial services in each country are shown with respect to the average of the four lowest national prices found. The latter is taken to be the competitive norm. Spain showed the highest prices of all the countries studied with an average mark-up of 34 per cent. Prices in Spain are particularly high for services to firms (foreign exchange drafts and commercial loans), mortgages and brokerage services.

Systematic econometric analysis of market conduct has only developed recently in Spain. For that matter, the banking industry has rarely been the subject of industry-specific econometric work that attempts to test the collusion hypothesis by attempting to measure market conduct for specific industries directly.[28]

In one paper Gual and Ricart (1989) test for collusive behaviour in the Spanish banking industry using quarterly data for the period 1974−84. They focus on a very specific submarket − term deposits (more than six-month maturity) − and attempt to test whether firms behave competitively when demanding deposits from atomized consumers. Data limitations preclude

Competition in Spanish Banking 303

firm-level analysis so that the authors work with industry-wide relationships. Estimation of the supply relation and the demand function yields a set-up where the market conduct parameter can be estimated due to the interest rate deregulation over the period (see section 8.2).

The authors cannot reject the null hypothesis of competitive behaviour. Although this might seem to disagree with the evidence presented so far, Gual and Ricart acknowledge that their results are only preliminary since they are working with aggregate data and the competition model proposed does not take proper account of the complexity of the banking business. However, the result is not so surprising since the study is restricted to a specific submarket, that of term deposits, where substitute products close to those of the banking industry exist, i.e. government bonds or commercial paper.

Another submarket where the possibility of collusive behaviour looms large is that of interest-bearing checking (money-market) accounts. Since 1987 interest rates on all accounts have been free, but the introduction of checking yielding market rates is very sluggish. Foreign banks, some small and medium-sized banks,[29] and some subsidiaries of the large banks[30] have introduced them. In fact there seems to be an inverse relationship between the interest given on checking accounts and the number of branches of an institution. Large banks offer them only to preferred customers without any publicity. It seems as if large banks and savings banks[31] are afraid of offering a new product that will necessarily make the financial cost of deposits more expensive. They know that a unilateral move would benefit the bank, but that other banks would follow suit and the outcome would be a transfer of surplus from the banks to the consumers. Therefore they do not introduce it through the main banks, but only through subsidiaries to respond to the competition of foreign and small banks. In other words, the (purely speculative) hypothesis would be that large institutions try to keep interest checking on the fringe of the market via a tacit agreement of non-aggression on this front.

Circumstantial evidence of anti-competitive behaviour has also been collected recently in anti-trust investigations by the EC Commission and the Spanish competition policy authorities. The EC investigation found no evidence of collusive behaviour and dropped the procedure, but the Spanish authorities are still examining the case against the banking industry, arguing for price fixing for some services.

The overall picture that emerges about the extent of market power is mixed. In certain dimensions of service and submarkets with non-bank substitute products competition seems vigorous; among others the collusion hypothesis cannot be dismissed. It is worth noting that this hypothesis is in fact consistent with the absence of correlation between size and profitability mentioned above. Such a correlation would appear from the 'efficiency hypothesis', for example.

8.2.4 **Other Issues**

It is well known that maintaining a leadership position in an industry such as banking, where managing information is one of the key strategic variables, requires a strong innovative activity at both the product (financial) and the process (operating) level. These innovative activities are themselves crucial determinants of the future market structure in view of the deregulation and disintermediation processes in financial markets. Commercial banks now have to compete in many markets with new competitors such as insurance companies, mutual funds and investment banks. This accentuates the multiproduct character of banking: money market accounts, mortgages, pension funds, cash management, underwriting, etc.

The Spanish financial sector has witnessed a recent explosion of new financial instruments fostered by the continuous move towards liberalization of the market. Foreign banks have led the way in introducing new financial products. However, the process is so recent that we only have scanty evidence of its main features.[32] There are many other issues worthy of empirical study. Among them we would like to mention the influence of reserve coefficients on banking competition (Romer, 1985; Repullo, 1988), and the role and extent of entry barriers in financial markets.

8.3   Competitive Analysis

The general picture that emerges from the data compiled in section 8.2 is as follows. There are six types of players, excluding the public institutions Banco Exterior, Banco Hipotecario (mortgages) and Caja Postal: the big bank groups, now numbering six, the medium-sized banks, the foreign banks (branches and subsidiaries), other banks, the two big savings banks and the other savings banks.[33] The new investment companies (there are about half a dozen) and small brokerage firms should be added to these when considering the securities business. The former tend to concentrate on doing business with foreigners and are trying to obtain foreign backing, particularly in terms of capital. The latter are composed of *agentes de cambio y bolsa*.

We shall now review the competitive position of the main types of players. In doing so it must be remembered that decisions are made by individual players and that in fact there may be substantial differences in the positions of players within the same group. Nevertheless players of the same type share the same basic structural parameters that condition their behaviour. Obviously there are factors that condition all the players in the market. The relatively low level of development and sophistication of the financial system is a very important general factor. In this sense an important fact is the lack of an adequate supply of qualified professionals in the field. There is a human capital problem in Spanish finance. Traditionally Spanish banks have not been interested in hiring people with university degrees for example. Things have changed, but only recently. Another factor that affects the Spanish players is the extensive branch network. This may prove to be a very important barrier to entry for foreign players in the retail business.

The big banks have been losing market share both in terms of deposits and loans because of the disintermediation process and in favour of the other players since the end of the banking crisis in 1983−4. Before that point they were increasing their market share through the consolidation process resulting from the crisis. Nevertheless, some of the mergers and absorptions involved banks in trouble that had to be put back into shape to compete.

The process of erosion of the position of the big banks including those affected by the 1978−83 crisis − first Hispano and later Banesto − has been met by different responses. Among the big seven the smaller are the relatively more efficient and better managed. In 1987 Bilbao and Vizcaya, with strong management, tried to merge with some of the larger banks − Banesto, Hispano and Central − with encouragement from the govenment. Bilbao in fact attempted a hostile take-over of Banesto but failed, and eventually merged with Vizcaya. The strength of the merged banks is in management and financial services (wholesale banking, corporate finance and stockbroking). This merger marked what seemed to be an end to the 'gentlemen's agreement' prevailing in the Spanish banking business. Later, Banesto and Central, the two larger banks, decided to merge. Their strength is in their industrial holdings with controlling interests in insurance, construction, electrical utilities and petroleum. Nevertheless the merger has failed recently in the midst of a struggle for control. Will mergers work? In any case they will need a lot of time to yield the desired results. Joint management problems and redundant branches and workers are not the least important issues. Other banks (Santander and Hispano) have made or are trying to make agreements with foreign banks in Belgium, Italy, France and the United Kingdom. The first merger attempts of Bilbao and Vizcaya were made with the idea of taking over banks which were poorly managed. It is important to note the active role played by the government in the merger process. Government intervention seems to be founded in the belief that a large size is necessary for competition in the European market and to prevent national banks from being taken over by foreigners.[34]

The merger projects can be interpreted in two ways. On the one hand they can be seen as an attempt to realize necessary economies of scale and scope and shake up inefficient management to face the competition of an integrated market. However, the mergers seem to have been made without much study of the economies that could be realized. If the results of Shaffer and David (1986) can be generalized to Spain, which is by no means clear, they imply that before the projected mergers the majority of the large Spanish banks were already of optimal size. After the two major mergers the resulting banks will be above this optimal size. On the other hand, mergers can be seen as a defensive reaction of large banks used to a regulated environment, in which they could easily coordinate their actions when faced with the prospect of fierce competition by more efficient and sophisticated institutions (that may also attempt to absorb them). On this view the idea would be to try to maintain high barriers to entry wherever possible and to pre-empt entry of foreign institutions. In this sense the extensive branching network and the ATM systems, together with consumer inertia and the goodwill of established institutions may prove to be formidable barriers to entry in the retail business. An open issue is whether the large banks will be able to maintain tacit agreements to keep profitability high (e.g. introducing interest checking only marginally) and to coordinate their actions to make entry of foreign institutions difficult (e.g. denying them easy access to the main ATM systems). A key aspect of future developments is up to what point banks will be able to compete in the new areas, particularly in providing services to consumers and firms. Large banks are now trying to develop capital market operations (Bilbao – Vizcaya and Santander seem to be ahead), build merchant bank units and launch pension funds for example. A potential problem for large banks in the development of investment banking activities is that they also have a major stake in industrial concerns and the question arises of how they are going to give independent investment advice. This issue may be important if we recall that one of the reasons for the severe banking crisis in Spain was the irregular and ill-founded practices of banks with controlled firms.

Large banks in Spain, as in most other countries, are caught in a situation of competing on all fronts − retail, wholesale, international and new financial operations − without, apparently, having a competitive edge in any of them. Perhaps some of the 1988 spin-offs or sales of medium-sized banks in Banesto, Hispano and Santander groups were a reflection of this state of affairs.

Savings banks seem to have a better competitive position in retail in terms of quality of service, which translates into a higher accumulated stock of goodwill, but this entails higher operating costs (operating expenses over assets; see table 8.3). The large savings banks also seem to have a more qualified staff than the banks. The financial cost of deposits has tended to become even with that of banks. The savings banks also have a more extended ATM system. For example, in 1987, the two private bank networks had shares of between 16 and 22 per cent of the national market (Servired had 26 per cent and 4B had 22 per cent), while La Caixa has 29 per cent of the Catalunya market and Cajamadrid had 52 per cent of the Madrid market (Ballarín et al., 1988, p. x−137). Savings banks can now compete on an equal footing with banks. As we have said before, savings banks were allowed to expand outside their local region from 1989.[35] This possibility of expansion induced a process of mergers and take-overs between savings banks which increased concentration in the sector. It also implied a higher degree of competition in the mass retail market and a geographic occupation of the few 'underbanked' areas left in Spanish cities (in Madrid for example).

Although convergence between banks and savings banks is rapid, particularly for the large savings banks, there are still some differences. Savings banks cannot issue equity capital but they can increase equity through reserves and provisions, subordinated bonds and, since 1988, participative shares. The only question is what influence will the fact that, in principle, they are not profit maximizers, having to pay dividends to stockholders, and with a board structure based on private and public representatives of local government, depositors, employees and representatives of the founding corporations, have on their behaviour. In summary, the competitive position of savings banks in the retail market is very strong, but perhaps lacks influence in the financial system because there is no 'central bank' of savings banks, which would increase their collective power.[36]

Medium-sized banks do well by specializing in particular market areas, such as the higher-income area of the retail market or servicing small and medium-sized firms including merchant bank operations, or on a regional basis. In fact some seem to follow a dual strategy, operating as a universal bank in their own region and as a specialized bank in the rest of the country.

Foreign banks have an edge in the wholesale business and in international operations in particular, and also seem to do well in the higher-income area offering, for example, checking accounts with high interest. Barclays and Citibank, for example, are expanding aggressively in well-to-do neighbourhoods in Spanish cities. Foreign banks are innovative in the Spanish context, but they try to accommodate the established business practices of national banks.

If we are to believe the Herfindhal index as an indicator of competitiveness in the broad markets for both loans and deposits, competition has been increasing since the end of the banking crisis in 1983−4. Prior to that it was declining owing to consolidation resulting from the crisis. The picture in 1988 was different, as we have seen (figures 8.6 and 8.7).

Nevertheless, the relevant concentration indices for an integrated market are global (European or even worldwide in this case) and not national. In those areas of the market where barriers to entry are low, national concentration levels do not mean much.

Apart from the fact that it is very risky to derive performance implications from structural measures like concentration indices, as we emphasized in section 8.3.3, it can also be argued that the relevant markets are not the large aggregates 'loans' and 'deposits'. This idea is reinforced by the fact that Spanish banking seems to be evolving into a segmented market with very different degrees of competitiveness. While higher-income retail business and servicing large firms are developing into highly competitive submarkets, owing to the disintermediation process and the increased competition of new entrants, other areas, like mass retail or servicing small firms, do not seem to be following this pattern. In any case the identified segments are probably still too broad, and a more refined analysis with well-specified products should be undertaken.

In summary, in wholesale banking competition will develop mainly between the large banks and the foreign banks, with some specialized smaller banks and some of the large savings banks as side players. This part of the market will be the most affected by the integration of financial markets, the development of the stock market and the disintermediation process. Competition will be fierce, with large banks having their industrial portfolio as an asset and foreign banks enjoying a better technological position. The high end of the customer retail market may develop similar levels of competition, particularly since new developments in communications technology may decrease the value of an extensive branching network and facilitate the entry of foreign and new players to compete with established institutions. The latter may include large commercial firms, mortgage societies and small investment companies. The degree of competition in the customer mass retail market will depend on the aggressiveness of the large savings banks and their willingness to play by the tacit rules established by the large banks or, on the contrary, behave non-cooperatively.

8.4 Speculative Remarks

What will the state of banking be in Spain after 1992? The first thing to note is that the answer depends on what happens in Europe. There are at least two important factors in this respect: first, the general development of financial markets and, in particular, the consolidation of financial centres in Europe; second, the degree of integration of the banking market in a variety of areas.

With regard to the first factor, will Spain develop a financial centre of any magnitude, say for stock and securities in Madrid and for options and futures in Barcelona? Or will Spanish financial centres be of second order, with most of the financial weight being concentrated in the large European centres (London, for example, absorbs about 40 per cent of the European stock capitalization while the Spanish market represents about 3 per cent). With regard to the second factor, will the European banking market be a system of national oligopolies with limited cross-participation or will it be more integrated? In particular, will barriers to entry in the retail and small-firm areas persist and be sufficient to deter foreign institutions from acquiring a substantial part of the national markets? At present market shares of foreign banks are high in the United Kingdom, Luxembourg and Belgium, modest in the Netherlands, Ireland, France and Spain, and very small in Germany, Italy, Portugal and Denmark.

An important issue in Spain is whether the present close interactions between banks and industry (recall that the large bank groups own substantial holdings in industry) will persist once the capital market develops. A closely related question is up to what point large banks will control the operation of capital markets. In any case it seems that in the near future the needs of financing the public deficit will continue to provide a central role for Treasury bonds in the securities markets, particularly since the compulsory investment coefficients will be phased out in the 1992 horizon.

Any exercise in prospective analysis must be taken with several grains of salt but let us try to describe a plausible scenario. The market is segmented. High barriers to entry, and high margins, remain in the customer retail area (with the possible exception of the high-income submarket) and the small-firm area. Barriers are maintained with the help of implicit coordination of the large Spanish institutions (e.g. by not selling pieces of the branching network, making access to ATM systems difficult etc.). Nevertheless, the large savings banks are growing through an expansion and merger process, profiting from their good competitive position in the mass retail market, and tend to operate like private banks. They are also entering lines of business which were previously closed to them. In the mass retail market competition will be essentially between banks and savings banks, and foreign banks will be only marginal. In the wholesale market, competition will be more intense and essentially between national and foreign banks. The close relationship between banks and industry continues. Large banks hold positions, control an important part of stock exchange operations, and consolidate a respectable market share in investment banking and some innovations (pension funds, for example). They are not the best in any particular area and they are not the most profitable institutions, but they are profitable enough. Nevertheless, some of the large banks may have trouble in coping with the new competitive conditions and may be taken over (by foreign banks?). Foreign and smaller banks increase their share in particular segments of retail and wholesale markets. In the mass retail market foreign banks have been mostly crowded out by the extensive network of banks and by the expansion of savings banks between 1989 and 1992.

In summary we can expect an increase in competitiveness in banking in Spain. This is already happening now, but will probably be moderate in some segments. It is also clear that the underdeveloped parts of the Spanish financial system, like the stock market, have a growth potential that will be realized in a few years. Nevertheless this does not mean that the Spanish capital market will increase its weight in Europe in any substantial way.

According to an EC report on the benefits of the integrated market Spain is the country which stands to benefit most in terms of reductions in the prices of financial services: potentially by 34 per cent on average. Our analysis seems to suggest that not all the potential price reductions will be realized. However, the effect of increased price competition on quality levels remains to be seen. In principle, high prices and high quality could be substituted by low prices and low quality, but 'quality' has many dimensions and the new product and service offerings (like ATM and home banking) may largely outweigh the decrease in service on other fronts (fewer tellers, for example). In any case, even moderate increases in the degree of competition which imply new product offerings and price decreases may have important welfare effects, given the starting conditions, in Spain.

8.5   Developments after 1989

Spanish banking had undergone very significant changes by the turn of the decade. These developments took place both with regard to regulation and in the competitive arena. This section briefly reviews the recent changes and highlights their implications within the prospect of further integration of European banking markets.

8.5.1   Regulatory changes

The trend towards deregulation of the Spanish banking system has continued and even accelerated over the period 1989−92. The hallmarks of this trend have been the substantial reduction of the compulsory reserve ratio and, even though it is not a banking regulation, the progressive reduction and final dismissal of capital controls. The reserve requirement was drastically reduced in February 1990 to 5 per cent with zero remuneration, down from 17.5 per cent with an average remuneration of about 4.5 per cent. In 1992 the reserves ratio was further reduced by an additional half percentage point for technical reasons.

At the time of the change banks were required to subscribe a special type of government debt ('certificados de depósitos') in proportion to the funds collected over the period 1989/III − 1990/I. This debt is only partially tradable among banks subject to the requirement, has a low rate of return similar to the previous average return on reserves, and is of variable maturity (ranging from March 1993 to September 2000). The mandatory investment established together with the new reserve requirement was essentially a lump-sum tax on banks, aimed at mitigating the effect of the reduction of the reserve ratio on public sector financing. Of course, by subscribing the debt the government was also able to soak the liquidity created by the reduction in the reserves ratio, but such a drain in liquidity could have been achieved by alternative means.

The second remarkable change in the policy environment has been the complete liberalization of capital flows, in the context of the entry (June 1989) of the Spanish peseta into the exchange mechanism of the EMS. Between 1987 and 1989 some temporary restrictions were introduced to limit capital inflows and prevent a further appreciation of the peseta due to high domestic interest rates. These restrictions were lifted between 1989 and 1991 along with some other restrictions concerning long-term borrowing. In 1991 some controls on short-term flows still remained; for instance, Spanish citizens could not hold checking accounts in foreign institutions or borrow short-term abroad. The final liberalization for these remaining controls was adopted in February 1992, ten months ahead of the schedule established by the European directive on the liberalization of capital flows.

In terms of deregulation, the introduction of credit ceilings was a temporary setback. These credit controls were introduced in July 1990 in the form of an advice by the monetary authorities on the recommended rate of growth of total assets. The rate was established at 17 per cent for 1990 (at the time of the introduction of the ceiling total assets were growing at a rate of 22 per cent), reduced to 10 per cent for 1991, and eliminated as of 1 January 1992.

Credit ceilings represented a crude instrument used by the monetary authorities to restrict aggregate spending at a point in time when the Spanish economy was overheated. Among other consequences, the introduction of the controls led to a temporary surge in the market for private debt ('pagarés de empresa'), which meant that financing could still flow to large firms that had access to capital markets.

8.5.2 Competitive Moves: Price Wars and Concentration

Two years after the introduction of deposit rates liberalization in 1987, an open price war broke out between the major firms in the Spanish banking system. Led by Banco de Santander and followed by Banco Bilbao Vizcaya, in the autumn of 1989 the major Spanish banks introduced high-return checking accounts (known as 'supercuentas') with aggressive marketing campaigns. Most large banks followed the Santander lead, and only a few months later similar competition emerged in savings accounts, the traditional stronghold of savings institutions which as a consequence were involved in the battle.

The consequences of the price wars in terms of margins, profitability and market shares have been significant and are partially illustrated in tables 8.7 and 8.8. Institutions that led the price war have, by and large, experienced a substantial increase in market share in total borrowed funds (even more in checking accounts, but, of course, that basically means transfers within the bank). However, in terms of cost of funds the differences among institutions have not changed significantly and, somewhat surprisingly, cost increases have been smallest among the most aggressive competitors in the price war.

Table 8.7 Market share of main banks in the deposits market 1989–1991 (market share as of June 1991 minus market share as of June 1989)

Bank	Change in market share (total deposits)	Change in market share (checking accounts)
Banesto	0.29	9.76
BBV	0.13	−1.71
Central	−0.11	−0.43
Exterior	0.12	−0.59
Hispano	−0.17	−0.64
Popular	−0.25	−0.92
Santander	1.09	3.56
Other banks	−1.45	−5.30
Total, banks	−0.35	3.73
Total, savings banks	0.35	−3.73
Total	0.00	0.00

Source: Gual (1992)

As recently as 1991 a new episode of competition took place as a result of fiscal changes in the market for investment funds. The new regulations allowed for the operation of highly liquid open-end mutual funds that enjoy significant tax advantages. The investment funds have to be managed by independent subsidiaries that, however, may be owned by a bank or a securities firm. This has shifted demand out of 'supercuentas' towards investment funds and further contributed to declining margins and some difficulties with loan financing as funds have been channelled away from traditional banking deposits. However, banks and savings banks have been able to maintain a substantial share of the investment fund business.

Increased competition in the deposit market has not substantially altered conditions in the loan market. Competition in this market has been dominated by the above mentioned credit ceilings which have limited competitive moves in the market for private lending (except for the public bank Exterior which was not subject to the limits). However, it is apparent from table 8.9 that the same does not hold for public sector loans where competition has led to a decline in the market share of official lending institutions. As a whole,

Table 8.8 Average financial costs of deposits by banks and groups 1989–1991 (as a percentage of total assets)

Bank	1989	1991	Change 1991–89
Banesto	6.47	8.56	2.09
Banesto Group	6.53	8.53	1.99
BBV	7.00	7.36	0.37
BBV Group	7.40	7.54	0.14
Central[a]	6.55	7.62	1.07
Central Group [a]	6.54	7.58	1.04
Exterior	7.32	8.67	1.36
Exterior Group	7.19	8.56	1.37
Hispano[a]	7.14	7.62	0.48
Hispano Group[a]	7.11	7.58	0.47
Popular	5.53	6.49	0.96
Popular Group	5.60	6.47	0.87
Santander	7.19	7.61	0.41
Santander Group	7.16	7.81	0.64
Large and subsidiaries[b]	6.91	7.77	0.87
7 medium size and subsidiaries[b]	7.18	8.25	1.07
Independent[b]	7.94	8.69	0.76
Large savings banks	6.61	7.52	0.91
Total, savings banks	6.41	6.86	0.44

[a] Data for 1991 correspond to the bank resulting from the merger of Banco Hispano Americano and Banco Central. As of 31 June 1991, the costs of both banks were the following: Hispano 4.28, Grupo Hispano 4.27; Central 3.62 and Grupo Central 3.64.
[b] Only commercial banks.
Source: Gual (1992).

restrictions in the loan market have contributed positively to profitability at a time when developments in the deposit market seriously affected some institutions.

Both as a result of the competitive moves just discussed and also as a consequence of the mergers attempted or completed in 1988, the period 1989–92 also witnessed several important mergers among the major Spanish banks, as well as some minor operations involving a large number of small savings banks. In the private sector two large savings banks merged in 1989, La Caixa and Caixa de Barcelona, and Banco Central and Banco Hispano Americano followed suit in 1991. As a result the Herfindahl index in terms of deposits (see figure 8.12 for bank groups) has gone up once more as it did with the Bilbao–Vizcaya merger in 1988, counteracting the underlying trend of less concentration resulting from the growth of medium to large banks.

Table 8.9   Market share in the credit market 1989–1991 (as a percentage)

Firm	Change 1989–91	Private sector loans 1991	Change 1989–91	Public sector loans 1991
Banesto	0.25	6.06	0.74	2.55
BBV	−0.99	6.89	0.77	3.94
Central Hispano Americano[a]	−0.45	9.90	0.99	6.42
Exterior	2.47	5.18	3.00	4.17
Popular	0.10	2.34	0.02	0.16
Santander	−0.18	4.41	0.63	1.31
Other banks	1.17	26.26	4.95	21.23
Public lending institutions	−3.18	6.45	−10.01	29.69
Savings banks	0.81	32.53	−1.08	30.53
Total		100.00		100.00
Pro-memoria Total credit (million ptas)	6,301,960	34,484,538	1,756,799	8,938,523

[a] To compute the change in market shares for this bank we have added the market shares of Banco Central and Banco Hispano Americano in 1989.

Source: Gual (1992).

An additional merger has involved two public institutions that operated as commercial banks and savings banks, and a set of public lending institutions, leading to a public conglomerate of a very significant size. Although the effect on this merger is small in terms of deposits because the public institutions do not collect deposits, the impact in the loan market is substantial (see figure 8.13).

The banking business has also been affected by regulatory changes in the financial industry at large completed over the last few years, as well as by the implications of the new regulation on the relation between banks and non-financial firms.

EC regulations will clearly tend to reduce the traditional presence of Spanish banks in non-financial firms, but the impact so far has been limited, partially because of the long adjusting period allowed for by these regulations. In the meantime some banks have rationalized their holdings selling some participations, most in foreign firms. Others are attempting to reduce their industrial holdings by the public offer of shares in their industrial corporations. However, the evolution of the stock market has not favoured these strategies thus far.

As for the reform of the stock exchange, the progressive liberalization of entry into the market as well as the gradual elimination of caps on fees, the introduction of continuous contracting and the low performance of the market in the downturn of 1990–92 have resulted in fierce competition. Transaction

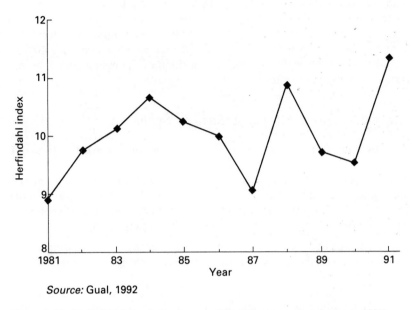

Source: Gual, 1992

Figure 8.12 Herfindahl index for banks consolidated in groups: deposits (up to 1991).

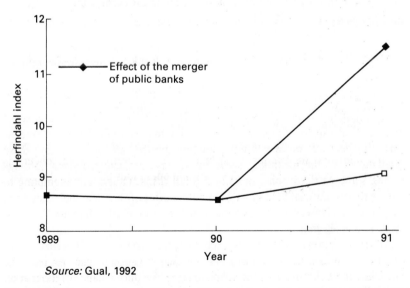

Source: Gual, 1992

Figure 8.13 Herfindahl index for banks consolidated in groups: loans (including public banks).

costs are declining and concentration in the market is steadily increasing, with a prominent role played by dealers and market makers owned or controlled by some of the main banks. The traditional control of the capital market by banking institutions has not declined and, although independent securities firms are present in the stock exchange, in other secondary markets and in the primary capital market, the position of the main banking groups continues to be predominant.

Appendix   Stock Market Reform in Spain

The government instigated a major reform of the stock market, reflected in the 1988 Reform Bill. According to de la Dehesa (1988): 'The central objective [of the stock exchange reform] is more transparency in all market operations: less insider trading, more security for the investor, easier conditions for Spanish companies to tap the market and the promotion of more competition.' The reform included the following aims:

1   the creation of a computerized national stock exchange – allowing a stock to be quoted either on one of the four stock exchanges or on the national stock exchange;
2   the establishment of two types of stock exchange member firms, *agencias* (single-capacity brokers) and *sociedades* (brokers/dealers) who are able to make markets as well as dealing direct with the public;
3   restrictions on ownership of the two types of firms (only individuals being allowed to take stakes in *agencias*, with no stake larger than 20 per cent – stakes in *sociedades* were also limited with different bounds until 1992, and might now be freed);
4   abolition of fixed commissions;
5   creation of a National Stock Exchange Commission, appointed by the Ministry of Economy, with wide powers and supervisory responsibilities;
6   centralization of all settlement procedures through a limited company jointly owned by the government, stock exchange member firms and banks (Servicio de Compensación y Liquidación de Valores);
7   the outlawing of insider trading.

An important issue still under discussion is the level of capital requirements for *agencias* and *sociedades* when markets are liberalized. The concern is that this level could be set so high for certain operations that only subsidiaries of large banks could afford to satisfy it.

Notes

1   This is not to say that there are no counter-examples. For instance, the competitive analysis of investment banking in the United States by Hayes et al. (1983).

2 See Neven (1989) for a discussion of the lessons for banking competition that can be derived from IO.
3 For a survey of existing models of the banking firm see Baltensperger (1980) and Santomero (1984).
4 In 1983, about 80 per cent of the financial wealth of households was held in the form of bank liabilities plus cash. In the United Kingdom and Germany this ratio was about 50 per cent.
5 These Treasury bills became the reference point in terms of maturity and return for other privately issued money market assets.
6 In 1977 the figure was 522.
7 The directive permits host countries to enforce their own rules on liquidity, business conduct and investor protection rules.
8 Theoretical analysis of banking crisis and regulatory measures to avoid them are given by Diamond and Dybvig (1983), Postlewaite and Vives (1987) and Baltensperger and Dermine (1987).
9 Nevertheless it was not unusual to give rates above the allowed level (*extratipos*) to large depositors. This practice was followed by new banks in particular in order to attract deposits, but the extent of competition in this sense was very limited.
10 This considers only foreign banks allowed into the country under the 1978 regulation. Previously existing foreign bank branches have a different legal regime and if included the foreign bank market share rises to around 11 per cent.
11 Sometimes the *H* index is multiplied by 10,000. This is done if market shares are expressed in percentage terms. In this chapter we shall multiply the index by 100 in our presentation of the results.
12 Deposits are taken to be customer resources in pesetas (*Acreedores*), which include mainly deposits and short-term bonds held by the public.
13 Loans are taken to be *Inversiones Crediticias*. Data from *Anuarios Estadísticos de la Banca Privada*, published by the Consejo Superior Bancario.
14 Results of the same type are obtained if we add savings banks to private banks and consider all of them individually. Other concentration measures such as concentration ratios give the same picture of the situation.
15 A group of banks usually includes the parent bank, regional banks, secondary trademarks (geared to different segments of the market) and investment banks, which are generally kept separate.
16 Figures on bank groups should be treated with caution because they have been computed simply by adding up individual bank figures. Nevertheless a limited check shows that the differences between the naive aggregation procedure and data from consolidated accounts for the 'big seven' banks are not generally large except in the case of the Banco Popular and, to a lesser extent, the Banco de Santander.
17 Savings banks include the public Caja Postal. Data taken from *Balances Estadísticos*, published by the CECA.
18 Banco Atlántico has been included with the foreign banks since 1984.
19 Market shares on loans have been computed excluding the public Banco Exterior. For deposits the Banco Exterior is included.

20 If the effect of the two projected mergers (recall that one has failed) is taken into account, the Spanish figure increases to 62.4 per cent (Gutiérrez and Campoy, 1988).

21 Three methodological notes are required at this point. First, a proxy measure of profitability (cash flow over assets) would probably be more appropriate for the period of the banking crisis since it is more difficult to manipulate. Second, if we were to compare real (inflation-adjusted) returns on equity Spanish institutions would fare very poorly, but the comparison is flawed since in bank balance sheets real assets are introduced at historical values. Third, comparisons for saving banks are more suspect because of differences in the methodology of interpreting the data in different countries. For example, in 1986 operating expenses for saving banks in Spain included provisions for pension funds.

22 Prime rates minus bank borrowing rates in per cent (deposits or saving certificates of one year) (Steinherr and Gilibert, 1988). We should use the real interest rate spread, i.e. the difference between the nominal interest rates on assets and liabilities with the same maturity, say one year, divided by the gross (annual) inflation rate. Nevertheless, performing this computation does not significantly modify the statement made in the text.

23 According to *The Economist Banking Survey*, March 1986.

24 Data provided by Steinherr and Gilibert (1988, p. 51) correspond to shares in total assets as of the end of 1987.

25 Previous work by Cuesta Torres (1983) dealt with saving banks.

26 If the projected merger between Banesto and Central, the two largest banks before the Bilbao–Vizcaya merger, had not failed, the predicted increase in margins would have been 65.06 per cent for deposits and 51.63 per cent for credits, when looking at groups of banks, and 52.94 per cent for deposits and 47.03 per cent for credits, when looking at both groups of banks and savings banks.

27 Econometric evidence of particular aspects of pricing in the Spanish equity market is provided by Rubio (1986) and Alonso and Rubio (1988).

28 Gelfand and Spiller (1985), following Spiller and Favaro (1984), have investigated the industry with a somewhat different aim. They tested for the presence of multiproduct oligopolistic interactions in the Uruguayan banking sector. The two products considered were loans denominated in local currency and US dollars. It was assumed that these multimarket strategies arose because of the existence of legal entry barriers. The relaxation of this legislation in the middle of the sample period provided a setting for testing the role of these barriers in the development of the multimarket strategies.

29 The medium-sized banks, as well as the small Banco de la Pequeña y Mediana Empresa, offer them in different degrees.

30 For example, Bankinter of the Santander group (now formally independent), Banc Catalá de Crédit of Banesto, Urquijo of Hispano (bought by March) and Banca Catalana of Vizcaya (now Bilbao–Vizcaya).

31 Some large saving banks also offer interest checking in a limited way.

32 See Polo (1988) for a study of the introduction of process innovations.

33 The division between the two big saving banks and the other savings banks is somewhat artificial. The former are definitely the leaders among the savings institutions, but the six major savings institutions are active and influential players.
34 The government is clearly worried about this possibility. Deutsche Bank's attempt to gain control of the Banco Comercial Transatlántico, which was unsuccessful owing to the intervention of the Bank of Spain, provides an example.
35 Nevertheless the government retained the possibility of introducing restrictions until 1992 and new out-of-region branches were not allowed to do business in insurance.
36 Their representative organ, the CECA, is itself a savings bank.

References

Aliber, R.Z. (1984) International banking, a survey. *Journal of Money, Credit and Banking*, 16, 661–95.

Alonso, A. and Rubio, G. (1988) Overreaction in the Spanish equity market. Southern Europe Economic Discussion Series, Discussion Paper 59.

Ballarín, E., Gual, J. and Ricart, J. (1988) Rentabilidad y competitividad en el sector bancario español. Un estudio sobre la distribución de servicios financieros en España, Universidad de Navarra, mimeo.

Baltensperger, E. (1980) Alternative approaches to the theory of the banking firm. *Journal of Monetary Economics*, 6, 1–37.

Baltensperger, E. and Dermine, J. (1987) Banking deregulation in Europe. *Economic Policy*, 4, 64–109.

Benston, G., Berger, A., Hanweck, G. and Humphreys, D. (1972) Economics of scale of financial institutions, *Journal of Money, Credit and Banking*, 4, 312–39.

Berger, A., Hanweck, G. and Humphrey, B. (1987) Competitive viability in banking: a restructuring and reassessment. *Journal of Money, Credit and Banking*, 14, 435–56.

Boletin Economico, Banco de España (March 1988) La rentabilidad del sistema bancario español.

Cuesta Torres, F. (1985) Sobre economias de escala en entidades financieras: panorama de la literatura existente. Documento N.8, Fundación FIES, Madrid.

de la Dehesa, G. (1988) *Euromoney*, 1.

Delgado, F.-L. (1989) Economías de escala en el sistema bancario español, mimeo.

Demsetz, H. (1973) Industry structure, market rivalry, and public policy. *Journal of Law and Economics*, 16, 1–10.

Diamond, D. and Dyvbig, P. (1983) Bank runs, deposit insurance, and liquidity. *Journal of Political Economy*, 91, 401–19.

Emerson, M. et al. (1988) The economics of 1992. *European Economy*, 35, 91–2.

Fanjul, O. and Maravall, F. (1985) *La eficiencia del sistema bancario español*, Alianza Universidad, Madrid.

Gelfand, M. and Spiller, P. (1985) Entry barriers and multiproduct oligopolistic strategies, mimeo.

Gilbert, R.A. (1984) Bank market structure and competition. *Journal of Money, Credit and Banking*, 16, 617−45.

Gilligan, T.W. and Smirlock, M. (1984) An empirical study of joint production and scale economies in commercial banking. *Journal of Banking and Finance*, 8, 67−77.

Gilligan, T.W., Smirlock, M. and Marshall, W. (1984) Scale and scope economies in the multi-product banking firm. *Journal of Monetary Economics*, 13, 393−405.

Gual, J. (1992) *Evolución de la competencia en el sector bancario español*. Report prepared for BBV Foundation, January.

Gual, J. and Ricart, J.E. (1989) Market power in the Spanish banking industry, IESE Research Paper 151B, May.

Gutiérrez, F.and Campoy, J. (1988) Eficiencia y competencia en el sistema bancario español. *Boletín Económico, Banco de España*, December.

Hayes, S., Spence, A.M. and Marks, D.P. (1983): *Competition in the Investment Banking Industry*. Cambridge, MA: Harvard University Press.

Humphrey, D. (1985) Costs and scale economies in bank intermediation. In Aspinwall, D. and Eisenbeis,B. (eds), *Handbook for Bank Strategy*. New York: Wiley.

Humphrey, D. (1987) Cost dispersion and the measurement of economies in banking, mimeo.

Lafuente, A. and Salas, V. (1983) Concentración y resultados de las empresas en la economia española. *Cuadernos Económicos del ICE*, no. 22−23.

Lindenberg, E. and Ross, S. (1981) Tobin's *q* ratio and industrial organization. *Journal of Business*, 1−32.

Mester, L. (1987) A multiproduct cost study of savings and loans associations. *Journal of Finance*, 62, 423−45.

Neven, D. (1989) Structural adjustment in European retail banking. Some views from industrial organization, mimeo.

OECD (1988) *Espagne, 1987-88, Etudes Economiques de l'OCDE*. Paris: OECD.

Polo, Y. (1988) *Desarrollo de nuevos productos: aplicaciones a la economia española*. Zaragoza: Prensas Universitarias ed. Zaragoza.

Postlewaite, A. and Vives, X. (1987) Bank runs as an equilibrium phenomenon. *Journal of Political Economy*, 95, 485−91.

Repullo, R. (1988) Los efectos ecconómicos de los coeficientes bancarios: un análisis teórico, *Investigaciones Economicas*, 13, (2), 227−44.

Romer, D. (1985) Financial intermediation, reserves requirements, and inside money. *Journal of Monetary Economics*, 16, 175−94.

Rubio, G. (1986) Size, liquidity and valuation. Southern Europe Economic Discussion Series, Discussion Paper 41.

Santomero, A. (1984) Modelling the banking firm. *Journal of Money, Credit and Banking*, 16 (4), 577−602.

Schmalensee, R. (1987) Collusion versus differential efficiency: testing alternative hypotheses. *Journal of Industrial Economics*, 35 (4), 399−426.

Schuster, L. (1984) Profitability and market share of banks. *Journal of Bank Research*, 15, 56−61.

Shaffer, S. and David, E. (1986) Economies of superscale and interstate expansion. Report 8612, Federal Reserve of New York.

Smirlock, M. (1985) Evidence of the (non)relationship between concentration and profitability in banking, *Journal of Money, Credit and Banking*, 17, February, 69−83.

Spiller, P. and Favaro, E. (1984) The effects of entry regulation on oligopolistic interaction: the Uruguayan banking sector. *Rand Journal*, 15 (2), 244−54.

Steinherr, A. and Gilibert, P. (1988) The impact of freeing trade in financial services and capital movements on the European banking industry, mimeo.

Termes, R. (1988) Informe del Presidente, Asociación Española de Banca Privada.

Trujillo, J., Cuervo-Árango, C. and Vargas, F. (1988) *El sistema financiero español* (3rd edn). Barcelona: Ariel Economia.

US Department of Justice (1984) *Merger Guidelines*. Washington, DC: US Government Printing Office.

Comment

Rafael Repullo

In this chapter the extent of competition in Spanish banking was discussed in order to assess the likely developments after 1992. The main conclusions of the chapter are contained in sections 8.3, 8.4 and 8.5, and I will come to these below. First, however, I will comment on some of the arguments leading to these conclusions.

It is claimed that the chapter is written in the spirit of what is called the 'industrial organization (IO) of banking'. I am afraid that this is rather an overstatement. With regard to the IO of banking, there is little more than the use of the Herfindahl concentration index in section 8.1, and the discussion in section 8.2 of the relationship between market power and profitability in terms of this index. I should add this is not entirely the authors' fault: there is at present no theoretical model of imperfect competition in banking which could be used to understand what might be going on in this area. Unfortunately, borrowing the traditional IO paradigm will not be enough.

Take, for example, the case of the various measures of concentration in Spanish banking, which are given some space in the chapter. We can ask ourselves: what do we learn from them? The answer is, I am afraid, not much. To support this claim, look at figures 8.4 or 8.5 which depict the evolution of the Herfindahl index for commercial banks (consolidated in bank groups) and savings banks. (Incidentally, given the operational convergence in recent years of commercial and savings banks, I think that it is more appropriate to take them together, as in figures 8.8 and 8.9, rather than to consider only commercial banks, as in figures 8.2 − 8.5.) Looking at these figures, it appears that not much happened in Spanish banking in the 1980s; in particular, for deposits (and similarly for loans) the equivalent number of banks increased from 24 in 1981 to 25 in 1988. Unfortunately, the measures of concentration tell us very little about competition in the banking industry, mainly because there is not a single market in which all these banks compete. (For example, at that time you could find in Spain banks paying almost zero interest on checking accounts located next to banks paying 10 per cent or more for the same type of account.) Thus, contrary to what is suggested by the evolution of the Herfindahl concentration index, I believe that in recent years there has been a significant increase in the degree of competition in Spanish banking which has been brought about mainly by the foreign banks in the wholesale market, and by the saving banks in retailing.

A feature of the prevailing regulation of banking in Spain which receives little attention in section 8.1, compared for example with chapter 7 on the Italian case, is the impact of reserve and investment requirements. The fact that Spanish banks in 1988 were required to keep 18 per cent of a subset of their liabilities as deposits in the Bank of Spain, and a further 10 per cent in Treasury notes is something that must have made a difference. The problem, as noted above, is that without a model of imperfect competition in banking it is difficult to assess the impact of these requirements (and of its gradual reduction as 1992 approached) on deposit and borrowing rates (who bears the cost?), on banks' profits and, last but not least, on bank competition.

Most of section 8.2 is devoted to summarizing various empirical findings about economies of scale (which seem to be present), size and profitability (which do not show any correlation) and market power (where the results are somewhat mixed but point towards some degree of non-competitive behaviour). Somewhat surprisingly, the study by Delgado (1989), estimating a translog cost function with two outputs (intermediation and services) for commercial banks, savings banks and foreign banks, receives too little attention in this section.

In sections 8.3, 8.4 and 8.5, which contain the main conclusions of the chapter, the authors review the competitive position of the principal players, namely the big banks, the medium-sized banks, the rest of the banks, the two large savings banks, the rest of the savings banks and the foreign banks. The only comments that I have on this are the following.

1 I do not agree with the statement that 'the relatively low level of development and sophistication of the financial system . . . is a very important general factor . . . that conditions all the players in the market'. This was certainly not the case for the Spanish banking system of 1989.
2 I do not agree with the statement that 'there is a human capital problem in Spanish finance'. This may be true for some institutions (in particular, some of the big banks), but is not the general rule.
3 I do not understand the statement about savings banks lacking more influence because 'there is no "central bank" of saving banks'. In fact, they have CECA, whereas the commercial banks have nothing of this sort.
4 Finally, I do not agree with the statement about 'the relevant indices of concentration being global (European or worldwide) and not national'. As I argued above, in many areas (in particular, in retailing) there is not a single market even at a regional level.

Leaving aside these minor comments, I basically agree with what is said about the principal players. They will be playing in three somewhat separated markets: the mass retail market, the high income retail market and the wholesale market. Competition will be particularly strong in the second and, particularly, the third of these markets, while high barriers to entry, in the form of an extensive branching network, will protect the margin of the incumbents in the first market. How long will this protection last? It is very difficult to say, but it seems that developments outside the banking system, in particular the evolution of the new market for public debt and the reform of the stock market, will play some role.

9

Portuguese Banking in the Single European Market

Antonio M. Borges

The Portuguese banking sector has been undergoing rapid change. Keeping up with the development of the financial sector, Portuguese banks have been preparing for a radically different context with many challenges and opportunities, but also with serious clouds on the horizon. The main component of this new context was the expected impact of increased competition. The authorization of new private banks, starting in 1984, began to introduce some aspects of a healthy competitive spirit. But, naturally, it was during the transition towards the European single market in financial services that the full impact of competition and deregulation was felt.

The development of the banking sector has been characterized by a rapid liberalization process, which led to an inevitable rationalization in the way that banks and other financial insititutions operate. The climate of competition that began to dominate the economic environment of banks necessitated a fundamental change in the factors which determine profitability. To survive and to continue its development, the Portuguese banking sector needed to compete with other financial institutions as well as with foreign banks, which for the most part start from much more solid competitive positions.

In this as in other elements of the Portuguese economy, competition in the long term will bring important gains in efficiency and a substantial increase in the rate of economic progress. In the particular case of the banking sector, however, profitability and competitiveness have been substantially curtailed by factors related to government intervention in the economy which damaged the sector's ability to develop and which were a serious source of concern about its capacity to face the impact of liberalization and foreign competition.

In assessing Portugal's integration in the single European market for financial services, it is important to analyse in some detail the impact of certain restrictions and distortions which have substantially constrained the

Many of the ideas presented in this chapter have benefited from discussions in Portugal at various seminars on banking after 1992 (Borges, 1988).

way that banks operate, reduced their ability to adapt and limited their competitiveness. Among these, the most important have been of three types:

1 the persistence of a system of intervention on the part of the government which is designed primarily to provide a simple and economic means of financing a large budget deficit;
2 the predominance of monetary policy as the only operative instrument of economic stabilization, with all its well-known consequences in terms of its impact on the banking sector;
3 the coexistence of fundamentally distinct economic objectives for nationalized and private banks and the obvious contrast between their respective competitive positions.

There is still a large potential for improvement in the efficiency and competitiveness of Portuguese banks; however, as long as these important sources of vulnerability persist, their chances of survival against foreign competition and their ability to keep up with a rapidly changing financial sector will always be limited. Each of these points will be covered separately in this chapter.

9.1   The Exceptional Taxation of the Banking Sector

Despite some recent progress, Portugal continues to live with a very large budget deficit (figure 9.1). In 1989 the public sector borrowing requirement (PSBR) remained above 8 per cent of gross national product (GNP). It was a rather low value — about half — relative to the peaks in some episodes of Portugal's economic policy, but it was still an unsustainable deficit.

Given such large borrowing requirements, only a limited set of options are available to the government to finance it. Clearly the monetization of the deficit or the increase in the public debt cannot be used indefinitely, since they lead to dramatic problems of instability, which the government is not prepared to accept.

An increase in the money supply may always be a natural way of financing part of any government deficit. In the case of Portugal, however, this should only be a small percentage of the total deficit, since otherwise the increase in liquidity would be sufficient to generate intolerable inflation levels and current account deficits which would be impossible to finance. Two recent experiences with very high inflation and large foreign deficits have convinced the authorities of the dangers of such a route.

Alternatively, an increase in the public debt in the hands of the public may look like a less dangerous approach. Indeed, this has been the approach followed since 1986, with a substantial percentage of the PSBR covered by

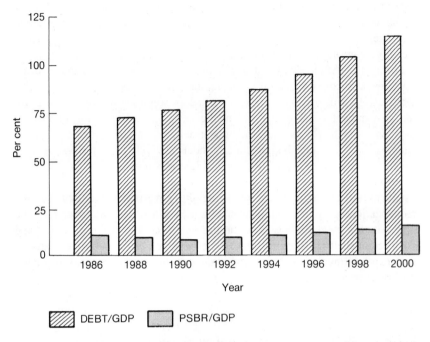

	1986	1988	1990	1992	1994	1996	1998	2000
GDP	4,418.8	5,909	7,177	8,718	10,589	12,861	15,622	18,974
Public debt (% GDP)	68.2	72.8	76.5	81.3	87.6	95.1	104.1	114.6
Interest (% GDP)	9.2	9.6	8.5	9.6	10.9	12.2	13.7	15.5
Primary deficit (% GDP)	−1.8	−0.2	−0.2	−0.2	−0.2	−0.2	−0.2	−0.2
PSBR (% GDP)	10.3	9.5	8.4	9.5	10.7	12.1	13.6	15.3

Assumptions for simulation: GDP real growth, 3%; domestic inflation, 7%; external inflation, 3; public expenses and revenues constant (in % GDP); real interest rate of Treasury bills (BTs), 4%; government borrowing from the banking sector at a real rate of 2%; constant proportion of financing, BTs 60%; and banking sector 40%.

Figure 9.1 Simulation of the development of public debt.

Treasury bills and, to a lesser extent, by long-term bonds. Treasury bills and bonds have obvious advantages as sources of government finance: they represent new instruments available for financial investors and lead to a more accurate estimate of the cost of the public debt. However, it is precisely because they have to pay an attractive interest that their utilization cannot exceed certain limits. In fact, once the budget deficit reaches levels similar to that of Portugal, if a large part of it is financed by issuing debt at positive real interest rates the deficit becomes explosive since interest payments will steadily grow more than revenues.

Portugal's deficit already exceeds interest payments; in other words, revenue exceeds expenditure, excluding interest on the public debt. Obviously it will become impossible to adopt solutions which will magnify the government's financial problems, generating an expansion of interest payments which will increase the budget deficit as a percentage of GNP. A simple projection of the budget deficit, under relatively plausible assumptions for real interest rates and GNP growth, illustrates how quickly the growth in government debt and interest payments reaches intolerable proportions.

Given the impossibility of financing the government's deficit through monetization or by increasing the public debt at a faster and faster rate, the only solution available has been the use of a tax, which is not explicit and not accounted for, which is paid by the banking sector and which falls on financial intermediation. In practice, this form of taxation consists in placing government debt with the Central Bank, with a corresponding increase in the monetary base coupled with a strict control of money creation through the imposition of credit ceilings on banks. This double intervention in the banking sector leads to a much faster growth in deposits than in credit, forcing banks to maintain an increasing proportion of their assets in idle applications as excess reserves, which are obviously available to finance the government deficit at a very low cost − in fact partly free of any cost. This is of course a tax like any other, which falls on banking activity in its main component − financial intermediation − and which is paid by depositors, who obtain a lower interest than otherwise, and borrowers, who pay more for credit than is desirable.[1]

In the absence of other alternatives and given the impossibility of solving the problem by a substantial reduction in the government deficit, this has been the only viable solution to financing the public sector. Clearly, however, the systematic increase in the level of taxation of an important sector of activity leads to cumulative distortions, the cost of which is much too high; naturally the consequence has been a substantial weakness of Portuguese banks relative to competitors which are not burdened with such a high level of taxation.

Two indicators display clearly the economic impact of this policy. First, the intermediation margin has increased steadily and is now at very high levels. Banks have to recover on a smaller and smaller base the cost of interest payments made to depositors. Thus borrowers pay a high price for funds, while depositors receive a poor return on their savings, and yet bank profitability has been very low or negative, since interest on loans net of interest paid to depositors has been either negative or too small to cover operating costs. Second, the imposition of strict credit controls, plus the priority given to government financial requirements, implies an insufficient growth in private sector credit, with obvious consequences for economic growth. In fact, in real terms, total credit has stagnated or even decreased since 1983 which, given the rate of economic growth achieved since then, represents a strong brake with costly consequences.

Since credit to the government sector has grown at a rapid pace, the productive sector − private plus nationalized industries − has had to survive with smaller and smaller levels of credit in real terms (figure 9.2). In

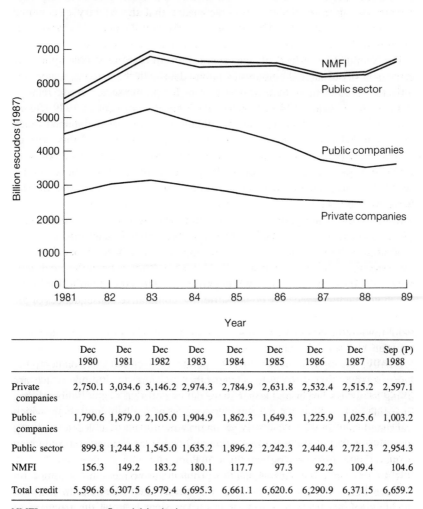

	Dec 1980	Dec 1981	Dec 1982	Dec 1983	Dec 1984	Dec 1985	Dec 1986	Dec 1987	Sep (P) 1988
Private companies	2,750.1	3,034.6	3,146.2	2,974.3	2,784.9	2,631.8	2,532.4	2,515.2	2,597.1
Public companies	1,790.6	1,879.0	2,105.0	1,904.9	1,862.3	1,649.3	1,225.9	1,025.6	1,003.2
Public sector	899.8	1,244.8	1,545.0	1,635.2	1,896.2	2,242.3	2,440.4	2,721.3	2,954.3
NMFI	156.3	149.2	183.2	180.1	117.7	97.3	92.2	109.4	104.6
Total credit	5,596.8	6,307.5	6,979.4	6,695.3	6,661.1	6,620.6	6,290.9	6,371.5	6,659.2

NMFI, non-monetary financial institutions.

Figure 9.2 Total credit in real terms in Portugal, 1980−1988 (1987 prices). *Source*: Banco de Portugal.

recent years the borrowing requirements of nationalized firms have been sharply reduced — thanks to marked improvements in efficiency — which has eased the situation somewhat for the private sector. However, the amount of credit available to private companies is still below what their growth would require.

When analysing Portugal's recent economic performance, it may seem that this problem is not too serious, since the level of investment in the last few years has been remarkably high. However, investment in Portugal, even in record years, remains far below what should be possible given the very high private savings rate, which of course means that the country's economic growth rate is significantly below what it could be if the public sector did not capture such a large share of the country's financial resources.

The cumulative effect of the application of credit ceilings plus the placement of substantial amounts of public debt with the banking sector was reflected in 1988 in a share of 43 per cent for public sector credit relative to total credit, against 34 per cent in 1985 and 12 per cent in 1979 (figure 9.3). It is easy to conclude that this policy could not be maintained much longer. In what concerns the banking sector, the impact of this type of taxation inevitably becomes unsustainable. In 1988, the banks' total portfolio of loans represented only around 40 per cent of assets, with a similar percentage invested in Treasury bills, bonds or deposits with the Central Bank (figure 9.4).

In addition, this policy had important discriminatory consequences. Clearly, a bank credit ceiling becomes the crucial determinant of its profitability. But credit ceilings were applied on a bank by bank basis, sometimes in ways which introduced substantial differences in the conditions under which banks had to operate. In particular, it is quite obvious that banks which were created recently do not suffer the cumulative consequences of the application of credit ceilings for more than ten years. They are in a much more favourable economic situation, which of course distorts the competition between new and old banks.

Finally, Portuguese banks do not operate in a closed environment, but rather have to face competition from other financial institutions which are trying to carve a larger and larger share out of Portugal's rapidly liberalizing financial sector. Thus the exceptional taxation of the banking sector, which translated into an excessively large intermediation margin, led to a strong incentive to financial disintermediation and therefore a substantial reduction or modification of banking activities in Portugal.

It is important to emphasize that this problem has no medium- or long-term solution other than the reduction in the government's deficit. In fact, we might conclude that the introduction of Treasury bills or the payment of interest on bank reserves would represent a viable solution to the problem of bank profitability; both measures have been introduced to alleviate the

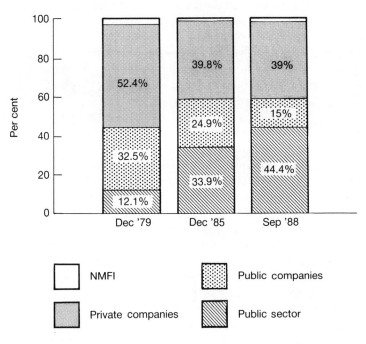

	Dec 1979	Dec 1980	Dec 1981	Dec 1982	Dec 1983	Dec 1984	Dec 1985	Dec 1986	Dec 1987	Sep (P) 1988
Private companies (%)	52.4	49.1	48.1	45.1	44.4	41.8	39.8	40.3	39.5	39.0
Public companies (%)	32.5	32.0	29.8	30.2	28.5	28.0	24.9	19.5	16.1	15.0
Public sector (%)	12.1	16.1	19.7	22.1	24.4	28.5	33.9	38.8	42.7	44.4
NMFI (%)	3.0	2.8	2.4	2.6	2.7	1.8	1.5	1.5	1.7	1.6
Total credit (%)	100.0	100.0	100.0	100.0	100.0	100.0	100.0	100.0	100.0	100.0

NMFI, non-monetary financial institutions.

Figure 9.3 Total credit composition in Portugal.
Source: Banco de Portugal.

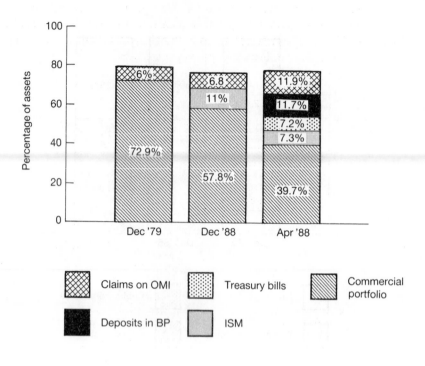

Figure 9.4 Credit structure of commercial banks in Portugal.
Source: Banco de Portugal.

	1979	1980	1981	1982	1983	1984	1985	1986	1987	Apr 1988
Commercial portfolio (%)	72.9	66.4	62.1	59.3	60.2	57.8	52.0	50.8	40.3	39.7
Applications in ISM (%)	0.1	5.4	6.3	5.1	3.1	11.0	16.0	17.4	8.4	7.2
Treasury bills (%)	0.0	0.0	0.0	0.0	0.0	0.0	1.1	3.1	5.6	7.2
Deposits in BP (%)	0.0	0.0	0.0	0.2	0.6	0.1	0.5	0.2	9.9	11.7
Claims on OMI (%)	6.0	7.6	8.5	10.2	8.6	6.8	6.5	8.2	14.5	11.9

ISM, Interbank Security Market; BP, Banco de Portugal; OMI, other monetary institutions.

squeeze on the banks' cash flow. Treasury bills provide an attractive application of funds which has induced depositors to use time deposits to buy the new instruments; the resulting disintermediation has benefited the banks considerably, since it has reduced the cost of funds by substantially increasing the share of inexpensive demand deposits (figure 9.5).

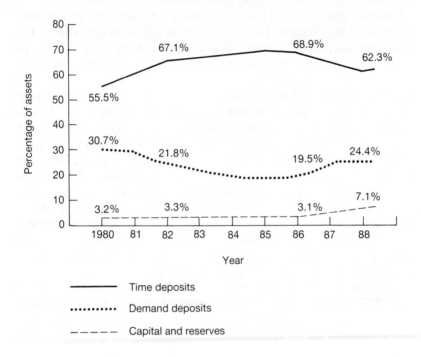

	1979	1980	1981	1982	1983	1984	1985	1986	1987	Apr 1988
Demand deposits (%)	30.7	29.2	24.7	21.8	19.6	18.5	19.5	24.4	25.7	24.4
Time deposits (%)	55.5	60.5	65.5	67.1	67.9	69.6	68.9	64.8	61.4	62.3
Non-monetary liabilities (%)	8.5	5.8	5.2	6.6	9.1	9.6	10.0	10.7	12.4	12.8
Capital and reserves (%)	3.2	3.1	2.9	3.3	3.0	2.9	3.1	4.8	6.5	7.1

Figure 9.5 Liabilities structure of commercial banks in Portugal, 1979–1988.

Source: Banco de Portugal.

Similarly, if banks' excess reserves receive interest, the burden of taxation is greatly reduced. In fact, the tax consists in the interest that banks could potentially receive on loans minus the interest that their reserves fetch, corrected for the administrative cost and risk premiums associated with credit. Thus, even with interest payments on reserves at a rate below what their clients are ready to pay, banks might bear no tax, since deposits with the Central Bank have negligible operating costs and no risk.

However, either solution can only be short-term medicine for a problem that requires deep surgery. In fact, if they were systematically adopted, they would increase the cost of government borrowing so much that the situation would quickly evolve towards an explosive deficit. Treasury bills have to pay market interest rates, which obviously the government cannot afford if it maintains its high level of borrowing requirements. The payment of interest on bank reserves also implies that government borrowing is costly, since placing debt with the Central Bank is no longer free of charge; in the medium or long run the budget cannot cope with the increase in interest costs.

Clearly, the situation can only improve if the PSBR is reduced to a level which can be met with debt placed with the public, but without debt service costs that will become an unbearable burden in the government's budget. Until this is achieved, either economic stability will always be at stake − since the inflationary or current account consequences of monetization would be dramatic − or the banking sector will continue bearing the cost of a very large tax, which of course will prevent it from developing a strong competitive position relative to post-1992 Europe.

Furthermore, the reduction in the budget deficit is certainly possible in Portugal's current fast-growth environment. A slow-down in the rate of growth of public spending plus a small increase in revenues through the modernization of the tax system should be sufficient to bring the deficit down to tolerable proportions. Integration in Europe's single market and the need for Portugal's banking sector to meet the associated increase in competition provide the strongest incentives to achieving rapid progress in this area.

In the short term, there were two solutions which could help alleviate the problem significantly: tax reform and privatization.

The 1989 comprehensive reform of direct taxation contributed to the modernization of the tax system. Although the intention of the government was to reduce marginal tax rates significantly, the increase in the tax base maintained the total level of revenue. Beyond this minimal objective, the government expected to reduce tax evasion and thus in fact increase tax collection above its previous levels.

The privatization of nationalized firms provided substantial government revenue, thus reducing borrowing requirements. The sale of assets on which the government received very little income translated into a reduction in public debt and the budget deficit was permanently reduced. The first substantial privatization took place in early 1989. The proceeds were used to retire public debt, and the government's financial position was improved markedly.

9.2 The Impact of Tight Monetary Policies

To the exceptional taxation of the banking sector must be added the impact of tight monetary policies as an additional constraint on the profitability and efficiency of Portuguese banks. The effectiveness of monetary policy in Portugal is beyond question. Its application in the stabilization programmes of the 1980s showed how swiftly it is possible to restore external balance in a relatively short time through tighter monetary policies (figure 9.6).

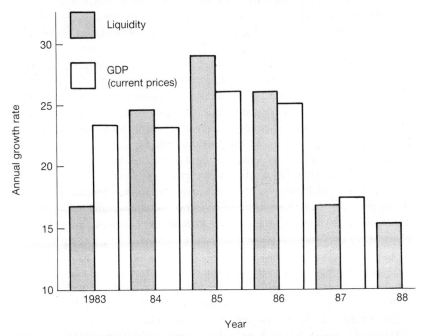

	Dec 1983	Dec 1984	Dec 1985	Dec 1986	Dec 1987	Dec 1988
Means of payment	16.4	24.7	24.6	19.3	13.5	14.4
Liquidity	16.8	24.6	29.0	25.9	16.8	15.3
GDP (current)	23.3	23.1	26.0	25.0	17.4	16.2[a]

[a] Estimate based on real growth and consumer price index.

Figure 9.6 Monetary policy in Portugal, 1983–1988.

Source: Banco de Portugal.

However, it is well known that monetary policy, if it is the only instrument of stabilization, has important limitations, and that one of the main costs of monetary policy is its uneven incidence on the economy, and in particular its costly impact on the banking sector. Portugal's integration in the European Community (EC) in January 1986 coincided with a significant shift in macro-economic policy. After the rather severe stabilization programme of 1983–5, the external accounts showed a marked improvement which, together with the more favourable external environment, induced the government to embark on a policy which must be considered to be relatively ambitious. While stimulating growth and investment, the government hoped to reduce inflation and maintain the current account under control. This policy was quite successful, since economic growth proceeded at a very fast pace; furthermore, the recovery was led by investment, which was unprecedented in recent Portuguese history. Today, Portuguese industry is operating at full capacity, unemployment is at very low levels and real wages have resumed growth.

The other side of the coin is that this very success could perhaps be excessive. The growth in investment, private consumption and exports in the late 1980s signalled an excessive expansion in aggregate demand. Inevitably, either the current account or the inflation rate, or both, would be hurt by the impact of such growth in spending. To avoid serious future imbalances, the government had to slow down the pace of demand growth.

Portugal's recent history indicates an inability to use fiscal instruments when it becomes necessary to slow down spending growth. After introducing a tax reform which was widely publicized as revenue neutral, and under strong pressure to increase spending in infrastructure to match EC funds, the government may find it very difficult to reduce the expansionary character of fiscal policy. Since exchange rate policy will not be of any help when the root of the problem is excess demand, only a tighter monetary policy will produce sufficient results in the immediate future. It is most likely that a strict programme of credit control will remain in place, leading to higher interest rates.

The consequences of this option − for which there seems to be no alternative − are quite predictable. Investment will probably be the variable most seriously affected and the slow-down in spending will be achieved through some sacrifice in terms of capacity growth. But it is the impact of tighter monetary policies on the banking sector that should be of particular interest at this point.

Credit restrictions and the increase in credit cost represent a substantial brake on the normal development of the activities of the banking sector. In sharp contrast with the rapid pace of growth in the late 1980s, banks will have to scale down their development plans, which naturally will not facilitate the desired transition towards higher levels of efficiency. It may even be that substantial projects undertaken recently will now prove to be detrimental to bank profitability, since they were based on scenarios of rapid growth. Although this type of uncertainty is no different from what can happen in any other sector of activity, it is regrettable that an excessively expansionary policy in recent years now has to be replaced by a more moderate approach, the impact of which is very uneven. Clearly, this will not be the best environment for the modernization of the banking sector and the preparation for stronger competition from abroad.

It is important to add that a tighter monetary programme has an additional implication of a different type. The increase in interest rates leads to a reduction in the total amount of credit but also to a change in its quality. In fact, the increase in price will lead to adverse selection: with higher rates, only high return projects will ask for credit, but these projects will naturally have higher risk as well, which of course forces the banks to operate with a group of clients biased in the direction of higher exposure to risk. The stability of bank profits will normally be affected.[2]

Finally, the continued utilization of monetary policy as the primary instrument of stabilization sooner or later generates important distortions, which reduce its efficiency and render its impact more costly. In the case of Portugal, three examples illustrate this point.

First, integration in the EC already implies stronger competition from foreign capital. Thus, by restricting domestic credit, monetary policy will induce an additional demand for foreign credit, which will become very attractive and easier to obtain. In this way, not only will it become difficult to control the growth in domestic liquidity, but there will also be discrimination against domestic banks and in favour of foreign competitors, which is of course the opposite of what Portuguese banks would want.

Second, the development of financial markets should normally lead to a stronger interdependence between monetary and capital markets. The somewhat tighter monetary policy that has been in place in Portugal is not unrelated to the lack of recovery from the 1987 crash in the Portuguese stock market. This of course represents an important obstacle to the continued development and modernization of Portugal's financial system.

Finally, since interest payments are a very large component of public spending, an increase, however limited, in market interest rates will have very unfavourable consequences on the government's budget, increasing the dimension of what is already Portugal's primary economic problem.

In the current environment, and despite all its limitations and drawbacks, there is no alternative to a tighter monetary policy. However, the costs associated with this dilemma are becoming so serious that it can only be hoped that the government will soon recover its ability to control public spending as a less costly means of slowing down aggregate demand.

9.3   The Structure of the Banking Sector and the Evolution of Competition

The opening up of the banking sector to private initiative, the creation of some new Portuguese banks and the entry of a few foreign banks into the Portuguese market were the dominant factors in the change in the structure and performance of the banking industry in the late 1980s. The new banks are still quite small and represent a limited share of total banking business in Portugal, but their presence modifies considerably the competitive context in which banks operate.

A quick comparison of profitability shows that small banks obtain much better results – in fact, extraordinarily high results in some cases (figure 9.7).

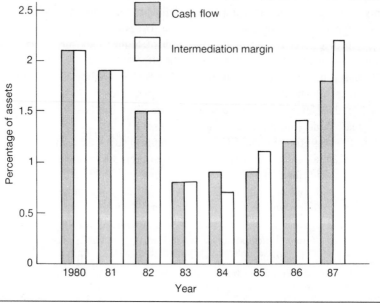

	1980	1981	1982	1983	1984	1985	1986	1987
Cash flow (in escudos)	26,349	35,423	45,784	39,971	42,668	54,030	76,810	142,908
Intermediation margin (in escudos)	30,853	36,936	38,237	24,556	33,406	64,526	90,461	174,895
Cash flow (% assets)	2.1	1.9	1.5	0.8	0.9	0.9	1.2	1.8
Intermediation margin (% assets)	2.1	1.9	1.5	0.8	0.7	1.1	1.4	2.2

Intermediation margin = revenues on loans – costs of deposits.
Cash flow = operating profit + depreciation + provisions.

Figure 9.7   Profitability of other monetary institutions in Portugal.
Source: Banco de Portugal.

It is easy to conclude that Portugal is another illustration of the irrelevance of scale economies in banking, since smaller banks actually outperform larger ones (figure 9.8).

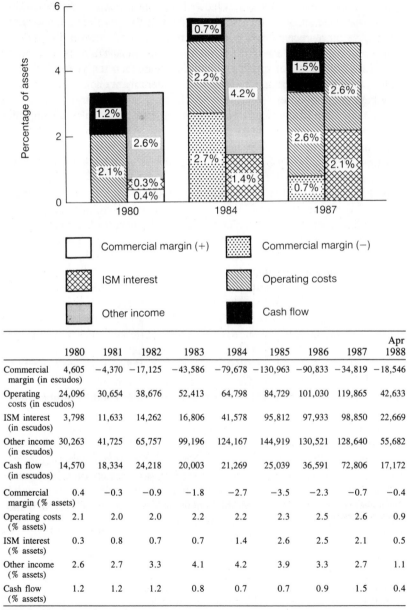

	1980	1981	1982	1983	1984	1985	1986	1987	Apr 1988
Commercial margin (in escudos)	4,605	−4,370	−17,125	−43,586	−79,678	−130,963	−90,833	−34,819	−18,546
Operating costs (in escudos)	24,096	30,654	38,676	52,413	64,798	84,729	101,030	119,865	42,633
ISM interest (in escudos)	3,798	11,633	14,262	16,806	41,578	95,812	97,933	98,850	22,669
Other income (in escudos)	30,263	41,725	65,757	99,196	124,167	144,919	130,521	128,640	55,682
Cash flow (in escudos)	14,570	18,334	24,218	20,003	21,269	25,039	36,591	72,806	17,172
Commercial margin (% assets)	0.4	−0.3	−0.9	−1.8	−2.7	−3.5	−2.3	−0.7	−0.4
Operating costs (% assets)	2.1	2.0	2.0	2.2	2.2	2.3	2.5	2.6	0.9
ISM interest (% assets)	0.3	0.8	0.7	0.7	1.4	2.6	2.5	2.1	0.5
Other income (% assets)	2.6	2.7	3.3	4.1	4.2	3.9	3.3	2.7	1.1
Cash flow (% assets)	1.2	1.2	1.2	0.8	0.7	0.7	0.9	1.5	0.4

ISM, interbank security market.

Figure 9.8 Commercial bank profitability in Portugal. *Source*: Banco de Portugal.

In the case of Portugal, however, it is legitimate to question whether the differences in profitability are simply explained by size, or whether they are due to other factors specific to the structure of the sector, which distort competition and damage the larger banks in particular because they are older.

The main factor of distortion in the competitive position of old banks relative to more recent ones is the historical cost of intervention policies which will continue to affect the economics of nationalized banks. First, the systematic utilization of credit controls for more than ten years puts older banks at a clear disadvantage relative to the more recent ones, which are only now beginning to suffer from these restrictions. Second, large nationalized banks have often been forced to offer credit to other nationalized companies in the past without much prospect of repayment. Although this problem has been magnified by careless management, the cost of non-performing loans remains largely a heavy burden which was imposed on banks without much alternative.

Without these impediments, private banks are in a much more favourable position to benefit from conditions which − particularly in what concerns intermediation margins − are determined by the need to keep nationalized banks afloat. It is not surprising that their results are far superior.

Private banks, however, have shown clear leadership in terms of managerial capacity and innovativeness, willingness to compete and a sense of opportunism, and are ready to take advantage of new possibilities that may emerge. In this sense, their higher profits also reflect the legitimate reward of more dynamic management. Their situation is by no means easy, since they face competitors which operate under different rules and have an enormous capacity to absorb losses. A private bank finds it more difficult to accept that its main competitors do not have the same requirements of profitability, but rather can afford to maintain very low profits, thanks to the indifference of their main shareholder. It is also a huge source of uncertainty to be reminded that, when in direct competition, nationalized banks can price below cost for periods of indefinite duration, without any undue concern on the part of managers or of the authorities responsible for proper competitive practices. Finally, if economies of scale are perhaps not very significant, other barriers to entry − such as the existence of large networks of branches or the importance of well-established client relationships − will certainly represent substantial assets in the hands of the large nationalized banks, which they should take advantage of in the future.

9.4 The Outlook

Given the unusual features of the pre-1992 situation, what perspectives can be identified for Portuguese banks entering a single European market of financial services?

A preliminary point requires clarification. The improvement in the profitability of the banking sector during the late 1980s, although extremely positive since it may provide more solid foundations for future development, was largely due to artificial factors. In fact, although the depressing trend towards lower and lower profitability had been reversed, it was mainly due to factors exogenous to the banking sector, essentially linked to a modification in the intervention of the monetary authorities. First, the effective intermediation margin was increased, thanks to a reduction in the average cost of deposits, which was due mostly to the process of disintermediation associated with the introduction of Treasury bills, as well as the channelling of funds to the stock market in 1987. Since interest rates on credit remained very high in real terms, the banks could benefit from a high intermediation margin for some time. However, it should be remembered that the availability of other financial instruments which will free the banks from the responsibility of remunerating time deposits at attractive levels − since they are the predominant form of holding savings − will not continue expanding indefinitely unless there is a substantial recovery of the capital market. Second, the significant increase in the remuneration of bank reserves by the monetary authorities cannot possibly continue to improve in proportion to the growth in the assets of the banking sector, given the consequences that such an increase would have for the effective cost of servicing the government debt. Thus the two main factors that have improved the profitability of the banking sector in Portugal are likely to be only temporary and to have a limited impact. In any case, the substantial increase in the cash flow of the banking sector made possible a large reinforcement of its own equity, with very positive implications for the stability of the banking sector and the adoption of the EC requirements in this respect.

A slightly deeper comparison of the performance of private and nationalized banks also leads to some conclusions with respect to the future perspectives for the banking sector as a whole. A strong contrast can be identified between the generality of smaller banks and the totality of larger ones in what concerns their competitive strategy and positioning. While most small private banks chose a strategy of wholesale banking, based on small margins and a strong economy of operating costs, nationalized banks continue to maintain the base of their operations in retailing, benefiting from positions acquired long ago and almost completely amortized. While smaller banks attempt to improve their results by the constant application of new technologies, in particular creating new products and introducing financial innovations which are attractive to large clients, nationalized banks rely on traditional activities, close to the mainstream of banking and depending on large volume and gradual improvements in productivity over time. Smaller banks often follow a 'cream-skimming' strategy, choosing their clients, products and markets carefully; nationalized banks do not have the freedom to withdraw from segments which they may not be interested in, but rather have to maintain a large client base. In the not too distant future, it is possible that the positions of large banks will prove to be the most solid, given the likely development of bank profitability. With the expected and desirable continued development of the financial system, strategies oriented towards a small number of very good large clients will be more and more vulnerable to competition from other operators in financial markets who may be in a better position than banks. For large companies or investors, with impeccable ratings and a position of pre-eminence in the financial markets, banks are a rather expensive source of funds. Either through capital markets or by issuing commercial paper, large investors can obtain the funds they need under better conditions than by borrowing from banks. For these investors, banks as financial intermediaries have very little to offer that would justify the higher cost of funds that they demand. In what concerns large clients it is quite possible that Portugal will follow the example of other more advanced countries, where direct access to the primary source of funds is preferred, leaving specialized activities in the area of financial engineering for the banks.

In this case, banks are left with the vast segment where their access to information and their ability to diversify risks become dominant. It is with small and medium-sized clients, perhaps very profitable but less well known or unable to go directly to the capital markets, that banks can build a solid base of operation, guaranteeing the stability required for long-term survival. For this it is necessary to start from a strong presence in the marketplace, to be close to clients and to be well informed of opportunities, and to benefit from an operating efficiency that will enable a large number of small and medium-sized transactions to be handled at low cost. This is of course very far from wholesale banking, which today concentrates the attention of private banks, while the more sophisticated approach linked to innovative and financial engineering will remain confined to a rather specialized segment of the market.

It is clear in any case that the survival of Portuguese banks will depend largely on how the regulatory environment is changed in Portugal. The spirit of the European Commission's 1992 initiative assumes not only a much more open and competitive market but also points to a much lower level of regulation. It is utopian to expect Portuguese banks to survive if credit ceilings remain the dominant instrument of monetary control. It is also unacceptable for banks to continue to be forced to finance large nationalized companies which are insolvent and will never repay interest or principal on most of their loans. In these, as in other aspects, a deeper integration in Europe will impose on Portugal a stronger discipline which will be highly beneficial for the economy.

However, it is important that existing opportunities for Portuguese banks are not underestimated. In an environment of more open competition, the existing positions of Portuguese banks will be important assets, which will remain a strong deterrent to entry for other banks. Also, the fact that today Portuguese banks are still quite inefficient in certain areas proves that there is a substantial potential for improvement, which will lead to stronger competitive positions.

What Portuguese banks must avoid at all costs is an attitude of indolence, which would neglect the very rapid changes which they will have to undergo, if they want to be ready for the impact of competition. It is essential that in the next few years a strong flow of innovation and improvement in management routines will take place, leading to more efficient operations and closer proximity to the client.

Notes

1 This is an example of the concept of financial repression described by McKinnon (1973).
2 See this argument in Stiglitz and Weiss (1981).

References

Borges, A. (1988) Problemas e perspectivas da Banca Portuguesa. *Revista da Banca*, July – September.

McKinnon, R. (1973) *Money and Capital in Economic Development*. Washington, DC: Brookings Institution.

Stiglitz, J. and Weiss, A. (1981) Credit rationing in markets with imperfect information. *American Economic Review*, 71, 393 – 410.

Comment

Jorge Braga de Macedo

My aim here is not so much to comment on Borges' chapter but to place the issue of European banking after 1992 in a perspective of structural adjustment of the Portuguese economy. The Portuguese banking experience is largely the story of how seven financial groups and a competitive fringe became eight nationalized banks. The adjustment to an open capital market, which has been delayed until 1995, will be accompanied by considerable competitive pressure from new private and foreign banks.

The eight commercial banks are known by their initials. Seven come from the large 'family' conglomerates of the 1960s. The eighth, Uniao de Bancos Portugueses (UBP), was a result of the merger in 1975 of three similar banks. The role of the seven 'family' groups was so central that the story of the transformation can serve as an account of financial development in Portugal. The delayed entry of new banks and the slow privatization of old ones are then easy to explain along revenue-seeking lines. Uncovering the fiscal roots of regulation certainly suggests a greater transparency of the role of the banking system in satisfying the PSBR. Such is the crucial element of banking policy towards 1995. Needless to say, the views expressed here are personal and do not affect the assessment of national economies carried out by the Commission Services.

Banking competition and the frozen public sector

In highly competitive markets, commercial banks tend to avoid the financing of medium and long-term investment and concentrate instead on short-term operations. In Portugal, internal and external regulations led firms to be committed to a particular commercial bank. The bank in turn took a longer-term view of the project's profitability than would be the case in a competitive environment. The creation of industrial groups which were able to provide their own finance was thus a consequence of tight financial regulation. The existence of a fringe of emerging industrial and financial groups allowed successful firms to shop around for more attractive sources of funding. The financing of some manufactured exports, particularly textiles, operated in this competitive way. However, these firms remained an enclave relative to the large industrial groups devoted to import substitution. Indeed, non-monetary financial intermediaries were limited to two state-owned savings and investment banks and a mortgage bank. It can be said that the seven groups and the state banks served as substitutes for a financial market.

Financial groups serving as markets alongside a textile export enclave suggest an ambiguity of objectives on the part of the government. This ambiguity undermined the social and political roots of the Portuguese economic miracle of the 1960s. It was therefore easy for the military coup of 25 April 1974 to reverse the strategy of economic development, less than a year after restoring democracy. The family groups were believed to control the state: thus a primary political objective of the revolutionary rulers was to own them. On 1 March 1975 they were nationalized with a vague promise of compensation. The eight commercial banks were among the dozens of so-called public enterprises formed in this way.

Despite the revolutionary euphoria, the elections of April 1975 marked a victory of the Socialist Party (PS) of Mario Soares over the more extreme leftist parties. However, the military rulers scored in the political constitution voted in 1976. According to the document (currently under review), the objective of the Portuguese State is to achieve what Article 1 calls a 'classless society'. To ensure the transition to socialism, Article 83, No. 1, froze the post-revolutionary nationalizations as 'irreversible conquests of the working classes'. The request for membership in the EC, presented by a minority PS government in 1977, was bound to collide with the course towards classlessness. In fact, the application simply restored the ambiguity of objectives of public policy characteristic of the 1960s, when catching up with Europe was constrained by the defence of colonial rule over the African territories. Instead, during the negotiations with Brussels, catching up was constrained by the defence of the socialist constitution (including the first amendment in 1982). Both defences originated in a suspicion of the market and a belief in the economic power of the state. Therefore the ambiguity has maintained a defensive approach in public administration. It remains to be seen whether the challenge of the single market will liberate the economy, rather than simply elevate the defensive approach to the EC level.

The defensive approach to public policy and the ambiguity of objectives had consequences for banking. Managers were nurtured in a type of financial intermediation where most of the operations were internal to the group. The closing down of the stock market was followed by widespread nationalization — the generally inexperienced successors of the group bankers probably viewed the nationalized sector as one large group. At the same time, the abnormally high level of gold and foreign exchange reserves available changed its nature. Urged by politicians to put banks 'at the service of the people', the new managers saw those reserves as a collateral against which the nationalized enterprises were borrowing. The rational response to a rise in the collateral is to lend to riskier borrowers. Unfortunately this rational response under equilibrium credit rationing does not carry over to a disequilibrium situation. How else can we describe an inflationary environment, where every borrower, especially the government, was facing negative real interest rates? With high wage inflation and controlled prices, profits and retained earnings fell. The repression of the financial market made private firms more dependent on bank credit. The system of credit ceilings on an individual bank basis prevented banking competition and kept the market shares of the eight roughly stable.

The combined share of the eight nationalized commercial banks in total credit has been falling, however. Between 1979 and 1985, the fall was due to foreign banks whose share rose from 2 to 6 per cent. Between 1985 and 1987 the fall was due to private domestic banks whose share rose from zero to 3 per cent. The share of private commercial banking is still small, especially on the liability side. However, the spectacular growth of private banks has had a strong demonstration effect on banking competition, stronger than the mere increase in the number of players. Measuring size by total assets, at the end of 1987 the new commercial banks were equivalent to an increase in the total number by one more bank of equal size. The process of catching up needs to be coupled with economic restructuring in the light of the objective of the single European market. Restructuring of the banking sector, through privatization or other means, will have to absorb the overhang of inefficiency. This is unlikely to be complete before 1995, even though a quicker readjustment cannot be ruled out.

Hidden deficits and implicit taxes

Banking competition − internationally as well as domestically − could not be addressed without recognizing that nationalized banks acted as forced buyers of public debt and also as (implicit) tax collectors. This situation is of course not unique to Portugal. It was identified in Italy before the so-called 'divorce' between the Bank and the Treasury in 1981 and can be seen in other EC member countries. However, it is typical of semi-industrialized countries subject to financial repression.

The relentless expansion of public debt made private firms the residual borrowers. Unlike the public sector, they were subject to recurrent squeezes due to stop−go macro-economic policies. These were often inversely correlated with the main trading partners. The inverse correlation occurred even within the same electoral majority. The first government led by the social democratic party (PSD) stabilized inflation in 1980 and the second government of the same coalition expanded during the world recession. Another coalition government, the PS−PSD, stabilized during the world boom. This involved a belated increase in domestic interest rates. The adverse selection effect towards riskier borrowers was probably offset by a less binding constraint on credit ceilings. This allowed banks a better mix of borrowers and projects. Nevertheless, the higher rates reduced the intermediation margin and the profitability of nationalized banks. The spreading of arrears and bad debts also became apparent. From being about twice as large as the equity of commercial banks in 1982, non-performing loans were three times as large in July 1985, at the end of stabilization. Bad debts then reached about 18 per cent of the commercial loan portfolio. The situation improved at year end. Moreover the stock market revived in 1987 and served as a substitute for bank credit, especially for firms with low collateral.

A successful anti-inflationary programme was initiated in late 1985 by a minority government led by former Minister of Finance Cavaco Silva. Paradoxically it lost force after PSD gained an electoral majority in mid-1987. The rate of increase of the GDP deflator dropped from 20 per cent in 1985 to 11 per cent in 1987, bringing *ex post* real interest rates on domestic public debt up from −10 per cent to +1 per cent. The primary budget deficit, including Treasury operations, fell from the equivalent of 11 per cent of GDP in 1981 to less than 1 per cent in the crash of October 1987. Public and private expenditure debt ended up rekindling inflation in 1988, requiring a credit crunch in early 1989. Take-overs of some commercial banks by stronger state-owned financial institutions happened during 1989. This did not necessarily enhance the transparency of fiscal policy, and we claim that disguised fiscal policy is largely responsible for the danger of returning to stop−go macro-economic policies in the near future.

In Portugal the debt-to-income ratio has been increasing at 4 per cent per annum for over ten years. Because of negative interest rates, this is associated with an implied deficit about twice as large. The implied deficit is in turn made up of a reported deficit and a hidden deficit. The difference is in part due to deficient data, but the bulk of it reflects disguised fiscal policy. Unreported lending operations by the Treasury and debt write-off and take-over operations by the government are acknowledged sources of discrepancy. Between 1977 and 1985 − leaving out 1980 because of a major debt write-off operation − the reported deficit was, on average, equal to the hidden deficit. Despite substantial year to year variations, the share of the hidden deficit reached a maximum of 90 per cent in 1986−7.

Before 1985, the revenue from seigniorage accounted on average for the same share of the implied deficit as net foreign borrowing. In 1985−7, the repayment of foreign debt accounted for close to 10 per cent of the implied deficit, and the share of private debt rose from zero to 80 per cent so that seigniorage revenue fell to about 30 per cent. In September 1988 the Treasury announced that it would cease to have automatic access to the Central Bank. To understand why tax anaesthesia was so considerable just before the 'divorce' requires an analysis of the role played by banks in collecting taxes. But it is clear that the demonstration effect of the entry of private banks was as strong on taxation as it was on competition.

In general, seigniorage and other anaesthesized taxes will be collected not only from borrowers or depositors, but also from bank shareholders. If the binding constraint is the existence of credit ceilings on private borrowers, the base of the implicit intermediate tax is the corresponding stock of loans. Here we assume this to be the case, even though private depositors may have been constrained occasionally. To compute the rate, take an average rate on deposits from figures on the stock of total deposits and the interest bill paid by banks. Then use the (administered until September 1988) loan rate for the 91 − 180 day maturity as the representative rate for loans extended by commercial banks during the sample period. Credit ceilings of course imply that this is a relatively small share of the total assets of banks. The tax rate is the spread between the loan rate and the deposit rate net of an assumed intermediation margin. If this is 2 per cent, then the estimated tax revenue peaks at about 10 per cent of GDP in 1982, falling to 4 per cent in 1987.

Commercial banks in Portugal are being forced to act as tax collectors. This requires a closed domestic financial market. It also greatly constrains monetary policy. The credit crunch of March 1989 relied mostly on tighter credit ceilings, and avoided the large increases in interest rates that would be required to cool off demand. A rise in interest rates would increase the burden of public debt. It might also reduce the revenue from the implicit intermediation tax. Disguised fiscal policy ends up determining monetary and exchange rate policy as well, at least if the effectiveness of capital controls is taken for granted. However, this will change before 1995.

Financial liberalization and fiscal adjustment

International capital mobility and free trade in financial services, by greatly increasing the competition among banks, is bound to make Portuguese banks unwilling and unable to finance the deficits of the public sector. Capital controls become less effective as barriers to bilateral trade in goods are dismantled according to the transition agreement with the EC. The difference between Spain (where the capital market is semi-open) and Portugal (where it is closed) can be illustrated by computing the real interest rate differential against the Eurodollar. Between September 1982 and January 1988, the average was 1 per cent p.a. and −4 per cent p.a. respectively, suggesting that the rates in Portugal were kept artificially low by virtue of exchange controls. Moreover, in economies with an open capital account, the country risk premium (given by the covered interest differential) is zero so that the real forward premium equals the real return differential. In Spain the country premium during the period was −2 per cent so that the currency premium contributed 3 per cent. In Portugal the real forward premium was 4 per cent and the covered interest differential reached −8 per cent, suggesting significant barriers to capital outflows.

With respect to exchange rate arrangements, there is an advantage for Portugal to explore forms of association which will enhance the credibility of domestic macro-economic management without excessive reliance on the policies of the Bundesbank. To experiment with some form of wider band, as in Italy, might facilitate early membership in the EMS. The system of credit ceilings has played a substantial role in stabilization packages. Otherwise, monetary policy has been largely determined by disguised fiscal policy and incomes policy. The divorce between the Bank of Portugal and the Portuguese Treasury may not last. Even if it does, how independent will the Central Bank be of the agreements about wages between the government and the mostly socialist trade union (UGT)? Certainly much less than if it were to follow the Bundesbank via membership in the EMS. How well the operation of monetary policy prepares this institutional change greatly affects the assessment of the costs and benefits from joining the EMS. Apart from the consolidation of the divorce, monetary policy must learn to operate without the strictures of implicit taxes. The announcement of the intention to introduce indirect monetary control in 1989 was certainly a step in the right direction.

The expectation of external financial liberalization in 1995 is not likely to validate a change in the domestic financial regime. Validation hinges essentially on the credibility attached to a fiscal adjustment strategy that will take the economy from here to there. As the programme for debt stabilization announced by the government in 1988 is not explicit about the means to achieve the objective, its credibility may be questioned. Apart from a better knowledge of the debt situation of the enlarged public sector, immediate steps may involve a rethinking of exchange rate policy along the lines of what might be called the shadow exchange rate mechanism of the EMS.

In 1987 and early 1988, the pound sterling was in the shadow EMS and did not remain too far from the major European currencies. Demand expansion made this strategy short lived. With this caveat in mind, a similar attempt on the part of Portugal may be appropriate. This would hold in particular if the expectation that Spain is to join relatively soon becomes widespread. A shadow exchange arrangement would of course be less rigid than one which would tie the Central Bank's hands. If the multi-annual fiscal adjustment strategy (MAFAS) is so gradual that for a time the frozen public sector will essentially be given, this shadow EMS may be the only alternative consistent with opening the capital markets by 1995. In short, experimentation with an informal peg may be more credible than either keeping the crawling peg or joining the EMS. To the extent that an explicit MAFAS is not forthcoming, the extra credibility would quickly disappear.

Conclusion

The preference for a sequencing of financial liberalization after real liberalization is now widely recognized. Clearly, the international mobility of capital brings pressures for the harmonization of regulation in banking services or insurance. However, the national, Community and world regulatory tiers may interact in perverse ways. The harmonization efforts currently carried out at the EC level find themselves in the centre of this regulatory interaction.

The financial regime in Portugal has changed a great deal since private commercial banks began opening the capital market. Nevertheless, domestic seigniorage and other implicit taxes remain significant sources of government revenue. The pressure of 1992 was not sufficient to affect the design of the comprehensive income tax introduced on 1 January 1989. The most important effect of the 1988 Tax Act may be an increase in the credibility of a future MAFAS. The ongoing tax reform will not be complete until tax anaesthesia is reduced to a level consistent with external financial liberalization. For this, the government has had to commit to restoring control of public finances via a MAFAS. This commitment was all the more required as the doubling of structural funds by 1992 agreed upon by the European Community was bound to bring additional pressure on public investment expenditure.

With inflation still substantially higher than the EC average and a serious overhang of bad debts, the shadow EMS seems to be the appropriate signal that the 1992 deadline will be met. The single market should not fail in Portugal because of the burden of a frozen public sector. Fiscal adjustment in the form of a MAFAS is thus an essential component of macro-economic stability. Stronger than that, it is a prerequisite for sustained economic growth and structural change. The longer it is before public sector reforms begin, the harsher the fiscal discipline must be.

10

Swiss Banking After 1992

Alexander K. Swoboda

It can be taken for granted that Swiss banking will be different after 1992. Whether the difference will be due mainly to steps taken by the European Community (EC) towards creating a unified internal market for banking and other financial services, and what precise role Switzerland will play in international financial markets by the end of the century, is another matter. What concerns the Swiss banking industry most is the general worldwide trend towards deregulation and increased competition of which '1992' is but a part. Thus, although in the following we attempt to discuss some of the implications of an integrated EC market for Swiss banking, we shall not always succeed in disentangling them from these broader developments.

The position of Switzerland in international financial markets during the lead up to 1992 must of necessity be our starting point and will be considered briefly in the next section, together with a brief discussion of the sources of Switzerland's apparent comparative advantage in the production and export of financial, particularly banking, services. In section 10.2 we discuss the main implications of recent and forthcoming changes in the international financial system for the competitive position of Swiss banks. This is followed, in section 10.3, by a consideration of the relationship between Switzerland and the EC, both generally and more specifically in the banking field; this section starts with a mention of the general issue of the relationship between the unified internal market and third countries. In section 10.4 we review these factors and issues that are likely to be particularly important in shaping the future place of Swiss banking in European and international financial markets. It turns out that these factors are internal (stamp duties, rules on the registration of shares, the structure of Swiss exchanges etc.) as well as external (reciprocity, right of establishment, international harmonization of capital ratios etc.).

The author would like to thank Christos Gortsos for his comments and suggestions.

10.1   Swiss Banking Before 1992

10.1.1   The Swiss Banking System

Switzerland is a small open economy with a banking and financial sector that is disproportionate to the country's size in terms of volume of transactions handled, balance-sheet totals and value added as a share of gross domestic product (GDP).

That Switzerland is an open economy is witnessed by the fact that imports represent almost 40 per cent of GDP, and exports only slightly less. Trade relations with the EC are particularly important as some 70 per cent of Swiss imports come from the EC while some 50 per cent of Swiss exports are absorbed by the EC. The openness of Switzerland extends to financial transactions; for instance, external assets of Swiss banks account for 40 per cent of their total assets, and external liabilities for some 30 per cent of total liabilities. A few figures illustrate the importance of the banking sector relative to the country's size. Although Switzerland's GNP only accounted for 1.1−1.3 per cent of the OECD GDP and its population for 0.8 per cent of OECD population, the share of Switzerland in international financial activity (as measured, for instance, by the external assets and liabilities of banks) has been estimated to range from 8 to 12 per cent (Bridel, 1984). As measured by transactions volumes, Zurich still seems to be the fourth international financial centre, after New York, London and Tokyo. Another indicator of the banking industry's importance is that the financial sector's contribution to total value added rose from 3.6 per cent in 1970 to 6.9 per cent in 1984, percentages that are significantly higher than those in most other countries over the period as indicated in a study of Switzerland by the OECD (1987) from which table 10.1 is reproduced.

There are some 600 banks and financial companies in Switzerland. The banks, with total assets of SFr 920 billion at end December 1988 (of which SFr 355 billion are in external assets), are officially divided into eight categories. Among these, the most important are the five large banks with 53 per cent of the total, the cantonal banks with 19.2 per cent, and the foreign banks with 12 per cent. These figures, however, do not reflect the importance of the activities of the various banking groups in Switzerland and abroad. In the first place, off-balance-sheet items have become increasingly important in the activities of the banks. Thus, fiduciary assets of banks in Switzerland amounted to SFr 265 billion, the lion's share going to the large banks (43 per cent) and the foreign banks (39 per cent). The growth in the market shares in terms of the balance sheets of various banking groups is shown in Figure 10.1, and that of total assets and fiduciary operations is shown in table 10.2. Moreover, the portfolio management activities of the Swiss banks−with an estimated total of assets under management of over SFr 1,500 billion−are an important source of revenue, and the main source for the private bankers.

Table 10.1 Value added and employment shares in the financial sector

	1970	1975	1980	1981	1982	1983	1984
Value added (% of total)							
Switzerland[a]	3.6	4.5	5.3	5.7	6.4	6.5	6.9
USA	2.5	2.3	2.6	2.8	2.8	3.0	–
Germany	2.5	3.4	3.5	3.9	4.4	4.6	–
Austria	3.1	3.9	4.3	4.8	4.8	4.6	4.5
Denmark	2.3	2.9	2.3	2.0	1.9	1.9	2.0
Finland	2.1	3.0	3.4	3.6	3.5	3.5	3.8
Netherlands	1.8	2.8	3.3	3.4	3.7	–	–
Norway	1.9	2.6	2.9	3.3	3.8	3.9	3.5
Sweden	2.6	3.1	4.6	5.5	5.8	5.8	5.9
Employment (% of total)							
Switzerland	1.9	2.4	2.7	2.9	3.0	3.1	3.1
USA	1.9	2.1	2.3	2.4	2.5	2.6	–
Germany	1.5	1.9	2.0	2.1	2.1	2.2	–
Sweden	1.1	1.2	1.3	1.3	1.3	1.3	1.4
Norway	1.3	1.5	1.6	1.7	1.7	1.8	1.8
Netherlands	–	2.2[b]	2.4	2.4	2.5	2.5	2.5
France	–	1.8	2.0	2.0	2.0	2.1	2.1
Finland	1.8	2.3	2.5	2.5	2.5	2.6	2.7
Denmark	1.7	2.3	2.7	2.8	2.8	–	–

Reproduced from OECD (1987, p. 48)
[a] Share in GNP.
[b] 1977.

Sources: OECD, *National Accounts*: estimates for value added in Switzerland computed by the Secretariat on the basis of balance-sheet data published in *Les Banques suisses en . . .* , various issues

Table 10.2 Balance-sheet totals and fiduciary operations: main banking groups

	Total assets (billion SFr (%))			Fiduciary assets (billion SFr (%))			Fiduciary/total assets (%)		
	1975	1981	1987	1975	1981	1987	1975	1981	1987
Large commercial banks	147 (45.5)	282 (50.4)	461 (51.0)	19 (36.0)	61 (38.5)	63 (33.3)	12.8	21.6	13.6
Foreign institutions	37 (11.3)	74 (13.2)	116 (12.9)	23 (44.1)	68 (42.8)	87 (46.0)	63.1	91.5	76.0
Private banks	2 (0.6)	3 (0.5)	5 (0.6)	2 (3.1)	7 (4.3)	10 (5.3)	75.9	238.2	184.1
Cantonal banks	74 (23.1)	111 (19.8)	167 (18.6)	0.5 (0.7)	3 (1.7)	3 (1.6)	0.5	2.4	1.7
Others	63 (19.4)	91 (16.1)	152 (16.9)	8 (16.0)	20 (12.6)	26 (13.7)	13.36	22.0	16.9
Total	323 (100)	560 (100)	902 (100)	52 (100)	158 (100)	188 (100)	16.2	28.2	20.8

Source: Swiss National Bank, *Monthly Bulletin*, various issues

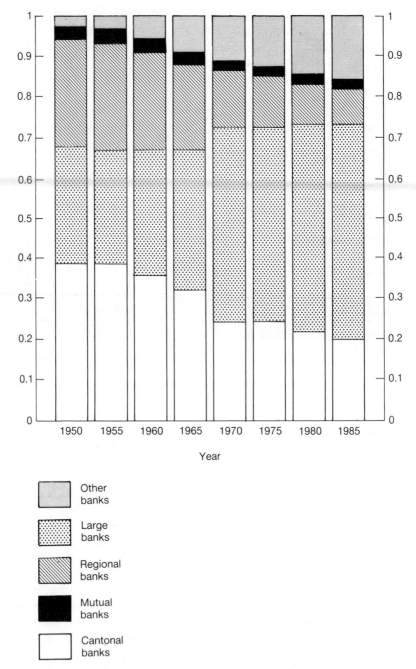

Figure 10.1 Market shares in the banking sector (from OECD, 1987, p. 62).
Source: Swiss National Bank.

Involvement in international business is concentrated in the large and foreign-owned banks (although a few of the 'other' Swiss banks are active but relatively small and the private bankers' portfolio management activities are heavily international in terms of both investments and clientele). Thus, the large Swiss banks have roughly 50 per cent and the foreign-owned banks approximately 70 per cent of their assets abroad. The two groups also dominate the fiduciary market, as noted above, as well as the interbank and foreign exchange market. Similarly, they dominate the new issues market, two-thirds of which are typically issues by foreign borrowers.

Switzerland and the Swiss franc also play an important role in medium- and long-term international capital markets. Since Swiss banks are universal banks which act as underwriters and brokers, a substantial part of their income is derived from international capital market activities. In recent years, the Swiss franc has been the main currency of denomination of foreign bond issues (48 per cent in 1985) and banks established in Switzerland (and particularly the large banks) have had a virtual monopoly of such issues (Christensen, 1986). Unfortunately for Swiss banks, Eurobonds have come to dominate international bond issues (from 39 per cent of a total of $8.6 billion in 1974 to 81 per cent of a total of $166 billion in 1985) and, because of stamp duties on securities sales, very few Eurobond issues have taken place in Switzerland. Still, the foreign branches of the Swiss banks have been active participants in Eurobond trading abroad, and gross medium- and long-term capital exports from Switzerland have been substantial, totalling SFr 46 billion for January to October 1988 for authorized public issues, note issues and bank credits.

A few features of the regulatory and supervisory framework are worth mentioning here. The supervisory authority is the Swiss Federal Banking Commission, an independent body which sets capital requirements, monitors risks and can require banks to make provisions for problem loans. Required capital-to-asset ratios are among the highest in Europe, actual ratios are higher yet and the banks have built up substantial hidden reserves which make their effective capital ratios even higher than those stated (see also section 10.3.1). Furthermore, Swiss banks have typically a lower direct exposure to problem countries than banks from other major industrial countries. Capital requirements, as well as limits on exposure to single customers, are applied on a consolidated basis. There are practically no restrictions on capital imports or exports. The restrictions on capital inflow which had been introduced starting in 1971 (to prevent, first, an unwanted expansion of the money supply and then too sharp an appreciation of the Swiss franc) began to be reversed in 1979, partly in view of their lack of effectiveness, and have since been abandoned for all practical purposes.

We conclude this picture of the Swiss banking system with four additional points. First, as mentioned in passing, Switzerland has a universal banking system; in fact, banks do tend to specialize, but the large banks are truly universal banks. Second, the celebrated Swiss banking secrecy is far from being unique to Switzerland. There are two differences, however: violations of banking secrecy constitute criminal offences and penalties are relatively severe, and banking secrecy can be lifted only for offences that constitute a crime in Switzerland, which tax evasion is not. Third, cartels, although regulated, are legal in Switzerland; a number of agreements (or 'conventions') governing fee structures are in force and limit competition, at least on the domestic side of the banking business. Finally, and somewhat paradoxically, a number of tax provisions are putting the Swiss banking industry at a disadvantage internationally: a turnover tax on precious metal transactions (now being removed) has driven the physical gold market away from Zurich; the withholding tax on interest and dividend income, at 35 per cent, is one of the highest in the industrialized countries, although it is waived on foreign bond issues and fiduciary deposits; there is a 3 per cent duty on new capital issues, a rate considerably higher than elsewhere, and there is a stamp duty of 0.15 − 0.30 per cent on all transactions (issue, sale or resale, including dealer transactions) in securities at whatever maturity. This last tax is partly responsible for the absence of a developed money market in Switzerland and for driving the Eurobond market abroad.

10.1.2   Sources of Switzerland's 'Comparative Advantage'

The position of Switzerland as a financial centre and the strength of its competitive position in banking derive in part from historical reasons. Briefly put, they find their roots first in the general Swiss social, political and economic environment, second in specific features of the financial industry, and third in the external environment. This is not the place to trace the history of the emergence of Switzerland as a financial centre, and we shall restrict this discussion to a few general remarks on the conditions for becoming an international financial centre (IFC).[1]

If a country is to become an IFC, its financial system must be part of an appropriate general national social and economic system that offers guarantees of stability, freedom of transactions and the endowments in physical and human capital required to sustain a competitive financial industry. The country's commitment to stability and freedom of transactions needs to be credible, i.e. economic agents need to believe that it will be adhered to in the future. A most important element in gaining such credibility is a long past history of stability and respect for freedom of transactions. Another important element is a record of macro-economic stability which stands as a guarantee that freedom of transactions will not be infringed for macro-economic or fiscal reasons.

It would indeed be difficult for a country that suffers from large government budget deficits, is a heavy borrower in international capital markets or has a habit of having an inflationary monetary policy to become an IFC. In all three cases, the temptation to resort to exchange controls that could easily spread from residents to non-residents is great. Such controls would serve to help place the government's bonds with the public, avoid capital flight or avoid seeing the base of the inflation tax shrinking together with holdings of the national currency. Thus a stable and sound monetary policy seems a prerequisite to accession to IFC status, both for its own sake and as a reflection of fiscal discipline.

Switzerland is of course a case in point. The performance of the Swiss economy has been remarkably good. In terms of GDP per capita it ranks either first, second or third depending on the exchange rate used. Inflation and unemployment in the post-war period have been among the lowest in the OECD countries. The Swiss franc has been devalued only once, in 1936, since the end of the First World War and until the breakdown of fixed exchange rates, and Switzerland was the only country, with the United States, to emerge from the Second World War with a convertible currency. At the root of this success, there is in part the good fortune of having escaped the devastations of war but also political (and legal) stability and a high degree of social consensus. These combine with conservative macro-economic policies, an unusual system of labour – management relations, and an outward oriented and adaptable industrial structure to explain the country's macro-economic performance.[2]

On the financial side, there is first the historical role of Swiss banking in international finance and the role of the country as a haven for refugee capital during the Second World War. In addition, the country's record and international reputation of exceptional political, monetary and economic stability have combined with the absence of controls over capital outflows (you can always get your money out which, once you are in, is more important than being able to come in) to lend attractiveness to doing banking business in Switzerland. At the same time the high net savings rate of the Swiss economy (including government budgetary balance or even surplus) has entailed a large net accumulation of foreign assets that has not only made continuation of a liberal policy towards capital movements credible but has also lent Swiss financial institutions their international outlook and made it imperative that they be able to adapt to a changing international financial environment.

Second, a number of specific features of the banking system and capital market have reinforced Switzerland's position as a financial centre. Some of these have been operative for a long time; others have come into play more recently. They include banking secrecy, the absence of legal obstacles to universal full-service banking, the placing power of the Swiss banks derived partly from their portfolio management activities, an early move towards fee income, a strong capital base and the absence of political pressure to engage in loans to high-risk−low-return sectors or countries. In addition, a highly educated labour force, more internationally minded than most, was in the past a source of qualified bank personnel.

Third, external factors have also contributed to the position of Switzerland as a financial centre. Put simply, *le malheur des uns fait le bonheur des autres*. In other words, Switzerland's comparative advantage was based partly on other countries' self-inflicted comparative disadvantage. Exchange controls and excessive regulations abroad created opportunities for the Swiss financial industry. The removal of these controls and regulations in turn is putting competitive pressures on the Swiss banking industry.

10.2   Changes in the International Financial System

10.2.1   The Global Environment

The catchwords for the changes that have swept international financial markets in the last ten years or so are 'deregulation', 'innovation', 'securitization' and 'globalization'. These trends have resulted in a decidedly more competitive environment for the financial industry in all industrialized countries. This competition, in turn, implies lower margins and return on capital for a number of banking systems and shifts in the pattern of comparative advantage.

It is difficult to predict how well Swiss banks will fare, and which Swiss banks will fare well, but a list of starting strengths and weaknesses can be offered. As far as the catchwords mentioned above are concerned, the Swiss banks (or at least the large banks, other banks (especially foreign banks) and private bankers to use the official classification) are, with one exception and one qualification, well placed. They have hardly been heavily regulated and protected in the past, and globalization is a long-established feature of their activities. A substantial part of the income of the more internationally minded banks is derived from securities-related activities and off-balance-sheet transactions; the qualifier is the stunting effect of stamp duties on securities business in Switzerland itself. The exception is innovation; few of the many innovations in financial techniques and instruments have originated in Switzerland, and its banks and financial companies have been slow in positioning themselves in markets for new financial instruments. The reasons include innate conservatism, the absence of a domestic test market, adequate profitability in other more traditional lines of business, lack of qualified personnel and failure to invest in the appropriate hardware and software. There have, however, been some changes. For instance, a fully electronic

Swiss Options and Financial Futures Exchange (SOFFEX) has been operating since mid-1988, and is handling a sizeable volume of transactions and making a contribution to increased market transparency.

Among further strengths, we can refer to the capital ratios of commercial and large banks mentioned above which, even without taking into account the major part of hidden reserves, are the highest of all the countries surveyed by J Revell (1985) in his OECD study (see table 10.3). At a time when the thrust of international banking supervision is on risk-weighted capital-to-asset ratios on a consolidated basis, as embodied in the 1988 Basle Capital Convergence Accord, Swiss banks thus seem well placed, especially since some of the lowest capital ratios are to be found in Japan, the most threatening new entrant on international capital markets. The Swiss banks, at least the larger ones, also seem to enjoy favourable cost ratios in international comparison. Thus, one study has found the Swiss banks to have comparatively low staff costs in relation to earnings, low total operating

Table 10.3 Capital ratios, average 1978–82 (per cent)

Large banks

Australia	5.16
Austria	2.42
Belgium	2.54
Canada	3.48
France	1.35
Germany	4.74
Greece	4.10
Italy	2.11
Japan	2.06
Netherlands	3.88
Norway	4.42
Spain	5.66
Switzerland	5.99
UK	5.26
USA	4.62

Commercial banks

Belgium	2.90
Denmark	8.19
Finland	7.18
France	2.28
Germany	4.63
Italy	2.42
Netherlands	3.21
Norway	4.73
Spain	5.98
Sweden	1.52
Switzerland	11.63
USA	5.81

Source: Revell, 1985, p.99, table 34

costs and hence one of the highest net earnings margin, a very favourable ratio of other income (mainly fee income from non-balance-sheet operations) to total assets and one of the highest ratios of pre-tax profit to gross earnings. In addition, the large Swiss banks appear to have among the lowest intermediation costs, presumably indicating high efficiency and competitiveness.[3] Some indications on comparative cost and efficiency ratios are given in table 10.4.

Table 10.4 Comparative indicators of cost and efficiency

	Interest margin/ FCNFE	Net bank income/ FCNFE	Operating costs/ FCNFE
Switzerland	1.6 (1.8)	3.1 (3.6)	1.7 (2.1)
Japan	1.8 (1.5)	2.1 (1.9)	1.5 (1.3)
Belgium	3.1 n.a.	3.9 n.a.	3.2 n.a.
Germany	3.3 (3.8)	4.5 (5.4)	3.0 (3.7)
USA	3.7 (3.2)	4.9 (4.6)	3.4 (3.2)
Italy	3.8 (2.8)	5.2 (4.3)	3.4 (3.3)
Spain	4.8 (5.7)	5.9 (6.9)	3.9 (4.4)
France	4.9 (4.7)	5.8 (5.5)	3.9 (3.8)
UK	n.a. (4.7)	n.a. (6.9)	n.a. (4.8)

FCNFE, funds committed to non-financial entities.
The first number of each indicator refers to all commercial banks; the second, in parentheses, refers to top commercial banks.
n.a., not available.
Source: chapter 6, tables 6.10−6.12

However, the picture is not entirely rosy. In addition to falling behind in the innovations race, the basis for the competitive advantage of Swiss banks is being eroded in a number of respects. In the first place, the role of banking secrecy is diminishing both because the share of institutional investors for whom it is not important is rising and because it is not, or appears to investors not to be, as absolute as in the past. Second, Swiss capital markets, in particular equity markets, have come under increasing and largely justified criticism; Swiss exchanges risk falling far behind their competitors in terms of transparency (inadequate prospectuses, lack of information on volumes and prices of transactions), liquidity (absence of market makers and specialists) and access (registration of shares etc.). The situation is not helped by stamp duties and a cartelized fee structure. Third, the increasing sophistication of the clientele has combined with more open competitive markets to produce a shift from relationship to transactions banking. This means a less secure clientele base, notably in the portfolio management sector of the industry, be it private individual or institutional management. Fourth, the Swiss labour pool is shrinking and salaries are high (but social charges are comparatively low though rising). Fifth, telecommunications costs are comparatively high and facilities are often backward mainly because of the monopoly of the Post Office (PTT), once the pride of the land. In brief, life has been a little too comfortable for too long, and what used to be minor distortions have become more severe handicaps with the advent of increased foreign competition.

10.2.2 1992 and All That

In many respects, the creation of a unified EC market in banking and financial services can be seen as part of the general trend towards deregulation, increased competitiveness and globalization. Mutual recognition, right of establishment, freedom to buy and sell financial services and liberalization of capital movements should all result in increased competition within the EC zone. Provided that no barriers are erected towards the outside world, trade creation should outweigh trade diversion (in the limit there should be no trade diversion).[4] There should thus be obvious efficiency gains from switching from high- to low-cost sources of supply, be they within or without the EC.

The increase in competition will affect various banks, be they in the EC or in third countries, in like manner but to a different extent depending in part on how protected they were initially. Presumably, Swiss banks should see a net gain in so far as they have been part of what was already a quite open system but were previously denied access (as were their EC competitors) to a number of individual highly protected national markets within the EC. That is, the change in environment brought about by 1992 might be much larger, and the adjustment problems correspondingly greater, for a number of national banking systems within the EC than for Swiss banks.

Things are of course not quite so simple. There is, first, the issue of how open the EC internal market will in fact be to third countries. There are also issues that are specific to the relationship between Switzerland and the EC. It is to these issues that we now turn.

10.3   Switzerland and the European Community

10.3.1   The European Community Financial Market and Third Countries

Summarily put, the Commission's strategy in creating a unified internal market in financial services followed a twofold approach: freedom of capital movement and liberalization of financial services. Although the EC set itself *erga omnes* liberalization as a goal for the first of these, this was not an obligation. As a matter of fact, there are explicit safeguard clauses that allow the imposition of controls on capital account transaction with third countries, in the case of foreign exchange market or monetary disturbances. Moreover, France made its approval conditional on the Commission presenting proposals aiming at avoiding tax evasion from countries with weak currencies. There are thus some grounds for worry on the part of third countries even if one accepts the intellectual argument of the Commission that full and *erga omnes* capital liberalization is in the interest of the EC if it wants to become, or remain, a major international financial centre.

There were three principal means by which the second and complementary part of the strategy − full liberalization in the provision of financial, notably banking, services − was to be achieved: freedom for credit institutions granted a banking licence in any member state to set up a branch in any other member state (right of establishment); freedom to supply financial services in any member country; home country prudential supervision on a consolidated basis. In addition, to ensure bank stability and a level playing field, minimum common standards in matters such as preventive and prudential regulation, notably with respect to capital-to-asset ratios were to be set up. However, once these minimum common standards have been met, every country has to accept the regulatory norms of the member state whose authorities are competent for the supervision of home banks.

The question for third countries concerns the conditions of their access to the financial services market thus created. Access, according to the Commission's proposals (e.g. Second Banking Directive) is to be granted on the basis of reciprocity. In addition, the EC seemed to want to use the reciprocity negotiations to obtain harmonization of the third country's legislation or practices concerning matters such as tax treatment, fiscal control or prudential rules with those of the EC.

Reciprocity is the main potential source of conflict with third countries. From an economic point of view, reciprocity is a strange concept; it implies that your partner cannot see the benefits to himself of liberalizing trade and that you have to force him to do good unto himself. As part of the political dynamics of the liberalization process it can, however, play a useful role. But it can also be used for protectionist purposes; hence the fear that it may be the main building block of 'fortress Europe'. Much depends on what is meant by reciprocity. At one extreme, reciprocity may mean simply conditional 'national treatment', identical operating conditions for domestic and foreign-owned establishments granted under certain conditions. At the other extreme, reciprocity may mean allowing third-country banks to do in the EC only what all the banks from any EC country are authorized to do in the third country. The Commission's position, as reflected in Article 7 of the Second Directive and in informal explanations, is disquieting. Article 7 seems to imply that, under the EC's interpretation of reciprocity, establishment will be granted under national treatment to third-country banks only if banks from any EC country are allowed to carry out in the third country all the activities that they are allowed to carry out in the EC within the confines of the single bank licence. For 'activities' read 'underwriting' and for 'third country' read the United States and you have the problem in a nutshell. Perhaps fortunately, the protectionist use of reciprocity is a double-edged sword as it invites reciprocal retaliation.

To close this brief discussion of the general problem of relations with third countries, it should perhaps be mentioned that a number of issues are still very unclear; for instance, the application of home country control or the extension of the principle of mutual recognition.

10.3.2 Switzerland's Relationship with the Community

Relations with the EC have recently been a matter of intense political discussion in Switzerland. 1992 focused the public's and the authorities' attention on the dangers of being left out and/or of missing a crucial economic opportunity. The government and Swiss diplomacy are actively working on trying to define the shape that economic and political relations with the EC should take. Swiss involvement in European economic organization is not new. Switzerland was a founding member of the European Free Trade Association (EFTA) (1960) and applied for Association with the EC in 1969. After rejection of its application, Switzerland concluded a bilateral Free Trade Agreement in industrial products with the EC in 1972. A joint Switzerland—EC Committee was created and over a hundred bilateral agreements have been concluded since 1972 on the basis of the 'future developments clause' of the original Agreement. As mentioned in section 10.1, the EC is Switzerland's major trading partner.

The issue of whether to apply for membership was discussed in the late 1980s; the government's position, which seems to represent the population's majority view, is that such membership would be inappropriate at the moment though every effort should be made to negotiate further agreements and to take into account the EC's development when drafting economic legislation. The basis for rejection of full membership at this stage is both political and economic. One political argument is that membership would be incompatible with the concept of permanent neutrality, although this may not be an overriding objection. Another is that membership would conflict with specific features of Swiss federalism, notably direct democracy. A third is that the European integration process is far from fully evolved and one would not know what one was joining. Of the economic arguments, let us mention three, of which the first two have strong political overtones. First, membership of the EC would imply accepting the free movement of labour from EC members, a prospect that scares (to some extent wrongly in our view) a population which already finds itself *überfremdet*; the enlargement of the EC has added to this concern. Second, Switzerland manages to have an agricultural protection system that is even more protectionist than that of the EC and which it wants to preserve to some extent. Third, some 40 per cent of its trade is still with non-EC countries.

One interesting question is whether there are strong economic grounds for rejecting membership as far as the changes that it would entail for the Swiss financial system are concerned. First, take capital adequacy requirements and harmonized prudential supervision; there are unlikely to be major problems here for the reasons already mentioned. Second, membership would entail a substantial change in the rules governing banking secrecy. Article 14.4 of the EC Banking Directive provides that competent authorities (which, in the meaning of the Article, include the bankers' external auditors) will be free, under certain circumstances including decisions subject to administrative appeal, to use information obtained confidentially. This runs counter to Swiss banking law which specifies that external auditors are addressees of Swiss banking secrecy. Application of Article 14.4 would thus constitute a major dent in Swiss banking secrecy. This would undoubtedly cause a significant decline in customers in the short run, but banking secrecy is in any event likely to play a diminishing role in the longer run. Third, tax harmonization with the EC may well entail a loss of fiscal revenue as Swiss withholding taxes may have to be lowered and stamp duties removed (the latter would be a good thing for the Swiss financial system anyway). Fourth, there is one change which would be strongly resisted in Switzerland and which might cause substantial losses to a number of financial institutions: the exchange of information with member country tax authorities. Fifth, there would be some substantial changes in the securities markets; for instance, legislation concerning the transferability of bearer stocks would have to be harmonized with the EC's companies directive. Similarly, the provisions contained in proposed directives concerning the winding up of credit institutions would require substantial changes in Swiss banking law. Finally, there might be some increase in competition from EC banks operating within Switzerland beyond the competition that already exists because of their current presence; the reason is that Swiss tolerance of cartel-like arrangements (subject to the so-called 'effective competition rule') would probably be challenged under EC anti-trust law.

All in all, it would not appear that EC membership would pose insurmountable problems for the Swiss banking system. *A fortiori*, Swiss banks should be able to adapt to the changes implied by 1992 even if competitive pressure, or reciprocity negotiations, brought about a certain amount of harmonization of Swiss and EC banking regulations.

10.4 Swiss Banks After 1992

How well the Swiss financial centre and its banks will fare in the long run will depend on how well they respond to three interrelated challenges: the EC's unified internal market for financial services, increased worldwide competition in the provision of such services and the challenge posed by some increasingly binding internal constraints. These three issues are taken up, albeit briefly, in turn.

10.4.1 The Challenge of 1992

The specific challenge of the unified internal EC market, beyond the general competitive pressures that increasing globalization and deregulation of competitors entail, manifests itself in two main forms: securing access to the EC's financial markets and finding a *modus vivendi* with the EC on tax matters to avoid discrimination against the Swiss financial system based on capital flight considerations.

Securing the right of establishment in the EC and non-discrimination against Swiss suppliers of financial services is conditional on being able to satisfy EC demands on reciprocity. This should not be overly difficult in so far as Switzerland has a universal banking system and is itself broadly open to the establishment of foreign, including EC, banks (the Swiss themselves require reciprocity in granting the right of establishment but their requirements for the granting of such reciprocity appear to be much more modest than those of the EC). However, Swiss bargaining power is somewhat limited by the fact that the gains for Swiss banks from access to the large EC internal market are likely to be higher than those of EC banks from access to the Swiss market. Some protection against EC discrimination is, however, available both from the OECD's code of liberalization on capital movements and from the General Agreement on Tariffs and Trade (GATT) Uruguay round of negotiations on the liberalization of trade in services, a route which Swiss economic diplomacy is actively pursuing. Harmonization with the EC's minimum common standards with respect to prudential supervision and protective regulation, although it will pose some problems in fields like deposit insurance, should not pose insuperable problems if only because Swiss requirements are already above minimum standards in most important cases.

Where a major conflict may arise is in the field of measures to prevent 'fiscal distortions and tax evasion'. Here the Commission argues that the risk of distortions in capital movements arising from differences in the taxation of capital and capital income will rise with freedom of capital movements, as will the risk of tax evasion. It, together with a number of member states, therefore proposes that some measures be taken to minimize such risks. Three types of measures are envisaged: a general obligation for banks to declare interest income to the tax authorities of the investor; a reinforcement of cooperation between tax authorities, with the tax authorities of a member state being given access to the interest receipts of its tax payers in other member states in the case of presumption of tax evasion; a generalization and harmonization of the withholding tax on interest income. The first two of these measures would be unacceptable to the Swiss authorities and would clearly be in contradiction with bank secrecy. The third might be acceptable, as in any event Switzerland has one of the highest withholding taxes on interest income; however, this tax is waived for fiduciary deposits and foreign bonds for the sake of the participation of Swiss banks in international capital markets. The saving grace for Switzerland is that these measures are unlikely to be unanimously approved by EC member countries, as they must be since countries such as Germany have a philosophical opposition to the first two and countries like the United Kingdom and Luxembourg fear that the third, in addition to the first two, would totally undermine their position in international financial markets unless exemptions are granted. The margin of manoeuvre for the EC if it wants to be an international financial centre open to the outside world, is thus seriously limited.

10.4.2   The Challenge of Worldwide Financial Competition

Worldwide financial competition challenges Swiss banks both in their home market and in third markets. At home, Swiss banks are likely to lose market share in a number of fields, both traditional, such as portfolio management, and newer, such as financial engineering, treasury management, mergers and acquisitions or sophisticated composite new instruments where they have been slow to develop an expertise. Cartel-like arrangements governing fee structures will increasingly be challenged and margins are likely to fall. However, we would not expect to find foreign establishments making deep inroads into the retail business of Swiss banks; regional characteristics, including language differences, in a national market which is still small by international standards constitute a substantial entry cost for new entrants. We would also expect to see increased international competition work to the detriment of medium-sized non-specialized banking institutions; here we would expect, within banks established in Switzerland, to see the large banks become larger and retain their universal character and to see the other banks, especially foreign banks, occupy increasingly specialized niches in which they could obtain a substantial market share, with both phenomena working to the detriment of the market share of the cantonal and regional banks.

A similar trend can be expected in the competitive position of Swiss banks in third markets or in the truly international portion of the Swiss market. The key here is being able to supply standard products at low cost or acquiring a comparative advantage, be it technological or management based, in a specialized market. A favourable regulatory, fiscal and socio-economic environment is also essential. How well Swiss banks will meet this international challenge thus essentially depends on the domestic constraints they face and on domestic responses to these challenges and constraints.

10.4.3   Domestic Constraints and Domestic Responses

We have argued that in many respects Switzerland enters the international competitive race in a good starting position. How well it will come out at the end depends on appropriate domestic responses to a number of constraints and problems.

Among these, we would single out first a set of factors that have driven a substantial portion of Swiss banking and capital market activities abroad. Carrying these activities out of foreign centres like London has not notably hampered the large Swiss banks in the short run. On the contrary, it has allowed them to some extent to act like profit-maximizing discriminating monopolists equating their marginal cost to marginal revenues in separate markets, charging low prices in the wholesale international market where price elasticity is high and high prices in the domestic market where price elasticity is low and entry is limited by cartel-like arrangements and neighbourhood effects. As well as being detrimental to the Swiss consumer of banking services, such displacement of banking activities abroad is detrimental in the long run to the Swiss financial centre as a whole and to the large banks themselves, as they increasingly recognize. The reason is that financial skills are partly acquired through learning by doing and learning by innovating. The displacement (or hiring) of highly qualified staff abroad acts as a brake on the creation and maintenance of a pool of talent and source of innovative capacity at home.

The factors that have driven banking activities abroad include prominently stamp duties on securities transactions but also the narrowness of the skilled labour pool. In addition, any arrangement that makes domestically supplied financial services uncompetitive for foreign customers is likely to act as an incentive to supply them from abroad (provided that the reason that they are expensively supplied at home is a monopoly power or a local regulatory/fiscal disadvantage that is absent abroad). Among such arrangements are an uncompetitive fee structure on Swiss exchanges and various conventions on fees as well as other cartel-type agreements including restrictions on membership in issuing syndicates. As a matter of fact, reform of the Swiss stock exchanges (see section 10.2.1) is becoming an urgent matter if trading is to take place in Switzerland rather than abroad. There is again an important externality here: trading in Switzerland would contribute to constituting a larger pool of skilled traders and increase the innovative capacity of the Swiss financial industry.

Ultimately the fate of the Swiss financial system is in the hands of the Swiss. Appropriate responses are required on the part of both the authorities and the industry. On the side of the authorities, removal of stamp duties and a more vigorous policy *vis-à-vis* cartels is the first order of business. In addition, but this is an issue that goes beyond the financial sector, the authorities could contribute to relieving labour market pressure both by helping to provide better business education and by adopting a work permit/immigration policy that is oriented more strongly towards industry's need for highly skilled personnel. The banking sector could also play a greater role in sponsoring research and education in finance and banking to help create and maintain the pool of talent and creativity that is indispensable to the maintenance of the competitive position of Switzerland as an international financial centre. After all, the financial industry is a service industry whose strength depends primarily on people. It is also becoming a high-technology service industry; investment in technology is the other main source of its strength. Here again, both the authorities, through removal of the Post Office's monopoly on telecommunications, and the banks, through investment in technology, have a role to play. Ultimately then, the fate of Swiss banking after 1992 will be, given a stable legal, economic and regulatory framework, in the hands of government and the banking industry.

Notes

1 The next two paragraphs are adapted from Swoboda (1987).
2 On the role of the labour market and macro-economic policy, see Danthine and Lambelet (1987).
3 These findings, based in large part on Revell's work, are reported in Braillard et al. (1988, 10).
4 Even if there were no barriers whatsoever anywhere on trade in financial services, trade diversion, or second-best, problems may still arise if there exist restrictions on other types of trade or domestic distortions. This raises some interesting issues that are analogous to those involved in the proper sequencing of liberalization in the development literature. These will not be pursued here.

References

Braillard, P., Betcher, O.G. and Lusenti, G. (1988) *Switzerland as a Financial Center*. Dordrecht: Kluwer.

Bridel, P. (1984) Essai d'estimation de la part Suisse à l'activité financière internationale, 1975–83. *Bulletin Trimestriel, Banque Nationale Suisse*, no. 3, September, 147–80.

Christensen, B.V. (1986) Switzerland's role as an international financial center. Occasional Paper 45, July, International Monetary Fund.

Danthine, J.P. and Lambelet, J.-C. (1987) The Swiss case: conservative policies ain't enough! *Economic Policy*, 5, October.

OECD (1987) *Switzerland, Economic Surveys 1986/87*. Paris: OECD.

Revell, J.R.S. (1985) *Costs and Margins in Banking: Statistical Supplement 1978–1982*. Paris: OECD.

Swoboda, A. (1987) *International Financial Centres, Proceedings of the 40th International Banking School, 1987*, pp. 173–4.

Comment

Jean-Pierre Danthine

I shall start my comments with a few methodological reflections on the various country studies presented in this book. The assignment can be viewed as follows: first, assess the health of the banking sector of the particular country before 1992; second, describe the nature of the expected change in the environment of this industry; third, try to guess how it will perform in the new environment.

Loosely speaking, this assignment is in the spirit of the economists' favourite comparative statics analysis. However, it has a few peculiarities which make the possible answers highly speculative.

1 The change envisaged is not of a repetitive nature and the past contains few hints, for the particular countries under review, of how it will be met.
2 The change is particularly complex, with many facets, quite the opposite of comparative statics analysis where the *ceteris paribus* fiction is maintained.
3 The nature of the environmental change is highly uncertain: without knowing for sure what the question is, it is impossible to eliminate vagueness in the answer.
4 In the case of Switzerland, there is a double layer of uncertainty: like everyone else, we have to guess how Europe 1992 will develop. Moreover, we have to estimate what the nature of Switzerland's association with Europe will be after 1992. Viewed in this light, Swoboda's conclusion, which in substance says that the Swiss banking sector is a fine athlete with a few weaknesses, does not fully make sense until we know whether our athlete will have to play rugby or badminton, and thus whether his shortcomings will be decisive or not.
5 Finally, placing this whole exercise in the context that we know best reveals that we have adopted the wrong perspective: by looking at each country individually we have taken a sort of partial equilibrium approach. However, the new environment is not going to be characterized only by new rules of the game. It is equally important to estimate the strength of the other players and a full evaluation of the future cannot be attempted until we have rounded out the tour of the different countries and attempted a synthesis. Swoboda acknowledges this when he asserts that one of the

strengths of the Swiss banking sector resides in the self-inflicted comparative disadvantage of other countries.

Swoboda paints a rosy picture of the Swiss situation with which I do not fundamentally disagree. It would be interesting to complete (or qualify) the static evaluation he proposes with some elements of a dynamic assessment. Has the industry been gaining or losing ground in the recent climate of increased competition to which 1992 will only be the sequel? I would like to add one important additional advantage among the strengths he identifies: a credible quality label, achieved from centuries of experience in conservative banking. I would also like to voice my scepticism regarding another point: the data indeed appear to show the Swiss banking sector as benefiting from low costs of operations (relative to international competitors). This would be a unique case among Swiss industries. Given the level of salaries and rents in Switzerland and the prices of other inputs, and given also the apparent absence of returns to scale in banking, we may wonder if this statement is not an aberration due to some peculiarities of the data.

That there are a number of weaknesses is in some sense reassuring: there is a lot of room to do better. Of course this is true for everyone; but more so for Switzerland, as the view often is that 'they've got the most to lose'. In fact, if these weak spots find a solution 'the others' may not be catching up so easily after all! The rewards of putting the Swiss equity markets in shape, removing the stamp duties (the required fiscal adjustment is of an order of magnitude that would bring a smile to the lips of the French finance minister) and creating the conditions for a larger skilled labour force, thus making it possible to retain at home some of the high value-added services that have emigrated outside Switzerland, should be great.

In order to assess the degree of preparedness of the Swiss banking industry in the perspective of 1992, it is useful to distinguish three areas of activity.

1 Production of services abroad: the prospects of new markets opening up should be entirely favourable as the (large) Swiss banks seem better prepared than most for international competition.
2 Purely domestic activities: the Swiss banks are strong in traditional businesses. Outsiders have been making inroads by introducing new services. Given the strong local implantation of the Swiss, we can question whether these are permanent. However, a decrease in the margins applied by Swiss banks may be necessary to restrict entry and protect their markets. All in all the Swiss consumer of banking services should benefit.
3 International business attracted to Switzerland: this is where there is the most to lose and where uncertainty is the largest. We do not know for sure what the reasons are for the Swiss success on this front: secrecy is one, but so are other attributes of the services provided as well as the

credibility of the general political and economic environment. It would be of interest to obtain some indication of the profits generated from managing the estimated SFr 1,500 billion portfolio of assets and thus form an idea of what is at stake.

The importance of banking secrecy is decreasing owing to the rise of institutional investors, US pressure on insider trading and domestic pressure on drug money. How much extra erosion will be forced on the Swiss by pressure from the EC is impossible to say at this point. Two remarks are in order.

1 The trend is clearly toward relying on other 'assets': the rumour is that return performance should be one of them, but information is scanty here also.
2 The secrecy issue should not be examined in a vacuum and the relative position with respect to competitors in the EC is also of importance. On this front, Luxembourg, in particular, may lose as much of its rent as Switzerland, if not more.

The climate of uncertainty with respect to negotiating with the EC is generating much fear in Switzerland: 'the worse is at hand'. The main point of concentration is cited by Swoboda: the benefits for the Swiss banks in gaining access to EC markets are likely to be larger than the benefits for the EC banks in gaining access to the Swiss market. This is sometimes expressed even more radically as 'They don't need us!'

It is useful here to notice that, as far as can be seen, there will be mutual gains and there is no reason to believe that those mutual gains will not be realized. There is thus ground for optimism rather than pessimism. Furthermore the statement about the prospects of the various banking sectors amounts to an admission that EC consumers stand to gain more than the Swiss consumers. Without being excessively naive we can hope that this will be the determining factor and that the spirit of 1992 will continue to be to the benefit of the consumers rather than the protection of an industry.

11

Capital Requirements of German Banks and the European Community Proposals on Banking Supervision

Bernd Rudolph

The German banking industry has seconded the proposal for a single European banking market and the establishment of a 'fair level playing field'. In banking services, this implies the harmonization of rules on capital adequacy. The Cooke committee at the Bank for International Settlements and the European Commission have been working on new capital guidelines and deposit protection schemes. It is argued in this chapter that capital adequacy regulations significantly affect the competitive positioning of the German banking industry.

The chapter is structured as follows. The German banking system, its supervisory controls and the deposit insurance mechanisms are described in section 11.1 and the effects of the new capital regulations are assessed in section 11.2.

11.1 The German Banking Industry and its Supervisory System

11.1.1 The Structure of the German Banking System

It is common practice to divide the German banking industry into three groups differing mainly with respect to the legal form of their member banks and to their connecting banking associations as well as their related regulations and deposit protection schemes. These three groups are the commercial banks, the savings banks and the credit cooperatives. Two of these groups, the savings banks and the credit cooperatives, operate within well defined areas (*Regionalprinzip*) and therefore do not compete with one another. But this *Regionalprinzip* no longer holds for their central institutions running branch offices in Frankfurt for instance. In many aspects the competing units are the banking groups, acting in joint competition (*Gruppenwettbewerb*), but competition in retail banking acts mainly on a local basis. The German unification process did not change the principal structure of the German banking system, but the groups and single banks showed definitive different strategies in penetrating the markets of the 'Neue Länder'.

Commercial banks are organized as stock corporations or limited liability companies. For statistical purposes they are usually divided into four sub-groups: the three big banks with their Berlin subsidiaries and a nationwide network of more than 3,000 branches; the very heterogeneous group of so-called regional banks operating nationwide with only a limited number of branches, or only in a certain region, or as single banks like most of the subsidiaries of foreign banks belonging to this group; the branches of foreign banks; the private bankers, the oldest group within the banking industry but nowadays with only a few independent houses neither owned nor controlled by other banks.

The *savings bank sector* consists of more than 750 local saving institutions and their 11 regional central institutions, the *Landesbanken/Girozentralen*, including a central institution, the Deutsche Girozentrale—Deutsche Kommunalbank, with similar functions. With a few exceptions savings banks are incorporated under public law and owned by their respective municipalities or districts. The *Landesbanken* are organized as public law corporations and owned by the state itself and/or the state savings banks association. At the moment the *Landesbanken* are considering building larger groups through mergers with other giro institutions or larger savings banks.

The last of the three sectors, the *credit cooperatives* consists of more than 3,000 local credit cooperatives, eight regional institutions and a central institution. The local institutions are organized in the legal form of cooper-atives, and the regional institutions are organized as stock corporations. Recently the central institution of the credit cooperatives sector, the Deutsche Genossenschaftsbank, planned to acquire all the regional institutions with the aim of building an only two-tiered system in this sector, but after high losses the position of the remaining institutions has been strengthened. However, as 1992 approached, merger activities were stimulated in all sectors of the German banking system.

While the savings banks and cooperative banks show a certain 'unity and harmony, as a result of the regional organization which practically excludes competition within each group, commercial banks work together only on general economic and public relations matters' (Scheidl, 1988). Therefore, the central organization of the commercial banks (Bundesverband deutscher Banken) is a loose association representing its members' interests whereas the association of savings banks (Deutscher Sparkassen-und Giroverband) and the association of credit cooperatives (Bundesverband der Deutschen Volks-banken und Raiffeisenbanken) undertake more central functions for their members.

The banks of all three banking groups are called *universal banks* because in principle they carry out the full range of commercial and investment banking services. This common characteristic does not exclude some specialization with respect to certain customers or business activities on the basis of historical, regional or strategic differences. Therefore we cannot speak of a uniform type of universal banks. Only the three large branch banks, some other large regional banks and the central institutions of the savings and corporate banks operate as universal banks in a definitive sense, i.e. as institutions offering the whole range of banking services and at the same time holding shares and supervisory board memberships in non-bank companies as well as exercising equity voting rights.[1] The same institutions or most of them (with obvious and noteworthy differences) have built up a European or global network of subsidiaries and affiliates. The other institutions called universal banks offer a wide range of services in their regional district (partly in connection with their central institutions) but do not exhibit any other features of the large banks.

In addition to the three groups of universal banks mentioned above, there are a number of specialized banks with different legal forms and sometimes with their own associations and regulations. Some of the specialized banks are included in the statistics of the German Central Bank, the Deutsche

Table 11.1 The institutional structure of the German banking system

	No. of reporting banks at end of 1990	Volume of business (billion DM)
Commercial banks	341	1,408,979
Big banks	6	468,554
Regional and other commercial banks	192	801,398
Branches of foreign banks	60	76,291
Private bankers	83	62,736
Savings banks	598	1,842,624
Central and regional giro institutions	11	761,769
Savings banks	771	1,080,855
Credit cooperatives	3,487	808,576
Central and regional institutions	4	216,687
Credit cooperatives	3,392	591,889
Mortgage banks	36	611,217
Private mortgage banks	27	456,721
Public mortgage banks	9	154,496
Special functions banks	18	490,570
Postal giro and savings banks	16	72,876
All categories of banks	4,589	5,243,842

Bundesbank, namely the mortgage banks, the special functions banks and the postal giro and postal savings banks. The grouping of these statistics gives a rough idea of the institutional structure of the German banking system (see table 11.1 for this grouping, together with data on the number of the banks in each sector and their respective business volumes at the end of 1990).

Other specialized banks, which are normally not included in the statistics of the Bundesbank, are the *Bausparkassen* (institutions similar to building and loans associations), investment companies, securities clearing houses and special guarantee banks. We shall not deal with these institutions here because, with one exception, they are not real competitors of the universal or specialized banks. The one exception are the building and loan associations which operate under a special law but nevertheless are central to the financial services industry. In the following we shall concentrate on the universal banks and only occasionally refer to related problems concerning the specialized banks.

11.1.2   The Development and Basic Structure of the Supervisory System

Development of the supervisory system

The fundamental law on the supervision of German banks is the *Banking Act* of 10 July 1961 (*Gesetz über das Kreditwesen, KWG*),[2] which replaced the Banking Act of 1934. The introduction of general supervision of banks was a consequence of the banking crisis of 1931, which culminated in the illiquidity of the Danatbank in 1931.[3] Prior to 1931 only partial legislation had existed with respect to banking supervision, for example the Mortgage Bank Act of 1899. In 1931 and 1932 a number of emergency orders set up for the first time a comprehensive system of governmental supervision of all banks. These orders were consolidated in the Banking Act of 1934 (*Reichsgesetz über das Kreditwesen*), which established the principle that banking had to be licensed and regulated following certain guidelines.

After the war bank supervision was carried out at state, as opposed to federal, level. A uniform regulatory framework did not exist until the passing of the Banking Act in 1961, which at the same time created the legal basis for the establishment of the Federal Banking Supervisory Office in Berlin.[4] The Banking Act of 1961, which remained essentially unaltered for 15 years, adopted the central elements of the pre-war legislation. The first substantial changes were brought about by the amendment of the Banking Act in 1976. This amendment act incorporated various attempts to remedy certain weaknesses in the banking system which had become particularly apparent in connection with the collapse of Bankhaus I.D. Herstatt on 26 June 1974 (stricter rules on the extension of large-scale credits, on the information required of borrowers and on the Banking Supervisory Office's rights of information and investigation). The 1976 amendments had been preceded and accompanied by other measures to improve the viability of the banking system. The developments following the Herstatt crisis support the thesis that the development of banking supervision is mainly a reaction to current political pressures: the introduction of Principle Ia to limit risks from open currency positions relative to the bank's liable capital in August 1974; the foundation of the *Liquiditätskonsortialbank* in September 1974 with the objective of standing by in cases of liquidity shortages; the establishment of the study group *Grundsatzfragen der Kreditwirtschaft* in November 1974;[5] the reform and further development of the deposit protection schemes by the savings banks in December 1975, by the commercial banks in May 1976 and by the credit cooperatives in April 1977.

The second larger revision of the Banking Act was brought about by the Third Act to Amend the Banking Act which came into effect on 1 January 1985. Legislative actions which led to the 1985 amendments were expedited by the financial difficulties of the private bankers Schroeder, Münchmeyer, Hengst & Co. (SMH-Bank) in the autumn of 1983, although this case resulted in a remarkable rescue operation by the private banking community in concert with the authorities.

The 1985 amendments produced extensive changes in the regulatory system. Most importantly, they prescribed consolidation of banking groups, including foreign subsidiaries, for the purpose of both capital adequacy ratios and large-scale credit ratios. Until then the banks could build up so-called credit pyramids through their subsidiaries without a corresponding increase in the capital base of the parent bank, thereby bypassing the restrictions on business based on the bank's liable capital. In addition to these consolidation requirements the 1985 amendments reduced the ceiling for large-scale credits from 75 to 50 per cent of the equity, supplemented the provisions on equity by establishing stricter requirements for silent capital participation and by recognizing special participation rights, the so-called *Genußscheine*, as equity capital.[6] Such capital must not, however, exceed 25 per cent of the other liable capital.

Aims and regulating instruments of banking supervision

Section 6 of the Banking Act quotes three functions of the supervisory authority which has the task of supervising banking institutions in accordance with the provisions of the Banking Act: the Federal Banking Supervisory Office shall counteract undesirable developments in banking which may endanger the safety of the assets entrusted to banks, adversely affect the orderly conduct of banking business or result in serious disadvantages for the domestic economy.

There is some debate as to whether the three functions are of equal importance or whether there are one or two main functions. In the past some authors seemed to give equal prominence to the protection of deposits and therefore to a special protection of the deposit owners on the one hand and the safeguarding of the orderly functioning of the banking system on the other hand. However, there has recently been a tendency to define the protection of the functioning of the banking system as the main task of banking supervision. The 1985 amendments to the Banking Act underline this position in explicitly stating in section 6 (3) that the supervisory authority shall exercise its functions exclusively in the public interest.[7] In addition to this debate, some hold the opinion that the instruments of the supervisory authority which serve the objective of deposit or lender protection also serve the objective of protecting the functioning of the banking system. This view can be legitimately held if one remembers that a bank collapse can be infectious.[8]

The instruments of the supervisory authority can be classified in several ways. One possibility is to distinguish the instruments regulating entry to and exit from the banking market (licensing, start-up capital, powers to intervene) and instruments governing banking operations. We shall only deal with the second class of instruments concerning ongoing banking activities. These instruments can be classified as the so-called structural norms and the informational rights and obligations.

Structural norms are as follows:

1 provisions regarding equity and liquidity;
2 limitations of investments;
3 rules governing the extension and diversification of large-scale loans;
4 rules governing loans to borrowers closely associated with the lending bank (Organkredite).

Informational norms are as follows:

1 reporting obligations;
2 annual financial statements;
3 credit information exchange concerning loans of a million DM or more;
4 bank audits;
5 rights of information and investigation.

Basic features of the structural norms

The structural norms on banking operations, which are set forth in sections 10–20 of the Banking Act, relate to the definition of bank equity, the maintenance of adequate capital and liquidity, consolidation for supervisory purposes, and finally to the limitations of investments and credits in relation to equity capital.

Section 10 of the Banking Act defines what is to be regarded as liable capital (paid-up share capital plus reserves plus certain elements according to the legal form of the bank). Section 10 also requires banks to maintain adequate liable capital in order to fulfil their obligations to their creditors and particularly in order to safeguard the assets entrusted to them. The Federal Banking Supervisory Office draws up Principles according to which it assesses as a rule whether the requirement of adequate liable capital is satisfied.

Principle I stipulates that a bank's loans and participations should not exceed eighteen times its liable capital. In accordance with the proposals of the EC, special financial instruments such as financial swaps, futures and options have also had to be counted in Principle I since October 1990. As banks are not exposed to credit risk for the full face value of their contracts, but only to the cost of replacing the cash flow if a counterparty defaults, those engagements will be converted to credit risk equivalents. Two different ways exist to calculate the 'credit equivalent amount', one incorporating a 'mark to market' element, the other one regarding the maturity of the contract. For calculating the Principle I ratio the loans and the credit equivalent amounts are weighted in accordance with various risk groups. The parent banks of banking groups must ensure that Principle I is also complied with on a consolidated basis.

Principle Ia limits the open positions in foreign exchange, precious metal trading and special off-balance-sheet instruments such as interest rate options and futures, forward rate agreements, stock options and futures, and index options and futures as a proportion of the bank's liable capital on a daily basis.

Section 11 of the Banking Act stipulates that banks invest their funds in such a way as to ensure adequate liquidity all the time. Liquidity is assessed according to principles II and III.

Principle II restricts the sum of the long-term assets to certain financial resources which are deemed to be long term.

According to Principle III the sum of various short- and medium-term assets should not exceed short- and medium-term financial resources.

In essence Principles II and III establish limitations on the banks' ability of maturity intermediation and transformation. Table 11.2 shows the average ratios of Principles I, II and III in the last ten years and makes clear that on average, banks can follow the requirements on capital and liquidity better today than in the past. However, there are marked differences between the banking groups, and we know that there are also large differences between the individual banks which cannot be obtained from the statistics.

Table 11.2   Average utilization of Principles I, II and III

	Principle I (limit 18)	Principle II (limit 100%)	Principle III (limit 100%)
All banks (average on an annual basis)			
1977	12.7	86.1	73.5
1980	14.0	91.7	82.9
1985	13,4	90.2	78.2
1986	12.7	87.9	71.3
1987	12.3	86.7	65.2
1988	12.4	88.4	65.6
1989	12.6	89.5	66.9
1990	12.6	88.8	69.6
Banking groups (averages on the basis of 1990)			
Commercial banks	12.7	85.5	88.0
Regional giro institutions	15.1	89.4	56.5
Regional institutions of the cooperative sector	7.1	86.9	57.1
Savings banks	12.4	91.6	56.2
Credit cooperatives	11.7	88.9	63.0
All banks	12.6	88.8	69.6

Section 12 of the Banking Act stipulates that a bank's fixed assets and shareholdings in other enterprises must not exceed its liable capital.

In section 13 of the Banking Act the loans to a single borrower exceeding 15 per cent of the bank's liable capital (large loans) are restricted in two ways to enforce diversification: no single loan may exceed 50 per cent of the liable capital (to be reduced to 25 per cent in the future according to the EC proposals), and all large loans taken together must not exceed eight times the liable capital. These limits also apply to banking groups as a whole. Finally, loans to borrowers closely linked to the lending bank (insider loans) must be granted on the basis of unanimous decisions by all managers of the bank and only with the explicit approval of the supervisory board (section 15 of the Banking Act).

11.1.3   Deposit Protection Schemes

All banks belong to one of the deposit guarantee funds set up on a voluntary basis by the banking associations. The fund established for the commercial banks aims primarily at protecting depositors, while the schemes operated by the savings banks and credit cooperatives are designed to avert insolvency of member banks.

The Deposit Guarantee Fund of the commercial bank sector safeguards non-securitized liabilities to non-bank creditors in cases of insolvency. The protected deposits per creditor amount to up to 30 per cent of the last published annual liable capital number. Larger liabilities are protected up to this guarantee limit. Protection covers both deposits in Germany and those at branches abroad, irrespective of the currency in which they are denominated and no matter whether the creditors are residents or non-residents. The banks have to pay a contribution of 0.3 per thousand of the balance-sheet item 'liabilities to other creditors arising from banking business'.

Although in the case of public savings banks responsibility for indemnifying depositors ultimately rests with the local authorities which set up the bank, the savings banks and giro associations have nevertheless set up guarantee funds. The by-laws of the credit cooperatives provide for a limited obligation of members to pay up further capital if called. However, the guarantee scheme operated by the credit cooperatives has ensured that not a single insolvency with full loss of value for one of the members has yet arisen in the credit cooperative sector.

11.2 The Development of the German Bank Supervisory System under the Second Banking Directive

German regulations concerning the soundness of individual banks as well as the stability of the banking system are currently being reviewed. Even though Principles I and Ia on capital adequacy do already regulate risks of financial swaps, futures and options they will have to be adjusted to account for banks' securities in order to incorporate the new EC proposals. In what follows, we give a short overview of these new rules and their effects on German law. More specifically, we focus on capital adequacy regulation.

As discussed in chapter 1, the driving force of the EC proposals is not the complete harmonization of national regulations, but rather the opening of financial markets guided by three principles: mutual recognition, home country control and minimal harmonization of the definition of own funds and capital rules.

11.2.1 The Regulation of Capital

The Commission followed closely the recommendations of the Cooke committee *International Convergence of Capital Measurement and Capital Standards*, with one major difference. The Cooke regulations concern international banks exclusively, while the EC proposals concern all credit institutions. In what follows, we consider the proposals of the Cooke committee and those of the Commission together.

The Cooke report deals with four topics: the definition of bank capital, the risk-weighting systems for assets, the solvency ratio and the timetable for implementation. The definition of capital is the most controversial issue.

Bank own funds are divided in two tiers, core capital and supplementary capital. Core capital includes equity (issued and fully paid ordinary shares as well as perpetual non-cumulative preference shares) and disclosed retained earnings. It is wholly visible in the published accounts and is the basis on which market judgements are made. The committee requires at least 50 per cent of capital to consist of core elements. Supplementary capital consists of the following elements which may be included by national authorities at their discretion. Elements not mentioned in the proposals cannot be included in the second tier.

Undisclosed reserves are unpublished or hidden reserves which can be included if they have passed through the profit and loss account and if they are accepted by the authority. In Germany, this reserve is identified by the so-called 26a reserve. According to section 26a of the Banking Act, banking firms are allowed to show accounts receivables and securities held as current assets at a lower value than actual ones. These reserves are a special vehicle to safeguard against the particular risks inherent in the business of banking institutions. According to the 1986 Council Directive on Annual Accounts, these reserves have to be limited to 4 per cent of assets. The reserves defined under section 26a will probably be included in supplementary capital.

Revaluation reserves may arise when a bank revalues certain assets to reflect current market values. The German associations are calling for the legal acceptance of revaluation, while the Bundesbank and the Federal Banking Supervisory Office want to exclude such reserves.[9]

General loss reserves are created by banks to absorb anticipated but as yet unidentified future credit losses. The effective accounting law for German banks does not recognize general loan provisions, but Article 38 of the European Directive on Annual Accounts defines such an item. Therefore, we can anticipate that German law will recognize general reserves.[10]

Hybrid debt capital instruments are instruments which combine some characteristics of debt and equity. In Germany *Genußcheine* do qualify for own funds (up to 25 per cent of the other components). Therefore, in this case, core capital as specified by Cooke is more narrowly defined.

11.2.2 Consequences of the New Capital Regulations for German Banks

Calculations by the Bundesbank have shown that the minimum solvency ratios of the Cooke guidelines − 4 per cent for core capital and 8 per cent in total − are being met by German banks with 5 per cent and 9 per cent respectively. However, these calculations take all capital elements into account, even if they are not accepted by German regulation. This is understandable, since, in the opinion of the Bundesbank, the Cooke ratio is only voluntary at present.

This voluntary basis cannot be maintained for the solvency ratios of the EC. Supplementary capital will only include those elements accepted by the German Banking Act. It is not yet clear what will be included, but it seems that the Bundesbank will follow a narrow definition of capital. This raises a question about the impact of the capital guidelines on the competitive positioning of the German banking industry.

In a pure Modigliani−Miller world, capital ratios will have no effect on profitability. Larger equity leading to higher solvency will be reflected in lower cost of deposits. However, this reasoning assumes full information, rationality of depositors and tax neutrality, three hypotheses which can be questioned. Our view is that capital is a costly resource.

So far, it is not clear whether the German regulatory authorities will adopt a more narrow or a more broad definition of capital. Of course, a compromise has to be found. It should be based on the concept of two-tier equity and abandon the current single definition of capital. Unfortunately, neither the Cooke report nor the EC directive offer a thorough explanation of the function of second-tier capital. A well-known study by the Committee on Financial Markets of the Organization for Economic Cooperation and Development (OECD) has come up with a useful definition: 'Core capital should include all elements permanently available to absorb losses; they must not impose contractual charges against earnings; they must not be redeemable at the holders' request' (Pecchioli, 1987). Revaluation and undisclosed reserves clearly meet these standards and should be included in core capital. The current capital ratio of 18, which can be converted into a capital-to-asset ratio of 5.5 per cent, will pose no problem for German banks since the current 5.5 per cent can include subordinated debt up to 20 per cent. Therefore Principle I is in line with the 4 per cent core capital ratio. The main issue lies with supplementary capital and the inclusion or exclusion of hidden reserves or revaluation of assets.

In conclusion, the supervisory authorities in Germany should avoid penalizing the German banks. This implies a revision of the Banking Act, the introduction of the concept of two-tier capital and a broad definition of supplementary capital.

Notes

1 Cable (1985) states that the German banking system is virtually indispensable to companies seeking external finance. This finding is somewhat outdated as far as debt financing is concerned. Bank control, through board membership, shareholding and proxy rights, relates mainly to large stock companies. These companies succeed in avoiding controls by maintaining about ten core relationships with banks. Moreover, large companies have access to the Euromarkets. However, the *hausbankprinzip* seems to play a larger role for external equity financing.

2 For a more detailed analysis of the development of bank supervision in Germany, see Deutsche Bundesbank, Banking Act of the Federal Republic of Germany, Deutsche Bundesbank Special series no. 2, Schneider (1984), Schneider et al. (1986) and Fitzenreiter (1988).

3 James (1985) states that the collapse of 1931 was immediately attributable to monetary conditions. The best known study on this topic is that of Born (1967).

4 The Banking Act provides for cooperation with the Deutsche Bundesbank. While the Federal Banking Supervisory Office is the only institution responsible for granting or withdrawing banking licences, the Bundesbank is involved in permanent supervision by collecting and processing data.

5 The study group published its report *Grundsatzfragen der Kreditwirtschaft* in 1979. The work and results of this extensive study of universal banking in Germany are outlined by Krummel (1980).

6 For a short description of the main characteristics of *Genußcheinkapital* see Rudolph (1988).

7 Therefore no depositor has the right of recourse to the supervisory authorities in the case of a bank failure.

8 See the article 'Bundesbank ist besorgt ueber EG-Beschluss', in *Frankfurter Allgemeine Zeitung*, 14 December 1988.

9 See Rudolph (1991).

10 Loan loss general reserves are part of core capital in the latest version of the EC proposal (Article 2).

References

Born, K.E. (1967) *Die Deutsche Bankenkrise 1931*. Munich.

Bahre, I.L. and Schneider, M. (1986) *KWG-Kommentar*. Munich.

Cable, J. (1985) Capital information and industrial performance: the role of West German banks. *Economic Journal*, 95, 118–32.

Fitzenreiter, J. (1988) Bank supervision. In *Germany's Financial Centre*. London: Euromoney Publication.

James, H. (1985) *The Reichsbank and Public Finance in Germany 1924–1933. A Study of the Politics of Economics During the Great Depression*. Frankfurt.

Krummel, H.J. (1980) German universal banking scrutinized. *Journal of Banking and Finance*, 4, 133–55.

Pecchioli, R. (1987) *Prudential Supervision in Banking*. Paris: OECD.

Rudolph, B. (1988) The market for *Genußscheine* of German banks. In *Frankfurt, Germany's Financial Centre*. London: Euromoney Publications.

Rudolph, B. (1991) *Das effektive Baukeigenkapital*. Frankfurt.

Scheidl, K. (1988) West Germany. In A. Hendrie (ed.), *Banking in the EEC*. London: Financial Times Business Information.

Schneider, H., Hellwig, H.J. and Kingsman,D. (1986) *The German Banking System* (4th edn). Frankfurt.

Schneider, U. (1984) Die Entwicklung des Bankenaufsichtsrechts. In Deutscher Sparkassen- und Giroverband (ed.) *Standortbestimmung: Entwicklungslinien der Deutschen Kreditwirtschaft*. Stuttgart.

Comment

Ernst-Moritz Lipp

If countries of the world were measured not by their land mass but by the size of their national product, then Europe would be about the same size as the United States. Japan would be much smaller, and if the four little tigers (Singapore, Hong Kong, Taiwan and Korea) were added together, the total combined national product would amount to about $3 billion which would still be $1 billion less than the European figure. This highlights the economic potential in the world and its distribution. However, the picture looks somewhat different for specific markets. For example, let us take the worldwide market for asset management. Here the North American market ranks well ahead of Europe, including Switzerland, while the European group manages about twice the volume of assets held in Japan.

In Europe there has been a band of growth extending from the Midlands of England through the north of France, the Benelux countries, and the western and southern regions of Germany to northern and central Italy. There have also been several other smaller centres of growth, but the point is that Europe does not represent an area of uniform growth. Rather, growth tends to be concentrated in specific regions, especially within the growth band referred to above. This conclusion is drawn from an analysis of per capita national product, savings volumes and density of companies. The aim must be to establish an appropriate presence within the growth axis.

Banks located in Germany enjoy a competitive advantage in so far as they have a central location in Europe. This advantage becomes clear when one realizes that most growth centres lie within a radius of 200−300 miles from Germany. This has made it possible to follow a twofold regional strategy. On the one hand, banks can expand their presence in the major European financial centres, i.e. expand along the major European growth axis. On the other hand, they can use their German business base, backed by a strong external presence, to expand around German borders within the radius mentioned above. Three other competitive advantages are enjoyed by German banks.

1 Competitive strength compared with foreign banks in the largest segment of the EC markets, namely Germany. This market has recently been characterized by vigorous growth.

2 There are large universal banks with great depth in investment banking. If an international universal bank has already acquired the quite special investment-banking mentality, it will have a better starting position than other competitors in the European arena.

3 The domestic and European presence of German banks is well developed compared with that of major competitors. The task will be to make this presence, which is based in part on commercial banking, effective in the investment services area also.

These are the strengths of the German banks; the disadvantages, as Professor Rudolph points out, are the costs imposed by capital regulations. These relate essentially to the definition of supplementary capital and the application of the risk-weighting system. For instance, the German Banking Act recognizes neither the revaluation of property nor general reserves. With regard to risk weights, it appears that the EC rules are more severe than the Cooke guidelines, while the German regulations are even more restrictive. At the end of January 1989, the German Banking Supervisory Authority presented a draft amendment to Principle I. It appeared to be fairly restrictive as, for instance, the weights used for swaps with banks from the OECD were twice as large as those used by the Federal Reserve or the Bank of England. Much work remains to be done to bring the Banking Act and the EC proposals in line with the international agreement reached by the Cooke committee.

Part IV

The Macro Perspective

12

The Euromarkets After 1992

Richard M. Levich

Financial markets and institutions hold a critical place in modern market-based economies. Through their pivotal role in the execution of money and credit policies, and their operation of the payments mechanism, many officials and academics consider firms within the financial services sector (and banks in particular) as 'special' institutions. Quite naturally, then, government officials who are held responsible for the performance of their domestic economies have seen fit to place their domestic banks and financial institutions under close regulatory scrutiny. The fiduciary nature of many financial transactions and the susceptibility of the financial sector to recurring crises have added to the argument for tight supervision.

Throughout most of the twentieth century, a complex set of regulations has evolved to circumscribe and monitor the activities of firms offering financial services. These regulations entail both costs and benefits for individual firms. As regulations act to promote public confidence in financial institutions, restrict entry into the industry or supply ancillary services (e.g. deposit insurance, wire transfers) below their costs, private firms benefit. On the other side of the equation are the costs that hit private firms, such as forgone interest on required reserves, forgone earnings from excessive capital requirements, and forgone revenues from limits (e.g. geographic and product line) on their activities. The difference between these costs and benefits measures the net regulatory burden (NRB) placed upon private firms.

In a single closed economy with a lone regulatory body we expect that private firms will use financial innovations, product repackaging and other strategies to minimize their NRB. A single economy may have many regulatory bodies at the federal level, complemented by a host of other regulatory groups at the state and local levels.[1] These regulators compete with one another to enhance the reach of their regulatory domains. Domestic

Comments from Daniel Gros, Jean Dermine and Lawrence Brainard on an earlier draft are appreciated. The author acknowledges responsibility for any errors that remain. This paper is part of the research programme of the National Bureau of Economic Research in international studies. Any opinions expressed are those of the author and not those of the National Bureau of Economic Research.

financial firms appreciate this competition which widens their scope for reducing the NRB. In this game-theoretic setting, domestic regulators are likely to respond to private initiatives with *re*regulations in an effort to recover part of their lost regulatory domain.

In the open world economy with many governments and many regulatory authorities, we find a still more fertile ground for firms to reduce their NRB. National regulatory authorities may compete on the basis of NRB. Again, private firms benefit from this international competition, especially if financial innovation and technological change allow them to operate success-fully at a distance from their home office.

The primary thesis of this paper is that the Eurocurrency market is a natural outgrowth of differential national regulation set in a world with declining barriers to capital movements and increasing capabilities in telecommuni-cations and data processing. The Eurocurrency market and its offspring (the Eurobond, Euro-commercial-paper and Euro-equity markets) comprise one of the most important financial innovations of the last 40 years. The key to the innovation is an example of 'unbundling', in this case taking the exchange risk of one currency (the US dollar, for example) and combining it with the regulatory climate and political risk of another financial centre. The Eurocurrency and Eurobond markets, which were virtually nonexistent until the late 1950s, have grown to become major centres of activity and influence.

My assigned task in this chapter is to assess the prospects for Euromarkets in the post-1992 era. I shall not attempt an unconditional forecast for the Euromarkets. The more valuable conclusion we reach is that the prospects for the Euromarkets are conditional on the regulatory balance, both among European Community (EC) countries and between EC and non-EC countries. In our context, it will be convenient to summarize the regulatory balance in terms of NRB in competing financial centres.

In reaching this conclusion, we draw out a number of other implications based on the dynamic interplay between regulators and regulatees in the open economy. First, our reading of the evidence suggests that the equilibrium NRB (NRB*) that can be assessed in any country has fallen because of increased competition among financial services firms and technological change. Second, if private firms feel that their regulatory burden is too high, one strategy open to them is to transfer some of their activities to another regulatory jurisdiction – i.e. 'structural arbitrage'. Financial innovation, technological change and the accumulated experience of financial services firms in dealing with change have very probably narrowed the 'neutral band' around the NRB* needed to induce structural arbitrage.

Together, the first two points suggest that the scope for maintaining a radically different regulatory regime is decreasing, as is the scope for inflexibility in policies, quantitative controls, taxes etc. for meeting domestic macro-economic – monetary policy objectives. Countries will be driven *de facto* and endogenously, towards harmonization. Active coordination of regulation may be useful, but there should be a continuing need for flexibility because of the dynamic nature of financial services. As a long-run proposition, the equilibrium sustainable NRB* is probably greater than zero, because of the uncertainties inherent in financial contracting, political risks, the value attached to promises of official regulatory authorities regarding their onshore markets and the convenience associated with onshore transactions. This suggests that even if transactions costs approach zero and an island state promotes an NRB that also approaches zero, that island state will not attract all the world's financial services business.

Regarding the Euromarkets in general, and the offshore markets for EC currencies in particular, our title suggests the question whether there will be a Euro-DM in London, a Euro-lira in Paris, and so forth in the post-1992 era. In this paper, we take '1992' as a metaphor for the bold plan adopted by the European Commission. The plan called for the abolition of all capital controls among participants in the European Monetary System by 1 July 1990 and this is really the key date for our analysis. It was after this date (rather than 31 December 1992) that all EC residents shared the flexibility to move capital freely between onshore and offshore markets.

After 1 July 1990, incentives for offshore markets dropped because of liberalization and relaxation of controls in onshore markets. Nevertheless, incentives still existed as the NRB for DM or lira *onshore* was higher than it was *offshore*, based on the need for onshore regulators to meet their domestic monetary policy objectives. As financial centres, however, London and Paris still faced competition within the EC (e.g. Luxembourg) and from outside the EC (e.g. Switzerland).

In the case of offshore markets for non-EC currencies, the incentives for a Euro-dollar market in London, Luxembourg or Paris have continued as before. The fact that non-EC centres (e.g. Singapore, Hong Kong etc.) have not taken over the Euro-dollar market suggests that these centres have pushed their regulatory competition to the limit. However, if the EC *re*regulates to increase its NRB (e.g. by new withholding tax laws or increased disclosure rules, such as have been discussed), migration of the Euro-dollar market to non-EC centres would be a likely outcome.

Our focus on the NRB is to facilitate the exposition of a stylized model. Holding other factors constant, we shall demonstrate the role played by the NRB. Both borrowers and lenders may be willing to trade off a high NRB against other factors – convenience of local transactions, market liquidity, local market expertise and so forth – which are not dealt with here. The optimal level of the NRB*, its relations to economywide systemic risks and the distribution of the NRB (across shareholders, depositors and taxpayers) are other interesting issues that are left as important but unanswered questions.

In the remainder of the paper, an overview of the Eurocurrency market including its origin, growth, pricing mechanics and important innovative features is presented in section 12.1. In section 12.2 we develop the theme of international competition in regulation; the NRB concept is defined and we discuss the notion of structural arbitrage. The main features of the plan for EC financial markets after 1992 are reviewed in section 12.3. We also discuss regulatory factors that were unresolved by 1992 and how they are likely to affect the Euromarkets. A concluding section presents our conditional forecasts about the Euromarkets and the development of European financial centres.

12.1   Origins and Essentials of the Eurocurrency Market

The Eurocurrency market – the market for deposits denominated in a currency different from the indigenous currency of the financial centre – took shape in the 1960s as something of an enigma, but unimportant enough to be overlooked. As the market expanded to financial centres outside Europe (such as the Bahamas, Singapore and Hong Kong), the term 'offshore' (as distinct from onshore) became more appropriate to describe its location. As the market grew in scale and in scope (to include currencies other than the dollar), officials saw it, at best, as a minor nuisance – something to make the formulation of monetary policy a bit more difficult – and, at worst, as a major policy issue – an unregulated and independent source of instability in world financial markets. Today the Eurocurrency markets are a common and well-accepted fixture of the international financial markets.

12.1.1   Historical Overview

The founders of the Eurocurrency market did not set out to create a market that would rival US financial markets in terms of size and importance. The objective of UK merchant banks in the late 1950s was simply to overcome Bank of England restrictions on the use of Sterling for external loans. Their solution was pragmatic – use the US dollar to conduct these transactions from accounts based in London. Since Bank of England regulations did not cover the US dollar, UK merchant banks could set competitive interest rates to attract deposits and offer external loans denominated in dollars.

But the solution was also innovative, not simply because it had never been done before, but because it gave the market an early illustration of 'unbundling' – in this case, taking the exchange risk of one currency and combining it with the regulatory climate and political risk of another financial centre. Perhaps some officials did see the genius of this innovation and the impending snowball about to be set loose. When Paul Einzig, a *Financial Times* journalist, first came across the market, he was asked not to write about it (quoted in Grabbe, 1986, p. 17).

The Eurocurrency market got an additional boost from the Russians, who at the time were reluctant to hold their US dollars (needed for international trade transactions) in US accounts. Instead, they deposited their dollars in London and Paris with affiliates of state-owned Russian banks.[2]

A more important, although temporary, stimulus to the Eurocurrency market was the set of credit restrictions and capital controls imposed by the United States during the 1963−74 period. In response to the undesired build-up of dollars overseas (dollars that the United States was obliged to convert into gold at $35 per ounce) the United States adopted the Interest Equalization Tax (IET), effectively an excise tax on US purchases of new or outstanding foreign securities. But the IET resulted in neither new tax revenues for the United States nor a halt to the accumulation of dollars abroad. Rather than pay the tax or halt dollar lending to foreigners, the borrowing activity simply shifted its locus to the Eurocurrency markets in London and Luxembourg. Other US regulations such as the Foreign Credit Restraint Program ('voluntary' in 1965 and mandatory in 1968) gave firms further incentives to investigate the Eurocurrency markets. These measures were eliminated in 1974.

European governments also experimented with capital controls during this period which similarly helped to promote the non-dollar segments of the Eurocurrency market. Bundesbank rules requiring foreigners to place funds at the Bardepot in non-interest-bearing accounts and the negative interest rates imposed on foreigners by the Swiss National Bank are two examples. The German capital controls expired in 1974, and the Swiss negative interest rates were abolished in December 1979.[3]

The lasting stimulus to the Eurocurrency market, then, has been the differential regulation between offshore and onshore banking operations. As we shall review, particular US banking regulations (i.e. interest rate ceilings on time deposits, mandatory reserve requirements held at zero interest and mandatory deposit insurance) became increasingly costly throughout the 1960s. By setting up their deposit-taking and lending operations offshore, banks were able to reduce their costs, passing on more favourable rates to both depositors and borrowers.

12.1.2 Growth of the Eurocurrency Market

The data in table 12.1 indicate the growth of the Eurocurrency deposit market, from essentially zero in 1960 to over $6.0 trillion on a gross basis and \$3.4 trillion on a net basis (netting out all interbank deposits) in September 1991. The market has grown at a compound annual rate of approximately 18 per cent over the last 18 years. The market, once exclusively dollar denominated, seemed to stabilize during the 1970s with a roughly 75–80 per cent dollar share. Recently, however, the dollar's share has fallen to about 50 per cent based on data collected by the Bank for International Settlements (BIS) from offshore centres in industrial countries. Simply as a matter of accounting, the dollar's share of the Eurocurrency market falls as the dollar depreciates against other currencies. But the use of other currency units has clearly grown, the DM and the Japanese yen holding 13 and 9 per cent market shares respectively in September 1991.

Table 12.1 Dimensions of the Eurocurrency deposit market (US\$ billions)

Year	Gross size	Net size	Eurodollars as a percentage of gross	US money stock (M2)
1973	315	160	74	861
1974	395	220	76	908
1975	485	255	78	1,023
1976	595	320	80	1,164
1977	740	390	76	1,287
1978	950	495	74	1,389
1979	1,235	590	72	1,500
1980	1,525	730	75	1,633
1981	1,954	1,018	79	1,796
1982	2,168	1,152	80	1,954
1983	2,278	1,237	81	2,185
1984	2,386	1,277	82	2,363
1985	2,846	1,480	75	2,563
1986	3,683	1,833	72	2,808
1987[a]	4,229	2,270	55[b]	2,910
1988	4,615	2,450	56	3,070
1989	5,476	2,830	54	3,223
1990	6,440	3,445	48	3,328
1991 (September)	6,058	3,390	49	3,392
Compound growth (%)	17.9	18.5		7.9

[a] Break in data sources as described below.
[b] Based on liabilities in industrial reporting countries only.

Sources: For years 1973–86, Morgan Guaranty Trust, *World Financial Markets*, various issues, and *Economic Report of the President*, 1989, Table B-67. For years 1987–91, Bank for International Settlements, *International Banking and Financial Market Developments*, various issues, and Federal Reserve Board, *Federal Reserve Bulletin*, various issues.

Data on the geographic reach of the market is reported in table 12.2. Europe has been the dominant region and the United Kingdom the dominant country. Europe and the United Kingdom appear to have lost market share, although some of the decline is spurious because the BIS has increased its reporting coverage. Japan has substantially increased its market share, coinciding with its capital market liberalizations of the past few years. At 14.9 per cent in 1991, Japan ranks second. The United States has roughly maintained its market share. The establishment of International Banking Facilities (IBFs) in 1981 which permit offshore transactions for non-US

Table 12.2 Major international banking centres (US$ billions)

External positions of banks in	End of 1975 Stock of liabilities	% share	End of 1980 Stock of liabilities	% share	End of 1985 Stock of liabilities	% share	End of 1990 Stock of liabilities	% share
Total European	297.5	66.4	928.4	69.6	1,331.5	53.8	3,366.9	52.3
UK	137.4	30.7	374.4	28.1	610.5	24.7	1,203.5	18.7
France	42.5	9.5	130.3	9.8	155.2	6.3	481.2	7.5
Belgium	40.5	9.0	65.9	4.9	106.7	4.3	217.3	3.4
Luxembourg			84.6	6.3	99.4	4.0	271.2	4.2
Germany	22.9	5.1	74.2	5.6	74.2	3.0	224.7	3.5
Netherlands	18.5	4.1	64.6	4.8	64.6	2.6	148.1	2.3
Switzerland	16.6	3.7	43.7	3.3	45.3	1.8	321.1	5.0
Other[a]	19.0	4.2	90.7	6.8	175.6	7.1	499.8	7.8
Total USA	58.7	13.1	138.2	10.4	365.5	14.8	653.7	10.2
US IBFs	n.a.	n.a.	n.a.	n.a	191.8	7.7	373.8	5.8
Other	58.7	13.1	138.2	10.4	173.7	7.0	279.9	4.3
Total Japan	26.7	6.0	80.2	6.0	179.3	7.2	958.5	14.9
Offshore	n.a.	n.a.	n.a.	n.a.	n.a.	n.a.	418.0	6.5
Other	n.a.	n.a.	n.a.	n.a.	n.a.	n.a.	540.5	8.4
Canada	14.1	3.1	43.6	3.3	65.7	2.7	81.0	1.3
Other reporting countries[b]	51.0	11.4	144.1	10.8	534.4	21.6	1,379.8	21.4
Grand total	448.0	100.0	1,334.6	100.0	2,476.4	100.0	6,439.8	100.0

n.a., not available.
[a] Includes Italy, Austria, Spain, Sweden, Demark, Finland, Ireland and Norway.
[b] Includes Bahrain, the Cayman Islands, Hong Kong, Singapore, Netherlands Antilles and US banks in Panama.

Source: Bank for International Settlements, *Annual Reports*, various years

residents helped the United States to attract deposits from the Caribbean and elsewhere.[4] The remaining 20 per cent of the cross-border deposit market is spread over a large number of other countries. Again, some of this increase is spurious because of improved reporting coverage.

In terms of several dimensions — scale of operations, number of currencies represented and geographic spread of financial centres — the Eurocurrency market has emerged as a world-class market.

12.1.3   Pricing of Eurocurrency Deposits and Loans

For our purposes, it will be convenient to imagine a world with n currencies and n countries or financial centres. To begin with, consider the case of one currency (the US dollar) and two financial centres (New York and London). The relationship between onshore and offshore interest rates can be easily developed within the context of a loanable funds framework.[5]

Suppose that, in the onshore market, the demand D for funds depends on the required rate of return on available projects, while the supply S of funds depends on individuals' rates of time preference. The curves take on the expected slopes as illustrated in figure 12.1. In the absence of transactions

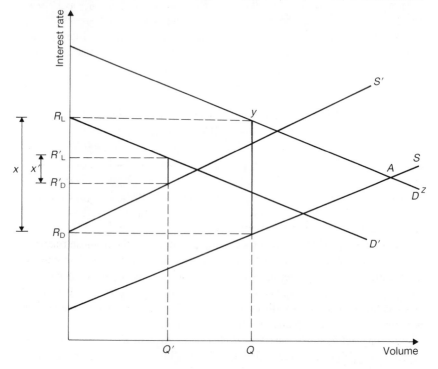

Figure 12.1   Determination of offshore interest rates: one currency, one offshore centre.

costs, equilibrium would be at point A. However, banks incur costs in collecting deposits and in servicing loans. The major categories of costs are (a) non-interest-bearing reserves at the Federal Reserve, (b) Federal Deposit Insurance Corporation (FDIC) insurance, (c) credit review, (d) asset – liability risk management, (e) taxes and (f) administrative overhead. If, after reaching a given scale, these costs can be summarized by an amount x, then the onshore market will reach an equilibrium with deposit rate R_D, lending rate R_L and market size Q.

Now assume that a new market in US dollar-denominated balances opens in London. Americans will supply dollars to the offshore market only if they are compensated for bearing the extra costs and risks associated with London. Since Americans can earn R_D with minimum inconvenience and no political risks in the onshore market, the supply curve to the offshore market (S') is hinged at R_D.[6] Similarly, in the absence of capital controls, no borrower would travel to London to pay a higher price for funds.[7] Therefore, the demand curve for offshore funds (D') must be hinged at R_L, reflecting the unfunded projects along segment yz of D.

Assuming that the cost of collecting deposits and servicing loans in the offshore market (x') is less than in the onshore market, we can determine the offshore deposit rate R'_D, lending rate R'_L and market size Q' as before. Since Eurobanks (a) earn interest on their voluntary level of reserves, (b) do not pay FDIC-like insurance, (c) deal primarily with known high-quality credits, (d) use floating interest rate arrangements and maturity matching to minimize interest rate risks, (e) often operate in tax havens, or under other special tax incentives, and (f) operate a wholesale business with lower overheads, we fully expect to find $x' \ll x$. Figure 12.1 illustrates the normal relationship between onshore and offshore interest rates, i.e. $R_L > R'_L > R'_D > R_D$.[8] In more familiar terms, this inequality states that the New York 'Prime' lending rate exceeds the London Interbank Offered Rate (LIBOR) which exceeds the London Interbank Bid Rate (LIBID) which in turn exceeds the cost of funds (say a Certificate of Deposit (CD) rate) of a New York Bank. In today's market, the LIBOR – LIBID spread may average about 0.25 per cent while the spread between the New York CD rate and Prime may approach 2.00 per cent.

The offshore market survives by driving a wedge into the onshore financial market – it provides a similar financial service at a lower cost. The interest differential $R'_D - R_D$ measures the extra compensation paid to depositors for bearing additional risk, taxes or inconvenience with deposits outside their home country. The interest differential $R_L - R'_L$ measures the incentives for borrowers to gain acceptance in the offshore market, where size and credit quality may act as entry barriers. Both $R'_D - R_D$ and $R_L - R'_L$ should be responsive to market forces, financial innovation and the accumulation of financial know-how. Domestic financial deregulation and money market mutual funds that channel funds from small investors offshore should reduce $R'_D - R_D$. Active corporate financing strategies that seek the lowest cost source of funds worldwide should lead to a reduction in $R_L - R'_L$.[9]

12.1.4 Market Share and Pricing in Competing Offshore Centres

Now consider the case of one currency (the US dollar) and several offshore centres (London, Germany, Singapore and Rio). In figure 12.2, we continue to assume that the demand for dollars offshore is described by D', which reflects the underlying set of projects. The supply of funds to each offshore centre depends on depositors' assessments of the costs of using the centre (i.e. known taxes and capital controls, as well as the cost of time zone differences) and the risks (i.e. future taxes and capital controls). In principle, each centre might have its own cost (x'_A, x'_B etc.) for collecting deposits and servicing loans. For convenience, assume that these costs are identical across centres and equal to 0.25 per cent. In figure 12.2, this selection of x' results in a London deposit rate of 8.0 per cent and a lending rate of 8.25 per cent and a London market size of Q_A.

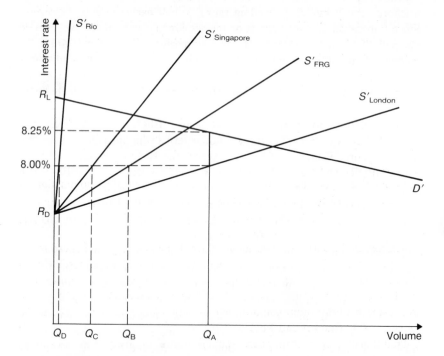

Figure 12.2 Determination of offshore interest rates and market shares: one currency, four offshore centres.

If a German offshore centre is to exist, it must offer loans at 8.25 per cent, which means that it must pay no more than 8.00 per cent on deposits and it must be satisfied with a market size of Q_B. A similar story applies to Singapore with a resulting market size Q_C and Rio with a market size of Q_D. In our example, once the most efficient and least risky financial centre has set the price of funds, other centres must follow suit and quantity is the only other variable left to adjust.[10]

In reality, if Germany or Singapore were saddled with higher operating costs, they might be able to set a higher R'_L and still attract borrowers. But their loan portfolios would have higher credit risks than London. Figure 12.2 also suggests that countries which are viewed by depositors as more risky will need more favourable regulations to lower their costs and reduce their lending rates.

Figure 12.3 offers a representation of the general case of n currencies and n financial centres. Regulatory costs and political risks vary as we move from column to column. Exchange risks vary as we move from row to row. The cells along the northeast – southwest diagonal represent the onshore market, and the remaining cells represent the offshore market. We have analysed the interest rate differential between New York dollars and London dollars using a loanable funds approach. Arbitrage and regulatory competition should keep the offshore interest rates for a single currency nearly equal. The market share of the offshore market earned by a financial centre depends on both the costs of using the centre and the perceived risks of capital controls and new taxes. The interest rate differential between offshore instruments should conform to the predictions of the interest rate parity relationship, as we review in the section 12.1.5.

12.1.5 Euromarkets, Innovation and Market Linkages

The link between assets that are alike in all respects (e.g. maturity, credit risk, political risk, etc.) except for their currency of denomination is described by the well-known interest rate parity relationship

$$F_t = S_t(1.0 + i)/(1.0 + i^*) \tag{12.1}$$

which relates the current forward rate F_t for delivery one period ahead to the current spot rate S_t and a pair of one-period interest rates on domestic (i) and foreign (i^*) currency. By providing a setting in which the assumption of similar risk instruments is satisfied, the Euromarkets have given us the cleanest tests of this important arbitrage pricing relationship (see for example Aliber, 1973; Frenkel and Levich, 1975).

Traditionally, interest rate parity has been used to describe the incentives for international capital flows, covered against exchange risk. But equation (12.1) can also be interpreted as an 'assignment statement'. Equation (12.1)

Country of issue

Currency of denomination	USA	UK	Germany	Switzerland	Singapore	Brazil
US dollars	New York dollars	London dollars	Frankfurt dollars	Zurich dollars	Singapore US dollars	
Sterling	New York IBF Sterling	London Sterling	Frankfurt Sterling	Zurich Sterling	Singapore Sterling	
DM	New York IBF DM	London DM	Frankfurt DM	Zurich DM	Singapore DM	
Swiss franc	New York IBF Swiss francs	London Swiss francs	Frankfurt Swiss francs	Zurich Swiss francs	Singapore Swiss francs	
Singapore dollar					Singapore Dollars	
Cruzeiro						Rio Cruzeiro

Figure 12.3 The structure of international financial markets: many currencies, many financial centres. In the United States, non-residents may hold offshore deposits with international banking facilities. Legislation effective from 1 January 1990 permits US residents to hold non-dollar accounts at US commercial banks.

suggests that a forward contract can be constructed by combining a spot contract with borrowing and lending in two currencies. The right-hand side of (12.1) is therefore a replicating portfolio; we can construct a synthetic forward contract when the market does not provide a forward contract directly (e.g. in the case of long-term forward contracts). This then explains why forward contracts do not exist for currencies in which borrowing and lending is restricted. Equation (12.1) also suggests that a forward contract is a redundant instrument, since it can be replicated perfectly by other contracts. Forward contracts exist, therefore, only because they reduce transaction costs in comparison with the replicating portfolio.

Equation (12.1) can be rearranged to produce

$$1.0 + i^* = (1.0 + i)S_t/F_t \qquad (12.2)$$

which suggests that the yield on a foreign security (with a particular maturity and credit risk, etc.) can be replicated by a dollar security (with similar attributes) combined with a forward exchange contract. Therefore, if yen commercial paper does not exist or if access to the Euro-DM bond market is temporarily blocked, a synthetic instrument can be constructed.[11]

Another rearrangement of equation (12.1) leads to

$$1.0 + i = (1.0 + i^*)F_t/S_t \qquad (12.3)$$

which suggests that US dollar financing can be replicated by a foreign security combined with a forward exchange contract. Equation (12.3) is the argument underpinning swap-driven bond issues which originate in one currency but when combined with a forward contract (or a set of forward contracts) have the attributes of a dollar security.

The integration of international financial markets through the quest for covered interest arbitrage profits is a powerful force. It has long been understood that covered interest arbitrage integrates the short-term Eurocurrency markets. But it is now becoming more apparent that longer-term Eurocurrency markets, commercial paper markets and onshore short-term financial markets are also being integrated by actual or potential arbitrage. Our equations (12.2) and (12.3) reveal how straightforward it is to use the Euromarkets to overcome prohibitions on particular markets or instruments, or to overcome quantity restrictions or restrictions on access. As a result, the incentive for onshore regulators to maintain these restrictions is decreasing. On the contrary, the incentives are toward *re*regulation in order to compete with offshore markets and synthetic instruments.

12.2 International Competition in Regulation

In the previous section, we demonstrated that compliance with regulations in the onshore banking market creates opportunities to develop a parallel offshore market for the delivery of similar services. Barriers must exist to keep all activity from migrating offshore. In this case, political risks and minimum transaction size temper the flow of deposits offshore, and credit quality and size perform a similar role for borrowers.[12] But in addition to the narrow provision of bank deposits and loans, we have also shown that Euromarkets can be used to replicate a variety of non-bank financial instruments (e.g. long-term forward contracts, short-term commercial paper, long-term bonds, Eurocurrency interest rate futures etc.), many of which may also be regulated by onshore financial authorities. Consequently, the offshore banking market raises a competitive threat to onshore financial services activities in general and not simply to onshore banking institutions.

12.2.1 Competition among Regulators and Contestable Markets

The rise of offshore markets underscores that market participants have the alternative to arrange transactions in any of several financial centres. Therefore, if domestic regulators desire to have transactions conducted within their centre (to maintain an adequate level of prudential regulation, to maximize their revenues from the taxation of financial services, or simply to maximize their regulatory domain), the regulatory requirements cannot be set arbitrarily. Indeed, as Edward Kane (1987) has recently argued, domestic financial regulations are determined competitively and endogenously after taking account of regulations (both present and prospective) in other financial centres.

The essence of Kane's (1987) analysis is that the market for suppliers of financial regulation is highly competitive. As such, the movement to liberalize regulations affecting financial institutions is not the result of a sudden outpouring of *laissez-faire* feeling, but rather the result of an endogenous process as national regulators vie for market share. The market for financial regulation is contestable in the sense that other national regulatory bodies offer (or threaten to offer) rules that may be more favourable than those of the domestic regulator. This actual or threatened competition serves to constrain the actions of suppliers of financial regulation.

This view results in what Kane refers to as a 'regulatory dialectic' − a dynamic interaction between the regulator and the regulatee, where there is continuous action and reaction by all parties. The players in this game-theoretic setting may behave aggressively or defensively. To the extent that the parties behave adaptively, even if underlying factors (e.g. communications technology, the level of financial transactions etc.) remain constant, it is likely to require considerable time for an equilibrium regulatory structure to emerge.

In a changing environment, players will adapt with varying speed and degrees of freedom. Kane (1987, p. 115) summarizes the 'average adaptive efficiencies' of various players as follows:

1 less-regulated players move faster and more freely than more tightly regulated players;
2 private players move faster and more freely than governmental players;
3 regulated players move faster and more freely than regulators;
4 international regulatory bodies move more slowly and less freely than all other players.

Given Kane's ordering of adaptive efficiencies, we expect that the lag between a regulation and its avoidance is on average shorter than the lag between avoidance and *re*regulation. The lag in reregulation may be shorter for industry-based self-regulatory groups than for governments, and it will probably be the longest when international regulatory groups are involved. Appreciation of this likelihood seems to have affected the style of regulatory harmonization that the EC has adopted, which we shall discuss shortly.

12.2.2 Net Regulatory Burden and Structural Arbitrage

A given regulatory regime bestows both benefits and costs on individual financial services firms. Regulations that (a) assure the stability and orderliness of the system over time and promote public confidence in financial institutions, (b) restrict entry into the industry and monitor anti-competitive pricing arrangements and (c) provide ancillary services, such as deposit insurance or wire transfers at below private cost, and other transaction cost savings measures, all benefit private firms. Regulations may also result in revenue losses from (a) forgone interest on required reserves, (b) forgone earnings on excessive capital requirements and (c) forgone revenues from limitations on geographic activity or product offerings, as well as explicit charges. The difference between these costs and benefits defines the NRB placed upon private firms.[13]

Private firms monitor their NRB and transfer activities into another regulatory regime when, *ceteris paribus*, their NRB can be reduced. In a perfect capital market with no entry or exit costs, no transaction costs, no barriers between countries and no sovereign risk, we predict that all banking activities would migrate to the country with the lowest NRB inclusive of taxes. In the real world, a variety of imperfections exist that permit some dispersion of NRB across countries. This dispersion among NRB cannot be too great or private firms will have an incentive to relocate their activities. Entry and exit costs, currency conversion costs and distance-related delivery costs, plus uncertainties surrounding these costs and other control measures, act as effective barriers to complete NRB equalization across countries. Technological change which has lowered communications and information processing costs and the rapid growth of international business have lowered the gap in NRB needed to induce arbitrage.

In a similar fashion, regulators have also become more willing to compete on the basis of their NRB. The regulator must ensure that his regulatory revenues (when combined with supplementary budgetary support that comes willingly from informed taxpayers) are sufficient to produce a given set of regulatory services. If this condition is not met, the regulatory burden is unsustainable, and reregulation will force it back into line. However, if the regulator is generating more than enough revenues to cover his costs, he needs to be concerned that private firms will migrate to lower NRB regions. In this case the regulator could either lower his NRB or impose taxes and controls to stop the migration of activity.

Since taxes and controls are easily avoided, the policymaker will probably alter his NRB. The question for policymakers then is: what is the long-run equilibrium sustainable value of the NRB (NRB*)?

12.2.3   Implications for Coordination of International Financial Regulation

Even within a single economy, the optimal design of financial regulation is a complex matter. Continuing to think of regulation as a tax, the issue we wish to consider is whether a government will necessarily be able to collect a tax that is 'excessive'.[14]

Regulations impose costs which, in part, will be transferred to clients. Costly regulations create incentives for financial firms to innovate in order to reduce their costs and capture a larger market share. Money market mutual funds and off-balance-sheet financing techniques are two well-known domestic examples. The greater the extent of regulatory costs, the greater is the incentive to innovate or avoid the domestic financial system. The 1,200-mile movement of Citibank's credit card operations from New York to South Dakota (in part to escape New York's interest rate ceilings) illustrates this kind of domestic mobility. The limiting case might be found in a country experiencing hyperinflation, in which case residents might shift into commodity monies or completely avoid domestic financial institutions.

In the international setting, the scope for governments to collect excessive regulatory taxes is reduced because there is greater competition among national regulatory environments. Each domestic financial centre faces competition from foreign and offshore financial centres. As transactions costs and information costs decline, the cost of using an offshore financial centre declines. The development of offshore currency and bond markets in the 1960s represents a case in which borrowers and lenders found that they could carry out the requisite market transactions more efficiently and with sufficient safety by operating offshore − in a parallel market. Capital flight from less developed countries is an extreme example of residents escaping the local inflationary tax or fleeing from low or highly variable real rates of return. While the capital flight example sounds dramatic, Dooley (1987) has argued that, under some definitions, the shift by Americans of $250 billion from domestic to Eurocurrency accounts in 1980−2 could usefully be interpreted as capital flight.

In the past, policymakers often set financial regulations as if there were no international feedback effects. The obvious point to make is that, in today's world, communications costs are low and capital mobility is high. It is becoming less feasible for a state or a nation to impose an NRB that stands too far from world norms. In the past 20 years, US and European financial institutions have moved a large part of their operations offshore, suggesting that they judged the cost of domestic financial regulations as excessive. If we assume that transaction costs and communication costs are declining, would it follow that the NRB* on financial institutions is zero − i.e. that a financial institution would migrate rather than pay any positive regulatory tax?

In our judgement, a long-run equilibrium can be maintained with a *positive* NRB. Financial transactions involve uncertainty − about the monetary unit of account, about the creditworthiness of the financial institutions and about the political stability of the financial centre. Financial institutions ought to value their access to lender of last resort facilities, the opportunity to be head-quartered in a stable political climate, and so forth. And in those markets that are largely unregulated, with an NRB approaching zero, we observe that they have not taken over a 100 per cent share of the Euromarkets. If financial institutions find it in their interest to pay some regulatory tax, the economic question then concerns the sustainable magnitude of this tax.

As we have stressed throughout, communications costs are falling and capital mobility is increasing. Whatever the cost of the regulatory burden placed on financial institutions, it seems clear that this cost must be roughly similar across the major countries of the world. Given the complexity of the financial system, accomplishing the necessary consistency, coverage and coordination of regulations represents a major undertaking. The approach to regulation in the Eurocurrency market provides some indication of the problems that might be faced and how they might be overcome.[15]

Eurocurrency operations occur 'offshore' but not beyond the reach of governments. Eurocurrency banks could be regulated on a 'territorial' basis. Under this approach, the country in which a deposit was issued would impose reserve requirements on both domestic banks and branches and subsidiaries of foreign banks. For the territorial approach to be effective an agreement would be required among all countries, small and large, that might potentially harbour Eurobanks. However, all the major players in this market are headquartered in a major industrial country − this is almost a criterion for success in attracting deposits in this market. Eurocurrency banks could instead be regulated on a 'domiciliary' approach requiring the country in which the headquarters of the bank is domiciled to impose consistent regulations across all offshore branches and subsidiaries. The domiciliary approach would 'only' require agreement across major industrial countries. A large bank might move its headquarters to a regulation-free mini-state, but this seems unlikely given *inter alia* the value of lender of last resort facilities, as argued earlier.

The approach taken by the BIS is along the lines of the domiciliary approach. In the Basle Concordat (1974), the United States and 30 other countries agreed to assume lender of last resort responsibility for their offshore banks. In 1980, the BIS announced an agreement among Central Banks requiring commercial banks headquartered within their territories to consolidate their worldwide accounts. This agreement enabled bank examiners to regulate offshore and onshore operations on a consistent basis.

The recent discussions at the BIS on capital adequacy requirements fit within the domiciliary framework. A recent study by Cumming and Sweet (1987–8) suggests that there is considerable variation in the financial structures across the Group of Ten countries with greater integration of banking and securities activities outside Japan and the United States. Whether the present level of diversity is consistent with stable financial markets is unclear. We can conclude that the 'one-market' hypothesis outlined in the Brady Commission report and elsewhere clearly needs to be interpreted internationally. Not only are there strong arbitrage price linkages between stocks, futures, options and various 'bank products' within one country, but these linkages extend between countries for similar products denominated in US dollars or in other currencies. Clearly, however, a consistent set of regulations will be necessary to prevent competitive distortions.[16]

12.3   Financial Services in the European Community after 1992

The current and proposed regulations that will affect the financial services industry in the EC after 1992 are addressed in detail in several of the chapters in this volume. In this section, we briefly review the key principles of the plan and then turn to several unresolved policy issues that could have a dramatic impact on the Euromarkets.[17]

12.3.1   **Basic Tenets of the Plan**

A scant seven paragraphs (numbers 101–7) of the European Commission's White Paper (1985) formed the basis of the plan to remove internal barriers affecting financial markets in the EC.[18] This, in itself, is consistent with the Commission's minimalist framework. The broad goals were (a) a minimal amount of regulation shared by all EC countries, (b) complete freedom to offer financial services throughout the EC based on mutual recognition of national laws, regulations and practices and (c) home country control over all activities supervised by firms headquartered in the home country.

The common core of regulation shared by all EC countries is intended to safeguard certain fundamental public goods dealing with the safety and solvency of the financial system, as well as to set minimum standards for investor, depositor and consumer protection. The principle of 'mutual recognition' leaves scope for accommodating differences in regulation across countries. Rather than 'straight-jacketing' regulation across the EC, this feature allows for competition and dynamic adjustment, as hypothesized by Kane (1987) and discussed earlier in section 12.2. The principle of home country control reflects a domiciliary approach, along the lines of the Basle Concordat. As such, home country control both preserves national sovereignty in these areas and exploits existing regulatory and supervisory bodies without the need for a new supranational Community-wide agency.

Taken together, these principles circumvent the need to homogenize a wide array of financial regulations and practices, thus speeding up the ultimate goal of unifying the internal financial markets. Furthermore, by exploiting competition among regulatory authorities, the EC will ultimately achieve a market-determined level of regulation that is more responsive to market conditions than one designed *ex ante* by a supranational body and then revised subject to long and variable lags.

12.3.2 Unresolved Policy Issues

With only seven paragraphs forming the foundation for a unified financial market, a great many details have been left unspecified. The resolution of these issues bears heavily on the Euromarkets.

The starting point of this discussion must be the specification of regulations that will reside in the common core. The expressed desire is to keep these regulations to a minimum, but which variables will be covered and will numerical values be a part of these regulations? Padoa-Schioppa (1988) has suggested that the directives which form the common regulatory framework need not specify every detail. Rather, it may suffice simply to list those variables which must be addressed in *national* regulations, perhaps specifying a range of acceptable values. This approach appears sensible as it would both speed up the process of agreement on a core and permit countries to preserve their national sovereignty relating to key issues (control of national monetary policy, national taxation policy etc.). However, it could well lead to a very minimal common core which in turn would permit a wider variety of national regulatory regimes with wider variability of NRBs.

410   *Richard M. Levich*

We now consider three policy variables the treatment of which in 1992 had a critical impact on the Euromarkets. The first is the reserve requirements on demand deposits held in banks. Reserve requirements represent a tax or a regulatory burden to the extent that required reserves (a) exceed actuarially sound reserves and (b) earn less than the market rate of interest. As we see in table 12.3, in 1988 reserve requirements ranged from zero or near zero in Belgium, Denmark, Luxembourg and the Netherlands to 15 per cent and higher in Italy, Portugal and Spain. This is a considerable variation, the effect of which is magnified with higher absolute levels of interest rates. Yet because reserve requirements are seen as an instrument of *domestic* monetary policy (where harmonization might infringe on national sovereignty) there are apparently no plans to harmonize reserve requirements across EC countries. By April 1992, reserve requirements were little changed – up slightly in three countries and down somewhat in three countries, including a sharp drop from 18.5 per cent to 5 per cent in Spain. As European financial markets integrate further, there should be pressures on central banks to reduce their reserve requirements and to rely on other instruments of monetary policy.

Table 12.3   Reserve requirements in selected countries (percentage of deposits)

| Country | Demand deposits | | Time deposits | Savings deposits |
	mid-1988	April 1992	April 1992	April 1992
EC countries				
Belgium	0.0	0.0	0.0	0.0
Denmark	0.0	0.0	0.0	0.0
France	5.0	5.5	0.5	2.0
Germany	6.6–12.1	6.6–12.1	4.95	4.15
Greece[a]	7.5	8.0	8.0	8.0
Ireland	10.0	6.0	6.0	6.0
Italy[a]	25.0[b]	22.5	22.5	22.5
Luxembourg	0.0	0.0	0.0	0.0
Netherlands	[c]	1.1	1.1	1.1
Portugal	15.0	17.0	17.0	17.0
Spain[a]	18.5	5.0	5.0	5.0
UK	0.5	0.5	0.5	0.5
Other countries				
Canada	n.a.	0.0	0.0	0.0
Japan	n.a.	0.1–1.3	0.05–1.2	0.05–1.2
Switzerland	n.a.	2.5	2.5	0.5
United States	n.a.	3.0–10.0	0.0	0.0

n.a., not available.
[a] Required reserves are remunerated to some degree.
[b] Applied against the increase in deposits since May 1984; the effective level of required reserves is close to 20 per cent.
[c] A small, variable and remunerated reserve requirement was introduced in May 1988.

Source: Mid-1988 data are from Morgan Guaranty Trust, 1988. April 1992 figures supplied by the BIS, private correspondence.

A second key area is harmonization of tax rates on interest, dividends and capital gains as well as withholding practices. As we see in table 12.4, the distinctions (a) between dividends, interest and capital gains and (b) between residents and non-residents often matter a great deal.[19] Again, practices pertaining to withholding tax rates vary considerably across nations.

Table 12.4 Tax treatments of dividends, interest and capital gains in the European Economic Community

Country	Withholding tax on interest paid to		Withholding tax on dividends paid to		Tax treatment of capital gains
	Residents	Non-residents	Residents	Non-residents	
Belgium	25	25	25	25	Yes, if speculative
Denmark	0[a]	0	30	30	Yes
France	[b]	0−51	0	25	Yes
Germany	0[c]	0[c]	25	25	Yes, for shares; no, for bonds
Greece	[d]	49	42−53	42−53	n.a.
Ireland	0−35	0−35	0	0	n.a.
Italy	12.5−30	12.5−30	10	32	No, except in particular cases
Luxembourg	0	0	15	15	Generally not taxed
Netherlands	0[a]	0	25	25	Yes, if speculative
Portugal	30	30	12	12	n.a.
Spain	20	20	20	20	n.a.
UK	25	25	0	0	Yes

n.a., not available.
[a] Banks report interest income to the tax authorities.
[b] Recipients can choose to pay 27 per cent or 47 per cent, depending on the savings instrument, or to lump interest income with other income. Banks report interest income to the tax authorities.
[c] Banks do not report interest income to the tax authorities; a 10 per cent withholding rate was in effect from 1 January to 1 July 1989.
[d] Corporations pay 25 per cent; individuals pay 8 per cent plus an amount linked to graduated rates applicable to income taxes.
Sources: Data on withholding taxes, Morgan Guaranty Trust, 1988, citing Arthur Andersen; information on taxation of capital gains, Micossi, 1988

In an environment with free capital mobility (the EC after 1 July 1990), table 12.4 suggests fertile ground for tax-motivated capital flows and new financial instruments designed to transform highly taxed capital flows into lesser taxed flows. In all EC countries (except Luxembourg), residents either pay a withholding tax on interest income or have their domestic interest income reported to the tax authorities. Non-residents, however, face no withholding taxes against interest income in Denmark, Luxembourg and the Netherlands. Residents incur no withholding tax against dividends in France, Ireland and the United Kingdom, and the last two countries follow the same treatment for non-residents. Luxembourg appears to offer the most favourable treatment of capital gains within the EC. However, Morgan Guaranty Trust (1988) reports that the capital gains tax rate on individuals is zero in Belgium and Greece, and in many circumstances it is zero in Italy and the Netherlands.

The third critical policy area related to taxation is harmonization of disclosure and reporting of interest and dividends to tax authorities (i.e. rules on secrecy). Even though there is no withholding tax on interest paid to residents of Denmark and the Netherlands, banks report interest income to the tax authorities. Luxembourg stands out as the only country with neither withholding tax nor reporting to authorities of interest paid to residents. However, for non-residents of Denmark, Luxembourg and the Netherlands there is neither withholding tax nor reporting to authorities of interest paid. No withholding tax and no reporting to authorities is also the practice for dividends paid to both residents and non-residents of Ireland and the United Kingdom.

The data in table 12.4 suggest that non-residents should prefer to hold interest-paying instruments (such as bank deposits or bonds) in Denmark, Luxembourg or the Netherlands. Given the precedent of reporting to the tax authorities for residents of Denmark and the Netherlands, Luxembourg stands out. Unless it can be persuaded to amend its secrecy laws or to impose withholding taxes on interest payments, Luxembourg is likely to gain considerable ground as a leading European financial centre.

12.4   Conclusions Regarding the Euromarkets and the Development of European Financial Centres

In three key areas − reserve requirements; tax and withholding treatment of interest, dividends and capital gains; and disclosure and secrecy laws − we currently observe considerable variation across EC countries. All these factors contribute to the NRB placed on financial institutions, which they in turn attempt to pass on to their customers. When the barriers to the free flow of capital and financial services finally dissolve, we expect to see tremendous competitive forces unleashed − forces that will induce the NRBs to converge across countries.

The main factor which retards the completion of the internal market is the perception of a trade-off between economic efficiency and national sovereignty. It is often argued that the stability of the European Monetary System depends heavily on the coordination of monetary policies, and if EC countries lose this degree of freedom concerning their national sovereignty they can rely on fiscal policies to meet their internal policy objectives. In this chapter we have argued that the loss of monetary policy independence is more substantial — i.e. the *tools* of monetary policy (such as reserve requirements) must be coordinated also. And the remaining independence of fiscal policy may be slightly exaggerated — i.e. while countries may be free to spend their tax revenues as they please, they can only collect taxes on mobile factors (financial services) if they are levied at a competitive rate. A country with an excessive NRB will experience a migration of financial activity and a decline in tax revenues.

While the policymakers of the EC are rightfully concerned about harmonization of critical policies across the EC and the creation of a 'level playing field' free from competitive distortions, this is only half the story. The NRB of the EC must be commensurate with that in other industrial countries. If not, there will be a migration of financial services offshore to Switzerland, to international banking facilities in the United States, to Liechtenstein or elsewhere. As the Europeans have been the beneficiaries of excess US financial market regulation, they can hardly question that this migration will occur. The only question can be how sensitive the migration will be in response to a given difference in net regulatory burdens.

The recent German experience offers some indication of the sensitivities of investors and policymakers. In 1988, about DM 120 billion flowed out of West Germany, in part because investors wanted to avoid the 10 per cent withholding tax on interest income that became effective on 1 January 1989. On 27 April the German government announced that the withholding tax would be abolished on 1 July 1989. Instead, the Germans will support some form of unified withholding tax of the sort proposed in February 1989 by the European Commission (Protzman, 1989).

The innovations that have taken place in communications technology, information processing and financial services strongly suggest that the equilibrium NRB is falling, as is the neutral band around it needed to induce arbitrage. In this environment, a minimal core of prudential regulation is a sound idea. EC countries will be driven, *de facto* and endogenously, towards harmonization. Active coordination of regulation may be useful, but there is a continuing need for flexibility because of the dynamic nature of financial services.

The treaty at Maastricht commits the EC to have the European Currency Unit (ECU) as its common currency and the European Central Bank (ECB) as its monetary authority by 1 January 1999 at the latest (and for a subset of EC countries that have met convergence requirements by as early as 1 January 1997).[20] Once a common currency and monetary authority are in place, differential reserve requirements will no longer be an effective element of monetary policy. If reserve requirements are indeed used, they will have to be imposed on a uniform basis. Once the ECU is the common currency of the EC, the Deutschmark, pound and other national currencies will vanish, and along with them the London-Deutschmark market, the Frankfurt-pound market and other such EC offshore markets will vanish as well. European financial centres will continue to harbour offshore markets for US dollars, Japanese yen, Canadian dollars, Australian dollars and other non-EC currencies, vying for market share on the basis of factors discussed earlier.

While the progression of recent EC developments threatens national sovereignty, it seems safe to say that for the foreseeable future (and even after 1999), national elections and national sovereignty will continue to be strong forces. National policymakers will monitor transactions by domestic residents and transactions in domestic currency (while these exist) more closely than others. The NRB for these transactions may remain relatively high, leaving incentives for offshore markets for EC currencies (again, while they exist) within the EC. Luxembourg stands out as a likely candidate to gain market share if its NRB is not increased. Not surprisingly, the government of Luxembourg has gone on the record to oppose unified EC rules raising withholding taxes and disclosure requirements.

But the EC also faces competition from outside the EC and for markets in non-EC currencies. As a long-run proposition, the equilibrium sustainable NRB* is probably greater than zero, because of the uncertainties inherent in financial contracting, political risks, the value attached to promises of official regulatory authorities regarding their onshore markets and the convenience associated with onshore transactions. The fact that non-EC centres (e.g. Singapore, Hong Kong etc.) have not taken over the Euro-dollar market suggests that these centres have pushed their regulatory competition to the limit. This suggests that, even if transactions costs approach zero, an island state with an NRB approaching zero will not attract all the world's financial services business. However, if the EC *re*regulates and raises its NRB, migration of the Euro-dollar market to non-EC countries is the likely outcome.

Notes

1 In the case of the United States, at the Federal level financial activities could fall under the domain of the Federal Reserve Board, the Comptroller on the Currency, the Securities and Exchange Commission and the Commodity Futures Trading Commission to name only the major bodies. Each of the 50 States would have its own regulatory bodies to deal with banking and insurance. Every city and municipality has a body responsible for local income taxes, real estate taxes, transfer taxes, stamp duties, etc., all of which affect the NRB on financial institutions.

2 The Paris bank *Banque Commerciale pour l'Europe du Nord* carried the cable address EUROBANK, which later became synonymous with the general activity of accepting deposits offshore. See Kvasnicka (1969).

3 For an analysis of the impact of German capital controls on the differential between onshore and offshore interest rates, see Dooley and Isard (1980). The Swiss control programme is described in various issues of the *International Letter*, Federal Reserve Bank of Chicago, over the 1974–9 period.

4 IBFs are exempt from reserve requirement, interest rate ceilings and deposit insurance. See Chrystal (1984) for a discussion of the regulations pertaining to IBFs and their significance. On 23 December 1988 the Federal Reserve Board passed a rule which allowed US commercial banks to offer foreign currency denominated deposits after 1 January 1990. Regulations for these deposits are still being formulated and so it is unclear whether the accounts will be competitive with other offshore centres.

5 This section draws on the presentation in Levich and Hawkins (1981).

6 We are assuming away the existence of Russians (say in the 1950s) or others who view the United States as risky and who would deposit funds offshore at rates below R_D.

7 For the case of offshore interest rate determination in the presence of capital controls, see Levich and Hawkins (1981, p. 398).

8 As mentioned, offshore lending rates may exceed onshore lending rates ($R'_L >$ R_L) when capital rationing or other restrictions affect the domestic market. Onshore deposit rates may exceed offshore deposit rates ($R_D > R'_D$) when there are controls or taxes on non-resident capital inflows, such as in Germany and Switzerland in the early 1970s. The onshore lending rate must exceed the offshore deposit rate ($R_L > R'_D$) for otherwise arbitragers will borrow in the onshore market and deposit their funds offshore.

9 A recent case study by Finnerty (1986) has documented that some firms have actually engaged in arbitrage – issuing their bonds in the Euromarket and purchasing US securities to earn the interest differential. In the same vein, Kim and Stulz (1988) show that corporations have behaved opportunistically by issuing in the lower cost Eurobond market and gaining an improvement in their equity share prices. However, the magnitude of this benefit has fallen to become insignificant.

10 An offshore centre might adjust its deposit rates higher than 8.00 per cent in our example, but this might signal to the market that it was a less convenient or more risky centre to hold deposits. See Stoakes (1985) for a discussion of Wells Fargo Bank's difficulties with offshore deposits placed in Citibank's Philippines branch.

11 The technique of solving for a replicating portfolio, writing down an arbitrage pricing relationship and then solving for the implied value of one variable is quite general. Brenner and Galai (1986) use put-call parity of option prices to solve for an implied interest rate on borrowed funds. Machayya (1989) develops an arbitrage model for pricing fixed-rate currency swaps as a function of forward contracts. Koh (1988) shows how to synthesize a Eurocurrency interest rate futures contract (which does not now exist) using a combination of Euro-dollar interest rate futures and currency futures contracts.

12 Money market funds that buy Euro-dollar deposits have enabled US investors to reduce some of these access barriers.

13 Note that because some regulations may not generate revenues and some regulations entail externalities, the value of net regulatory benefits received by firms need not equal the net regulatory costs collected by the regulatory authorities.
14 This section draws heavily on Levich and Walter (1988, pp. 71–4).
15 For a thorough discussion of this issue, see Dam (1982, pp. 320–8). A related problem is that countries may coordinate on a set of financial regulations that are excessively strict or liberal. In this regard, it would be preferable to maintain competition among regulatory authorities. See Kane (1987) for a complete discussion of this theme.
16 Competitive distortions in international financial services are discussed by Levich and Walter (1988, pp. 74–82).
17 These issues have also been reviewed by Micossi (1988), Morgan Guaranty Trust (1988) and Padoa-Schioppa (1988).
18 The European Commission's February 1988 proposal for a Second Banking Directive contained language identical with that in the 1985 White Paper.
19 In contrast with table 12.4 Buchan (1989), citing European Commission sources, reports that the withholding tax on interest paid to non-residents is zero in Belgium, France and Greece. He also reports that the withholding tax on interest paid to both residents and non-residents in Portugal was 25 per cent.
20 For a thorough discussion of the Maastricht Treaty and its implications, see Kenen (1992).

References

Aliber, R.Z. (1973) The interest rate parity theory: a reinterpretation. *Journal of Political Economy*, 81, 1451–9.
Bank for International Settlements, *Annual Report*, various years.
Brenner, M. and Galai, D. (1986) Implied interest rates. *Journal of Business*, 59 (3), 493–507.
Buchan, D. (1989) Brussels spreads the pain of tax on savers. *Financial Times*, 9 February.
Chrystal, K.A. (1984) International Banking Facilities. *Monthly Review, Federal Reserve Bank of St Louis*, April, 5–11.
Commission of the European Communities (1985) *Completing the Internal Market: White Paper to the European Council*. Brussels: Commission of the European Communities.
Cumming, C.M. and Sweet, L.M. (1987–8) Financial structure of the G-10 countries: how does the United States compare? *Quarterly Review, Federal Reserve Bank of New York*, 12 (4) Winter, 14–25.
Dam, K.W. (1982) *The Rules of the Game*. Chicago, IL: University of Chicago Press.
Dooley, M. (1987) Comment. In D. Lessard and J. Williamson (eds) *Capital Flight and Third World Debt*. Washington, DC: Institute for International Economics.
Dooley, M.P. and Isard, P. (1980) Capital controls, political risk and deviations for interest rate parity. *Journal of Political Economy*, 88 (2), April, 370–84.

Economic Report of the President (1989). Washington, DC: US Government Printing Office.

Finnerty, J.D. (1986) Zero coupon bond arbitrage: an illustration of the regulatory dialectic at work. *Financial Management*, Winter, 13–17.

Frenkel, J.A. and Levich, R.M. (1975) Covered interest arbitrage: unexploited profits? *Journal of Political Economy*, 83, 325–38.

Grabbe, J.O. (1986) *International Financial Markets*. New York: Elsevier.

Kane, E.J. (1987) Competitive financial reregulation: an international perspective. In R. Portes and A. Swoboda (eds), *Threats to International Financial Stability*. London: Cambridge University Press.

Kenen, P.B. (1992) *EMU After Maastricht*. Washington, DC: Group of Thirty.

Kim, Y.C. and Stulz, R.M. (1988) The Eurobond market and corporate financial policy: a test of the clientele hypothesis. *Journal of Financial Economics*, 22, December, 189–205.

Koh, A. (1988) A study of the effectiveness of hedging dollar and non-dollar borrowing costs using Eurodollar and currency futures, unpublished Ph.D. dissertation, New York University, June.

Kvasnicka, J.G. (1969) Eurodollars – an important source of funds for American banks. *Business Condition, Federal Reserve Bank of Chicago*, June.

Levich, R.M. and Hawkins, R.G. (1981) Foreign investment. In M. Polakoff and T. Durkin (eds), *Financial Markets and Institutions*, 2nd edn. Boston: Houghton Mifflin, ch. 18.

Levich, R.M. and Walter, I. (1988) The regulation of global financial markets. In T. Noyelle (ed.) *New York's Financial Markets*. Boulder, CO: Westview Press.

Machayya, M. (1989) Efficiency of the currency swap market: theoretical pricing and empirical evidence, unpublished Ph.D. dissertation, New York University, February.

Micossi, S. (1988) The single European market: finance. *Quarterly Review, Banco Nazional del Lavoro*, June, 217–35.

Morgan Guaranty Trust (1988) Financial markets in Europe: toward 1992. In *World Financial Markets*. New York: Morgan Guaranty Trust.

Padoa-Schioppa, T. (1988) Towards a European banking regulatory framework. *Economic Bulletin, Banca D'Italia*, No. 6, February, 49–53.

Protzman, F. (1989) 10% withholding tax abolished by Germany. *New York Times*, 28 April.

Stoakes, C. (1985) Eurodollar deposits on trial. *Euromoney*, August, 25.

Comment

Daniel Gros

My remarks will concentrate on the title of the chapter, 'The Euromarkets after 1992'. But before discussing this general topic I would like to comment on the theory of the Euromarkets that is used by the author. Using the concept of the NRB the author argues that Euromarkets exist only because they can perform certain financial services cheaper than the domestic market. This implies that the interest rate spread on the Euromarkets should be smaller than the spread on the domestic market. In section 12.1.3 this is formally expressed by the inequalities

$$R_L \quad > \quad R'_L \quad > \quad R'_D \quad > \quad R_D \qquad (12C.1)$$

New York Prime rate (\$)	LIBOR (\$)	LIBID (\$)	New York CD (\$)

One immediate remark is that it is not fair to compare the New York Prime rate with the LIBOR rate. The former applies to lending to non-banks and the latter to the interbank market, with obvious differences in risk. An additional remark is that this series of inequalities does not hold for currencies of countries with capital controls, e.g. the French franc or the Italian lira. During times of tension, when the Italian and French capital controls are operating, one can observe a quite different relationship:

$$R'_L \quad > \quad R'_D \quad > > \quad R_L \quad > \quad R_D \qquad (12C.2)$$

Euro-interbank		Domestic interbank	

It is therefore not necessarily true that the Euro-lending rate is always below the domestic lending rate.

Observation of the Euro-DM rates and the domestic German interbank rates show that these inequalities do not always hold for currencies not subject to capital controls also. For example, on 14 February 1989 Dow Jones/telerate reported the following rates for DM deposits on the interbank market:

$$R_L = 6.35 \qquad R'_L = 6.5625 \qquad R'_D = 6.4375 \qquad R_D = 6.25$$

It is apparent that the inequalities (12C.1) do not hold in this case since the spread on the domestic market is approximately the same as the spread on the Euromarket and both Euro-rates exceed the domestic rates.

What is the reason for this discrepancy between theory and reality? It is, in my opinion, that for his theory the author assumes that the demand and supply of deposits in the currency considered comes only from domestic residents. However, this is not necessarily the case. There will be a demand and supply of deposits from non-residents as well, especially for currencies that are to some extent vehicle currencies in international trade. A large UK firm might therefore hold some Euro-dollar balances in London even if it could earn a higher return in New York, because going to the United States involves an additional cost for the UK firm. If there is a substantial demand for deposits from non-residents for these reasons the inequalities (12C.1) do not always have to hold. Another reason for the apparent discrepancy might be that to check his theory the author should not look at the interbank markets where the NRB is zero in most countries since these markets are not regulated and deposits on them are not subject to reserve requirements.

However, this specific comment aside, it is difficult to disagree with the main propositions of the paper, namely

1   Euromarkets arise because activities are transferred abroad if the domestic NRB becomes too large;
2   the sustainable long-run equilibrium NRB is positive.

In his discussions of the Euromarkets and 1992, the author has not looked at all the implications of his analysis, however. The remainder of my comments will try to show that he should have drawn some strong conclusions from his own analysis.

The starting point has to be the 'fact of life' that, as shown by the author, most taxes and regulations apply only to the production of financial services if residents are involved (as consumers or producers) and/or if a foreign currency is involved. This 'fact of life' will not be affected by 1992, and it follows immediately that 1992 will have no effect on the Euro-dollar market or all non-EC currency Euromarkets. Developments in the Euro-dollar market will therefore be independent of 1992. A change in the US NRB, however, could have a strong impact. For example, reregulation in the United States should strengthen the Euro-dollar market with or without 1992. And the share of the US dollar in the Euromarkets may have declined recently also because of the deregulation in the United States in the late 1980s.

The reason for the lenient attitude of regulators towards non-residents is presumably that Central Banks are concerned with the determination of their *domestic* monetary aggregates and the stability of their *domestic* banking system. Deposits for or by foreigners in a foreign currency have presumably no relation to the demand for the domestic currency and losses by a foreign depositor would presumably not affect confidence in the domestic banking system.

The interesting issue that remains is therefore the effect of 1992 on the Euro−Euro markets, i.e. the Euromarkets in EC currencies. In this respect, however, 1 July 1990 is the more important date, since at this date capital controls were completely abolished among all members of the European Monetary System (with Spain following one year later). This abolition of capital control led to a real Euro-lira and Euro-French-franc market and also allowed the Italians and French to participate much more in other Euromarkets. In contrast, 1992 has only allowed banks to offer financial services in other countries under their own domestic NRB. Therefore 1992 did not allow banks to escape their domestic NRB and had no *direct* effect on the Euromarkets. An indirect effect should come from the competition in regulation that will arise after 1992, however, and this should lead to a reduction in the average NRB in EC member countries. If this happens the Euro−Euro market would lose part of its competitive advantage and might contract.

The abolition of capital control therefore had a much stronger direct effect on the Euro−Euro markets than 1992. Italy seems to stand out as the country with the highest NRB, if only because of the 22.5 per cent marginal reserve requirement.[1] After the abolition of capital controls it can therefore be expected that substantial amounts of wholesale deposits in lira go to either Luxembourg or London. How much will depend on the reaction of the Banca d'Italia and on the behaviour of nominal interest rates because the latter determine the effective tax implicit in the reserve requirement.

One might argue that, if an EC country has a near-zero NRB on domestic operation (e.g. Luxembourg), banks headquartered in this country might use the home country rule of 1992 to transfer some of the Euro-business from Luxembourg to the country of origin (e.g. DM business back to Frankfurt). However, this will happen only if the main elements that make up the competitive advantage of the Luxembourg financial centre fall under the home country rule and can therefore be exported by Luxembourg banks. As argued by the author, the three main elements of most NRBs are

1   reserve requirements,
2   taxes on interest, especially withholding taxes,
3   reporting requirements.

The first element belongs to monetary control procedures and therefore does not fall under the home country rule, and the second and third are not specific to banking regulation and therefore do not come under the home country rule either. 1992 will therefore not lead to 'repatriation' of Euro−Euro market activity.

But if 1992 is irrelevant for the Euromarkets, what could have an impact? The answer is centralization of monetary control procedures in the context of the movement towards a common European currency and a European

Central Bank. If the European Central Banking Institution (whatever form or name it takes) that might be created by 1992 starts to treat all business by and for EC residents in the EC as domestic and imposes some reserve requirements or other monetary control procedures, there would be an incentive for the Euro−Euro markets to leave the EC and migrate to other places, such as Switzerland or some islands. In this sense, the results of the so-called Delors Committee, which is studying concrete steps towards economic and monetary union, will be more important for the Euromarkets than 1992.

The predictions of the 'NRB escape' theory of the Euromarkets can therefore be summarized as follows.

1 Euromarkets in *non-EC currencies* should not be affected by 1992.
2 The Euromarkets in *EC currencies* should:
   (a) not be affected directly by 1992,
   (b) lose some business if the competition in regulation caused by 1992 lowers the average NRB in the EC,
   (c) leave the EC if increasing monetary unification leads national regulators to regard all EC business as domestic.

Note

1 Which is remunerated at 5.5 per cent, however.

13

Macro-economic Implications of 1992

Charles Wyplosz

The Single Act is clearly a set of micro-economic policy measures. Yet the Cecchini report prepared for the European Commission concluded that its effects would be to add the equivalent of 5 percentage points of gross domestic product (GDP) to the European Community (EC) as a whole over the first five years. This is a sizeable aggregate effect which cannot fail to have macro-economic implications. As for any micro-economic policy measure, it is tempting to attribute the growth-enhancing effect to the supply side of the economy. Stopping there, though, would be misleading in two respects at least. First, faster growth will not materialize fully if the demand side is not validating the supply-side boost. Second, the expected changes in the micro-economic structure will affect the conduct of macro-economic policy. In particular, exchange rate and monetary policies are likely to face different constraints after 1992, with a further reduction in the degree of national independence. This in turn should strengthen the strategic importance of national fiscal policies.

From a macro-economic viewpoint it is useful to separate the implications of 1992 into the effects on the goods markets and those concerning financial markets. By and large, the EC countries have already achieved a considerable degree of goods market integration. The exceptions are the more recent members — Greece, Portugal and Spain — which are still in the process of integrating into the EC with particular timetables so that for them 1992 makes only a limited difference. For all the other countries, the remaining trade barriers have all but vanished, being now more in the nature of local regulations, fixed costs or particular restrictions targeted at non-EC countries. While 1992 may well lead to a shake-up of particular industries and deeply affect particular firms, it is hard to believe that the global macro-economic effects will be large. The Commission's estimate is that the EC GDP should be increased by 3.2−5.7 per cent over a five-year period with consumer prices lowered (relative to trend) by 4.5−7.7 per cent. About half these effects are expected to come from a more efficient supply side, the next-largest effect coming from the elimination of rents in the financial sector (primarily banking).

I thank José Viñals for making data available to me, and Jean Dermine for comments.

These numbers can be looked at from two quite different perspectives. On one hand, raising GDP by 5 per cent in one step is quite impressive, even if the Commission's numbers are generous. On the other hand, the orders of magnitude are those achievable through standard macro-economic policies. Thus the Reagan expansion brought up the GDP growth rate from an average of 2.7 per cent over the 1970s to 6.6 per cent in 1984. To be sure, some regions or countries may benefit – or lose – more than others as overall welfare gains may be accompanied by particular losses. These are normal micro-economic effects which may well amount in size and scope to macro-economic effects, particularly at the regional level. This issue will be considered at some length in section 13.3 within the broader context of fiscal policies.

The picture is altogether different when it comes to financial markets. Until 1985, European financial markets were mostly characterized by capital controls, considerable protection, heavy regulations and a well-known absence of price competition. Of course, some countries stand out, most notably the United Kingdom. By and large, however, 1992 implies the opening up to trade of highly protected and segmented financial markets. In contrast with the goods markets, then, this is where large effects are to be expected. Will such effects have macro-economic implications? On the one hand, it is possible to express doubts. After all, the crash of October 1987, a real-life experience of the potential macro-economic effects of large-scale financial disturbances, did not dent growth in the late 1980s. On the other hand, even if financial markets do not seriously affect the real economy (an admittedly extreme view), they provide the background against which macro-economic policies are conducted. In this respect, 1992 will usher in major changes which cannot fail to modify policymaking profoundly.

In Section 13.1 the effects of goods market integration are considered, and three main points are made. First, as noted by several authors (e.g. Commission of the European Communities, 1988a; Bean et al., 1988), the supply-side benefits may lag behind the temporary adjustment costs. Second, the distribution of gains may be unevenly spread. Third, while the aggregate effects are likely to be limited at the individual firm or industry levels, there may be considerable changes. In section 13.2, the focus is on financial integration and the resulting strengthening of interest rate linkages. It is argued that monetary policy independence will be severely curtailed, thus creating a challenge for the European Monetary System (EMS) which is likely to require more explicit coordination than has been the case so far. In particular, the monetary union option is considered as a long-run prospect but several possible steps in this direction are examined. Financial integration will also affect the financing of public debts, which is a very important issue for some countries.

This consideration naturally leads to the issue of how fiscal policies will be affected. In section 13.3 the facts are reviewed and particular attention is paid to the EC-wide redistributive aspects. Many of the issues have been extensively discussed in two reports prepared by the EC Commission: the McDougall report (1977) and the Padoa-Schioppa report (1987). The chapter draws attention to serious risks of capture by interest groups.

13.1 Goods Market Integration

13.1.1 Existing Trade Restrictions before 1992

Border costs

Border costs were incurred by the simple need to check goods at border crossings. These were mostly waiting time costs plus, of course, the services of custom officers. These costs simply cumulated over the regular transportation costs and implicit convenience delays of shipping. Even though they were not wholly negligible, it has been hard to get excited about the savings to accrue from the elimination of border posts: the Cecchini report put the estimates at 0.4 per cent of GDP. The economic effect has been to make goods manufactured in different EC countries (slightly) more substitutable and hence increase competition.

Local preference buying and regulations

Local preference buying and regulations existed in most countries. They included such items as national preference clauses on purchases of goods and services by administrations and the existence of particular 'safety' or 'quality' regulations which were costly or lengthy for foreign producers to adopt. Such restrictions were used to protect local champions (such as the French computer company Bull) or state-owned companies (such as many airlines) and were quick to come under attack, as in the German purity laws concerning beer. Because these restrictions have been pervasive and numerous, they are still likely to be significant. Quite often they occur in markets which require some form of regulation anyway, e.g. airlines, telecommunications and insurance, so that trade liberalization may be a powerful tool to lead to deregulation. In other cases (e.g. public works) such regulations are often implicit and concern the process of tenders which can be made more open, but those markets are likely to be contestable whenever they are not competitive already.

Quotas or voluntary export restraints

Quotas or voluntary export restraints (VERs) *vis-à-vis* non-EC countries exist in a number of sensitive industries such as automobiles, electronic equipment and textiles. To be effective, such quotas had to be enforced at all border posts. The removal of these posts will necessitate that country-specific restrictions be harmonized at the EC level. Because these restrictions were unambiguously set up to restrict trade, and did so quite powerfully, the relaxation will be quantitatively important. Of course, harmonization may occur at the more restrictive level and thus increase the overall degree of protection. While such an outcome cannot be ruled out for some industries, harmonization is more likely to regress to the least restrictive stand. Pressure exerted on the EC via the General Agreement on Tariffs and Trade (GATT) by the United States, Japan and other countries should be understood as designed mainly to influence this aspect. It is ironic that these pressures remain the best hope for European consumers in the face of the European Commission's likely tendency to give in to industry demands in a quid pro quo arrangement whereby more intra-European trade is swapped against more protection *vis-à-vis* the rest of the world.

13.1.2   Hecksher−Ohlin Trade

For the part of trade that relies on comparative advantage in factors of production, a number of standard results are readily applicable. A crucial result is the equalization of factor costs. For the original EC members, much of this convergence has already occurred. Direct comparisons are difficult because of exchange rate fluctuations, differences in tax treatments and income distributions. Table 13.1 provides some partial information: it shows the levels of GDP per capita once GDPs have been converted into a common currency. Dispersion, as measured by the standard deviation, was

Table 13.1 Gross domestic product per capita (gross domestic product for the European Community 12 = 100)

	1960	1970	1987
Belgium	116	114	109
Denmark	123	140	153
Germany	123	132	140
Greece	40	49	34
Spain	35	48	54
France	124	120	118
Ireland	59	57	61
Italy	81	94	102
Netherlands	96	112	110
Portugal	28	32	27
UK	130	96	86
Standard deviations			
EEC 6	19	14	15
EEC 9	25	26	29

GDPs are converted at current prices and exchange rates into ECUs.
Source: European Economy, 33, July 1987, table 7

never large among the original six EEC members (Belgium, Luxembourg, Germany, France, Italy and the Netherlands) and decreased during the 1960s after they concluded the Treaty of Rome in 1957. The next three entrants (Denmark, Ireland and the United Kingdom) brought in more diversity when they joined in 1973. If anything, the data show increased dispersion, but the combination of the Danish Krone overvaluation and slow UK growth play an important role here.

Overall these results suggest that there are few Hecksher–Ohlin gains in store for the EC nine. This is probably why the Cecchini report never considers this aspect of integration. Against this, for the most recent members, Spain, Portugal and Greece, Hecksher–Ohlin trade is likely to play an important role, although factor price equalization will no doubt take time. The changes in these countries will often be dramatic because they start from a very different position from the rest of the EC. In the original core of the EC, given the relatively small size of the new entrants, the changes will be globally subdued but concentrated at first in the most labour-intensive industries. A prime candidate for shake-up would be agriculture if it were not for the Common Agricultural Policy (CAP). By setting minimum prices, the CAP transforms downward relative price adjustments into inter-country transfers and excess supplies. Thus less visible transfers to the new EC members will replace the tensions which existed over low price imports from these countries.

An important part of the process should be the change in specialization towards labour-intensive industries in the south and, on a limited scale, towards labour-saving industries in the north. This reallocation improves welfare in the long run, but is potentially painful during the transition period, the more so as it takes place at a time of generalized mass unemployment throughout the EC. This is not the place to review the unemployment situation in Europe, but current knowledge suggests that improvement on that front would require, among other things, a moderation of labour costs and a halt to the shift towards labour-saving growth. The integration of the south is thus found to occur at a particularly awkward period with rising labour costs in the south and labour saving in the north being an undesirable implication of the enlargement of the EC. The result is likely to be the setting up of regional policies which run against the purposes of 1992, an issue reviewed in section 13.1.4 below.

While most of the effects of Hecksher–Ohlin specialization may occur through trade in goods in the absence of movements of the production factors, the actual process may well include some factor mobility. As is well known, the two types of mobility are, in theory, substitutable. Labour is not very mobile among EC countries for a number of well-known reasons: language, cultures, traditions etc. differ considerably. At the same time, migration has been observed for decades already, suggesting that these barriers are not so powerful in the face of very large income differentials. The most plausible outcome is that trade in goods will gradually replace labour mobility in the process of arbitrage in labour income. It is even possible to envision in the medium run a reverse flow, of the type observed in recent years within Italy, as southern European workers seek to enjoy increased standards of living in their home countries.

Against this, physical capital mobility may rise on account of Hecksher – Ohlin-type comparative advantage. An extreme example of this process can be observed in the case of Spain since this country is undergoing the sharper change of joining the EC after years of protection and heavy-handed regulations and because this is a case where Hecksher – Ohlin trade is likely to be more important than within the group of the EC nine countries (see table 13.1 for evidence that factor prices differ markedly). Table 13.2 documents a clear acceleration of foreign direct investment in Spain, partly from the EC, since it joined the EC in 1986. Whether capital mobility substitutes for trade in goods or merely accompanies it is of interest. Once again, we turn to Spain. Table 13.3 shows a dramatic increase in financial services and a moderate decrease in such traded-good industries as mining, chemicals and metals. While other cases are less clear cut, there is an indication that whenever possible (i.e. in traded-good industries), trade substitutes for capital mobility and vice versa.

Of particular interest is the role of trade diversion: as with any regional trade integration (as opposed to global protection reductions of the type worked out through GATT), more trade within the zone leads to the displacement of some trade with the rest of the world. In this sense, some negative effect on non-EC countries is hardly avoidable. A natural way to reduce such an effect is to replace trade in goods by capital mobility. This is a particularly attractive option for multinational corporations (MNCs). It will raise (it already has) thorny questions about what defines a locally produced good. It is important to note that while non-EC based MNCs can thus avoid being victims of trade diversion, non-EC countries do not escape: the very relocation of MNC activities within the EC amounts to a transfer of capital, jobs and technology.

13.1.3   Intra-industry trade

Even limited reductions in barriers to trade may have sizeable effects on intra-industry trade. From the producer's viewpoint, reduced direct or implicit costs mean that economies of scale and scope can be more fully exploited. From the consumer's vantage point, more competition is always good news in markets characterized by monopolistic competitions.

Table 13.2   Foreign direct investment in Spain (billion pesetas, current prices)

	1982	1983	1984	1985	1986	1987
(1) Foreign direct investment	183	158	267	280	401	727
(2) Total investment[a]	3,597	3,967	3,987	4,279	5,083	6,121
Ratio (1)/(2) (%)	5.1	4.0	6.7	6.5	7.9	11.9
Share of foreign direct investment originating in the EC (%)	45.4	63.7	48.3	54.4	72.1	74.8

[a] Non-government fixed capital formation.

Sources: Ministerio de Económia y Hacienda; *Cuentes Nacionales*

Table 13.3   Foreign direct investment by industry (per cent of total)

	1960−79	1979−81	1985−7
Agriculture	0.5	1.7	1.1
Energy and water	0.5	0.8	0.3
Mining and chemical	22.8	18.1	20.0
Metal industries	33.5	33.2	23.2
Other manufacturing	14.4	16.4	16.0
Building	1.6	1.5	0.4
Commerce, restaurants and hotels	17.8	17.9	16.1
Transport and communications	0.6	0.4	0.8
Financial institutions	3.4	9.7	20.5
Other services	0.1	0.4	1.4
Total	100.0	100.0	100.0

Source: Ministerio de Económia y Hacienda

While Hecksher−Ohlin gains are likely to be limited because the (original) EC countries exhibit limited differences in endowments − except for agriculture of course − gains from increased intra-industry trade may be more significant. This is because probably most of the competition within the EC is monopolistic and intra-EC trade is mostly intra-industry. Either the Single Act leads to more intense (monopolistic) competition or it leads to a restructuring of various industries through mergers and acquisitions or exit. In the first case, the gains come from lower prices and a wider choice of goods. In the second case, we should observe the advantages of increasing returns to scale.

A key feature of monopolistic competition is that the outcome is not unique. Depending on the timing of moves and the actual history of these moves, market shares among competing firms and the actual number of firms in a particular market may take a priori an infinite number of values. The observed situation is the result of a particular history, and the resulting equilibrium itself is at best locally stable. This result has important implications for the years to come. Because the completion of the internal market will change several parameters which determine the current situation, a shake-up is unavoidable. Because the outcome is not uniquely determined, it is a priori impossible to specify what the post-1992 equilibrium will look like. The size and activity of existing firms, indeed their very survival, will depend on the choice and timing of their moves.

While the effect is likely to improve social welfare globally, the distribution of gains across firms is bound to be uneven and unpredictable. Since some firms are large relative to the regions or countries where they are based, the uneven distribution of gains and losses shifts from the area of competitive efficiency to the area of region or country-wide imbalances. This aspect makes intra-industry trade fundamentally different from Hecksher – Ohlin trade and brings to the forefront the need to organize some transfer payments which will make the Pareto gains to be achieved at the EC level acceptable to all regions and countries.

13.1.4 Regional Policies

The EC has decided to double the regional funds in the coming years. While the amounts will remain limited, they will represent the second major transfer organized by the EC, after the ill-famed CAP. Several factors have led to this decision. First, there is the view that 'social cohesion' is needed to cement the enlarged EC. This is meant to imply some effort at promoting equity. Second, because of adjustment costs in labour markets, employment may decrease before it benefits from the growth push. Third, as noted above, the outcome of the modified monopolistic competition is unknown. It is likely to lead to a 'redistribution of cards' among large firms, which may be large enough to affect significantly whole regions or possibly even countries. Fourth, it is conceivable that, in the future, some disturbances affect some particular regions or countries. If such disturbances are permanent, the regions or countries have no choice but to bear the associated costs. An exchange rate correction and some increase in inflation (a one-shot price increase) are often the most efficient responses. If the Single Act so restricts policymaking as to prevent such responses, the EC membership may imply a cost which is not acceptable from the affected country's point of view.

Of course, similar effects affecting particular regions occur within any single country. This is a misleading analogy. One reason is that the adjustment to permanent shocks often takes the form of displacement of labour. Migration is bound to be much costlier across countries and entail serious intangible welfare costs. It cannot be thought of as a desirable implication of 1992. The other reason is that, within any country, there exists a large number of transfer schemes organized through the central government budget. These transfers are generally an implication of national solidarity and accepted (sometimes grudgingly, e.g. the unemployment compensations) as such. Within the EC, such a sense of solidarity is likely to be slow to emerge and, more importantly perhaps, there is no channel to organize these transfers. Indeed, for inter-regional transfers to be politically viable, they must be a reasonably small fraction of the overall budget: if they are too conspicuous they inevitably prompt recriminations on the part of those regions which are frequent net payers. The current situation of the EC budget is such that it is particularly ill-fitted to play the required role. As table 13.4 makes abundantly clear, even the most decentralized countries maintain a central budget largely in excess of the local budgets. These observations should make it clear why comparisons with the United States are wide of the mark.

Table 13.4 Share of central government expenditures, 1984 (percentage of general government expenditures)

Belgium	92.5
Denmark	75.3
Germany[a]	64.0
France	89.4
Ireland[a]	91.4
Italy[b]	90.6
Netherlands	96.2
Spain[a]	86.1
UK[a]	84.1
USA[a]	68.0
EC[c]	2.1

[a] 1983.
[b] 1975.
[c] EC institutions' expenditures as a percentage of total member states' general government expenditures.

Sources: IMF, *Supplement on Government Finance*, No. 11, 1986; EC, *Eurostat*

These points have been recognized for a long time and were explicity discussed in the McDougall report (1977), and they form the basis of the European version of fiscal federalism studied in the Padoa-Schioppa report (1987). The required transfers will take the form of a regional fund. Regions including some entire countries, such as Greece and Portugal, and a large portion of Spain, have been identified as recipients.

There is no valid economic argument to subsidize whole regions or countries unless the losses are correctly measured and the victims identified, the regional or national authorities being merely used as channels.[1] What is needed is a permanent system of insurance providing support to the individual victims (households or firms) of either the transition process or, in the longer run, adverse disturbances. Bean et al. (1988) propose an EC-wide system of unemployment benefits which goes a long way towards satisfying these criteria.

13.2   Financial Market Integration

13.2.1   Framework of Analysis

A number of factors have so far limited a complete integration of most European financial centres into the world markets. Of course, the City of London *is* a key component of the global financial market. As for the other countries, many still retained until very recently a variety of capital controls (France, Italy, Belgium, the southern EC) which at times prevented arbitrage operations. These restrictions were lifted in July 1990 as part of the run up to a full implementation of the Single Act. It must be noted, however, that, even for the countries that dismantled all restrictions to capital movements some time ago, a number of local regulations and traditions still hamper competition and maintain less than full integration as illustrated in the country studies in this volume.

Not only will the Single Act eliminate all restrictions to capital movements, it will also introduce a heavy dose of competition in all financial markets. In this section I do not consider the market structure implications, since these are the principal concern of the present volume. Instead, I focus on the macro-economic implications, chiefly the new conditions under which monetary policies will be conducted.

In order to understand this issue, we need to clarify a number of technical issues. The reader impatient with technicalities may skip them and proceed to the next section directly. The degree of financial integration is most easily observed via the so-called interest parity conditions. The first condition, the *covered* interest parity condition, relates to arbitrage activities on assets denominated in different currencies; arbitrage being riskless, this condition is always verified unless restrictions to capital movements inhibit arbitrage. The covered interest parity condition obtains when the difference in interest yields on similar (in terms of risk) assets denominated in two different currencies is equal to the forward discount at the same maturity. Failures of this condition are well documented and occur when capital controls are binding restrictions to capital movements. When this occurs, it means that the monetary authorities are able to move the domestic interest rate away from the level implied by international arbitrage, i.e. they retain some degree of independence even though they maintain a fixed exchange rate. Typically, this occurs in pre-realignment periods of the EMS, when devaluation-prone countries would normally face high domestic interest rates. The main, maybe the only, use of capital controls is to shield domestic financial markets in crisis periods (Wyplosz, 1986).

A different relationship, the *uncovered* interest parity, establishes equality between the interest differential and the (market) expectation of exchange rate change. This results from speculative activity designed to take advantage of profitable opportunities by borrowing in one currency and investing in another. Such a relationship ties the domestic interest rate to the foreign rate and to market sentiment. It implies a complete loss of monetary independence.

In principle, for the uncovered condition to hold, the covered condition must hold first. Capital controls destroy both, at least in crisis periods. Even if the covered parity condition is verified, the uncovered condition may fail to hold because risk-averse speculators require a risk premium. Empirically, the risk premium is usually found to be small and volatile (Hodrick, 1987; Frankel, 1986). Even though the premium may react to policy actions, its behaviour has never been found to be systematically related to any known variable, so that it is reasonable to conclude that it is not possible for monetary authorities to affect the risk premium.

The above discussion may be summarized using the uncovered parity condition:

$$i_t + e_t = i_t^* + E_t e_{t+1} + \psi_t \qquad (13.1)$$

where i_t and i_t^* are the domestic and foreign interest rates, e_t is the logarithm of the spot exchange rate, $E_t e_{t+1}$ is its one-period-ahead forecast, and ψ_t is the risk premium; it is clear that the right-hand side is not open to control by the monetary authorities.

13.2.2 Monetary Policy and the European Monetary System

Relation 13.1 makes it clear that individual countries are able to set independently either the interest rate or the exchange rate, but certainly not both. This is the limitation of monetary policy independence for countries which operate under a fixed exchange rate. The United Kingdom is the only EC country with a freely floating exchange rate, and it has been fully integrated in the world market for many years now. The other EC countries are part of the EMS, so it is natural therefore to focus on the link between financial integration and the EMS. Two main considerations apply. The first is the fact that in the absence of full convergence of inflation rates realignments are unavoidable. The second concerns the operating of monetary policy between realignments.

Over its first ten years of existence the EMS went through 12 realignments. Most of these were preceded by speculative crises. A key lesson from the theory of balance-of-payments crises is that an attack exhausts foreign exchange reserves of a weak currency country, thus making it unable to peg immediately to a new, devalued, parity (Krugman, 1979; Flood and Garber, 1984; Obstfeld, 1984). Yet the experience so far does not correspond to the theory's prediction that crises lead to a temporary period of free float.

A likely interpretation is that capital controls put a ceiling on the volume of speculative funds available to exhaust the foreign exchange reserves (Wyplosz, 1986).

Under this view, restrictions of capital movements have played a key role in the very survival of the EMS. The implication is that the Single Act constitutes a direct threat to the EMS. Such a view is widely shared and is developed in the Padoa-Schioppa report as well as by the Commission of the European Communities (1988b).[2] It implies that the rules of the game governing the EMS must be modified.

The conduct of monetary policy when the parity condition (13.1) holds is the central implication of 1992. In 1989, the only countries operating in the EMS under these conditions were Germany and the Netherlands, two countries without capital controls. Given the relative size of these two countries, the Netherlands sets $i_t = i_t^* + \psi_t$ and simply pegs its currency to the DM. This is an instance of a total loss of monetary independence. Does it prefigure post-1992 Europe?

To organize the discussion, subtracting expected inflation on both sides of rates (13.1), we get the *real* interest rate parity condition:

$$r_t - r_t^* = E_t q_{t+1} - q_t + \psi_t \qquad (13.2)$$

where r_t and r_t^* are the real domestic and foreign interest rates and q_t is the logarithm of the real exchange rate. In the foregoing, I take the view that monetary policy works through the real interest rate.[3] One key objective – and success so far – of the EMS is to avoid large fluctuations in relative competitiveness (see figure 13.1). This implies a commitment to keep the real exchange rate q_t stable, and therefore amounts to pegging the domestic real interest rate to the foreign level. In effect, it eliminates the ability to conduct an independent monetary policy.

There seem to be only two possibilities to recover some independence. Suppose that a country wants to reduce its real interest rate. This requires engineering the expectation of a real appreciation. One possibility is to accept, indeed publicize, a positive inflation differential at a constant nominal exchange rate. Thus rising inflation becomes a condition of monetary policy effectiveness, in effect quickly worsening the very effectiveness of monetary policy based on some degree of price stickiness. This is hardly a promising route. The other possibility is to devalue immediately to the point where the currency is clearly undervalued: monetary policy boils down to exchange rate policy. Once capital is fully mobile and (13.2) holds, there will be no monetary policy independence left within the EMS if individual member countries are not allowed occasionally to move their exchange rates away from the purchasing power parity (PPP) rule which has prevailed so far, as shown in figure 13.1.

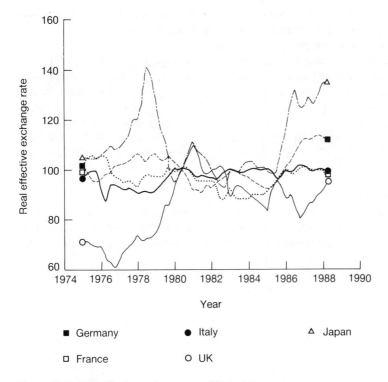

Figure 13.1 Real effective exchange rates (1980=100).

13.2.3 Distribution of Power and Asymmetries

From what precedes it is clear that, short of introducing more real exchange rate flexibility, the only practical way for one country to retain some monetary policy independence is to affect simultaneously its own real interest rate and that of the other EMS members. Put differently, a country's ability to conduct its chosen monetary policy is limited to its influence on the other countries. This brings to the forefront the issue of distribution of power within the EMS. The prevailing view is that Germany is the only country in a position to impose its monetary policy stance on the rest of the EMS zone (see for example Giavazzi and Giovannini, 1989). While formal evidence in support of this view is not compelling,[4] it is important to understand why the view might be correct.

Borrowing the Bundesbank's credibility

The most widely quoted reason for the hegemony of Germany within the EMS is based on the so-called credibility argument. This view starts from the literature on time inconsistency, which makes the point that the authorities cannot precommit themselves to a path of policy actions which is understood by the public as likely to become less desirable in the future. The traditional example which is relevant to the EMS concerns inflation (Barro and Gordon, 1983). Because of a number of market inefficiencies (taxation, labour market restrictions etc.) an economy typically operates at a level of activity below the social optimum. Consequently the authorities are looking for ways to boost the level of activity and can do so through occasional inflation surprises. Naturally the public expect them to do just that and accordingly set prices and wages, thus introducing an inflationary bias. The best course of action left to the authorities is simply to accommodate the inflation drift – no more, no less – and operate at the below-optimum level of activity. The more inflation prone the monetary authorities are known to be, the larger the drift, with no gain whatsoever in output. Clearly then, the best position is to have no drift at all, which requires that the public believes that this is indeed the most preferred strategy of the authorities. Hence the result is obtained that the more credible are the authorities in their determination to resist inflation, the lower the actual inflation rate is, with no output cost at all.

Under such conditions it pays to have a Central Bank which enjoys a 'conservative' reputation (Rogoff, 1985). What if that is not the case? One solution is for the monetary authorities to acquire such a reputation by investing in tough-minded policies until the public recognizes the seriousness of the Central Bank's commitment to resist inflation. The benefits come in the longer run. In the interim, as long as the public's perceptions remain unswayed the cost comes in terms of a recession: it is precisely the authorities' willingness to pay such costs that will shift the public's perception. An alternative is to peg the currency to the currency of a country whose Central Bank has already acquired such a reputation. If that commitment is credible, or can become credible faster because it is more easily verifiable, the interim costs are reduced.

It is fairly obvious to see how this literature can be applied to the case of the EMS. The Bundesbank is credited with full credibility as an inflation-averse Central Bank. This is not the case for other countries' authorities whose best course of action at the height of inflation in the late 1970s may then have been to borrow the Bundesbank's credibility by tying their currencies to the DM. Once the investment has been made, it is only natural to carry on and reap the benefits of low inflation, strong currency status with no further output cost.

Such is the prevailing interpretation of the view that the EMS is a DM zone. This interpretation suffers from a number of defects, however (Wyplosz, 1989). First it must be shown that the output costs of disinflation have been lower under an EMS regime than outside. Evidence is quite lacking. De Grauwe and Verfaille (1987) have shown that disinflation seems to have been more efficient in those European countries which did not belong to the EMS. Second, it must be established that inflationary expectations have shifted as a consequence of EMS membership. Some of the most ardent proponents of the credibility view have tried to detect these shifts and found that they occurred long after the EMS was started (1983 in France, 1985 in Italy) and, most importantly, as a result of a highly visible change in domestic policies (Giavazzi and Giovannini, 1989). Of course, it is always possible to view a policy regime change as endogenous to the exchange rate regime. In particular, it is true that both in France and in Italy EMS membership has been presented as the reason for a turnaround of monetary policies. However, these countries (and others as well) have been able to operate within the EMS for several years before the policy change: this indicates that the EMS by itself does not require a change in regime.

A third objection is that no reason has been given as to why a government intent on confronting inflation, and willing to bear the costs required to achieve credibility, would prefer to depend to that end upon a *foreign* Central Bank. Leaving aside the political aspects − which cut both ways − there is no generally valid argument that monetary policy should be set according to immutable rules. The reason is that there exists a trade-off between the advantages of rules (reduction in policy uncertainty, time consistency, no capture by interest groups) and the lack of responsiveness to contingencies. Surely, even the most enthusiastic supporter of rules must recognize that there may exist some particularly large shocks which warrant exceptional use of discretion. Under such circumstances it must be preferable to rely on one's own suitably independent Central Bank than on a foreign Central Bank unlikely to react optimally.

This naturally leads to a fourth objection. The argument presumes that once credibility has been achieved the output costs of keeping inflation low disappear. While this may be a property of some models, it is by no means general. To take just one example, the employment − and possibly output − effects of both nominal and real disturbances depend on the degree of real wage rigidity, which in turn depends upon the wage-setting mechanism. If the German labour institutions differ from, say, the French labour institutions, a given disturbance will elicit different costs in the two countries. Under such circumstances it may be inefficient for the French authorities to take their cues from the Bundesbank.

There is some evidence that the EMS is imposing a continued output cost on a country like France. This can be gathered from table 13.5 in which the French and UK output performances over the last two decades are compared. This is an interesting comparison as the United Kingdom remained outside the EMS precisely to safeguard its policy independence. During the nine-year period preceding the creation of the EMS, France grew much faster than the United Kingdom and Germany. Over the following nine years, while growth went down in all three countries, the United Kingdom has managed to do significantly better than both France and Germany. This is partly due to the end period, though. When we cumulate the GDPs over each period — thus measuring total creation of value added — we find that France and the United Kingdom have behaved similarly, outperforming Germany by 1 per cent of total cumulated output. Yet, the marked worsening of France's performance is quite impressive, and cannot be attributed to disinflation, as is clear from the bottom part of the table.

Table 13.5 Growth and inflation in France, Germany and the United Kingdom (per cent)

	Jan 1970 to Apr 1978	Jan 1979 to Apr 1987
Total growth over 9 years (real GDP)		
France	42.4	16.9
Germany	31.9	16.1
UK	33.5	28.1
Cumulated growth: in excess of Germany[a]		
France	4.2	1.0
UK	0.5	1.0
Total CPI increase over 9 years		
France	110.5	100.1
Germany	51.5	30.2
UK	185.5	95.1

CPI, consumer price index.
[a] Let Y_t^i be the real GDP of country i. The measure is $(\Sigma_t Y_t^i / \Sigma_t Y_t^j) - 1$ where i is France or the United Kingdom and j is Germany.
Source: *International Financial Statistics*

A temporary and unstable arrangement

Another explanation of the leadership by Germany emphasizes the nature of policy objectives which prevailed at the end of the 1970s and in the early 1980s (Begg and Wyplosz, 1987; Melitz, 1987). Apparently, this was the time when most countries came to recognize that inflation had to be brought down. With parallel objectives, the EMS countries have spontaneously espoused German-type policies, thus creating the *impression* of a German leadership, perhaps even using the EMS as a scapegoat for unpopular measures. The implication of this view is that once inflation has been stabilized at acceptable levels, each country should revert to its self-styled system of policy preferences. Put differently, the success of the EMS, a surprise to many early sceptics, is the outcome of a rare coincidence of policy objectives. Under this view the outlook is now more problematic. In particular, the mirage of German leadership should dissipate.

It is too early of course to assess this explanation. The result, reported above, that it has taken many years to observe a change in expectations can be seen as an indication that indeed the policy shift has not occurred simultaneously in all countries, which would have represented an incredible coincidence. If true, this explanation should predict growing policy divergences in the post-inflation era. So far, there are faint signs that it is happening, which may mean simply that governments do not feel that inflation is low enough or has not been low for long enough to be considered as stabilized.

The systemic bias

A third explanation attempts to disentangle policy objectives from policy constraints (Wyplosz, 1989). This explanation emphasizes the implication of exchange market interventions on the domestic money supply. One of the virtues of the EMS experience has been the dedramatization of realignments, in contrast with the practice (and probably the spirit) of the Bretton Woods system. By allowing frequent realignments, the EMS has shown great tolerance for steady-state inflation differentials. This is the extent of monetary policy independence enjoyed in this fixed exchange rate arrangement: a country can sustain indefinitely an inflation rate different from the rest of the EMS countries. All that is required is that the country intervenes on the exchange markets to keep its currency within the agreed-upon band and realigns when external competitiveness considerations so require. Importantly, this is true for both below average and above average inflation rates.

In practice, however, the situation is different, a point which had been emphasized much earlier (e.g. Nurkse, 1945) but had been quite underplayed in more recent academic discussions. In order to sustain a given target inflation rate, the exchange market interventions must be sterilized. A country with lower than average inflation thus accumulates foreign exchange reserves and reduces its domestic assets. Conversely, a country with above average inflation loses reserves and increases its domestic lending. When seen this way, it becomes fairly clear that the process is not quite symmetric, for losses of reserves are likely to become seriously binding long before the reduction of domestic assets creates a difficulty for the monetary authorities.

This asymmetry has a profound influence. Indeed the management of exchange rates within the EMS is overdetermined as there is one free exchange rate less than the number of member countries. This overdetermination − sometimes referred to as the $N-1$ problem − can be solved in a number of ways. One way is to free one country from its exchange rate obligation: this country becomes the centre of the system, as was the United States in the Bretton Woods arrangement and as the Germany hegemony view interprets the EMS. Another possibility is for member countries to agree on their parities jointly, a solution to which I shall return in the discussion of possible transitions towards a European Monetary Union (EMU). Yet another plausible outcome is a non-cooperative management of the system whereby each country – or a subset of member countries, two being enough – plays the intervention game in an effort to influence the system's overall money growth. The outcome of such a game – surely not optimal from a global welfare point of veiw – is very much a function of the respective powers of the players. This clearly eliminates the smaller countries. Among the largest ones, it is clear that the country with lowest inflation enjoys a strategic advantage as it can sustain the process of intervention-cum-sterilization much longer. Once this asymmetry is recognized by the players, their strategy must be adapted accordingly, which implies a fundamental systemic asymmetry: Germany can dominate its large and small EMS partners.[5]

As far as I know, no empirical support has been adduced for this interpretation. Evidence is likely to be scarce since the proposed interpretation amounts to asserting that inflation-prone countries end up converging more towards the inflation-averse countries than the other way around. One observable prediction of this view is that monetary policy should become more restrictive for an inflation-prone country once it enters an EMS-type arrangement. Evidence to this effect has been reported in the literature as noted above. Unfortunately this does not discriminate the present interpretation from the two previous ones. It is quite unfortunate, because the three interpretations have quite different policy implications. In particular, the present interpretation, by suggesting the existence of a systemic asymmetric *constraint* on policy choices, implies that the EMS may become too costly to some member countries, especially as financial liberalization strengthens interest linkages and the limits on monetary policy independence.

13.2.4 Effects on Fiscal Policy

With much of the ability to conduct an independent monetary policy gone, the role of fiscal policy is likely to grow after the liberalization of capital flows. In principle, fiscal policy independence is preserved in the new regime. Yet it is becoming apparent that fiscal policy will not stay unaffected. Early analyses – as yet mostly informal – do not come to a clear unambiguous conclusion on whether fiscal policy is likely to become more, or less, restrictive. Those who believe that fiscal discipline will be reduced argue that, with exchange rates credibly fixed and total financial integration, all interest rates will be equalized ($i_t = i_t^*$ as $\psi_t = E_t e_{t+1} - e_t = 0$ in (13.1)). Consequently, fiscal recklessness will not face an interest or exchange rate sanction. Of course, each government bond issue may be priced differently by the markets, thus confronting profligate treasuries with bad ratings. The experience of local governments in most federal countries (the United States, Germany, Canada) indicate the absence of such a market signal or, at best, very small risk premiums. Furthermore, it may be good tactics to finance budgetary deficits with money. Indeed, with all EMS monies becoming close substitutes, one country's expansion wll simply add to the global EMS money stock or force the most inflation-adverse countries to compensate fiscal-cum-money laxity elsewhere with an added dose of stringency.

A number of other arguments were presented to suggest that fiscal policy would in fact become restricted after July 1990. The first obvious reason concerns the monetary financing of budget deficits. Clearly, the constraints on monetary policy are bound to affect the ability to raise seigniorage taxes. Much has been said about this issue (Dornbusch, 1988; Drazen, 1988; Giavazzi, 1988). Yet in most cases the numbers are trivial (Cohen and Wyplosz, 1988). Indeed, seigniorage income has rarely exceeded 1 per cent of GDP in the EMS countries. True, there have been in all countries some occasional inflation 'blips', but they are by definition short lived. The only countries which seem to be able to derive sizeable (i.e. above 1 per cent GDP) seigniorage income are those which impose on their banking systems various regulations which result in large monetary bases. However, one important implication of 1992 will be the introduction of competition among national regulations. The most likely possibility is that, as far as banking regulations are concerned, competition will result in reduced monetary bases throughout the EC. Consequently, income seigniorage will decline wherever it is currently significant.

The second reason is closely related to the previous discussion concerning the real interest rate. In most EC countries the public debt represents more than 40 per cent of GDP, this proportion rising to above 100 per cent in Belgium, Italy and Ireland. Debt service thus represents some 5−15 per cent of GDP and is therefore closely related to the real interest rate. In many countries, a number of regulations have been used to lower the real interest rates, at least those applying to the public debt. These regulations will not survive long after 1992 − if all goes as announced − and the difficulty of influencing the real interest rate will imply, therefore, that the cost of the public debt will be largely beyond governmental control. This will certainly tighten up the directly perceived budget constraint, most probably pushing governments further in the direction of caution in their discretionary use of fiscal policy. For the existing debts, with servicing costs rising, the pressure to generate primary (i.e. net of interest payments) budget surpluses will grow. Whether this pressure leads to spending cuts or explicit tax increases, fiscal policy is bound to become more restrictive. Thus 1992 is likely to strengthen the contractionary bias already imparted by the EMS.

13.3   The Options for the Transition

Post-1992 Europe will differ markedly from what we knew before. From a macro-economic perspective, it has been argued in this chapter that the most important effect will be the loss of monetary independence, i.e. the ability to set an interest or exchange rate independently of the other EMS members.[6] As noted, technically this amounts to the fact that $N-1$ monetary policies become fully endogenous or, more properly, that one degree of freedom has to be managed. In this section, I review the options.

13.3.1   The European Monetary Union

The EMU option amounts to attributing the available degree of freedom to a European Central Bank to be created. The merit of this option is that it solves the problem at hand radically. Of course, it does not come without drawbacks.

The pros

The EMU will solve the asymmetry problem discussed in section 13.2.3.[7] There are many institutional issues involved, regarding the decision-making process, the statute of the European Central Bank, seigniorage and the financing of budget deficits (for discussions of these issues see Cohen, 1986, and Mathieu and Sterdyniak, 1989). None of them seems insuperable. An additional benefit is that it would lead to a much more credible monetary policy. This is true even if the new Central Bank is not fully independent and if it is instructed to use discretion rather than rules. The reason is that, irrespective of the decision-making rules, the new authority will be considerably less sensitive to particular interests, simply because it will have a great many constituencies. In particular, and paradoxically, it will be in a much stronger position than the US Federal Reserve Board which is accountable to one powerful congress and deals with one powerful government. The paradox is that the inversion of the usual historical process, which requires political unification before monetary unification, will result in a European-wide institution with no political counterpart.[8]

An additional benefit concerns the interest rates. Currently, real interest rates in a country reflect the exchange risk premium. This risk is a consequence of (possibly unjustified) expectations of a devaluation, the devaluation itself being predicted upon a lax monetary policy. Thus the suspicion that the government will resort to this form of taxation implies a cost surcharge for all borrowers. Once a monetary union is created, the interest rate will be the same everywhere. If a particular government is suspected of being unable to raise standard (i.e. not inflationary) tax revenue, so that its longer-run solvency is questioned, it will have to pay an interest premium. Thus there is an advantage in shifting the premium to the borrower whose credit rating is suspect, not to the whole country.

The cons

Because the EMU involves an irremediable decision to give up exchange rate policy it implies that, even under exceptional circumstances when a country might have invoked particular escape clauses, the adjustment will need to take place differently, possibly at a higher cost. Once again, the example of a wage shock in a particular country provides an adequate illustration. Faced with such an occurrence, the only solution is a recession long and deep enough to force a downward adjustment of real wages.

With a proper set of redistributive policies, such difficulties can be relatively easily overcome. In the current situation this is not the case, as discussed in section 13.1.4. The EMU might well, then, increase the risks of misguided regional policies, in particular raising serious issues of moral hazard. The point is that economic 'misbehaviour' may be able to elicit transfers from the rest of the EMU, if only to avoid the risk of a break-up.

Contrary to a widely held view, the EMU would not entirely solve the coordination problem. The policy coordination literature, in the tradition of Hamada (1974), has emphasized the exchange rate externality and the risk of beggar-thy-neighbour policies (e.g. to reduce inflation via an exchange rate appreciation) in the absence of coordination. This risk would be eliminated with the EMU, of course. But there are other externalities. Cohen and Wyplosz (1988) show the role of the balance of trade. Each country faces an intertemporal balance-of-trade constraint, but so does the EMU zone as a whole. A set of policies which yield the optimal trade imbalance for each individual country may well result in a conflict over the aggregate trade balance. The EMU does not solve this important difficulty.

These potential economic costs are quite formidable. They come on top of political − or symbolic − aspects. This is why it is probably unrealistic to expect an early shift to the EMU.[9] Accordingly, we now explore some of the possible steps which could deal with the challenges underlined in section 13.2.

13.3.2 Realignments within the Band

It has been argued in section 13.2 that the liberalization of capital movements threatens to render realignments within the EMS unmanageable. The reason, it was suggested, is that speculative crises are likely to erupt in anticipation of discrete exchange rate changes. One possible solution to cope with this difficulty is to organize realignments in such a way as to avoid jumps in the exchange rate. This can be done by exploiting the flexibility provided by the bands of fluctuation around the declared parity. The normal pattern so far has been for the exchange rate to drift within the band towards one of its limits, stay close to that limit for a while and be allowed to jump out of the pre-existing band at the time of the realignment. The jump is merely the consequence of the fact that the new and old bands do not overlap. If the new central parity were inside the previous band, however, the jump would not have to occur and could be avoided by the authorities. In fact, the mere (credible) commitment that bands would overlap and that no jump would be tolerated would be sufficient to eliminate speculative crises.

Of course, such an advantage does not come free. The realignments would have to be smaller than the band of fluctuation (4.5 per cent), probably much smaller. The cost would be that realignments would be more frequent, thus apparently weakening the exchange rate stability property of the system. This cost is more apparent than real. The existence of the bands already allows fluctuations of the exchange rates of up to 4.5 per cent (12 per cent for Italy). Frequently changing the central parity need not therefore add to exchange rate instability. Furthermore, given the convergence to moderate inflation rates achieved over the last years, realignments are now bound to be much less frequent than in the early 1980s. Finally, by eliminating the threat of crises, the modified system is likely to operate in a quieter way.

13.3.3　Towards More Symmetry

While there is some uncertainty about why the EMS may be operating asymmetrically as a DM zone, a number of steps may be taken to eliminate at least some of the potential sources of asymmetry, particularly as the competing explanations are not mutually exclusive so that addressing all of them is a distinct possibility.[10] The first source of asymmetry mentioned in the previous discussion was related to the superior credibility achieved by the Bundesbank. Most observers seem to consider that this credibility is largely due to the formal independence of the Bundesbank. Increasing the independence of the other EMS Central Banks could be a test of the joint proposition that independence brings credibility and that credibility is the source of the asymmetry. While none of these propositions is clearly established, there seems to be little risk in this kind of experimentation. Most governments now seem to be ready to move in that direction and a number of ways exist to guarantee that the independent Central Banker does not become a malevolent dictator.[11]

The second source of asymmetry of interest here is the possibility of a systemic bias related to the mechanics of intervention-cum-sterilization. The asymmetry is related to the fact that inflation-prone countries exhaust their foreign exchange reserves long before the inflation-averse countries face a constraint in the balance sheet of their Central Banks. In order to correct this asymmetry, we need to establish a system of interventions whereby the inflation-averse countries do more of the work to stabilize their bilateral exchange rate *vis-à-vis* the inflation-prone country. In fact, available evidence on interventions has shown that Germany has so far been considerably less active in interventions concerning the EMS parities, thus magnifying the systemic source of asymmetry (Matropasqua et al., 1988). The first, minimum, solution is then to seek a more even distribution of responsibilities. This step has already been informally taken at the European Summit in Nyborg in August 1987. The next step would be to make more use of the existing arrangement for sharing exchange reserves. In principle, short-term swaps are unlimited under the EMS agreement. Dedramatizing and publicizing large-scale borrowings, and making it easy to roll them over, would go a long way towards correcting the systemic bias.[12] The last step, related to the previous one, is technically more difficult to set up. The objective would be to ascertain that bilateral interventions are asymmetric, the inflation-averse country undertaking a larger share than the inflation-prone country.

13.3.4 Giving up the Purchasing Power Parity Rule

One of the key achievements of the EMS is also its weakness. By stabilizing the real exchange rates among its member countries (see figure 13.1), the EMS has eradicated the wide misalignments that have occurred outside the zone. This has largely been by design since it is now well known that realignments are negotiated on the basis of PPP rules. The negative implication is that it has eliminated exchange rate policy from the list of available instruments. Quite clearly, history has shown the dangers of exchange rate manipulations. However, there is no theoretical basis to justify PPP as a long-run rule. On the contrary, for all we know, permanent real disturbances require changes in the real exchange rate. In the shorter run, temporary nominal disturbances can sometimes be eased out by a judicious adjustment of the terms of trade. Moreover, disagreements on policy objectives may be most easily reconciled by allowing deviations from PPP (the argument is spelled out in some detail in section 13.2.2).

As the opportunity for national policy independence decreases, the elimination of exchange rate policies is becoming more binding. In the long-run world of EMU, such restrictions will be compensated by the so-called regional policies. In the coming years, though, we may find ourselves in the worst of all worlds with insufficient intra-European solidarity and yet under the iron fist of PPP. The obvious solution, then, is to agree informally to move away from the implicit PPP rule.[13] Of course, there is no support for beggar-thy-neighbour actions: deviations from the rule must be based either on evidence (which may be hard to establish) of real permanent disturbances or on well-specified policy objectives: the Swedish devaluation of 1981 provides an example of a successful manipulation of the exchange rate.

Notes

1   Identifying the three latest EC members as recipients of aid is illogical from an economic point of view. These countries joined the EC presumably because they expected to benefit as a whole. Transfers should thus be organized within each country to compensate those who bear costs more than their benefits. It might well be that the latest members should actually compensate some of the EC nine for bearing the costs of the new round of integration. In any case, there is no economic efficiency reason to ask the rich to support the poor. There are equity reasons, of course, but it should work from individual to individual.

2   This view, however, is dismissed by Gros and Thygesen (1988).

3   This is of course a gross simplification excluding, among others, the effects on agents' expectations about inflation and therefore their pricing decisions. I shall return to these issues.

4   For some conflicting evidence see De Grauwe (1988) and Cohen and Wyplosz (1988).

5   The asymmetry may even go deeper in a world where speculative attacks can be self-sustaining as noted by Obstfeld (1988). Such attacks can only be prevented if the countries with low inflation always stand ready to contract their money supply, or raise their interest rates, more than they wish. The argument is formally developed by Wyplosz (1989).

6   It can be emphasized that the EC members which stay out of the EMS do not face this problem. The cost comes in terms of interest or exchange rate volatility instead.

7   This is why the Bundesbank is cool and France is warm to the EMU.

8   Unless, of course, the creation of the EMU speeds up the process of political unification. Undoubtedly, this possibility must be one of the reasons why Mrs Thatcher opposed the EMU, seen as a Trojan horse ushering in a powerful European Commission and a powerful European Parliament.

9   There is a view, popular among bankers, that the industry could go ahead and create a *de facto* monetary union by issuing ECU-denominated instruments. This revival of the parallel currency theory misses the essential point that a monetary union is, above all, about the coordination of monetary policies. As long as the various governments are not ready to merge their monetary policies, the ECU may spread as a unit of account, although it is not obvious how it would dislodge the national currencies on a quantitatively significant scale. The example of countries with hyperinflation shows that national currencies are extremely resilient.

10   A complex proposal explicitly designed to promote more symmetry has been put forward by Russo and Tullio (1988). It is based on a McKinnon proposal transposed at the EMS level. The proposal implies an agreed-upon aggregate money supply target coupled with national intervention rules.

11 For a proposition along these lines, based on a politico-economic analysis of Central Banks' behaviour, see Alesina (1989).
12 Of course, it raises a moral hazard issue to which potential lenders are understandably very sensitive. The difficulty is not hopeless, however, since the borrower's actions are actually observable. It is enough, then, to build in safeguard clauses allowing the lender to refuse further assistance whenever the borrower deviates too far and too long from accepted norms, an action possibly decided jointly by all EMS members.
13 The main apparent deviation from the PPP rule in the first ten years of the EMS has been the moderate real appreciation of the Italian lira in 1981−2. This has been the result of the Italian authorities' own wish to use the exchange rate to accompany their anti-inflationary policies. It has been achieved through a number of lira devaluations short of the accumulated inflation differential. Quite symptomatically, such deviations from the implicit norm which are apparently easily accepted work towards a contractionary stance.

References

Alesina, A. (1989) Politics and business cycles in industrial democracies. *Economic Policy*, 8 April.

Barro, R. and Gordon, D. (1983) Rules, discretions and reputation in a model of monetary policy. *Journal of Monetary Economics*, 12 (1), July.

Bean, C., Malinvaud, E., Bernholz, P., Giavazzi, F. and Wyplosz, C. (1988) Macroeconomic policies for 1992: the transition and the long-run. Unpublished paper, Center for European Policy Studies, Brussels.

Begg, D. and Wyplosz, C. (1987) Why the EMS? Dynamic games and the equilibrium policy regime. In R. Bryant and R. Portes (eds), *Global Macroeconomics, Policy Conflicts and Cooperation*. London: Macmillan.

Cohen, D. (1986) Imaginer la monnaie unique. In *L'Ecu et la Vieille Dame*. Paris: Economica.

Cohen, D. and Wyplosz, C. (1988) The European Monetary Union: an agnostic evaluation, paper presented at the IMF−CEPR−Brookings Conference on Macroeconomic Policies in an Interdependent World, Washington, DC, December.

Commission of the European Communities (1988a) The economics of 1992. *European Economy*, 35, March.

Commission of the European Communities (1988b) Creation of a European financial area. *European Economy*, 36, May.

De Grauwe, P. (1988) Is the European Monetary System a DM zone?, Working Paper No. 297, Centre for Economic Policy Research.

De Grauwe, P. and Verfaille, G. (1987) Exchange rate variability, misalignment, and the European Monetary System. Unpublished paper, University of Leuven.

Dornbusch, R. (1988) The European Monetary System, the dollar and the yen. In F. Giavazzi, S. Micossi and M. Miller (eds), *The European Monetary System*. Cambridge: Cambridge University Press.

Drazen, A. (1988) Inflation tax revenue in open economies, paper presented at the CEPR Conference on Monetary Regimes and Monetary Institutions: Issues and Perspectives in Europe, Castelgandolfo, June.

Flood, R. and Garber, P. (1984) Collapsing exchange-rate regimes: some linear examples. *Journal of International Economics*, 17, 1−14.

Frankel, J. (1986) The implications of mean−variance optimization for four questions in international macroeconomics. *Journal of International Money and Finance*, 5, 553−76.

Giavazzi, F. (1988) The exchange rate question in Europe. Discussion Paper, Centre for Economic Policy Research.

Giavazzi, F. and Giovannini, A. (1989) *Limiting Exchange Rate Flexibility: The European Monetary System*. Cambridge, MA: MIT Press.

Gros, D. and Thygesen, N. (1988) The EMS: achievements, current issues and directions for the future. Paper No. 35, Center for European Policy Studies.

Hamada, K. (1974) Alternative exchange rate systems and the interdependence of monetary policies. In R.A. Aliber (ed), *National Monetary Policies and the International Financial System*. Chicago, IL: Chicago University Press.

Hodrick, J. (1987) *The Empirical Evidence on the Efficiency of Forward and Futures Foreign Exchange Markets*. Chur: Harwood Academic.

Krugman, P. (1979) A model of balance-of-payments crises. *Journal of Money, Credit and Banking*, 11, 311−25.

Matropasqua, C., Micossi, S. and Rinaldi, R. (1988) Intervention, sterilization, and monetary policy in EMS countries (1979−1987). In F. Giavazzi, S. Micossi and M. Miller (eds), *The European Monetary System*. Cambridge: Cambridge University Press.

Mathieu, C. and Sterdyniak, H. (1989) Vers une monnaie commune en Europe? *Observations et Diagnostics Économiques*, No. 26, January.

Melítz, J. (1987) Discipline monétaire, République fédérale allemande et Systeme monétaire européen. *Annales d'Economie et Statistiques*, 8, 59−88.

Nurkse, R. (1945) Conditions of international monetary equilibrium. *Essays in International Finance*, 4, Spring.

Obstfeld, M. (1984) Balance-of-payments crises and devaluation. *Journal of Money, Credit and Banking*, 16, 208−17.

Obstfeld, M. (1988) Competitiveness, realignment, and speculation: the role of financial markets. In F. Giavazzi, S. Micossi and M. Miller (eds), *The European Monetary System*. Cambridge: Cambridge University Press.

Rogoff, K. (1985) The optimal degree of commitment to an intermediate target. *Quarterly Journal of Economics*, 4, 69−89.

Russo, M. and Tullio, G. (1988) Monetary policy coordination within the European Monetary System: is there a rule? In F. Giavazzi, S. Micossi and M. Miller (eds), *The European Monetary System*. Cambridge: Cambridge University Press.

Wyplosz, C. (1986) Capital controls and balance of payments crises. *Journal of International Money and Finance*, 5, 167−79.

Wyplosz, C. (1989) Asymmetry in the EMS: intentional or systemic?, paper presented at the Third Annual Congress of the European Economic Association, Bologna, August 1988; INSEAD Working Paper No. 88/41; *European Economic Review, Papers and Proceedings*, 33, (2−3), March.

Comment

Wolfgang Rieke

I believe that we can all agree that the potential benefits from full economic and financial integration in Europe are considerable, even though they cannot be measured precisely. But perhaps exact estimates are not of the essence, just as East—West disarmament is not simply a matter of agreeing on precise numbers for tanks, aeroplanes, soldiers etc. In other words, there are important qualitative aspects to the integration process and the political dimension is only one. Two further points should perhaps be made at the outset.

Firstly, the lack of progress towards an internal European market, and towards greater economic and financial integration, probably contributed to the lack of economic dynamism in Europe in the 1970s and early 1980s, and it deprived Europe of the weight it should have been able to bring into play during the period of instability as reflected in the sharp ups and downs of exchange rates. Giscard d'Estaing and Helmut Schmidt correctly diagnosed the weakness of Europe when confronted with the US monetary 'benign neglect' and the Japanese challenge. They set up the EMS as a means to deal with one important aspect of this weakness.

Secondly, Europe would badly miss a unique opportunity if it were to set up the internal market as a 'Fortress Europe'. It is indeed desirable to use this opportunity to create a truly free market Community, both internally *and* externally. Perhaps the German experience shortly after the Second World War could serve as an example: Ludwig Erhard used the unique chances offered by the 'currency reform' of 1948 to set up a liberal free market system and thus created the foundations of what became known as the German economic 'miracle' of the 1950s and 1960s. Even if that miracle cannot be repeated and the gains to prosperity, if measured in terms of gross national product per head or otherwise, remain more limited, the effects could be considerable. It would be highly desirable for the overall effects to be significant, because only then will the temporary adjustment costs that will arise in various areas, as well as the unevenly distributed gains, be accepted without too much noise. The more the effort is seen as a positive sum game, the better are its success and chances of acceptance.

A quick glance at some rough growth figures in the EEC and elsewhere leaves some doubt as to the benefits that countries were able to reap so far from participation in the exchange rate mechanism (ERM). Germany averaged only 1.1 per cent real growth in the pre-1983 EMS period, but 2.3 per cent in the years 1983−7 and 3.5 per cent in 1988. France had a moderately higher growth rate in the earlier period than in the later period (2.1 per cent against 1.6 per cent); the growth rate in Italy was similar. Against that the United Kingdom, a non-participant in the ERM, was stagnant in the early phase but achieved 3.5 per cent on average in the later phase, and the United States, a non-ERM and non-EMS participant, did even better. A positive aspect for the ERM countries is that growth was somewhat more stable in the 1980s than earlier, but then there are special reasons that may account for this.

The question is, of course, how the ERM countries would have done without the EMS and what their policies would have had to be like to achieve it. Could France or Italy have pursued the kind of policy mix that the United States pursued in a floating exchange rate environment under President Reagan, or would they have had to pursue an even more rigorous fiscal regime of the Thatcher type? And would this have produced results that would also prove sustainable in the years ahead, or on the contrary would it confront them with dilemmas no less palatable than those which confronted the US and UK authorities?

It seems to me that the governments and Central Banks of the major ERM partners, as well as of the smaller ones, are correctly adhering to the stability option.

With this I turn to some aspects that relate to the removal of capital restrictions to financial market integration, monetary policy and exchange rate management. These are at the core of the debate which has been under way for some time. The debate is about the need for closer coordination, or even common decision-making, in the field of monetary policy in a system of virtually fixed exchange rates and increasingly free capital movements.

It has always been doubtful whether restrictions on capital movements are a cost-effective means to achieve the ends sought by individual countries, namely faster economic growth and employment based on the exclusive use of domestic savings for domestic use. In an environment where major high saving countries have forgone capital restrictions, the application of such restrictions by low saving countries may have been of doubtful value as they may have repelled capital inflows as much as, or more than, they prevented undesirable capital outflows. Their short-term effectiveness may have encouraged reliance on them for extended periods in place of more appropriate measures that would reap longer-term benefits.

It would be disappointing if one had to conclude that restrictions on capital movements have played a key role in the very survival of the EMS. Recent experience may warrant a different conclusion. Countries that have dismantled capital restrictions have not systematically confronted greater difficulties in the ERM. On the contrary, interest rate action may have gained in effectiveness, and greater public confidence in the determination of the monetary authorites to deal with the real causes of exchange rate tensions rather than the symptoms may have helped to increase the effectiveness of the measures taken.

There is another aspect: Will the country whose currency serves as the key currency in the EMS, and whose monetary policy is said to provide the stable 'anchor' for the system, face greater difficulties in a new environment without widespread recourse to capital restriction by its partner countries? And would close coordination of monetary policy or EC-based decision-making be an acceptable answer? There is no question that closer coordination and eventual decision-making at EC level (entrusted to a European Central Banking System that is independent *vis-à-vis* national governments and EC institutions) will be both desirable and necessary, but it is not the right time for that. As long as the system relies on the monetary policy of the partner whose currency is most widely used for intervention and reserve purposes as its 'anchor' of stability, any infringement on the ability of the Bundesbank to pursue such a policy could be highly risky for the system as a whole.

I have the impression that Professor Wyplosz himself is not particularly confident that a common objective function would be realistic as an alternative to the current practice of pegging to the most stable currency. He prefers to discuss what can be done to minimize the potential losses if objectives differ rather than what regime would be optimal with a given common objective in place. He appears to want to retain as much room for manoeuvre as possible in macro policy, which would seem to argue for managed floating rather than a system of regionally fixed but adjustable exchange rates.

Much has been said about the question of asymmetry, German hegemony or dominance or even the Bundesbank's 'Diktat' over other countries' policies. The debate is somewhat unfortunate, even potentially poisoning. Simple logic suggests that, if there is a common commitment to a particular objective, then those partners who are still furthest away from that objective will have to make an asymmetric effort to move closer to it. The prime commitment in the EMS is to internal and external stability, meaning domestic price stability and exchange rate stability. The commitment to exchange rate stability is formal, but it is fully recognized that it rests on countries' willingness and ability to maintain conditions that will allow that formal commitment to be met. Convergence towards the highest possible measure of price stability is the main condition here. This being so, it is also the major convergence indicator in the system. Thus countries that still have higher inflation rates than the most stable partner will have to make an asymmetric policy effort to converge towards the common objective.

Borrowing the Bundesbank's credibility has been of some help in achieving this, but it has also involved some of the partners of Germany in maintaining a somewhat overvalued exchange rate as a means to compress the domestic forces of inflation. As a consequence, German net exports tend to be inflated to levels that lead to complaints about insufficient domestic demand growth in Germany as a means to keep export surpluses in check and stimulate overall growth. There seems to be a dilemma here.

It may be true that Germany could allow faster growth of domestic demand without incurring inflation risks, if only its supply side were more responsive than it actually is for a lot of well-known reasons. But, lacking this constraint, positive stimulation of domestic demand would in the present circumstances be risky, unless other partners stand ready to restrain domestic demand growth more readily than they have done so far in order to keep their inflation in check.

In other words, reliance on the import of stability from Germany would have to be replaced by home-made stability to a greater extent than has been the case so far. The alternative would mean toleration of more inflation in Germany which is highly unlikely as a matter of policy, although circumstances may in fact make somewhat higher inflation rates unavoidable temporarily. Like other countries, including non-EMS countries such as the United States and Switzerland but also including its EMS partners, Germany has seen market interest rates rising lately. And the monetary authorities have themselves acted to move interest rates higher in response to growing evidence of accelerating inflation. There can hardly be any doubt that strong demand from abroad especially for investment goods is a factor in this development. There is also the fact that the DM exchange rate depreciated in real terms during 1988−9 by a considerable margin.

Hence there is at present no policy dilemma in the sense that both price stability and exchange rate stability call for a somewhat more restrictive monetary policy stance. But there is a potential dilemma in so far as any effective dampening of demand may curtail domestic demand more than export demand, thus impairing the chances of a correction of the external imbalances within the EC. There are those who look at the pattern of exchange rates as an instrument to deal with the situation. Others have called for more effective recycling of the German surpluses as a solution. Unfortunately there is insufficient space to discuss these subjects here.

Part V

Lessons From the United States

14

European Banking Post-1992: Lessons From the United States

Anthony M. Santomero

As Europe enters the post-1992 era its financial services industry looks to the United States for some insight into what will happen in its future. Europeans correctly recognize that the United States has undergone a similar evolution over the last several decades. Its experience may illuminate the change that is an inevitable part of the reduction in national boundaries in the European banking community. Accordingly, in this chapter we shall review the process of change in the US financial structure and relate it to lessons that may be useful to the European financial community.

At the outset it should be clear that, while there are many similarities between European and US banking, the dissimilarities are at least as important. To begin with the dissimilarities, the United States has had a tradition of regulation centring upon both product restrictions and geographic limitations. The first of these, epitomized by the separation of the banking business into commercial and investment banking during the Great Depression, is a polar extreme in the worldwide industry. The Glass – Steagall Act of 1933 had made separation of functions a hallmark of US banking just as universal banking was synonymous with Germany. Accordingly, much of the innovation which has taken place over the last several decades has centred around product expansion, innovation and regulatory avoidance which has little counterpart outside the United States.

Notwithstanding the above, similarities do exist in the two financial structures. Perhaps the most relevant are the historical and deep-seated geographic restrictions that have played a central part in bank evolution in the United States. Since its infancy the United States has been committed to a dual banking system with dual regulatory controls. States' rights are more than a historical accident: they are an important part of an understanding of the evolution of the US banking structure. State legislators dealing in isolation and truly oblivious to the rest of the country forged unique banking systems on a state by state basis. These ranged everywhere from unit banking restrictions to state-wide branching activity. The net result was a fragmented industry with too many participants of unequal size and focus. Prior to 1970 this system was presumed to be acceptable and the prognosis had been for its continuation.

However, since that time the forces of change have altered the structure of geographic restrictions dramatically and moved the US banking market closer to full interstate banking. This was not easily done nor was it directly debated. Rather, this evolution was achieved in fits and starts by a combination of market forces, declining barriers to entry and 'beggar-my-neighbour' state policies. To the Europeans this aspect of the evolution of US banking is perhaps the most interesting for it forecasts changes that are subtle, political and at times discrete. Nonetheless they will change the financial structure rather dramatically.

This review of the US system will begin with a discussion of the evolution of the industry in terms of both product expansion and geographic broadening. In section 14.1 details of this process of change are given as an aid to understanding the long and tortuous road the industry has followed. In section 14.2 an attempt is made to gain some perspective from the catalogue of structural alterations and some key reasons for the evolution are offered. Finally, some highly subjective forecasts of future issues that will be debated in European banking circles are listed in section 14.3.

14.1   The Evolution of the US Banking System

The US financial services industry in general and the depository institutions specifically have gone through a period of transition from a highly regulated structure to a structure with less constraints on both their product and geographic markets. This section will briefly review its evolution using a historical perspective in each area.

14.1.1   Product Market Expansion of US Banks

The mid-twentieth-century US banking structure which included substantial product market restrictions on commercial banks can be traced back to the Glass–Steagall Act of 1933. This law, more properly titled the Banking Act of 1933, separated commercial and investment banking and is the root of product-price regulation. In terms of the separation of commercial and investment banking, the Act effectively established product market barriers to entry in the commercial and investment banking businesses by separating deposit-taking activity from securities and underwriting. It divided a once-combined industry by severely restricting product lines that could be offered by commercial banks and forbidding banking activity within their investment banking counterparts. After much discussion trust activity, which was also subject to divestiture, was retained by the commercial banking sector.

In the subsequent decade little was done to challenge this division of the banking industry as the economy of the 1930s and the following war period did not lend itself to experimentation. Thus it was not until the late 1950s that banking firms tried to broaden their markets through product expansion and limited innovation within the bank itself. Once begun, however, the process accelerated, but always within the severe restrictions of allowable activity. It was with the advent of the widespread use of the holding company form, however, that substantive relief and flexibility were made possible. Then, banks wishing to expand their activity could do so through the establishment of a holding company which transcended the restrictions and regulations that were relevant to the wholly owned banking subsidiaries.

In 1956, the passage of the Bank Holding Company Act gave the Federal Reserve Board the authority to determine the permissible activities (products) of these multibank holding companies. To some, this was seen as the first step in the regulators' attempt to control the expansion of this form of financial firm. However, to avoid such restrictions imposed on multibank holding companies, many banks exploited a loophole in the law and maintained a one-bank holding company structure which allowed continued expansion of its non-banking activities without regard to national regulatory approval. The 1970 Amendment closed this loophole by restricting one-bank holding companies to adherence to all provisions of the 1956 Bank Holding Company Act. This new law enabled the Federal Reserve Board to maintain closer control over the activities of commercial bank holding companies, which were in turn restricted to the product areas that were consistent with or equivalent to the business of banking. Yet, to a large extent, the law sanctioned the use of a holding company structure to broaden bank activity. It eliminated the incentives to maintain a one-bank holding company structure and prompted several banks to expand by acquiring additional banks both domestically, where possible, and internationally. At the same time, interpretation of federal regulation during the 1960s and 1970s tended to reduce the prohibitions on merger activity in the banking industry and ratified the ongoing product development of bank holding companies. Accordingly the post-1970 Amendment period was one of rapid expansion for major US banking firms.

Spurred on by the new-found freedom under the bank holding company regulation, banking firms, particularly in New York City, California and Chicago, increased their presence on the national scene. This very fact attracted the attention of out-of-state legislators who sought to bring the increased employment potential of money centre bank activity to their economically stagnant markets. Accordingly, South Dakota welcomed out-of-state bank holding companies in 1980 to the extent that they provided employment for more than 100 persons. Likewise, Delaware passed the Financial Center Development Act in 1981 to attract out-of-state institutions into the Wilmington area. The desirability of Delaware was increased by a regressive tax schedule which was in marked contrast with the corresponding statute in New York State. South Dakota and Delaware are only the most visible states in the set of locations that have attempted to attract financial service employment and tax dollars by preferential legislation. By all accounts such attempts have been remarkably successful. Delaware alone has become a major financial centre attracting not only money centre institutions but also large regional banks into the state. Other areas such as South Dakota have continued to increase their employment as a result of the presence of banking firms from outside the state.

The key elements that such locations offered large banking institutions were attractive regulation and low operating costs in terms of land, labour and taxation. By design, they passed legislation aimed at expanding permissible activities and out-of-state bank presence, frequently requiring that such activities be conducted only with out-of-state clients. But beyond the regulatory issues, cost swings have been a significant factor. When compared with alternatives in New York City or San Francisco, out-of-state land and labour costs provide a needed competitive edge in the increasingly aggressive market for financial services. Taxation issues merely add to the tangible operating cost savings of the move.

As the above trend continued, the movement towards the elimination of the boundary between commercial and investment banking continued. The product lines of each part of the financial services industry were becoming more intertwined. Investment banks expanded into a relatively large segment of the retail banking market with the introduction of money market mutual funds, cash management accounts and most recently non-bank-banks, an oddity of the US market. Likewise commercial banks have expanded their activities in private placements, corporate finance and commercial paper. The main recipients of this expansion have been money centre banks, but major regional firms have also garnered an appreciable market share.

At the beginning of this decade, then, the US industry was quite different from how it had been only 50 years earlier. Banks had expanded through holding company structures to a substantially larger product area. This included a wider array of corporate banking services and a larger set of retail customers. Corporate banking services operating through a subsidiary of the bank or holding company offered commercial clients advice, the *de facto* underwriting of commercial paper and private placement, to mention just a few. These groups, commonly referred to as a capital markets division, looked increasingly like an investment banking subsidiary. At the consumer level, trust activity expanded and investment services flourished. So too did expanded liability products aimed at a broader segment of household savings. On the credit side, open lines of credit, credit cards and mortgages of various types all added to the bankers' options. Indeed it can be argued that there is a surplus of credit available at the consumer level.

However, this did not end the industry's evolution. Banks continued to push the boundaries of Glass—Steagall in the move to become full service institutions. Recently, this received a substantial boost by interpretations of the 1933 Act which would allow the major banks to be engaged in limited security underwriting business through affiliates. On 13 June 1988 the Supreme Court let stand the Federal Reserve Board's approval for commercial bank affiliates to underwrite commercial paper, municipal revenue bonds and securities backed by mortgages and consumer debt under the condition that a bank affiliate's underwriting is limited to 5 per cent of the affiliate's gross revenue. The ruling was based on the interpretation of the Banking Act which prohibits bank affiliation with firms that are 'principally engaged' in securities activities. The percentage limits on underwriting which would keep bank affiliates from being 'principally engaged' in securities became the determining factor on permissible association. Although this makes the new powers useful only to the largest banks which can develop huge affiliates engaging in government securities trading or other non-banking activities, 12 banks were quickly affected by this ruling and some of them announced an immediate plan for such security underwriting activity.

However, this prospect has not been met with universal approval. The US Congress viewed the ruling as a clear usurping of legislative prerogative and asked for a stay. Yet by the close of the 1988 session, no legislation had been forthcoming. To many this was viewed as good news as the industry had been evolving around these prohibitions successfully for nearly two decades. Any legislation would include a quid pro quo for new powers which would be met with suspicion. One such condition being discussed was the separation of securities activity to a segmented affiliate to ensure the integrity and stability of the banking entities in the holding company.

Even without such safeguards one must recognize that the evolution of bank product lines was a necessary and critical feature of the financial service industry in the United States. Such changes prevented the industry from slipping further behind its investment banking counterparts in the intensely competitive financial services market. In addition, these changes allowed US institutions some degree of competitive response to a world market in which universal banking is the norm.

14.1.2 Expansion of Geographic Markets

The control of geographic expansion of US commercial banks can be traced to the 1927 McFadden Act in which the historical tradition of the state's right over the allowable expansion of commercial banks was reaffirmed. The 1956 Douglas Amendment of the Bank Holding Company Act continued the deference to state policy on geographic expansion of both nationally chartered and state-chartered institutions. Specifically it indicated that out-of-state expansion could not occur unless the host state expressly permitted such entry. The 1960 Bank Merger Act continued the tradition of the state's right on this issue. Together, these three Acts had effectively erected barriers to entry in interstate banking by prohibiting banks from operating branches outside their home state (McFadden Act), by forbidding banks from purchasing banks outside their home state, unless the laws of the acquired bank's state expressly permitted such an acquisition (Douglas Amendment), and by establishing guidelines for the approval of mergers between federally insured banks (Merger Act).

In the interim, large banks and bank holding companies wishing to expand their geographic presence did so through holding company non-bank subsidiaries which would provide a variety of services across the state lines. These services were offered through facilities such as loan production offices, and international branches referred to as Edge Act offices, as well as a variety of bank holding company non-bank subsidiaries that ranged from leasing companies and real estate appraisal firms to investment management groups that provided trust services.

As this process of non-bank product expansion continued, the basic vehicle of financial product distribution began to change. Telecommunications and electronics began to replace brick and mortar as a delivery system of retail products. An example of the technology-driven changes in the delivery of retail products is the emergence of the automatic teller machine (ATM) which expanded the potential service area beyond arbitrary branching restrictions. ATMs allowed customers to gain access to cash and give instructions from anywhere in the area network. Similarly, banks located in the 41 standard metropolitan statistical areas (SMSAs) which cross state boundaries allowed customers to access their bank relationships anywhere in the SMSA through the use of switching systems even if such transactions crossed state lines. However, branches were branches and branching was restricted by state legislation.

State control was nearly complete, and yet it was eroding. Legislation passed in 1960 and 1966 permitted bank mergers that provided benefits to the community which outweigh the potential competititve aspects of a merger. The Bank Merger Act provided the Justice Department with a basis for developing compromise guidelines to be employed in evaluating bank merger proposals. In addition, the emergency provisions of the Garn–St. Germain Act of 1982 provided that banks could cross state boundaries to acquire failing domestic institutions under certain circumstances. As a result of this legislation, California's Bank of America acquired Seafirst of Washington. The latter was shaken by problems associated with energy and foreign lending activities.

The issue of interstate mergers to aid troubled institutions across state lines was the first of a growing number of areas in which the previously sacred state boundary began to be crossed in the new wave of mergers. The once clear limitation of geographic expansion, made official in the Douglas Amendment to the McFadden Act, has undergone significant erosion over the last decade or so. This development added new dimensions and opportunities to the geographic expansion potential of the bank holding company.

The year 1975 was the beginning of formal state legislation which changed the perception of exclusivity of explicitly intrastate banking. Then, Maine enacted the first state law permitting general entry of out-of-state banking units. The result was a period of rapid acquisition of Maine holding companies by banking firms in New York, Rhode Island and Connecticut.

After considering the results of this experiment, additional states did not follow Maine's lead until seven years later. At that point both New York and Massachusetts passed interstate banking laws. The law in Massachusetts was considerably different from the law in New York however. While New York authorized out-of-state bank activity within its borders without reciprocity, Massachusetts established a regional banking statute providing access on a limited basis based upon the home state of the holding company. In essence, Massachusetts argued for regional banking by differentially treating outside banks and explicitly discriminating against one group over another.

Litigation followed quickly, with the future of regional pacts subject to considerable debate. In addition, Congressional action on various broadly based interstate banking proposals and other local interstate banking bills had been slowed in anticipation of the Supreme Court's decision in the test case, Northeast Bancorp Inc. et al., Petitioners, v. Board of Governors of the Federal Reserve System et al. (hereafter, the Northeast Bancorp case).

On 10 June 1985 the Supreme Court of the United States delivered its opinion on the Northeast Bancorp case as follows:

> We hold that the state statutes here in question comply with the Douglas Amendment and that they do not violate the Commerce Clause, the Compact Clause, or the Equal Protection Clause of the United States Constitution (Northeast Bancorp Inc. et al., Petitioners, v. Board of Governors of the Federal Reserve System).

The eight—nil court ruling upholding regional banking implied that state geographic barriers to entry would be replaced by regional barriers to entry. While these regional barriers to entry provided a reduction in the constraints on merger activity, they unquestionably fuelled the interstate banking trend before it.

Table 14.1   Interstate banking legislation by state

State	Area covered by interstate legislation
Alabama	Reciprocal, 12 states (AR, FL, GA, KY, LA, MD, MS, NC, SC, TN, VA, WV) and DC
Alaska	National, no reciprocity
Arizona	National, no reciprocity
Arkansas	Reciprocal, 15 states (AL, FL, GA, KS, LA, MD, MS, NE, NC, OK, SC, TN, TX, VA, WV) and DC
California	National, reciprocity
Colorado	National, no reciprocity
Connecticut	Reciprocal, 5 states (MA, ME, NH, RI, VT)
Delaware	National, reciprocity
District of Columbia	Reciprocal, 11 states (AL, FL, GA, LA, MD, MS, NC, SC, TN, VA, WV)
Florida	Reciprocal, 11 states (AL, AR, GA, LA, MD, MS, NC, SC, TN, VA, WV) and DC
Georgia	Reciprocal, 9 states (AL, FL, KY, LA, MS, NC, SC, TN, VA)
Idaho	National, no reciprocity
Illinois	National, reciprocity
Indiana	National, reciprocity
Kentucky	National, reciprocity
Louisiana	National, reciprocity
Maine	National, no reciprocity
Maryland	Reciprocal, 14 states (AL, AR, DE, FL, GA, KY, LA, MS, NC, PA, SC, TN, VA, WV) and DC
Massachusetts	Reciprocal, 5 states (CT, ME, NH, RI, VT)
Michigan	National, reciprocity
Minnesota	Reciprocal, 12 states (IA, ND, SD, WI, ID, IL, KS, MO, MN, NE, WA, WY)
Mississippi	Reciprocal, 12 states (AL, AR, FL, KY, LA, MO, NC, SC, TN, TX, VA, WV)
Missouri	Reciprocal, 8 states (AL, IA, IL, KS, KY, NE, OK, TN)
Nebraska	National, reciprocity
Nevada	National, no reciprocity
New Hampshire	Reciprocal, 5 states (CT, RI, ME, MA, VT)
New Jersey	National, reciprocity
New York	National, reciprocity
North Carolina	Reciprocal, 12 states (AL, AR, FL, GA, KY, LA, MD, MS, SC, TN, VA, WV) and DC
Ohio	National, reciprocity
Oklahoma	National, after initial entry BHC must be from state offering reciprocity or wait 4 years to expand
Oregon	National, no reciprocity
Pennsylvania	National, reciprocity
Rhode Island	National, reciprocity

Table 14.1 *continued*

State	Area covered by interstate legislation
South Carolina	Reciprocal, 11 states (AL, AR, FL, GA, KY, LA, MD, NC, TN, VA, WV) and DC
South Dakota	National, reciprocity
Tennessee	Reciprocal, 13 states (AL, AR, FL, GA, IN, KY, LA, MO, MS, NC, SC, VA, WV)
Texas	National, no reciprocity
Utah	National, no reciprocity
Vermont	National, reciprocity
Virginia	Reciprocal, 12 states (AL, AR, FL, GA, KY, LA, MD, MS, NC, SC, TN, WV) and DC
Washington	National, reciprocity
West Virginia	National, reciprocity
Wisconsin	Reciprocal, 8 states (IA, IL, IN, KY, MI, MN, MO, OH)
Wyoming	National, no reciprocity

Several states prohibit acquisition of banks in operation for less than a specified number of years. Some allow out-of-state firms to acquire problem institutions.

Sources: *Federal Reserve Bulletin*, February 1987, updated by *American Banker*, 31 January 1989

The results of states opening up their borders were immediate, in some cases, with substantial cross-boundary acquisitions and regionalization. During the time leading up to fully open access, completed in the early 1990s, the market was very active. From 1986−9 over 250 institutions were involved in merger activity *each year*. This level of activity was a testament to continued reorganization. However, this number grossly underestimated the impact of the forthcoming legislation; in many states the regional compacts included nationwide trigger dates, which fostered further consolidation and merger activity.

The merger activity before 1990 is analysed in a study from the Salomon Brothers Center, Beatty et al. (1987). Examining a bank merger sample of all deals completed over a period of nearly two years covering 1984 and 1985 they find several important features when comparing the two sides of merger deals. Their data indicate that acquiring banks are inevitably larger institutions − on average nine times the size of the acquired firm. They possess a portfolio that is riskier as measured by asset category ratios and loss experience, suggesting greater risk tolerance by managers and/or stockholders of the acquiring firm. This is substantiated by a higher leverage ratio and a higher *ex post* return on capital. In sum, they portray the merger market as a market in which higher risk banks acquire their smaller more conservative counterparts to exploit the potential of their assets. For this opportunity, acquiring firms paid on average a 40 per cent premium over book value for the equity of the acquired firm, with substantial variation around this average figure.

Since the period covered in this study, merger activity accelerated. Regional banks seeking to gain sufficient size to compete rapidly expanded their network of affiliates and their total asset size. This was facilitated by a relative stock value for super-regionals which until December 1988 substantially favoured these firms over their money centre counterparts. The First Fidelity losses, however, caused some to question the wisdom of the market's previous view of these banking firms.

Nonetheless, it is interesting to note that New York State is conspicuously absent from those states in which only regional expansion is permitted. The adjoining states of Connecticut, New Jersey and Pennsylvania do not allow New York State access to their markets. Indeed, the prominent explanation offered for the existence of regional compacts is the support of local banks at the expense of their New York money centre counterparts. For these purposes all New York State institutions are viewed with suspicion as potential predators of local banking firms. Local market perspectives remain.

14.2   A Distillation of the US Experience

As is evident from the above review, much has changed in the US banking scene. The old lines dividing commercial from investment banking are quickly eroding. State boundaries too have fallen to regional banking trends and the quick evolution to interstate banking. This is a fairly idiosyncratic experience brought about by the historical structure and regulation of US banking. Yet the forces that led to the decline in the regulation of both product and geography are universal. Understanding them is a prerequisite for understanding the institutional evolution reported. To the extent that these forces are truly universal, such an understanding will focus the European debate concerning financial structure on the few important factors that are the root causes of change in the US experience. Accordingly, in section 14.2.1 an attempt is made to discuss the forces that brought about the changes, while the discussion in section 14.2.2 centres upon the institutional implications of these evolutionary forces.

14.2.1   The Forces of Change in US Financial Markets

The motive forces behind the evolution of the US banking system appear to centre around two fundamental issues that were previously not understood in the financial service sector. First, the product line offered to the industry's natural constituents, firms and households, cannot be arbitrarily segmented across industry lines. The US attempts to do so were inherently inefficient and opened the way for economic forces consistent with an expansion in the product line offered by various financial entities. Second, technology ultimately made geography less meaningful as a constraint on the delivery system of financial services. This led to an inevitable trend to expand product markets and substitute technology, telecommunications or mail service for physical space. In most cases, this has resulted in increased competition and a reduction in the number of competitors in the industry as a whole.

Addressing the first of these forces, it should have been apparent as early as 1933 that the arbitrary division of products offered to the corporate sector was doomed to failure. Yet faced with a contraction of the US banking system by 50 per cent in the 1920s, US lawmakers were committed to adding security and stability to the US financial system. Searching for a market definition which would narrow the risks inherent in the monetary trans- mission mechanism, legislators embraced the suggestions of Messrs Glass and Steagall that there was something natural about the division between short-term commercial lending and other commercial borrowing needs. Enamoured of the real bills doctrine, these legislators arbitrarily sorted the industry by maturity of debt instrument, presuming that commercial banks were relegated to the short end of the spectrum. As is evident from the above, this division was arbitrary and not long lived. Carter Golembe once suggested that it was an ill-conceived deviation from the norm in US banking. In any case, as is recounted in the previous sections, banks sought to expand their product menu to satisfy customer needs. This was done first by an expansion into investment banking areas with longer duration, such as private placement middle market and venture pools. It was followed by a realization that a substantial portion of investment banking activity was essentially a substitute for the lending function even at the short end of the maturity spectrum. Commercial paper facilitation and Euromarket syndication are clear cases of loan alternatives into which commercial banks have sought entrance.

It should be pointed out that commercial banks were not the predators in this expanding product line process. Indeed, it could be argued that our investment banking community, subject to much less explicit regulation, was the first to see the opportunity to expand its product franchise into commercial banking products. Its success led to a further decline in the already minor position of commercial banks in the US financial system. Junk bonds, commercial paper and venture capital pools were the product alternatives used by investment banking firms to enter the traditional bank market of major industrial lending, and these were successful. Their position was further advanced by the process of securitization in which a substantial portion of standard bank portfolio could be initiated and sold without the need of a depository source.

The result of this confrontation between the two divided parts of the banking industry was the virtual elimination of the division proposed in the Glass–Steagall Act. Major participants are no longer defined along industry lines but by their chosen strategy of market concentration. In commercial lending, Goldman Sachs, Bankers Trust and Morgan Guaranty are more alike than are regional and money centre commercial banks, for example.

At the consumer level the same process was at work. Increasingly, household portfolio choice was viewed as hampered by arbitrary restrictions along industry activity lines. The simple savings account gave way to a complex array of portfolio options, only a few of which were previously viewed as allowable activities for commercial banks. Institutions which refused to innovate found themselves losing household market shares to a securities industry that adapted well to the consumer's desire for participation in a wider array of debt instruments and access to the equity market. Mutual funds, money market funds, tax-deferred or tax-exempt instruments all developed as an alternative to the previous rather staid and increasingly obsolete bank savings vehicles. Banks had little choice but to evolve so as to follow their customers' needs for greater savings vehicle flexibility.

At the same time technology was changing the face of the industry and its delivery system. Corporate banking shifted from a simple single bank relationship and passive corporate finance to unbundled product marketing. Roll-over financing directly from the market substituted for bank seasonal borrowing, as lenders were linked more easily with the corporate treasurer's office. Cash management moved from manual systems to on-line real-time cash controls.

On the consumer side the telephone became a substitute for location in retail deposit gathering. Home banking, wire transfer and the mail box slowly replaced the teller line. In a search for higher yields, portfolios shifted from one bank to another or from banks to their counterparts in the mutual funds industry or the brokered deposit market.

Credit instruments also evolved. Spearheaded by some aggressive banking firms looking for market share and a different distribution network, electronic banking, credit cards and point-of-sale products developed. In each case the institution offering the new product saw it as an opportunity to harness new technology and substitute telecommunications for geographic presence. This in turn led to increasing concentration of certain product lines and increasing emphasis on off-site operation centres to achieve low cost production. As location became less central, the need for efficient production increased.

Interestingly, as the portfolio offered by banks expanded, the number of institutions with whom a consumer dealt grew rather than fell. The new products caused price competition and fragmentation of the customer relationship even as a wider relationship was made possible by the new product.

Consumers became much more price, as well as product, conscious. This led the institutions that offered the wider array of products to decentralize the production of these specialized products and expand their geographic presence. This resulted in lower delivery costs due to both increases in technical efficiency and lower unit costs (economies of scale). This cost cutting and relocation had dramatic effects on employment concentration in the industry and the very functioning of the organizations in question. For example, Citicorp is at present the preeminent retail banker in the United States. Yet, its headquarters' location of New York is not the site for its multi-million dollar credit card operation nor its top tier mortgage subsidiary.

14.2.2 The Institutional Effects of the Changes

The net result of these economic forces is the development of a different kind of banking system in the United States. The holding company structure, which began as a device to circumvent regulation, is developing into a model of bank organization. The holding company is becoming a portmanteau for a highly diversified financial service firm which does not necessarily enter and engage in all financial market activity. Instead, it selects a product line or subsegment of the industry and functions in a fully diversified manner within this area. For example, Citicorp is increasingly concentrating in retail banking and has developed a number of subsidiaries supporting its major thrusts in mortgages, credit cards and transaction services. PNC Financial, a major regional bank, has concentrated in consumer portfolio services from trusts, investments and upscale retail banking; it operates major regional banks in three states and ranks in the top 20 banking holding companies in the United States. J.P. Morgan and Company has become the premier institutional bank with major wholesale thrusts in syndication, cash management and upscale commercial relationships. It does so with US locations in New York and Delaware as well as foreign offices in major centres around the world. The above examples are not meant to be complete but are symptomatic of the evolution of the industry.

Concentration has increased as smaller regional forces disappeared or were accumulated by growing super-regionals seeking a geographic presence for their product niche. Holding companies have emerged as a major force above the retail level with occasional attempts to minimize their presence by maintaining local names and control. This raises the familiar issues of concentration of power in the industry. For the United States we have minimized the likelihood of debate on this issue by asserting that horizontal integration maintains local competition and gains in delivery efficiency. Indeed regulatory standards and anti-trust considerations have increasingly moved from local concentration ratios to national or global ones. This has increased the freedom of participants to expand geographically either directly or through the use of an alternative distribution mechanism to gain the efficiency of size. However, there is little evidence to support this contention of production efficiencies in the literature. Economy of scale studies have yet to isolate the cost efficiencies that are alleged.

Yet as bank size continues to grow there is a second process under way. Forced by competitive pressure of new entrants to be low cost producers, major financial entities are increasingly shifting the actual production process associated with financial transactions away from financial centres. This has resulted in a relative decline in employment at centres of financial activity as production and cyclical employment expands in low cost areas such as the midwest, the south and mountain states. This issue has become so serious that New York State, the presumed financial capital of the United States, has actively studied its future role within the industry. It produced reports demonstrating a relative decline in employment within its boundaries as other regions compete for employment opportunities via regulatory relief or outright financial weapons such as tax abatement.

It could be argued that this trend towards the decentralization of the industry's production process is a desirable characteristic of the evolution. I am quite certain that this position would be taken by the governors of Delaware and South Dakota. On the macro-economic level too there are advantages. Slumps in economic activity in this industry will be less deleterious to one state or city because of the diversification that has developed.

Employment diversification, however, does not fully equate with political and corporate power diversification. Indeed, the US scene is changing rather dramatically as a result of the super-regional bank movement. To be parochial, the Philadelphia market is the fourth largest metropolitan area in the United States. Prior to deregulation it had five regional banks of substantial note: First Pennsylvania, Philadelphia National Bank, Girard Bank, Fidelity Bank and Provident Bank. It is currently home to only one small super-regional, Corestates, a transmutation of its lead bank Philadelphia National Bank. This process is being duplicated throughout the United States.

14.3   Some Issues that will Surface in Europe

If the US experience is any guide, there are interesting times ahead in the European banking community. To conclude, I shall suggest some topics that may be part of the future debate about its evolution. First, one should expect to find the same type of political considerations that developed in the US emerging as issues in the EC. To an outsider this seems fairly evident. Pan-European banking will quickly give way to regional bias and preferences.

A casual reading of the *Financial Times* suggests that this is already occurring. Using the US example, national officials will find legitimate reasons to protect the market shares gained by home country banks. Issues of local autonomy, the need for a net inflow of funds into the country and a long history as a banking community will all be offered as reasons for preferential treatment for local banks. Attempts will be made to increase the phase-in time for equal treatment and local banks will be afforded preferential access to intranational financings if only because of better access to the political process.

Second, names will become important. Even more than in the United States, local recognition is a major issue in Europe, to say nothing of language. Accordingly, there will be an attempt to develop trans-European names on bank holding companies to allow for easier access and acceptance into local economies.

Third, at the same time it will be interesting to see the evolution of major national institutions within the EC. In the United States there is much speculation whether any super-regionals will merge into a new breed of national bank. The European counterpart of this issue is whether major institutions in the lead economies of Europe will merge into single entities. Of equal interest is whether small members of the EC will allow the acquisition of their lead banks by outside banking firms. In Europe, as in the United States, lead banks in different regions are of different size. In the United States this led to the acquisition of smaller banks by larger ones. Will this be acceptable across national lines in Europe?

Fourth, one can expect the acquisition of smaller banks by lead institutions even within national markets. Indeed, the Spanish bank mergers may be viewed as an attempt to start this process. We shall see more such consolidations as national banking systems further concentrate to reach some critical size which is viewed as less vulnerable to acquisition. It should be noted that the US experience suggests that, in general, this is folly. In fact, institutions that are acquired generally are those that have reached a critical size so that merged entities actually have an increased probability of outside acquisition.

Fifth and finally, employment issues in the industry, which have yet to receive any attention in Europe, will become highly political. As institutions seek low-cost production points, one can expect to find them considering alternative site relocations to reduce operating costs. Some nations will cater to the industry and seek such employment. Indeed, we should expect to find an increase in employment opportunities in the relatively less developed portions of the EC as they are seen as a low-cost production area. Such decisions which will inevitably be made by some industry participants will be unpopular and generally cause local governments to behave aggressively and consider reregulation.

The only force working against the dissipation of the concentration of financial employment away from more developed urban sectors of Europe will be the need for an advanced infrastructure including such things as transportation and telecommunications capability. Indeed such development projects may have substantial social benefits to some members of the Common Market as a mechanism to attract financial service employment.

Overall, the situation will change. The transition will be more burdensome than many will expect because industrial restructuring is always difficult, but we can be sure that it will be exciting.

Reference

Beatty, R., Santomero, A. and Smirlock, M. (1987) *Bank Merger Premiums, Analysis and Evidence*. New York: Salomon Brothers Center, New York University.

Comment

Greg Udell

The continuing deregulation of the financial services industry in the United States provides a logical analogue to post-1992 European banking. The similarities between the introduction of cross-country banking in Europe and the advent of interstate banking in the United States make for an appealing comparison. However, as Santomero points out, the dissimilarities may be equally important. This chapter provides a valuable road map for those who wish to use the US experience as a predictor of the future of European banking.

In the chapter, it is stated that the most relevant similarity between the two financial structures stems from 'historical and deep-seated geographic restrictions' that have characterized the regulation of banking in the United States. Market forces, however, have exerted pressure in the opposite direction to push back these geographic constraints with varying degrees of force over time. Recently technology and interindustry competition made the breakdown of interstate banking restrictions inevitable. To apply the US experience to post-1992 European banking, however, requires a careful analysis of the idiosyncratic nature of the US experience. Even the process itself is idiosyncratic. Rather than a discrete shift the 'evolution [of interstate banking] was achieved in fits and starts by a combination of market forces, declining barriers to entry and "beggar-my-neighbour" state policies'. The approach taken in this chapter is first to offer the reader a portrait of the peculiarly American regulatory landscape. Then the author distils from this the forces behind the recent change in the US financial services industry. I find this approach particularly helpful because it is motivated by a search for a common denominator − potentially universal forces that may jointly guide and shape the evolution of the two financial systems.

In addition to geographic constraints, the regulation of US banking has been characterized for most of this century by extensive product restrictions. To some extent the historical regulatory quid pro quo for this constraint has been the federal safety net provided by Federal Deposit Insurance Corporation (FDIC) deposit insurance and the Federal Reserve discount window. What this paper implicitly suggests is that this arrangement was not a stable long-run equilibrium. The combination of competition and innovation has worked to undermine the era of protected banking in the

United States. While the safety net remains intact, regulatory constraints have
been significantly relaxed with respect to both geographic restrictions and
product restrictions. In January 1989, for example, the Federal Reserve
Board approved limited commercial bank underwriting of corporate debt.
This represented a significant and fundamental reinterpretation of the Glass –
Steagall barrier between commercial and investment banking.

Santomero identifies two forces behind the erosion of the regulatory wall
erected around commercial banking. First, he argues that arbitrary segmentation of financial product lines across industries is unnatural and inherently
inefficient. As a consequence, competition will inevitably exert pressure to
redefine the walls themselves. The second force, technology, altered the
economics of the delivery of financial services by providing substitutes for
interstate banking.

Closely related to these two forces is the process of financial innovation.
Financial innovation can be motivated by a desire to circumvent regulatory
constraints, to reduce transactions costs or to improve risk-sharing – or a
combination of these (e.g. securitization). Often an exogenous shock
provides the impetus. For example, rising and increasingly volatile interest
rates put depository institutions at a regulation-imposed disadvantage as non-
depository intermediaries offered newly created substitutes for bank
liabilities such as the money market mutual fund. (This ultimately led to
congressional approval of money market deposit accounts.) Sometimes the
motivation for financial innovation is hard to identify. A good example is the
leveraged buyout (LBO). While it has become popular to view the LBO as
a phenomenon of the 1980s, the LBO had its true origin a decade earlier in
the 'bootstrap' financing offered to middle market borrowers by commercial
finance companies. In response most large banks started competing 'asset-
based' lending departments in the 1970s. Then Drexel Burnham Lambert
elevated the LBO to capital market status by introducing junk bond financing.
Even in junk-bond-financed LBOs commercial banks are often still involved
in either the bridge loan or other senior debt. The LBO provides a good
illustration of a key point made by Santomero: defining a bank by the type
of product it sells is arbitrary and 'unnatural'. In an economic sense, financial
innovation dooms product restrictions to eventual economic irrelevance.
When Glass – Steagall was authored in 1933, products such as junk bonds and
collateralized mortgage obligations did not exist.

As the author points out, applying the US experience to Europe is difficult
because the recent evolution of US banking has been driven to a large extent
by a combination of 'product expansion, innovation and regulatory avoidance
which has little counterpart outside the United States'. Moreover, deregulation of banking in the United States differs from the European
deregulation of 1992 in at least two other ways. First, the elimination of
geographic restrictions in the United States occurred in an environment in

which restrictions on interstate commerce were relatively minimal. The 1992 programme, in contrast, involves a concomitant deregulation of commerce and finance. Consequently, the benefits to cross-border banking may depend to a certain extent on the realized benefits to cross-border commercial trade. Efficiency in the payments system provides a good example of this point. A study by Berger and Humphrey (1988) demonstrates that full interstate banking in the United States will reduce clearing costs in several ways: transportation economies; transformation of transit checks to 'on-us' items due to greater concentration; and greater efficiency in interstate clearing because nationwide banks can clear through multiple clearing houses. The Berger and Humphrey model of cheque clearing under interstate banking assumed static payer–payee behaviour. However, a European model of cheque clearing must necessarily take into account that payer–payee behaviour will be affected by the concomitant deregulation of commerce as cross-border trade is substituted for local trade. Therefore the payments system benefits to cross-country banking will depend on the increase in cross-border clearing items produced by this substitution.

The other major difference between the European and US experience is the nature of bank regulation. The chartering and supervision of banking in the United States involves a combination of state and federal regulators – a system which has come to be referred to as *dual* banking. However, when compared with post-1992 European banking, the US system is *relatively* centralized. Every US bank is examined and supervised by at least one federal bank regulator: the Comptroller of the Currency; the Federal Reserve; or the FDIC (although state-chartered banks are generally also examined and supervised by the state banking authority). While these agencies do not always act in perfect concert with each other, their actions are generally coordinated. Moreover, the authority to issue a government deposit guarantee is vested in a single federal agency for banks (the FDIC) and a single federal agency for savings and loans (the Federal Savings and Loan Insurance Corporation (FSLIC)). The EC, in contrast, is still wrestling with the trade-off between harmonized EC-wide regulation and mutual recognition. As pointed out in a presentation by Sir George Blunden (1988) the 'principle of home control, however, arguably runs the risk of encouraging a migration of business to the member state with the lowest supervisory standards'. In the presence of implicit government guarantees, these differences in supervisory standards may also induce differences in bank risk taking across member states. A US counterpart to this problem is the differential regulation of the savings and loan and the commercial banking industries. The evidence seems fairly clear that the relative leniency of savings and loan supervision greatly exacerbated the magnitude of the savings and loan crisis and the FSLIC's current exposure.

The deregulation of banking in the United States provides some interesting lessons for post-1992 European banking. One must be careful, however, in applying the US model too literally. The author does an excellent job of identifying the idiosyncratic nature of the US experience as well as the underlying (and potentially universal) forces at work. In so doing he has provided the reader with a valuable resource with which to assess the nature of a single financial market in Europe.

References

Berger, N. and Humphrey, D.B. (1988) Interstate banking and the payments system. *Journal of Financial Services Research*, 1, 131–45.

Blunden, G. (1988) Presentation at the Italian Chamber of Commerce Conference, September 1988; published in *The World of Banking* (November–December).

Index